MBA'S GUIDE TO WINDOWS XP PROFESSIONAL

The Essential Windows Reference for Business Professionals

MBA'S GUIDE TO

The Essential Windows Reference for Business Professionals

WINDOWS XP PROFESSIONAL

Pat Coleman
Peter Dyson
Stephen L. Nelson

NEW AGE INTERNATIONAL (P) LIMITED, PUBLISHERS

Contents at a Glance

Contents

INTRODUCTION

You are unique among readers. Almost nobody reads the introduction to a book like this. However, you'll richly benefit by taking a few minutes to read through this information. Its purpose is to help you maximize your return on the investment you've made in this book—your investment in money and especially your even more costly investment in time.

Why This Book

The purpose of this book is to help you acquire the skills you need to get started with, use, and continue to learn about Microsoft Windows XP Professional. Other books give you a great deal of information about Windows XP Professional, but don't (in our opinion) give the sorts of detailed commentary and advice useful to business people. Business users of Windows XP Professional benefit by having a reference that emphasizes, talks from the point of view, and focuses on the business aspects of the software. In short, business users of Windows XP Professional need a book that talks about software as a business tool.

MBA's Guide to Windows XP Professional is the only book that specifically describes how you can more easily, more productively, and more powerfully use the software in business.

Although this book's title references the popular business professional degree, MBA, this book will also be of use to people without MBAs. MBA students, for example, will find this book useful. People with graduate degrees in accounting, public administration, economics, and related fields will find this book useful as well.

In addition, anyone who's finished a good undergraduate program in business or a related field (like accounting) will feel comfortable and gain skills using this book as a desktop reference.

What Is Windows XP?

An operating system is the set of programs responsible for the basic operation of a computer. Without an operating system, you can't run a word processor, a spreadsheet program, or a device such as a printer or a modem. The operating system establishes rules that applications must follow in order to function correctly, for example, how many characters a filename can have and the procedure for saving and opening files.

Windows XP is a family of three operating systems:

- Windows XP Home Edition
- Windows XP Professional
- Windows .NET Server

Each operating system serves a specific purpose and is appropriate for use in particular situations.

Windows XP Home Edition is, obviously, for home computers, and it contains features that let you easily network computers, connect to the Internet, and work with media files such as photos, recordings, movies, and the like.

Windows XP Professional looks much like Windows XP Home Edition, and you can run it on a standalone computer, on a small network, or on a large network. It can act as a client or as a server, as you will see in this book.

Windows .NET Server is an operating system that will be released some time in 2002. It will run on a network server machine. You can run Windows .NET Server on anything from a small network to a network of several hundred users.

This book focuses on Windows XP Professional, which you may be using in a variety of situations:

- On your desktop connected to a corporate network that uses Windows 2000 Server.
- On your desktop connected to a corporate network that uses Windows 2000 Server or Windows NT 4 Server.
- On a small network that includes both Windows XP Professional and Windows 2000 Professional, Windows 95, Windows 98 or only Windows XP Professional machines.
- On a standalone computer.

Regardless of the situation, Windows XP Professional is in use because it is a more reliable and a more secure operating system than any previous versions of Windows. If you've used previous versions of Windows, the skills you acquired apply directly and immediately to using Windows XP Professional. You'll see quickly, though, that you'll need additional skills to function at top speed in this new environment.

In order to get information to you as quickly as possible about this new operating system, we wrote this book using pre-release software. Consequently, what you see on your desktop and how certain features work on your computer may not correspond exactly with the illustrations in this book, and sometimes a procedure may vary from what we describe. In addition, if you bought a new computer on which Windows XP Professional was already installed, the manufacturer of that computer may have customized the desktop, installed additional features, or substituted some programs for the original programs released by Microsoft. Windows XP Professional is in many ways an evolving operating system. First, as is the case with any new operating system or application, it will continue to be refined. Second, a feature called Windows Update lets you immediately and automatically (if you choose to let it) install any new features or fixes as they are made available by Microsoft. Obviously, any updates to Windows that were released after this book was in production are not reflected here. As you know, the world of technology is characterized by nothing more than by rapid change. This characteristic sometimes makes using a computer a frustrating experience, but it also keeps our minds nimble, and that can't be a bad thing. With this caveat in mind, take a look at what we've included in the *MBA's Guide to Windows XP Professional.*

What's in This Book

The easiest way to see what's in this book is to turn to the table of contents. It lists each chapter and each chapter's contents in rich detail.

The chapters in this book fall into three categories:

Chapters 1 through 4 provide fast-paced but friendly tutorials on Windows XP Professional basics such as using the interface, working with files and folders, printing, and using Control Panel. In a nutshell, these four QuickPrimers™ move you to professional proficiency in using Windows XP Professional—even if you're new to Windows. If you don't need this help, of course, you can easily skip these primers. We suggest, however, that even if you already know how to use a previous version of Windows, you peruse these chapters because Windows XP Professional is totally redesigned.

Chapters 5 through 11 provide rich, detailed coverage of topics of interest to business users of Windows XP Professional—topics that are short-changed in books that have to be everything to everybody. Chapter 5, for example, explains how to use the accessories and utilities as business tools, and Chapters 7, 9, and 10 explain how to connect to the Internet and use it, an increasingly vital skill in today's business settings.

Chapters 12 through 16 describe real-life business projects involving Windows XP Professional—installing the system, setting up a network, troubleshooting, and creating a disaster recovery plan.

Conventions Used in This Book

To identify screen elements, the first letter of each word in the description is capitalized. This convention may look a bit strange at first, but it makes it easier to understand some instruction as "click the Print Table Of Links check box."

You'll also find Notes, Tips, and Warnings, which point out tidbits of useful information. Pay attention to Warnings; they help you avoid potential problems. A few sidebars are also scattered throughout. Sidebars contain helpful information that is not necessarily directly related to the topic at hand, or they may discuss in detail a subject that is mentioned in the running text but is not elaborated on.

Part 1

Business QuickPrimers™

In This Part

Chapter 1

USING THE WINDOWS INTERFACE AND DESKTOP

Featuring:

- Logging On
- Changing Your User Account Picture
- Fast Switching Between Users
- Getting Started
- Searching and Finding
- Getting Help
- Using the Run Dialog Box
- Logging Off and Shutting Down
- Using the Taskbar
- Using the Recycle Bin
- Using and Creating Shortcuts

The most important thing about any software you run on your computer is that it helps you to get your job done easier, better, or faster or all three. Windows XP Professional can certainly help you do your job easier, better, and faster, as well as give you a great deal of comfort about how safe the information on your computer is—but that is the case only if you know how to use it.

This chapter introduces you to the *desktop*, what you see after you first log on to your Windows XP Professional system. Theoretically, the Windows desktop is analogous to your physical desktop. Opinions vary as to how far this analogy extends without breaking down, and some techie types refer to the desktop as a *shell*, a term that normally refers to the user's environment as opposed to what's really going on inside a system that makes it work.

Nevertheless, this book calls the desktop the desktop, and this chapter describes its parts and pieces, tells you what each was designed to do, and shows you how to use it. If you've used other versions of Windows—Windows NT, Windows 2000, or Windows 95/98—the Windows XP desktop will not look familiar but rather strangely empty. One of the design goals for this operating system was to get rid of clutter. If your computer came with Windows XP already installed, the manufacturer may have placed several icons on the desktop. But if you performed a clean installation, you'll probably see only one desktop icon—the Recycle Bin. (For all the information about installing Windows XP Professional, see Chapter 12.)

Before getting started, though, a reminder is in order: the primary difference between Windows XP Professional and Windows 95/98 is security. In Windows XP Professional, you can't do anything unless you have permission to do so. Broadly speaking, the Windows XP Professional universe is divided into Computer Administrators and users. Simply put, if you want to make a configuration change to your system, for example, installing new software, you need to be logged on as a Computer Administrator. If you are working on a corporate local area network (LAN), you most likely do not have Computer Administrator privileges, but you have a system administrator who does. If you are running your own small network at home or in a small business, you do have Computer Administrator privileges because you set yourself up as a Computer Administrator when you installed Windows XP Professional. You'll want to keep these security features in mind as this chapter explores the desktop.

Logging On

If you've used Windows 95/98, you may be accustomed to seeing a logon dialog box when you start your computer. You also may be accustomed to simply pressing Escape or Enter to bypass this seeming inconvenience. You can't do this in Windows XP Professional. If you don't have a valid user name and password and enter them correctly, you can't do anything on a Windows XP Professional system. And if you are connected to a corporate LAN, you may also need the name of a domain if you're supposed to log on to a domain other than the default.

NOTE *A domain can be the description of a single computer, a department, or a complete network and is used for administrative and naming purposes.*

If your computer is a member of a network workgroup or is a standalone machine, by default you log on using the Welcome screen. Select your user name, enter your password, and press Enter to log on. If your computer is a member of a network domain, you won't see the Welcome screen, but instead the standard Log On To Windows dialog box. Enter your user name and your password, and press Enter to log on. As an added security measure, a Computer Administrator may also require you to press Ctrl+Alt+Del to display the Log On To Windows dialog box.

In Windows XP Professional, a user name can be a maximum of 20 characters and is not case sensitive. A password can be a maximum of 127 characters and *is* case sensitive. If you are on a mixed network, for example, you have both Windows XP Professional and Windows 95/98 machines, keep the password to a maximum of 14 characters, which is the maximum that Windows 95/98 will recognize.

If you are on a corporate LAN, your Computer Administrator will probably initially assign your user name and your password, and you can then change your password to some favorite expression. Most corporate Computer Administrators set your password to expire after 30 days, and they set password history so that you can't reuse a password until you've used 12 or 13 other passwords.

Passwords are an important part of the security of a network system. Here are some guidelines that lead to the creation of strong passwords and, thus, make it difficult for someone to break into your system using the usual cracking tools:

- Never use any term available in a dictionary.
- Your password should be at least seven characters in length and contain letters, numbers, and symbols.
- Your password should not contain your name or your user name. Children's names, pets' names, or any names or expressions that people associate with you are also not going to make a strong password.
- Don't continue to use the same password for long periods even if you can.

TIP *If your password isn't accepted, check the Caps Lock key. Remember, your password is case sensitive. If you originally entered it using all lowercase or a combination of upper- and lowercase and the Caps Lock key is on, your password obviously won't be accepted.*

Changing Your User Account Picture

If you work on a system that uses the Welcome screen, you can change your own picture that displays next to your user account name. If you are the Computer Administrator, you can change the pictures of other users of the system. Remember, the Welcome screen is available only if your computer is a member of a workgroup or is a standalone machine. To change your own picture, follow these steps:

1. Open Control Panel, which is shown in Figure 1-1.

Click the Start button, and then click Control Panel.

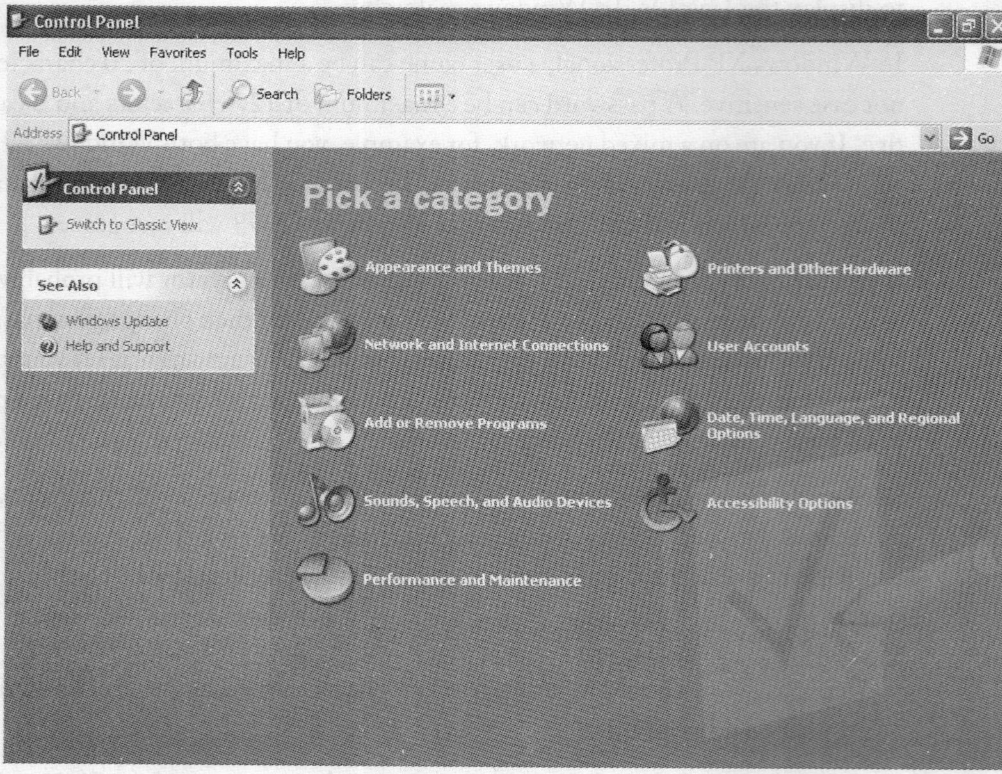

Figure 1-1 The Windows XP Control Panel.

NOTE *Control Panel in Windows XP is quite different from Control Panel in previous versions of Windows. Chapter 4 looks at Control Panel in detail.*

2. Open the User Accounts dialog box, which is shown in Figure 1-2.

Click User Accounts.

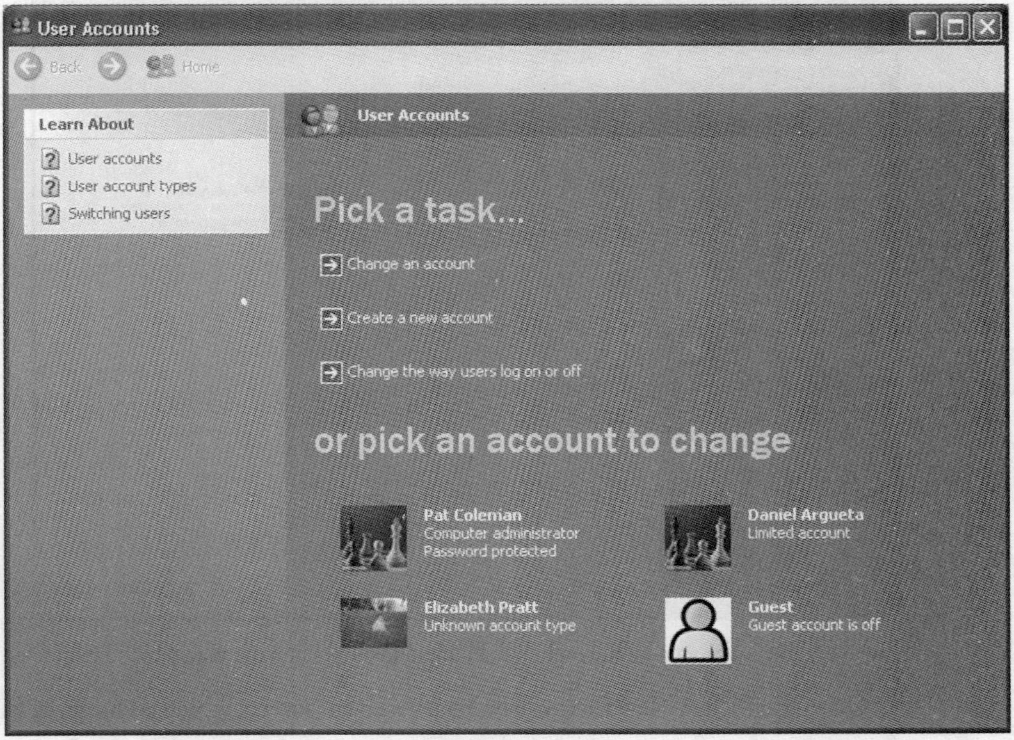

Figure 1-2 The User Accounts dialog box.

3. Open the What Do You Want To Change About Your Account? screen, which is shown in Figure 1-3.

Select your account, and in the Pick A Task section, click the Change An Account link.

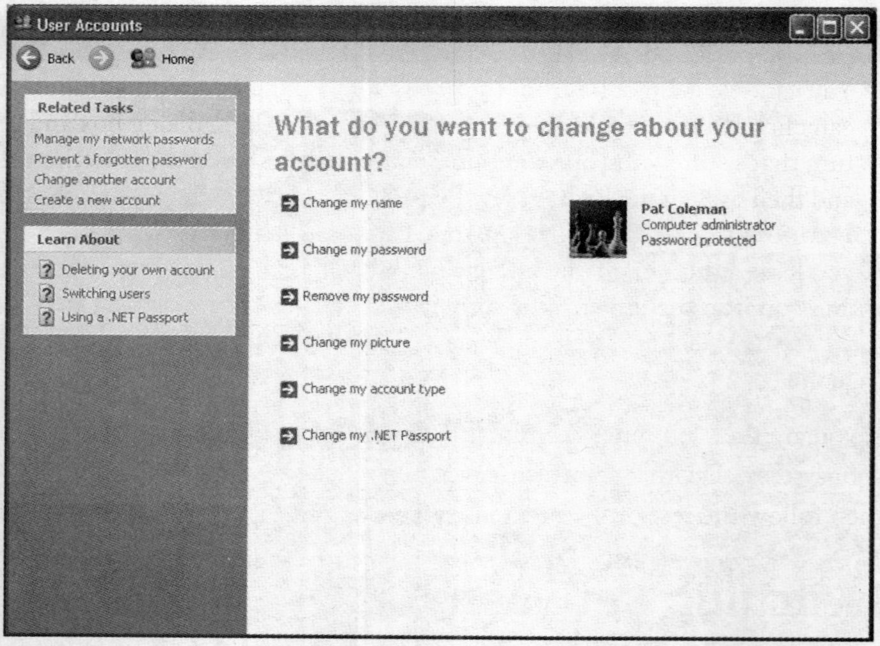

Figure 1-3 Telling Windows XP Professional what you want to change.

4. **Open the Pick A New Picture For Your Account screen, which is shown in Figure 1-4.**

   Click the Change My Picture link.

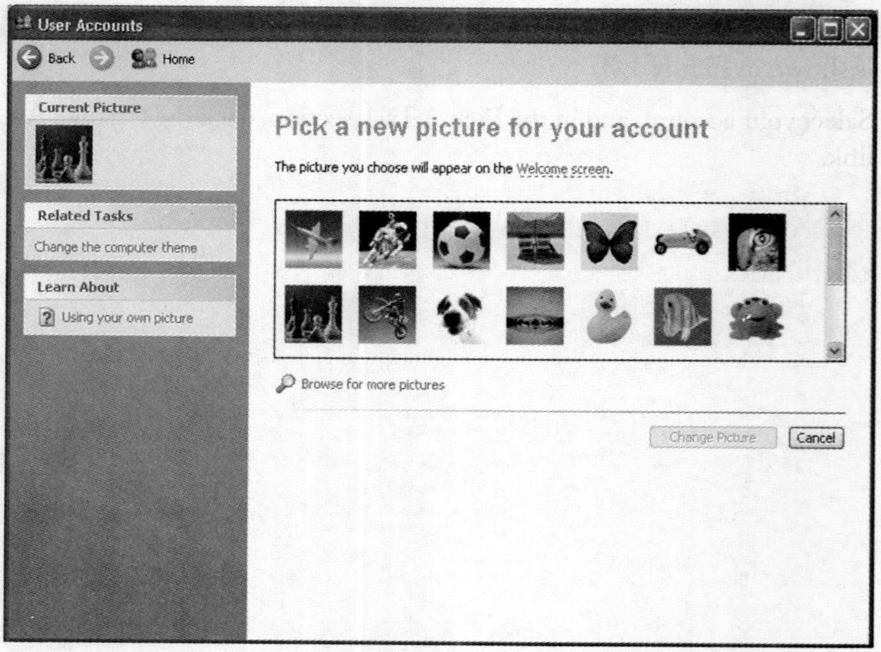

Figure 1-4 Selecting a picture for your account.

5. Select a picture.

You can select a picture from the group that is included with Windows XP, or you can click Browse For More Pictures to open the Open dialog box and select a picture that's stored on your computer. When you've made the selection, click Open, and then back in the Pick A New Picture For Your Account screen, click the Change Picture button. In the What Do You Want To Change About Your Account? screen, you'll see a thumbnail of your new picture. Click the Close button (the button with an X on it in the upper right corner) to close the User Accounts dialog box. Now, when the Welcome screen appears, your new picture will be displayed next to your name.

If you are the Computer Administrator and want to change the picture of a user on your system, click that person's user account name in the User Accounts dialog box, and then follow the rest of the previous steps.

Fast Switching Between Users

If multiple users share a computer, they can use the Fast User Switching feature to open their individual accounts without logging on or off the computer and without closing any applications that the previous user was running. (Fast User Switching is not available on computers that are connected to a network domain.)

To enable Fast User Switching, follow these steps:

1. Open the User Accounts dialog box.

Click the Start button, click Control Panel, and then click User Accounts.

2. Open the Select Logon And Logoff Options screen, which is shown in Figure 1-5.

In the Pick A Task section of the User Accounts dialog box, click the Change The Way Users Log On Or Off link.

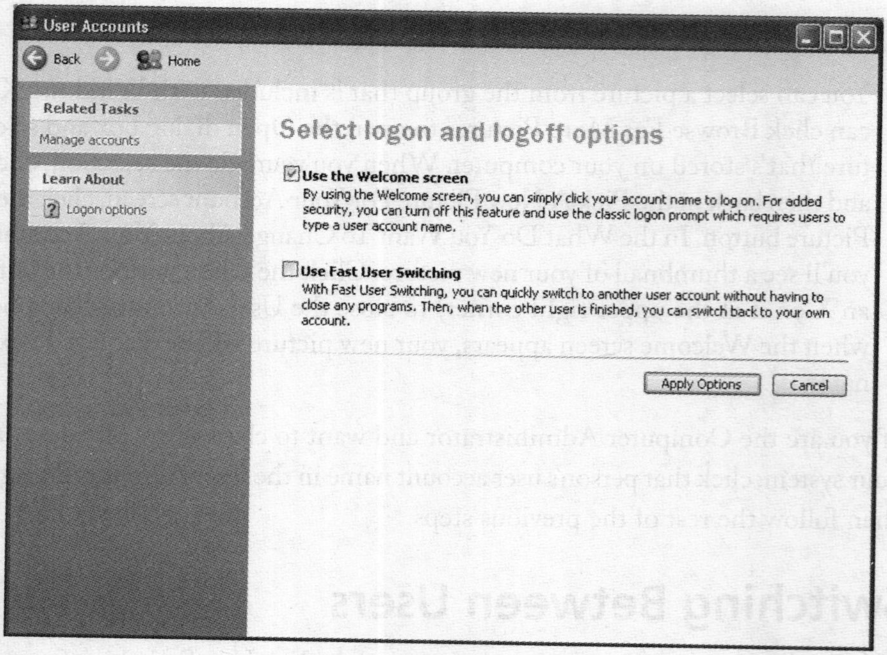

Figure 1-5 Enabling Fast User Switching.

3. **Enable Fast User Switching.**

   Click the Use Fast User Switching check box, and then click Apply Options. Close the User Accounts dialog box, and then close Control Panel.

Now to switch users, click the Start button, click Log Off to open the Log Off Windows dialog box, and click Switch User. In the Welcome screen, click the user account that you want to use, enter your password, and press Enter. When you click the user name, you'll see a message that tells you whether you have any unread e-mail messages and how many programs you are running.

Getting Started

If you've been following along at your computer, you've already located and used the Start button. As you've seen, the Start button is located on the far left end of the taskbar (discussed shortly), and you click it to open a menu from which you can navigate to various resources on your system. Before you click the Start button, though, your desktop looks similar to that in Figure 1-6.

Figure 1-6 The Windows XP Professional desktop.

The desktop in Figure 1-6 is what you'll see the first time you start Windows XP Professional if you, your Computer Administrator, or your computer manufacturer hasn't installed additional applications.

Now, click the Start button, and you'll see something similar to Figure 1-7.

TIP *If you don't see the Start button, move your cursor to the bottom of the screen.*

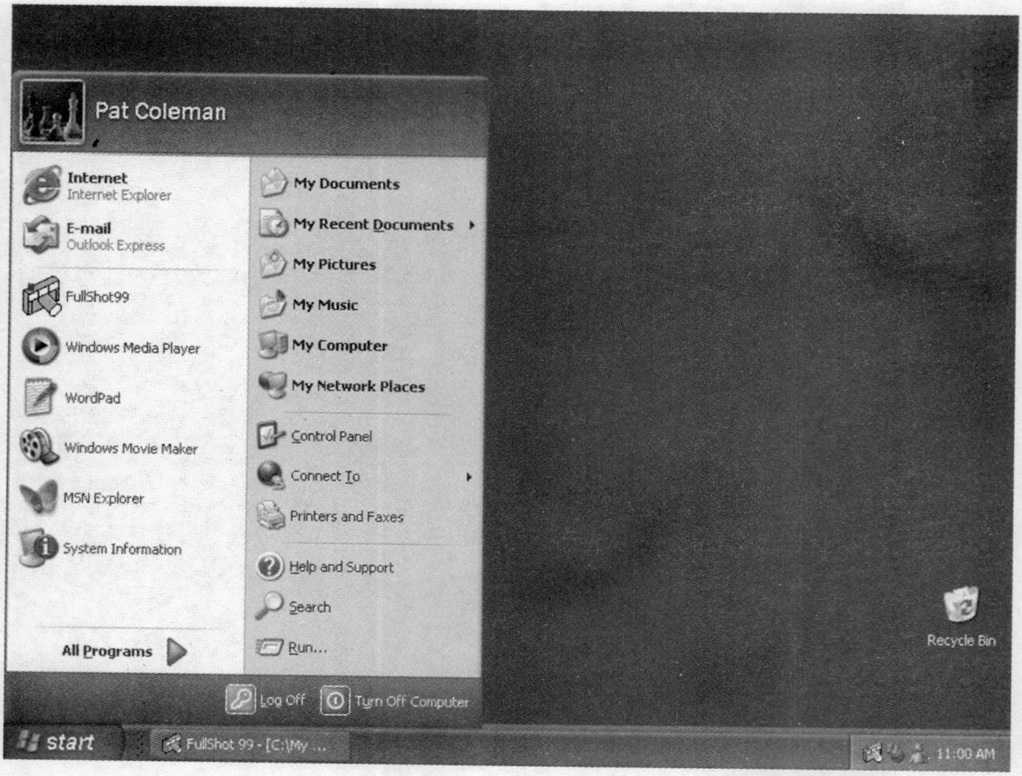

Figure 1-7 The Windows XP Professional desktop and the Start menu.

The Start menu in Windows XP is the primary tool for accessing programs and documents on your computer. Some items on the Start menu are permanent, and others display according to your use of programs. The following describes what you open when you click the items on the Start menu:

- Clicking Internet opens Internet Explorer, the Windows Web browser. Chapter 9 discusses Internet Explorer.
- Clicking E-Mail opens Outlook Express, the e-mail and news reader. Chapter 10 discusses Outlook Express.
- Clicking My Documents opens the My Documents folder, which, in addition to documents, stores your My Music and My Pictures folders. Chapter 2 discusses how to work with files and folders.
- Clicking My Recent Documents opens a list of the documents you have most recently accessed.
- Clicking My Pictures opens your My Pictures folder.

- Clicking My Music opens your My Music folder.
- Clicking My Computer opens the My Computer folder, which displays the contents of your local computer. Figure 1-8 shows a sample My Computer folder.

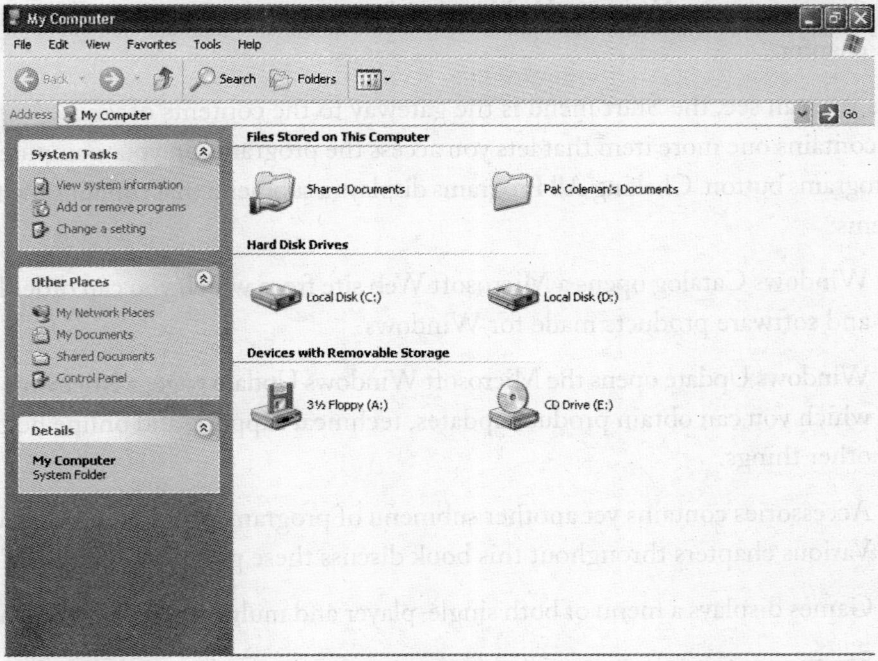

Figure 1-8 A sample My Computer folder.

- If your computer is part of a network, you'll see the My Network Places item. Clicking My Network Places opens the My Network Places folder, which shows your network connections. Chapters 13 and 14 discuss how to set up a network and work on a network.
- Clicking the Control Panel item opens Control Panel, as you saw earlier in this chapter.
- Clicking Connect To opens a submenu that contains two items: My ISP and Show All Connections. If you have a dial-up connection to the Internet, clicking My ISP opens the Dialing My ISP dialog box and dials the phone number for your connection. Clicking Show All Connections opens your Network Connections folder.
- Clicking Printers And Faxes opens your Printers And Faxes folder.
- Clicking Help And Support opens the Windows XP help program, Help And Support Center, which has been radically redesigned and expanded in this version of the operating system. Later in this chapter, we'll look in detail at Help And Support Center.

- Clicking Search opens the Search Results folder, which includes the Search Companion. Later in this chapter, we'll look at how to use this bar.
- Clicking Run opens the Run dialog box, which you can use to access programs, documents, or a Web site. We'll look at how to use the Run dialog box later in this chapter.

As you can see, the Start menu is the gateway to the contents of your computer, but it contains one more item that lets you access the programs on your computer, the All Programs button. Clicking All Programs displays a submenu that contains the following items:

- Windows Catalog opens a Microsoft Web site from which you can order hardware and software products made for Windows.
- Windows Update opens the Microsoft Windows Update page, a Microsoft site from which you can obtain product updates, technical support, and online help, among other things.
- Accessories contains yet another submenu of programs that come with Windows. Various chapters throughout this book discuss these programs.
- Games displays a menu of both single-player and multiplayer games for Windows.
- Startup contains the names of programs you want to use every time you start Windows XP. Initially, this list is empty.
- Internet Explorer opens the Internet Explorer Web browser.
- MSN Explorer starts a service that you can use to connect to the Internet via Microsoft Network, Hotmail, or an existing Internet service provider. Chapter 7 discusses Internet connections.
- Outlook Express opens Outlook Express.
- Remote Assistance starts a program you can use to allow others to connect to your computer and help you with a task. We'll look at this feature in detail later in this chapter.
- Windows Media Player starts a program you can use to play CDs, DVDs, and audio and video files and listen to the radio over the Internet.
- Windows Messenger opens an instant messaging program that you can use to chat and contact others while online.

Right-Clicking in Windows XP Professional

If you used an earlier version of Windows, you're familiar with shortcut menus, but you might have heard them referred to as *context menus* or even *right-click menus*. The reason for the alternate terms is that you can right-click any number of items in Windows XP Professional to display a menu of context-sensitive commands that are appropriate for the item you clicked.

For example, if you right-click most of the items on the Start menu, you'll see a shortcut menu that contains the most common commands for the item. You can right-click almost anywhere in Windows XP Professional and display something useful. In some cases, you won't display a shortcut menu but a What's This? box that you can click to get help on the item you clicked. If you're ever in doubt, just right-click. You can never hurt anything, and worst case, you'll get nothing.

If you're still not a believer in the virtues of right-clicking, consider this example which shows how it can save you time and effort. Suppose you want to open Windows Explorer, the program you use to manage your files and folders. You can do so in the following ways:

- Click the Start button, click All Programs, click Accessories to open the Accessories menu, and then click Windows Explorer.
- Right-click the Start button, and click Explore.

No contest which is quicker, right?

NOTE *You'll get a good look at how to use Windows Explorer in the next chapter.*

Searching and Finding

A feature that is new in Windows XP is Explorer bars. You'll see them primarily in Internet Explorer (discussed in Chapter 9), but you'll find them in other places as well. When you click Search on the Start menu, you open the Search Results folder, and as you can see in Figure 1-9, the Search Companion bar is in the pane on the left.

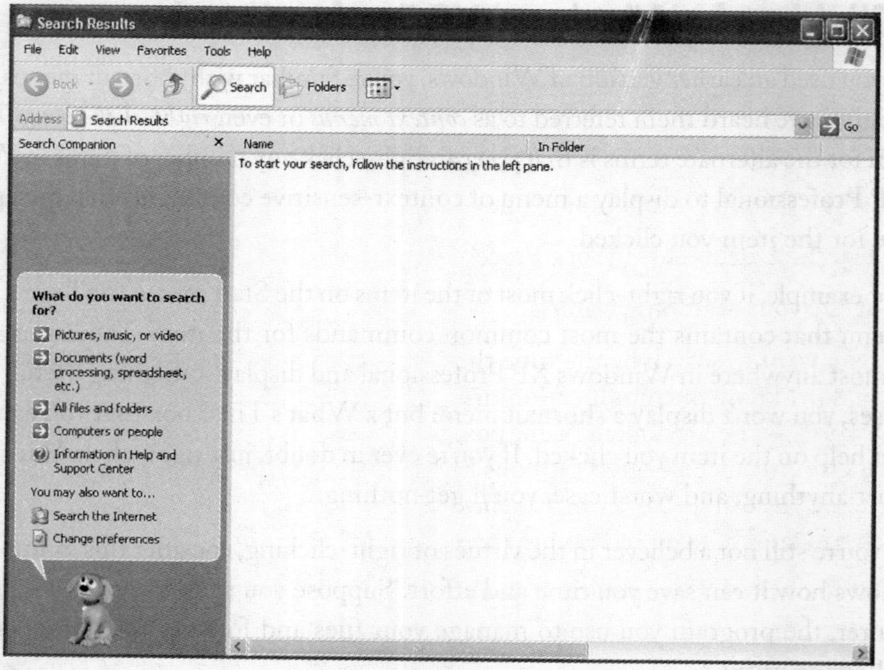

Figure 1-9 The Search Results folder includes the Search Companion bar.

You can use the Search Companion to look for files on your local computer or network, computers or people, a topic in Help And Support Center, or resources on the Internet (if you are connected to the Internet). Before getting into how you use the Search Companion, though, we need to take a look at what you can do to increase the speed at which the Search Companion retrieves results from your local computer.

Indexing Service extracts information from documents, document properties, and other resources and then creates an index. Searching this index is much faster than searching the documents and properties themselves. This feature is similar to the way that help files have traditionally worked in Windows. You might have noticed that often before you use a particular section of Help for the first time, you see a message that it has to be indexed first. This usually occurs very quickly. Thereafter, when you are searching the help files, the search service looks in the index rather than searching all the text in Help.

Indexing Service is not enabled by default. To enable it in Windows XP, in the Search Companion bar click the Change Preferences link. Then, in the next Search Companion bar, click the With Indexing Service (For Faster Local Searches) link. In the next Search Companion bar, click the Yes, Enable Indexing Service link, and click OK.

Back in the How Do You Want To Use Search Companion? bar, you can customize the Search Companion in some other ways. Click a link to change that behavior.

Now, let's do a search to see how the Search Companion works. Let's search for a document on your local computer. Follow these steps:

1. **Tell the Search Companion what you want to search for.**

   Click the Documents (Word Processing, Spreadsheet, Etc.) link.

2. **Specify your searching criteria.**

   If you want to search by the time the file was modified, click an option button. If you don't know the modification time, leave Don't Remember selected. In the All Or Part OfThe Document Name box, enter all or part of the document's name. Click the Use Advanced Search Options link to display more options for specifying the criteria. You can specify a word or phrase in a document, the drive to search and which drive to search if you have more than one drive.

3. **Tell the Search Companion to look for your document.**

   Click the Search button.

The results of your search are displayed in the pane on the right in the Search Results window.

TIP *Click the Back button in any of the Search Companion bars to return to the bar you were previously viewing.*

Getting Help

When you click the Start button and then click Help And Support, you'll see immediately that Help in Windows XP is entirely different from Help in previous versions of Windows. Figure 1-10 shows the home page of Help And Support Center, with which you can search the help files for a topic, connect directly to a Microsoft support professional if your license agreement permits it, contact a knowledgeable office colleague or friend who can then connect and see exactly what's on your computer screen, search the Microsoft Product Support Services online database for an article that deals with your topic, and much more.

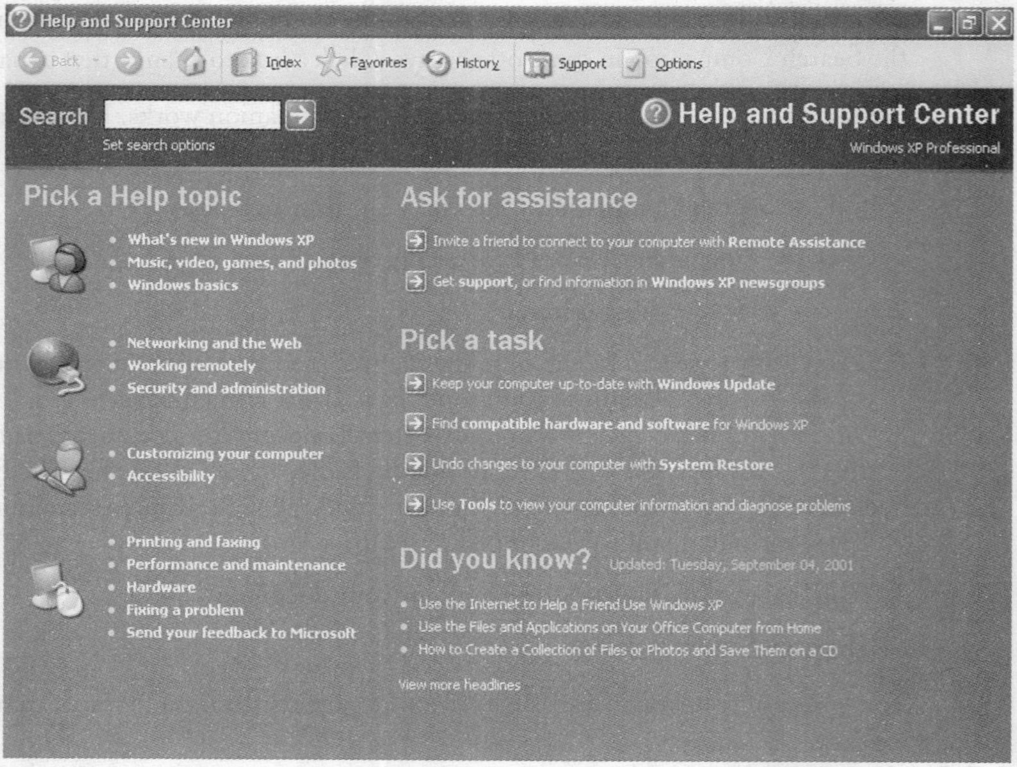

Figure 1-10 Help And Support Center in Windows XP Professional.

This section gives you an overview of the rich feature set in Help And Support Center, and we'll start by examining the buttons on the Standard toolbar, from left to right:

- Clicking the Back and the Forward buttons display the previous or next page you were viewing, as is the case in any window that displays these buttons.
- Clicking the Home button at any time when Help And Support Center is open displays the home page shown in Figure 1-10.
- Clicking Index opens the window shown in Figure 1-11, which will look familiar to users of previous versions of Windows. Enter a search term in the Type In The Keyword To Find box, and the list moves to the alphabetic area that contains the keyword. Double-click a topic to display its contents in the pane on the right.

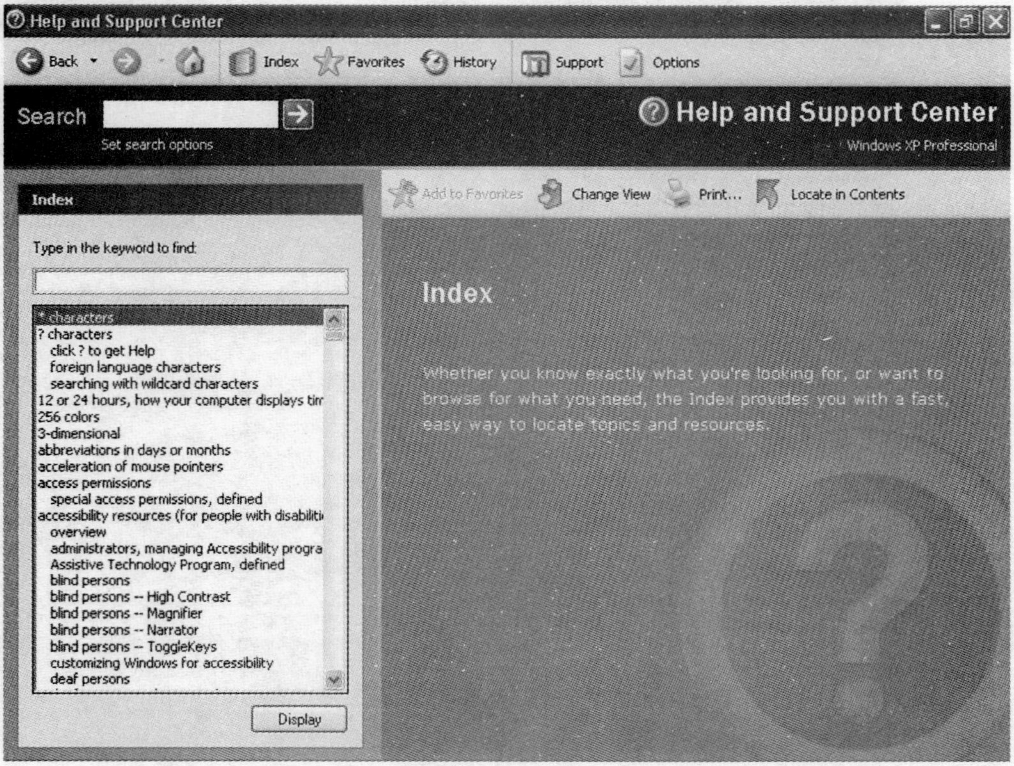

Figure 1-11 Searching the Index in Help And Support Center.

- Clicking Favorites opens the Favorites bar in a pane on the left of the window, which displays any help topics you've added to this list. The Favorites list is a handy device with which you can quickly access a topic rather than searching again for it. Once a topic is on the Favorites list, all you need to do to open it is to click it. We'll look at how you add a topic to the Favorites list later in this section.
- Clicking History displays the History bar, which shows a list of the items you most recently opened. Figure 1-12 shows a sample History bar.

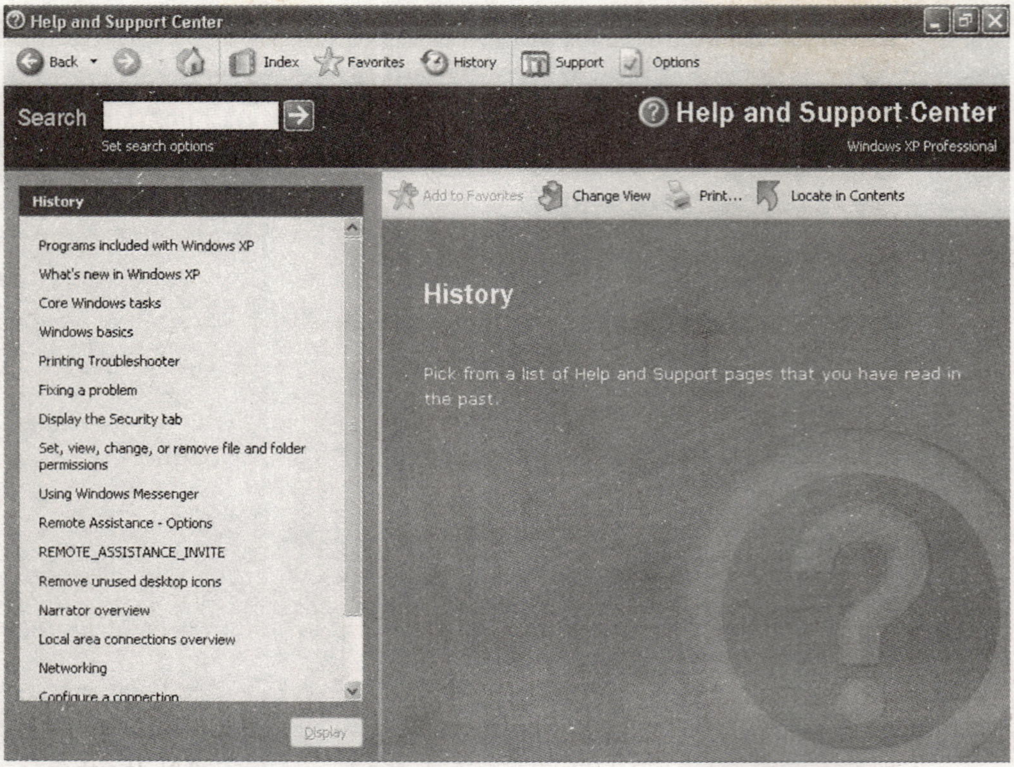

Figure 1-12 The History bar.

- Clicking Support displays a screen that describes the various ways you can get online and personal support for Windows XP.
- Clicking Options opens a screen that you can use to define settings and configure Help And Support Center.

Accessing Help Topics

The Help And Support Center home page is divided into four sections:

- Pick A Help Topic
- Ask For Assistance
- Pick A Task
- Did You Know?

Pick A Help Topic lists categories of topics. Click a category to display its contents in a pane on the right. To add a topic to your Favorites bar, click Add To Favorites. You'll then see a message box that tells you the page will be added to the list. Click OK to continue.

Getting Online Help

You can get online help and support in the following forms:

- Using the items in the Ask For Assistance section, you can contact a colleague or friend who can then access your computer directly if you are connected to the Internet. You can also contact a support professional if your license agreement allows it, and you can access Windows XP newsgroups.
- Using the items in the Did You Know? section, you can access Web sites that provide information about the topics listed. If you are connected to the Internet, simply click an item to go to that site. The items in this section change from time to time.

Let's look in detail at how to get remote assistance from a friend or colleague. To use this feature, both you and the other person must be running Windows XP, and both must be connected to the Internet or connected to the same LAN. If either one of you is behind a firewall, check with your network administrator for further instructions.

NOTE *A* firewall *is a device (it can be either hardware or software or both) that establishes a barrier that controls the traffic between a couple of networks, usually a private LAN and the Internet.*

For example, let's suppose you need a colleague's help walking through the steps to complete a task. Follow these steps to get his remote assistance:

1. Start Remote Assistance, which is shown in Figure 1-13.

In the Help And Support Center home page, click the Invite A Friend To Connect To Your Computer With Remote Assistance link in the Ask For Assistance section.

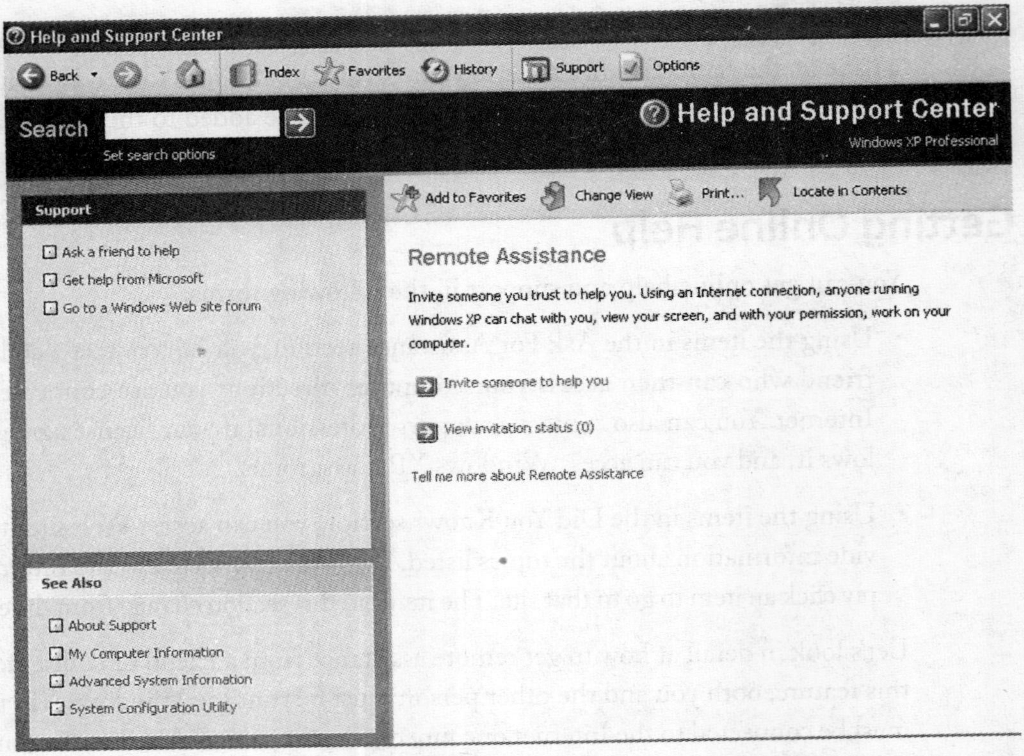

Figure 1-13 Starting Remote Assistance.

2. **Invite someone to help you with the task.**

   Click the Invite Someone To Help You link, and then select how you want the invitation to be sent. You can use Windows Messenger to extend the invitation, or you can send the person an e-mail message. In this example, we'll send an e-mail message, so in the Type An E-Mail Address box, enter the person's e-mail address, as shown in Figure 1-14, and click the Invite This Person link.

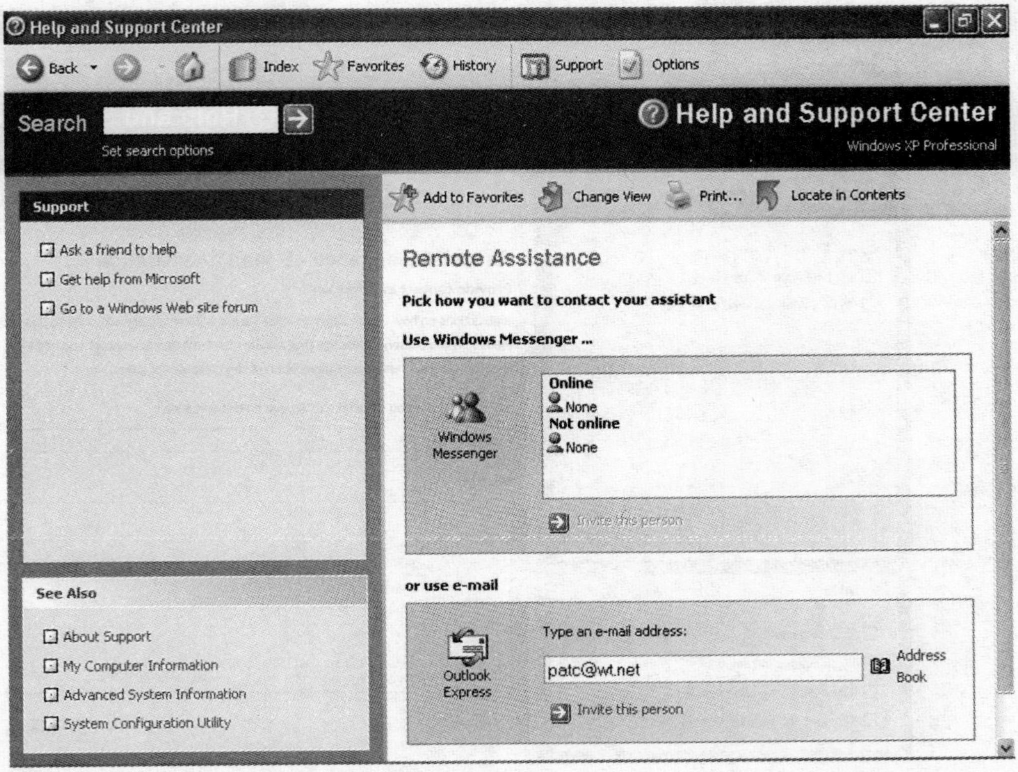

Figure 1-14 Sending an invitation via e-mail.

3. Complete the invitation.

In the next step, which is shown in Figure 1-15, provide information about what you need help with in the Message box, and then click Continue.

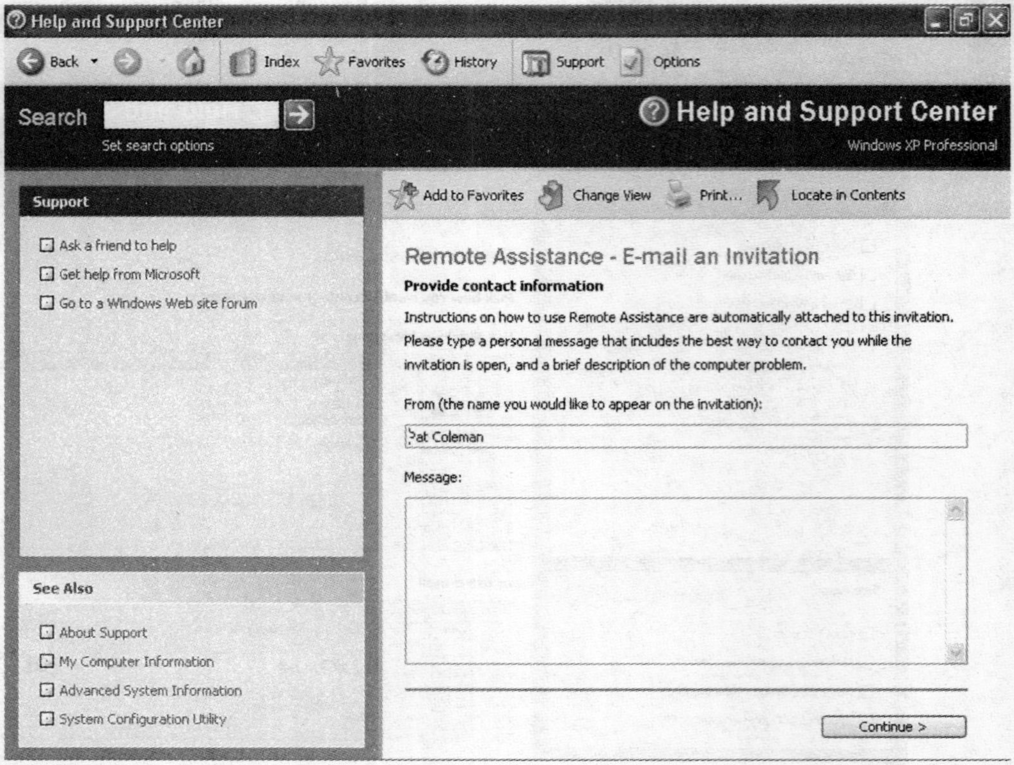

Figure 1-15 Completing the invitation.

4. Secure your invitation.

In the next screen, which is shown in Figure 1-16, click the Set The Invitation To Expire drop-down list boxes to specify a time by which you want the recipient to respond. Now if you want to require a password for security purposes, leave the Require The Recipient To Use A Password check box checked. Enter a password in the Type Password box, and enter it again in the Confirm Password box. As suggested, don't use your network or logon password or include the password in the message. Any unauthorized person that obtains this password may be able to connect to your computer. Inform your recipient of the password in a separate e-mail message, by phone, or in some other way. All the guidelines for creating good passwords discussed earlier in this chapter apply. When you've finished setting security, click Send Invitation.

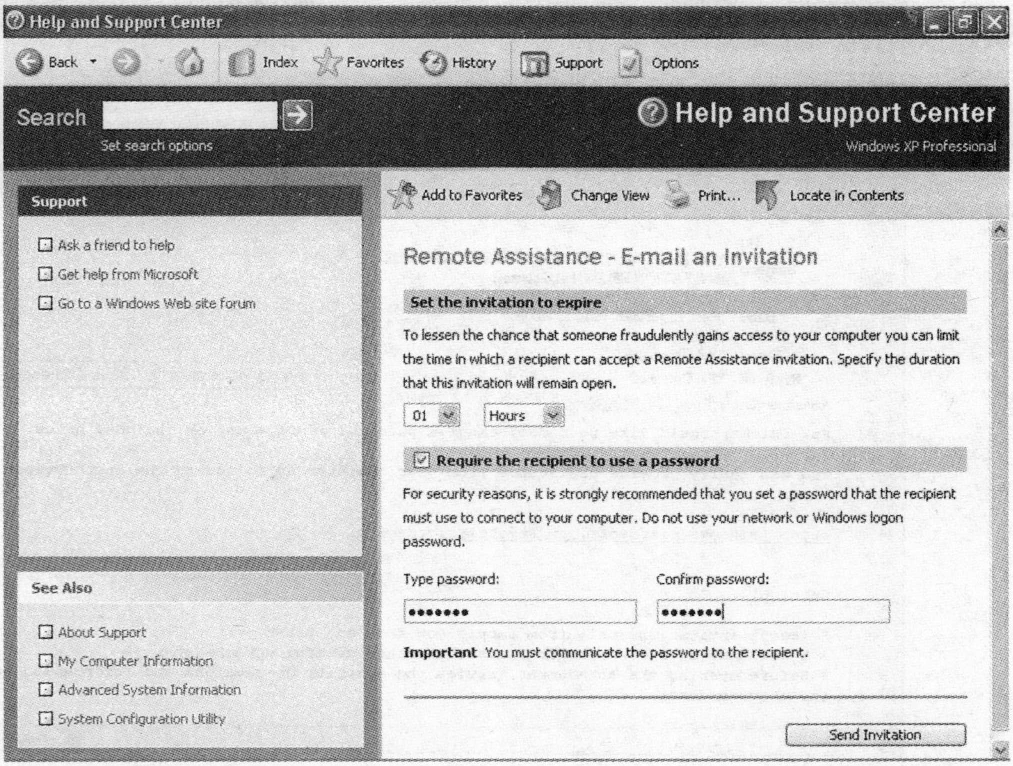

Figure 1-16 Setting invitation security.

Your request for assistance will now be sent, and if your invitation is accepted, you'll be notified that the recipient is ready to connect to your computer. Your request will include the instructions your recipient will need to connect to your computer. Figure 1-17 shows a typical message open in the recipient's mailbox.

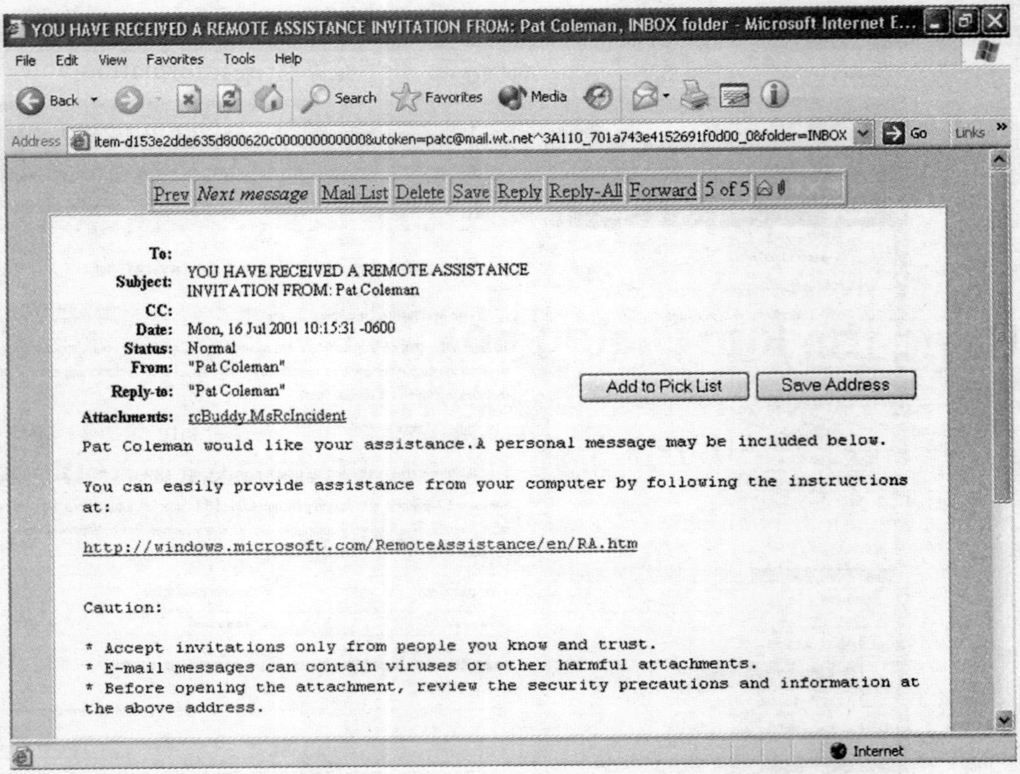

Figure 1-17 A Remote Assistance invitation.

When the recipient clicks the link in the body of the message, he will see the instructions to follow for connecting to your computer. Once you are both connected, you will see a chat box on the desktop, and your assistant sees your screen on his computer. He can chat with you, take a look at your work, and, with your permission, control your computer.

NOTE *Chapter 7 discusses how to connect to the Internet, and Chapter 10 deals with sending and receiving e-mail.*

Getting Help with a Task

The Pick A Task section in the Help And Support Center home page contains links to information that will help you take care of some specific tasks on your computer, including:

- How to use Windows Update
- How to find hardware and software that are compatible with Windows XP

- How to use System Restore
- How to use the Windows XP tools to find system information and diagnose problems

Click a link to display a screen that provides this information. In some cases, you'll need to be connected to the Internet because the link opens a page at the Microsoft Web site.

Using the Run Dialog Box

In Windows XP Professional, there's almost always more than one way to do something—start a program, open a document, go to an Internet site, and so on. Although the Run dialog box might not necessarily be your first choice, it is one of the many tools at your disposal for accessing programs, documents, folders, and Internet sites. Click the Start button, and then click Run to open the Run dialog box, as shown in Figure 1-18.

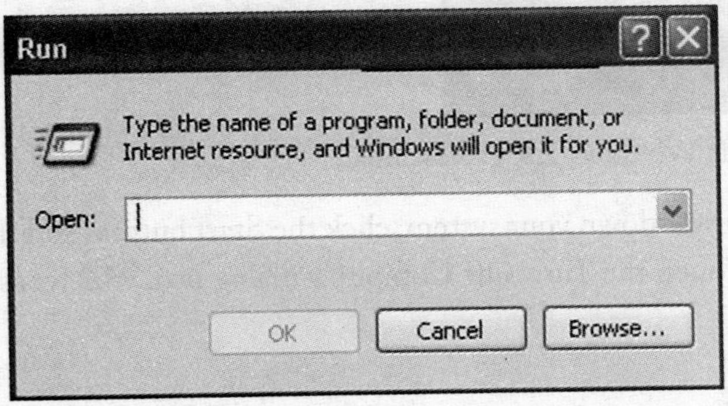

Figure 1-18 The Run dialog box.

To open a resource, you can type its name in the Open box or you can click Browse to look for it. When you've entered the name, press Enter or click OK.

Logging Off and Shutting Down

One of the most important features of Windows XP Professional is security. But, of course, you have to use security features properly in order to protect your system and the valuable information that you store on it. For example, suppose you're working on a document that concerns an employee's compensation. It's in a folder on your network drive that you have access to, and it's open on your screen. You're not quite finished with it, but it's almost noon, and somebody drops by to see if you're interested in going to lunch. You close the document, grab your coat, and take off.

Now, you are still logged on to your computer and the network, and anybody who cares to can sit down at your computer and open that document or any others to which you have access. But if you log off before you leave for lunch, somebody has to know your user name and password to get back onto your system and mess with your files. To log off, click the Start button, and then click Log Off to open the Log Off Windows dialog box, as shown in Figure 1-19. When you click Log Off, you end your current session and leave the computer running.

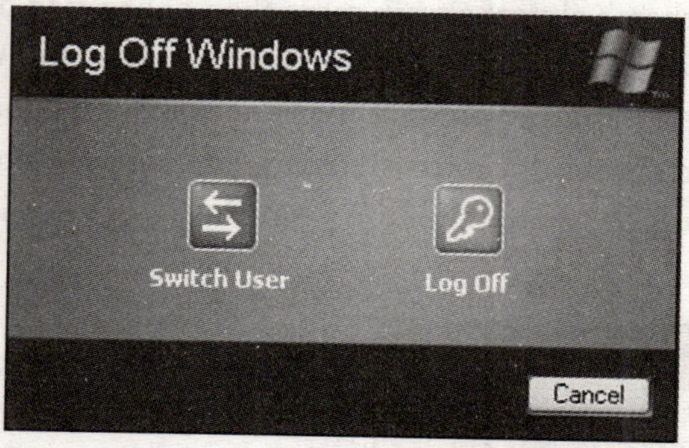

Figure 1-19 Logging off Windows XP Professional.

When you're ready to power down your system, click the Start button, and then click Turn Off Computer to open the Turn Off Computer dialog box, which is shown in Figure 1-20.

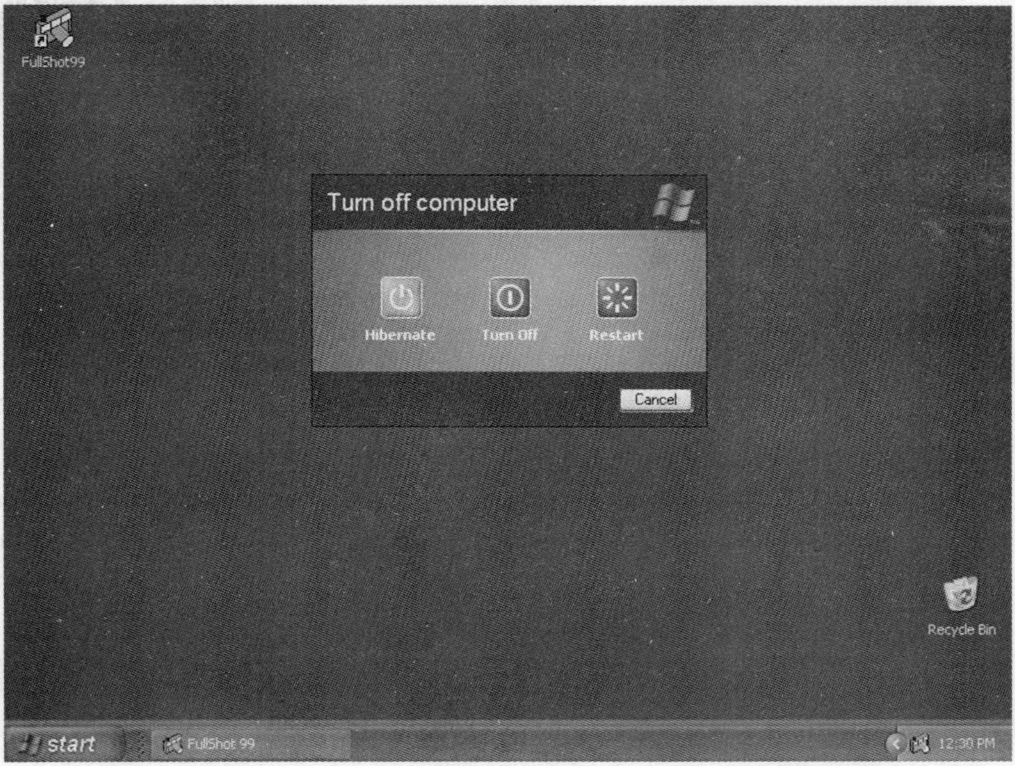

Figure 1-20 The Turn Off Computer dialog box.

In addition to using this dialog box to power down your computer, you have two other options:

- Clicking Hibernate shuts down your computer after saving everything in memory to your hard drive. The computer is completely off when in Hibernation mode.
- Clicking Restart restarts the system. You choose Restart when you dual-boot Windows XP and another operating system and want to close Windows XP and boot the other system.

You'll find out soon enough, if you haven't already, that it's to your advantage to shut the system down properly. If you don't, the next time you start up, you'll have to wait while Windows XP Professional does some file checking and some maintenance, and you may even lose some data or some configuration settings.

TIP *A common misconception is that you're in less danger of losing data on a computer if you just keep it running all the time. Although this was true in the past, today's machines are built so that you risk nothing by powering them down when you're ready for bed or ready to leave the office. You may also find that your office is a lot more comfortable in the morning if your computers were shut down the night before. Computers generate a substantial amount of heat, and if you live in a hot climate, the longer they are up and running, the more you're tempted to crank down the thermostat on your AC.*

Using the Taskbar

The taskbar is the toolbar at the bottom of the desktop, and it includes the *notification area* (the portion on the far right). Figure 1-21 shows the taskbar on one of our systems. Your taskbar should look similar, minus the FullShot99 icon, which is the program we use to create the illustrations in this book. When you have a program open, you'll see an icon for it on the taskbar.

Figure 1-21 The taskbar in Windows XP Professional.

Using the Notification Area

If you are connected to a corporate network that has upgraded from Windows NT to Windows XP, you'll probably hear the notification area referred to as the *system tray,* and in some other earlier versions of Windows it was called the *status area.* Regardless of what it's called, by default, the notification area contains the time. If you hover the mouse cursor over the time, the current date is displayed.

You may also see icons for other currently running services on your system, such as Task Scheduler. If your computer is connected to a LAN, you may see a little computer icon that indicates the network is up and running, and when you connect to the Internet, you may see another computer icon for that connection. If you hover the mouse over either of these icons, you'll see a description that shows the speed and other aspects of the connection. To disconnect from the Internet, right-click its icon and choose Disconnect from the shortcut menu. To disable your network connection, right-click its icon and then choose Disable from the shortcut menu.

To change the date or time, double-click the time to open the Date And Time Properties dialog box. Chapter 4 discusses this in detail.

Hiding and Displaying the Taskbar

Unless the taskbar is locked (more on this shortly), you can completely hide the taskbar, always display it, or choose to hide it unless you move the mouse cursor over it. To hide the taskbar completely, click its top edge and then drag the top edge down to the bottom edge. To display it once again, drag the visible edge upward.

To specify how and when the taskbar is displayed, right-click an empty area of the taskbar and choose Properties from the shortcut menu to open the Taskbar And Start Menu Properties dialog box, as shown in Figure 1-22.

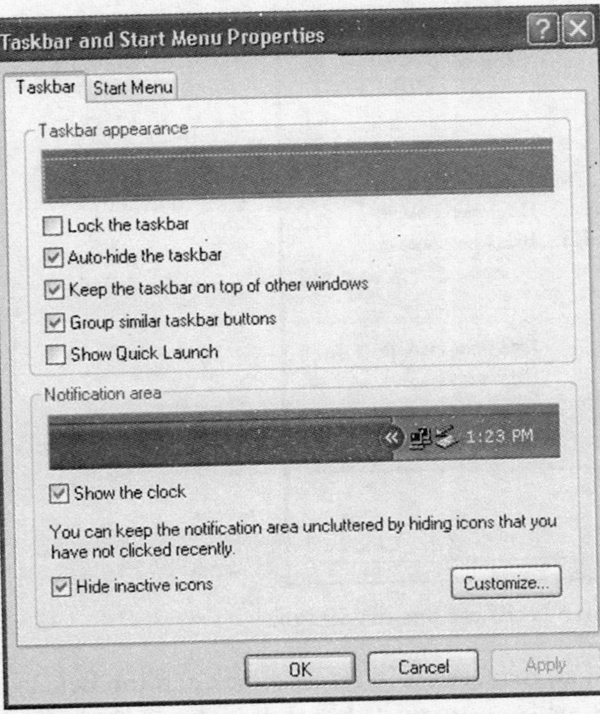

Figure 1-22 The Taskbar And Start Menu Properties dialog box open at the Taskbar tab.

If you want the taskbar visible at all times, even when you are working in an application program and have it maximized, click the Keep The Taskbar On Top Of Other Windows check box only. If you want the taskbar hidden unless you move the mouse cursor over it, click both the Keep The Taskbar On Top Of Other Windows check box and the Auto-Hide The Taskbar check box.

If you want, you can move the taskbar by clicking it in an empty area and dragging it. To prevent the taskbar from being moved to a new location on the desktop, click the Lock The Taskbar check box. If you prefer not to display the time in the notification area, clear the Show The Clock check box.

By default, Windows XP clears icons from the notification area when they are inactive. If you prefer to always display icons regardless of whether they are active, clear the Hide Inactive Icons check box. If you want to hide or display only certain icons, click the Customize button to open the Customize Notifications dialog box, which is shown in Figure 1-23.

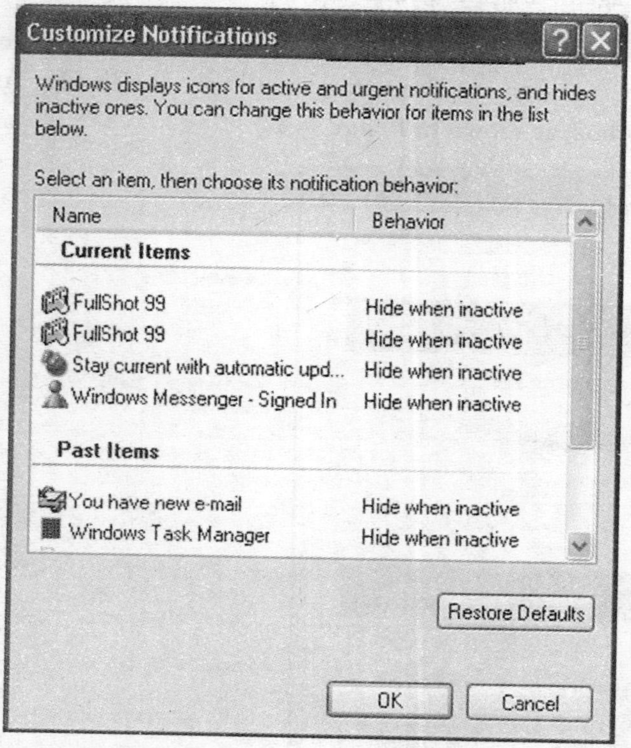

Figure 1-23 The Customize Notifications dialog box.

To specify the behavior of an item, select it. Its description in the Behavior column becomes a drop-down list, which you can click and then choose from the following:

- Hide When Inactive
- Always Hide
- Always Show

Choose a behavior, and then click OK. To restore the default behaviors, click the Restore Defaults button.

Using the Recycle Bin

The one icon you will always see on your desktop is the Recycle Bin. When you delete a file, a folder, or a program in Windows XP Professional, it's not really removed from your hard drive—it goes to the Recycle Bin. The Recycle Bin is a safety net, because, up to a point, you can retrieve items from it. By default, the Recycle Bin is set to exist on 10 percent of each drive on your system. When the Recycle Bin is full, the files least recently sent to it are automatically deleted to make room for other files. Until this point or until you manually empty the Recycle Bin, you can retrieve a file or folder.

WARNING *When you delete files from floppy disks, Zip disks, and network drives, they are immediately deleted. They don't go to the Recycle Bin first.*

To retrieve a file or folder from the Recycle Bin, follow these steps:

1. **Open the Recycle Bin folder.**

   Click the Recycle Bin icon on the desktop. You'll see something similar to Figure 1-24.

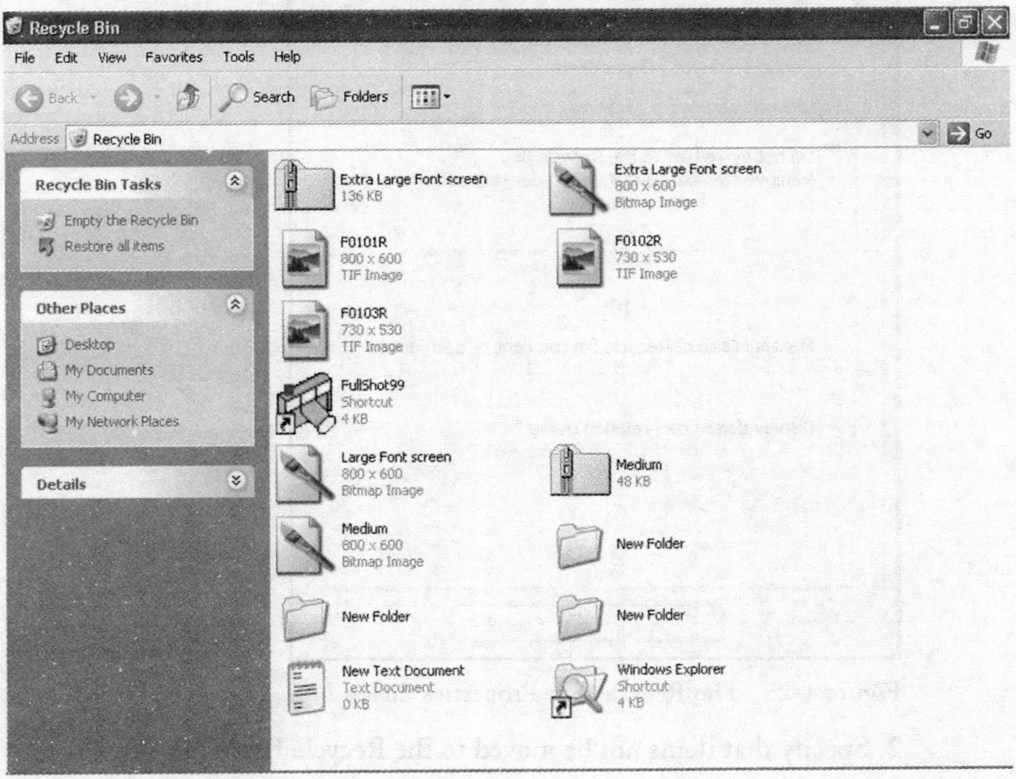

Figure 1-24 The Recycle Bin folder.

2. **Retrieve the file or folder.**

   Select the file or folder you want to retrieve, and then click Restore This Item in the Recycle Bin Tasks bar to send it back to its original location.

To restore all items in the Recycle Bin folder to their original locations, click Restore All Items in the Recycle Bin Tasks bar. To empty the Recycle Bin manually, click Empty The Recycle Bin in the Recycle Bin Tasks bar. To delete a single item from the Recycle Bin folder, right-click it and then choose Delete from the shortcut menu.

If you want to bypass the Recycle Bin and remove files and folders immediately when you choose or press Delete, follow these steps:

1. **Open the Recycle Bin Properties dialog box, which is shown in Figure 1-25.**

   Right-click the Recycle Bin icon on the desktop, and choose Properties from the shortcut menu.

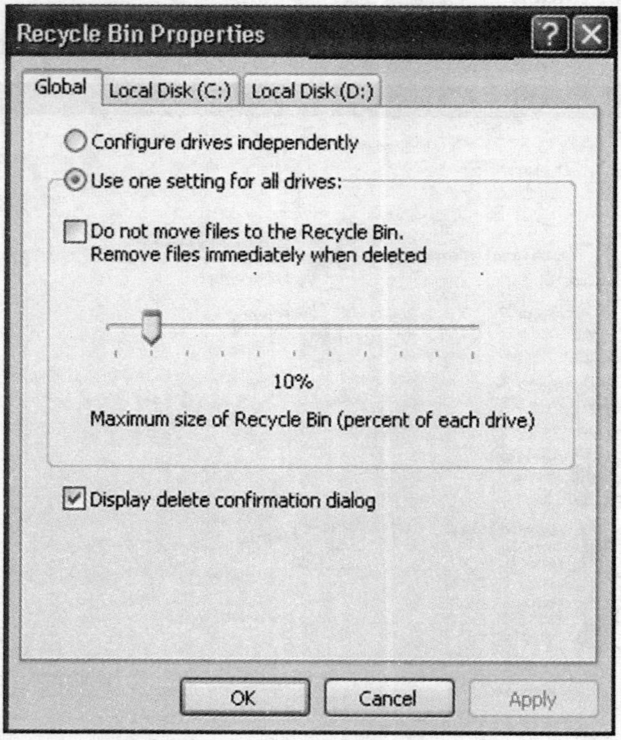

Figure 1-25 The Recycle Bin Properties dialog box.

2. **Specify that items not be moved to the Recycle Bin.**

   Click the Global tab, and then click the Do Not Move Files To The Recycle Bin check box.

3. Close the Recycle Bin Properties dialog box.

Click OK.

To change the size of the Recycle Bin, move the slider on the Global tab of the Recycle Bin Properties dialog box. If you have more than one hard drive and want to specify a size for the Recycle Bin for each drive, click the Configure Drives Independently option button, and then click the tab that corresponds to each drive and set the percentage of each drive by moving the slider bar.

Using and Creating Shortcuts

Because shortcuts have been mentioned several times in this chapter, you might have the impression that shortcuts are handy devices, and they are indeed. You can create a shortcut on the desktop to just about anything you want to access easily and frequently—Web sites, files, folders, programs, Windows Explorer, and so on. Sometimes when you install an application, the application's setup program even places a shortcut to the application on the desktop.

To create a shortcut for an item that you can see, follow these steps:

1. Open the All Programs menu (or any other menu).

Click the Start button, and then click All Programs.

2. Create the shortcut.

Select the item, and drag it to the desktop. Or right-click the item, and if the shortcut menu contains a Show On Desktop item, click that item to create the shortcut on the desktop.

To create a shortcut for an item that you can't see, follow these steps:

1. Start the Create Shortcut Wizard, which is shown in Figure 1-26.

Right-click an empty area of the desktop, choose New from the shortcut menu, and then click Shortcut. You'll see an icon on the desktop labeled New Shortcut, and the Create Shortcut Wizard will start.

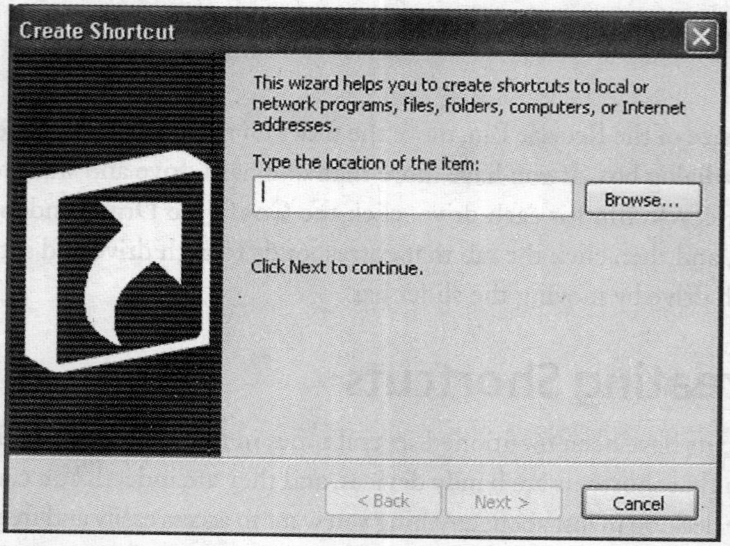

Figure 1-26 The Create Shortcut Wizard.

2. **Identify the item.**

   In the Type The Location Of The Item box, enter the pathname for the item, or click Browse to find it.

3. **Give the item a name.**

   Click Next to open the Select A Title For The Program screen, and in the Type A Name For This Shortcut box, enter a name.

4. **Close the wizard.**

   Click Finish to close the wizard and create the shortcut on the desktop.

To delete a shortcut, you can drag it to the Recycle Bin or right-click it and choose Delete from the shortcut menu. To rename a shortcut, right-click it, choose Rename from the shortcut menu, type the new name, and then click outside the name box.

TIP *When you delete a shortcut, you delete only the representation of the item on the desktop, not the item itself.*

You can change the icons associated with some shortcuts. Follow these steps:

1. Open the Properties dialog box for the icon, which is shown in Figure 1-27.

Right-click the icon, and choose Properties from the shortcut menu.

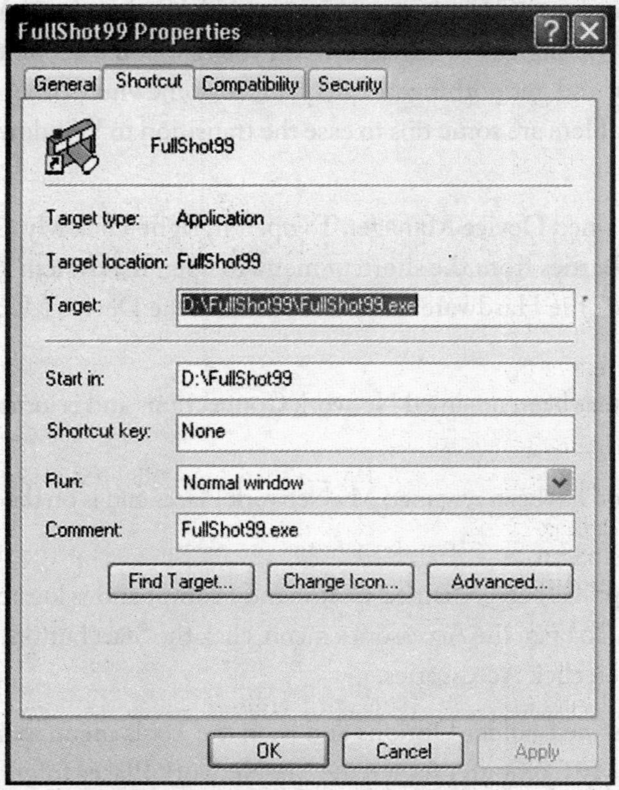

Figure 1-27 The Properties dialog box.

2. Open the Change Icon dialog box.

Click the Change Icon button.

3. Select a new icon.

Click a new icon, and then click OK.

NOTE *If you don't see a Change Icon button in the Properties dialog box for an icon, you can't change the icon associated with that item.*

Tips for Users of Previous Versions of Windows

If you've used previous versions of Windows—Windows NT Workstation 4, Windows 95/98—you might be slightly bewildered when you take some action that's just about second nature and get nothing or find yourself somewhere other than where you wanted to be. Here are some tips to ease the transition to Windows XP Professional:

- Devices has been renamed Device Manager. To open it, right-click My Computer and choose Properties from the shortcut menu to open the System Properties dialog box. Click the Hardware tab, and then click the Device Manager button.
- Dial-Up Networking has been renamed Network Connections and is located in Control Panel.
- Network Neighborhood has been renamed My Network Places and is on the Start menu.
- The MS-DOS prompt has been renamed Command Prompt and is located on the Accessories menu. To open the Accessories menu, click the Start button, click All Programs, and then click Accessories.
- Options has been renamed Folder Options and is on the Tools menu in many places, including the My Computer folder, the My Network Places folder, and Control Panel.
- Power Management has been renamed Power Options and is located in Control Panel.
- By default, Control Panel opens in Category view. If you prefer the Classic view, click Switch To Classic View in the Control Panel bar.

Summary

This chapter has given you a brisk tour of what you see when you start up Windows XP Professional. Now you can log on and off successfully, create a strong password, access the items on the Start menu, use the taskbar to navigate quickly and easily among running programs, and use, create, and remove shortcuts, as well as change the icon associated with shortcuts.

Chapter 2

WORKING WITH FILES AND FOLDERS

Featuring:

- Organizing Documents in Windows Explorer
- Setting File and Folder Permissions
- Understanding the Shared Documents Folder
- Working with Offline Files
- Specifying Folder Options
- Associating Files and Programs
- Working with Floppy Disks
- Working with Digital Camera Files

We've always been rather fascinated with people's work styles—how they decorate their offices, how they organize their files, what they keep on the top of their desks, what kinds of notes are posted on their computer monitors, and so on. It seems to us that all these things tell you a lot about how a person thinks and works. But does a messy office indicate a fuzzy head? Not necessarily. Some of the most efficient business people we know need a guide and a map to find their briefcase when they shut down for the day.

How you organize your office, though, is probably a pretty good indication of how you organize the information you keep on your computer. Our main point here is that it doesn't matter too much what kind of system you impose as long as you have a system that lets you get at stuff easily and quickly. Not knowing where you've saved a document and using the Search Companion every time you want to work on something is a system, but it's not a system that lets you find stuff easily and quickly. Understanding Windows Explorer and knowing how to use it to organize your programs and documents is an efficient system for quickly and easily retrieving what you need.

And while we're on our soapbox here, we're continually amazed at the number of people who work all day every day on their computer and don't know a thing about Windows Explorer. If you're a busy professional, you'll do yourself a huge favor by taking a few minutes to get on speaking terms with Explorer. In fact, this information alone will probably save you in time and aggravation many times the cost of this book.

This chapter starts with step-by-step instructions for how to manage your files and folders using Windows Explorer. We'll then take a look at how to compress files, how to use offline files, and how to use the Folder Options dialog box to display the kind of information you want.

NOTE *An important concept in working with files and folders is understanding the file system in Windows XP Professional. Because you need that information when you install this operating system, we've placed it in Chapter 12, "Installing Windows XP Professional."*

Organizing Documents in Windows Explorer

Although Windows Explorer is the underlying mechanism you use to impose a sense of organization on your documents, in Windows XP you will never see a window with the words *Windows Explorer* or *Exploring* in the title bar. One way to open Windows Explorer is to click the Start button, click All Programs, click Accessories, and then click Windows Explorer, which opens your My Documents folder.

You can also right-click any of the following in the Start menu to open an Explorer-like window with that item's folder selected:

- My Pictures
- My Music
- My Computer
- My Network Places

Regardless of how you open Explorer, you can navigate to any file, folder, or drive, but perhaps the best way to start is with the display you see when you right-click My Computer and choose Explore. Figure 2-1 shows this display.

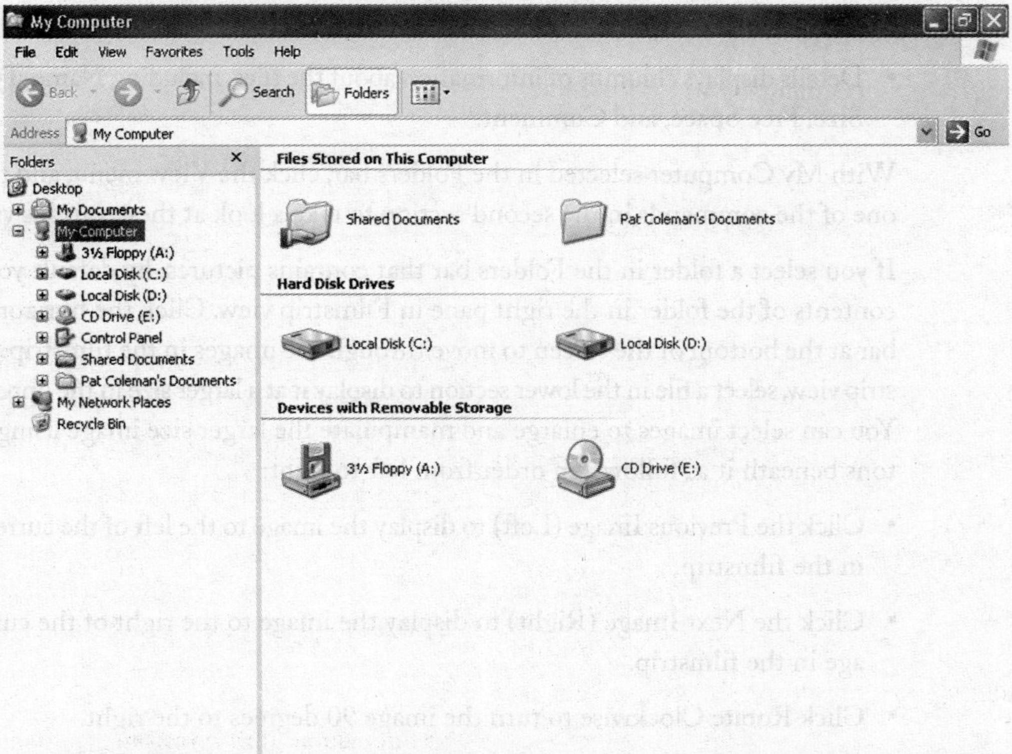

Figure 2-1 The My Computer view of Explorer.

In the Folders bar, select a folder to display its contents in the right pane. Click the plus sign (+) next to an item to display a list of what it contains. In the right pane, double-click a folder to display its subfolders or files. If you can't see all the items in the Folder pane, drag the horizontal scroll bar to the right, or drag the vertical scroll bar up or down.

NOTE *If you use Explorer frequently, you can place a shortcut to it on the desktop. Click the Start button, click All Programs, click Accessories, and then right-click Windows Explorer. From the shortcut menu, click Send To, and then click Desktop (Create Shortcut).*

Viewing Explorer in Various Ways

By default, the My Computer display of Explorer opens in Tiles view, but you can display it in the following ways using commands on the View menu:

- Thumbnails displays small pictures of the file folders.
- Icons displays files as even smaller pictures.

- List displays files in a list that is similar to the list in the Folders bar.
- Details displays columns of information about the files, including Name, Type, Total Size, Free Space, and Comment.

With My Computer selected in the Folders bar, click the View menu, and then click one of the commands in the second section to take a look at these various views.

If you select a folder in the Folders bar that contains pictures, by default you see the contents of the folder in the right pane in Filmstrip view. Click the horizontal scroll bar at the bottom of the screen to move through the images in the filmstrip. In Filmstrip view, select a file in the lower section to display it at a larger size in the upper section. You can select images to enlarge and manipulate the larger size image using the buttons beneath it as follows, in order from left to right:

- Click the Previous Image (Left) to display the image to the left of the current image in the filmstrip.
- Click the Next Image (Right) to display the image to the right of the current image in the filmstrip.
- Click Rotate Clockwise to turn the image 90 degrees to the right.
- Click Rotate Counterclockwise to turn the image 90 degrees to the left.

TIP *Point to a button to display a ScreenTip that tells you what it is.*

When you manipulate images using these buttons, the image is stored in the state in which you last displayed it.

If you are not in Filmstrip view, double-clicking an image file opens the image in Image Preview.

Opening Files and Folders

To open any file or folder in Explorer, simply double-click it. In most cases, it will open in the application in which it was created. To open a file on your network, follow these steps:

1. Navigate to My Network Places.

In the Folders bar, scroll down to My Network Places.

2. Find the file you want to open.

Expand My Network Places, and then click the disk, click the folder, and double-click the filename to open the file.

Creating a Folder

Whether you're working on a standalone machine or on a network, you have a user folder that was created during installation. You'll find that folder in the Documents And Settings folder. Inside your user folder is a My Documents folder. Although you can create a folder just about anywhere in the folder hierarchy that you want, we always suggest for starters that you keep your documents in subfolders of the My Documents folder. And if you are on a corporate network, that may be the only place you have permission to store documents, or your Computer Administrator may have created a folder on a specific drive for you.

We create subfolders for each of our projects in the My Documents folder, and then sometimes we create sub-subfolders and store documents in those. For example, we have a folder in the My Documents folder for this book, and then within that folder we have subfolders for each chapter. In those subfolders, we keep the art files and the document files that we create for each chapter.

You can create a folder from the desktop, from within Explorer, and from within a Windows application.

Creating a Folder on the Desktop

To create a folder on the desktop, follow these steps:

1. Open a shortcut menu.

Right-click an empty area on the desktop, choose New from the shortcut menu, and then click Folder. You'll see a folder icon on the desktop and a box beneath it containing the words *New Folder*.

2. Name the folder.

Type a name for the new folder, and then click outside the box.

Your new folder will be stored in the Desktop subfolder in your user folder. You can leave it there or move it, as you'll see later in this section.

Creating a Folder from Within Explorer

To create a folder inside another folder in Explorer, follow these steps:

1. Locate the parent folder.

Expand a folder or navigate to the folder inside which you want to create a new folder.

2. **Use the commands on the File menu to create the folder.**

   Click the File menu, click New, and then click Folder. You'll see a folder icon in the right pane and a box beside it that contains the words *New Folder,* as shown in Figure 2-2.

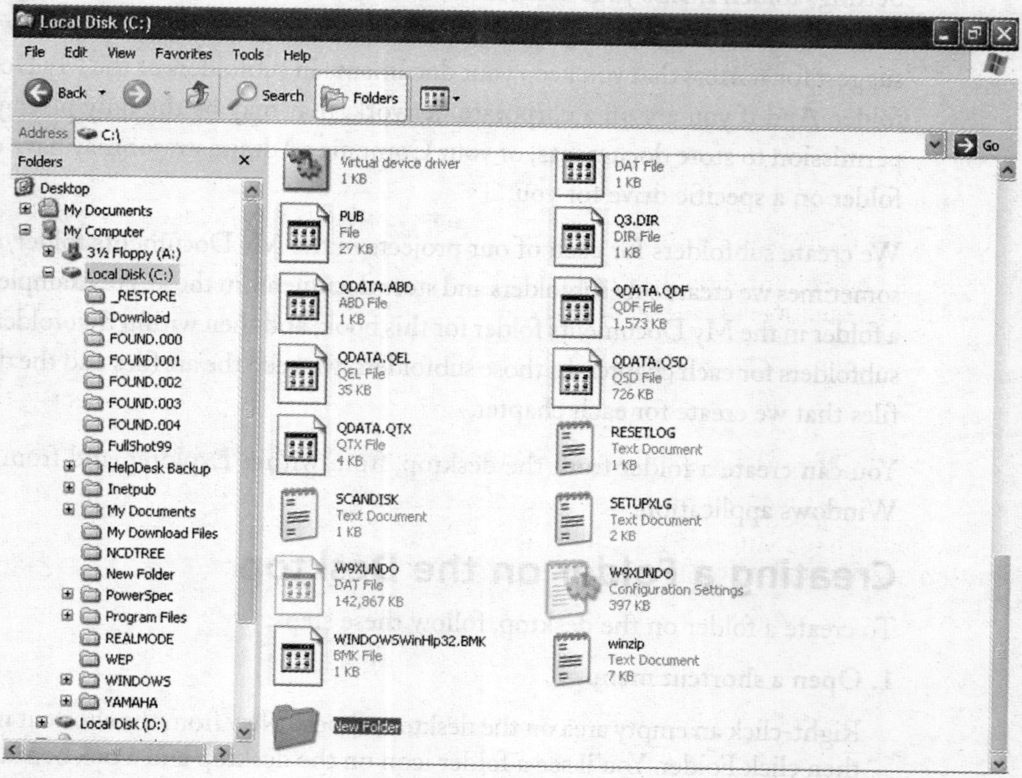

Figure 2-2 Creating a new folder in Explorer.

3. **Give the folder a name.**

   Type a name for the folder, and then click outside the box.

Creating a Folder from Within an Application

This method is often the handiest way to create a folder. Here are the steps for creating a folder in WordPad, an application that is included with Windows XP Professional, but a similar procedure works in most Windows applications:

1. **Open WordPad.**

   Click the Start button, click All Programs, click Accessories, and then click WordPad. Figure 2-3 shows WordPad open with a blank document screen.

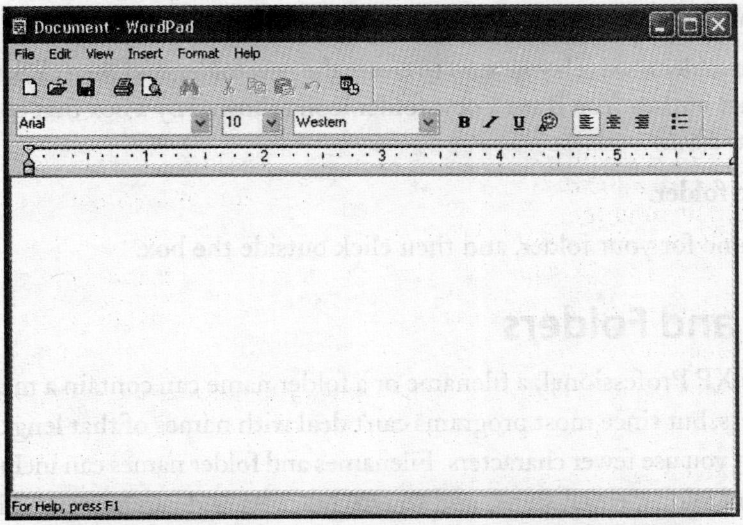

Figure 2-3 WordPad is a word-processing application that comes with Windows XP Professional.

2. Open the Save As dialog box.

Click the File menu, and then click Save. Figure 2-4 shows the Save As dialog box.

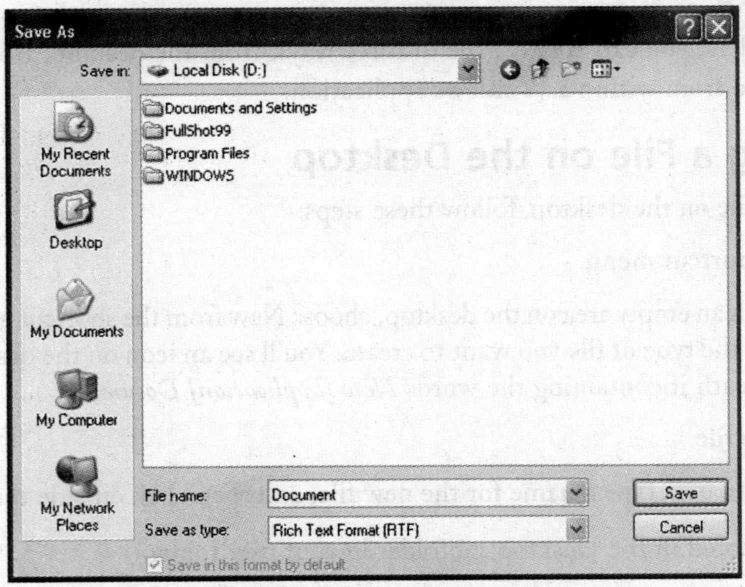

Figure 2-4 The Save As dialog box.

3. **Create the folder.**

   Locate the folder in which you want to create the new folder, and then click the Create New Folder button. You'll see a new folder icon followed by a box that contains the words *New Folder*.

4. **Name the folder.**

   Type a name for your folder, and then click outside the box.

Naming Files and Folders

In Windows XP Professional, a filename or a folder name can contain a maximum of 255 characters, but since most programs can't deal with names of that length, we recommend that you use fewer characters. Filenames and folder names can include spaces, commas, semicolons, equal signs, and square brackets and can be a combination of upper- and lowercase letters.

Be sure to give your files and folders names that are descriptive and that will make sense some time in the future when you're trying to locate something in particular.

Creating a File

As with folders, you can create a file in three ways: from the desktop, from within Explorer, and from within a Windows application.

Creating a File on the Desktop

To create a file on the desktop, follow these steps:

1. **Open a shortcut menu.**

   Right-click an empty area on the desktop, choose New from the shortcut menu, and then click the type of file you want to create. You'll see an icon on the desktop and a box beneath it containing the words *New [application] Document*.

2. **Name the file.**

   Click in the box, type a name for the new file, and then click outside the box.

This file is stored in the Desktop subfolder in your user folder.

In Windows XP Professional, each file has an extension that identifies its type, although you don't normally see that extension. For example, if you create a text document in WordPad the extension is DOC. To see a file's type in Explorer, click the View menu, and then click Details. Each file's type is listed in the Type column. Following are some common file types and their associated extensions in Windows XP:

- AVI, a video clip
- BMP, a bitmap image
- CDP, a CDBURN file
- CLP, a Clipboard clip
- CUR, a cursor
- FON, a font file
- HTML, a HyperText Markup Language document
- M1V, a movie file
- MP3, an MP3 format sound
- RTF, a rich text document

Creating a File in Explorer

To create a file in Explorer, follow these steps:

1. Open Explorer.

Click the Start button, right-click My Computer, and choose Explore from the shortcut menu.

2. Select a folder.

Open the folder that will contain the new file.

3. Create the file.

Click the File menu, click New, and then select a file type. You'll see an icon representing the file type and a box in the right pane.

4. Name the file.

Type a name for the new file, and then click outside the box.

Creating a File from Within an Application

Here are the steps for creating a file in WordPad. Creating a file in most Windows applications follows the same procedure.

1. Open WordPad.

Click the Start button, click All Programs, click Accessories, and then click WordPad.

2. Open the Save As dialog box.

Click the File menu, and then click Save.

3. **Choose where you want to store the file.**

   Click the folder in which you want to save the file you're creating.

4. **Name and save the file.**

   In the File Name box, enter a name for the file, and then select the file type in the Save As Type dialog box. Click Save.

Copying and Moving Files and Folders

As mentioned earlier in this chapter, regardless of where you create a file or a folder, you can always move it to another location. In addition, you can copy it to another location. When you move a file, you remove it from its current location and place it in another location. When you copy a file, the original remains in place, and a copy is placed in another location.

As with a number of tasks in Windows XP Professional, you can move and copy a file or a folder in several ways:

- By dragging and dropping with the right mouse button
- By dragging and dropping with the left mouse button
- By copying and pasting or by cutting and pasting
- By using the Send To command

Which method you use depends on the situation and your personal preference.

Using the Right Mouse Button

To copy or move a file or a folder with the right mouse button, follow these steps:

1. **Open Explorer.**

   Click the Start button, right-click My Computer, and then choose Explore from the shortcut menu.

2. **Drag the file to its new location.**

   Locate the file or folder, right-click it, and, while holding down the mouse button, drag the file or folder to its new location.

3. **Choose whether to copy or move the file or folder.**

   Release the right mouse button, and choose Copy Here or Move Here from the shortcut menu.

If you change your mind in the middle of a copy or a move, press the Escape key.

Using the Left Mouse Button

If the source and destination for a copy are on different drives, left-click the file, and then drag it to its new location. If the source and destination are on the same drive, left-clicking and dragging the file or folder moves it. To move a file or a folder to a different drive, click the file or folder with the left mouse button and hold down the Shift key while you drag the item.

Using the Cut, Copy, and Paste Commands

To copy or move a file using the Cut, Copy, and Paste commands, follow these steps:

1. **Open Explorer.**

   Click the Start button, right-click My Computer, and choose Explore from the shortcut menu.

2. **Locate what you want to copy or move.**

   Find the source file or folder.

3. **Open the shortcut menu.**

   Right-click the source file or folder, and choose Cut or Copy from the shortcut menu.

4. **Place the item in its new location.**

   Right-click the destination folder, and choose Paste from the shortcut menu.

Using Send To

A quick way to copy files and folders is to use the Send To command, which you'll find on the shortcut menu. Simply right-click the file or folder, choose Send To, and then select a destination. By default, you can send a file or a folder to a floppy disk, a compressed folder, the desktop, a mail recipient, or the My Documents folder. We'll look in detail at how to send a file or folder to a compressed folder later in this section.

If you frequently want to copy files to a destination that's not on the Send To menu, you can add that destination. For example, you might want to back up your files on another computer's hard drive on your network. To add a destination to the Send To menu, follow these steps:

1. **Open Explorer.**

   Right-click the Start button, and choose Explore from the shortcut menu.

2. **Find your Send To folder.**

   Locate your user folder, and then locate and select your Send To folder within it.

TIP *If you don't see your Send To folder, it's probably hidden. To display it, click the Tools menu, click Folder Options to open the Folder Options dialog box, and click the View tab. In the Hidden Files And Folders folder, click the Show Hidden Files And Folders option button, and then click OK. If you still don't see your Send To folder, close and then reopen Explorer.*

3. Start the Create Shortcut Wizard, which is shown in Figure 2-5.

Click the File menu, click New, and then click Shortcut.

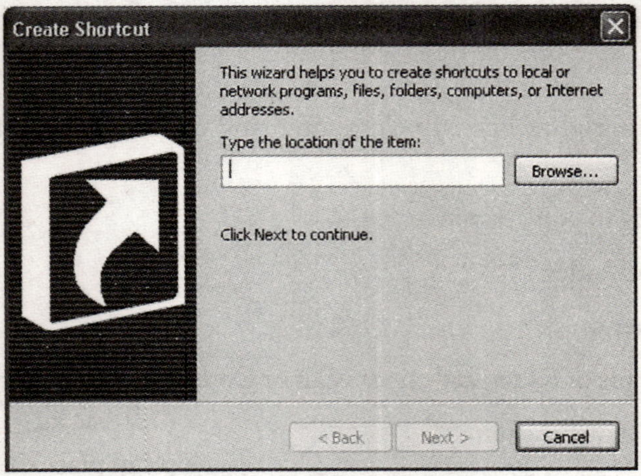

Figure 2-5 The Create Shortcut Wizard.

4. Enter the destination you want to add.

In the Type The Location Of The Item box, enter the filename for your new destination, or click Browse to locate it.

5. Enter a name for the destination.

Click Next, and in the Select A Title For The Program screen, type a name for the destination. Click Finish.

TIP *You'll also find the Send To command on the File menu of many Windows XP Professional applications.*

Sending a File or a Folder to a Compressed Folder

When you compress a file, you decrease its size so that it takes up less space on a drive or transfers quicker. At present, a number of compression programs are available through third-party vendors as shareware or commercial products. Included with Windows XP Professional, however, is WinZip7, a popular compression utility that has been widely distributed in previous versions.

If you've used WinZip or another compression utility when running an earlier version of Windows, you know that you open the program and then follow a series of steps to "zip" a file. In most cases, if you send a zipped file, the recipient needs the same program you used to compress it to decompress it. That's not the case when you compress a file or folder in Windows XP Professional. WinZip7 is compatible with almost any other compression utility, and a recipient can easily unzip the file or folder by double-clicking it.

In Windows XP Professional, you click the Compressed Folder item on the Send To menu to zip a file or a folder with no intervention from you. To zip a file, right-click it, click Send To, and then click Compressed Folder. A compressed copy is placed in the folder that contains the original file. You can easily identify it because its file folder icon displays a closed zipper. Once you create a zipped folder, you can place other files in it by simply dragging them to the folder.

When you zip a folder that is in a subfolder, a zipped folder is placed in the parent folder. To uncompress a zipped folder, simply double-click it. If you want a compressed folder in a location other than where the program places it, simply drag it there or use the Cut and Paste commands described earlier in this chapter. Figure 2-6 shows a couple of zipped folders.

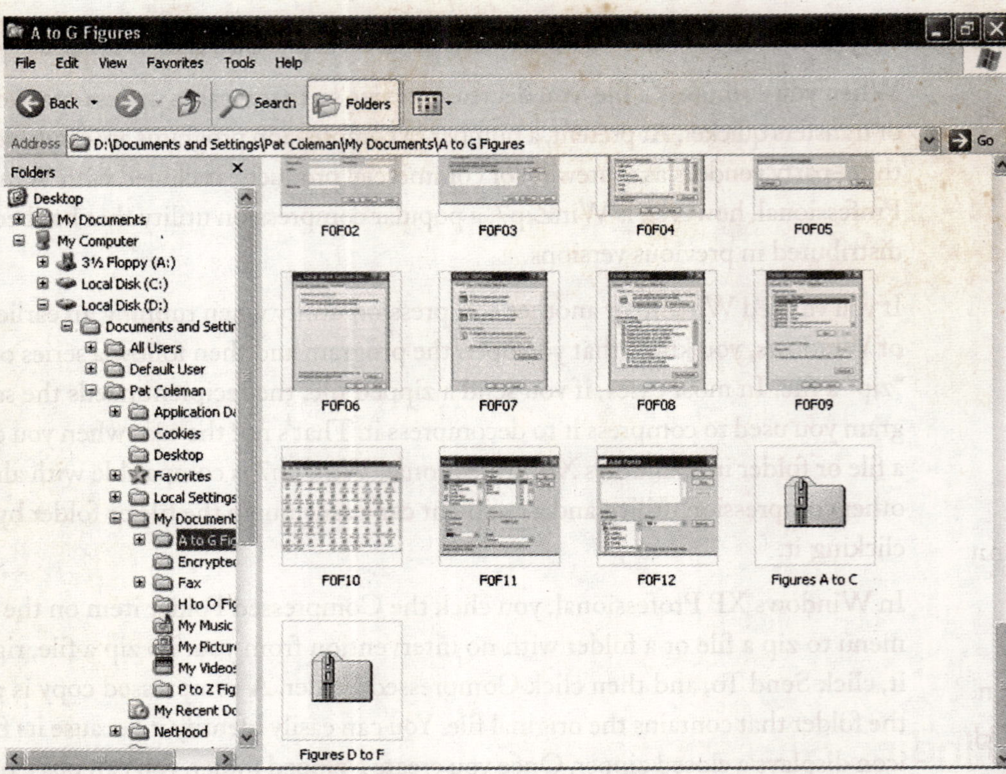

Figure 2-6 Compressed folders are identified by a zipper.

You can also compress files and folders in Windows applications. We'll look at how to do so using Outlook Express in Chapter 10.

Renaming Files and Folders

Renaming files and folders is simple. In Explorer, right-click a file or a folder, choose Rename from the shortcut menu, type a new name in the box that appears, and then click outside the box. You can also rename a file or a folder from within a Windows application. Open the Save As dialog box, right-click the file or folder, choose Rename from the shortcut menu, type a new name, and click outside the box.

Deleting Files and Folders

As Chapter 1 mentioned, when you delete a file or a folder, it goes to the Recycle Bin by default. It is not permanently deleted from your system until the Recycle Bin is emptied. You can delete a file or folder in several ways:

- In Explorer, right-click the file or folder name, and choose Delete from the shortcut menu.
- In the Save As dialog box in a Windows XP Professional application, right-click the name of a file or a folder, and choose Delete from the shortcut menu.
- In Explorer, left-click the file or folder name, and then press the Delete key or click the Delete button on the toolbar. (The Delete button has an X on it.)
- If the file or folder is visible on the desktop, click it, and then drag it to the Recycle Bin.

TIP *To bypass the Recycle Bin, hold down the Shift key while choosing the Delete command or pressing the Delete key.*

Finding Files and Folders

If you follow the guidelines in this chapter, you shouldn't lose track of the documents, files, and folders you create—although we all do from time to time. In that situation, you can use the Search Companion to look for a file, a folder, or text within a document. Look back in Chapter 1 if you need to refresh you memory about the steps.

Setting File and Folder Permissions

As this book continues to point out, one of the reasons that you choose to use Windows XP Professional is its security features. You can restrict access to your system right down to the file and folder level if you are using the NTFS file system. Even if someone walks into your office and makes off with your computer, he or she won't be able to access the files and folders unless he or she has permission.

Assigning permissions to a file or folder is a straightforward process, so we'll look at the steps to do that first. Understanding the types of permissions that you can assign is a bit more complicated, and this section gives you a brief rundown on that subject.

Assigning Permissions

To assign permissions to a file or a folder, follow these steps:

1. Open Windows Explorer.

Right-click the Start button, and then choose Explore from the shortcut menu.

2. Specify the file or folder to which you want to attach permissions.

Right-click the file or folder, and choose Properties from the shortcut menu to open the Properties dialog box for that folder. Click the Security tab, which is shown in Figure 2-7.

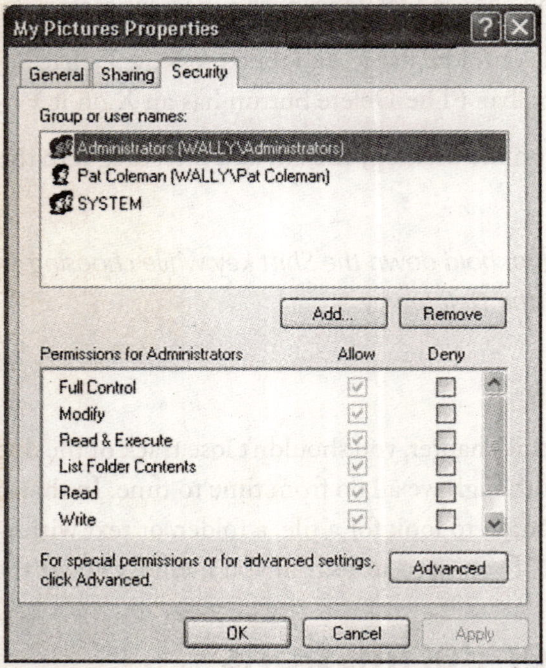

Figure 2-7 The Properties dialog box open at the Security tab.

NOTE *If you don't see the Security tab, click the Start button, and then click Control Panel to open Control Panel. Click the Appearances And Themes link, and then click the Folder Options link. In the Folder Options dialog box, click the View tab, and in the Advanced Settings list, clear the Use Simple File Sharing (Recommended) check box.*

3. Specify who can have access to this file.

Click Add to open the Select Users Or Groups dialog box, as shown in Figure 2-8. Enter the names of the user or group to whom you want to give permission in the Enter The Object Names To Select box, and click OK.

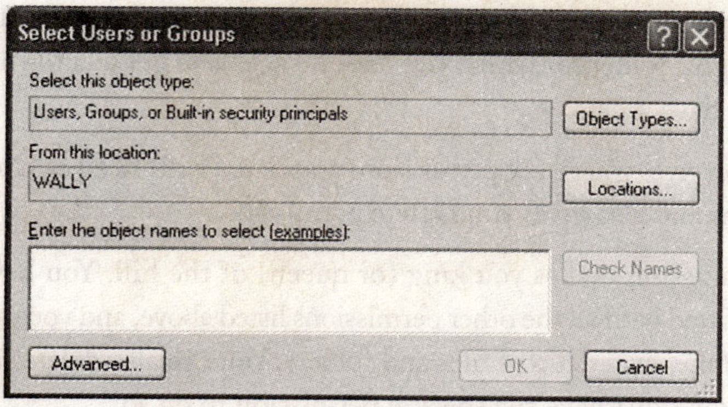

Figure 2-8 The Select Users Or Groups dialog box.

TIP *Although you can assign permissions to individual users and it is tempting to do so, don't. Assign permissions to groups of users, and place individual users in these groups. For example, if you set the permissions on drive C to give Full Control to Computer Administrators and create a new account name in the Computer Administrators group, that person automatically has Full Control on drive C. You need not manually give her that permission. This can save a lot of time in the long run.*

4. Specify what kinds of permission these users will have.

Back in the Properties dialog box, you'll see that the users you specified have been added to the list. Now click the Allow or Deny check boxes to specify the type of permissions that these users will have. When you're finished, click OK.

Types of Permissions

The types of permissions you can assign to files and folders are extensive, and in addition to the primary types described here, you can assign special access permissions. A discussion of special access permissions is beyond the scope of this book, but if you're interested in knowing more, check with your system administrator or look in Help And Support Center.

You can assign the following primary types of permissions to files and folders:

- Read permission allows you to view the contents, permissions, and attributes associated with a file or a folder.
- Write permission allows you to create a new file or a subfolder in a folder. To change a file, you must also have Read permission.

- Read & Execute permission gives you Read and Write permissions and also allows you to pass through a folder for which you have no access to get to a file or a folder for which you do have access.
- Modify permission gives you all the permissions associated with Read & Execute and Write permissions and also gives you Delete permission.
- Full Control permission makes you king (or queen) of the hill. You have all the permissions associated with all the other permissions listed above, and you can change permissions and take ownership of files and folders. You can also delete subfolders and files even if you don't have the specific permission to do so.
- List Folder Contents permission gives you permission to view filenames and subfolder names within that folder.

Understanding the Shared Documents Folder

In the My Computer window you will see a Shared Documents folder. The purpose of this folder is to store documents that you want to share with others on your system. You can copy or move a document to the Shared Documents folder. To copy a document, click it, hold down the Ctrl key, and then drag it to the Shared Documents folder. To move the document, click it and then drag it to the Shared Documents folder. Any document in the Shared Documents folder is available to anyone working on your computer or network.

As you've seen, there are other, better ways to give others access to resources that you want to share, and Chapters 13 and 14 describe how to set up users and groups and share resources. Advanced users may consider the Shared Documents folder an annoyance, and unfortunately there is no easy way to get rid of it. If you are a Computer Administrator, however, and if you are familiar with the Registry and have experience using it, you can permanently remove the Shared Documents folder.

WARNING *Do not attempt the following procedure unless you absolutely know what you are doing. One wrong click when working with the Registry can bring your system or your network to its knees.*

To remove the Shared Documents folder, follow these steps:

1. Open the Registry Editor.

Click the Start button, and then click Run to open the Run dialog box. In the Open box, type *regedit*, and then press Enter. You'll see a screen similar to that in Figure 2-9.

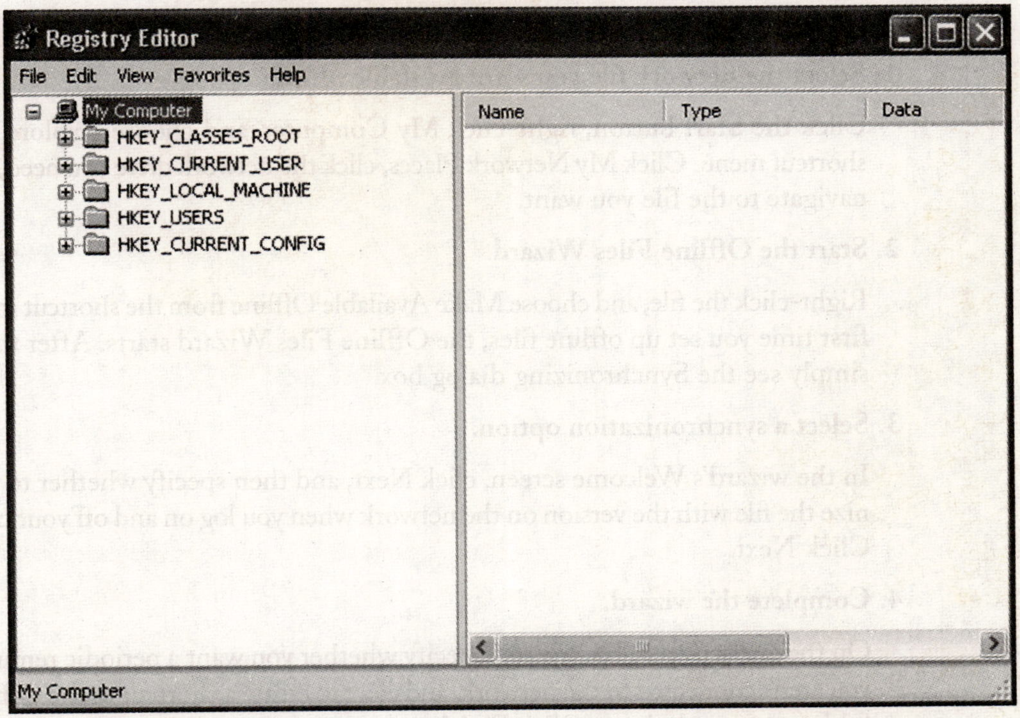

Figure 2-9 The Registry Editor.

2. Navigate to the Delegate Folders key.

Click the plus sign (+) next to HKEY_LOCAL_MACHINE, and then click the plus sign next to the following keys in order: SOFTWARE\Microsoft\Windows\CurrentVersion\Explorer\My Computer\NameSpace\Delegate Folders.

3. Tell the Registry Editor to remove the Shared Documents folder.

In the Delegate Folders key, select the subkey {59031a47-3f72-44a7-89c5-5595fe6b30ee} and delete it. Close the Registry Editor. You don't need to restart your computer. When you open My Computer, you'll no longer see the Shared Documents folder.

Working with Offline Files

If you work on a laptop or on a network that tends to be on the slow side, you'll want to know about using offline files. When you do so, you can work with a network or an Internet file even when you aren't connected to the network.

To make a network file available offline, follow these steps:

1. **Select the network file you want available offline.**

   Click the Start button, right-click My Computer, and choose Explore from the shortcut menu. Click My Network Places, click the network drive you need, and then navigate to the file you want.

2. **Start the Offline Files Wizard.**

   Right-click the file, and choose Make Available Offline from the shortcut menu. The first time you set up offline files, the Offline Files Wizard starts. After that, you'll simply see the Synchronizing dialog box.

3. **Select a synchronization option.**

   In the wizard's Welcome screen, click Next, and then specify whether to synchronize the file with the version on the network when you log on and off your computer. Click Next.

4. **Complete the wizard.**

   On the last screen of the wizard, specify whether you want a periodic reminder that you aren't connected to the network, and elect to create a shortcut to the Offline Files folder on your desktop. Click Finish.

The Synchronizing dialog box will show the file's progress.

Specifying Folder Options

Earlier this chapter looked briefly at using the Folder Options dialog box to display hidden files. Now it's time to take a longer look and see how you can use the options in this dialog box to specify how folders look and work. Figure 2-10 shows the Folder Options dialog box open at the General tab. To open the Folder Options dialog box, click the Tools menu and then click Folder Options in any folder or in Explorer.

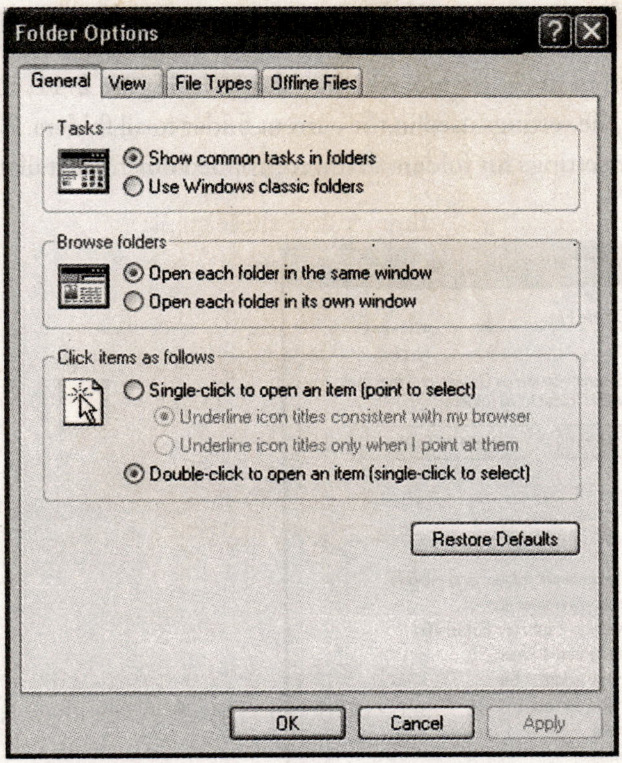

Figure 2-10 The Folder Options dialog box open at the General tab.

Displaying Folders

In the Tasks section of the General tab, you can specify that folders display a common tasks bar or to use classic Windows folders.

In the Browse Folders section, click the Open Each Folder In The Same Window option button if you want the window to stay put if you open a folder within another folder. Click the Open Each Folder In Its Own Window option button if you want a new window to appear each time you open a folder within an existing folder. Although selecting this option tends to clutter the screen, it's useful when you want to drag and drop items.

In the Click Items As Follows section, you can choose whether to single- or double-click to open items.

Specifying Views

Select a folder, and then in the View tab, which is shown in Figure 2-11, click Apply To All Folders to apply the settings used in the current folder to all folders. Click Reset All Folders to apply the settings for folders that were applied during installation of the operating system.

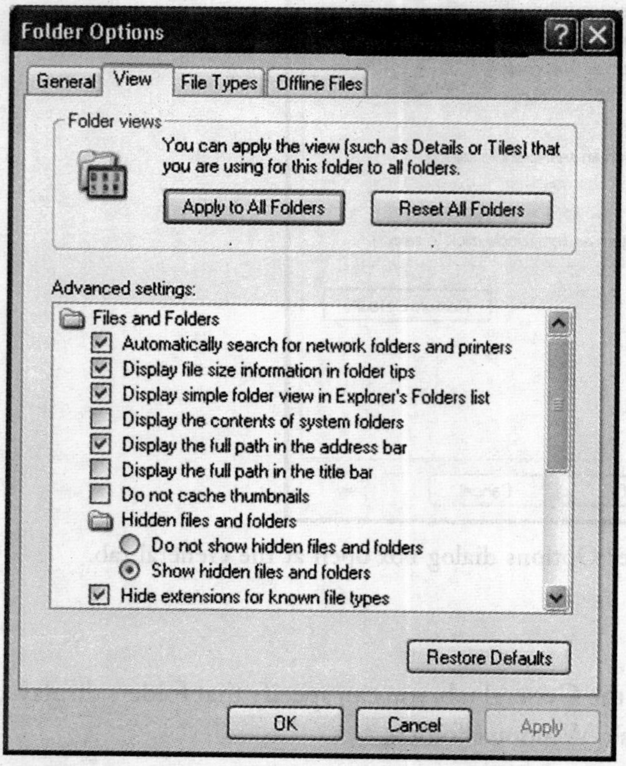

Figure 2-11 The Folder Options dialog box open at the View tab.

Scroll down the list in the Advanced Settings section of the View tab to check out the other options. For a description of each item, click the Help button (the one with the question mark), and then click the item. Clear a check box to disable that option; check a check box to enable that option. When you've made your choices, click OK. To restore all settings to the default, click Restore Defaults.

Viewing the File Types on Your System

The File Types tab, which is shown in Figure 2-12, is primarily for information only. It lists the filename extensions, their associated file type, and applications that are registered with Windows XP Professional. Unless you know what you are doing and have a good reason for doing it, you shouldn't experiment with this list. In fact, if you're on a corporate network, you probably don't even have permission to do so.

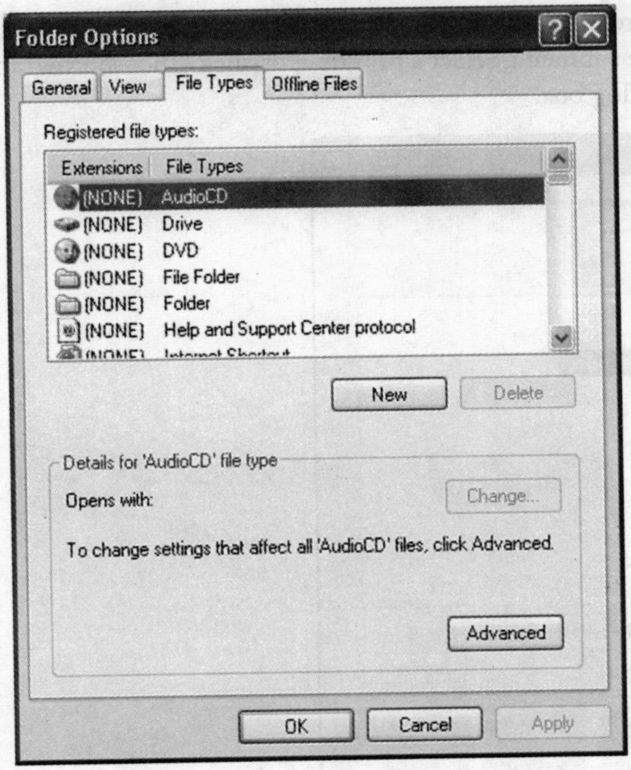

Figure 2-12 The File Types tab of the Folder Options dialog box.

Reprise: Setting Up Offline Files

Earlier in this chapter, we set up offline files using the Offline Files Wizard. You can also do this using the Offline Files tab in the Folder Options dialog box.

Associating Files and Programs

When you open a file by clicking it in Windows Explorer, it opens in the program with which it is associated by default. For example, a .jpg image opens in Image Preview, and a .doc file opens in WordPad if you have not installed Microsoft Word. You may want to change the program that is associated with a file type. To do so, follow these steps:

1. **Open the Open With dialog box, which is shown in Figure 2-13.**

   In Windows Explorer, right-click the file, and choose Open With from the shortcut menu. From the submenu, select a program, or click Choose Program to open the Open With dialog box.

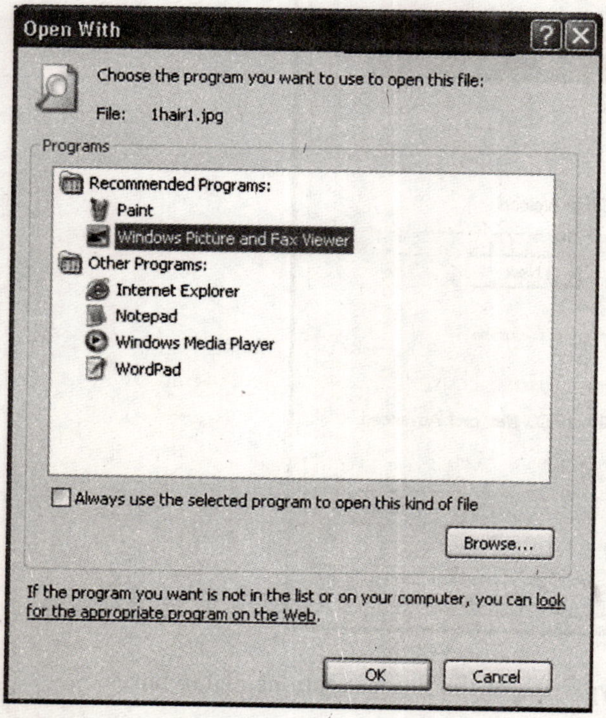

Figure 2-13 The Open With dialog box.

2. **Select a program.**

   In the list of programs, select a program. If you want all files of this type to open with this program, click the Always Use The Selected Program To Open This Kind Of File check box. Click OK.

TIP *If you don't see the program you want listed, click the Look For The Appropriate Program On The Web link to go to the Windows File Associations site, where you can find information about other programs for this file type.*

Working with Floppy Disks

These days most business professionals rely heavily on a corporate network and the Internet and seldom need to deal with a floppy disk. In fact, for security reasons, many network computers in large organizations don't even have floppy drives. Nevertheless, we'll close this chapter by looking at how to format and copy a floppy disk—just in case you ever need to copy a file to a floppy and give it to a coworker or colleague. This process, by the way, is sometimes referred to as sneakernet.

Formatting a Floppy Disk

Before you can use a floppy disk, it must be formatted. If you use floppy disks, you probably purchase formatted disks, which are widely available. But if you happen to have some unformatted disks or if you want to delete the files on a floppy you've been using, you need to format the disk. Follow these steps:

1. **Select the drive.**

   Insert the disk in the floppy drive. Open Windows Explorer, and right-click 3½ Floppy (A:) in the Folders bar.

2. **Tell Windows to format the disk.**

   From the shortcut menu, choose Format to open the Format 3½ Floppy (A:) dialog box, which is shown in Figure 2-14.

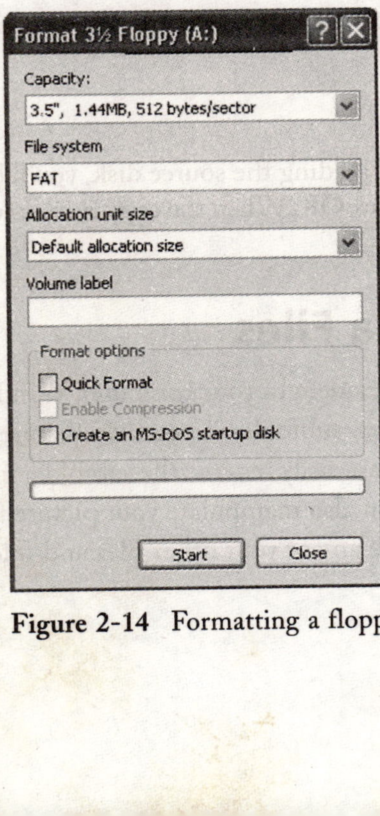

Figure 2-14 Formatting a floppy disk.

3. **Specify your options.**

   Give your disk a label, if you want, and then specify whether to use Quick Format. When you choose Quick Format, files are removed from the disk but the disk is not scanned for bad sectors. It is recommended that you use this option only if the disk has been previously formatted and you're sure the disk isn't damaged. When you're ready, click Start.

The bar at the bottom of the dialog box indicates the progress of the format. When you see a message that the format is complete, click OK, and close the dialog box.

Copying a Floppy Disk

To copy a floppy disk to another floppy, follow these steps:

1. **Open the Copy Disk dialog box, which is shown in Figure 2-15.**

   Insert the disk to be copied in the drive, right-click 3½ Floppy (A:) in the Folders bar, and choose Copy Disk from the shortcut menu.

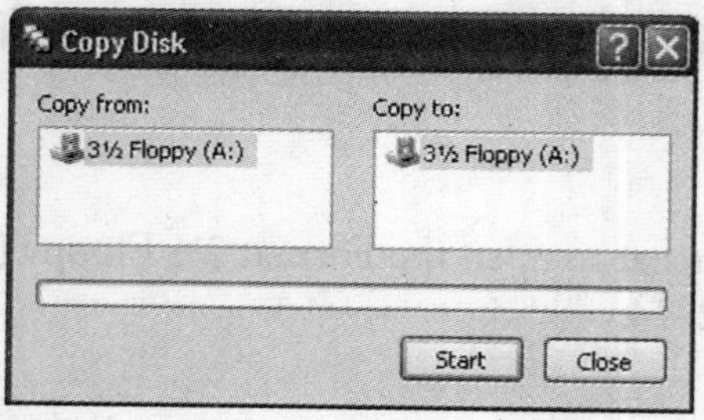

Figure 2-15 The Copy Disk dialog box.

2. **Start the process.**

   Click Start. When Windows has finished reading the source disk, you'll be asked to insert the destination disk. Do so, and click OK. When the copy is complete, click Close.

Working with Digital Camera Files

When you transfer photos from your digital camera to your computer, Windows XP Professional automatically places them in a new subfolder in your My Pictures folder. The new subfolder is given a name, but you can easily rename the subfolder using the technique you learned in this chapter. You can also manipulate your picture files and folders in the same ways that you manipulate any of your other files and folders.

Summary

This chapter has given you lots of information you can use to organize and protect your files and folders. We've looked at how to work with Windows Explorer, how to set file and folder permissions, how to work with offline files, how to specify folder options, and how to format and copy floppy disks. Acquiring these skills will make you more efficient in the workplace, but if you take away only one thing from this chapter, it should be how to use Windows Explorer. Explorer is your primary tool for organizing your computer system.

Chapter 3

PRINTING

Featuring:

- Installing a Local Printer
- Printing Documents
- Managing the Printer
- Customizing the Printing Process
- Installing and Using Fonts

The vision of a paperless office is not a reality, and probably it never will be, but we seem to be getting closer every year. The emergence of the Internet has contributed to the current state of affairs in a major way.

For example, five years ago an author submitting something for publication typically copied the document file and the illustrations to a floppy disk, printed the text, printed the illustrations, and, because printers were rather slow at the time, photocopied everything that was printed so that he or she had a reference copy. Then the printed copies and the floppy were sent to the publisher via an overnight delivery service. Today, all the files are compressed and sent as an attachment to e-mail. The author can keep a backup copy of files on the network and maintain almost no paper files in the office.

In the meantime, printers have become cheaper and cheaper, are easier to use and maintain, and are substantially faster. Using some of the features that are available with Windows XP Professional or a small, rather inexpensive software package, you can print your own business cards, greetings cards, photographs, newsletters, brochures, and so on.

In this chapter, we'll look at the steps to install and use a local printer with Windows XP Professional. A *local printer* is one that is physically attached to your computer by a cable. A *network printer* is a printer that is attached to another computer on a network or to the network hub and is known as a *print server*.

Installing a Local Printer

If you upgraded to Windows XP Professional rather than doing a clean install on a new machine or a new partition on your hard drive, you may not have needed to install your printer. Windows XP Professional should have recognized it during installation in the same way that it recognized your keyboard, your monitor, and so on. If you acquire a new printer, though, or if you do a clean install of Windows XP Professional, you'll need to install your printer. You do so using the Add Printer Wizard, which you access from the Printers folder.

To install a local printer that is Plug and Play, follow these steps:

1. Prepare the printer.

Be sure that the printer cable is securely connected to both the printer and your computer, follow any preparatory instructions that came with the printer, and turn on the printer.

2. Start the Add Printer Wizard.

Click the Start button, click Printers And Faxes to open the Printers And Faxes folder, and then in the Printer Tasks bar, click Add A Printer to open the Welcome screen, as shown in Figure 3-1.

Figure 3-1 The Add Printer Wizard.

3. **Specify a local printer.**

   Click Next, and click the Local Printer Attached To This Computer option button. Also click the Automatically Detect And Install My Plug And Play Printer. Click Next.

Windows will now locate and install your local Plug and Play printer. Follow any instructions that appear on your screen.

To install a local printer that is not Plug and Play, perform steps 1 and 2 for installing a Plug and Play printer, and then follow these steps:

1. **Specify a local printer.**

   Click the Local Printer Attached To This Computer option button, but leave the Automatically Detect And Install My Plug And Play Printer check box blank. Click Next.

2. **Specify the port to be used.**

   In the Select A Printer Port screen, tell the wizard whether to use an existing port and which one or to create a new port. Normally, printers use LPT1, which is selected by default. Unless you have a good reason to do otherwise, accept the default port.

NOTE *A printer port is the interface through which information between the computer and the printer passes.*

3. **Specify the manufacturer and model of your printer.**

   Click Next. In the Manufacturers list, select the manufacturer of your printer; in the Printers list, select the model.

4. **Name your printer.**

   Click Next. In the Printer Name box, enter a name that will be associated with the icon for your printer in the Printers And Faxes folder. If you want this printer to be used automatically when you print from a Windows application, click the Yes option button.

5. **Specify whether to share your printer.**

   Click Next. In this screen, you can specify whether to share your printer. If you work on a network and you want other users to be able to use your local printer, type a name for your printer in the Share Name box. If you share your printer, you'll see the Location And Comment dialog box when you click Next. In the Location box, you can specify where the printer is located, such as Room 323 on the third floor. In the

Comments box, you can specify anything particular about the printer, such as it is only for printing on legal-size paper.

6. **Print a test page.**

   Click Next. It's always a good idea to print a test page so that you can verify that your printer is up and running. Click the Yes option button to display the summary screen of the Add Printer Wizard.

7. **Complete the wizard.**

   On the summary screen, verify that all your printer settings are correct. If they are not, click the Back button to retrace your steps and change them. If the settings are correct, click Finish to complete the wizard and print your test page.

When you click Finish, Windows XP Professional copies the printer driver for your printer, and you'll see an icon for this printer in the Printers folder.

NOTE *A printer driver is a little program that lets a computer communicate with and control a printer. Windows XP Professional includes more than 300 printer drivers and probably found yours in the list automatically.*

Your Test Page Didn't Print?

If your test page didn't print or didn't print correctly, you are not out of luck. Here are some things you can do:

- In the dialog box that asks if your test page printed correctly, click No. You'll see a list of troubleshooting steps. Work through them to see whether you can locate the problem. (To do this, select an option and then click Next.)
- If you work through the Troubleshooter and still can't print, make sure that your printer is on the Hardware Compatibility List (HCL) at *www.microsoft.com/hcl*.
- If your printer is not on the list, contact the manufacturer of your printer to see whether it has a driver compatible with Windows XP Professional. If you can't obtain a compatible driver, you most likely will need to acquire a printer that is compatible with Windows XP Professional. Again, check the HCL before you go shopping.

Taking Care of Printer-Related Tasks

When you install a new printer and no longer need the driver for a previous printer, you can easily delete it. Open the Printers And Faxes folder, which is shown in Figure 3-2, by clicking the Start button and then clicking Printers And Faxes. Now, right-click the icon for the old printer, and choose Delete from the shortcut menu.

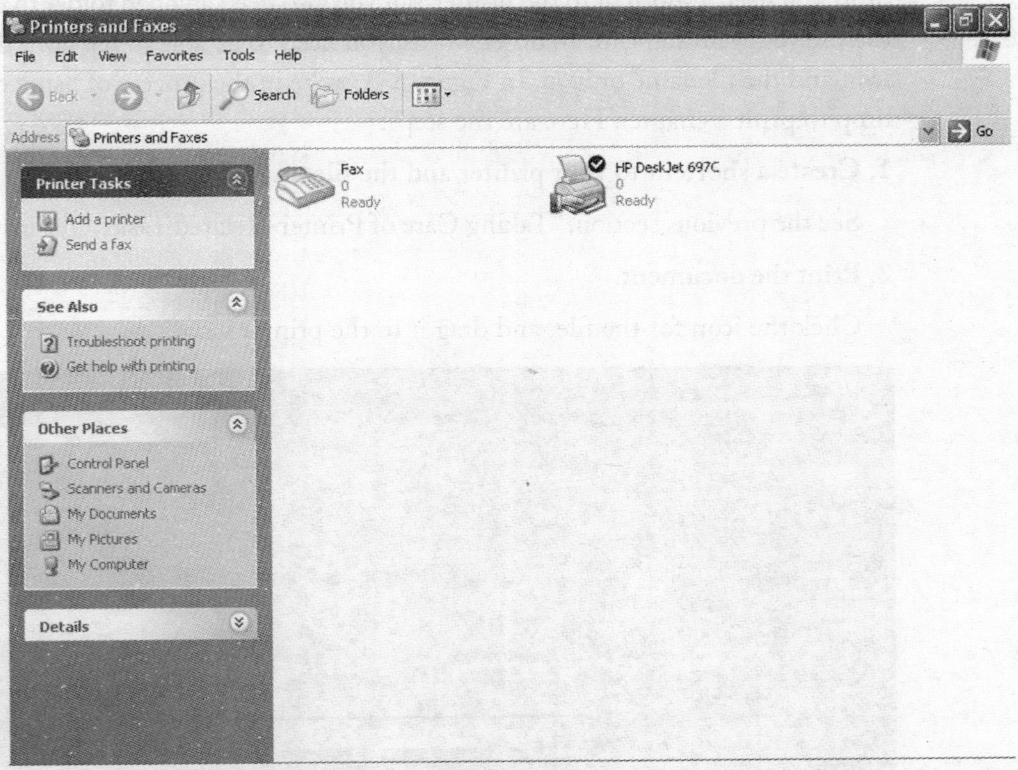

Figure 3-2 The Printers And Faxes folder.

To create a shortcut to a printer on the desktop, right-click the printer's icon in the Printers And Faxes folder, choose Create Shortcut from the shortcut menu, and in the Shortcut dialog box, click Yes. As you'll see in a later section in this chapter, you'll need a shortcut to your printer on the desktop if you want to use drag-and-drop to print.

Printing Documents

You can print from the desktop or from an application. In either case, Windows XP Professional is actually doing the printing. The print spooler program accepts the document and holds it on disk or in memory until the printer is free, and then the printer prints the document.

From the Desktop

You can print from the desktop using drag-and-drop, or you can right-click.

Using Drag-and-Drop

As we mentioned in the previous section, to print from the desktop using drag-and-drop, you need a shortcut to the printer, but you also need an open folder that contains the file you want to print. In other words, you need to be able to see both the printer icon and the filename or icon. In Figure 3-3, we're in the process of using drag-and-drop to print a chapter. Here are the steps:

1. **Create a shortcut to your printer and the file on the desktop.**

   See the previous section, "Taking Care of Printer-Related Tasks," for instructions.

2. **Print the document.**

   Click the icon for the file, and drag it to the printer icon.

Figure 3-3 Printing with drag-and-drop.

The file opens in its associated application and then prints, using the default options in the Print dialog box, which we'll look at shortly.

Using Right-Click

To print using the right-click method, follow these steps:

1. **Locate the file.**

   In Explorer, open a folder that contains the file you want to print.

2. **Print the file.**

   Right-click the file's icon, and choose Print from the shortcut menu.

As is the case when you use drag-and-drop to print, the file opens in its associated application and prints using the default options in the Print dialog box.

From Within a Windows Application

To print from an application easily and quickly, open the application, open the document, and click the Print button on the toolbar. Using the Print button, using drag-and-drop, and using the right-click method all print a document quickly, but, as we've mentioned, you pick up the default print settings when you use any of these methods. In other words, the entire file is printed, only one copy is printed, the printed output is portrait orientation (vertical), and the default paper size and paper tray are used.

To exercise finer control over how a document is printed, you need to print from an application. To print in WordPad, for example, follow these steps:

1. **Open WordPad.**

   Click the Start button, click All Programs, click Accessories, and then click WordPad.

2. **Open a document.**

   Click the File menu, click Open to open the Open dialog box, select the file you want to print, and click Open.

3. **Open the Print dialog box, which is shown in Figure 3-4.**

   Click the File menu, and then click Print.

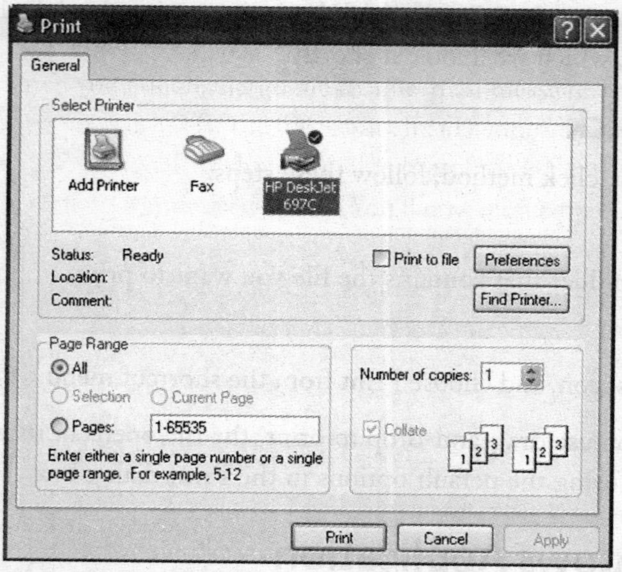

Figure 3-4 The Print dialog box.

4. **Select a printer.**

   The printer you selected as a default is already selected. To select another printer, click it. Move the mouse cursor over a printer to display its status in a ScreenTip.

5. **Choose what to print.**

   In the Page Range section, choose whether to print the entire file, only a selection (what you selected before you opened the Print dialog box), or selected pages.

6. **Specify the number of copies to print.**

   In the Number Of Copies spin box, select the number of copies you want to print. By default, multiple copies are collated. If you don't want them collated, clear the Collate check box.

7. **Specify the orientation of the printed page.**

   Click the Preferences button to open the Printing Preferences dialog box, which is shown in Figure 3-5. In the Layout tab, select Portrait to print vertically, or select Landscape to print horizontally.

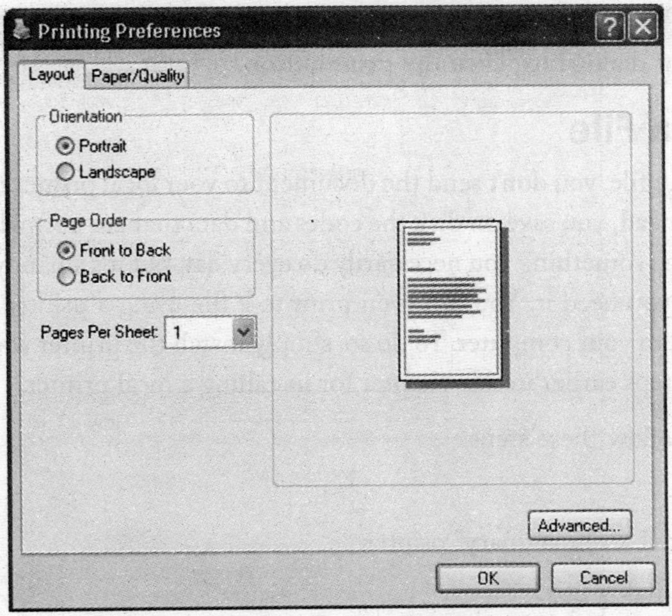

Figure 3-5 The Layout tab in the Printing Preferences dialog box.

8. Set the paper source and quality of the print.

Click the Paper/Quality tab, which is shown in Figure 3-6. Use the buttons and lists to set your specifications, and then click OK.

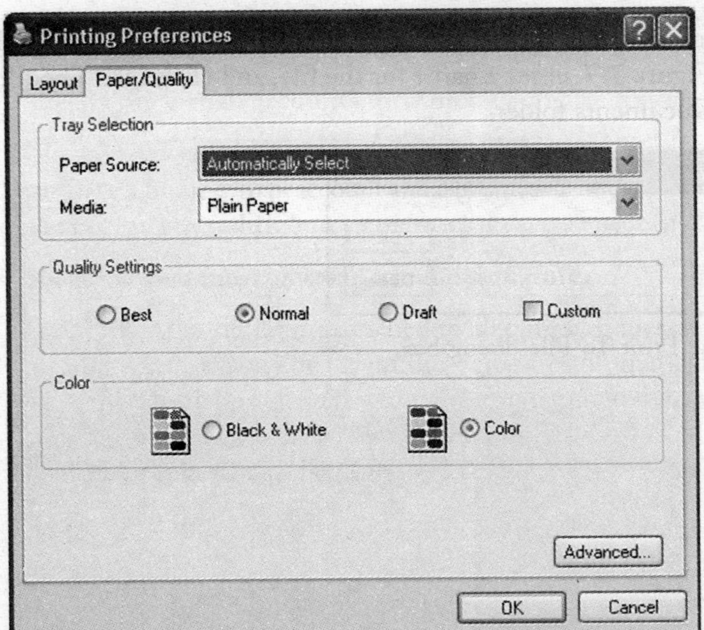

Figure 3-6 The Paper/Quality tab in the Printing Preferences dialog box.

9. **Print the document.**

   Back in the Print dialog box, click the Print button.

Printing to a File

When you print to a file, you don't send the document to your local printer or see any printed output. Instead, you save on disk the codes and data that are normally sent to the printer. This isn't something you necessarily do every day, but it's a handy thing to know about when you need it. You can even print to a file using a printer that isn't physically attached to your computer. To do so, simply install the printer you want to use following the steps earlier in this chapter for installing a local printer.

To print to a file, follow these steps:

1. **Install a printer.**

   If necessary, install an "imaginary" printer.

2. **Open the Print dialog box.**

   In the application, click the File menu, and then click Print.

3. **Choose a printer.**

   In the General tab of the Print dialog box, select a printer.

4. **Print the document to a file.**

   Click the Print To File check box, click Print to open the Print To File dialog box, as shown in Figure 3-7, enter a name for the file, and click OK. The file is stored in your My Documents folder.

Figure 3-7 The Print To File dialog box.

Printing Photos

Windows XP Professional includes a Photo Printing Wizard that you can use to print photographs from a digital camera or a scanner or photographs or other images stored on your computer. To start the wizard, click the Start button, click My Pictures, select a picture, and then click Print Pictures from the Picture Tasks bar. At the Welcome screen, click Next, and then follow these steps:

1. **Select the photos to print.**

   In the Picture Selection screen as shown below, click the photo or photos you want to print to check mark them, and then click Next.

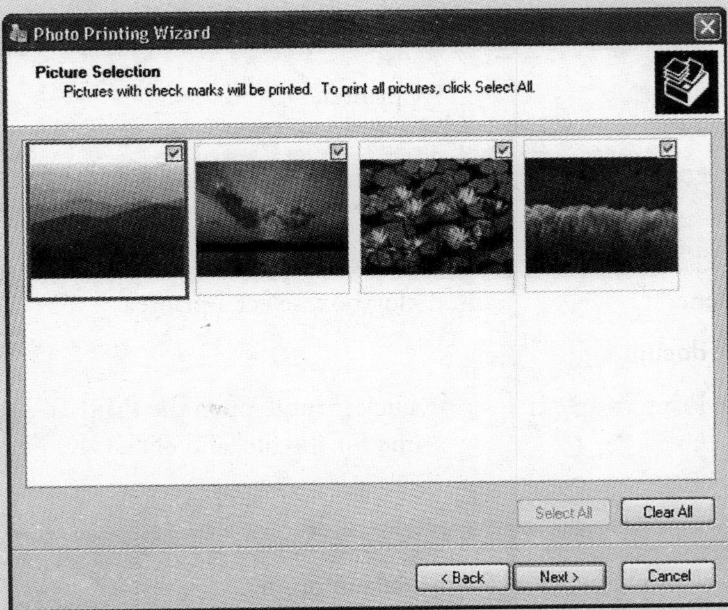

2. **Select the printer and the paper.**

   In the Printing Options screen, tell the wizard which printer to use and the type of paper, and then click Next.

3. **Format your photo(s).**

   In the Layout Selection screen, tell the wizard how to size and format your photo(s). Scroll down the Available Layouts list to see your options. The Print Preview box will show you how your selection will look when printed. Click Next.

The wizard then sends your photo(s) to the printer, and they are printed.

Managing the Printer

Once you click Print, your document wends its way through the printing process. But what if you suddenly realize that you've sent the wrong document to the printer and it's some 100 plus pages? You can reach over and turn off the printer, but that's not the best solution, and sometimes the printer isn't close at hand. The best way to manage the printer is to use the window that opens when you double-click the printer's icon in the Printers And Faxes folder. The printer window is shown in Figure 3-8.

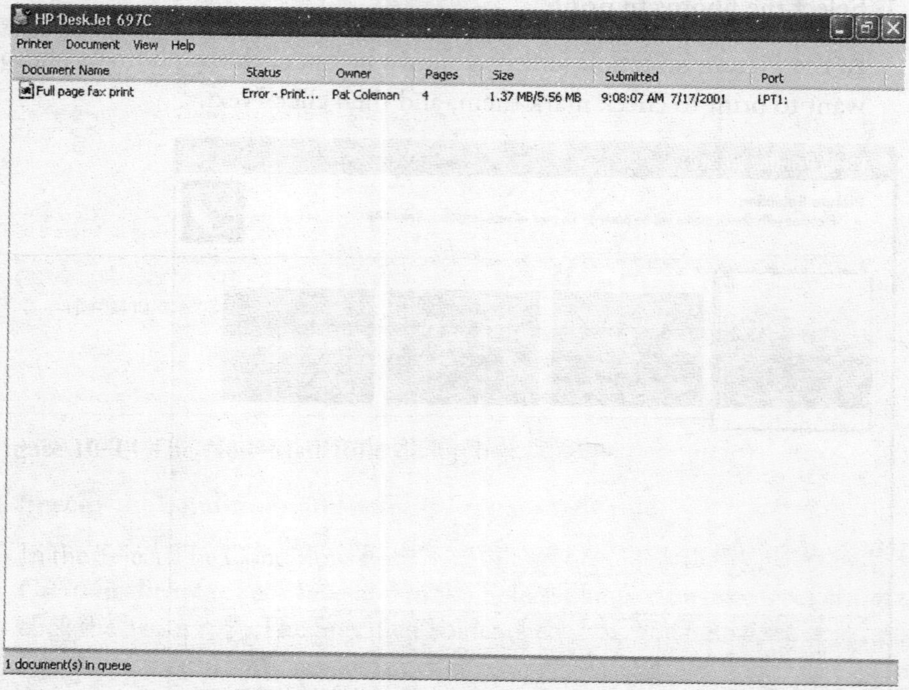

Figure 3-8 The printer window for the default printer.

Here's a description of what each column in the printer window displays:

- The Document Name column displays the name of the document and its associated application.
- The Status column indicates whether the document is being printed, paused, deleted, or, as is the case with the document in Figure 3-12, failed to print.
- The Owner column displays the name of the person who sent the document to the printer.
- The Pages column indicates the number of pages currently printed.
- The Size column displays the size of the document in bytes.

- The Submitted column displays the time and the date the document was sent to the printer.
- The Port column reports the port being used.

Use the following techniques to manage a printer in the printer's window:

- To cancel the printing of a document, right-click it and choose Cancel from the shortcut menu.
- To cancel the printing of all documents in the print queue, click the Printer menu and then click Cancel All Documents.
- To temporarily halt the printing of a document, right-click it and choose Pause from the shortcut menu.
- To resume printing a document, right-click it and choose Resume from the shortcut menu.

You'll notice that printing doesn't cease the second you choose Pause or Cancel. Whatever pages have already been spooled to the printer's buffer must print before the printing is halted.

Customizing the Printing Process

Earlier in this chapter we looked at how to specify such settings as the paper source for a printer, the print quality, and so on, using the printer's Properties dialog box. In this section, we'll look at the other ways you can use the options in this dialog box to customize the printing process.

Figure 3-9 shows the Properties dialog box for an HP DeskJet printer. As you can see, it has eight tabs. The number of tabs and the options within each depend on the printer. This DeskJet can print in color and in black and white, so its Properties dialog box contains a Color Management tab. It's also on a network, so we have a Sharing tab. Depending on your printer and its capabilities, you may have more or fewer tabs.

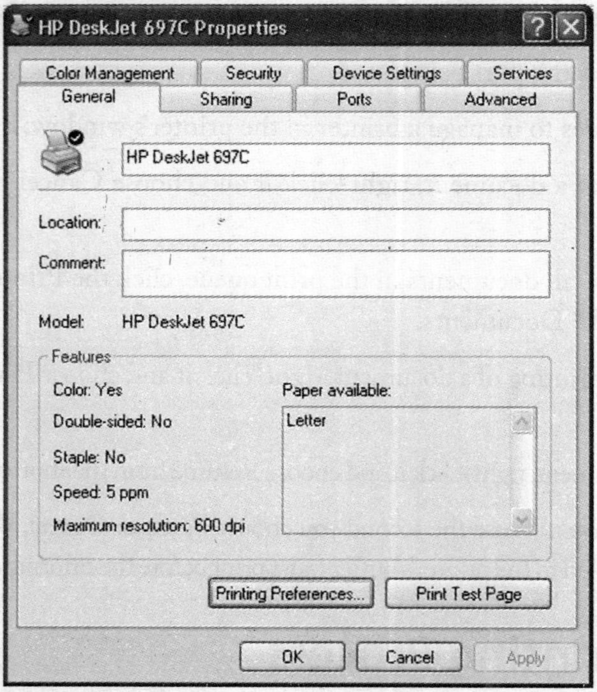

Figure 3-9 The Properties dialog box for an HP DeskJet printer.

Earlier in this chapter we looked at the Security tab and the Sharing tab. In this section, we'll look at the other options you can use on the tabs in the printer's Properties dialog box to customize your printer so that it's appropriate for your environment. The settings you establish in a printer's Properties dialog box become the default for that printer.

Using the General Tab

On the face of the General tab, you can change only a couple of settings—Location and Comment. Both are typically used for printers on a network, as you saw earlier in this chapter. To specify orientation, click the Printing Preferences button to open the Printing Preferences dialog box for your printer. In the Printing Preferences dialog box, click the Advanced button to open the Advanced Options dialog box, which is shown in Figure 3-10. You use the options in this dialog box to specify the default paper size, copy count, print quality of graphics, and so on. When you click an underlined option, you'll see a drop-down list box from which you can make selections.

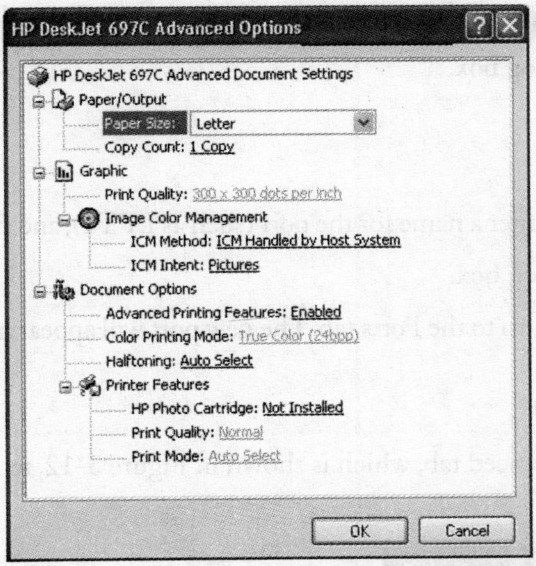

Figure 3-10 The Advanced Options dialog box for an HP DeskJet printer.

Using the Ports Tab

You use the settings on the Ports tab, which is shown in Figure 3-11, to add, delete, and configure ports. Most people never need to fiddle with the settings in this tab, but in the event that by accident your printer port gets deleted, we'll tell you how to add it back.

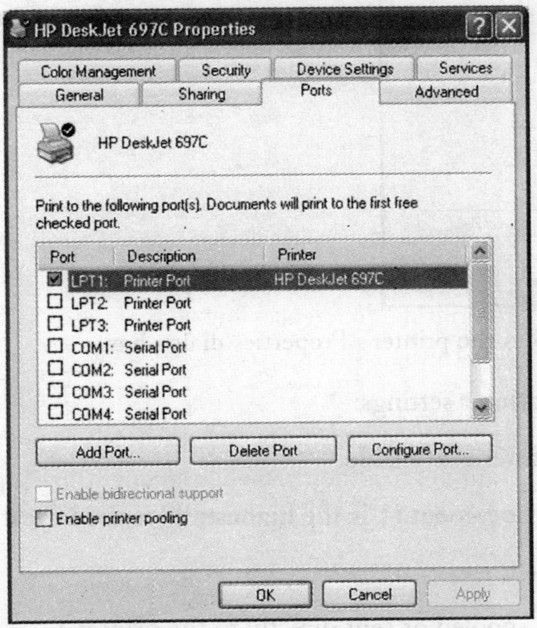

Figure 3-11 The Ports tab in the printer's Properties dialog box.

To add a port, follow these steps:

1. **Open the Printer Ports dialog box.**

   Click the Add Port button.

2. **Add a local port.**

   Click the New Port button, enter a name for the port (such as LPT1), and click OK.

3. **Close the Printer Ports dialog box.**

   Click the Close button to return to the Ports tab. The new port will appear in the list.

Using the Advanced Tab

You use the options in the Advanced tab, which is shown in Figure 3-12, to specify a number of settings.

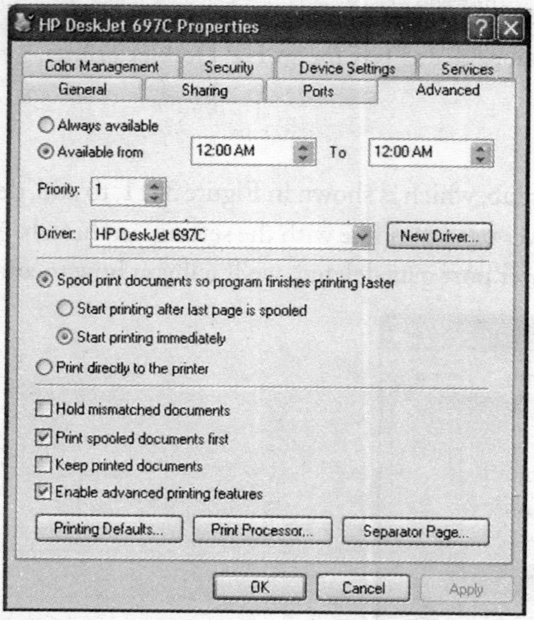

Figure 3-12 The Advanced tab in the printer's Properties dialog box.

You can specify the following printer settings:

- The times when a shared printer is available.
- The priority of the printing document (1 is the highest; 99 is the lowest).
- A new printer driver.
- Whether documents will be spooled or sent directly to the printer.

- Whether mismatched documents will be held. (Mismatched documents are those whose setup doesn't match the printer setup.)
- Whether documents will be stored in the print queue.

By default, documents are spooled and start printing immediately, and the Enable Advanced Printing Features check box is checked. Which features are enabled depends on the features available with your printer.

If you are having problems with your printer and think they might be connected to your printer driver, you may be able to download a printer driver from the manufacturer's Web site or obtain a driver on floppy disk from the manufacturer. In either case, click the New Driver button to start the Add Printer Driver Wizard and install the new driver.

Clicking the Printing Defaults button opens the Printing Defaults dialog box, which contains the same Layout and Paper/Quality tabs you saw earlier in the Printing Preferences dialog box. Clicking the Print Processor button opens the Print Processor dialog box, which lists the available print processors and the default data types. Don't mess with the options in this dialog box unless you are told to do so by an informed technician.

Using the Services Tab

The Services tab for an HP DeskJet is shown in Figure 3-13. Whether you have such a tab and which options are on it depend on your printer. As you can see, this tab has buttons you can click to align or clean the print cartridges.

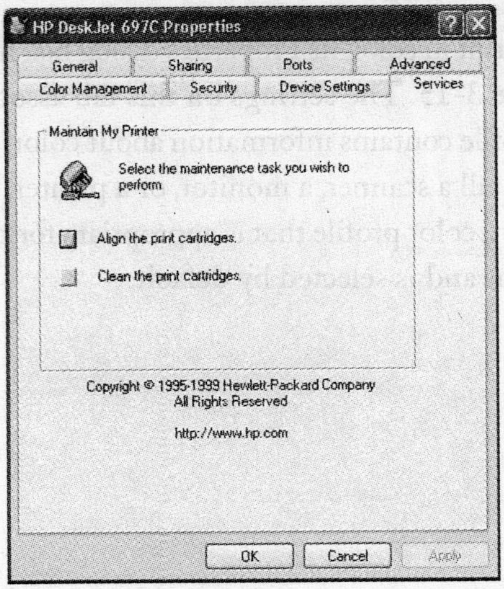

Figure 3-13 The Services tab in the printer's Properties dialog box.

Using the Device Settings Tab

If you have more than one paper tray on your printer, click the Device Settings tab, which is shown in Figure 3-14, to specify which size paper is printed from which tray. You can select a tray in the Print dialog box when you print from an application.

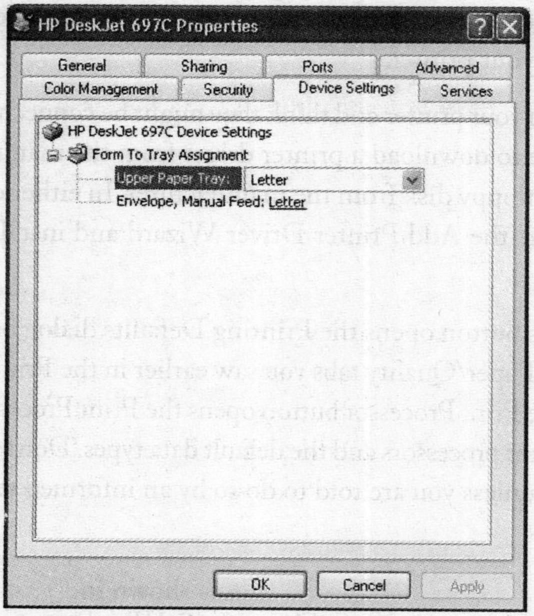

Figure 3-14 The Device Settings tab in the printer's Properties dialog box.

Using the Color Management Tab

Because the HP DeskJet printer can print in color, its Properties dialog box has a Color Management tab, as shown in Figure 3-15. The settings on this tab associate color profiles with your printer. A color profile contains information about color, hue, saturation, and brightness. When you install a scanner, a monitor, or a printer, Windows XP Professional automatically installs a color profile that is appropriate for the device. For most uses, this profile is sufficient and is selected by default.

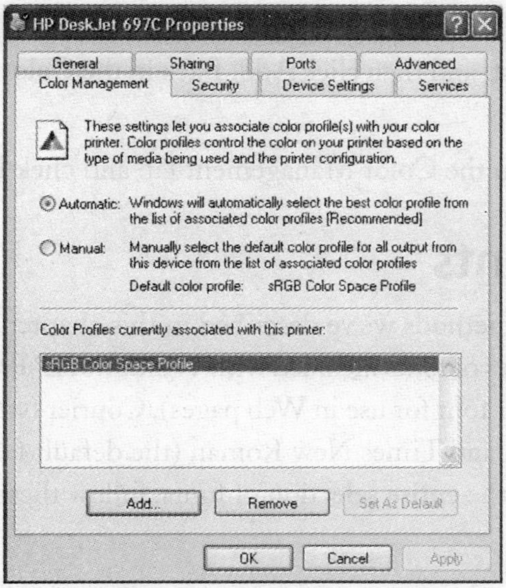

Figure 3-15 The Color Management tab in the printer's Properties dialog box.

If you are a graphic artist or if you produce complex color publications, you might want to install another color profile that lets you better control how colors are printed on your printer. To do so, follow these steps:

1. **Open the Add Profile Association dialog box, which is shown in Figure 3-16.**

   Click the Add button.

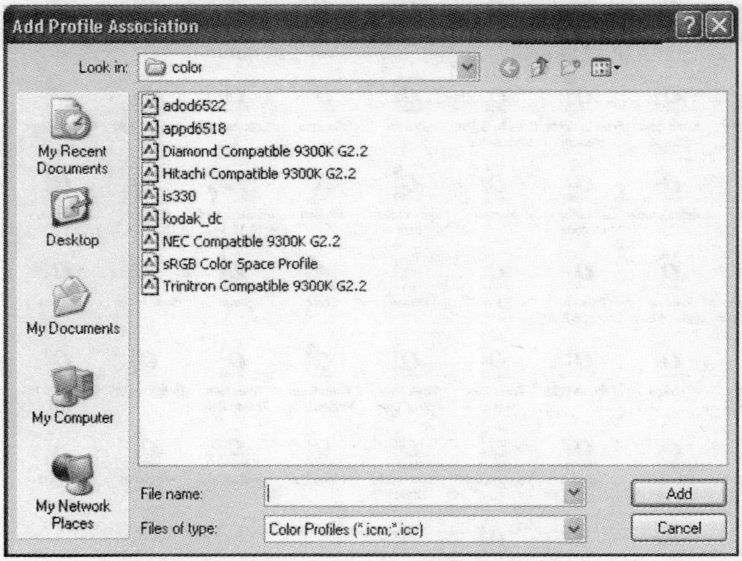

Figure 3-16 The Add Profile Association dialog box.

2. **Select a new profile.**

   Select a color profile from the list, and then click Add. Back in the Color Management tab, click OK.

To delete a color profile, select it in the Color Management tab and click Remove.

Installing and Using Fonts

When you print using any of the methods we've described in this chapter, you use a particular typeface, or *font*. Examples of fonts included with Windows XP Professional include Comic Sans MS (a popular font for use in Web pages), Courier (which looks like a typewriter did the printing), and Times New Roman (the default for printing in Windows applications). To see the entire selection of fonts, follow these steps:

1. **Open Control Panel.**

   Click the Start button, and then click Control Panel.

2. **Open the Fonts folder, which is shown in Figure 3-17.**

   In the Control Panel bar, click Switch To Classic View, and then double-click the Fonts icon.

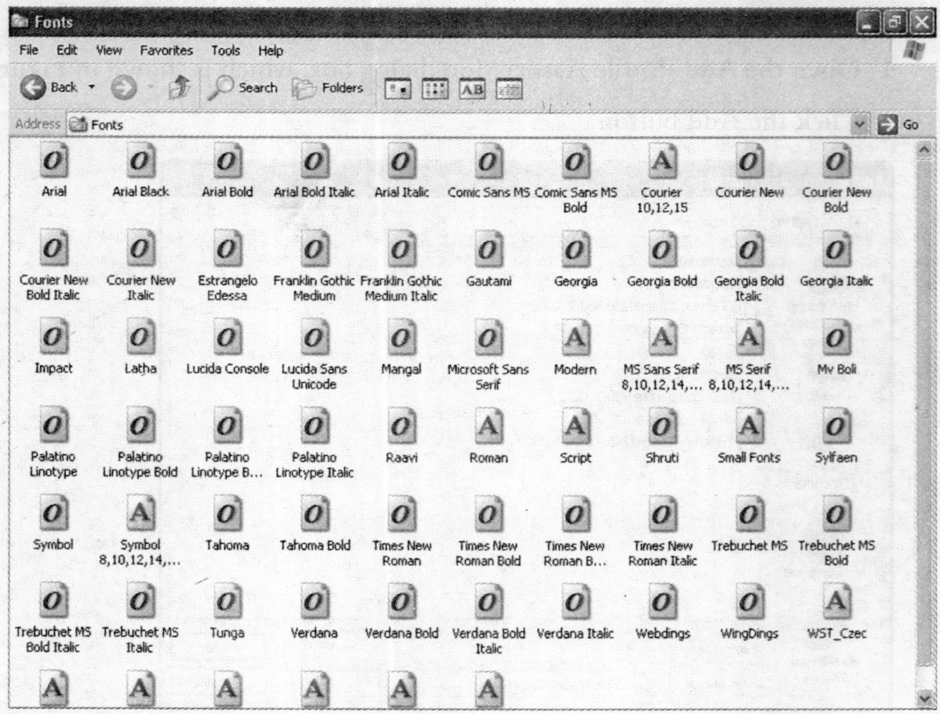

Figure 3-17 The Fonts folder.

You'll notice that fonts are identified with a lettered icon, which indicates the type of a font:

- The icon containing the letter O indicates an OpenType font, which is an extension of TrueType. An OpenType font also looks the same on the screen and when printed, and it can be rotated and scaled to various sizes.
- The icon containing the letter A indicates either a vector font or a raster font. Vector fonts are used primarily with plotters. Raster fonts are stored as bitmap images. They cannot be scaled or rotated and won't print if your printer doesn't support them.

A font can have size, which is measured in points (1 point is 1/72 inch), and style (for example, italic or boldface). To see what a particular font looks like in various sizes, double-click its icon. Figure 3-18 shows how Comic Sans MS looks in various sizes. To print this screen, click the Print button.

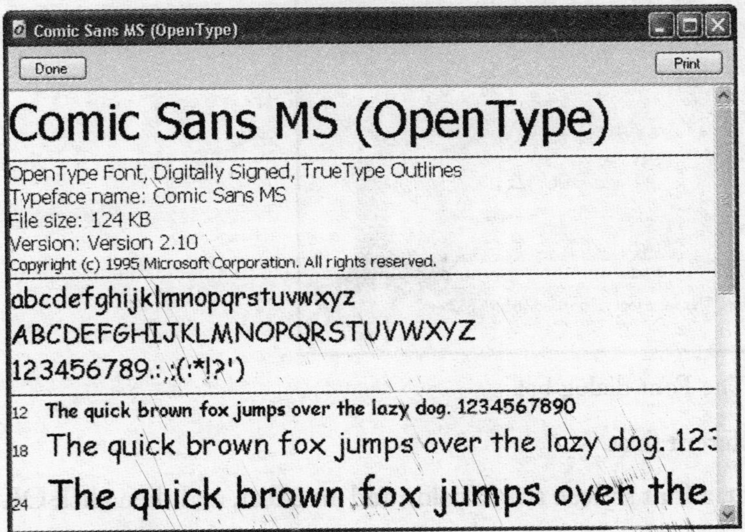

Figure 3-18 Checking out the look of a font at several sizes.

To display a list of fonts that are similar, select a font, click the View menu, and then click List Fonts By Similarity. To display only the basic fonts and not all variations—roman, italic, bold, bold italic, and so on—click the View menu and then click Hide Variations.

Changing the Font in an Application

To change the default font and print a document in a font that you specify, you must print from an application. The steps are the same in most Windows applications. Follow these steps to specify the font for a printed document in WordPad:

1. Open WordPad.

Click the Start button, click All Programs, click Accessories, and then click WordPad.

2. Open the Font dialog box, which is shown in Figure 3-19.

Click the Format menu, and then click Font.

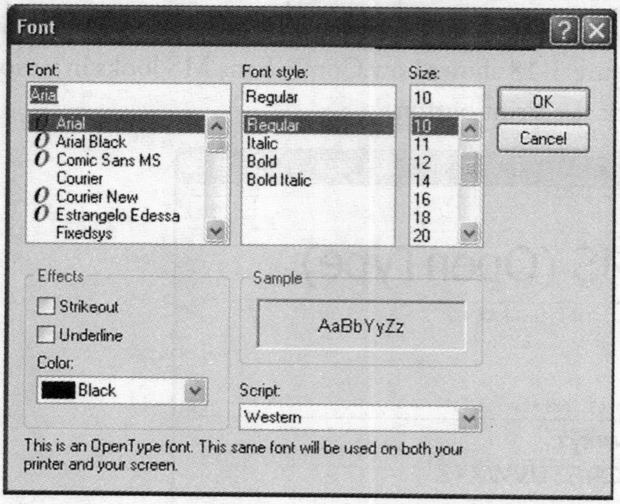

Figure 3-19 The Font dialog box.

3. Select a different font.

Select a font, a font style, a size, a color, and an effect, and then click OK.

Installing a New Font

Although Windows XP Professional comes with a great many fonts in all sorts of styles and sizes, you may want to install other fonts for particular purposes. Follow these steps:

1. Open the Add Fonts dialog box, which is shown in Figure 3-20.

In the Fonts folder, click the File menu, and then click Install New Font.

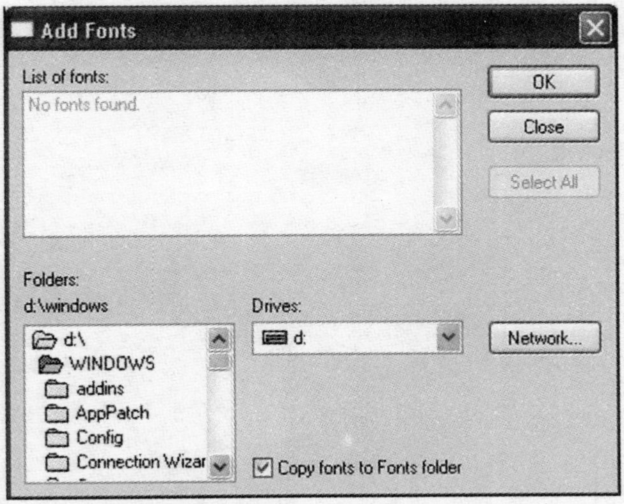

Figure 3-20 The Add Fonts dialog box.

2. **Locate and install the font.**

   In the Drives drop-down list box, select the drive where the font is stored, and click OK. By default, fonts are copied to the Fonts folder.

Summary

In this chapter, we've looked at how to install a local printer and a network printer, at the various ways to print in Windows XP Professional, at how to manage the printing process, at how to customize the way your printer works, and at how to use and install fonts.

Chapter 4

USING THE CONTROL PANEL TOOLS

Featuring:

- Understanding Control Panel
- Making Windows XP Professional More Accessible
- Setting the Date and Time
- Customizing the Display
- Adjusting the Mouse
- Adjusting the Keyboard
- Setting the Regional and Language Options
- Adding Hardware to Your System
- Adding and Removing Programs
- Personalizing the Start Menu
- Understanding User Profiles
- Looking at the Registry

You can use Windows XP Professional just as it comes out of the box, but as you become familiar with it, you'll probably want to tinker a bit—or maybe a lot. If you're working on a corporate network, your system administrator may have set things up so that you can't tinker with certain features. In addition, you must have permission to change some features, such as the date and time. To modify other features, you need to be logged on as Computer Administrator. Of course, if you have a network set up in your business, you probably are the Computer Administrator, and you can do anything you want.

In Windows XP Professional, you use Control Panel to customize features. Any changes you make are stored in the *Registry*, which is a database that contains all the configuration information about your system. (You'll find a brief discussion of the Registry at the end of this chapter.) If you are a knowledgeable user and have some technical background, you could make the changes directly in the Registry, but that is a risky undertaking. You can inadvertently bring down your entire system if you don't know exactly what you are doing.

Instead of using the Registry, use the applets in Control Panel to customize your system. This chapter will start with an overview of Control Panel and then tell you step by step how to personalize certain features so that you can set up Windows XP Professional to work the way you want to work.

Understanding Control Panel

If you've been following along with the previous chapters, you've already used Control Panel several times. The applets in Control Panel are theoretically small applications, but as you will see some of them are anything but small, and many are extremely powerful.

As you already know, to open Control Panel you click the Start button and then click Control Panel. Chapter 1 explained that in Windows XP Professional, Control Panel is available in two views: Category view and Classic view. The default view is Category view, which is shown in Figure 4-1.

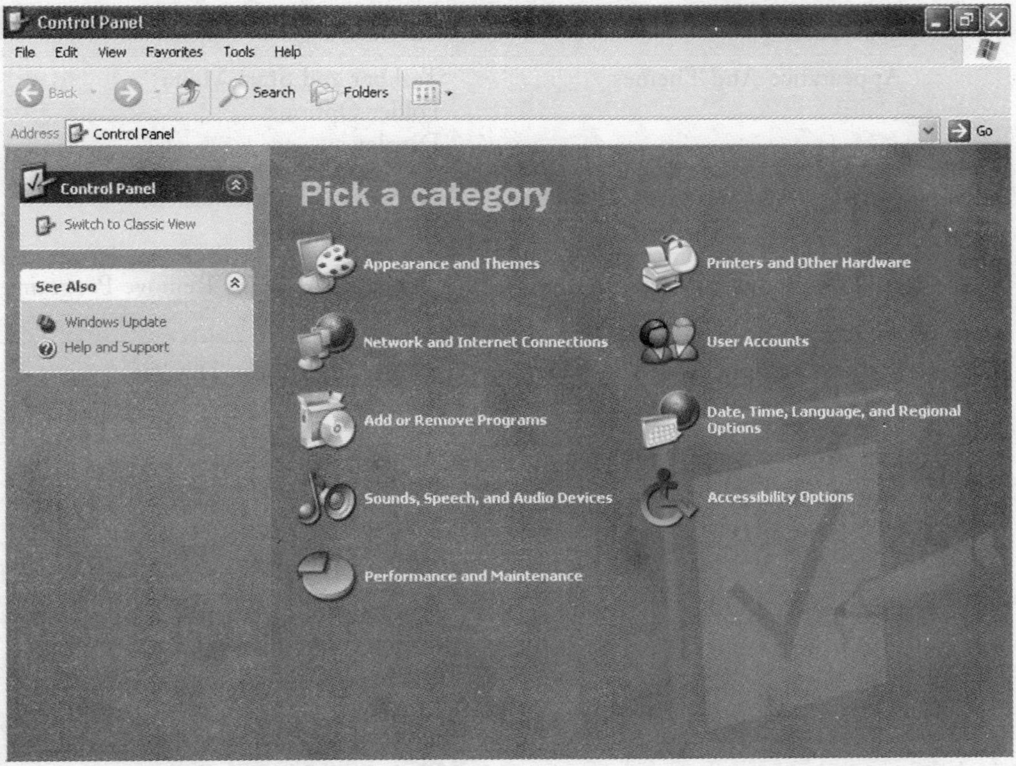

Figure 4-1 Control Panel in Category view.

If you've used previous versions of Windows, you may find this view of Control Panel puzzling. It's not immediately obvious which applets are in which category, and to open an applet, you must first select the category and then select the applet. Table 4-1 shows what you'll find in each category.

CATEGORY	CONTENTS
Appearance And Themes	Taskbar and Start Menu Folder Options Display
Network And Internet Connections	Network Connections Internet Options
Add Or Remove Programs	Opens the Add Or Remove Programs dialog box
Sounds, Speech, And Audio Devices	Sounds and Audio Devices Speech
Performance And Maintenance	Administrative Tools Scheduled Tasks System Power Options
Printers And Other Hardware	Printers and Faxes Scanners and Cameras Game Controllers Mouse Keyboard Phone and Modem Options
User Accounts	Opens the User Accounts folder
Date, Time, Language, And Regional Options	Regional and Language Options Date and Time
Accessibility Options	Accessibility Options

Table 4-1 Category contents in Control Panel.

As you will see when we look at some individual applets in the categories, the category folder, in many cases, also contains a list of tasks that are related to the applets in that category.

Notice that on the left of Control Panel in Category view is a See Also bar that contains links to Windows Update and Help And Support. If you are connected to the Internet, clicking Windows Update takes you to the Microsoft Windows Update site at *http://windowsupdate.microsoft.com/*. Clicking Help And Support opens Help And Support Center, which was discussed in Chapter 1.

If you don't find Category view to your liking, you can switch to Classic view of Control Panel, which is shown in Figure 4-2. To do so, click the Switch To Classic View link in the Control Panel bar.

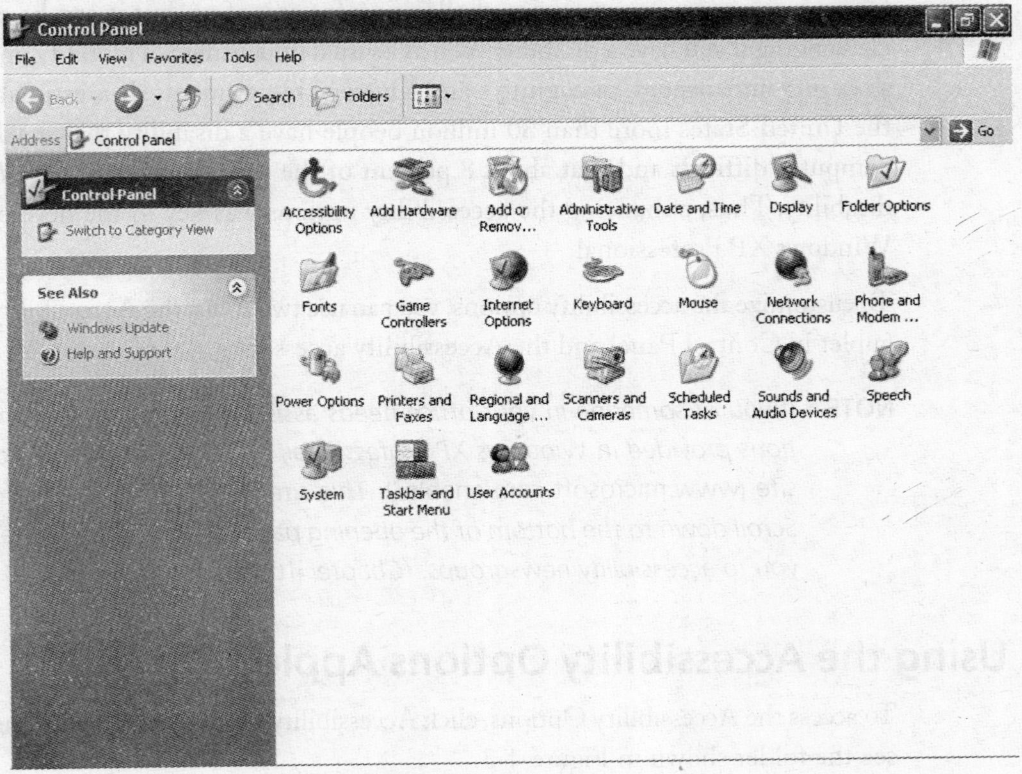

Figure 4-2 Control Panel in Classic view.

Figure 4-2 shows Control Panel in Classic view and in Icons view. You can also display Classic view in Thumbnails, Tiles, List, and Details view. Click the View menu, and then choose a view. Notice that in Classic view you also have the See Also bar that contains Windows Update and Help And Support links.

Because Windows XP Professional displays Control Panel in Category view by default, this chapter will use that view. We won't discuss how every single applet works (some are discussed in other chapters), but we will discuss those that you're likely to use most often.

Making Windows XP Professional More Accessible

Using a computer is sometimes challenging for any of us, but it can be even more challenging if you have a disability such as a visual impairment, a mobility impairment, a hearing impairment, or cognitive and language impairments. It is estimated that in the United States more than 30 million people have a disability that makes using a computer difficult and that about 8 percent of the people who use the Web have a disability. Thus, enhancing the accessibility options was key in the development of Windows XP Professional.

To customize the accessibility options, you can use two tools: the Accessibility Options applet in Control Panel and the Accessibility accessories.

NOTE *If you or someone in your office needs assistive technology beyond the options provided in Windows XP Professional, go to the Microsoft Accessibility site (www.microsoft.com/enable/). This site is a gold mine of information. Scroll down to the bottom of the opening page to click on a link that will take you to accessibility newsgroups. (Chapter 10 discusses newsgroups in detail.)*

Using the Accessibility Options Applet

To access the Accessibility Options, click Accessibility Options in Control Panel. You'll see the folder shown in Figure 4-3.

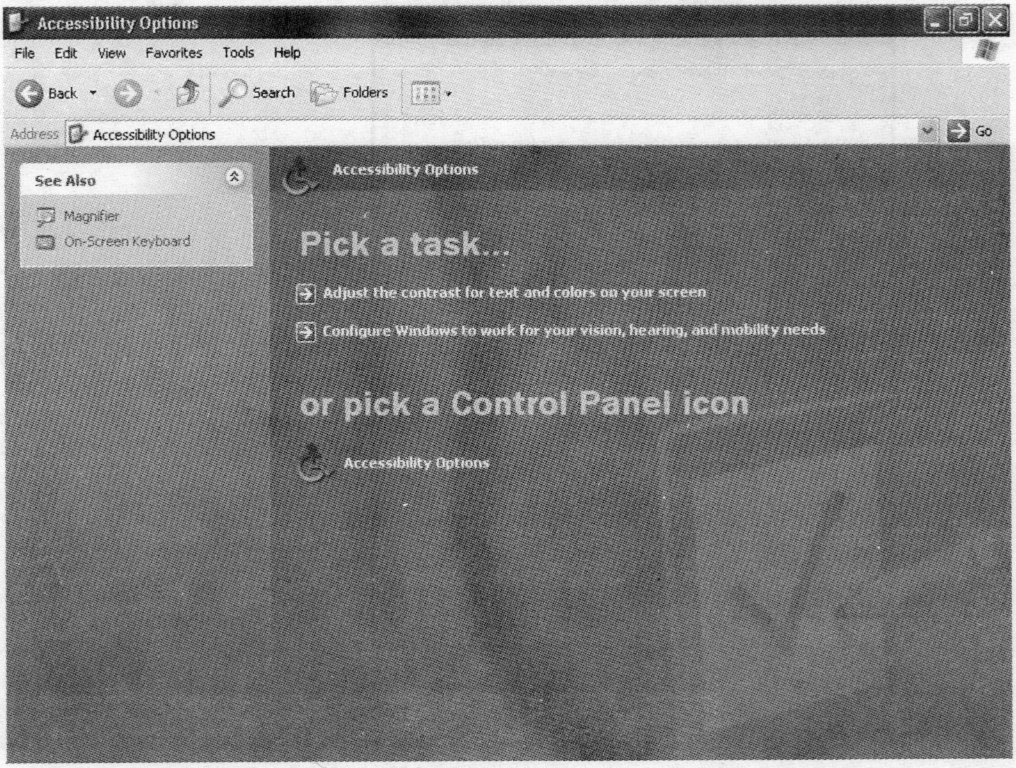

Figure 4-3 The Accessibility Options folder.

If you have difficulty seeing screen elements, you can display Windows colors in high contrast. Clicking the first task in the Accessibility Options folder, Adjust The Contrast For Text And Colors On Your Screen, opens the Accessibility Options dialog box at the Display tab, which is shown in Figure 4-4. Click the Use High Contrast check box to turn on high contrast. Click the Settings button in the High Contrast section to open the Settings For High Contrast dialog box, in which you can create a keyboard shortcut that enables high contrast and select a high contrast appearance scheme. You use the Cursor Options section of the Display tab to change the blink rate and width of the cursor.

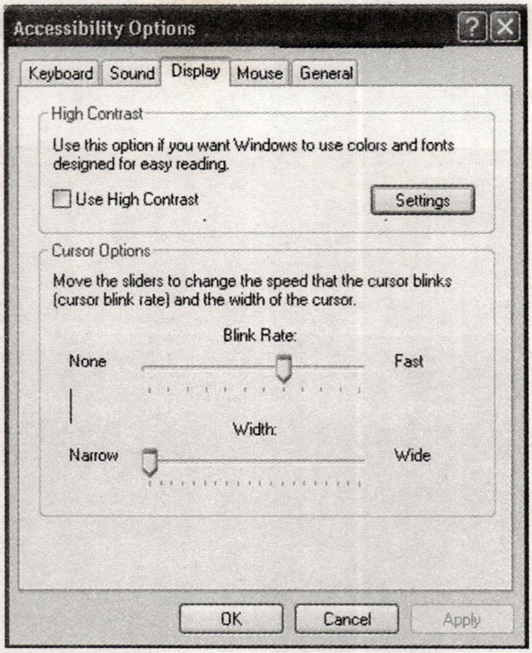

Figure 4-4 The Accessibility Options dialog box open at the Display tab.

Clicking the second task, Configure Windows To Work For Your Vision, Hearing And Mobility Needs, starts the Accessibility Wizard, which is an easy way to set up accessibility options, including some that you can also set in the Accessibility Options dialog box, which we'll look at next. You can tell the wizard what your particular disability is, and then you can follow simple onscreen instructions for ways to modify your computer for Windows XP Professional accordingly.

For example, start the wizard and click Next until you reach the Set Wizard Options screen, as shown in Figure 4-5. Click the I Am Blind Or Have Difficulty Seeing Things On Screen check box, and then click Next. The wizard will then step you through selecting how you want to view components such as scroll bars, icons, colors, the mouse cursor, and so on.

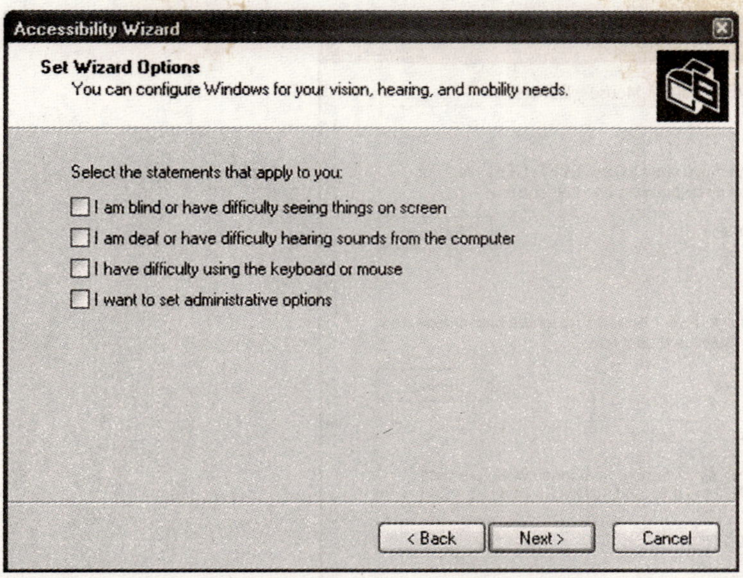

Figure 4-5 Informing the Accessibility Wizard of your particular disability.

TIP *When you select to save your settings in the wizard, you can take the file and apply those settings to another computer.*

Clicking the Accessibility Options link in the Or Pick A Control Panel Icon section of the Accessibility Options folder opens the Accessibility Options dialog box at the Keyboard tab, which is shown in Figure 4-6.

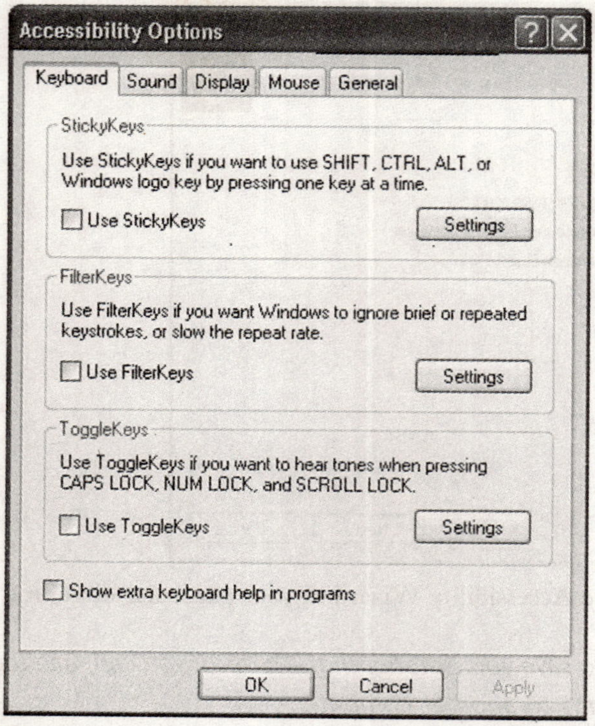

Figure 4-6 The Accessibility Options dialog box open at the Keyboard tab.

In the Keyboard tab, you can customize your keyboard in the following ways:

- Click the Use StickyKeys check box if you have difficulty pressing two keys at once, such as Ctrl+Alt. To fine-tune the use of StickyKeys, click the Settings button and use the options in the Settings For StickyKeys dialog box.
- Click the Use FilterKeys check box if you want Windows XP Professional to ignore short or repeated keystrokes or to slow the repeat rate. To fine-tune the use of FilterKeys, click the Settings button and use the options in the Settings For FilterKeys dialog box.
- Click the Use ToggleKeys check box if you want to hear a sound when you press Caps Lock, Num Lock, and Scroll Lock. Click the Settings button to open the Settings For ToggleKeys dialog box, in which you can enable or disable a shortcut that activates ToggleKeys.

Earlier you saw how to use the Display tab to adjust contrast and cursor options. You can use the other tabs in the Accessibility Options dialog box to adjust the sound and the mouse as follows:

- Click the Sound tab, and then click the Use SoundSentry check box if you want a visual cue when your system generates a sound. Click the Use ShowSounds check box if you want captions for speech and sounds that an application makes.
- Click the Mouse tab, and then click the Use MouseKeys check box if you want to control the mouse pointer from the numeric keypad.
- Click the General tab to specify an idle time interval after which accessibility features are turned off, to enable warning messages or sounds that signal the turning on or off of a feature, to enable an alternative mouse or keyboard device, and to select administrative options.

Using Magnifier

As you were clicking through screens in the Accessibility Wizard, you may have noticed a screen that let you select to use Microsoft Magnifier. Magnifier is a utility that displays a magnified portion of your screen in a separate window, as shown in Figure 4-7.

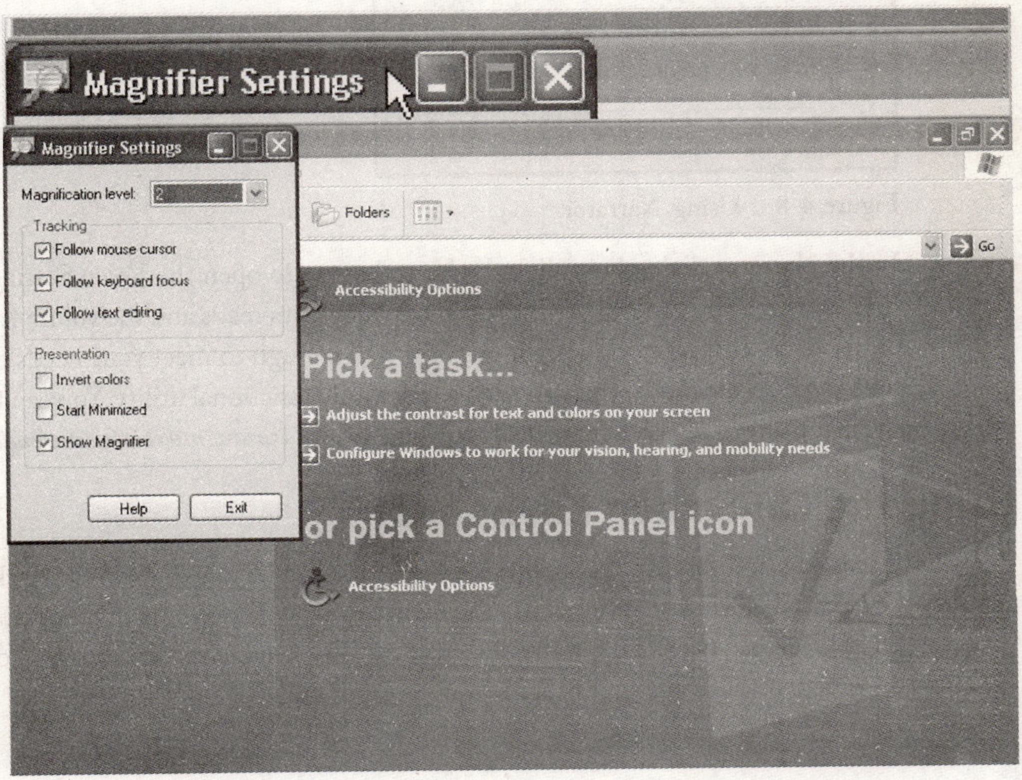

Figure 4-7 Setting up Magnifier.

To set up Magnifier, select it from the See Also bar in the Accessibility Options folder. In the Magnifier Settings dialog box, you can tell Magnifier to follow the mouse, the keyboard focus, or text editing. To return to normal view, click the Close button in the Magnifier Settings dialog box.

Running Narrator

If you have difficulty reading the screen or if you are assisting a user who is blind, you can enable Sam, the Windows XP Professional Narrator. Sam reads aloud menu commands, dialog box options, and so on. To open the Narrator dialog box, which is shown in Figure 4-8, click the Start button, click All Programs, click Accessories, click Accessibility, and then click Narrator. Sam reads aloud the contents of this dialog box.

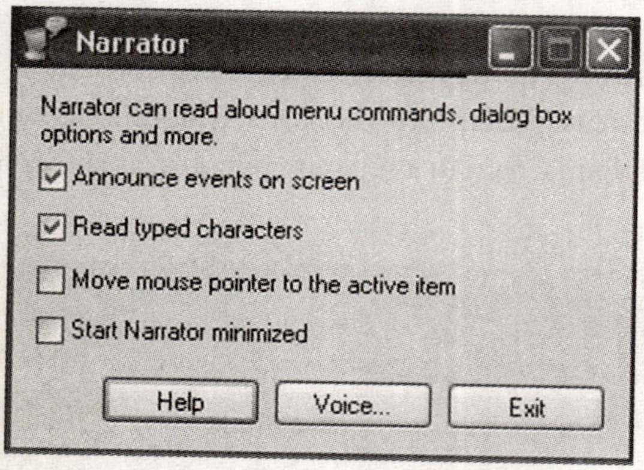

Figure 4-8 Using Narrator.

In the Narrator dialog box, click the Voice button to open the Voice Settings dialog box, in which you can modify the speed at which Sam reads and the volume and pitch of his voice. If Narrator does not perform well enough to meet your needs or cannot read some applications, you will need a more fully functional utility. You can find a list of such utilities at the Microsoft Accessibility site (*www.microsoft.com/enable/*).

Using the On-Screen Keyboard

If you have a disability that makes typing difficult, you might want to check out the On-Screen Keyboard. You can use the mouse to type. To see how this works, click the On-Screen Keyboard link in the See Also bar. The On-Screen Keyboard is displayed on your screen, as shown in Figure 4-9.

Figure 4-9 The On-Screen Keyboard.

Click the keys with your mouse. You can alternate between "typing" and choosing menu commands. When you're finished, click the Close button.

TIP *If you can't see a portion of the screen where you need to type, click the keyboard's title bar and drag the keyboard to a new location.*

Using Utility Manager

You use Utility Manager, which is shown in Figure 4-10, to start and stop Magnifier, Narrator, and the On-Screen Keyboard and to specify that any of the three start automatically when Windows starts or when you start Utility Manager. To open Utility Manager, click the Start button, click All Programs, click Accessories, click Accessibility, and then click Utility Manager, or press the Windows logo key+U.

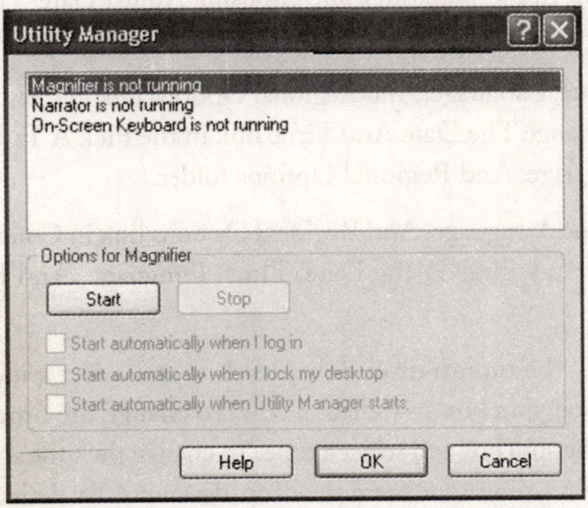

Figure 4-10 Utility Manager.

NOTE *From the Accessibility menu, you can also open the Accessibility Wizard, Magnifier, Narrator, and the On-Screen Keyboard.*

Setting the Date and Time

You set the date and time in Windows XP Professional in the Date And Time Properties dialog box, as shown in Figure 4-11.

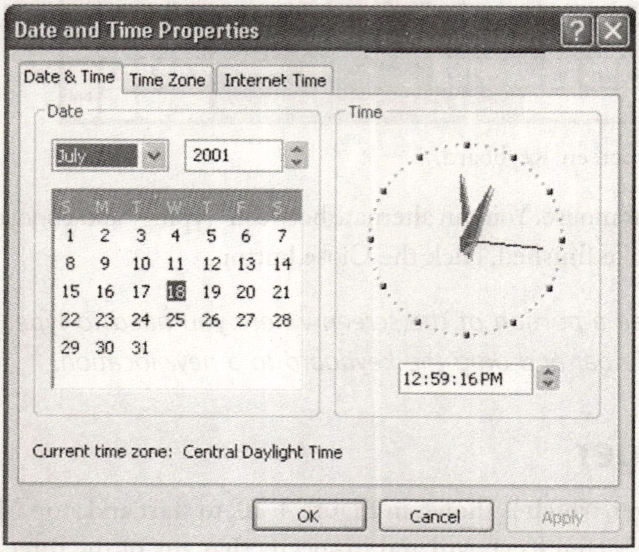

Figure 4-11 Adjusting the date and time.

You can open this dialog box in the following ways:

- By right-clicking the time in the status area and choosing Adjust Date/Time from the shortcut menu.
- By clicking the Date, Time, Language, And Regional Options link in Control Panel and then clicking the Change The Date And Time link in the Pick A Task section of the Date, Time, Language, And Regional Options folder.
- By clicking the Date, Time, Language, And Regional Options link in Control Panel and then clicking Date And Time in the Date, Time, Language, And Regional Options folder.

To change the month, click the month drop-down list box and select a month. To change the year, click the year spin box and select a year. To change the time, enter a time, or click the arrows in the spin box and select a time. To change the time zone, click the Time Zone tab and select a time zone from the drop-down list. By default, Windows XP Professional adjusts the time when the date arrives to go on daylight or standard time. If you don't want this to happen, clear the Automatically Adjust Clock For Daylight Saving Changes check box.

Click the Internet Time tab, which is shown in Figure 4-12, to synchronize your computer clock with a time server on the Internet. When you select this option, which is enabled by default, clocks are synchronized on a schedule that is determined by Windows (once a week) or by your computer manufacturer, which usually synchronizes clocks more frequently. In the Server drop-down list, you can choose from the time.windows.com server, which is operated by Microsoft, or time.nist.gov, which is operated by the U.S. government. You can also enter the name of another time server if it uses the Simple Network Time Protocol (SNTP). A server that uses Hypertext Transfer Protocol (HTTP) will not work for this purpose.

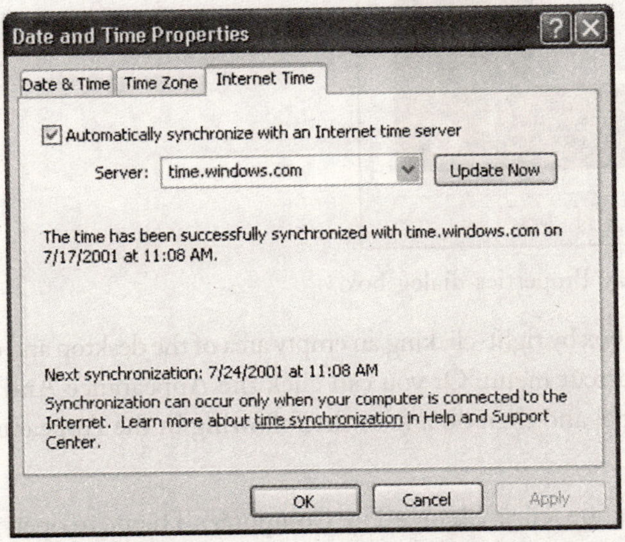

Figure 4-12 The Date And Time Properties dialog box open at the Internet Time tab.

NOTE *Remember, you must have permission to change the date and time if you are working on a network.*

Customizing the Display

The illustrations thus far in this book have used a standard Windows XP Professional theme on the desktop and a standard Windows color scheme for windows and buttons. You can customize these elements using the options in the Display Properties dialog box, which is shown in Figure 4-13.

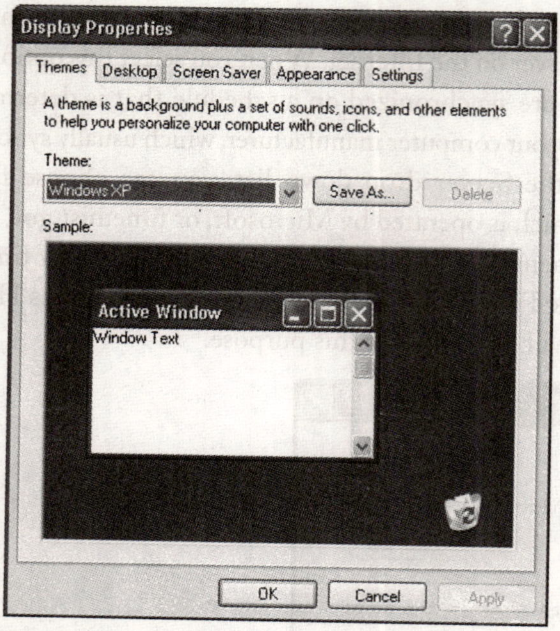

Figure 4-13 The Display Properties dialog box.

You can open this dialog box by right-clicking an empty area of the desktop and choosing Properties from the shortcut menu. Or you can click the Appearance And Themes category in Control Panel and then do any of the following in the Appearance And Themes folder:

- In the Pick A Task section, click Change The Computer's Theme to open the Display Properties dialog box at the Themes tab. A theme is a collection of display elements such as background, sounds, icons, and so on.
- In the Pick A Task section, click Change The Desktop Background to open the Display Properties dialog box at the Desktop tab.
- In the Pick A Task section, click Choose A Screen Saver to open the Display Properties dialog box at the Screen Saver tab.
- In the Pick A Task section, click Change The Screen Resolution to open the Display Properties dialog box at the Settings tab.
- In the Or Pick A Control Panel Icon section, click Display to open the Display Properties dialog box at the Theme tab.

Selecting a Theme

A theme is a collection of icons, colors, backgrounds, and so on that you can display on your desktop. By default, Windows XP Professional uses the Windows XP (Modified) theme, but you can choose from others that are included with the operating system or download a theme from the Microsoft site.

To see your choices, click the Theme drop-down list. Select an item, and then click OK to apply that theme. The Sample box will show what your theme will look like, so you can preview a theme before clicking OK.

To check out the themes available at the Microsoft site, be sure you are connected to the Internet and then click the More Themes Online item.

Customizing the Desktop

You have many options when it comes to choosing the background for your desktop and specifying which icons are displayed and for how long. The desktop background can be anything from a picture created in a drawing program to a piece of art that you download from the Internet. You can place a single picture in the center of the screen, you can tile the picture so that multiple identical images cover the screen, or you can stretch a picture so that it covers the entire screen.

Choosing a Background

In the Desktop tab of the Display Properties dialog box, which is shown in Figure 4-14, you can choose a background from any of the items in the Background list box. After you select a background, click the Position drop-down list to center it, tile it, or stretch it. You'll see the effect of your choice in the monitor. If you select Center, you can change the color of the surrounding background by clicking the Color drop-down list and making a selection from the list.

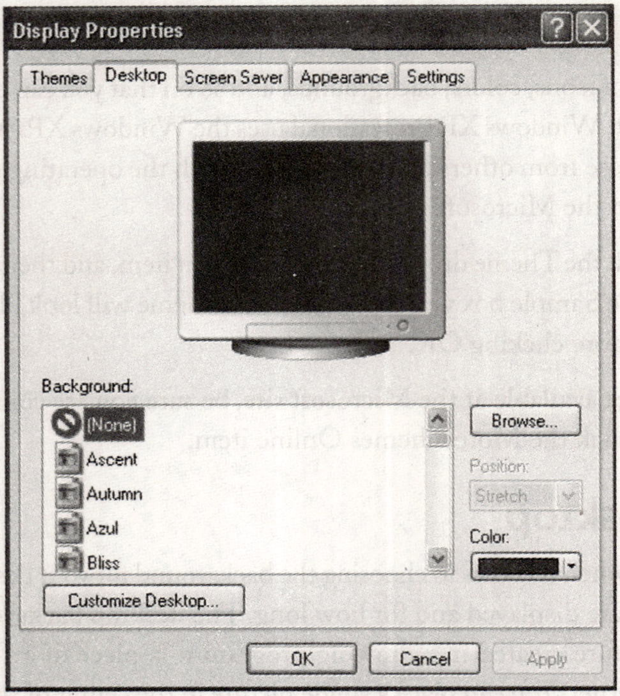

Figure 4-14 The Display Properties dialog box open at the Desktop tab.

You can use any kind of digital art as background. To use art you find on the Internet as background, right-click it and choose Set As Wallpaper from the shortcut menu. (The desktop background is also referred to as *wallpaper.*) To load a new file as wallpaper, follow these steps:

1. **Locate the file.**

   In the Display Properties dialog box, click the Browse button to open the Browse dialog box. Switch to the folder containing the bitmap file, select it, and click OK.

2. **Apply the new wallpaper.**

   Click OK in the Display Properties dialog box.

To specify desktop icons and to select a Web page to display on your desktop, click the Customize Desktop button to open the Desktop Items dialog box, as shown in Figure 4-15.

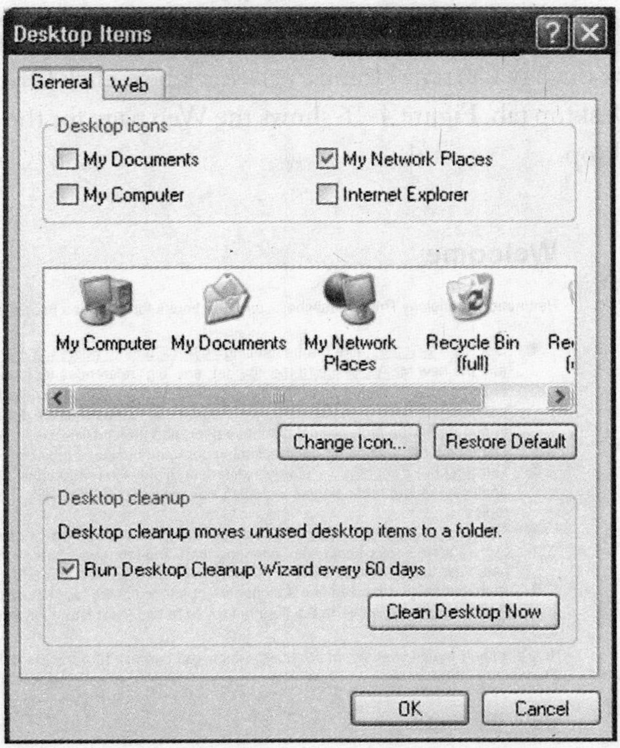

Figure 4-15 The Desktop Items dialog box open at the General tab.

Unless the manufacturer of your computer has added icons to the desktop, the only icon you'll see after first installing Windows XP Professional is the Recycle Bin. If you want to display an icon for My Documents, My Computer, or My Network Places, check that item in the Desktop Icons section of the General tab. If you want to change the icon for one of these items, select it, and click the Change Icon button to open the Change Icon dialog box. Select a different icon, and click OK.

TIP *To remove icons from the desktop, simply drag them to the Recycle Bin. Clearing an icon from the desktop removes only the visual representation, not the real thing, that is, the program itself.*

By default, Windows XP Professional removes any desktop icons that haven't been used during the last 60 days. To disable this feature, clear the Run Desktop Cleanup Wizard Every 60 Days check box. To remove any unused desktop icons now, click the Clean Desktop Now button.

If you want to display a Web page on your desktop, click the Web tab. To display your current home page, click the My Current Home Page check box, click OK, and then click OK again in the Desktop tab. Figure 4-16 shows the Web page for the publisher of this book on the desktop.

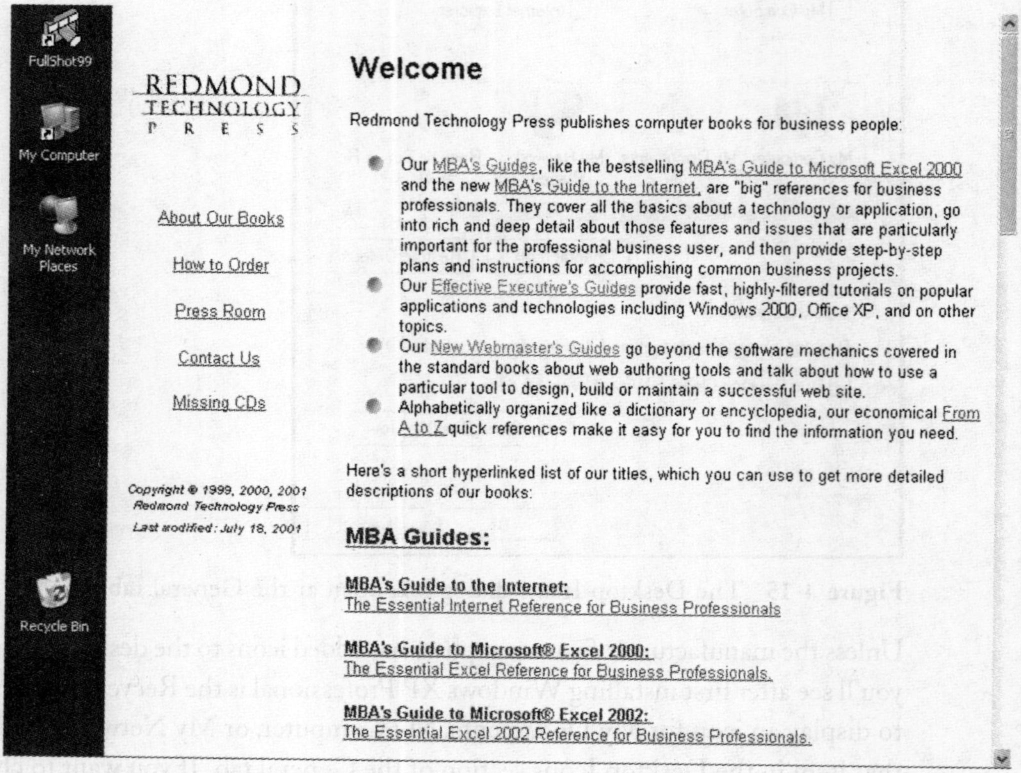

Figure 4-16 Displaying a Web page on the desktop.

To display a Web page other than your current home page, click the New button to open the New Desktop Item dialog box, enter the uniform resource locator (URL) of the page or browse for it, and then click OK.

Using a Screen Saver

A screen saver is a utility that displays a specified image on the screen after the computer has been idle for a certain amount of time. Originally, screen savers were used to prevent images from being permanently imprinted on the monitor's screen. Today's monitors need no such protection, but many people continue to use screen savers because they're decorative and fun.

To set up a screen saver, follow these steps:

1. **Select a screen saver.**

   In the Display Properties dialog box, click the Screen Saver tab, as shown in Figure 4-17, and then click the Screen Saver drop-down list to make a selection.

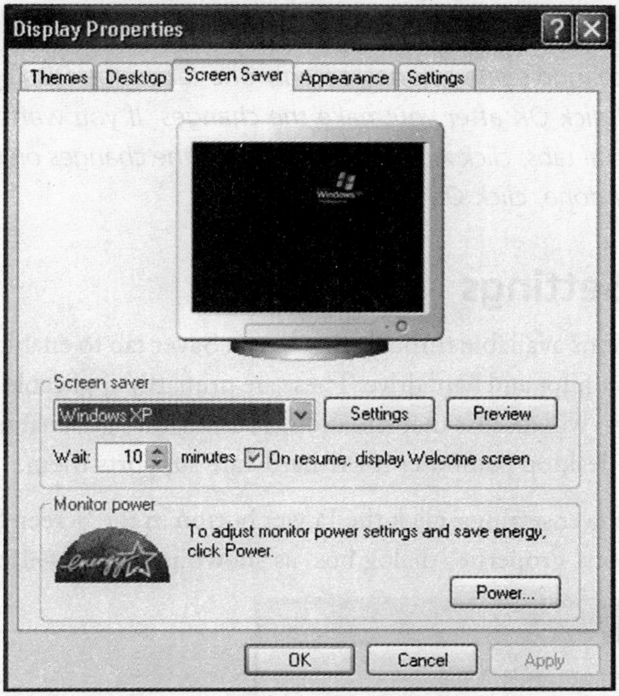

Figure 4-17 The Display Properties dialog box open at the Screen Saver tab.

TIP *If you've stored photos or other digital art in your My Pictures folder, you can display them as a slideshow screen saver by selecting My Pictures Slideshow from the Screen Saver drop-down list box. You might want to do this if you have a collection of new product illustrations or photos of award-winning employees, for example.*

2. **Set options for the screen saver.**

   You can customize some screen savers. To do so, click the Settings button to open the Settings dialog box. If the screen saver cannot be customized, you'll see a message box to that effect.

3. **Specify the idle time before the screen saver kicks in.**

   In the Wait spin box, click the arrows to specify the number of minutes your computer will be idle before displaying the screen saver.

During the display of a screen saver, you can click the mouse or press any key to return to what was on the screen before the screen saver kicked in. If a password is set for your logon account, you (or any other user) will have to log on again and enter that password to close the screen saver and return to what you were working on.

NOTE *If you want to change some settings on only one tab in the Display Properties dialog box, click OK after you make the changes. If you want to make changes on several tabs, click Apply after you make the changes on each tab. When you're all done, click OK.*

Establishing Power Settings

You can also use the options available through the Screen Saver tab to enable energy-saving features for your monitor and hard drive. These are primarily applicable to laptop computers, and Chapter 6 will discuss that situation. You can, though, enable energy-saving features for your desktop computer if the hardware supports them.

To set up or adjust the power settings, click the Power button in the Screen Saver tab to open the Power Options Properties dialog box, as shown in Figure 4-18.

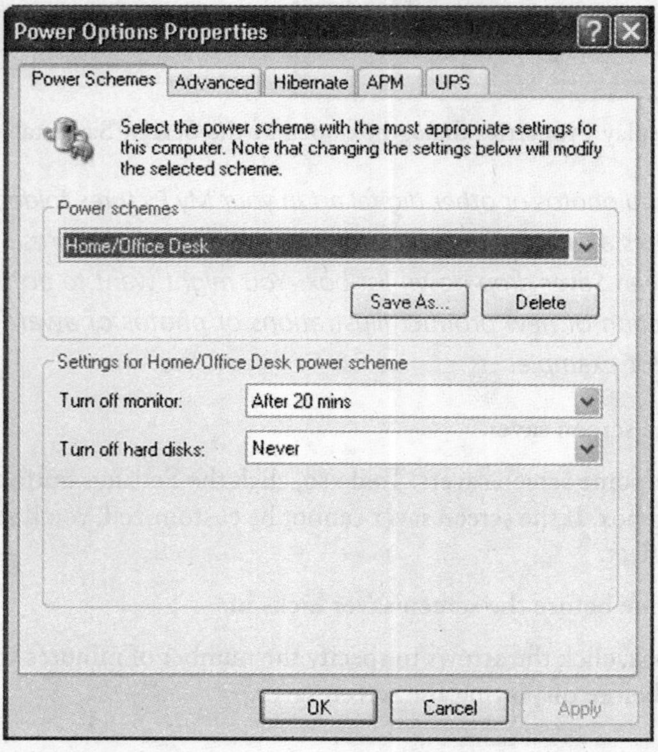

Figure 4-18 The Power Options Properties dialog box.

On the Power Schemes tab, you can do the following:

- Click the Power Schemes drop-down list to select a power scheme.
- Click the Turn Off Monitor drop-down list to specify when or whether to turn off the monitor.
- Click the Turn Off Hard Disks drop-down list to specify when or whether to turn off the hard disks.

Click the APM tab to enable Advanced Power Management if your hardware supports it, and click the UPS tab to configure an Uninterruptible Power Supply if one is installed on your system. In Chapter 6, I'll discuss the other options in this dialog box.

Changing Color and Fonts

Earlier, this chapter discussed how to change the background of the desktop. You can also change the color scheme and fonts for title bars, dialog boxes, menus, and so on. To do so, you use the options in the Appearance tab of the Display Properties dialog box, which is shown in Figure 4-19.

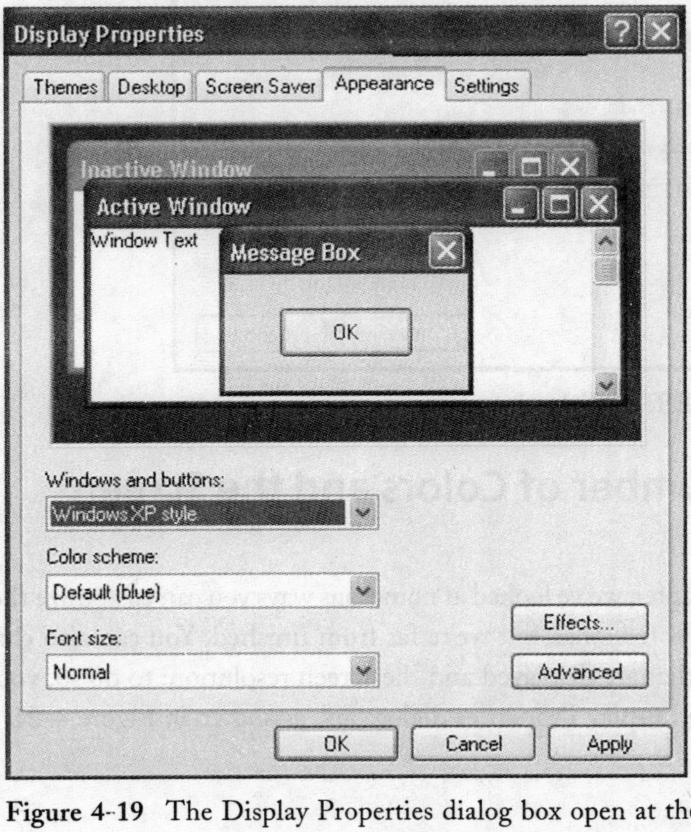

Figure 4-19 The Display Properties dialog box open at the Appearance tab.

- To change the style of windows and buttons, click the Windows And Buttons drop-down list and select a style.
- To change the color scheme, click the Color Scheme drop-down list and select a new color scheme. The box displays Windows elements in the color scheme you've selected, so you can preview before you commit to use it.
- To change the size of the display font, click the Font Size drop-down list and make a selection. Your choices are Normal, Large Fonts, and Extra Large Fonts.

By default, Windows XP Professional uses a fade effect when displaying menus and ScreenTips. To use a scroll effect instead and to customize the appearance of other elements, click the Effects button to open the Effects dialog box, which is shown in Figure 4-20. Clear or check an option to disable or enable it.

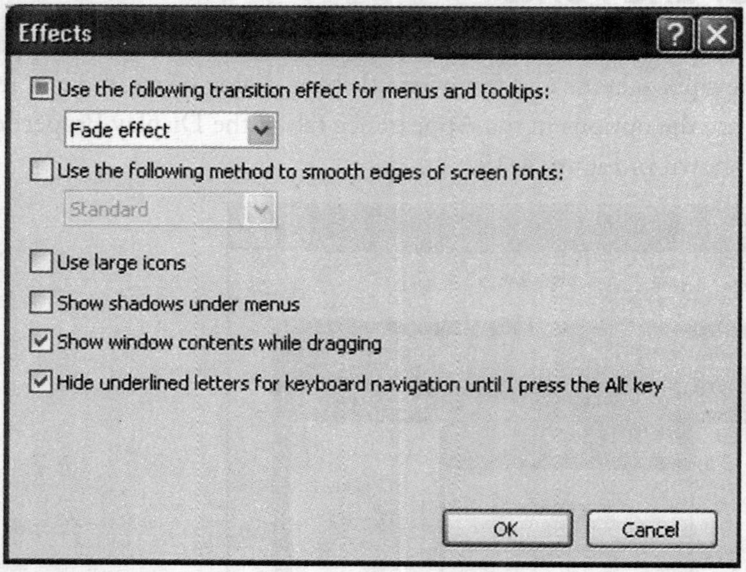

Figure 4-20 The Effects dialog box.

Changing the Number of Colors and the Screen Resolution

Thus far in this chapter, we've looked at numerous ways you can customize the display in Windows XP Professional, but we're far from finished. You can also change the number of colors that are displayed and the screen resolution; to do so, you use the Settings tab in the Display Properties dialog box, as shown in Figure 4-21.

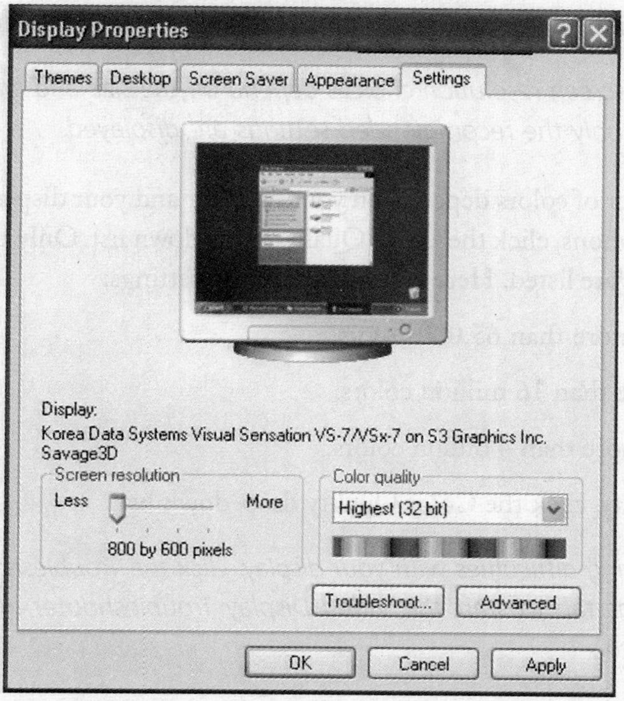

Figure 4-21 The Display Properties dialog box open at the Settings tab.

Resolution is the number of pixels (dots) on the screen. The higher the resolution, the smaller elements appear on the screen. So if you have a small monitor, you'll want to stick with a lower resolution. Here are some common settings and the monitors on which they display best:

- 640 by 480 is a standard Video Graphics Adapter (VGA) display, which is quite readable for most people on a 15-inch monitor.
- 800 by 600 is a super VGA display. On a 15-inch monitor, this is really small, but it's quite readable on a 17-inch monitor.
- 1024 by 768 is the upper limit of super VGA, and it's readable on a 17-inch monitor if you have good eyesight.
- 1280 by 1024 is a resolution for large monitors. You can hardly read the text at this resolution on a 17-inch monitor.

To change the resolution, you simply move the slider on the Screen Resolution bar.

NOTE *The available screen resolution choices depend on the size and type of your monitor, and only the recommended settings are displayed.*

The maximum number of colors depends on your monitor and your display adapter. To see the available options, click the Color Quality drop-down list. Only the recommended color settings are listed. Here are some common settings:

- Medium displays more than 65,000 colors.
- High displays more than 16 million colors.
- Highest displays more than 4 billion colors.

To select a color quality, click the Color Quality drop-down list.

TIP *If you are having difficulties with your display, click the Troubleshoot button in the Settings tab to start the Video Display Troubleshooter in Help and Support Center.*

If the screen resolution you use makes items too small to see comfortably, you can change the dots per inch (DPI) setting. Click the Advanced button in the Settings tab to open a Properties dialog box for your monitor. In the DPI Setting drop-down list box, select a larger size or click the Custom Setting item to open the Custom DPI Setting dialog box. Use the slider to scale the display to a percentage of normal size, which is 100 percent.

By default, Windows XP Professional does not restart when you change the display settings. This is usually okay, but if you find that some programs aren't operating properly, reboot your computer. If you always want the computer to reboot when you change the display settings, click that option in the Compatibility section of the General tab in the Properties dialog box for your monitor.

Using Multiple Monitors

When you are running Windows XP Professional, you can connect as many as 10 individual monitors to your system. You can attach multiple monitors to individual graphics adapters or to a single adapter if it supports multiple outputs.

When you are using multiple monitors, one monitor is primary, and that monitor displays the logon dialog box when you start your computer. The advantage to using multiple monitors is that you can run and work on numerous programs simultaneously and see them all at the same time. You can even stretch a huge Microsoft Excel worksheet across two monitors and view the entire worksheet without scrolling. When you open most programs, they are displayed first on the primary monitor.

If you have multiple monitors, you will see options for setting the resolution and color quality for all of them in the Display Properties dialog box. You can establish different settings for each monitor if you want.

Adjusting the Mouse

You can make some adjustments to the mouse using the Accessibility Wizard, which we looked at earlier in this chapter. Most often, though, you'll use the Mouse applet in Control Panel.

If you are left-handed, your first step after installing Windows XP Professional may have been to switch the mouse buttons, and you quickly found that you do this by clicking Printers And Other Hardware in Control Panel and then clicking Mouse to open the Mouse Properties dialog box, as shown in Figure 4-22.

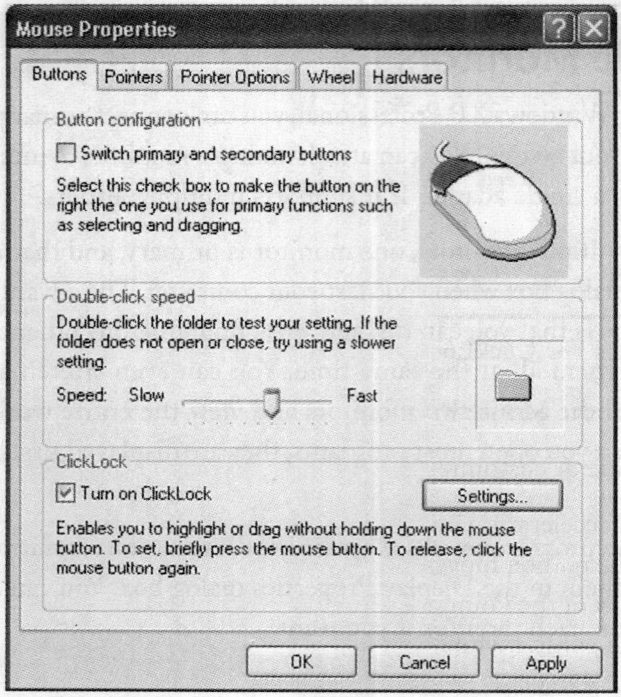

Figure 4-22 The Mouse Properties dialog box open at the Buttons tab.

To switch the mouse buttons, simply click the Switch Primary And Secondary Buttons check box. To adjust the double-click speed, move the pointer on the slider bar. You'll see the speed change in the test area, so you can preview before you implement the change. Double-clicking once opens the folder, and double-clicking again closes it.

ClickLock is a feature that lets you select or drag without holding down the mouse button continuously. If you enable ClickLock (by checking the Turn On ClickLock check box), simply press and hold down a mouse button or a trackball button for a moment. You can then drag objects or make multiple selections, for example. When the operation is complete, click the mouse or trackball button again to release ClickLock. To decrease or increase the time you need to hold down a button before your click is locked, click the Settings button in the ClickLock section of the Button tab to open the Settings For ClickLock dialog box, which is shown in Figure 4-23. Move the slider, and then click OK. You'll probably want to experiment with this feature. If you find you don't like using it, simply clear the Turn On ClickLock check box to disable ClickLock.

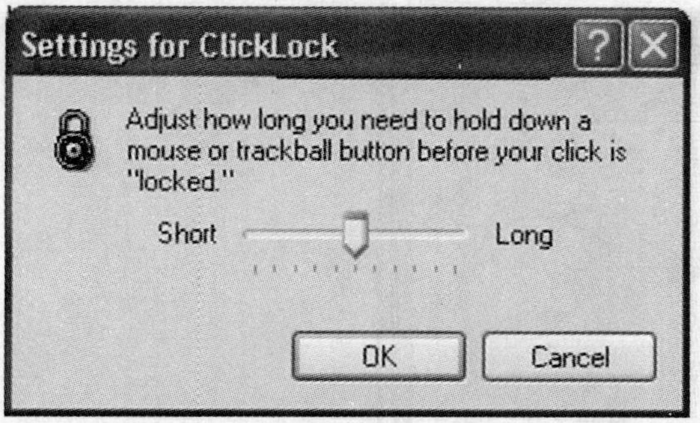

Figure 4-23 The Settings For ClickLock dialog box.

You use the other tabs in the Mouse Properties dialog box to do the following:

- Select a pointer scheme or customize a pointer in the Pointers tab.
- Adjust the speed and acceleration of your pointer in the Pointer Options tab. You can also specify that the pointer moves directly to the default button in dialog boxes. In the Visibility section of the Pointer Options dialog box, you can select to display pointer trails, hide the pointer while you are typing, and show the pointer location when you press the Ctrl key.
- In the Wheel tab, you can specify how many lines are scrolled per wheel notch.
- If your mouse isn't behaving properly, click the Hardware tab, and then click Troubleshoot to start the Mouse Troubleshooter in Help and Support Center.

Adjusting the Keyboard

When you install Windows XP Professional, the operating system recognizes your keyboard, and you don't normally need to tinker with the keyboard settings. You can, however, use the options in the Keyboard Properties dialog box, which is shown in Figure 4-24, to adjust the character repeat rate, the cursor blink rate, and to troubleshoot your keyboard. To open the Keyboard Properties dialog box, in Control Panel click Printers And Other Hardware and then click Keyboard.

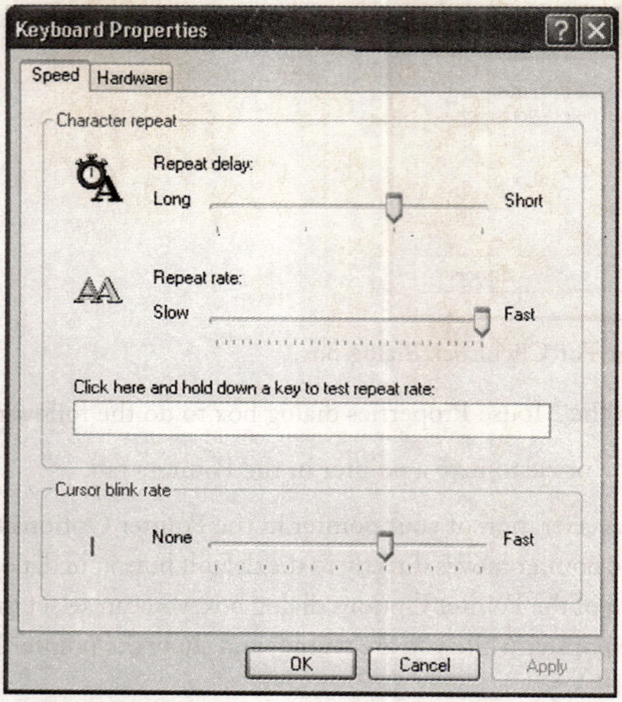

Figure 4-24 The Keyboard Properties dialog box.

In the Speed tab, click the pointer on the slider bars to set the repeat delay, the repeat rate, and the cursor blink rate. The Hardware tab contains information about your keyboard. If you are having problems with your keyboard, press the Troubleshoot button to start the Keyboard Troubleshooter in Help. Click Properties to display the Properties dialog box for your keyboard.

NOTE *If you have a digital camera, a scanner, or other imaging device attached to your computer, it is in all likelihood Plug and Play, and Windows XP Professional automatically recognized it, installed it, and configured it when you installed the operating system. To add, remove, or configure one of these devices, you can use the options in the Scanners And Cameras applet. Click Scanners And Cameras in the Printers And Other Hardware category in Control Panel.*

Setting the Regional and Language Options

During installation of Windows XP Professional, you chose a location, and then settings were established for that locale, including the language and the display of numbers, currencies, times, and dates. To change the locale, and thus these settings, you use the Regional And Language Options applet, which is shown in Figure 4-25. In Control Panel, click the Date, Time, Language, And Regional Options category, and then click Regional And Language Options.

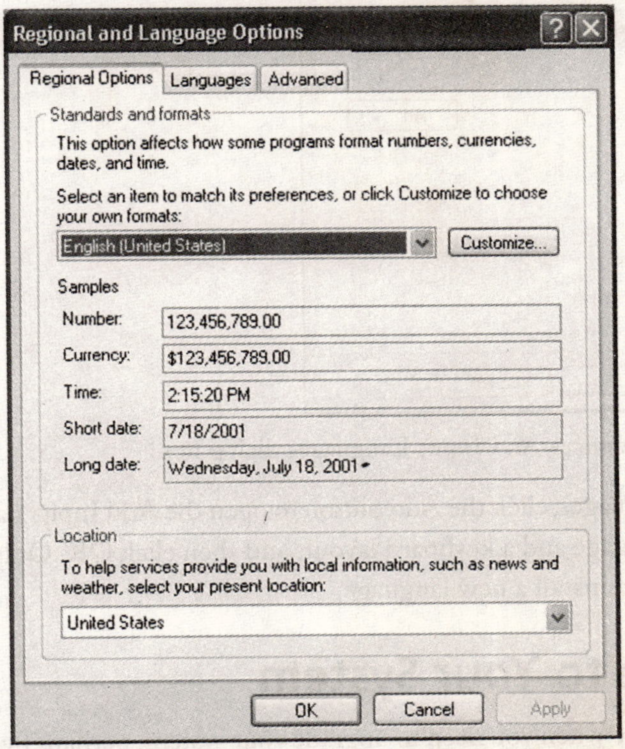

Figure 4-25 The Regional And Language Options dialog box open at the Regional Options tab.

To change the settings for dates and numbers, click the drop-down list box in the Standards And Formats section of the Regional Options tab. When you select a region, the boxes in the Samples section will display the associated formats. To change the formatting of individual items, click Customize to open the Customize Regional Options dialog box.

To view or change the language you selected during installation, click the Languages tab and then click the Details button to open the Text Services And Input Languages dialog box, which is shown in Figure 4-26.

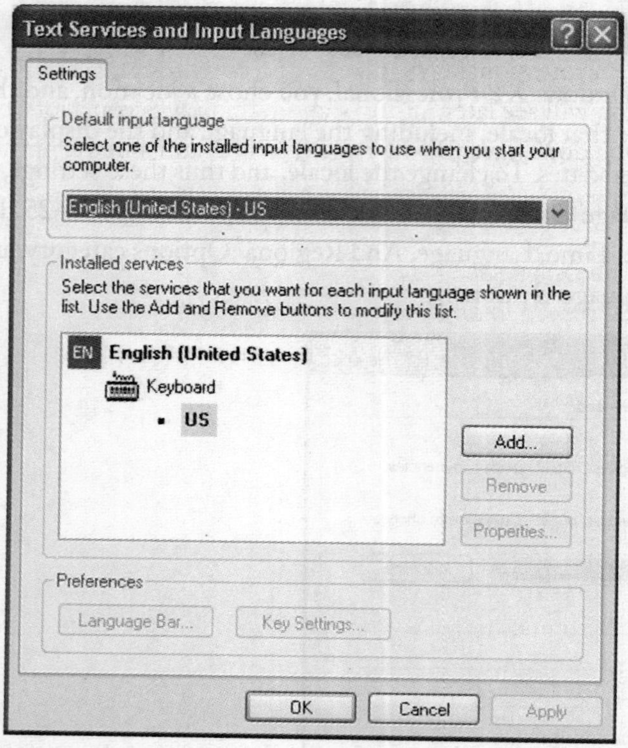

Figure 4-26 The Text Services And Input Languages dialog box.

To install additional languages, click the Add button to open the Add Input Language dialog box. Select a language and a keyboard layout, and then click OK. Only Computer Administrators can install a new language.

Adding Hardware to Your System

The time will surely come when you need to upgrade your system, perhaps by adding another hard drive, a faster modem, a scanner, and so on. If you work on a corporate network, your system administrator and some technicians will in all likelihood handle this. If you are your own system administrator in a small organization, it will be up to you.

Adding a piece of hardware to your system involves four main steps:

1. Acquiring the hardware
2. Connecting the hardware to your computer and turning it on
3. Loading the appropriate device driver
4. Configuring the hardware

A piece of advice about step 1: if at all possible, obtain a device that is Plug and Play–compliant. Windows XP Professional recognizes and configures Plug and Play devices automatically. And as you will see later in this section, that saves you a lot of time and aggravation. Basically, you don't have to bother with steps 3 and 4 in the preceding list.

To install new Plug and Play hardware, first turn off your computer.

TIP *If you're adding a Universal Serial Bus (USB) or Firewire device, all you need to do is plug the device in and turn it on. You don't need to turn your computer off first.*

Follow these steps:

1. **Connect the device.**

   Follow the manufacturer's instructions.

2. **Let Windows XP Professional do the rest.**

   Turn your computer back on to restart Windows XP Professional, which will locate the new hardware and configure it.

If for whatever reason you're installing a device that is not Plug and Play, you'll need to use the Add Hardware Wizard. First, turn off your computer, connect the device, and then turn your computer back on to restart Windows XP Professional. In Control Panel click the Printers And Other Hardware category, and then in the See Also bar, click Add Hardware to start the wizard, which is shown in Figure 4-27.

NOTE *You must log on as a Computer Administrator to run the Add Hardware Wizard.*

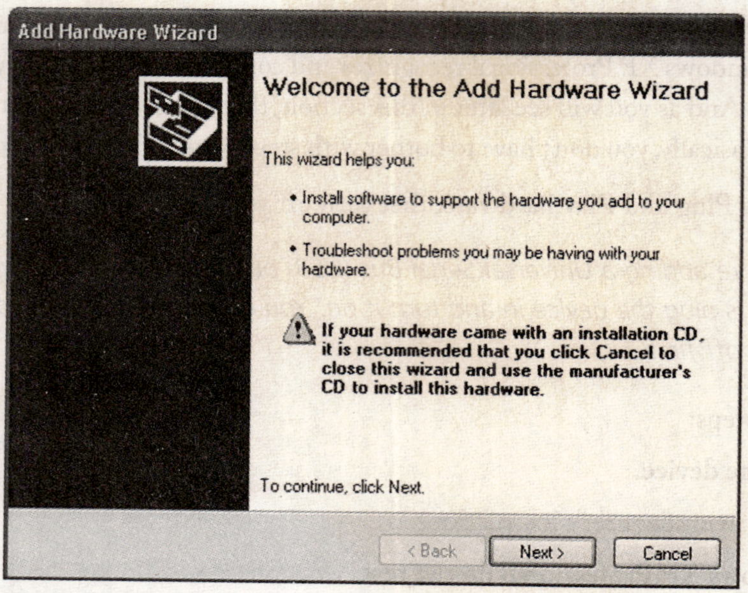

Figure 4-27 The Add Hardware Wizard.

At the Welcome screen, click Next, and then follow the onscreen instructions.

Adding and Removing Programs

To add and remove Windows applications and Windows components, you use the Add Or Remove Programs applet in Control Panel. To add an application that everyone on your system can use, you need to log on as a Computer Administrator. To add an application for a particular user on the system, log on with that person's user name.

NOTE *To add non-Windows programs, follow the instructions that are included with the application.*

Adding a New Program

To add a new program, follow these steps:

1. Open the Add Or Remove Programs dialog box.

In Control Panel, click the Add Or Remove Programs category link. You'll see the screen shown in Figure 4-28.

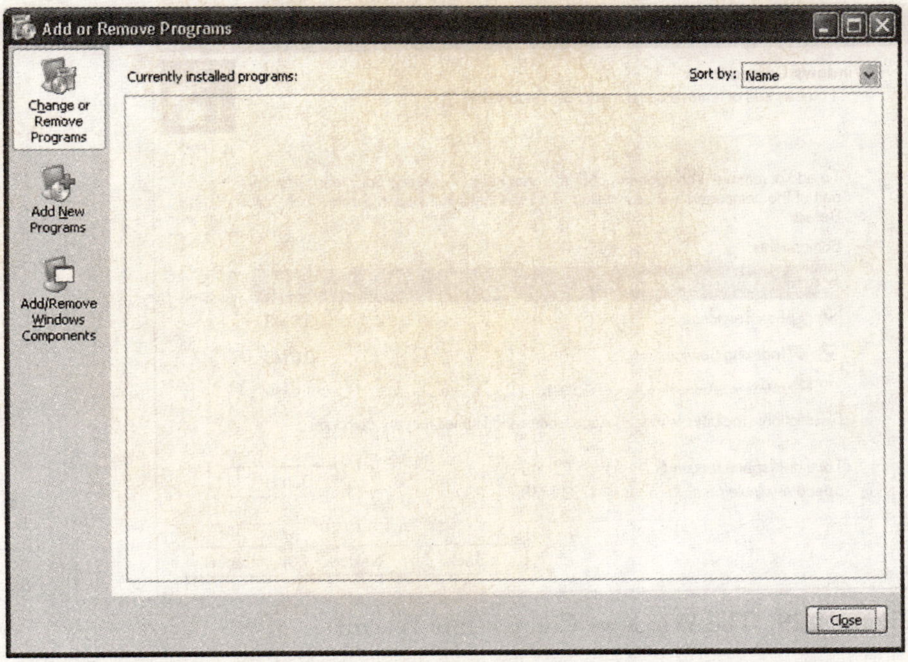

Figure 4-28 The Add Or Remove Programs dialog box.

2. **Install from a CD or a floppy disk.**

   Click the CD Or Floppy button. A wizard then guides you through installing and configuring the new application. Follow the onscreen instructions.

Changing and Removing Programs

From time to time, you will want to get rid of existing programs that you've installed or change them. If you've been a long-time user of Windows, you may remember the day when you could simply locate the executable file for a program and delete it. The only safe way to remove a program in Windows XP Professional is to click the Change Or Remove Programs button in the Add Or Remove Programs dialog box, select the program you want to remove, and then click the Change/Remove button.

Adding and Removing Windows Components

To add or remove a Windows XP Professional component, you will need to be logged on as a Computer Administrator, and you will need your installation CD at hand. Insert it in the drive, and then click Add/Remove Windows Components in the Add Or Remove Programs dialog box to start the Windows Components Wizard, as shown in Figure 4-29. To add or remove a component, follow the onscreen instructions.

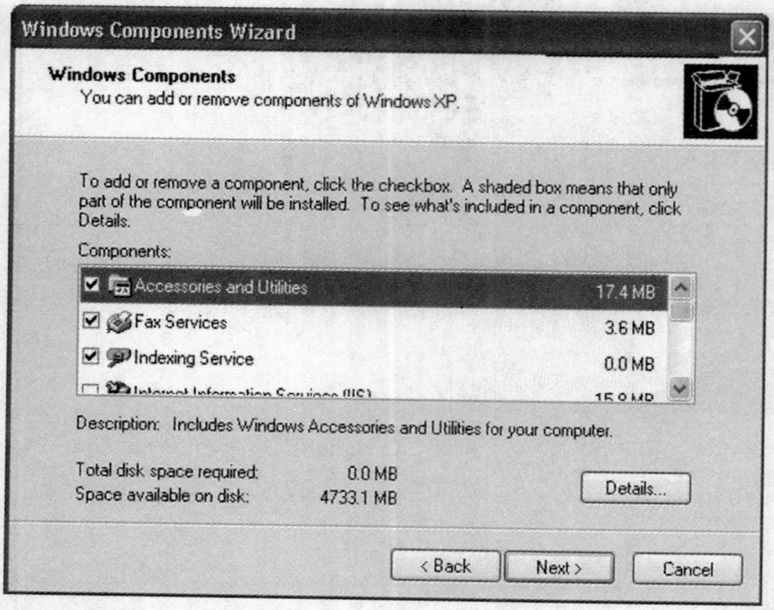

Figure 4-29 The Windows Components Wizard.

Personalizing the Start Menu

You can personalize your Start menu in many ways. To do so, follow these steps:

1. **Open the Taskbar And Start Menu Properties dialog box at the Start Menu tab, which is shown in Figure 4-30.**

   Right-click an empty area of the taskbar, choose Properties from the shortcut menu, and then click the Start Menu tab.

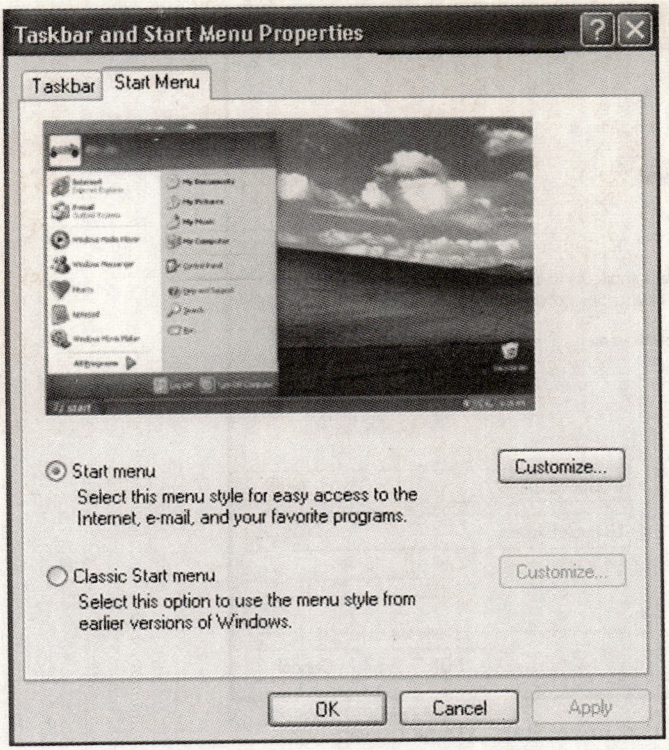

Figure 4-30 The Taskbar And Start Menu Properties dialog box open at the Start Menu tab.

2. Revert to the Classic Start menu.

If you prefer the Start menu as it appeared in previous versions of Windows, click the Classic Start Menu option button, and then click OK.

3. Open the Customize Start Menu dialog box, which is shown in Figure 4-31.

Be sure that the Start Menu option is selected, and then click the Customize button.

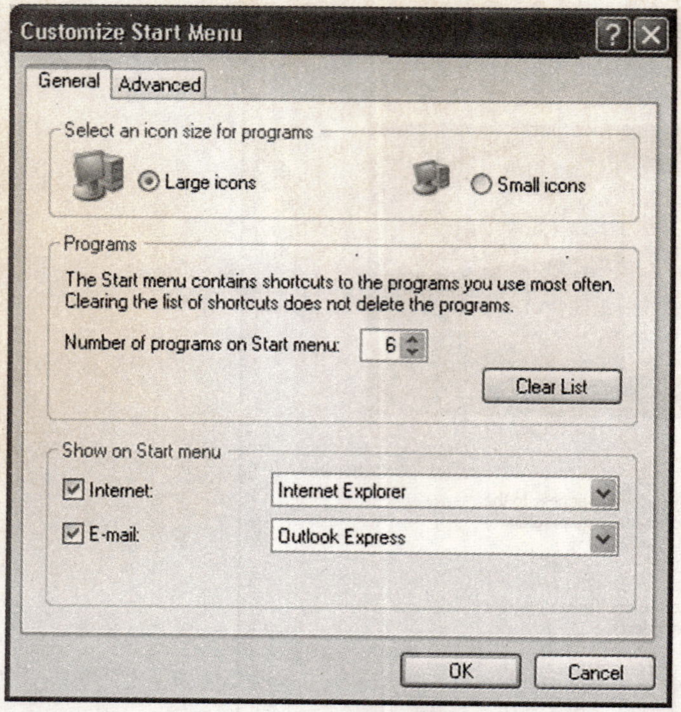

Figure 4-31 The Customize Start Menu dialog box.

4. **Select options in the General tab.**

   In the Select An Icon Size For Programs section, click either Large Icons or Small Icons. In the Programs section, click the Number Of Programs On Start Menu drop-down list box to select how many programs will be displayed. You can choose none to a maximum of 30. In the Show On Start Menu section, select whether you want to display an Internet or an e-mail program, and then click the drop-down lists to select the specific program.

5. **Select options in the Advanced tab.**

   Click the Advanced tab, and tell Windows the settings you want for the Start menu, which items to show, and whether to include a Recent Documents item. Click OK.

Understanding User Profiles

A user profile is a collection of settings that are applied each time you log on to the system. These settings include the following:

- Your Start menu options.
- The desktop icons you've selected.

- The display colors you've specified.
- The wallpaper, background, and screen saver you chose.
- Any accessibility options you've set up.
- Sounds that you've chosen to associate with system events.
- A special mouse cursor you want to use.

In other words, a user profile contains the settings for all the customization you've put in place using any of the tools discussed already in this chapter.

You can set up three types of user profiles:

- A *local* user profile was created the first time you logged on to your local hard drive after installing Windows XP Professional. When you then logged off, any changes you made to the display, accessibility options, and so on were stored in your user profile. If more than one user has logged on to your system, you will find multiple user profiles displayed in the list in the User Profiles dialog box. (More about this in a moment.) User profiles are commonly used on standalone and peer-to-peer systems.
- A *roaming* user profile is created for you by the Computer Administrator, and it follows you to any computer on the network that you log on to. Roaming user profiles are common on client/server networks.
- A *mandatory* user profile is also created by the Computer Administrator. It specifies settings for individuals and groups. If mandatory user profiles are in use, you cannot log on to the system until the appropriate mandatory user profile is found and loaded.

If you are the Computer Administrator and new users use your machine, you can create a user profile for a new user. Follow these steps:

1. **Set up a custom profile on the user's computer.**

   Log on as the new user; modify the display, wallpaper, and so on; and then log off.

2. **Open the System Properties dialog box.**

   Log back on to your computer as Computer Administrator, click the Start button, and then right-click My Computer to open the System Properties dialog box. Click the Advanced tab, and then click the Settings button in the User Profiles section to open the User Profiles dialog box, which is shown in Figure 4-32.

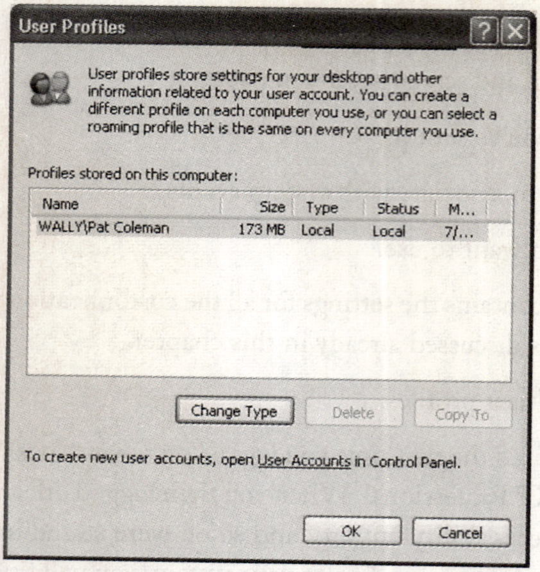

Figure 4-32 The User Profiles dialog box.

3. **Copy the new user profile to the default user profile.**

   Highlight the profile that you want to copy, and click the Copy To button to open the Copy To dialog box.

4. **Enter the path.**

   In the Copy Profile To box, enter *%SYSTEMROOT%\Documents & Settings\Default User*, and then click OK.

Looking at the Registry

The beginning of this chapter mentioned that all the customization changes you make using the Control Panel applets are stored in the Registry, and you were warned about tinkering directly with the Registry. But to be an informed user of Windows XP Professional, you should at least know what it looks like and what it contains. Besides, it is definitely not risky to simply open the Registry, take a peek, and close it back up.

Follow these steps to open the Registry:

1. **Open the Run dialog box.**

   Click the Start button, and then click Run.

2. **Open the Registry.**

   In the Open box, type *regedit*, and press Enter. You'll see something similar to Figure 4-33.

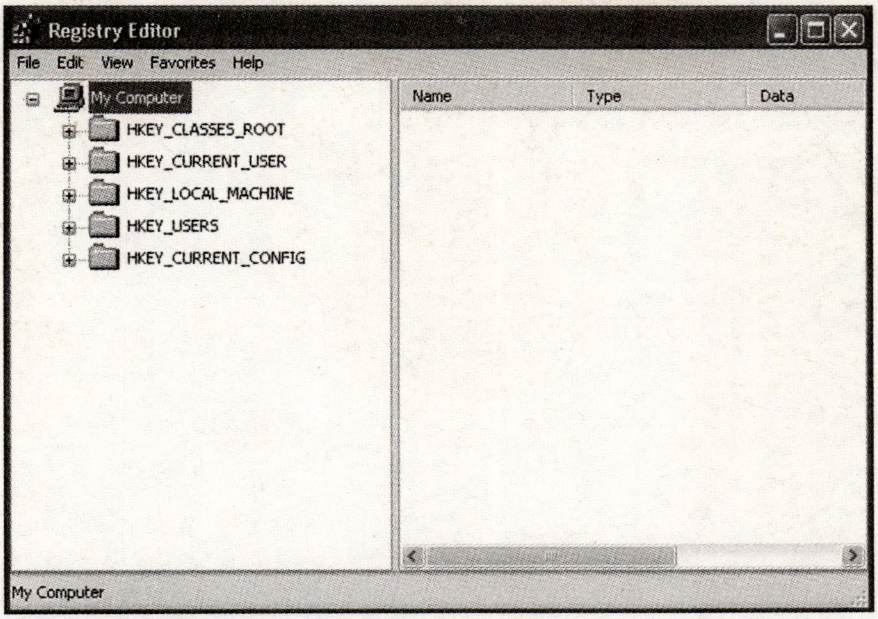

Figure 4-33 The Windows Registry.

In the pane on the left are five folders, and each contains specific information about your computer system. To see the contents of a folder, click the plus sign to expand it Now, to be on the safe side, click the Close button.

Summary

Now you have a lot of information at your fingertips if you want to get busy customizing Windows XP Professional. This chapter has covered some of the Control Panel applets and also looked at a few other ways to customize the system—modifying the Start menu and using user profiles.

Part 2

Business Tools

In This Part

Chapter 5

USING THE BUSINESS ACCESSORIES

Featuring:

- Using Calculator
- Using Media Player
- Using Movie Maker
- Using Notepad
- Using Paint
- Using WordPad

Windows XP Professional comes with more than three dozen accessory programs. These programs are rarely as powerful or useful as application programs that Microsoft and other software makers sell. Still, these accessories often come in handy when a more fully featured program isn't available. This chapter describes the accessories that aren't covered elsewhere in this book: Calculator, Media Player, Movie Maker, Notepad, Paint, and WordPad.

NOTE *Chapter 4 describes the Accessibility accessories, Chapter 8 describes Windows' Communication accessories, and Chapter 11 describes the System Tool accessories.*

Using Calculator

The Windows XP Calculator, which you open by clicking the Start button, clicking All Programs, clicking Accessories, and then clicking Calculator, is a very simple calculator, as shown in Figure 5-1. But in a pinch, you can use this tool to make several standard financial and statistical calculations.

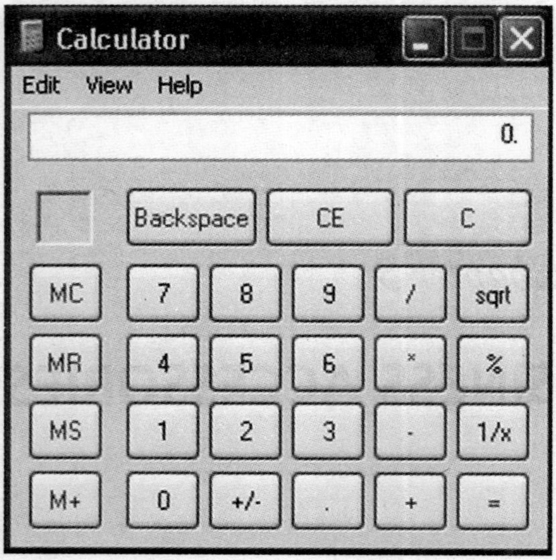

Figure 5-1 The Standard view of Calculator.

Using the Standard Calculator

The Calculator program works in almost the same way as a handheld calculator. To calculate some formula, you press the appropriate sequence of number and operator keys. Calculator also supplies some other standard keys, as listed in Table 5-1.

KEY	DESCRIPTION
/	Divide.
*	Multiply.
-	Subtract.
+	Add.
=	Equals.
+/-	Change sign.
.	Decimal point.
C	Clears every operator and operand you've entered.
CE	Clears the last operand you entered.
Backspace	Clears the last digit you entered.
MC	Clears Calculator's memory.

KEY	DESCRIPTION
MR	Recalls the value stored in Calculator's memory.
MS	Stores the displayed value in Calculator's memory.
M+	Adds the displayed value to the value stored in Calculator's memory, storing the new result in memory.
Sqrt	Calculates the square root of the register value.
%	Identifies the value just entered as a percentage.

Table 5-1 Operator keys supplied by the Standard Calculator view.

TIP *Click the View menu, and click Digital Grouping to direct Calculator to punctuate numbers with commas.*

Reviewing the Scientific View

To make financial calculations with Calculator, you use the Scientific view, which you can display by clicking the View menu and clicking Scientific, as shown in Figure 5-2. Although the Scientific view of Calculator looks very different from the Standard view, the Scientific view of Calculator simply provides a superset of statistical and mathematical operator keys.

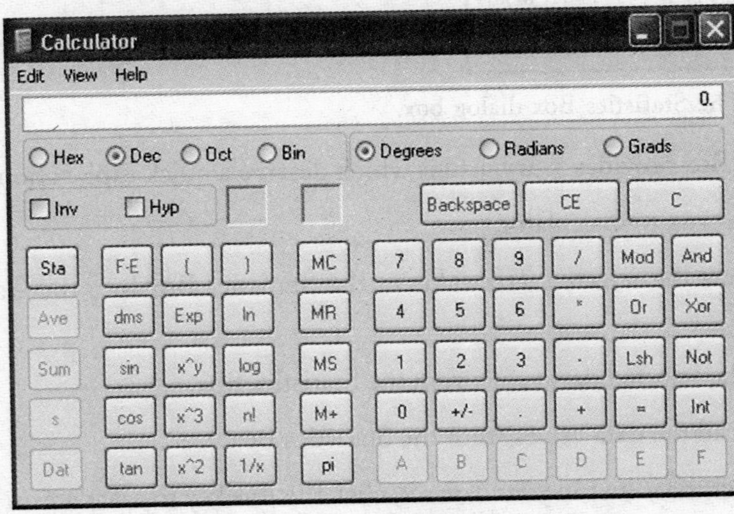

Figure 5-2 The Scientific view of Calculator.

NOTE *The Scientific view of Calculator lets you work in four different number systems: decimal, hexadecimal, octal, and binary. Use the Hex, Dec, Oct, and Bin buttons to choose the number system. If you choose to work with hexadecimal numbers, Calculator makes A, B, C, D, E, and F operand keys available so you can enter hexadecimal values.*

Making Statistical Calculations

To calculate a standard statistical measure using the Scientific view, click the Sta key so that Calculator opens the Statistics Box shown in Figure 5-3. Then enter each of the values in your data set followed by the Dat key. For example, to calculate statistical measures on a data set that includes the values 23, 34, 11, 65, 39, and 36; enter *23,* click Dat, enter *34,* click Dat, enter *11,* click Dat, and so on. As you enter the values and click Dat, Calculator lists the values in the Statistics Box.

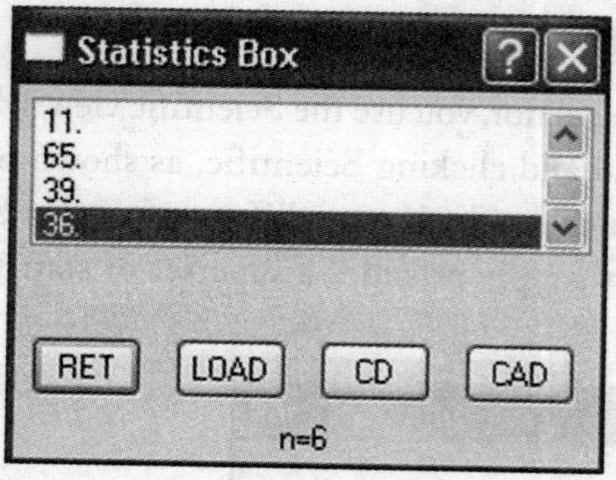

Figure 5-3 The Statistics Box dialog box.

The Statistics Box provides four buttons which deserve a quick explanation:

- RET returns you to Calculator.
- LOAD enters the selected data value in the Statistics Box into the Calculator display.
- CD clears the selected data value from the Statistics Box.
- CAD clears all the data values from the Statistics Box.

After you collect the values in your data set, click the Ave key to calculate an average, click the Sum key to sum the values, and click the s key to calculate a standard deviation. Calculator displays the statistical result.

Making Financial Calculations

Although the Scientific view doesn't provide financial operators, you can still use it for many common financial calculations.

Loan Payments in Arrears

To calculate a loan payment in arrears given the loan's balance, number of payments (or term), and periodic interest rate, you use the following formula:

*pv**i/(1-(1+i)^(-n))

where:

pv equals the loan balance

i equals the periodic interest rate

n equals the number of payments

NOTE *A loan payment in arrears is a loan payment made at the end of the payment period.*

Suppose, for example, that you want to calculate the loan payment on a $25,000 car loan that charges 6% annual interest and requires five years, or 60 months, of payments. If you first convert the 6% annual interest rate to a monthly interest rate of .5%—you make this calculation by dividing 6% by 12—your loan payment formula looks like this:

25000*.005/(1-(1+.005)^(-60))

To calculate this loan payment, enter this formula using the operator and operand keys:

25000*.005/(1-(1+.005)x^y(60+/-))=

Use the x^y operator key for the exponential operation, use the +/- sign change operator key to change the sign of the term argument, and end the formula with the equals sign. When you click the Equals key after entering the formula, Calculator returns the loan payment, which in the preceding example is 483.32 rounded to two decimal places.

TIP *The only real trick to making loan payment calculations with Calculator is to be sure you use the actual number of periods and the periodic interest rate. For example, if a loan has monthly payments, you need to input the loan term in months and use a monthly interest rate.*

Loan Payments in Advance

To calculate a loan payment in advance, first calculate the loan payment in arrears as described in the preceding paragraphs. Then divide that amount by the (1+periodic interest rate).

In the preceding paragraphs, for example, we explained how to calculate the monthly loan payment on a $25,000 car loan with 60 monthly payments and a 6% annual interest rate. If the loan payments are in arrears, the payment is 483.32. If the payment is in advance, the payment is 480.92, which is calculated as 483.32/(1+.005).

Balances on Loans with Payments in Arrears

To calculate the balance on a loan with payments in arrears, use the following formula:

(1-(1+i)^(-n))/i*pmt

where:

i equals the periodic interest rate

n equals the number of payments

pmt equals the loan payment

Suppose, for example, that you want to calculate the loan payment on a $25,000 car loan that charges 6% annual interest and requires five years, or 60 months, of payments equal to $483.32. Further suppose that the borrower has already made the first 12 payments, which means that there are 48 payments remaining. If you first convert the 6% annual interest rate to a monthly interest rate of .5%, your loan balance formula looks like this:

(1-(1+.005)^(-48))/.005*483.32

To calculate this loan payment, enter this formula using the operator and operand keys:

(1-(1+.005)x^y(48+/-))/.005*483.32=

Use the x^y operator key for performing the exponential operation, use the +/- sign change operator key to change the sign of the term argument, and end the formula with the equals sign. When you click the Equals key after entering the formula, Calculator returns the loan payment, which in the preceding example is 20,579.92 rounded to two decimal places.

Balances on Loans with Payments in Advance

To calculate a loan balance when the payments are made in advance, first calculate the loan balance as if the payments are made in arrears as described in the preceding paragraphs. Then multiply that amount by the (1+periodic interest rate).

The preceding paragraphs, for example, explain how to calculate the loan balance on a loan with 48 monthly loan payments equal to $483.32 left if the loan charges 6% annually. If the loan payments are in arrears, the balance is 20,579.92. If the payment is in advance, the loan balance is 20,682.82, which is calculated as 20579.92*(1+.005).

Future Value of a Lump Sum

To calculate the future value of a lump sum, use the following formula:

*pv**(1+i)^n

where:

pv equals the lump sum

i equals the periodic interest rate

n equals the number of payments

To calculate the future value of a $50,000 lump sum invested for 20 years at 10%, for example, you use the following formula:

50000*(1+.10)^20

To calculate this future value, enter this formula using the operator and operand keys:

50000*(1+.10)x^y20=

Use the x^y operator key for performing the exponential operation and end the formula with the equals sign. When you click the Equals key after entering the formula, Calculator returns the future value, which in the preceding example is 33,6375.00 rounded to two decimal places.

Future Value of an Annuity with Payments in Arrears

To calculate the future value of an annuity with payments in arrears, use the following formula:

((1+i)^n-1)/i*pmt

where

n equals the number of payments

i equals the periodic interest rate

pmt equals the payment

To calculate the future value of a $2,000 annual payment made for 40 years and invested at 10%, for example, you use the following formula:

((1+.1)^40-1)/.1*2000

To calculate this future value, enter this formula using the operator and operand keys:

((1+.1)x^y40-1)/.1*2000=

Use the x^y operator key for performing the exponential operation and end the formula with the equals sign. When you click the Equals key after entering the formula, Calculator returns the future value, which in the preceding example is 885,185.11 rounded to two decimal places.

Future Value of Annuities with Payments in Advance

To calculate the future value of an annuity when the payments are made in advance, first calculate the future value of the annuity as if the payments are made in arrears as described in the preceding paragraphs. Then multiply that amount by the (1+periodic interest rate).

The preceding paragraphs, for example, explain how to calculate the future value of an annuity of 40 annual payments equal to $2,000 if the annual interest rate is 10%. If the annuity's payments are in arrears, the future value equals 885,185.11. If the payment is in advance, the future value equals 973,703.62, which is calculated as 885185.11*(1+.10).

Term of a Lump Sum

To calculate the term of a lump sum that grows into a specified future value of lump sum, use the following formula:

Natural logarithm of (fv/pv) / Natural logarithm of (1/i)

where:

pv equals the present value

fv equals the future value

i equals the periodic interest rate

To calculate the term when a present value of $1,000,000 grows to a future value of $3,000,000 by earning 10% annually, for example, you use the following formula:

Natural logarithm of (3000000/1000000) / Natural logarithm of (1/.1)

To calculate the term using Calculator, enter this formula using the operator and operand keys:

(3000000/1000000)ln/(1+.1)ln

Use the ln operator key for calculating the natural logarithm and end the formula with the equals sign. When you click the Equals key after entering the formula, Calculator returns the term, which in the preceding example is 11.5 rounded to the nearest decimal place.

Term of an Annuity with Payments in Arrears

To calculate how long it takes for an annuity with payments in arrears to grow to a specified future value, use the following formula:

Natural logarithm of (1+(i*fv)/pmt) / Natural logarithm of (1+i)

where:

i equals the present value

fv equals the future value

pmt equals the payment

To calculate the term when the future value equals $1,000,000, annual payments equal $5,000, and the annual interest rate equals 12%, for example, you use the following formula:

Natural logarithm of (1+(.12*1000000)/5000) / Natural logarithm of (1+.12)

To calculate this formula using Calculator, enter this formula using the operator and operand keys:

(1+(.12*1000000)/5000)ln/(1+.12)ln

Use the ln operator key for calculating the natural logarithm and end the formula with the equals sign. When you click the Equals key after entering the formula, Calculator returns the term, which in the preceding example is 28.4 rounded to the nearest decimal place.

Term of an Annuity with Payments in Advance

To calculate how long it takes for an annuity with payments in advance to grow to a specified future value, use the following formula:

Natural logarithm of (1+(i*(fv/(1+i)))/pmt) / Natural logarithm of (1+i)

where:

i equals the periodic interest rate

fv equals the future value

pmt equals the payment

To calculate the term when the future value equals $1,000,000, annual payments equal $5,000, and the annual interest rate equals 12%, for example, you use the following formula:

Natural logarithm of (1+(.12*(1000000/(1+.12)))/5000) / Natural logarithm of (1+.12)

To calculate this formula using Calculator, enter this formula using the operator and operand keys:

(1+(.12*(1000000/(1+.12)))/5000)ln/(1+.12)ln

Use the ln operator key for calculating the natural logarithm and end the formula with the equals sign. When you click the Equals key after entering the formula, Calculator returns the term, which in the preceding example is 27.4 rounded to the nearest decimal place.

Periodic Interest Rate

Most interest rate calculations require iteration and, therefore, can't be solved using Calculator to calculate a single formula. You can, however, calculate the interest rate required for present value amount to grow into a specified future value amount with this formula:

(fv/pv)^(1/n)-1

where:

fv equals the future value

pv equals the present value

n equals the number of periods of compounding

To calculate the interest rate required to grow $1,000,000 into $2,000,000 in 10 years, for example, you use the following formula:

(2000000/1000000)^(1/10)-1

To calculate this formula using Calculator, enter this formula using the operator and operand keys:

(2000000/1000000)x^y(1/10)-1

Use the x^y operator key for performing the exponential operation and end the formula with the equals sign. When you click the Equals key after entering the formula, Calculator returns the future value, which in the preceding example is .072 (7.2%) rounded to three decimal places.

Copying and Pasting Values

Calculator supplies Copy and Paste commands on its Edit menu, which you can use to paste values to and from the Calculator display. These commands work like other applications' Copy and Paste commands, so they don't require explanation.

One noteworthy feature of Calculator's Paste command, however, is that you can paste not only values but also strings of operands and operators created using Notepad. If you paste the string *2+2=* into Calculator, it calculates the formula.

NOTE *Calculator's online help file lists the characters used to represent Calculator keys in copied text strings.*

Using Media Player

Media Player plays and organizes digital sound and video files stored either on your computer or on the Internet. You can use Media Player to listen to Internet radio stations, watch videos and DVDs, listen to music CDs—and collect and store information about these items.

Because the new Media Player supplies many new features and tools as compared to earlier versions, let's quickly review the Media Player window, which is shown in Figure 5-4.

Figure 5-4 The Media Player window in Full mode.

Along the left edge of the Media Player window is the Features area. The Features area supplies the clickable tabs Now Playing, Media Guide, Copy From CD, Media Library, Radio Tuner, Copy To CD Or Device, and Skin Chooser. You use the Now Playing tab to play a CD, DVD, or video. The Media Guide retrieves information from the Internet. You use the Copy From CD tab to copy tracks from the music CD in your CD drive. You use the Media Library tab to see and maintain a list of the media files on your computer and the media hyperlinks that you've saved. You use the Radio Tuner tab to listen to an Internet radio station. Click the Copy To CD Or Device tab to see a list of storage devices (such as recordable and rewriteable CDs) that you can use for copying music to CDs. Click the Skin Chooser tab to display a list of looks you can choose for the Media Player window.

Along the bottom edge of the Media Player window are the Playback Controls. These controls, which we briefly describe in the next section "Playing CDs and DVDs," let you play, pause, adjust the volume, fast forward, and rewind a video, CD, or DVD.

Just above the Playback Controls is the Playing Tools area. This area provides options for adjusting the equalization, choosing a video quality, selecting a DVD playback speed, and so on.

Along the right edge of the Media Player window is the Playlist area. The Playlist area displays a list of the items you can play or watch. If you've inserted a music CD in the CD drive, for example, the Playlist area lists the music tracks. If you've inserted a DVD, the Playlist area lists the chapters. If you've indicated you want to listen to an Internet radio station, the Playlist area lists the radio stations on the Presets list (which is just a list of memorized radio stations).

Playing CDs and DVDs

To play a music CD or watch a DVD, insert the CD or DVD in your CD or DVD drive. Windows XP starts Media Player and opens the Media Player window shown in Figure 5-5.

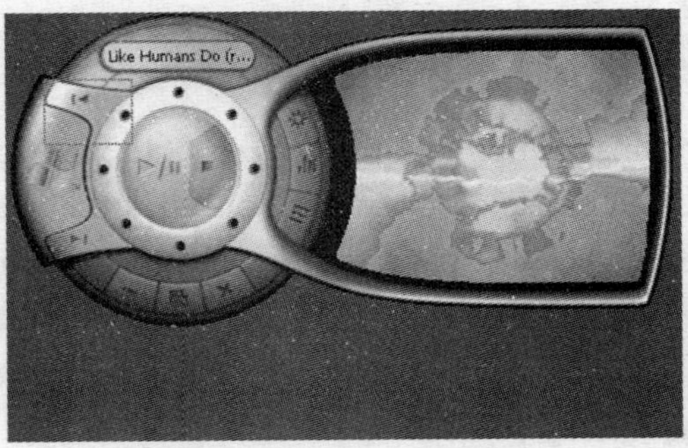

Figure 5-5 The Media Player window in Skin mode.

NOTE *Media Player lets you work with two versions of the Media Player window: Full mode, shown in Figure 5-4, and Skin mode, shown in Figure 5-5. To switch between these two modes, click the View menu and click Full Mode or Skin Mode.*

Using the Playback Controls

Using Media Player to listen to a music CD or watch a DVD is very easy. The Media Player window provides buttons and controls that mimic those available on the typical CD player or DVD player:

- To start the CD or DVD, click the Play/Pause button. To pause the music, click the Play/Pause button again.
- To stop the CD or DVD, click the Stop button.
- To move ahead or back to a track or chapter, click the Previous or Next buttons.
- To skip ahead or back up, click the Rewind or Fast Forward buttons.
- To adjust the volume, drag the Volume slider.

TIP *You can also use the Play menu's commands to specify how a music CD or DVD should play. Most of the commands on the Play menu correspond to buttons described in the preceding list. Only three new commands, in fact, appear: Shuffle, which randomly plays tracks on the music CD; Repeat, which tells Media Player to repeat playing a track; and Eject, which ejects the music CD or DVD from the CD or DVD drive.*

Using Visualizations for Music CDs

Media Player includes visualizations (sometimes called *skins*) of the music that you can watch as you listen to a music CD. To display a visualization, click the View menu and click Visualization. When Media Player displays the Visualization submenu, choose a visualization theme from the first submenu and then a visualization effect from the second submenu. A picture in a book doesn't do justice to the visualizations, so you'll want to experiment with visualizations yourself to see how they work.

TIP *The Media Player window also includes buttons for working with visualization effects: Click the Select Visualization button to display a menu of visualization themes. To try the next or previous visualization effect, click the Next Visualization or Previous Visualization button.*

Using the Now Playing Tools

Click the View menu, click Now Playing Tools, and then click Show Equalizer And Settings to add controls to Media Player for adjusting the equalization of the music and for displaying additional information about the music CD or DVD you're playing, as shown in Figure 5-6.

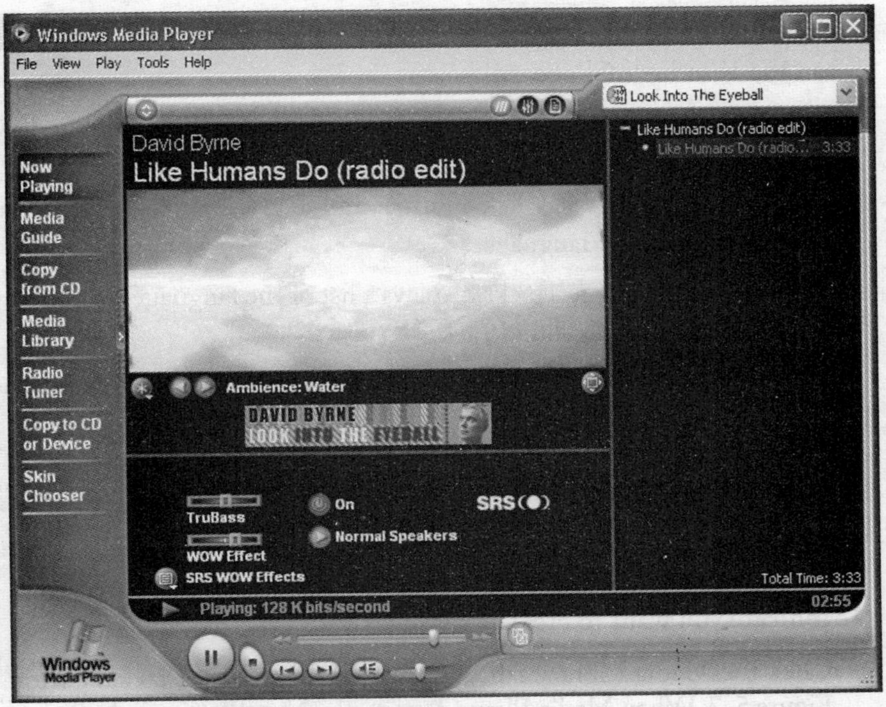

Figure 5-6 The Media Player window with the Equalizer and Setting controls.

Media Player supplies six sets of Equalizer and Setting controls:

- SRS WOW Effects, shown in Figure 5-6, lets you turn on and off the surround sound (SRS) effect, select a speaker size, and adjust the bass and WOW effect.
- Graphic Equalizer lets you adjust the equalization of the music by dragging slider buttons. The Graphic Equalizer controls also include a button for selecting equalizer settings appropriate to different styles of music: jazz, rock, swing, opera, and so on.
- Video Settings provides slider buttons you can use to adjust the Brightness, Contrast, Hue, and Saturation of the video played by Media Player.
- Media Information displays information about the CD, DVD, or video you're playing.
- Captions displays captions for a video when this information is available.
- Lyrics displays the words of a song when this information is available.
- DVD Controls provides a slider button for adjusting the play speed of the DVD and a button for moving to the next frame of the DVD.

Using the DVD Features Menu

The View menu's DVD Features command displays a submenu of commands you can use to work with DVDs:

- Capture Image takes a picture of the current frame's image and places the picture on the Windows Clipboard.
- Subtitles And Closed Captions displays a menu with two commands: Closed Captions and Subtitles. Click Closed Captions to add closed captioning to the DVD (if captioning is available). Click Subtitles and then select a language if you want to see subtitles in another language.
- Audio And Language Tracks displays a list of the languages in which you can hear a DVD's or a movie's soundtrack.
- Camera Angle lets you choose the angle from which you want to view the DVD.

Working with Playlists

Playlists list media items you can play or watch. For example, a playlist can list tracks on a music CD or identify video clips stored on your local drive.

To create a playlist, follow these steps:

1. Indicate you want to create a new playlist.

Click the Media Library tab, and then click the New Playlist button as shown in Figure 5-7. When Media Player displays the New Playlist dialog box, name the new playlist by entering a name in the box shown in Figure 5-8.

Figure 5-7 The Media Library tab.

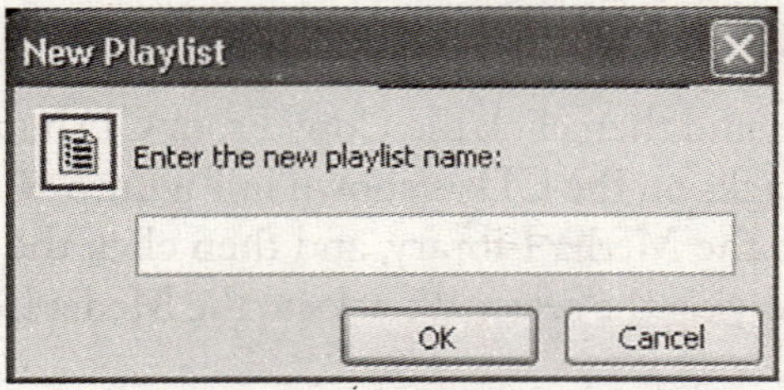

Figure 5-8 The New Playlist dialog box.

2. **Select the items you want to add to the playlist by clicking.**

   To select multiple items, hold down the Ctrl key as you click.

3. **Tell Media Player which media items go on the playlist.**

   Click the Add To Playlist button. When Media Player displays a list of the available playlists, click the playlist to which the selected items should be added.

You can edit the list of items on a playlist. To add a new item to the playlist, display the Media Library, right-click the item you want to add, choose Add To Playlist from the shortcut menu, and then select the playlist to which you want to add the item. To remove an item on the playlist, click the Media Library tab, click the playlist you want to change, right-click the item you want to remove, and choose Delete From Playlist from the shortcut menu.

To play the items in a playlist, select the playlist from the Playlist box. The Playlist box appears in the upper right corner of the Media Player window.

Creating a Music CD

If your computer includes a writeable or recordable CD, you can create your own music CDs. To do so, follow these steps:

1. **Copy the music tracks to the Media Library.**

   Insert the music CD in the CD drive, and then click the Copy From CD button in the Features area to see a list of the tracks on the CD as shown in Figure 5-9. Next, check the tracks you want to copy to the Media Library, and then click the Copy Music button. Media Player begins copying the selected tracks to the Media Library. This step may take several minutes.

Figure 5-9 The Copy From CD tab.

TIP *To stop copying a track, click the Stop Copy button. The Stop Copy button replaces the Copy Music button when Media Player is copying tracks.*

2. **Identify the tracks you want to put on the new CD.**

   Click the Media Library tab, open the track's folder, and then select the tracks that you want. To copy more than one track, hold down the Ctrl key as you click the tracks.

3. **Copy the selected tracks to the music CD.**

   Click the File menu, and click Copy To CD Or Device. When Media Player displays a list of the storage devices to which you can copy music tracks, select the CD drive. Then click Copy Music.

NOTE *If you click the Tools menu, click Options, and then click the Copy Music tab, Media Player displays a tab of options you can use to specify how Media Player copies the music. The Copy Music tab, for example, lets you specify where copied music is stored, choose a file format, and select a music quality setting.*

Listening to Internet Radio Stations

Media Player allows you to find and listen to Internet radio stations. To locate an Internet radio station, click the Radio Tuner tab in the Features area shown in Figure 5-10. You can double-click one of the stations listed in the Presets box. Or you can use the Station Finder boxes to provide search criteria for building a list of stations, click Search, and then double-click one of the stations your search returns.

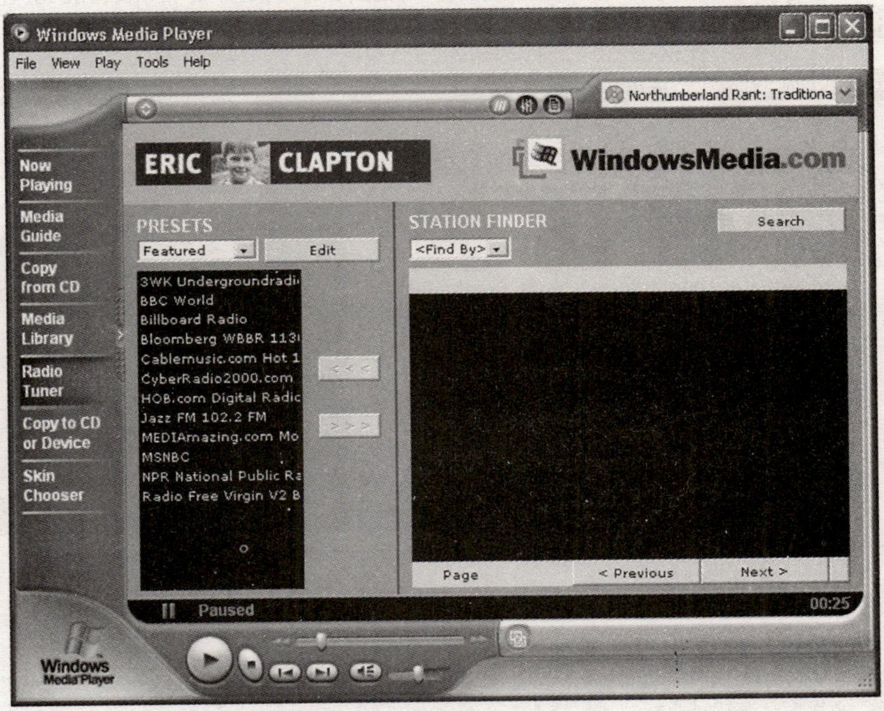

Figure 5-10 The Radio Tuner.

TIP *To add a new station to the list of Presets, click the station and then click the Add The Station You Have Selected To Your Preset List button. To delete a station from your list of Presets, click the station and then click the Delete A Station From Your Preset List button.*

Using Movie Maker

Movie Maker creates movies by piecing together video-clip files stored on your computer or on the Internet, video clips you shoot with a home video or camera, and narration you record with a microphone. Once you've created your movie, you can store the movie as a file on your computer, send the movie file in an e-mail message, or post the movie file to a Web server. You and anyone else can then view the movie using Media Player.

Setting Up a Movie Project

To set up a movie project, start the Movie Maker accessory by clicking the Start button, clicking All Programs, clicking Accessories, and then clicking Windows Movie Maker, as shown in Figure 5-11. After you start Movie Maker, create a movie project file for the new movie by clicking the File menu, clicking New, and then clicking Project.

re 5-11 The Movie Maker window.

Collecting Video Clips

After you set up a movie project, you collect video clips for your movie. You can collect video clips from a digital video camera or by importing video-clip files stored on your computer.

To collect video clips from a digital video camera, click the File menu and click Record. After Movie Maker opens the Record dialog box, select Video from the Record list box shown in Figure 5-12. You can use the Record Time Limit box to specify a time length for the video clip you want to record. Then click Record, and play the video on your digital camera. Movie Maker adds video clips to the clip area.

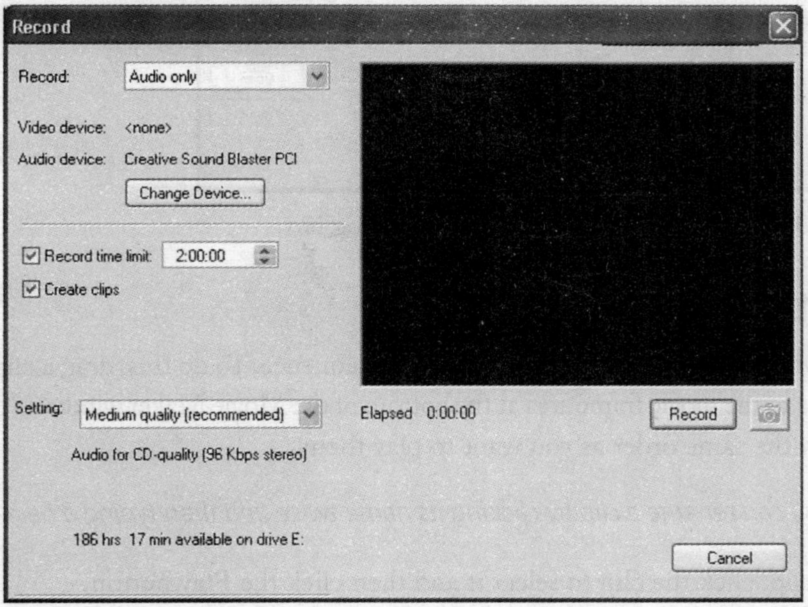

Figure 5-12 The Record dialog box.

TIP *Click the Create Clips check box to direct Movie Maker to create individual clips from a single video file or recording. Movie Maker detects clips in a video file each time an entirely different frame appears. Movie Maker detects clips in a video recording based on the digital camera's clock.*

To add a video clip stored on your computer, click the File menu and then click Import. When Movie Maker opens the Select The File To Import dialog box, use the Look In and File Name boxes to identify the video-clip location and file, as shown in Figure 5-13. Click Open. Movie Maker adds video clips to the Movie Maker clip area.

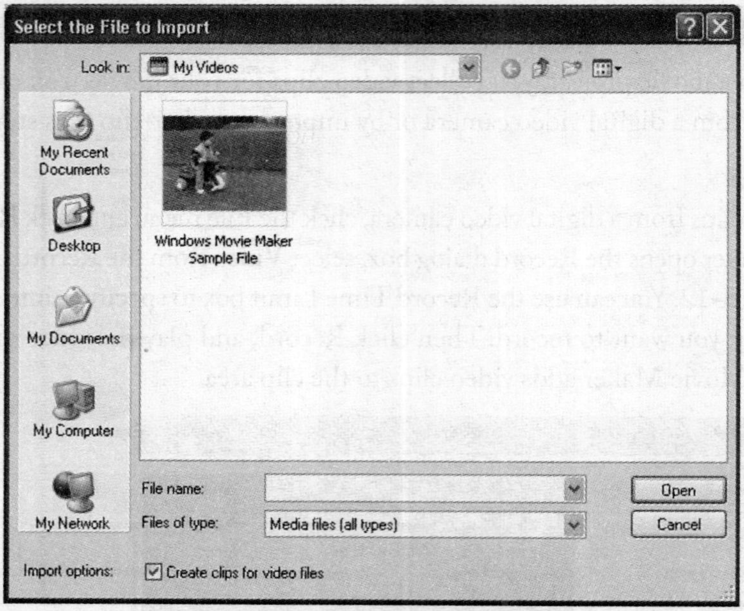

Figure 5-13 The Select The File To Import dialog box.

Working with Clips

To create your movie, you arrange the clips in a sequence. To do this, drag a clip from the clip area to the movie frame area at the bottom of the Movie Maker window. Arrange the clips in the same order as you want to play them.

TIP *You can rename a clip by clicking its name twice and then typing a new name.*

To play a clip, click the clip to select it and then click the Play button.

If you want to use only part of a clip, you can split the clip into two clips by clicking the clip, playing the clip until the frame where you want to split the clip, and then clicking the Split Clip button.

TIP *You can use the Next Frame and Previous Frame buttons to move one frame at a time through the clip.*

You can combine two clips into a single clip by selecting the clips, right-clicking the selected clips, and then choosing Combine from the shortcut menu.

You can play your sequence of movie clips by right-clicking the storyboard and choosing Play Entire Storyboard/Timeline from the shortcut menu.

Adding Narration

You can add narration to a movie. Click the View menu, and click Timeline to add a timeline to the storyboard pane. Then click the File menu, and click Record Narration. Movie Maker displays the Record Narration Track dialog box shown in Figure 5-14.

Figure 5-14 The Record Narration Track dialog box.

To begin recording, click the Record button and then narrate the movie. When you finish, click Stop. When Movie Maker displays the Save Narration Track Sound File dialog box, name the sound file and click Save, as shown in Figure 5-15. Movie Maker saves your sound file as a .wav file and imports the file into the open movie project.

Figure 5-15 The Save Narration Track Sound File dialog box.

Saving a Movie

After you arrange your clips and add any sound, you can save your movie by clicking the File menu and clicking Save Movie. When Movie Maker displays the Save Movie dialog box, use the Setting box to pick a movie quality. Then, as appropriate, describe the movie using the Title, Author, Date, Rating, and Description boxes shown in Figure 5-16. Click OK when you finish providing this information.

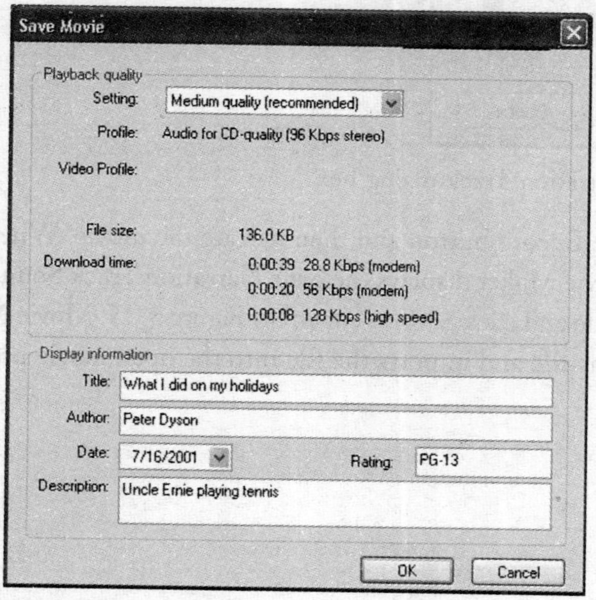

Figure 5-16 The Save Movie dialog box.

When Movie Maker displays the Save As dialog box, specify where the movie should be saved using the Save In box, pick a format for the movie using the Save File As Type box, and name the movie using the File Name box shown in Figure 5-17.

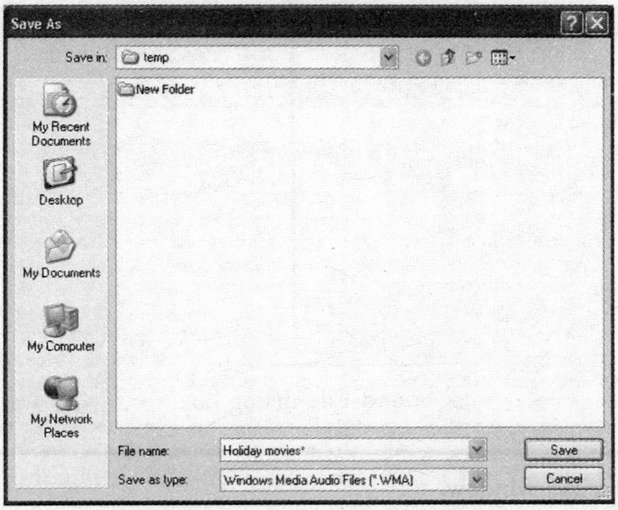

Figure 5-17 The Save As dialog box.

NOTE *Movie Maker takes several minutes to create your movie.*

Playing the Movie

You play movies using Media Player. To do this, click the File menu and click Open to open the movie file. Then click the Play button. To view your movie in a full-screen window, click the View menu and click Full Screen.

Using Notepad

Using the Notepad text editor is often the easiest way to create and edit small text files. To start Notepad, click the Start button, click All Programs, click Accessories, and then click Notepad. Windows opens a Notepad window, as shown in Figure 5-18. To create a text file, click in the window and then type your text. You edit Notepad text in the same way that you edit text in Windows text boxes.

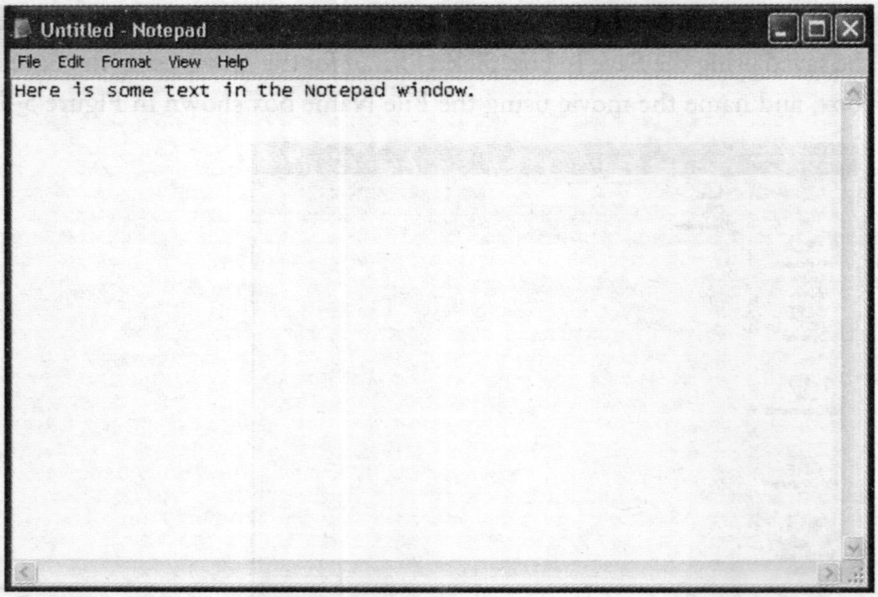

Figure 5-18 The Notepad window.

Working with Notepad Text Files

The Notepad File menu provides several useful and predictable commands for working with text files:

- New creates a new text file.
- Open displays the Open dialog box, which you use to locate and identify a text file you want to open.
- Save saves the text file using the same name and location as the last time that you saved the file. Or, if you haven't yet saved the file, the command displays the Save As dialog box so you can name and choose a folder location for the file.
- Save As displays the Save As dialog box, which you use to save the open text file in a specified location and using a specified filename.
- Page Setup displays a dialog box you can use to specify how the text file should be printed, as shown in Figure 5-19. For example, you can choose page margins (using the Margins boxes), specify whether the text file should be printed in a portrait or landscape orientation (using the Portrait and Landscape option buttons), and select a header and footer for the printed pages (using the Header and Footer boxes).

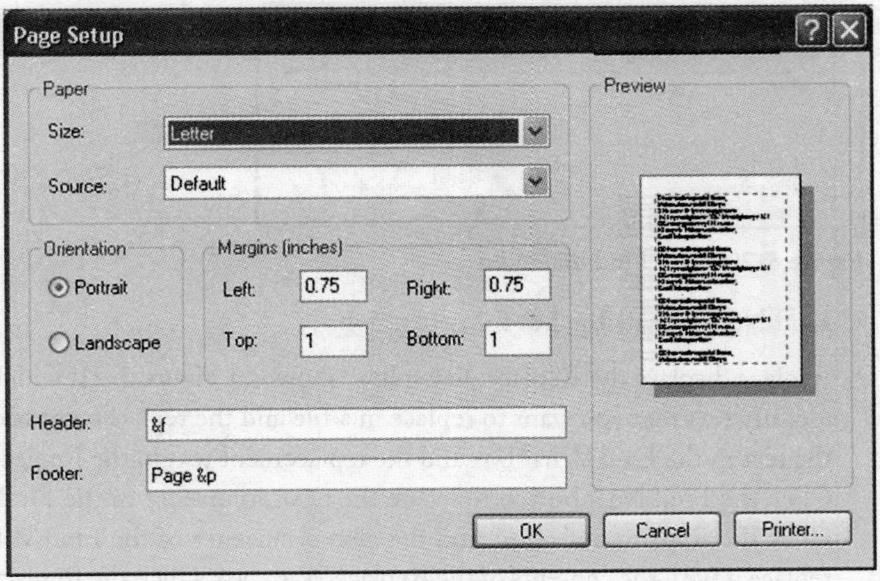

Figure 5-19 Notepad's Page Setup dialog box.

- Print displays a dialog box you use to describe how Windows should print the text file.
- Exit, of course, closes the Notepad program.

Text Editing in Notepad

The Edit menu provides commands for working with the text in a Notepad file:

- Undo undoes the effect of your most recent command or editing action.
- Copy moves a copy of the selected text to the Clipboard, so the text can be pasted.
- Cut moves the selected text to the Clipboard, so the text can be pasted.
- Paste moves a copy of the contents of the Clipboard to the insertion point location.
- Delete erases the selected text.
- Find displays the Find dialog box, shown in Figure 5-20, which you use to identify text you want to locate within the file. After you enter the text in the Find What box, use the Direction option buttons to indicate in which direction you want to search and then click the Find Next button.

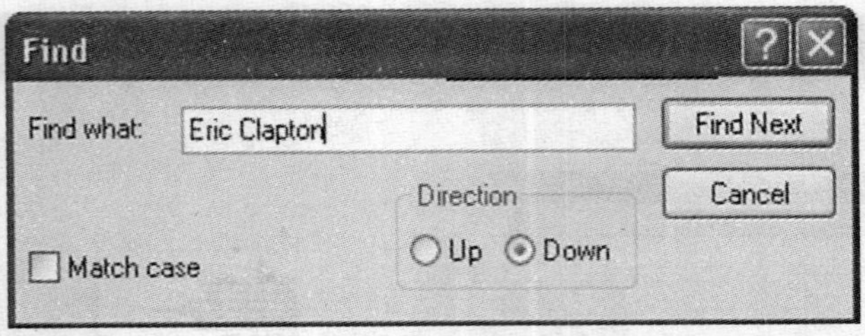

Figure 5-20 The Find dialog box.

- Find Next repeats the last find operation.
- Replace displays the Replace dialog box, shown in Figure 5-21, which you use to identify text that you want to replace in a file and the replacement text. You enter the text in the Find What box and the replacement text in the Replace With box. Click the Find Next button to locate the next occurrence of the Find What text. Click the Replace button to find the next occurrence of the Find What text and replace it with the contents of the Replace With box. Click the Replace All button to replace all occurrences of the Find What text with the contents of the Replace With box.

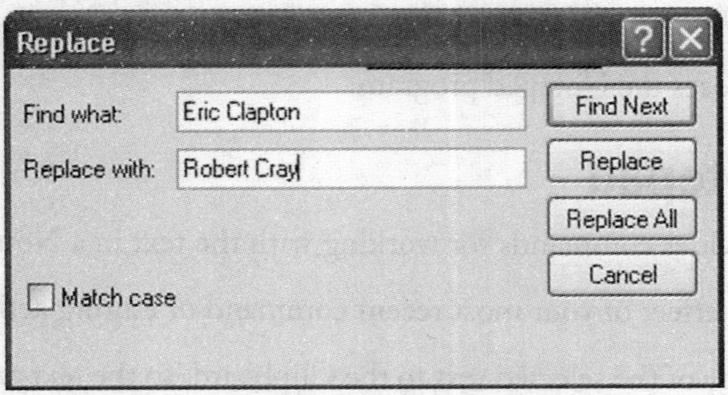

Figure 5-21 The Replace dialog box.

- Go To displays the Go To Line dialog box, which you use to move the insertion point to the specified line of the text file.
- Select All selects all the text in the file.
- Time/Date inserts the current system time and date at the insertion point location.

Formatting in Notepad

The Notepad Format menu provides two commands. WordWrap is a toggle switch that turns the wrapping of text on and off in the Notepad window. Font displays the Font dialog box, shown in Figure 5-22, which you can use to select the font, font style, and point size used for text.

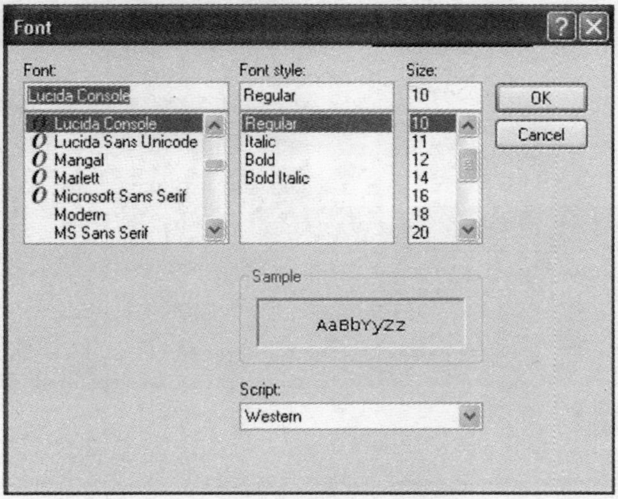

Figure 5-22 The Font dialog box.

Using Paint

Paint lets you create and edit bitmap images. To start Paint, click the Start button, click All Programs, click Accessories, and then click Paint. Windows opens the Paint window, as shown in Figure 5-23. To create a bitmap image with Paint, you draw shapes and lines using the Paint toolbar tools.

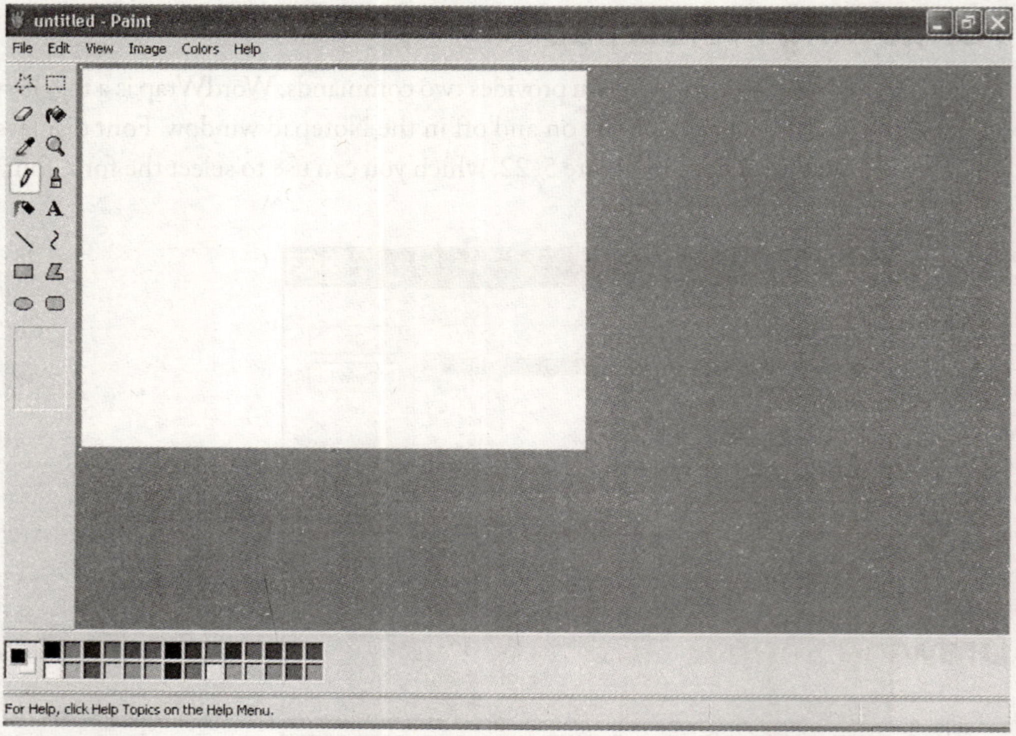

Figure 5-23 The Paint window.

Drawing Lines

You can draw, paint, and airbrush lines using the Pencil, Brush, Airbrush, Line, and Curve tools:

- To draw a line with the Pencil tool, click the Pencil button, click a color square, and then drag the mouse to draw a line.
- To paint a line with the Brush tool, click the Brush button, click a brush end, click a color, and then drag the mouse to draw a brushstroke.
- To spray a line with the Airbrush tool, click the Airbrush button, click a spray pattern, click a color, and then drag the mouse to spray the color.
- To draw a line, click the Line tool, click the line thickness, click a color square, and then drag the mouse from one line endpoint to the other line endpoint.
- To draw a curved line, click the Curve tool, click the line thickness, click a color square, drag the mouse from one line endpoint to the other line endpoint, and then drag the line to create its curve.

TIP *Remember that you can learn any tool's name by pointing to the tool with the mouse pointer. When you point to a tool, Windows displays the tool name in a pop-up box called a ScreenTip.*

Adding Text

To add text to the image, click the Text tool, drag the mouse to create a square in the image, and then type your text. When you add a text box to the image, Paint opens a Text toolbar, as shown in Figure 5-24. The Text toolbar provides boxes for selecting a font, point size, and font script as well as providing buttons for boldfacing, italicizing, and underlining.

Figure 5-24 The Text toolbar in the Paint window.

Drawing Shapes

To draw a rectangle, click the Rectangle tool, click the line thickness, click a color square, and then drag the mouse from one corner to the other corner of the rectangle. To make the rectangle square, hold down the Shift key as you draw.

To draw an ellipse, click the Ellipse tool, click the line thickness, click a color square, and then drag the mouse. To make the ellipse a circle, hold down the Shift key as you draw.

To drag a polygon, click the Polygon tool, click the line thickness, click a color square, and then draw the polygon's lines, clicking the mouse at each corner.

To draw a rounded corner rectangle, click the Rounded Rectangle tool, click the line thickness, click a color square, and then drag the mouse from one corner to the other corner of the rectangle. To make the rounded rectangle square, hold down the Shift key as you draw.

Coloring Lines and Shapes

You can color a line or shape before you draw by clicking a color square.

You can also color a line or shape after it's been drawn by clicking a color square, clicking the Fill With Color button, and then clicking the line or shape you want to recolor.

You can fill a shape with a color by clicking a color square, clicking the Fill With Color button, and then clicking inside the shape you want to fill.

To use an existing color, click the Pick Color button shown in the bitmap image, click the Pick Color tool, and then make the line or shape the color you want.

To change which colors Paint supplies using the Color Box's color squares, click the Colors menu and click Edit Colors. When Paint displays the Edit Colors dialog box, click the Define Custom Colors button to expand the Edit Colors box, as shown in Figure 5-25. Then identify the new color you want by clicking the rainbow-colored box or by entering values in the Hue, Sat, and Lum boxes or the Red, Green, and Blue boxes. After you identify or describe the color, click the Add To Custom Colors button.

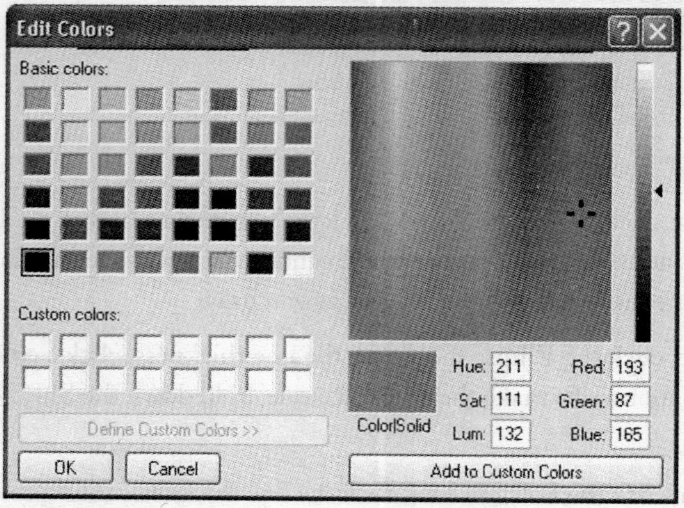

Figure 5-25 The Edit Colors dialog box.

Editing Bitmap Images

You can erase part of an image by clicking the Erase/Color Erase tool, clicking the eraser thickness, and then dragging the mouse over the image.

You can select a part of the image for deletion, copying, or cutting by using the Select or Free-Form Select tools. To use the Select tool, click the tool and then draw a rectangle around the part of the image you want to edit. To use the Free-Form Select tool, click the tool and then draw around the part of the image you want to edit. After you select the part of the image you want to edit, you can copy, cut, or delete the selection using Edit menu commands.

Paint's Edit menu provides the following commands for editing bitmap images:

- Undo undoes the effect of your most recent command or editing action.
- Copy moves a copy of the image selection to the Clipboard, so the selection can be pasted.
- Cut moves the image selection to the Clipboard, so the selection can be pasted.
- Paste moves the contents of the Clipboard to the upper left corner of the bitmap image. To move the pasted selection to the appropriate location, drag it.
- Clear Selection erases the image selection.
- Select All selects all of the lines and shapes in the images.
- Copy To displays the Copy To dialog box, shown in Figure 5-26, which you use to create a new bitmap image file from the current image selection.

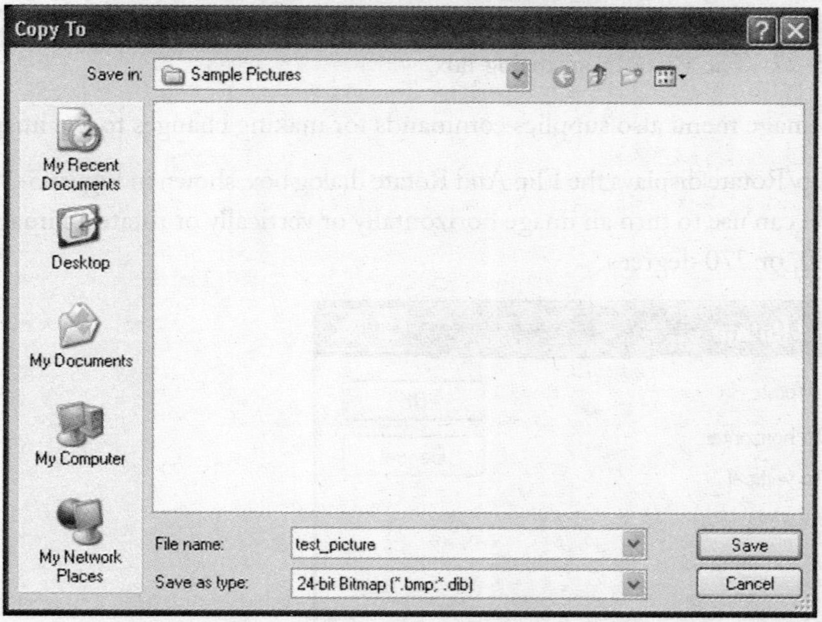

Figure 5-26 The Copy To dialog box.

- Paste From displays the Paste From dialog box, shown in Figure 5-27, which you use to select a bitmap image file you want to paste into the open bitmap image.

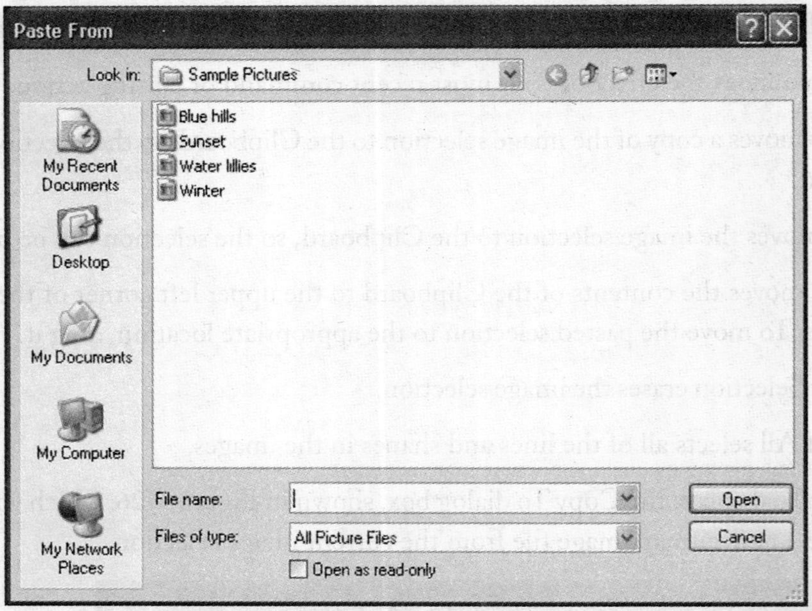

Figure 5-27 The Paste From dialog box.

Paint's Image menu also supplies commands for making changes to the image:

- Flip/Rotate displays the Flip And Rotate dialog box, shown in Figure 5-28, which you can use to turn an image horizontally or vertically or rotate an image by 90, 180, or 270 degrees.

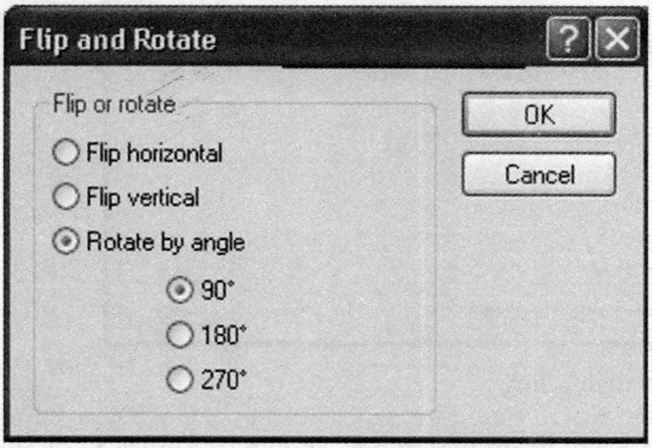

Figure 5-28 The Flip And Rotate dialog box.

- Stretch/Skew displays the Stretch And Skew dialog box, which you can use to stretch the image horizontally or vertically or skew the image horizontally or vertically by entering percentage or degree values in the boxes provided.

- Invert Colors inverts the colors used in the image, turning white to black, black to white, and so on.
- Attributes displays the Attributes dialog box, which you can use to specify what size the image should be (in inches, centimeters, or pixels), whether the image is in color or black and white, and whether the image should use a transparent background color.
- Clear Image erases the image, so you can start over.
- Draw Opaque is a toggle switch. If a check mark appears in front of the command, what you draw in an image is opaque. If a check mark doesn't appear, what you draw in an image is transparent. To add or remove the check mark, just click the command.

Working with Bitmap Image Files

The Paint File menu provides traditional commands for saving, opening, and printing bitmap image files:

- New creates a new bitmap image file.
- Open displays the Open dialog box, which you use to locate and identify a bitmap image file you want to open.
- Save saves the bitmap image file using the same name and location as the last time you saved the file. Or, if you haven't yet saved the file, the command displays the Save As dialog box so you can name and choose a folder location for the file.
- Save As displays the Save As dialog box, which you use to save the open bitmap image in a specified location and using a specified filename. By default, Paint saves bitmap image files using the 24-bit bitmap file format. You can also use the Save Files As Type box to indicate that you want Paint to save the bitmap file using some other bitmap image format or even a GIF or JPEG file format.
- Print Preview displays the Print Preview window, which shows how your bitmap image prints. To print the previewed bitmap image, click Print. Click the Zoom In and Zoom Out buttons to magnify the previewed page.
- Page Setup displays a dialog box you can use to choose a paper option (using the Size and Source boxes), specify whether the image should be printed in a portrait or landscape orientation (using the Portrait and Landscape option buttons), and specify page margins (using the Margins boxes).
- Print displays a dialog box you use to describe how Windows should print the image.

- Send opens your default e-mail program and attaches the image file as an e-mail attachment so you can e-mail the file.
- Set As Wallpaper (Tiled) and Set As Wallpaper (Centered) tell Windows to use the open bitmap image to create wallpaper for your desktop—either by using the image as a repeating tile or as an image centered in the middle of the desktop.
- Exit closes the Paint program.

Customizing Paint

Paint's View menu provides toggle-switch commands for adding and removing the toolbox, Color bar, status bar, and Text toolbar. Paint places a check mark in front of the command when the referenced item appears in the program window. To remove the item, click the command and Paint removes both the item and the check mark. To add the item, click the command and Paint adds the item and the check mark.

Clicking the View menu, and clicking Zoom displays a submenu of commands that you can use to magnify or reduce the size of the image shown in the Paint window. To increase the image size, click Large Size. To decrease the image size, click Normal Size.

NOTE *If you use the Large Size view of an image, you can click Zoom and then click Show Grid to add a grid that shows individual pixels in your image. Clicking Zoom and then clicking Thumbnail opens a small window that shows a thumbnail picture of the image.*

If you want to choose a specific size for your image, click Custom and then use the Custom Zoom dialog box to specify the desired size, as shown in Figure 5-29.

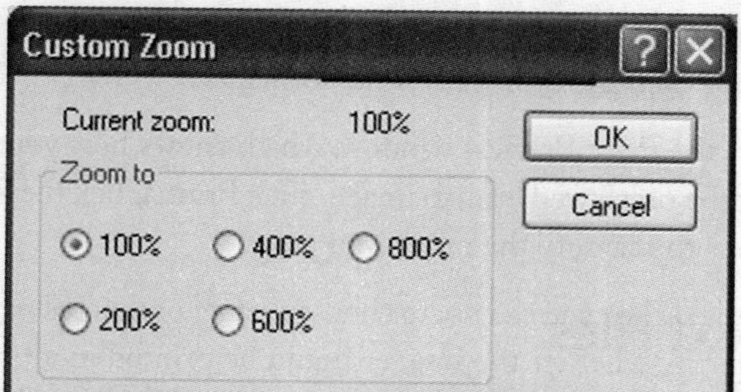

Figure 5-29 The Custom Zoom dialog box.

TIP *You can also click the View menu and click View Bitmap to see a large picture of the bitmap image.*

Using WordPad

The WordPad program performs simple word processing. WordPad doesn't include the word-processing tools available in a full-featured program, such as Microsoft Word. (You can't spell-check your document in WordPad, for example.) But WordPad does let you create richly formatted text files and even simple Word documents.

Creating a WordPad File

To create a WordPad file, first start the WordPad program by clicking the Start button, clicking All Programs, clicking Accessories, and then clicking WordPad. WordPad starts, and you begin creating your file by typing, as shown in Figure 5-30.

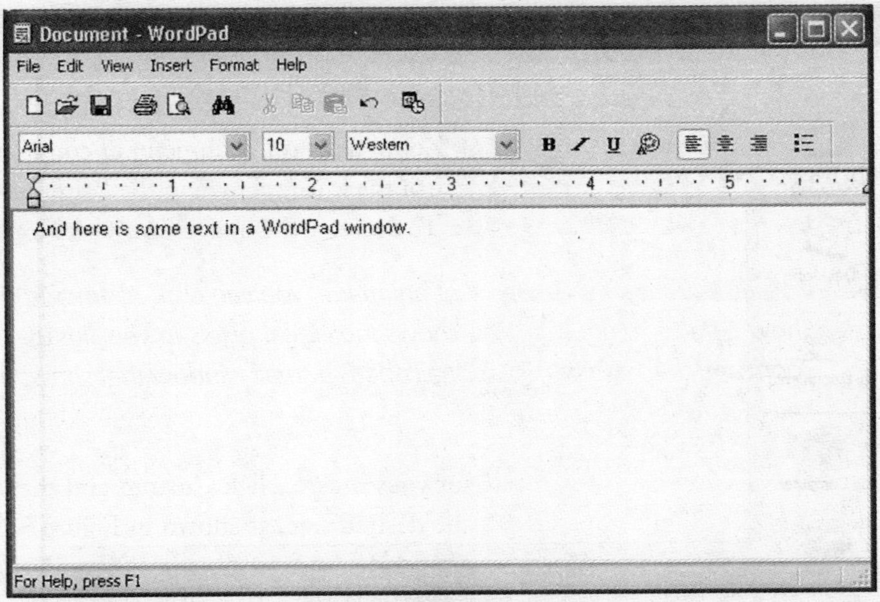

Figure 5-30 The WordPad window.

NOTE *WordPad creates and lets you work with rich text files, which are simply formatted text files.*

Working with Rich Text Files

The File menu provides several useful and predictable commands for working with WordPad files:

- New creates a new rich text file.

- Open displays the Open dialog box, which you use to locate and identify a rich text file you want to open.
- Save saves the rich text file using the same name and location as the last time you saved the file. Or, if you haven't yet saved the file, the command displays the Save As dialog box so you can name and choose a folder location for the file.
- Save As displays the Save As dialog box, which you use to save the open file in a specified location and using a specified filename, as shown in Figure 5-31. By default, WordPad saves rich text files using the RTF file format. You can also use the Save As Type box to indicate that you want WordPad to save the file as a Word document.

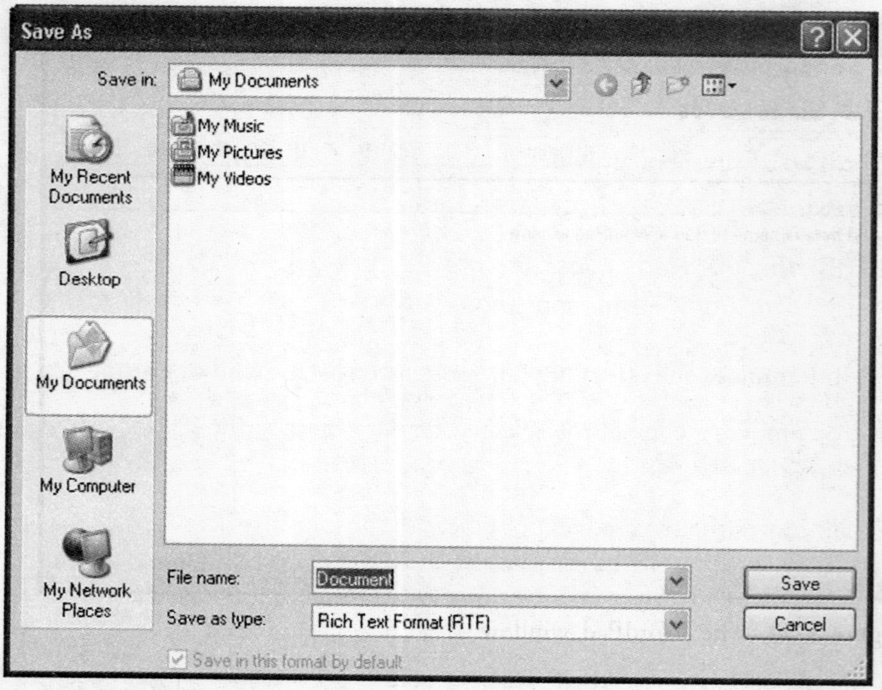

Figure 5-31 The Save As dialog box.

- Print Preview displays the Print Preview window, which shows how your file looks in printed pages. To print the previewed text file, click Print. You can use the Next Page and Prev Page buttons to page through the file, forward and backward. Click the Two Page button to preview two pages at a time. Click the Zoom In and Zoom Out buttons to alternately magnify and reduce the size of the previewed file.

- Page Setup displays a dialog box you can use to choose a paper option (using the Size and Source boxes), specify whether the rich text file should be printed in a portrait or landscape orientation (using the Portrait and Landscape option buttons), and specify page margins (using the Margins boxes).
- Print displays a dialog box you use to describe how Windows should print the file.
- Send opens your default e-mail program and attaches the WordPad file as an e-mail attachment so you can e-mail the document.
- Exit, of course, closes the WordPad program.

NOTE *The WordPad toolbar also provides buttons you can click to choose the New, Open, Save, Print, and Print Preview commands.*

Editing Rich Text Files

WordPad's Edit menu provides commands for editing and working with the contents of a rich text file:

NOTE *The WordPad toolbar also provides buttons you can click to choose the Find, Cut, Copy, Paste, and Undo commands.*

- Undo undoes the effect of your most recent command or editing action.
- Copy moves a copy of the selected text or object to the Clipboard, so the text can be pasted.
- Cut moves the selected text or object to the Clipboard, so the text or object can be pasted.
- Paste moves a copy of the contents of the Clipboard to the insertion point location.
- Paste Special displays the Paste Special dialog box which lets you specify exactly what gets pasted from the Clipboard. The Paste Special dialog box, for example, includes options for pasting only the text on the clipboard (rather than the formatting applied to the text) or the contents of the Clipboard. If you're pasting an object, you can also choose to specify whether the object or a link pointing to the object gets pasted.
- Clear erases the selected text or object.
- Select All selects all the text and objects in the file.

- Find displays the Find dialog box, shown in Figure 5-32, which you use to identify text that you want to locate within the file. The Find dialog box provides check boxes you use to indicate that WordPad should only find whole word occurrences of what you enter in the Find What box and that WordPad should consider case in its search.

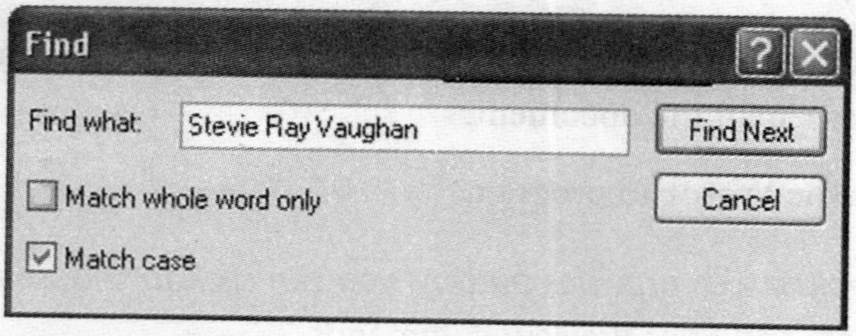

Figure 5-32 The Find dialog box.

- Find Next repeats the last find operation.
- Replace displays the Replace dialog box, shown in Figure 5-33, which you use to identify text you want to replace and the replacement text. You enter the text in the Find What box and the replacement text into the Replace With box. Click the Find Next button to locate the next occurrence of the Find What text. Click the Replace button to find the next occurrence of the Find What text and replace it with the contents of the Replace With box. Click the Replace All button to replace all occurrences of the Find What text with the contents of the Replace With box. As does the Find dialog box, the Replace dialog box provides check boxes you use to indicate that WordPad should only find whole word occurrences of what you enter in the Find What box and that WordPad should consider case in its search.

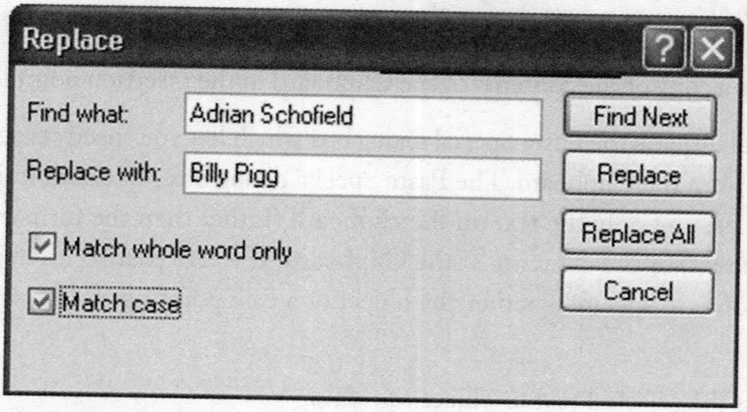

Figure 5-33 The Replace dialog box.

- Links displays the Links dialog box, which you can use to edit and update a link you've created with the Edit menu's Paste Special command.
- Object Properties displays a dialog box that provides information about the selected object.
- Object displays a menu that provides commands for editing or opening an object that you've inserted in a WordPad document using the Insert menu's Object command. Note that the precise name of the Object command depends on the selected object. If you select a chart object, for example, the command name is Chart Object.

Customizing WordPad

WordPad's View menu provides toggle-switch commands for adding and removing the WordPad toolbar, the Formatting toolbar, the Ruler, and the status bar. WordPad places a check mark in front of the command when the referenced item appears in the program window. To remove the item, click the command and WordPad removes the item and the check mark. To add the item, click the command and WordPad adds the item and the check mark.

Clicking the View menu and clicking Options displays the Options dialog box shown in Figure 5-34. The Options dialog box provides tabs for specifying units of measurement (the Options tab) and for specifying how word wrapping works and which toolbars should appear when you're working with plain text, rich text, Word documents, Windows write documents, and embedded objects (the Text, Rich Text, Word, Write, and Embedded tabs).

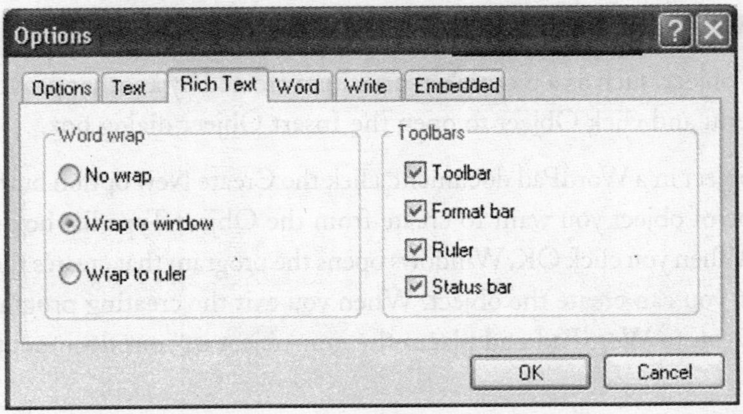

Figure 5-34 The Options dialog box.

Inserting Date and Time in WordPad Files

WordPad's Insert menu provides two useful commands for adding to and editing rich text files: Date And Time and Object.

If you click the Insert menu and click Date And Time, for example, WordPad displays the Date And Time dialog box shown in Figure 5-35. To insert a date or time at the insertion point, select the time or date entry that uses the formatting you want and then click OK.

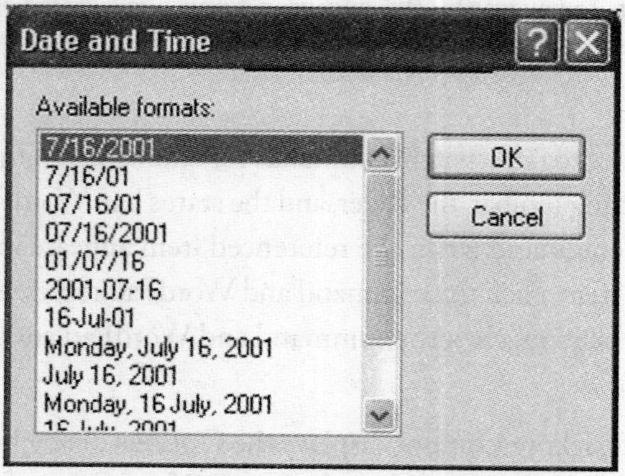

Figure 5-35 The Date And Time dialog box.

NOTE *The WordPad toolbar provides a Date And Time button you can click to choose the Insert menu's Date And Time command.*

Inserting Objects in WordPad Files

To embed an object, such as a picture or some item created by another program, click the Insert menu and click Object to open the Insert Object dialog box.

To insert an object in a WordPad document, click the Create New option button. Then select the type of object you want to create from the Object Type list box shown in Figure 5-36. When you click OK, Windows opens the program that creates the selected object type so you can create the object. When you exit the creating program, Windows returns you to WordPad and places the new object in your document.

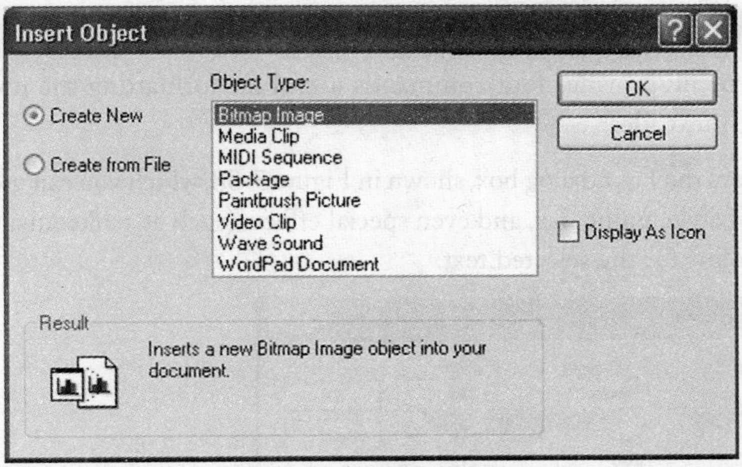

Figure 5-36 The Insert Object dialog box with the Create New option selected.

To create an object by using an existing file, click the Create From File option button shown in Figure 5-37. Then enter the complete path name for the file in the File Name box. If you don't know the complete path name, click the Browse button to display the Browse window, which you can use to navigate through your computer's and network's folders and locate the file.

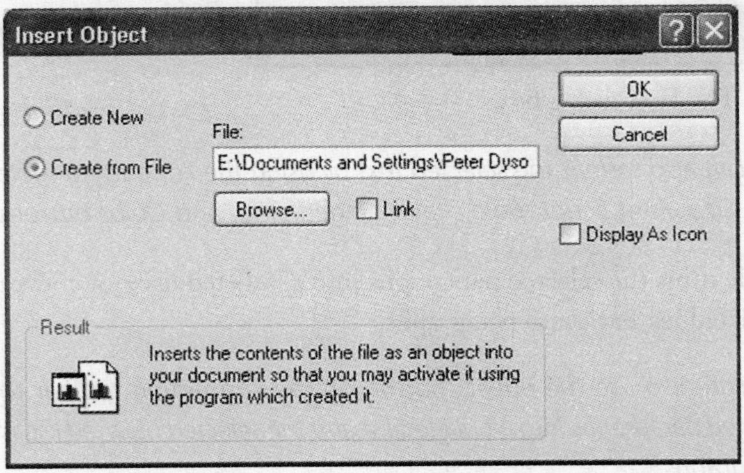

Figure 5-37 The Insert Object dialog box with the Create From File option selected.

NOTE *Click the Display As Icon check box to display an icon rather than a picture of the embedded object in the document.*

Formatting WordPad Rich Text Files

The Format menu provides four commands useful for formatting the text in your WordPad rich text files:

- Font displays the Font dialog box, shown in Figure 5-38, which you can use to select a font, font style, point size, and even special effects (such as strikeouts, underlining, and color) for the selected text.

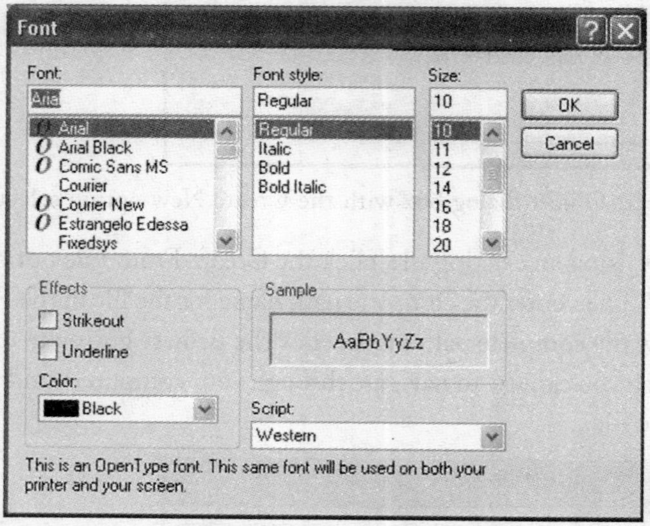

Figure 5-38 The Font dialog box.

NOTE *You can also format the selected text by using the Formatting toolbar's Font, Font Size, Font Script, Bold, Italic, Underlining, and Color buttons.*

- Bullet Style turns the selected paragraphs into a bulleted list—or converts the selected bulleted list back into paragraphs.

NOTE *You can also use the Bullets button on the Formatting toolbar to turn the selected paragraphs into a bulleted list and the selected bulleted list into regular paragraphs.*

- Paragraph displays the Paragraph dialog box, which you use to specify what indentation and alignment WordPad should use for the selected paragraphs, as shown in Figure 5-39.

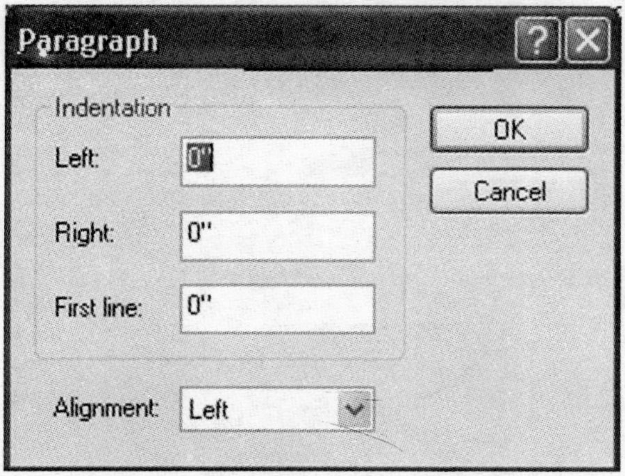

Figure 5-39 The Paragraph dialog box.

NOTE *You can also use the Align Left, Center, and Align Right buttons on the Formatting toolbar to align the selected text.*

- Tabs displays the Tabs dialog box, which you use to specify where WordPad should place tab stops, as shown in Figure 5-40.

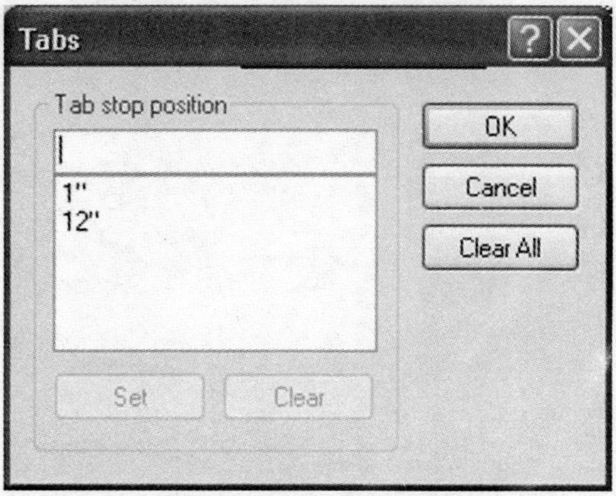

Figure 5-40 The Tabs dialog box.

Summary

The accessories described in this chapter don't provide a rich set of features. Nevertheless, their availability and simplicity make them worth knowing about. As a business user of Windows XP, you'll probably find the tools useful on occasion—especially when a more fully featured application such as Microsoft Word or Excel is unavailable.

Figure 5.39 The Paragraph dialog box.

NOTE: You can also use the Align Left, Center, and Align Right buttons on the Formatting toolbar to align the selected text.

- Tabs displays the Tabs dialog box, which you use to specify where WordPad should place tab stops, as shown in Figure 5.40.

Figure 5.40 The Tabs dialog box.

Summary

The accessories described in this chapter don't provide a rich set of features. Nevertheless, their availability and simplicity make them worth knowing about. As a business user of Windows XP, you'll probably find the tools useful on occasion—especially when a more fully featured application such as Microsoft Word or Excel is unavailable.

Chapter 6

USING WINDOWS XP ON A PORTABLE COMPUTER

Featuring:

- Installing Windows XP on a Portable Computer
- Enabling ClearType
- Using Shortcut Keys
- Securing Your Files
- Working with Offline Files
- Docking and Undocking
- Conserving Battery Life
- Remote Computing
- Accessing the Internet with a Wireless Laptop

If you are running Windows on a portable computer, as many, many business users do, you have some concerns that are not important to the desktop world. In this chapter, we'll look briefly at some Windows techniques that are specific to portable machines and point out some Windows features that can improve your comfort and efficiency when working on a portable computer.

Installing Windows XP on a Portable Computer

If you have Windows XP installed on a computer in your office, check your End-User License Agreement before installing it on your portable computer. In most cases, you are allowed to make a second copy that you can install on more than a portable computer.

Once you are sure that you are not violating the license agreement, follow the general instructions in Chapter 12. Of course, before you begin, be sure that your portable complies with the hardware requirements described in that chapter.

Enabling ClearType

ClearType is a Windows feature that triples the horizontal resolution of text on a Liquid Crystal Display (LCD) screen. In short, your screen display will be much clearer if you use ClearType. ClearType is not enabled by default. To turn on ClearType, follow these steps:

1. **Open the Display Properties dialog box at the Appearance tab, as shown in Figure 6-1.**

   Right-click the desktop, and choose Properties from the shortcut menu. Then in the Display Properties dialog box, click the Appearance tab.

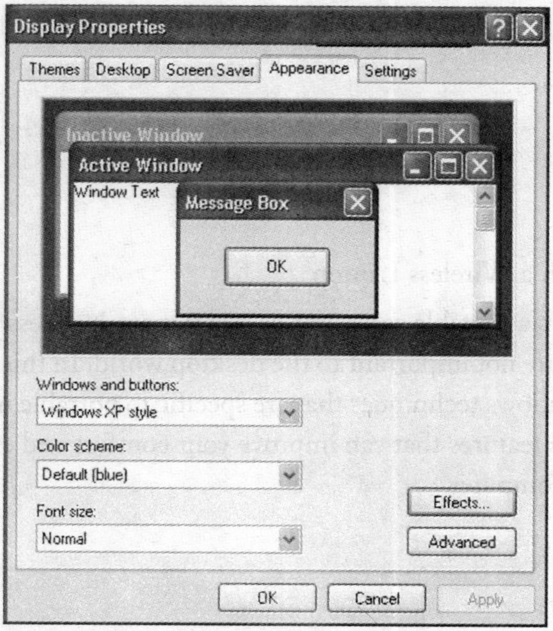

Figure 6-1 The Display Properties dialog box open at the Appearance tab.

2. **Open the Effects dialog box, which is shown in Figure 6-2.**

   In the Appearance tab, click the Effects button.

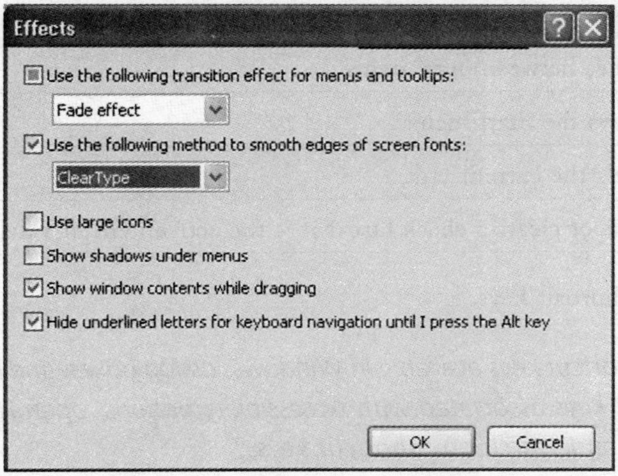

Figure 6-2 The Effects dialog box.

3. **Tell Windows to use ClearType.**

   Click the Use The Following Method To Smooth Edges Of Screen Fonts drop-down list, select ClearType, and then click OK. Click OK again in the Display Properties dialog box.

Using Shortcut Keys

When you're working on a portable computer, it's often much easier to use the keyboard instead of a pointing device. Table 6-1 shows the shortcut keys for some common Windows operations, but you can also create your own shortcut keys. We'll look at how to do that next.

SHORTCUT KEY	WHAT IT DOES
Ctrl+C	Copies the selection.
Ctrl+X	Cuts the selection.
Ctrl+V	Pastes the selection.
Ctrl+Z	Undoes the previous action.
F2	Renames the selected item.
F3	Searches for a file or a folder.

SHORTCUT KEY	WHAT IT DOES
Alt+Enter	Displays the properties for a selected item.
Alt+Spacebar	Opens the shortcut menu for the selected item.
Alt+Tab	Switches between open items.
Ctrl+Esc	Displays the Start menu.
Esc	Cancels the current task.
Spacebar	Checks or clears a check box if it is the active item in a dialog box.

Table 6-1 Windows shortcut keys.

TIP *For additional shortcut keys available in Windows, dialog boxes, and Explorer, and for shortcut keys associated with Accessibility options, open Help And Support Center and search on "shortcut keys."*

You can create your own shortcut keys for specific programs. These keys always begin with Ctrl+Alt. To illustrate, we'll create a shortcut key to WordPad. Follow these steps:

1. Open the WordPad Properties dialog box at the Shortcut tab, which is shown in Figure 6-3.

Click the Start button, click All Programs, click Accessories, right-click WordPad, and then choose Properties from the shortcut menu.

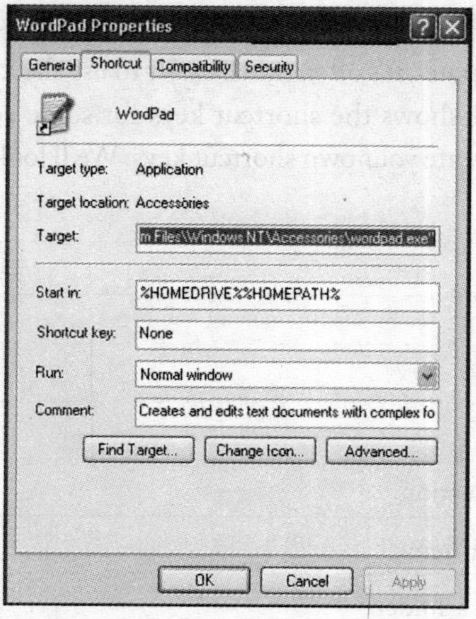

Figure 6-3 The WordPad Properties dialog box open at the Shortcut tab.

NOTE *You can also open the Properties dialog box for a program by right-clicking the program file (it has a .exe extension) in any Explorer-like window or by right-clicking a program's desktop shortcut.*

2. **Specify the key you want to use.**

   Click in the Shortcut Key box, and type the key. Windows then displays the key in addition to Ctrl+Alt. For example, if you type *w*, you'll see Ctrl+Alt+W in the Shortcut Key box. Click OK.

Now instead of clicking your way through the menus to open WordPad, simply press Ctrl+Alt+W.

Securing Your Files

In addition to taking full advantage of all the security features of Windows XP Professional, including user accounts, passwords, file and folder permissions, and so on, you can further protect your most sensitive data by encrypting it if you are using the NTFS file system. Then, only someone logged on to your computer with your user account can decrypt that data.

Experts recommend encrypting folders, not files, because a file can become decrypted when modified. The best approach is to create a special folder, perhaps naming it Encrypted Files, and then save sensitive files to that folder. They are automatically encrypted when you save them.

To create and encrypt a folder, follow these steps:

1. **Open Windows Explorer.**

   Click the Start button, right-click My Computer, and choose Explore from the shortcut menu.

2. **Create a new folder.**

   Select a parent folder for the new folder, click the File menu, click New, and then click Folder. Type a name for the folder in the box beneath it, and then click outside the box.

3. **Open the folder's Properties dialog box.**

   Right-click the folder, and choose Properties from the shortcut menu. Figure 6-4 shows the Properties dialog box for a folder named Encrypted Files.

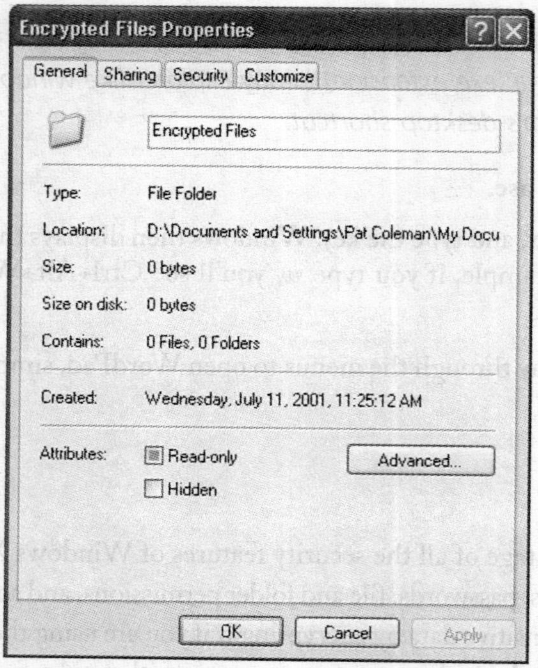

Figure 6-4 The Encrypted Files Properties dialog box.

4. Open the Advanced Attributes dialog box, which is shown in Figure 6-5.

In the Properties dialog box, click the Advanced button.

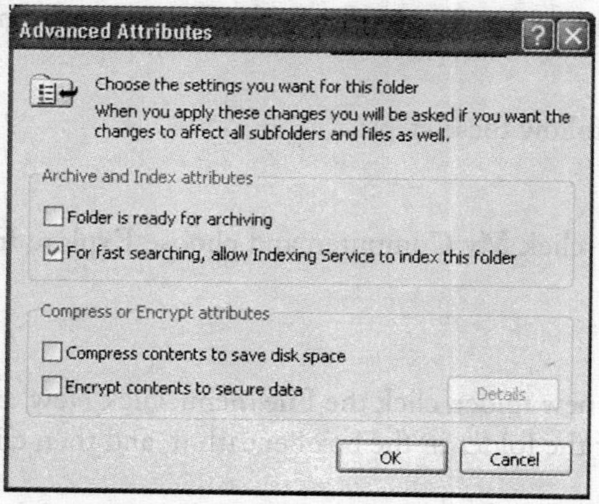

Figure 6-5 The Advanced Attributes dialog box.

5. Tell Windows to encrypt the folder.

Click the Encrypt Contents To Secure Data check box, and then click OK. Click OK again in the folder's Properties dialog box.

NOTE *You can compress a file or encrypt it, but you cannot encrypt a compressed file or compress an encrypted file.*

You access your encrypted files just as you access unencrypted files. When you open an encrypted file, you can read it and modify it just as you would if it weren't encrypted. When you then save it back to the encrypted folder, it is once again encrypted. To decrypt a file, select it, open its Properties dialog box, click the Advanced button to open the Advanced Attributes dialog box, and then clear the Encrypt Contents To Secure Data check box in the Advanced Attributes dialog box.

In addition to encrypting your most sensitive data, you need to take some practical steps to protect your portable and its data when you're on the road:

- Mark your computer with your name, address, and phone number. If possible, engrave this information right on the case.
- Back up regularly. Chapter 16 tells you how to back up using Windows XP.
- Carry insurance to cover the loss of your hardware and your data. If your standard homeowner's, renter's, or business owner's policies don't provide adequate coverage with reasonable deductibles, you might want to check Safeware, a company that specializes in computer insurance. You can find Safeware on the Web at *www.safeware.com*.

Working with Offline Files

When you work with offline files, you can work with a network or an Internet file even when you aren't connected to the network.

To make a network file available offline, follow these steps:

1. **Select the network file you want available offline.**

   Click the Start button, and then click My Network Places. Click the network drive you need, and then navigate to the file you want.

2. **Start the Offline Files Wizard.**

   Right-click the file, and choose Make Available Offline from the shortcut menu. The first time you set up offline files, the Offline Files Wizard starts. After that, you'll simply see the Synchronizing dialog box.

3. **Select a synchronization option.**

   In the wizard's Welcome screen, click Next, and then specify whether to synchronize the file with the version on the network when you log on and off your computer. Click Next.

4. **Complete the wizard.**

   On the last screen of the wizard, specify whether you want a periodic reminder that you aren't connected to the network, and elect to create a shortcut to the Offline Files folder on your desktop. Click Finish.

The Synchronizing dialog box will show the file's progress.

Docking and Undocking

If you have a portable computer that you regularly use at the office and at home or on the road, you probably know about docking stations and docking and undocking. When you're using Windows XP, you don't need to shut down or restart your computer when docking or undocking. When you dock the computer, Windows XP automatically detects the hardware change. To use automatically docking and undocking, however, both your application programs and hardware must support hot docking.

NOTE *A docking station consists of a monitor and other peripherals, such as a keyboard, that you plug a portable computer into. The portable then resembles a desktop computer. A docking station is also known as a docking bay and a port replicator.*

Conserving Battery Life

If you've just undocked your portable computer, it is now running on battery power, which is great because you can now use it on the train going home, while lounging on your back deck, during a cross-country airline flight, and in other situations where an electric power source is not available. You'll find out soon enough, if you don't know already, though, that batteries are expensive. Fortunately, you can use the power management features of your portable computer and Windows XP Professional to conserve battery power.

NOTE *When you run Windows XP Professional on a portable computer, shutting the computer's lid turns off the display.*

Windows XP Professional supports Advanced Configuration and Power Interface (ACPI), which is an industry standard that is designed to direct power management on a portable computer, on desktop computers, and also on server computers and peripherals that are ACPI-compliant. To access ACPI features, you use the Power Options applet. In Control Panel, click Performance And Maintenance, and then click Power Options to open the Power Options Properties dialog box, which is shown in Figure 6-6.

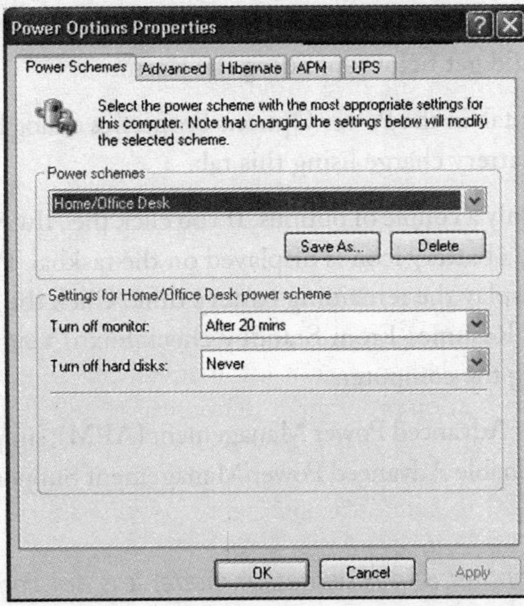

Figure 6-6 The Power Options Properties dialog box.

The tabs and options displayed in this dialog box depend on the hardware configuration of your portable computer. A *power scheme* is a group of options that describe your power settings. To define a power scheme, click the Power Schemes tab, if necessary, and follow these steps:

1. Specify the type of computer you are using.

In the Power Schemes drop-down list box, select Portable/Laptop.

2. Specify the idle time before a power scheme goes into effect.

In the Settings For Portable/Laptop Power Scheme section, select the idle time period after which the monitor is turned off and the idle time period after which your hard disk is turned off. Click Apply if you want to specify further options; otherwise, click OK.

If your system supports Hibernation, you will also see a Hibernate tab. Click it, and then click the Enable Hibernation check box to turn on Hibernation.

NOTE *In Hibernation, the computer stores the system state to the hard disk, and the computer completely shuts down. When power is restored, you can resume working exactly where you left off.*

If your portable computer has an alarm feature, you'll see an Alarms tab on which you can set a warning alarm that will alert you when your battery is low. Drag the slider to specify how low the battery should get before sounding the alarm.

You may also have a Power Meter tab in the Power Options Properties dialog box. You can check the condition of the battery charge using this tab.

Typically, the Advanced tab has only a couple of options. If you click the Always Show Icon On The Taskbar check box, a battery icon is displayed on the taskbar. Place the mouse cursor over this icon to display the remaining battery time. Click the Prompt For Password When Computer Resumes From Standby check box if you want to require a password before starting the computer.

If your portable computer supports Advanced Power Management (APM), simply click the APM tab and then click the Enable Advanced Power Management Support check box to enable this feature.

NOTE *When your portable computer is in Hibernation mode, it is not completely powered down. Therefore, when an airline asks that you turn it off during takeoff and landing, you will need to shut down completely.*

Remote Computing

When you're using your portable computer on the road, for example, when staying in a motel or connecting from a client's site, you may want to establish different dialing rules than those that apply in your home location. You can also set up your system to use a calling card.

Changing the Dialing Rules

To change the dialing rules so that you can dial out from a new location, follow these steps:

1. **Open the Phone And Modem Options dialog box, which is shown in Figure 6-7.**

   Click the Start button, click Control Panel, click the Printers And Other Hardware link, and then click Phone And Modem Options.

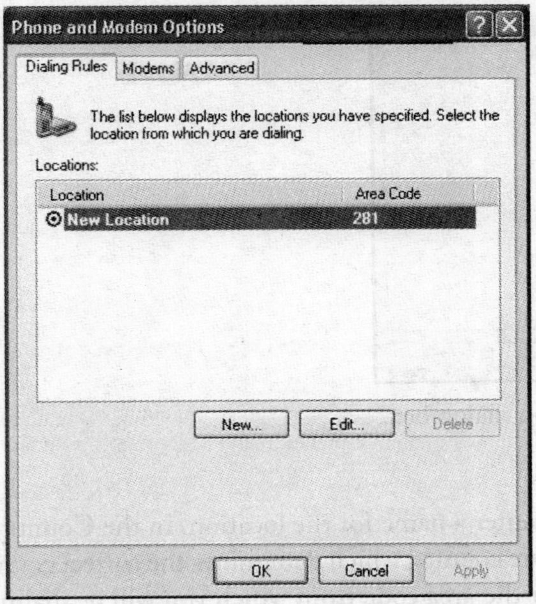

Figure 6-7 The Phone And Modem Options dialog box.

2. **Add a new location or edit an existing location.**

   Click New to open the New Location dialog box, or click Edit to open the Edit Location dialog box. The options are identical in both dialog boxes. Figure 6-8 shows the New Location dialog box.

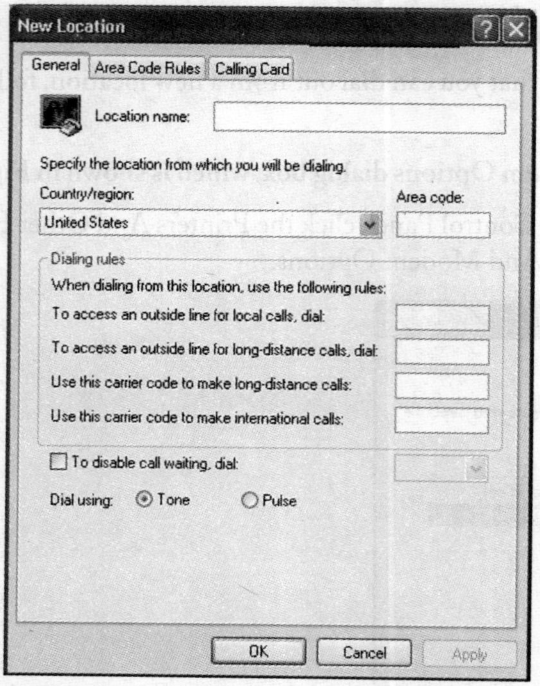

Figure 6-8 The New Location dialog box.

3. **Identify the location.**

   In the Location Name box, enter a name for the location. In the Country/Region list box, specify the appropriate country, which determines the correct country code. In the Area Code box, enter the area code from which you will be dialing.

4. **Specify the dialing rules.**

   If you need to dial a number to reach an outside line (such as 9), enter that number in the first text box. If you need to dial an additional number to access long distance service, enter that number in the second text box. If you need to enter a carrier code to make long distance or international calls, enter it in the appropriate box. To disable call waiting, click that check box, and enter the correct numeric code. You'll find it in the local phone book. Specify tone or pulse dialing, and then click Apply.

If you're in an area that uses 10-digit dialing for local calls, you'll need to separate long distance from local calling. You do this by creating a new area code rule. Click the Area Code Rules tab in the New Location (or Edit Location) dialog box, and follow these steps:

1. **Open the New Area Code Rule dialog box, which is shown in Figure 6-9.**

   Click the New button.

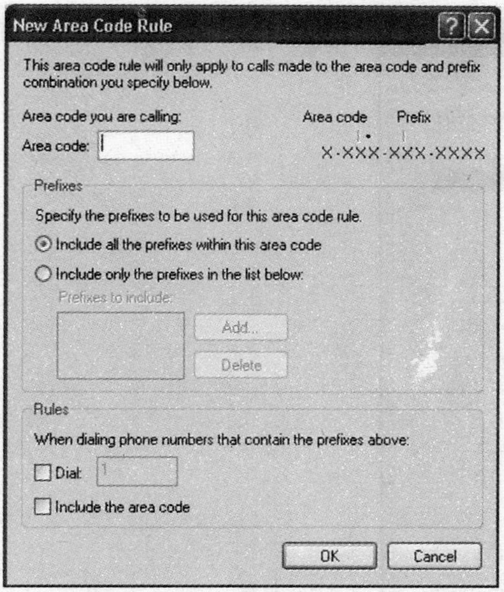

Figure 6-9 The New Area Code Rule dialog box.

2. **Specify the dialing rules.**

   In the Area Code box, enter the area code you will be calling. In the Prefixes section, specify what to do about prefixes. In the Rules section, specify whether to use the country code (1, which is for the United States, is the default) and whether to include the area code when dialing any prefix in the list. Click OK.

Setting Up a Calling Card

A calling card is a handy device when you're traveling, especially if you will be billing expenses back to your employer. If you are using a calling card that is in common use and thus is listed in the Calling Card tab, click the Calling Card tab, and then follow these steps to set it up:

1. **Specify the card type.**

   In the Calling Card tab, which is shown in Figure 6-10, select the card from the Card Types list.

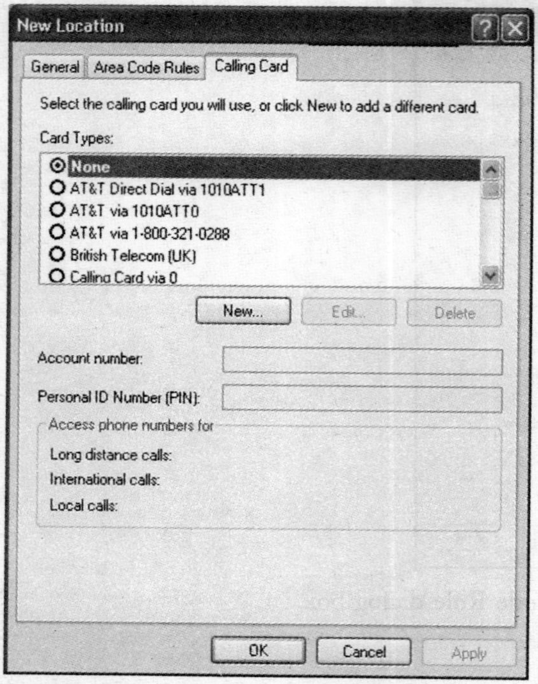

Figure 6-10 The New Location dialog box open at the Calling Card tab.

2. **Enter the information about your card.**

   Enter your account number, and then enter your PIN number. Access numbers are entered automatically when you select the card type. Click OK.

If your card is not listed in the Card types list, follow these steps:

1. **Open the New Calling Card dialog box, which is shown in Figure 6-11.**

   In the Calling Card tab, click New.

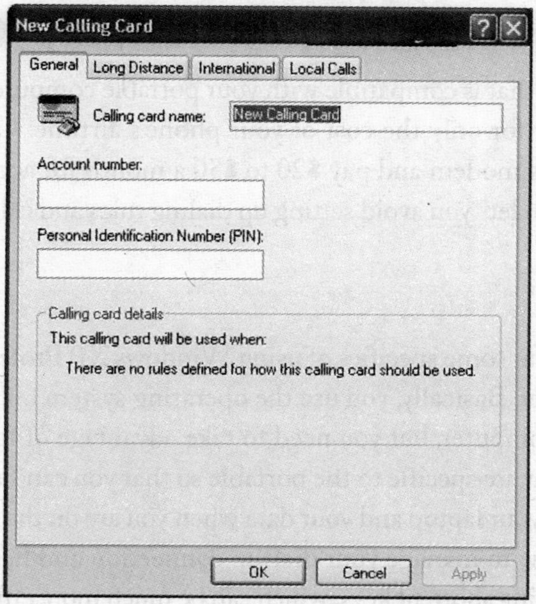

Figure 6-11 The New Calling Card dialog box.

2. **Enter information about the card.**

   In the Calling Card Name box, enter a name for the card, and then enter your account number and your PIN number.

3. **Enter the steps you must follow to make a call.**

   Click the Long Distance tab, enter the access number, and then in the Calling Card Dialing Steps box, enter the numbers in the exact order that you must enter them to make a call. For example, click the Access Number button, click the Wait For Prompt button, click the PIN button, click the Wait For Prompt button again, and then click the Destination Number button. To change the order of a step, click the Move Up or Move Down button. Click OK.

To use your calling card to make international or local calls, click the corresponding tab and follow step 3 above.

Accessing the Internet with a Wireless Laptop

If you travel with a cell phone that is compatible with your portable computer, you can access the Internet wirelessly for only the cost of your phone's airtime. Or you can purchase and install a wireless modem and pay $20 to $50 a month for access. In either case, a wireless connection lets you avoid setting up dialing rules and calling cards.

Summary

This chapter has taken a look at some specifics of using Windows XP Professional on a portable, or laptop, computer. Basically, you use the operating system on a portable just as you do on a desktop computer, but you need to take advantage of features included with Windows XP that are specific to the portable so that you can save battery life and ensure the security of your laptop and your data when you are on the road. This chapter has also looked at how to manage your dial-up connection and has included a section about using and creating shortcut keys, which can be much more efficient than a pointing device when you're using a portable computer.

Chapter 7

CONNECTING TO THE INTERNET

Featuring:

- Connecting to the Internet via Modem
- Connecting to the Internet via Cable Modem
- Protecting Your Computer System from the Outside World
- Connecting to the Internet via DSL
- Connecting to the Internet via ISDN

Assume you're in the market for a new computer and that you have only two choices: one computer has all the latest bells and whistles you could ever imagine on a standalone machine; the other has the fastest connection on the planet to the Internet. Cost is not an issue. Which computer would you buy?

Well, if you spend as much time on the Internet every day as we do, this decision is a no-brainer. In an ideal world, we'd take the computer with the great connection, and it would never go down. As the business world increasingly relies on the Internet and the services it provides, we yearn for faster and more reliable connections.

In this chapter, we'll take a look at some of the options you might consider when selecting a connection for your home office or for a small- to medium-sized business. If you work for a big firm, you may connect at the office to a very high-speed device, such as a T1. A T1 is a long-distance point-to-point communications circuit that transfers data at incredibly fast speeds (1.5 megabits per second, or Mbps) and is very expensive, somewhere in the neighborhood of $2,000 a month.

Although a T1 is not generally an option for most of us, present and emerging technologies are delivering faster Internet connections to many areas in the United States and at affordable prices. If you live in an outlying area, providers may be touting what is on the horizon rather than what is actually available in your neighborhood, but even that is progress.

We'll start by discussing the modem, and then we'll look at some high-speed connections that are becoming more common, depending on your location. We'll also look at how to share these connections and how to connect to your office when you're on the road or at home.

Connecting to the Internet via Modem

A modem is the most common device in use for connecting to the Internet, but it is also the slowest.

How Does a Modem Work?

A modem is a device that lets a computer transfer information over a telephone line. A computer is a digital device, and a telephone line is an analog device; therefore, a mechanism is needed that can convert digital signals to analog signals and vice versa, and that's what a modem does. A modem is connected to a computer on one end and plugs into a phone jack on the other end; a modem can be external, that is, on the outside of the computer, or internal, on the inside of the computer.

Modem speed is measured in kilobits per second, which is abbreviated Kbps, but people commonly refer to this speed in "bauds" and speak of modem speed as "baud rate." Modems can typically transfer information over a standard telephone line at a rate of up to 56 Kbps, but this is a theoretical maximum because of electrical noise on the phone line. Another speed limitation concerns whether you are downloading information (for example, receiving e-mail or accessing a Web page) or uploading information (for example, sending e-mail or posting a Web page to a Web server). Downloading information is faster than uploading for the fastest modems, with the 33.6 Kbps the fastest speed you can upload over a modem.

Installing a Modem

If your modem is Plug and Play, and most are today, Windows XP Professional recognizes and installs it when you install the operating system. It also installs the modem if you later upgrade or change modems. Windows XP Professional includes many more device drivers than were available in previous versions of Windows, so it's quite likely that the installation program will find the appropriate driver for your modem. If your modem was working properly before installing Windows XP but does not function afterward, you have several choices as to your course of action. One choice is to use the Roll Back Driver feature, which is new in Windows XP. During installation, the previous device driver is saved if Windows installs a new driver. Thus, you can return to the driver you were previously using. Follow these steps to use Roll Back Driver:

1. **Open the System Properties dialog box at the Hardware tab, which is shown in Figure 7-1.**

   Click the Start button, right-click My Computer, and then choose Properties from the shortcut menu. In the System Properties dialog box, click the Hardware tab.

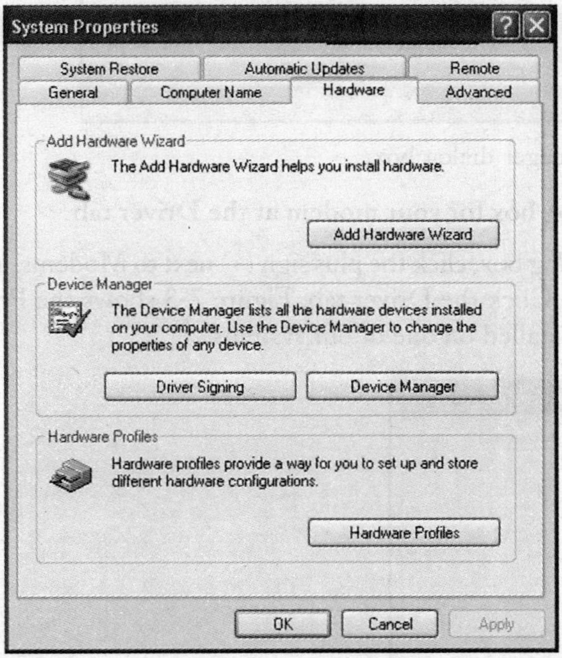

Figure 7-1 The System Properties dialog box open at the Hardware tab.

2. **Open the Device Manager dialog box, which is shown in Figure 7-2.**

   In the Device Manager section of the Hardware tab, click Device Manager.

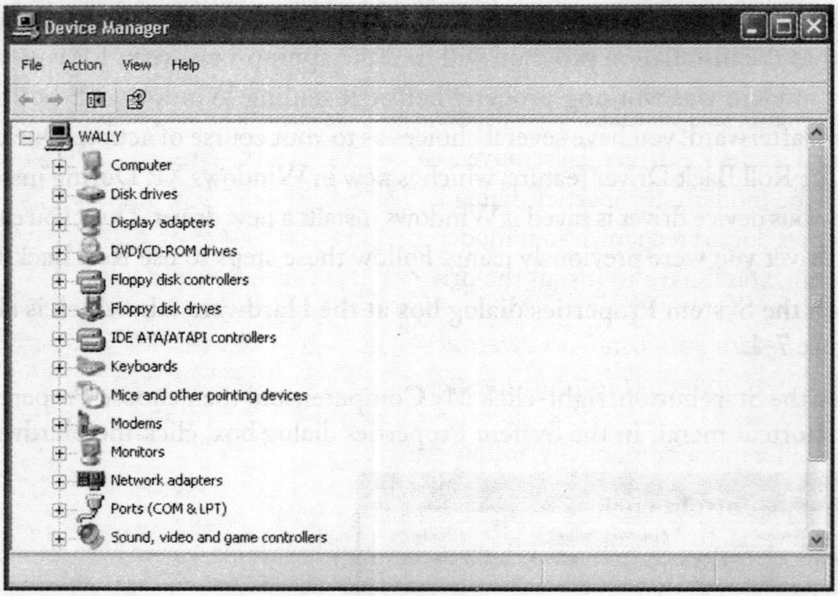

Figure 7-2 The Device Manager dialog box.

3. Open the Properties dialog box for your modem at the Driver tab.

In the Device Manager dialog box, click the plus sign (+) next to Modems, and then double-click your modem. Click the Driver tab. Figure 7-3 shows the Properties dialog box for a modem installed on one of our systems.

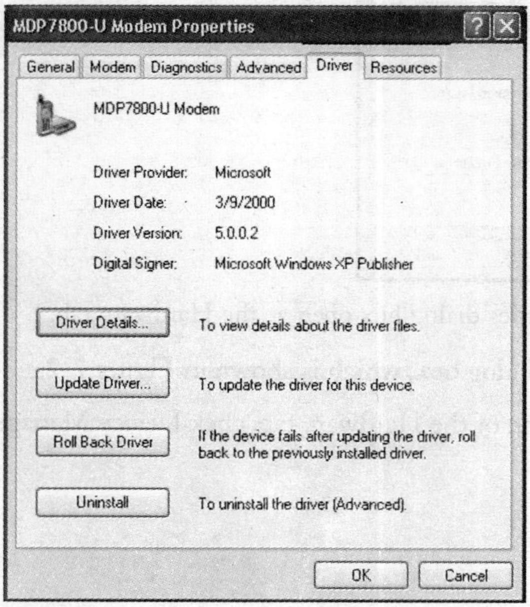

Figure 7-3 The Properties dialog box for an MDP 7800-U Modem open at the Driver tab.

4. **Tell Windows to use your previous driver.**

   Click the Roll Back Driver button.

Another approach to take if your modem isn't working properly is to remove it and then reinstall its device driver. To remove a driver, click the Uninstall button on the Driver tab of the modem's Properties dialog box and follow the onscreen instructions. Or if Windows doesn't recognize your modem and, thus, doesn't have the proper device driver to install, you'll have to install the driver and the modem manually.

TIP *Before you install an external modem, be sure that it is turned on and that it's connected to both the telephone line and your computer.*

To install a modem manually, follow these steps:

1. **Open Control Panel.**

   Click the Start button, and then click Control Panel.

2. **Open the Phone And Modem Options dialog box at the Modems tab, which is shown in Figure 7-4.**

   Click the Printers And Other Hardware category, click Phone And Modem Options, and then click the Modems tab.

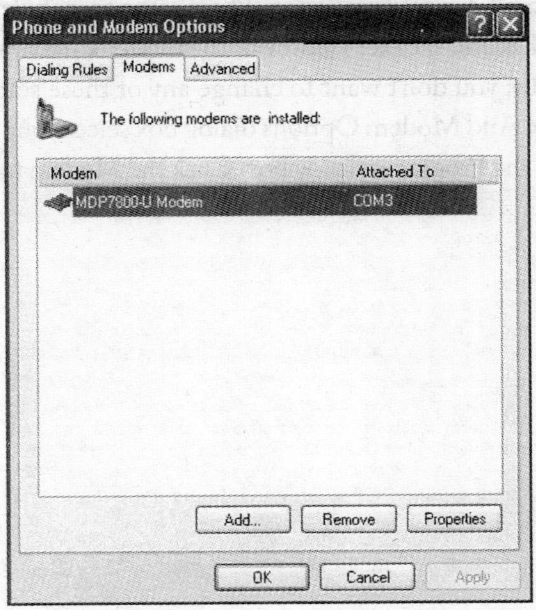

Figure 7-4 The Phone And Modem Options dialog box open at the Modems tab.

3. **Start the Add Hardware Wizard.**

   Click the Add button.

4. **Follow the onscreen instructions.**

   Click the Don't Detect My Modem; I Will Select It From A List check box. Click Next. You'll be asked to choose your modem's make and model from a list. If the list doesn't contain the make or model of your modem, look in the manual that came with your modem to see whether an equivalent type is listed. If you don't find an equivalent type, you can do one of the following:

   - Check the disk that was provided with your modem. If it contains a driver, click the Have Disk button to open the Install From Disk dialog box, and install the driver.
   - Select one of the standard modem types in the Models list.
   - Contact the manufacturer of your modem to see whether it has an updated driver.

Setting Up a Modem

When you install a modem or when it's installed automatically, all your communications programs, such as Microsoft Outlook Express, Fax, HyperTerminal, and so on, use the settings that were configured during installation. These settings include the port on which the modem was installed, the speaker volume of the modem, maximum port speed, and dial control. Normally, you don't want to change any of these settings. To take a look at them, in the Phone And Modem Options dialog box select your modem, and then click Properties to open the Properties dialog box. Click the Modem tab, which is shown in Figure 7-5.

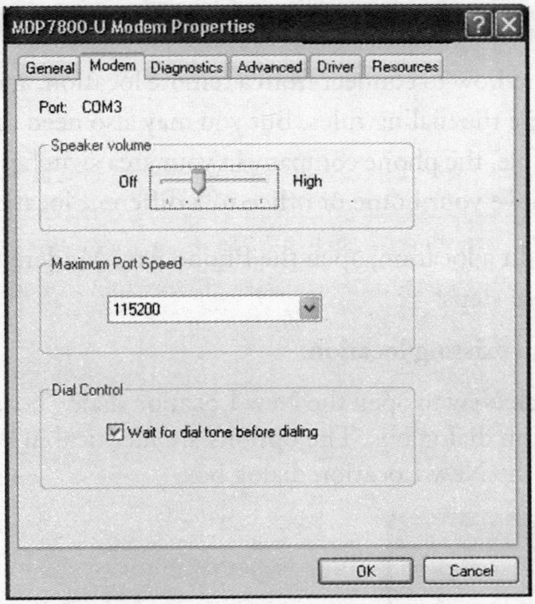

Figure 7-5 The Properties dialog box for a modem open at the Modem tab.

Internal modems are usually installed on COM port 3 or 4. External modems are normally installed on COM port 2. If you are an advanced user and really know what you are doing, you can change the port setting using the options on the Advanced tab.

When you connect using your modem, you'll hear the modem dialing out—unless the volume of the speaker inside your modem is set too low (or your modem doesn't have a speaker). To increase or decrease the volume, move the Speaker Volume slider bar.

When your modem connects with the modem at your Internet service provider (ISP), it tries to connect at the maximum speed. In general, set the maximum port speed at three or four times the rated modem speed to take advantage of the modem's built-in data compression.

Clear the Wait For Dial Tone Before Dialing check box if you need to manually dial your modem connection or if your modem doesn't recognize the dial tone used by your current location.

To see if your modem is responding to Windows, click the Diagnostics tab and then click the Query Modem button. If the modem is not responding, you've got a problem, and you should probably get some help from a professional technician.

Setting Up Dialing Rules

Later in this chapter, we'll look at how to connect from a remote location, and in that situation you may want to change the dialing rules. But you may also need to change the dialing rules when, for example, the phone company in your area switches to a 10-digit dialing system or if you move your home or office to a different location.

To create a new location or to edit a location, open the Phone And Modem Options dialog box, and then follow these steps:

1. Add a new location or edit an existing location.

On the Dialing Rules tab, click New to open the New Location dialog box, or click Edit to open the Edit Location dialog box. The options are identical in both dialog boxes. Figure 7-6 shows the New Location dialog box.

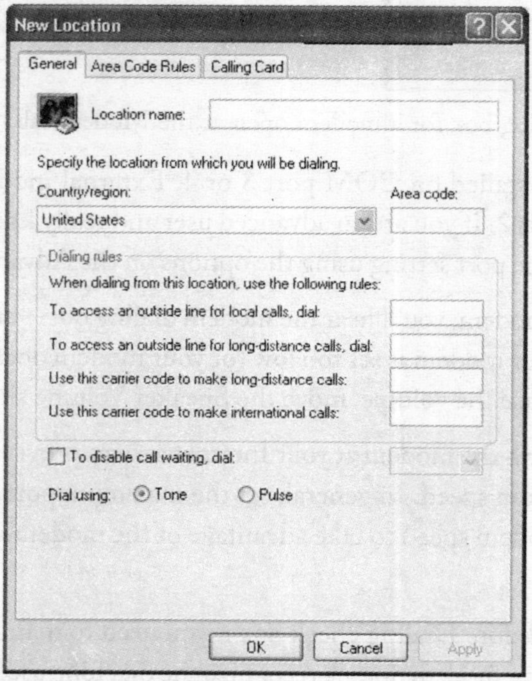

Figure 7-6 The New Location dialog box.

2. Identify the location.

In the Location Name box on the General tab, enter a name for the location. In the Country/Region box, specify the appropriate country, which determines the correct country code. In the Area Code box, enter the area code from which you will be dialing.

3. **Specify the dialing rules.**

   If you need to dial a number to reach an outside line (such as 9), enter that number in the first text box. If you need to dial an additional number to access long-distance service, enter that number in the second text box. If you use a carrier code to make long-distance or international calls, enter it in the appropriate box. To disable call waiting, select that check box and enter the correct numeric code. You'll find it in your local phone book. Specify tone or pulse dialing, and then click Apply.

If you're in an area that uses 10-digit dialing for local calls, you'll need to separate long-distance from local calling. You do this by creating a new area code rule. Click the Area Code Rules tab in the New Location (or Edit Location) dialog box, and follow these steps:

1. **Open the New Area Code Rule dialog box, which is shown in Figure 7-7.**

   Click the New button.

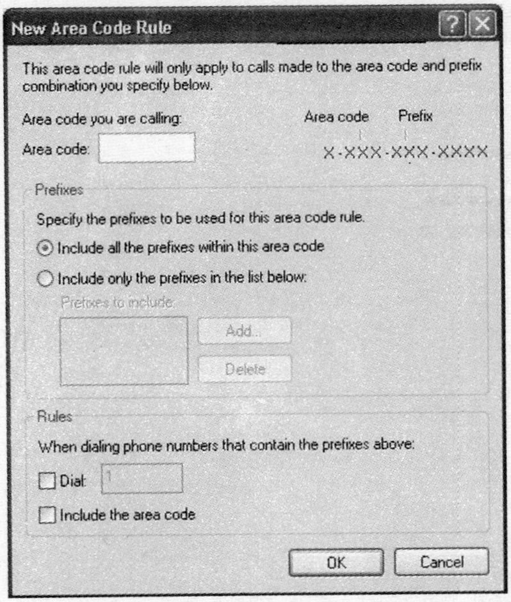

Figure 7-7 The New Area Code Rule dialog box.

2. **Specify the dialing rules.**

   In the Area Code box, enter the area code you will be calling. If the entire area code is a local call, click the Dial 1 and the Include The Area Code check boxes. If only numbers with certain prefixes are local calls within this area code, click the Include Only The Prefixes In The List Below option button and add the local prefixes. Click OK.

Setting Up Your Internet Connection

When you installed Windows XP, you were given an opportunity to set up your Internet connection. If you didn't do so then, you can do so now. But first you need an account with an ISP and the following information:

- User name and password
- The phone number to dial in to your ISP

To set up your connection, you use the New Connection Wizard. Click the Start button, click Connect To, and then click Show All Connections to open the Network Connections folder shown in Figure 7-8.

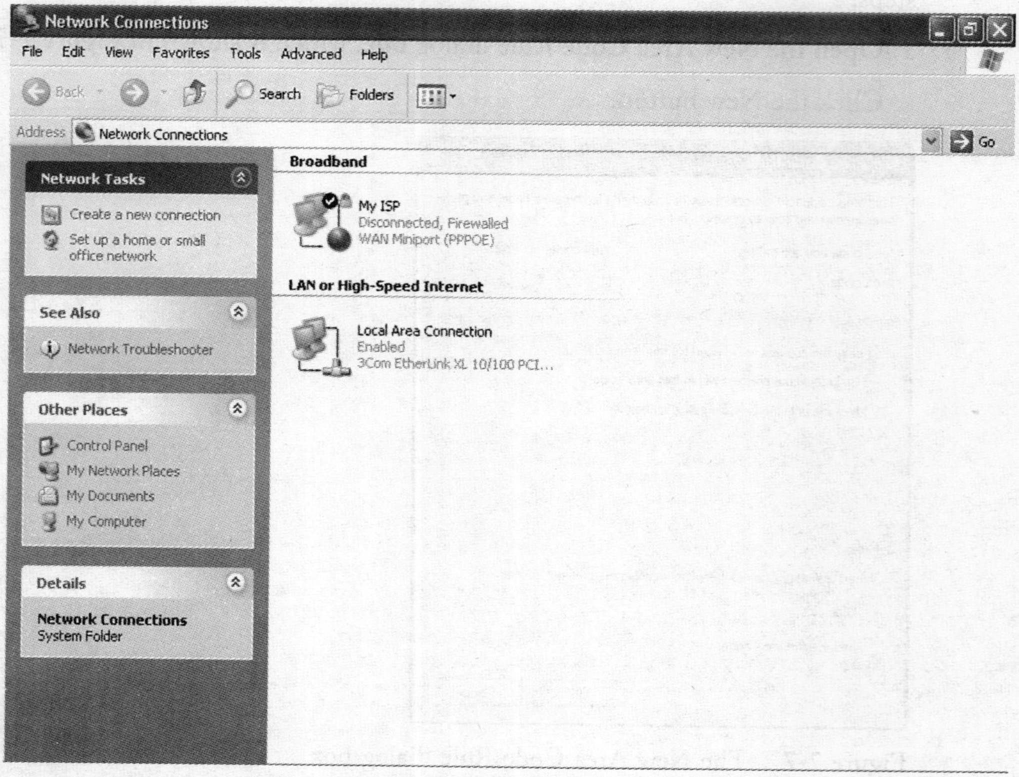

Figure 7-8 The Network Connections folder.

To start the wizard, click the Create A New Connection link in the Network Tasks bar. You'll see the Welcome screen shown in Figure 7-9. Click Next.

Figure 7-9 The New Connection Wizard.

To create a new dial-up connection, follow these steps:

1. Specify the type of connection you want to create.

In the Network Connection Type screen, which is shown in Figure 7-10, click the Connect To The Internet option button, and then click Next.

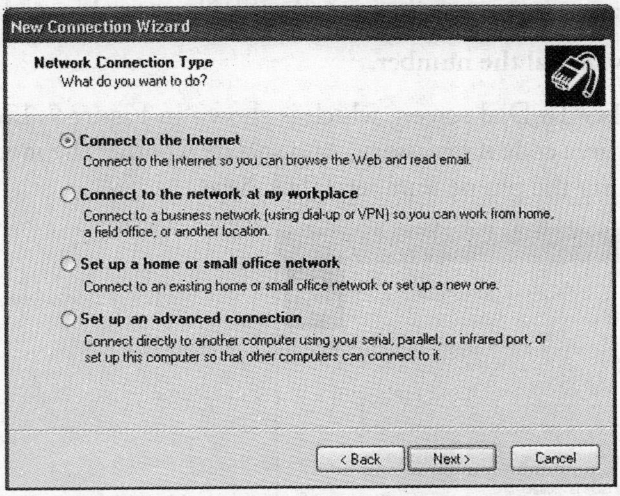

Figure 7-10 Selecting a connection type.

2. Tell the wizard how you want to connect.

In the Getting Ready screen, select the option that most accurately describes how you want to connect, and then click Next. Assuming you have an account with an ISP and the information you need, click Set Up My Connection Manually.

3. **Specify how you connect.**

   In the Internet Connection screen, which is shown in Figure 7-11, click the Connect Using A Dial-Up Modem option button, and then click Next.

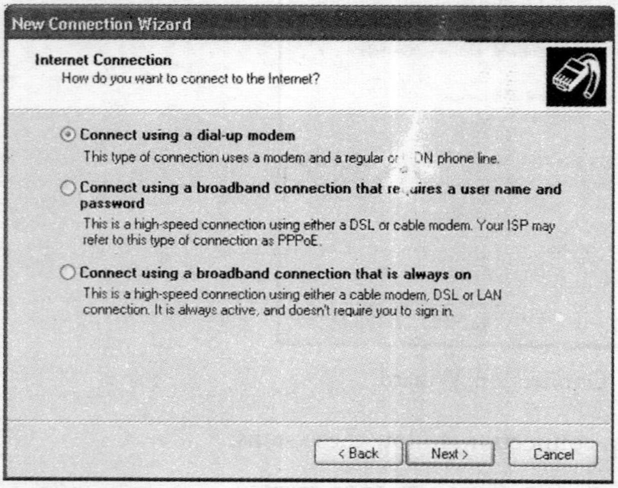

Figure 7-11 Selecting how you connect to the Internet.

4. **Name the connection.**

   In the Connection Name screen, enter a name in the ISP Name text box, and click Next.

5. **Tell the wizard how to dial the number.**

   In the Phone Number To Dial screen, which is shown in Figure 7-12, enter the phone number (and area code if necessary), and specify whether the modem needs to dial 1 before dialing the phone number. Click Next.

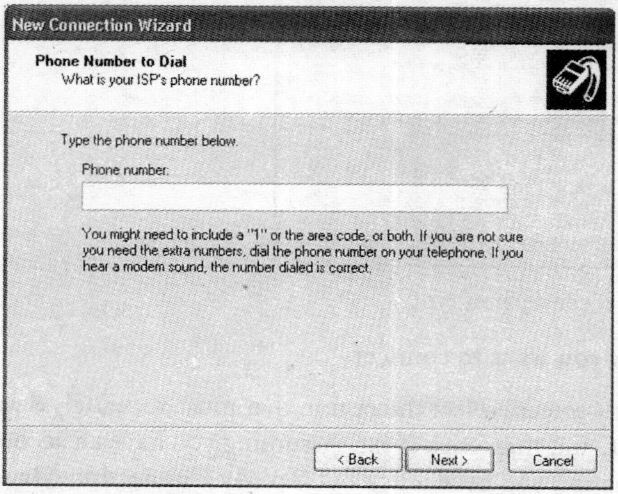

Figure 7-12 Specifying how to dial your ISP's number.

6. **Supply information about your account.**

   In the Internet Account Information screen, which is shown in Figure 7-13, enter your name and password and reconfirm your password. If you want any user who logs on to your computer to be able to use your connection information, leave the first check box selected. If you always want to dial out using this connection, leave the second check box selected. And if you want to keep the Internet Connection Firewall enabled, leave that check box selected. Click Next.

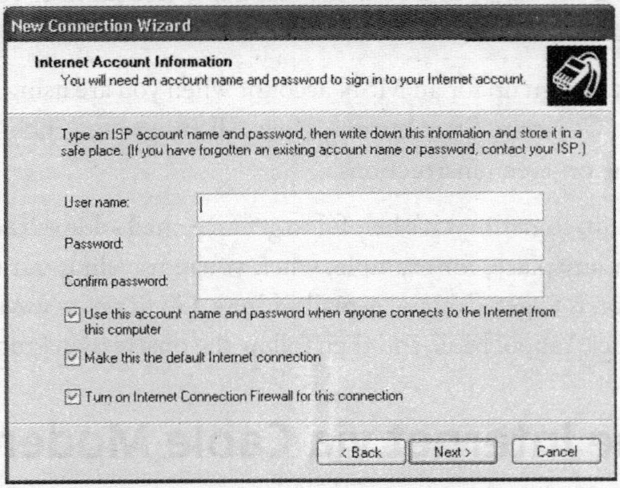

Figure 7-13 The Internet Account Information screen in the New Connection Wizard.

7. **Complete the connection.**

   In the final screen, verify that the information is correct. If you want to change any of it, click the Back button to go to that screen. If you want a shortcut to this connection on your desktop, click that check box. Click Finish.

Obtaining an Internet Account

As you will see in the next section, if you have a cable modem, your Internet account will be with your cable provider. If you have an analog modem, a digital subscriber line (DSL) modem, or an Integrated Services Digital Network (ISDN) modem, you can choose your ISP. You'll find information about ISPs in your local newspaper, local phone book, computer publications, and so on. You may also find start-up disks for providers such as America Online (AOL) and CompuServe in newspapers, magazines, and other publications.

In some cases, to set up your account you simply pop in the CD or floppy disk that you've acquired and follow the onscreen instructions. You'll usually need a credit card, and often you'll get a number of free connection days. The fee depends on the type of account, but often you pay only a set amount for unlimited Internet and e-mail services. Many ISPs also allow you to post a home page on their Web server and, for a fee, provide development services. If you travel on business and use a laptop computer, be sure to verify that your ISP has a toll-free number you can access while on the road.

Microsoft makes it easy to sign up for an MSN account when you are using Windows XP Professional. Click the Start button, click All Programs, click MSN Explorer, and follow the onscreen instructions.

After you have an account, sometimes it's helpful to get an e-mail address that you can access from almost any place, for example, when you're traveling out of the country. One such option is to get a Yahoo! e-mail address. Go to *www.yahoo.com*, click Personal Email, click Yahoo! Mail, and then follow the onscreen instructions.

Connecting to the Internet via Cable Modem

Most people who use the Internet outside a corporate environment probably start out using a modem. If you spend a lot of time accessing the Web or if you send and receive lots of files, as we do, you soon become dissatisfied with the speed of your connection and start looking for alternatives. One alternative that may be available to you is a cable modem, which uses the same wiring that brings cable TV into your home or office.

Today, more than 100 million homes are wired for cable TV, so if your cable provider also provides cable modem service, it might make sense to use a cable modem. We say *might* because there's a catch. Downloading over a cable modem can be 4 to 40 times faster (256 Kbps to 2 Mbps) than downloading over a 56-Kbps modem, but uploading is only about four times faster (usually 128 Kbps). What this means in practical terms is that if you're primarily interested in accessing Web resources, a cable modem is going to bring them to your screen much, much faster than a modem. On the other hand, if you want fast transmission rates when you're uploading files, you're probably better off with DSL, if it's available in your area. In the plus column, however, a cable modem is usually more affordable than other high-speed options.

NOTE *Not all cable companies provide Internet access, although many are in the process of adding this service. If you haven't seen a flyer advertising cable modem service in the envelope with your monthly cable bill, you can, of course, simply call the cable company and ask.*

How Does a Cable Modem Work?

Once you're connected via a cable modem (and we'll look at getting connected next), data between your computer and the Internet travels along the following path:

- The coaxial cable that comes into your home or office from a pole is divided into two connections by a splitter. One connection goes to your TV, and the other goes to your cable modem, a little box that is external to your computer.
- The cable modem connects to the network card inside your computer or to the USB adapter on your computer. Data traveling to your computer from the Internet goes through the coaxial cable, through your cable modem, and into your computer. Data traveling from your computer to the Internet follow this path in reverse.
- Once data is inside the coaxial cable, its next stop is a node, which is also the next spot on the route for cable television signals. Each cable company divides its region into nodes, or neighborhoods, of about 500 subscribers. All 500 subscribers share one node, which can become a bottleneck if all access the Internet at the same time.
- From the node, data passes through high-speed fiber-optic lines to a head-end cable facility, which handles the nodes for some four to ten regions.
- The head end accesses the Internet by means of high-speed links, and the head end also has high-speed Internet servers for mail, newsgroups, the Web, and so on. Thus, your cable company becomes your ISP as well as your connection to the Internet.

Getting Connected

The most difficult part of getting connected via cable modem may be getting your cable company to actually come to your home or place of business in a timely fashion. That said, once a technician arrives on the premises, he or she will fiddle with the main cable a bit, attach the splitter, and then run the cable to the cable modem.

If your computer already has a network card, the technician will attach the cable modem to the network card with another cable. If your computer doesn't have a network card, the cable company will probably provide one and configure it—perhaps for an additional fee.

Now you can use the New Connection Wizard to configure your connection in short order, following these steps:

1. **Open the Network Connections folder.**

   Click the Start button, click Connect To, and then click Show All Connections.

2. **Start the wizard.**

   Click the Create A New Connection link in the Network Tasks bar. You'll see the Welcome screen, as shown earlier in this chapter. Click Next.

3. **Tell the wizard your connection type.**

   In the Network Connection Type screen, click the Connect To The Internet option button, and then click Next.

4. **Tell the wizard how you want to connect.**

   In the Getting Ready screen, click Set Up My Connection Manually, and then click Next.

5. **Specify how you connect.**

   In the Internet Connection screen, click the second option if you have to log on with a user name and a password. Click Next, and then complete the rest of the following steps. If your cable modem connection is always on and you don't need to log on, select the third option, click Next, and click Finish.

6. **Name your connection.**

   In the Connection Name screen, which is shown in Figure 7-14, enter a name in the ISP Name box. Click Next.

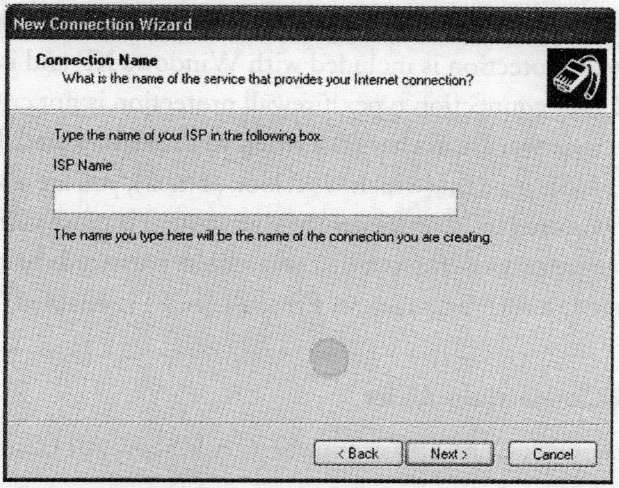

Figure 7-14 Naming your connection.

7. **Supply information about your account.**

   In the Internet Account Information screen, enter your name and password and reconfirm your password. If you want any user who logs on to your computer to be able to use your connection information, leave the first check box selected. If you always want to dial out using this connection, leave the second check box selected. And if you want to keep the Internet Connection Firewall enabled, leave that check box selected. Click Next.

8. **Complete the connection.**

   In the final screen, verify that the information is correct. If you want to change any of it, click the Back button to go to that screen. If you want a shortcut to this connection on your desktop, click that check box. Click Finish.

You can now do a couple of things—you can log on to the Internet, or you can call your telephone company and cancel the second line you've been using for Internet access, if you had one.

Protecting Your Computer System from the Outside World

A *firewall* is a security system that prevents unauthorized users from accessing your computer system when you are connected to the Internet. With a firewall installed, users can always reach the Internet, but only safe network traffic can pass through the firewall into your system or network.

In the past, that is, before the release of Windows XP, you had to obtain a firewall from a third party. Now firewall protection is included with Windows XP and is installed by default, regardless of your connection type. Firewall protection is not critical with a dial-up connection because you are in charge of when you are connected. However, with a cable modem or a DSL modem (which we'll look at next), you are always connected if your system is powered up. Consequently, your system is more vulnerable to the possibility of unauthorized access. Be sure that you require passwords to any shared resources, and verify that Internet Connection Firewall (ICF) is enabled. To do so, follow these steps:

1. **Open your Network Connections folder.**

   Click the Start button, click Connect To, and then click Show All Connections.

2. **Open the Properties dialog box for your cable modem connection at the Advanced tab, which is shown in Figure 7-15.**

   Right-click your cable modem connection, choose Properties from the shortcut menu, and then click the Advanced tab.

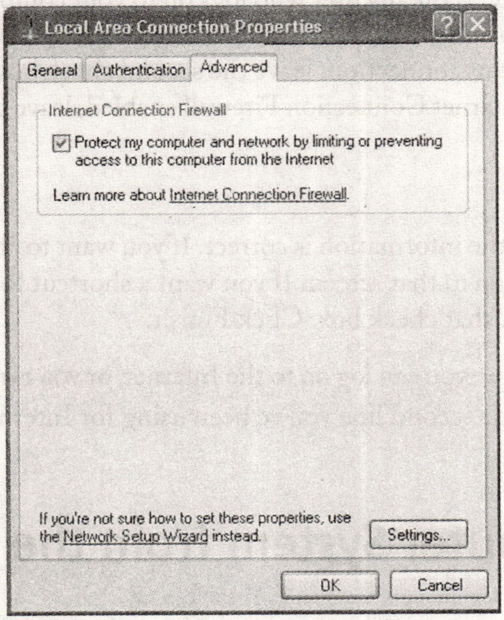

Figure 7-15 Using the Advanced tab to enable or disable ICF.

3. **Check that firewall protection is enabled.**

   Be sure that the check box in the Internet Connection Firewall section is checked. Click OK.

Connecting to the Internet via DSL

Another popular high-speed option is a digital subscriber line (DSL) modem. DSL comes in two basic flavors—asymmetric and symmetric. DSL service providers often refer to asymmetric DSL as "home" DSL and refer to symmetric DSL as "business" DSL. Here's why. With asymmetric DSL, download speeds are much faster than upload speeds, which means that you can access a Web page at much higher speeds than you can transmit a document over e-mail. Service providers seem to have collectively decided that home users access Web resources much more often than they transfer files, and so they deem asymmetric DSL the most appropriate for home use. Asymmetric DSL is also usually a good deal cheaper than symmetric DSL.

With symmetric DSL, upload and download speeds are the same, and the more you are willing to pay, the faster the speed. For example, at our ISP, asymmetric DSL is available for about $60 a month. This yields download rates of 640 Kbps and upload rates of 256 Kbps. Symmetric DSL is available at speeds ranging from 144 Kbps to 7 Mbps (7000 Kbps) and at prices ranging from about $100 a month to $400 a month. The speed available to your home or office depends on location, as you will see shortly.

How Does DSL Work?

DSL uses your existing telephone lines, but transmits data at higher frequencies than those used to transmit voice. Therefore, you can use your fax machine, your telephone, or even a modem at the same time that you are accessing the Internet with your computer.

The DSL modem attached to your computer must be the proper type for your DSL provider, and the telephone Central Office must be within a certain distance of your home or office. The exact distance depends on the type of DSL and the speed.

A DSL modem is external to the computer and looks similar to a cable modem, only it really isn't a modem in the true sense of the word. A modem converts digital signals to analog signals and vice versa. A so-called DSL modem transmits and receives all data as digital signals.

Getting Connected

The process of getting connected with DSL is very similar to the process for getting connected with cable modem. Once a technician arrives on the premises, he or she may fiddle with the phone lines a bit and then connect the phone line to the DSL modem.

If your computer already has a network card, the technician will attach the DSL modem to the network card with another cable. If your computer doesn't have a network card, the technician will probably provide one and configure it—perhaps for an additional fee.

And that's it. You don't even need to run the New Connection Wizard. If you need to log on to your account, you may have to configure your network protocols. Follow the instruction provided by your ISP. Once that's complete, you can now do a couple of things—you can log on to the Internet, or you can call your telephone company and cancel the second line you've been using for Internet access, if you had one.

WARNING *DSL modem is "always on," as is cable modem. Therefore, be sure that Internet Connection Firewall is enabled by following the steps in the "Protecting Your Computer System from the Outside World" section earlier in this chapter.*

TIP *If you want to check the speed of your Internet connection, go to* http:// computingcentral.msn.com/internet/speedtest.asp. *Enter your area code, and then click Test It. The Bandwidth Meter Results page will show your connection speed.*

Connecting to the Internet via ISDN

Integrated Services Digital Network (ISDN) is not a new technology, but it has become a popular way to connect to the Internet for several reasons. For starters, it was one of the first alternatives to the analog modem. It continues to be popular because it is more universally available than other high-speed connections, though it tends to be more expensive.

How Does ISDN Work?

ISDN uses existing telephone wires and requires an ISDN modem. As is the case with a DSL modem, an ISDN modem isn't really a modem. Although it looks like one, it is actually an adapter that lets you send and receive digital signals over ISDN phone lines. For ISDN to work, the telephone company must have digital-switching equipment.

The most common kind of ISDN access is called Basic Rate Interface (BRI). The ISDN modem sends a digital signal over the telephone wire, which is divided into three channels. A channel is not a wire but a way in which data travels. Two channels transmit data, and the third channel sends routing information. Using ISDN, you can access the Internet while talking on the phone over the same connection; thus, you can disconnect the second phone line you might have been using for Internet access.

Getting Connected

After contracting with your phone company for ISDN service, you need to install your ISDN modem. The process is exactly the same as installing an analog modem, and if the ISDN modem is Plug and Play (and it certainly should be), Windows will recognize it and install the necessary driver.

To configure an ISDN modem, follow these steps:

1. **Open the Network Connections folder.**

   Click the Start button, click Connect To, and then click Show All Connections.

2. **Open the Properties dialog box for your ISDN connection.**

   Right-click the dial-up connection that uses ISDN, and choose Properties from the shortcut menu.

3. **Open the ISDN Configure dialog box.**

   Click the General tab, select the ISDN device, and then click Configure.

NOTE *Depending on the type of ISDN modem that you have, clicking the Configure button may open the Modem Configurations dialog box.*

4. **Select a line type.**

   In the Line Type section, select the type of line you will be using. If you want to negotiate for a line type, click the Negotiate Line Type check box. Click OK.

How Fast Is Fast Enough?

If all these high-speed options leave you wondering which is best for you, which is fastest, and so on, here are some points to consider:

- The fastest analog modem transmits data at 53 Kbps. DSL ranges from 144 Kbps to 7 Mbps. Cable modem access generally peaks at 1 to 10 Mbps, but during slow times may be as slow as 256 Kbps or slower, and ISDN access maximum access speed is 128 Kbps.
- With cable modems, DSL modems, and ISDN, you don't need a second phone line.
- With cable modems, you can't use a separate ISP.
- ISDN is usually more expensive than the other high-speed options. Some providers even charge by the minute, but if you want something faster than an analog modem and neither DSL nor cable modem are available in your area, ISDN may be your only choice.
- Cable modem speed can be impeded if all the subscribers in your so-called neighborhood are simultaneously accessing the Internet.
- In some situations, you can start with a lower speed DSL connection and upgrade to a higher speed.
- Cable modems and DSL modems are always on. Be sure to enable Internet Connection Firewall.

Summary

With the information in this chapter, you should be equipped to make an effective decision about which kind of Internet connection will work best for you. You also have at your fingertips the steps you need to take to set up that connection. We've looked at analog and ISDN modems, at DSL connections, and at cable modems. In addition, we've looked at how to protect your computer system that is connected to the Internet from unauthorized outside users.

Chapter 8

USING THE COMMUNICATIONS TOOLS

Featuring:

- Faxing from Your Computer
- Using Fax Console
- Using HyperTerminal
- Conferencing with NetMeeting
- Setting Up Your .NET Passport
- Instant Messaging with Windows Messenger
- Downloading Files with FTP
- Connecting via Telnet

The terms *Web* and *Internet* are often used interchangeably, and we have done so in this book, but technically they are not the same at all. The World Wide Web is an Internet service that uses the Hypertext Transfer Protocol (HTTP), and as you will see in this chapter and in Chapter 10, there are other Internet protocols used for e-mail and other Internet services. In this chapter, we're going to look at some of those other services as well as some programs you can use to send a fax, access remote computers, make phone calls, and conference over the Internet.

Faxing from Your Computer

To send and receive faxes from your computer, all you need is a fax modem. If you bought your computer within the last couple of years, your modem is probably also a fax modem. To verify that your modem can be used to send and receive faxes, open the Printers And Faxes folder (click the Start button, click Control Panel, click Printers And Other Hardware, and then click Printers And Faxes). If you see a Fax icon, your modem is a fax modem.

If you upgraded from an earlier version of Windows that already included fax, the operating system automatically detected your fax modem, installed the fax service, and installed the associated printer. If you made a new installation of Windows, you may have to install the fax components of Windows separately. Insert your Windows CD into the drive, and click Start, click Control Panel, click Add Or Remove Programs, and then click the Add/Remove Windows Components button. In the Windows Components dialog box, check the option for Fax Services (and any other additional elements you want to add to your system), and click Next. When the wizard has copied all the component files to your computer, click Finish.

Once Windows fax services are installed, you can perform the following tasks:

- Send faxes, including cover pages and attachments, to single or multiple recipients.
- Receive faxes.
- View and annotate faxes.
- Configure fax resources.
- Archive sent and received faxes.

The easiest way to get started quickly is to use the Fax Configuration Wizard, so we'll look at that next.

Configuring Your Fax

The first time you use the fax service, though, you need to do some configuration; here are the steps:

1. **Start the Fax Configuration Wizard.**

   Click the Start button, click All Programs, click Accessories, click Communications, click Fax, and finally click Send A Fax. When the wizard starts, click Next.

2. Enter user information.

Enter the information you want to use on your fax cover page, including your name, address, fax number, e-mail address, and so on, as shown in Figure 8-1. Click Next.

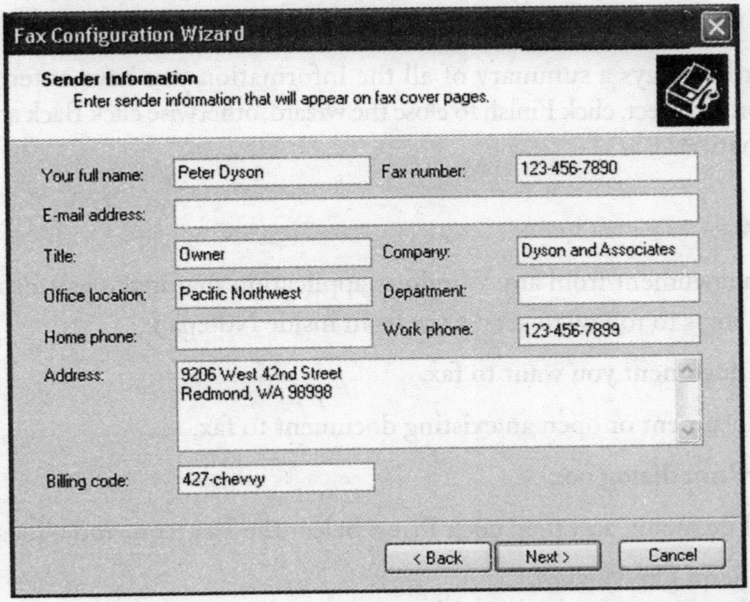

Figure 8-1 Entering user information in the Fax Configuration Wizard.

3. Choose a modem for sending a fax.

Use the up and down arrows to select the modem you want to use. Most people have only one modem installed in their computer, so this is usually an easy choice. Specify how many rings you want the fax modem to wait before answering. Two rings is a pretty typical setting, but it depends on how you use the telephone line and whether the line is shared with other devices or a handset for voice calls.

4. Enter your Transmitting Station Identifier (TSID).

Enter either your fax number or your company name in this box. This information will be sent along with your fax and will be printed at the top of each page as your fax is printed out at the receiving location. Click Next.

5. Enter your Called Station Identifier (CSID).

Enter either your fax number or your company name in this box. This information will be sent to the sending fax machine. Click Next.

6. **Choose a routing option.**

   When you receive a fax, you can send it to a printer or you can store a copy of the fax in a folder to work on later. Click Next.

7. **Close the wizard.**

   The wizard displays a summary of all the information you have entered. If the information is correct, click Finish to close the wizard, otherwise click Back and correct the information.

Sending a Fax

You can fax a document from any Windows application that includes a Print menu. Here are the steps to follow to send a fax from inside Notepad:

1. **Open the document you want to fax.**

   Create a document or open an existing document to fax.

2. **Open the Print dialog box.**

   Click the File menu, and then click Print. Select the Fax icon, and choose Print.

3. **Open the Send Fax Wizard.**

   The Send Fax Wizard opens; click Next.

4. **Enter the recipient and dialing information.**

   Fill in the To, Fax Number, and dialing information, as shown in Figure 8-2, and click Next. If you are sending the same fax to several recipients, enter information for each of the recipients and then click Add. You can also select a recipient from the list and click Remove to remove them from this list. Click Next.

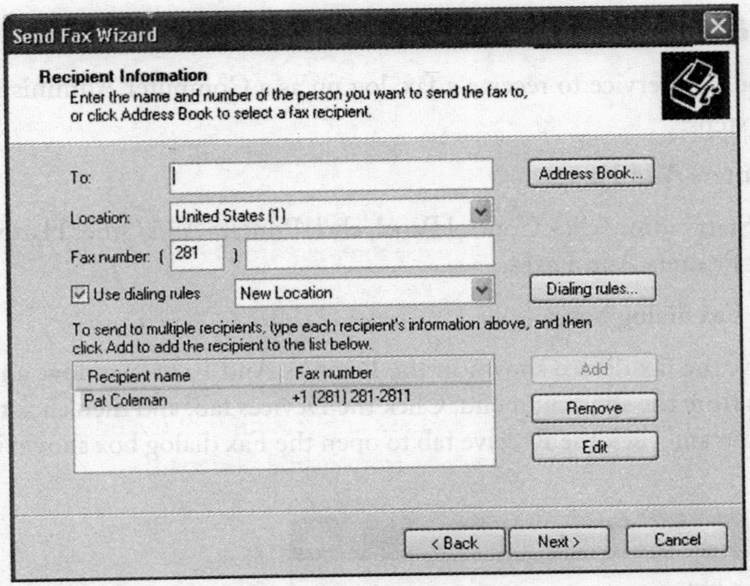

Figure 8-2 Entering recipient and dialing information.

5. **Enter information for your cover page.**

   In the Adding A Cover Page screen of the wizard, specify whether you want to include a cover page and, if so, what it should contain. Use the Cover Page Template drop-down list box to select a type of cover page. Add text for the subject line. When you're finished, click Next.

6. **Specify when to send the fax.**

   Click an option button, and click Next. At the summary screen, click Finish.

7. **Close the wizard.**

   The wizard displays a summary of all the information you have entered. If the information is correct, click Finish to close the wizard; otherwise, click Back and correct the information. You can also click Preview to see an onscreen image of your fax. This is a very convenient way to check that you will be sending exactly what you thought you would be sending.

You can track the progress of the fax using the Fax Monitor dialog box, which appears on your screen as the fax is dispatched.

Receiving a Fax

To set up your fax service to receive a fax, log on as a Computer Administrator and follow these steps:

1. **Open Printers And Faxes.**

   Click the Start button, click Control Panel, click Printers And Other Hardware, and then click Printers And Faxes.

2. **Open the Fax dialog box.**

   Right-click the fax device shown in the Printers And Faxes window, and choose Properties from the shortcut menu. Click the Devices tab, and then click the Properties button and click the Receive tab to open the Fax dialog box shown in Figure 8-3.

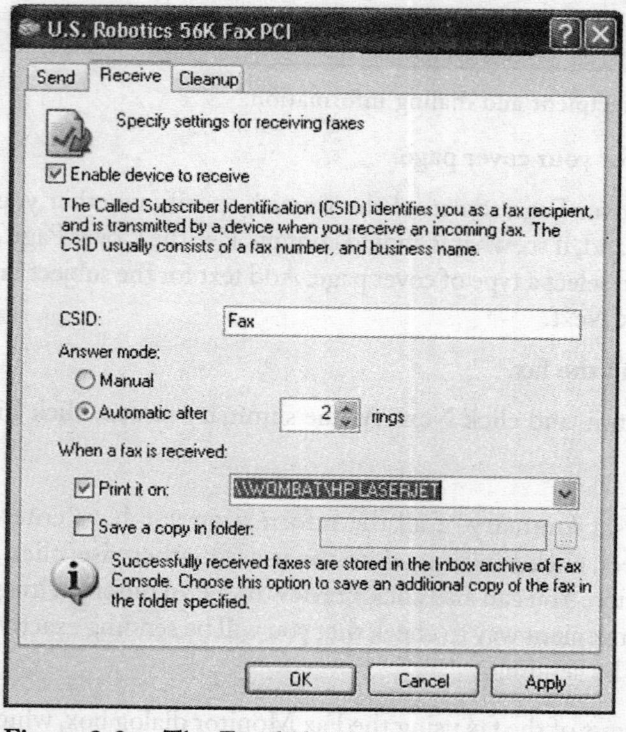

Figure 8-3 The Fax dialog box open at the Receive tab.

3. **Allow the fax to receive.**

   Click the Enable Device To Receive check box to allow the fax to accept incoming faxes. Choose either the manual or the automatic answer mode, choose the number of rings to wait before the modem answers (usually two rings), and specify where the incoming fax should be printed after it has been received. Click Apply, and then click OK.

When a fax arrives, you may or may not hear the initial two rings, it depends on your modem's settings, including the modem volume you have specified.

Local or Remote Fax

A fax modem attached to your computer is known as a *local fax* (called a local fax resource in Help And Support Center); a fax machine available on a network is called a *remote fax* (again, in Help And Support Center this is called a remote fax resource). You can control all the options, properties, and settings for your local fax, but a Computer Administrator will specify the configuration details for a fax attached to the network. The security settings established by the Computer Administrator will affect how (and perhaps when) you can use a remote fax, including the types of fax you can send and how you can look at incoming and outgoing faxes.

Using Fax Console

The Fax Console is a central management tool you can use to send and receive faxes, look at fax activity, and open fax archives. Click the Start button, click All Programs, click Communications, click Fax, and then click Fax Console. You will see a window similar to the one shown in Figure 8-4.

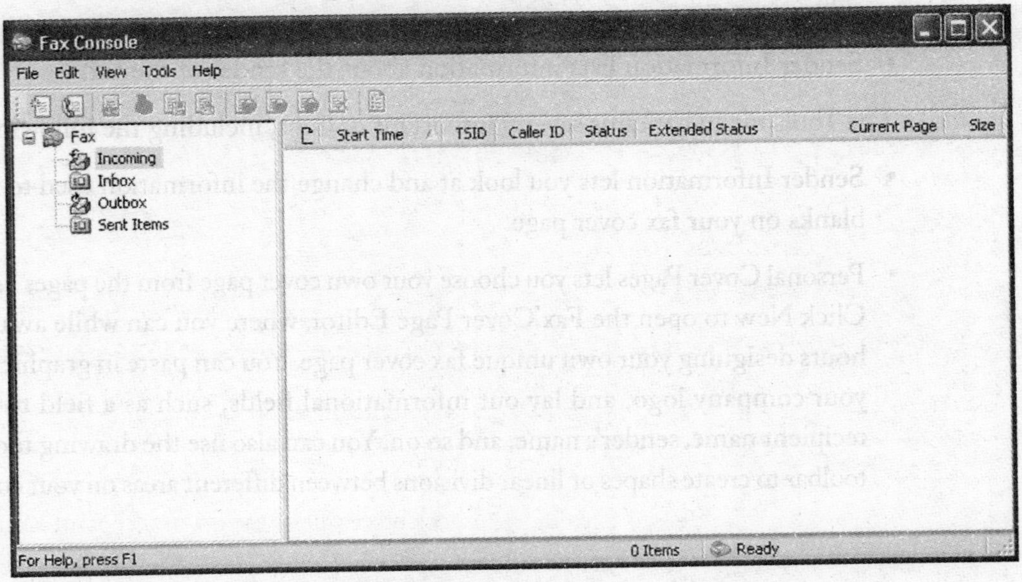

Figure 8-4 The Fax Console window.

In the tree pane on the left you will see a group of folders:

- Incoming holds faxes that are in the process of arriving. Once the fax is complete, it is automatically moved to the Inbox.
- Inbox holds all complete incoming faxes. If you use a local fax, you will be able to see all the faxes in this folder. If you use a remote fax, you will see only the faxes for which you have the appropriate permissions.
- Outbox holds outgoing faxes until it is time to send them, as well as faxes in the process of being sent. Once the fax has been successfully sent, it is moved automatically to the Sent Items folder.
- Sent Items holds the faxes you have sent.

When you click a folder in the left pane, you will see a list of the faxes it contains displayed in the right pane. Each outgoing fax, for example, is listed with its submission time, recipient name, recipient fax number, and an icon indicating whether the fax is paused, has been resumed, deleted, or has been restarted. Right-click a fax, and choose Properties from the shortcut menu. You'll see the following three tabs:

- General lists the fax name, subject, the size and the number of pages, as well as recipient information.
- Details lists job and broadcast ID numbers, as well as the billing code and original submission time.
- Sender Information lists information about the sender of the fax.

The Tools menu contains several important options, including the following:

- Sender Information lets you look at and change the information used to fill in the blanks on your fax cover page.
- Personal Cover Pages lets you choose your own cover page from the pages listed here. Click New to open the Fax Cover Page Editor, where you can while away endless hours designing your own unique fax cover page. You can paste in graphics, such as your company logo, and lay out informational fields, such as a field to hold the recipient name, sender's name, and so on. You can also use the drawing tools on the toolbar to create shapes or linear divisions between different areas on your cover page.

- Fax Printer Status displays a list of the fax printers, along with their current status.
- Configure Fax starts the Fax Configuration Wizard we looked at earlier in this chapter.
- Fax Printer Configuration opens the Fax Properties dialog box, which you can use to look at or change fax configuration settings.
- Fax Monitor lets you look at current fax activity information. If you are not in the process of sending or receiving a fax, this option will be grayed out and unavailable.

Using HyperTerminal

HyperTerminal is terminal emulation software, and in English that means it is a program that mimics the attributes of a piece of hardware, in this case a computer terminal, in software. HyperTerminal is text-based and is useful for connecting to public access servers, especially those running operating systems other than Windows, and for running text-based applications. In university settings, students and faculty often have Windows computers, and the main computer system runs Unix. In this case, students and faculty can use HyperTerminal to connect to the main Unix system and run Unix applications. Typically, HyperTerminal is also used to connect to a bulletin board or the catalog at a local library.

Establishing a HyperTerminal Connection

Before you can use HyperTerminal, you need to configure a connection. Obtain the phone number for the computer you'll connect to, and then follow these steps to configure the connection and to connect:

1. Start HyperTerminal.

Click the Start button, click All Programs, click Accessories, click Communications, and then click HyperTerminal to open the Connection Description dialog box, shown in Figure 8-5, in the foreground and the HyperTerminal window in the background.

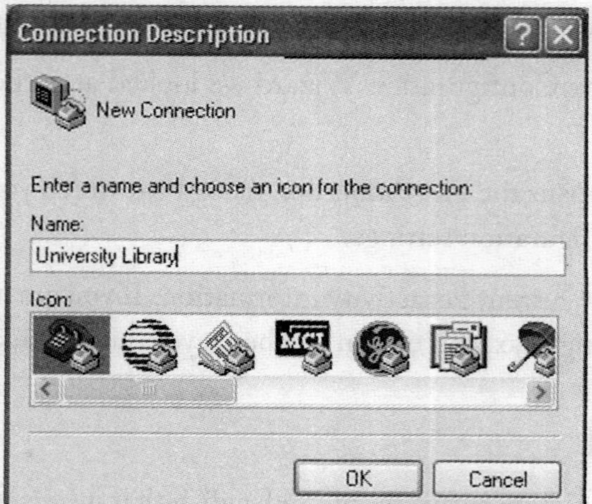

Figure 8-5 The Connection Description dialog box.

2. **Choose a name and an icon for your connection.**

   In the Name box, enter a name, select an icon, and click OK to open the Connect To dialog box, as shown in Figure 8-6.

Figure 8-6 The Connect To dialog box.

3. **Open the Connect dialog box, which is shown in Figure 8-7.**

   Verify that the country, area code, and modem are correct, enter the phone number, and click OK.

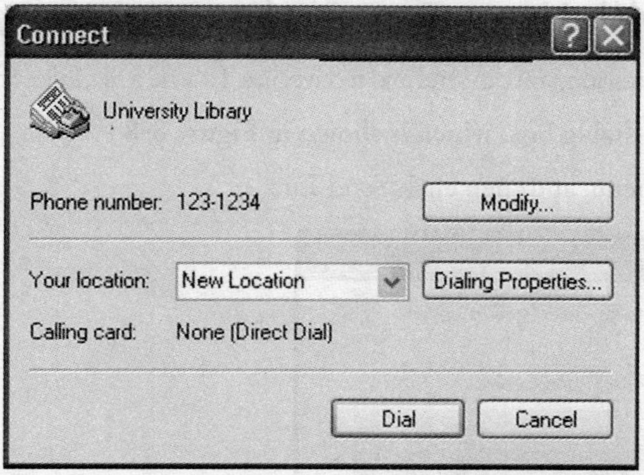

Figure 8-7 The Connect dialog box.

4. Get connected.

Verify that the phone number is correct. If it is not, click the Modify button to open the Properties dialog box for this connection, and change the phone number. To look at or change any of the options associated with your modem setup, click the Dialing Properties button to open the Phone And Modem Options dialog box. When everything is correct, click Dial.

You'll now be connected to the remote computer system that you dialed. What you see next depends on the system to which you are connecting. You might be asked for a terminal type, to enter a password, or to choose from a menu. When you complete this HyperTerminal session, log off from the remote computer according to the instructions provided you by that system. When you close the HyperTerminal window, you'll be asked if you want to save the session. Click Yes, and the next time you want to make that connection, you can use a submenu item for it that is added to the HyperTerminal menu item. Clicking the menu item for your connection opens the Connect dialog box, and you simply click Dial to connect.

TIP *To save a HyperTerminal session as a text file, click the Transfer menu and then click Capture Text to open the Capture Text dialog box. Enter a name for the file, and click Start.*

Transferring Files with HyperTerminal

During a HyperTerminal session, you can send and receive files. To send a file, follow these steps:

1. **Open the Send File dialog box, which is shown in Figure 8-8.**

   Click the Transfer menu, and then click Send File.

Figure 8-8 The Send File dialog box.

2. **Specify the filename and protocol.**

   In the Filename box, enter a filename or browse to locate it. In the Protocol box, accept the protocol that HyperTerminal suggests, or choose another protocol from the drop-down list. If you don't know the protocol that the other computer requires, use the protocol that HyperTerminal suggests—Zmodem With Crash Recovery—which is a commonly used and fast protocol. Click Send to start the file transfer.

To receive a file during a HyperTerminal session, click the Transfer menu and then click Receive File to open the Receive File dialog box. Enter the name of the folder into which to place the file, verify the protocol, and click Receive.

Using HyperTerminal as a Telnet Client

We will be looking at the Windows Telnet client in some detail toward the end of this chapter, but you can also use HyperTerminal to do the same thing, that is, to act as a Telnet client to a remote Telnet server.

Here's how. Start HyperTerminal, enter an appropriately descriptive name in the New Connections dialog box, and click OK. When the Connect To dialog box opens, choose TCP/IP (Winsock) from the Connect Using drop-down list as Figure 8-9 shows, and then enter either the name of the server you want to connect to or the Internet Protocol (IP) address of the server in the Host Address box. Telnet connects by default on port 23. Click OK. When the remote computer answers, you can enter your login ID and start your Telnet session.

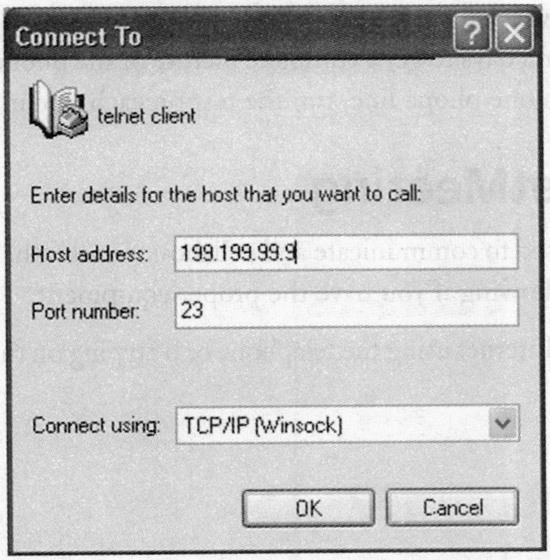

Figure 8-9 The Connect To dialog box in Telnet mode.

Checking the Speed of Your Internet Connection

You can also use HyperTerminal to check the actual speed of your Internet connection when using a modem. This particular line test is provided by modem-maker US Robotics; other tests are available, and they all do pretty much the same thing. Here are the steps:

1. **Dial the number.**

   Open a HyperTerminal window, click Dial, enter *1-847-330-2780*, and click OK.

2. **Log on.**

   When you connect to the Line Test system, you will be asked if your system supports graphics; press Enter. Then you will be prompted for your first name. Type *line*, and press Enter. When prompted for your last name, type *test* and press Enter.

3. **Check the statistics.**

   When a prompt appears on your screen, press Enter to view the first screen of line statistics. Press Enter again to see a second screen of statistics.

4. **Disconnect.**

   Type the letter *g*, and press Enter to disconnect.

Because phone line conditions vary due to all sorts of external factors, you should run this test several times over several days to get a complete picture of the phone lines in your area. If you use more than one phone line, run the test on each line in turn.

Conferencing with NetMeeting

NetMeeting is an application used to communicate and collaborate with other people, and you can use it to do the following if you have the proper equipment:

- Chat with someone over the Internet using the telephone or by typing on the screen.
- Hold an audio conference.
- Hold a video conference.
- Share applications.
- Collaborate on documents.
- Transfer files.
- Draw on the whiteboard.

NOTE *NetMeeting allows you to hold audio- and videoconferences, and in the sections that follow, to keep it simple, we'll just simply refer to conferences.*

To open NetMeeting, click the Start button, click All Programs, click Accessories, click Communications, and then click NetMeeting. A wizard takes you through the steps of filling in your name, e-mail address, specifying the Internet Locator Service (ILS) directory that will list you, specifying your connection speed, adjusting microphone and speaker volume levels, and so on.

An ILS directory is a service on the Internet with which you register. Once you have registered, you can communicate with any other registered users. You don't have to use an ILS directory, and if you are working on a local area network you can connect directly. To connect with someone over the Internet, all you need to know is their IP address.

When the wizard's work is done, the main NetMeeting window opens, as shown in Figure 8-10. None of the buttons in this window have labels but you can place the mouse cursor over a button to display a ScreenTip that describes what the button does.

Figure 8-10 The main NetMeeting window.

Placing a Call

To use NetMeeting to make a call, both the sender and the receiver need microphones, sound cards, and speakers. To place a call, follow these steps:

1. Open the Place A Call dialog box, which is shown in Figure 8-11.

In the NetMeeting main window, click the Place Call button. You can also open the Call menu and choose New Call.

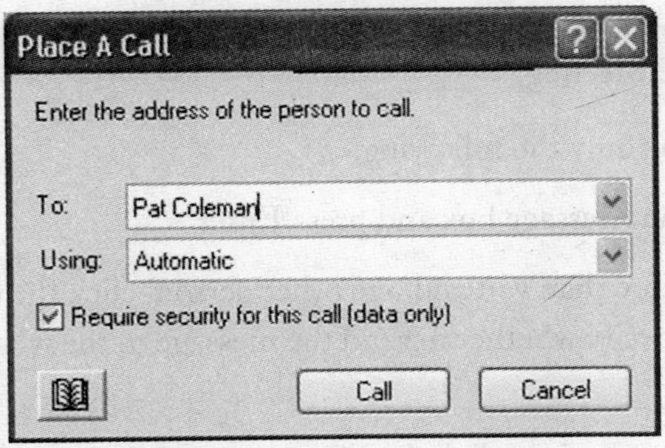

Figure 8-11 The Place A Call dialog box.

2. **Enter an address.**

   In the To box, enter a name, an e-mail address, a computer name, a computer IP address, or a telephone number.

3. **Place the call.**

   Click Call.

Chatting on the Screen

Once you are connected to another computer, you can also use the other NetMeeting applications, such as Chat where you type messages to other people just like an Internet chat room (more on Internet chat rooms in a moment). Figure 8-12 shows the Chat window. To open it, click the Chat button in the main NetMeeting window.

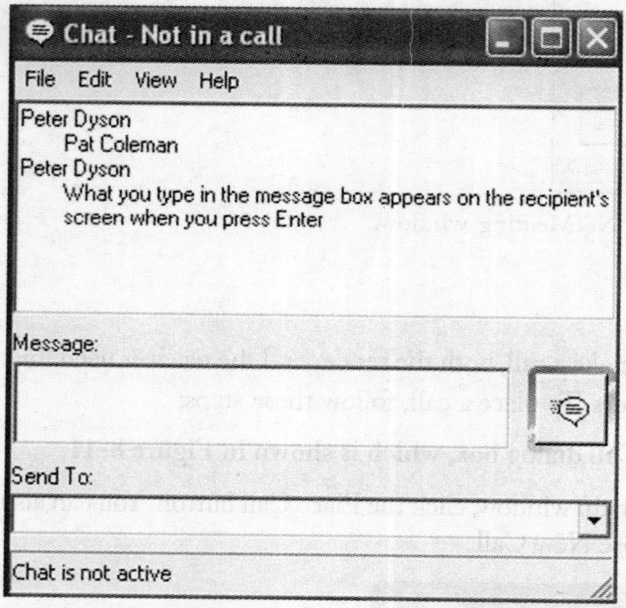

Figure 8-12 Using Chat in NetMeeting.

To use Chat, you need to know only the following:

- To communicate, type in the Message box and press Enter.
- If a Chat session involves more than you and one other person, click the down arrow in the Send To box to specify whether to send the message to the whole group or only one person.
- To save the contents of a Chat session, click the File menu and then click Save As.
- To end a Chat session, click Close.

Sharing Applications

One of the best aspects of NetMeeting is the way it lets you share an application with other people in a conference. Other people taking part in the conference can use your applications, they can edit your newest Word document or enter their data into your Excel spreadsheet, even though they don't have these applications on their own computer. Only the person actually opening the file is required to have a copy of the application installed on their computer. Here are the steps to follow:

1. Open the application.

Start the program you want other people in the conference to be able to see or use. Click the Sharing button (the one at the bottom left) on the main NetMeeting window. The Sharing dialog box opens as shown in Figure 8-13.

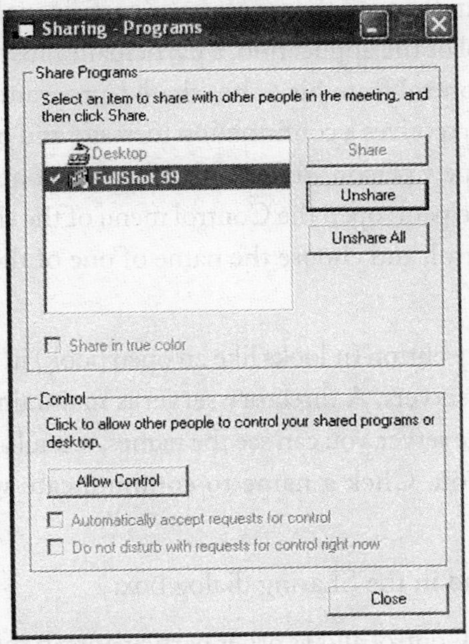

Figure 8-13 The NetMeeting Sharing dialog box.

2. Share the application.

Select the program you want to share from the list, and click the Share button. You will see the Windows Desktop listed in the Sharing dialog box. This is because NetMeeting treats your desktop as just another application you can share if you wish. If you do share the desktop, all of the participants in your conference will be able to watch everything you do. And that can be a great teaching aid if you have to demonstrate applications as a part of your job.

NOTE *If you do decide to share your desktop and you click Allow Control, be aware that other participants in the conference can now copy, move, and delete files; create new folders; and so on. In fact, they can do anything on your computer that you can do, no matter where they are located physically.*

3. **Allow control.**

   Normally, the other people in the conference will just be able to look at the application you are running, but if you want to allow other people to actually use the application, open menus and enter data, and so on, click the Allow Control button. A new window opens on the other participants' computers, showing the same view of the application that you see on your own computer.

Only one person can be in control of a shared document at a time, and if the mouse pointer becomes a box with initials by it, then another conference participant has taken control of the program. To take control of the application, a participant must open the Control menu and choose Request Control from his or her shared-program window. The person who shared the application receives a confirmation message and must click Accept before control is passed to the new person. You can also forward control of the application to another conference participant; open the Control menu of the shared application window, click Forward Control, and choose the name of one of the conference participants from the list.

Click the Find Someone In A Directory button (it looks like an open book) in the main NetMeeting window to use directory servers. A directory server is maintained by an organization, and when you log on to the server, you can see the names, e-mail addresses, and so on of others who are logged on. Click a name to communicate with that person.

Two other important options are found in the Sharing dialog box:

- Automatically Accept Requests For Control allows other participants in the conference to take control of the application using the Control menu in the shared-program window.
- Do Not Disturb With Requests For Control Right Now allows you to decline attempts by other conference participants to take control of the application.

NOTE *If the conference results in the creation of a new application data file, say a new spreadsheet file, only the person who originally shared the program can distribute the file.*

Sharing an application like this can be tremendously useful when several people scattered over a wide geographical area want to collaborate on a project, but NetMeeting does impose a significant overhead. If you are using a dial-up modem over a normal telephone line, you will notice that things run slower than usual on your computer, and sometimes the cursor seems jerky and hard to control. This is nothing to be concerned about, and things will return to normal as soon as you close the conference and end NetMeeting.

Tips for a Successful Conference

According to a recent survey performed by Gartner, by the year 2004 up to 80 percent of workers who have permanently assigned workstations will be away from their desks for up to 50 percent of their day. So audio- and videoconferencing meetings will become more and more common. Here are some tips you can use to make sure you get the most out of these virtual meetings:

- Identify yourself, the other conference participants, and the purpose of the meeting as soon as the conference starts.
- E-mail an agenda to the participants well before the conference starts.
- Summarize the decisions taken during the meeting at the end or in a follow-up e-mail.
- Give conference participants aural clues if you do not have a video link; if they can't see you, they can't see your hand gestures and they can't pick up on other nonverbal clues.
- Keep to the point.
- Don't play the radio in the background; your microphone may pick up more than your voice, confusing other conference participants.
- Don't multitask. Concentrate on the conference, and ignore the other 100 vital assignments screaming at you from your desk.
- Keep it short.

And don't forget; rules are meant to be broken.

Using the Whiteboard

Click the Whiteboard button in the main NetMeeting window to open the NetMeeting whiteboard shown in Figure 8-14, which looks and works a lot like the Windows Paint application. You can use the NetMeeting whiteboard during a conference just as you would use the whiteboard hanging on the real conference room wall. All participants can add notes or drawings using the toolbars or selections from the Tools menu.

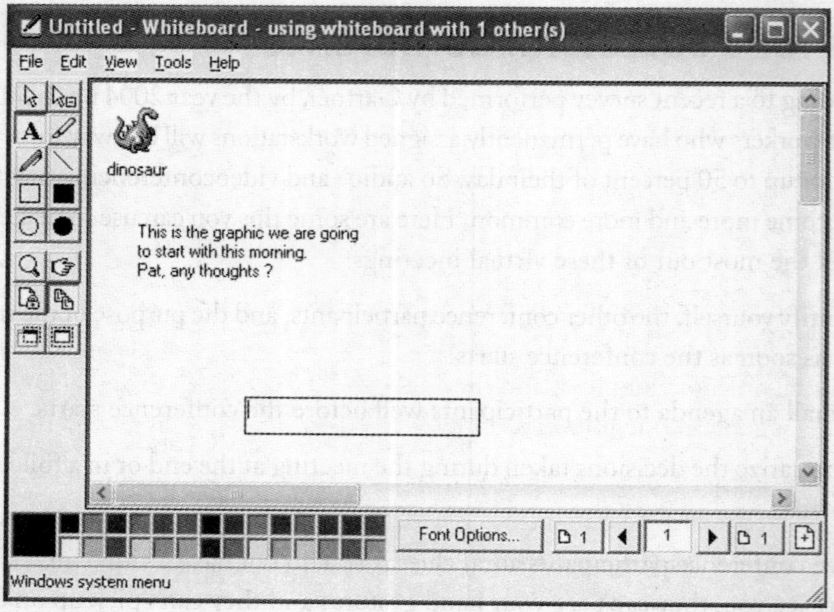

Figure 8-14 The NetMeeting whiteboard window.

To copy a graphic or a part of another application to the whiteboard, click the Tools menu and click Select Area. Your mouse cursor changes to a set of crosshairs; drag it to the area you want to capture. You will have to do some juggling here to get the right window in the right place on your desktop so you can see all of the area you want to copy and still have access to the NetMeeting Tools menu. When you release the mouse button, the area you selected appears on the whiteboard. If you want to copy a whole window to the whiteboard, use Select Window from the Tools menu.

If the whiteboard gets very cluttered during a conference, check with the other conference participants before you clear it or close it. When you open the Edit menu and select Clear Page, you will see a dialog box asking if you are sure you want to clear the page; other users will not see this dialog box, and if you click Yes, their own copies of the whiteboard will simply go blank.

Transferring Files

If you want to send a file to one or more of the conference participants, click the Transfer Files button (at the bottom right of the main NetMeeting window), or click the Tools menu and click File Transfer. When the File Transfer dialog box opens, choose the conference participant or participants you want to send the file to; click the File menu and click Add Files to select the file to send. And finally, click the Send All button to dispatch the file, or right-click the file and choose Send A File from the shortcut menu.

When another conference participant sends you a file, click Accept in the File Transfer dialog box that opens automatically as the file arrives. Once the file transfer is complete, the Accept button changes to the Close button. Click Close to close the dialog box. To reject the file, click the Delete button.

Fine-Tuning Audio and Video in NetMeeting

As we said a few paragraphs back, if you are using a dial-up modem over a normal telephone line to hold a NetMeeting conference, you will notice that things run slower than usual on your computer, and the video may seem jerky. On a local area network, a DSL- or cable-modem link, you won't have these problems.

If your computer has a microphone and speakers, audio is automatically turned on during a NetMeeting conference and everyone can hear you speak. However, not everyone may be able to hear you while someone else is speaking. Some sound cards provide only half-duplex audio capabilities (only one person can speak at a time), while others offer full-duplex capabilities (two people can speak at the same time, just like in a normal meeting).

To fine-tune your audio settings, click the Tools menu, click Audio Tuning Wizard, and then follow the instructions on the screen; you can't use this wizard during a conference, and you will have to close any other applications you have running that play or record sound. The wizard adjusts volume and microphone sounds levels to their optimum, and it is a good idea to run the wizard before your first NetMeeting conference, just so you know what to expect.

You can send video to just one other person in the NetMeeting conference, and over a normal dial-up connection, the image you see will be small, grainy, and jerky; more like a set of related still images than the latest installment of your favorite television show. Click the Start Video button (on the left in the middle of the NetMeeting window) to begin your video transmission; click Stop Video when you end the conference.

To take more control of your NetMeeting settings, click the Tools menu and click Options. The Options dialog box contains four tabs: General, Security, Audio, and Video. Let's take a closer look.

General Tab

The General tab shown in Figure 8-15 lists your identification information, specifies whether or not you will use a directory, and if so, which one, and other NetMeeting configuration settings. Click the Bandwidth Settings button to open the Network Bandwidth dialog box, where you can specify the type of connection you will be using. In order of increasing speed, you can choose 14400 bps Modem, 28800 bps or Faster Modem, Cable, xDSL or ISDN, or Local Area Network.

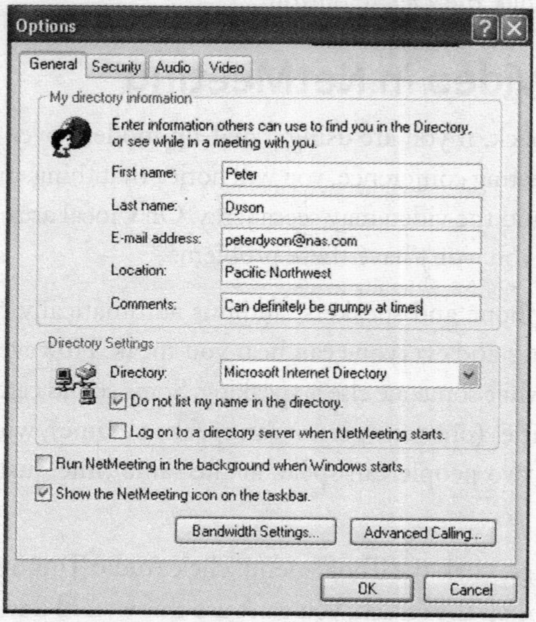

Figure 8-15 The Options dialog box open at the General tab.

Security Tab

The Security tab shown in Figure 8-16 lets you specify that incoming or outgoing calls are secure, and whether to use a digital certificate for encryption or encryption and authentication.

In a NetMeeting conference, all calls must be of the same type, either secure or not secure; calls are nonsecure by default. In a secure call, any information you exchange is encrypted, so only the intended recipients can read it, but you are limited to using chat, the whiteboard, and sharing applications; you can't use audio or video as these transmissions are not encrypted.

A digital certificate is a mechanism used to identify a specific person or organization and is issued only by a trusted entity known as a Certificate Authority. Digital certificates are used to prove that the person with whom you are in communication actually is the person you think it is. NetMeeting has one privacy certificate by default when you start the program, but you can add others as required.

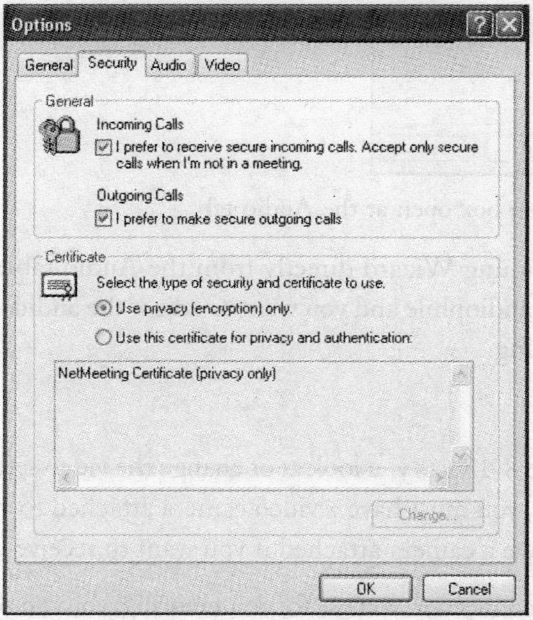

Figure 8-16 The Options dialog box open at the Security tab.

Audio Tab

The Audio tab shown in Figure 8-17 allows you to specify full-duplex audio (if your sound card supports only half-duplex audio, this option will not be available), as well as auto-gain microphone volume adjustment (which again, is not available on all sound cards). The Automatically Adjust Microphone Volume While In A Call setting can achieve similar results if your sound card does not have auto-gain volume adjustment.

NOTE *If your computer doesn't have a sound card, you won't see an Audio tab in the Options dialog box.*

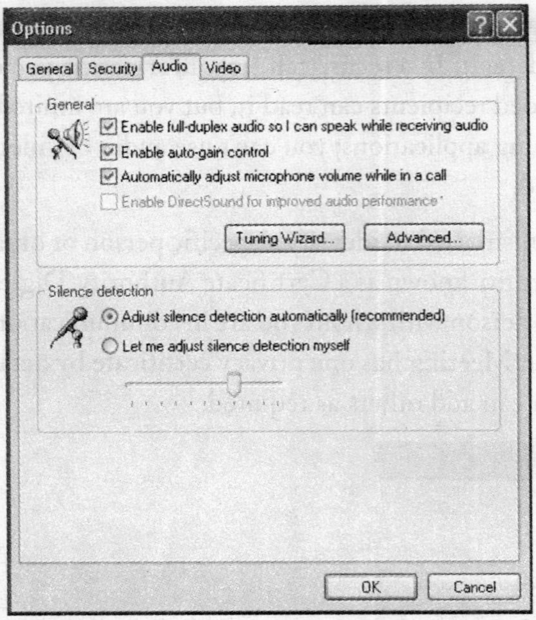

Figure 8-17 The Options dialog box open at the Audio tab.

You can also run the Audio Tuning Wizard directly from the Audio tab. Click the Advanced button if you are an audiophile and you want to adjust the audio-compression settings used in NetMeeting.

Video Tab

The Video tab shown in Figure 8-18 lets you look at or change the video settings used in NetMeeting. To send video, you must have a video camera attached to your computer, but you don't have to have a camera attached if you want to receive video.

Depending on the speed of the connection you use for conferencing, you can adjust both the size of the image (choose Small, Medium, or Large) and also the video quality by choosing between Faster Video and Better Quality. So by tweaking these settings, you can arrive at the best possible video image for your own particular set of circumstances.

Figure 8-18 The Options dialog box open at the Video tab.

Setting Up Your .NET Passport

A Microsoft .NET Passport, just as its name implies, gets you in. A Passport contains your personal information and a password, and you use it to gain access to Passport-enabled services and Web sites. Instead of having a password and user name for every single secure Web site you visit, you enter your information into Passport, and when you arrive at a Web site, you just click the green Sign In link. Your Passport profile information is sent to the site automatically, so there is no more retyping the same old information over and over each time you access a new site.

NOTE *You can also get a Passport when you sign up for the MSN Messenger service.*

Using the .NET Passport Wizard on a Standalone Computer

The steps you use to set up your Passport on a computer, attached to a network are slightly different from the steps you use on a standalone computer, so we'll look at how to use the Passport Wizard on a single computer first. Here are the steps:

1. **Open User Accounts in Control Panel.**

   Click the Start button, click Control Panel, and open User Accounts.

2. **Select an account.**

   On the Pick A Task page, select your account.

3. **Start the Passport Wizard.**

   On the What Do You Want To Change About Your Account page, click Set Up My Account To Use A .NET Passport. When the .NET Passport Wizard starts, you can review the Passport privacy statement if you wish; click Next when you are ready to move on to the next step.

4. **Select an e-mail account.**

   Passports are based on e-mail accounts, and if you already have an account you can use it with your Passport; otherwise, you can sign up for a free Hotmail account. Make sure your modem is connected to your phone line if you select this option, as you will be taken to the Hotmail registration site to open an account. Click Next, or go to the Hotmail site, create an e-mail account, return to this page, click Yes, Use An Existing E-Mail Account, and then click Next.

5. **Enter your information.**

   Enter your e-mail address, which Passport will use as your sign-in name, and click Next. Enter and then confirm a password of your choice, which must be at least eight characters (letters or numbers, but no spaces). Complete the rest of the account information, including your location and ZIP code. Click Finish to close the wizard and create your .NET Passport.

Using the .NET Passport Wizard on a Network

Starting the Passport Wizard on a computer attached to a network or a domain is just a little different. Make sure you are logged on as a Computer Administrator, click the Start button, click Control Panel, and then click User Accounts. Click the Advanced tab, and in the Passwords And .NET Passports section, click .NET Passport Wizard. Follow the steps outlined in the section above to enter your information and complete the wizard.

Using Your .NET Passport

Once you have created your Passport, you will receive an e-mail welcoming you to Passport Member Services. This e-mail also lists the benefits of using your Passport. Next time you arrive at a Passport-enabled Web site, just click the green Passport Sign-In icon, enter your Passport user name and password, and all of your information is made available to the Web site. And your information is sent in encrypted form so it is secure from prying eyes. Once you have signed in at one Passport Web site, you can sign in to the next participating site with a single click; no need to retype your information. When it is time to leave, click the purple Sign-Out icon to sign out from all the Web sites you accessed using your Passport. You can find out more about Passport at *www.passport.com.*

Instant Messaging with Windows Messenger

According to a recent survey by Forrester Research, instant messaging is among the hottest Internet applications, even rivaling e-mail for speed and convenience. When you send an e-mail to someone, the message is sent to the appropriate mail server, where it sits and sits and sits, until the person it is addressed to logs on to the server and accesses their mail. With instant messaging, you know immediately whether someone is logged on, so when you click the Send button, the message goes straight to their screen.

Instant messaging is much more direct than a phone call because you can tell straight away if someone is available. Also, instant messaging is fast enough that you can keep a proper conversation going, and that is almost impossible with e-mail.

NOTE *Instant messages are temporary; unless you deliberately save them, when you close the window, they are gone.*

Windows Messenger lets you do several things that you can't do with e-mail:

- Send instant messages.
- Receive instant messages.
- See if your friends or business associates are online.
- Specify who can contact you.

NOTE *Windows Messenger is also compatible with Outlook Express and NetMeeting.*

With the Windows Messenger contact list you can create your own online world and add anyone you like to that world; and your friends and associates can add you to their world too, as long as you agree to be added. The first step is to get a .NET Passport, which we covered in the last section. Once you have your Passport, you are ready to start.

NOTE *To participate in the Microsoft instant messaging community, everyone must have a Passport.*

RUReD4this?

To do instant messaging properly, you have to learn the lingo. Some of the wireless devices that can receive instant messages are limited in the number of characters that they can display. Some can display up to 160 characters (about two dozen words), while others can display more. This has led to the evolution of a new dialect that consists of abbreviated words and numbers to get the message across. For example, "want to talk" becomes "wan2tlk" and "see you later" turns into "cul8r." Capital letters can signify the beginning of a new word, and spaces are just ignored. A capital letter in the middle of a word indicates a double letter (as in "CaTl" for "cattle"), and a dollar sign indicates double S (as in "SC$" for "Success"). Whether or not this dialect is suitable for business purposes is something you will have to decide for yourself. But it sure is fun.

Using Instant Messaging

Once you have signed up for the Passport service, the first thing to take care of is to go online and set up your contact list or buddy list. When you click the Start button and open Windows Messenger, you will see a window similar to the one shown in Figure 8-19. If you are not connected to the Internet, you will see a Click Here To Sign In link in the center of the window. Click the link, enter your .NET Passport e-mail address and password, and you will connect to the instant messaging service. If you are already connected to the Internet, these steps process automatically.

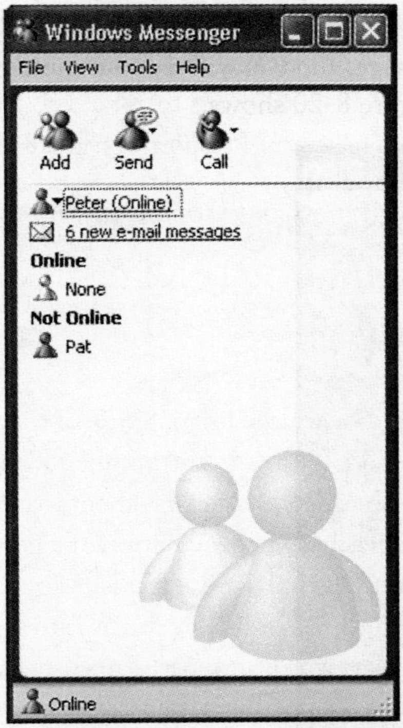

Figure 8-19 The Windows Messenger window.

To start adding people to your contact list, click the Add button to find them by e-mail address or sign-in name, or to search for a contact. Others can add you to their contact list by the same process, as long as you agree to be added. Once added, you will see their names and icons down the left side of the window whenever they are online.

NOTE *Once you have signed up for the service, you can open a Windows Messenger window by clicking the Messenger icon on the Internet Explorer toolbar.*

Sending a Message

To send an instant message to a person in your contact list, follow these steps:

1. Choose a person.

Double-click the name of the person to whom you want to send a message, and the instant messaging window opens.

2. Type your message.

Type your message in the lower part of the window. Your message can be up to 400 characters long if you are sending a message to another computer, or about 160 characters if you are sending a message to a mobile device, such as a cell phone.

3. **Send your message.**

   Click the Send button to send your message, and you will see your message appear in the top portion of the window as Figure 8-20 shows.

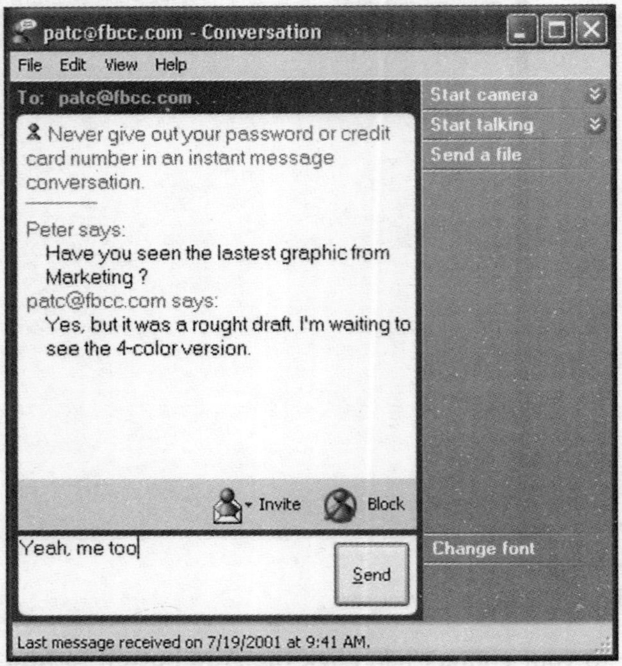

Figure 8-20 The instant messaging window.

In the instant-messaging window status bar, you will be able to see when the other person is typing, as well as the date and time of the last message you received.

You start an instant message conversation with only one person, but once you have made contact with that person and the instant messaging window is open, you can add other people to your conversation. In the instant messaging window, click the Invite button, click To Join This Conversation, and then click the name of the person you want to add. A total of five people can participate in a conversation.

To send a message to a person who is not on your contact list, type your message and click the Send button, then click Other and enter their Passport address. To participate in an instant message conversation, everyone must have Windows Messenger installed on their computer.

Sending a Message to a Mobile Device

If you want to send a message to a wireless device, such as a Web-enabled cell phone, a Palm device, a Windows CE device, or a pager, click the Page button, and then click the name of the person you want to receive the message. For the Callback Number, click the phone number where you can be reached. Type in your message, and click the Send button.

Your message, your e-mail address, and the phone number where you can be reached are all sent to your contact's mobile device. Remember that if their cell phone or pager is turned off, they may not see your message until later when they turn their mobile device on again.

Setting Your Status

You can set the status others see associated with your name in their MSN Messenger Service window to one of the following:

- Online
- Busy
- Be Right Back
- Away
- On The Phone
- Out To Lunch
- Appear Offline

Click the File menu, click My Status, and then select one of the options from the list shown above. Your status, as it appears on other peoples' computers, will be changed to reflect your choice.

Allowing and Blocking Contacts

You can select which of your contacts can see your online status and which of them can send you an instant message using the Privacy tab of the Options dialog box. Click the Tools menu and click Options to open the Options dialog box shown in Figure 8-21.

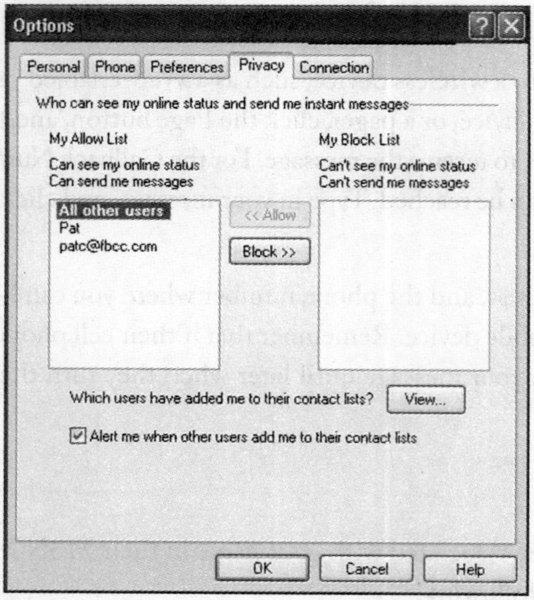

Figure 8-21 The Options dialog box open at the Privacy tab.

By default, everyone on your contact list can see your status and can send you instant messages. People on your Allow list appear in the left pane of the Privacy tab, and people on your Block list appear in the right pane. You can use the Allow and Block buttons to move contacts from one pane to the other.

Click the View button to see a list of your contacts who have added you to their own contact lists. Click the check box at the bottom of the Privacy tab to alert you when others add you to their own lists; when they do so, you can accept or reject their request.

Sending a File

You can also attach a file to an instant message. Start by choosing the person to whom you want to send the file using one of the following methods:

- In the instant messaging window, click the File menu and click Send A File.
- In the main window, click the File menu, click Send A File To, and then click your contact's name.
- In the main window, right-click your online contact's name, and choose Send A File from the shortcut menu.

When the Send A File dialog box opens, select the file you want to send in the usual way, and then click Open. While the file is being transferred, you may click Cancel to stop the transfer. Once the transfer is complete, you will be notified that it has been received successfully by the recipient.

NOTE *If you are on a corporate network behind a firewall, you may not be able to attach a file to an instant message. If this is the case, use Outlook Express to send the file instead.*

If the person to whom you want to send the file is not on your contact list, click the File menu, click Send A File To, click Other, and then enter their Passport address.

When you receive a file from someone else, a dialog box opens displaying the sender's name and the name and size of the file; you can choose to accept or reject the file. When you click the Accept button, the file is stored in the folder specified on the Preferences tab of the Options dialog box. To open the Options dialog box, click the Tools menu and click Options.

Using Audio and Video

Click Start Camera or Start Talking in the instant messaging window to run the Audio And Video Tuning Wizard; you can also start the wizard from the Tools menu. This wizard will help you to ensure your microphone, speakers, and video camera are all working properly. We stand by the caveat we mentioned in the NetMeeting section earlier in this chapter; if you are using a dial-up connection, the video will be grainy and jerky and the sound quality will probably be poor. If you can use a DSL or cable modem connection, the overall quality will be much better. Follow the instructions on the screen to complete the wizard.

Sharing Applications and the Whiteboard

You can also use Windows Messenger to share applications between two or more users, and you can also open and use a whiteboard. Click the Invite button at the bottom of the instant messaging window and select one of the following:

- To Start Application Sharing.
- To Start Remote Assistance.
- To Start Whiteboard.

Application sharing and the whiteboard work in a very similar fashion to these same functions described in an earlier section in this chapter for NetMeeting, so we won't cover them again here

A Final Cautionary Note

Instant messaging with Windows Messenger lets you set up a business community quickly and easily, joining people from different geographical locations. It can also reach out past the edges of the company local area network to people using wireless devices, and it can restrict messaging to a specific group of users. However, the questions of reliability and long-term security are both wide open. You, as a manager, will hope that messages stay focussed on business issues, but you have little control over the kind of business information that may be leaking out of your company through instant messaging. So apply its use in your business with care.

Using Internet Chat Rooms

To chat or not to chat, that is the question. You can certainly find a number of reputable business chat rooms on the Internet. In general, you'll probably want to use Internet chat rooms primarily to attend special online chat events that relate to your business or an area of interest. Many chat rooms require that you register, and that means, at the least, providing your real name and your e-mail address, which you may very well not want to do—we don't.

For a list of sites that have or link to business chat rooms on the Internet, use your favorite search engine to search on *business chat.* You'll find some business chat rooms at Yahoo! Some chat rooms are voice enabled, though you can turn off this feature. We found it particularly annoying.

Although we have not made an exhaustive survey, we're sorry to report that every time we visited a so-called business chat room, we were less than pleased with the quality of the conversation, and often the chat was interrupted by offensive personal advertisements. If you stick to the special purpose chat events and topics, you'll probably have a good experience, but you can, of course, judge for yourself.

Downloading Files with FTP

File Transfer Protocol (FTP) is an Internet protocol that you can use to download files from or upload files to an FTP site. The address of an FTP site starts with *ftp://*.

Although you can use Internet Explorer to find and download files at an FTP site, you may prefer to use special FTP client software.

Here's how FTP works:

- Using FTP client software, you connect to an FTP server on the Internet. The commands that you give to the FTP client are translated into instructions that the server executes for you.
- Log on to the server with a user name and a password. Some FTP sites are private, and you will need an authorized user name and password to access these sites. Other sites are known as anonymous FTP sites because you can log on with the user name of "anonymous" and use your e-mail address as the password.
- Browse through the available files. When you spot a file you want to download, use the commands in your FTP client software to do so.

NOTE *For security reasons, you can normally only download files from anonymous FTP sites; you cannot upload.*

If you have large files that you need to transfer among dispersed groups at your company, you might want to consider setting up an FTP site. Transferring files with FTP can be considerably faster than attaching them to an e-mail message. Consult your technical professional for how to do this.

To start FTP and connect to the Microsoft FTP site, click the Start button, click Run, type *ftp ftp.microsoft.com* in the Open box, and click OK. A text window opens displaying your FTP session. You can become an FTP expert with just a few commands:

- ascii sets the file transfer mode to text so you can transfer text files.
- binary sets the mode to binary so you can transfer executable files.
- get followed by a filename transfers that file to your computer.
- quit terminates your FTP session and breaks the communications link.

Figure 8-22 shows the contents of an FTP site at Microsoft (*ftp://ftp.microsoft.com*). You won't find any banners and glitz at an FTP site, but you will be able to quickly find and download information that you need.

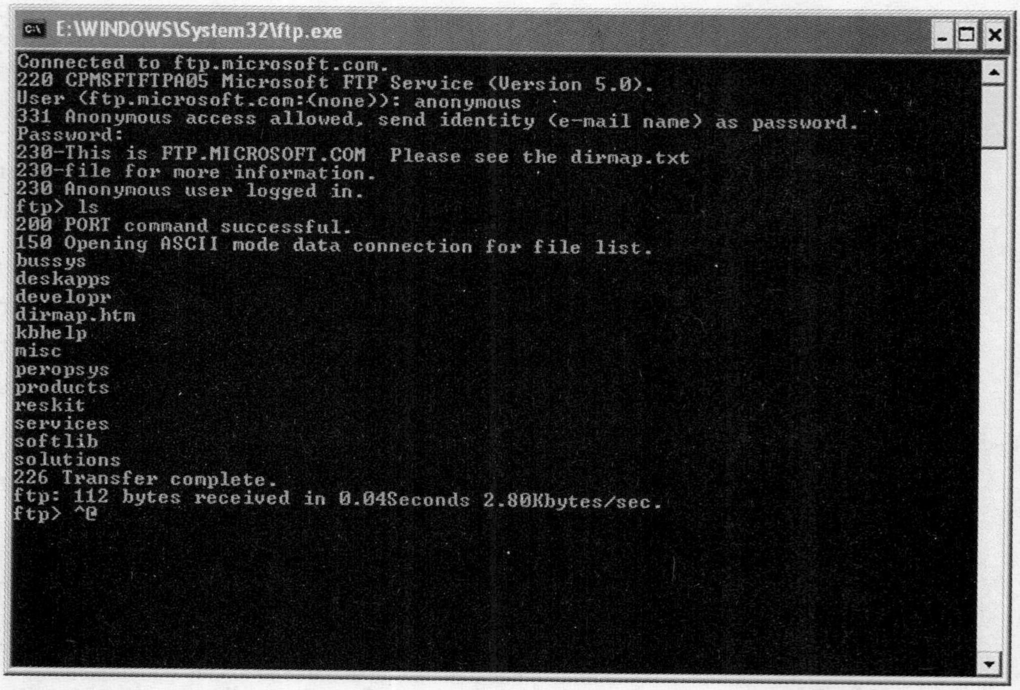

Figure 8-22 The Microsoft FTP site.

Connecting via Telnet

Telnet is a terminal emulation protocol that you use to log on to another computer on the Internet. Your computer actually becomes part of that computer, which is called the *host*. Depending on your level of access, you can use the host's services, memory capacity, disk storage, and so on. In other words, your computer emulates a terminal attached to the host computer.

Telnet has long been used in educational institutions to connect students and teachers with resources such as a library or a bulletin board system. Today's Telnet software is even being used on palm-size computers to connect to a remote system and check e-mail, transfer files, and talk to another person.

TIP *Besides Window's built-in Telnet client, Telnet, you can also use HyperTerminal to perform the same tasks.*

Here's how Telnet works:

- Click the Start button, and then click Run. In the Run dialog box, enter *telnet* followed by the Internet address of the computer you want to contact—for example, *telnet dante.u.washington.edu*.
- The remote computer and your computer determine which type of terminal emulation will be used. The most common type is VT-100. Terminal emulation ensures that your keyboard and monitor will function as the host computer expects.
- Text that you type on your computer accumulates in a buffer until you press the Enter key. It is then sent to the host computer, along with the host's Internet address and your Internet address.
- The host computer then returns the data you requested or the results of a command you sent.

NOTE *VT-100 is one of a series of terminals that was manufactured by DEC. Many communications and terminal-emulation programs emulate or mimic the VT-100.*

Summary

In this chapter we have looked at the communications tools found in Windows XP Professional. We looked at how to send and receive faxes, how to use HyperTerminal, and how to run a virtual conference with NetMeeting. Then we looked at the .NET Passport service and at instant messaging with Windows Messenger. And although most business users are familiar with e-mail and the Web, not everyone is aware of the other services that you can use to become a more effective user of the Internet, and in this chapter we looked at FTP and Telnet.

Chapter 9

USING INTERNET EXPLORER

Featuring:

- Understanding How a Web Browser Works
- Opening Internet Explorer
- Exploring the Web
- Using the Favorites Bar
- Using the History Bar
- E-Mailing Pages and Links
- Using the Media Bar
- Saving and Printing Web Pages
- Searching the Web
- Dealing with Cookies and Temporary Internet Files
- Customizing Internet Explorer

To access resources on the World Wide Web you need a client program called a *Web browser*. The Web browser's primary job is to let you view Web pages and move from one resource to another, although these days most browsers provide much more functionality than that. In this chapter, we focus on Microsoft Internet Explorer, the Web browser that's included with Windows XP Professional.

Understanding How a Web Browser Works

Before getting into Internet Explorer specifics, we want to explain how a Web browser works. You don't need this information to use a Web browser, of course, but knowing the process will help you understand why access is sometimes slow, give you a clue as to the meaning of some of the cryptic messages you sometimes see on your screen, and, in general, help you to become a more informed business user of the Internet.

When you enter a Web address in the Web browser application on your computer, here is an overview of what happens:

- The browser software on your computer sends the address to your Internet service provider (ISP).
- Your ISP then sends the address to the nearest node of the Domain Name Service (DNS). The DNS is a set of databases, distributed among servers, that stores the numeric addresses of Web sites. (The section "A Word About URLs" explains URLs and numeric addresses.)
- The DNS returns the site's numeric address to your Web browser.
- Your Web browser sends the numeric address to a router, which checks the traffic on the Internet and finds a path that is the least busy to the server that contains the resource you are requesting.
- The server receives the address, acknowledges this receipt, and places the request in a queue to wait until the server fulfills earlier requests. When the server acknowledges the receipt, you'll see a message in the browser's status line that tells you the connection is successful.
- The server then sends the resource back over the Internet to your ISP, which then sends it to your computer.

This process may sound time-consuming, but even with a slow Internet connection, it can take only seconds, and with a fast Internet connection, it can happen almost instantaneously, whether the resource is stored on a server halfway around the world or on a server in the next building in your office complex.

Opening Internet Explorer

You can open Internet Explorer in the following ways:

- Click the Start button, and then click Internet.
- Click the Start button, click All Programs, and then click Internet Explorer.

The first time you open Internet Explorer, you'll see something similar to Figure 9-1, which shows the MSN page. You can retain this start page or select any other. You'll find the steps later in this chapter.

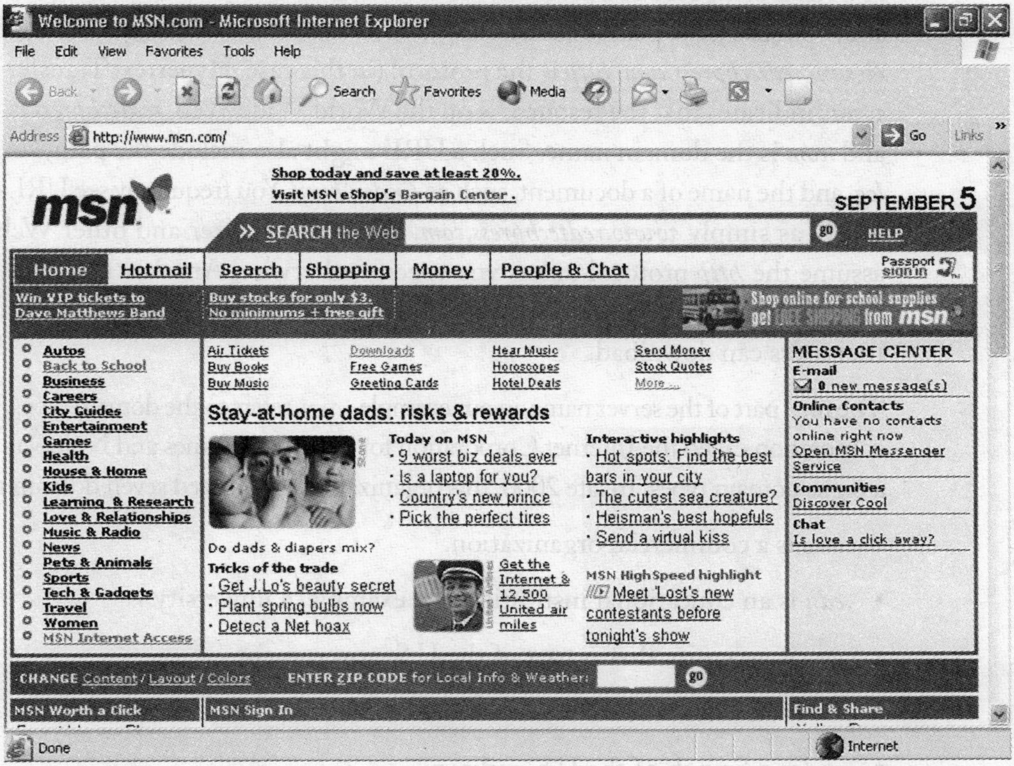

Figure 9-1 The default start page.

You can also open Internet Explorer from any document that includes a hyperlink. For example, if you receive an e-mail message that contains a URL in the body, simply click the URL to open that page in Internet Explorer. In addition, in Windows Explorer, clicking a filename that ends in .htm or .html opens that file in Internet Explorer.

NOTE *HyperText Markup Language (HTML) is the programming language that is used to create Web pages. To take a look at the underlying HTML for a Web page, open the page in Internet Explorer, click the View menu, and then click Source.*

A Word About URLs

URL stands for Uniform Resource Locator and is an address for a resource on the Internet. It actually represents a string of numbers called an Internet Protocol (IP) address, for example, 169.254.69.104. Since it's much easier for humans to remember names instead of numbers, we typically use URLs.

A URL is composed of a protocol, the name of the server on which the resource resides, and, optionally, the path to the resource and its filename. For example, in the URL *http://www.redtechpress.com*, *http* is the protocol (in this case, Hypertext Transfer Protocol), *www* indicates that the resource is on the World Wide Web, *redtechpress* is the server, and *.com* is the domain name. Such a URL might also include the path, such as */catalog*, and the name of a document, such as */index.html.* You frequently see URLs in various media as simply *www.redtechpress.com*. Internet Explorer and other Web browsers assume the *http* protocol unless you specify otherwise. Another less frequently seen protocol is the File Transfer Protocol (FTP); an FTP server contains programs and files that users can download.

The final part of the server name, in our example, *.com*, refers to the domain type. A nonprofit corporation called the Internet Corporation for Assigned Names and Numbers (ICANN) assigns domain types. In late 2000, this organization recognized seven domain types:

- *.com* is a commercial organization.
- *.edu* is an educational institution, for example, a university.
- *.gov* is an entity that is part of the U.S. government.
- *.int* is an international organization, such as the United Nations.
- *.mil* is a branch of the U.S. military.
- *.net* is a network organization.
- *.org* is a nonprofit organization.

By mid-2001, however, ICANN will begin issuing URLs that incorporate seven new domain types. These new suffixes were designed as alternatives to *.com*, which is currently crowded with 20 million registrations. Think of it as similar to adding area codes to the phone system to accommodate growth. Here are the new domain names you can expect to see:

- *.aero* will indicate airlines, airports, computer reservation systems, and related industries.
- *.biz* will be specifically for businesses.
- *.coop* will designate business cooperatives such as credit unions and rural electric coops.
- *.info* will be a more global identifier. Currently, most *.com* registrations are in the United States.

- *.museum* will indicate accredited museums worldwide.
- *.name* will be a category for individuals.
- *.pro* would indicate a professional status such as doctor or lawyer.

You pronounce the domain part of a URL as "dot com," "dot e-d-u," "dot gov," and so on. You have, no doubt, though seen references to *dot-coms,* which are businesses that in recent years have sprung up on the Internet. These are not simply businesses that have a Web site, but businesses that exist entirely on the Internet.

Mid-2000 found many dot-coms in trouble, and by 2001 many dot-coms were out of business. The reason, according to some dot-com CEOs, is that the focus was on acquiring an audience at all costs—regardless of the costs.

The Internet is a seductive medium, but it's probably safe to assume that there's no substitute for a well-designed and carefully thought out business plan.

Understanding the Internet Explorer Window

The components of the Internet Explorer window are much like those in other Windows applications. You'll see vertical and horizontal scroll bars as necessary, you can size portions of the window by clicking and dragging, and you can display a ScreenTip by pointing to a button. Here is a list of some other components:

- The title bar is at the top of the window, and it displays the name of the current Web page or other file that is open.
- The menu bar is just beneath the title bar, and it contains a set of menus, many of which appear in other Windows applications.
- The Standard toolbar is just beneath the menu bar, and it contains several buttons that correspond to items on the menu bar, as well as the Back, Forward, and Home navigation buttons.
- The Address bar is beneath the Standard toolbar, and you use it to enter a URL or filename. You can also click the drop-down arrow to select a URL.
- The Links bar is a drop-down list on the far right of the Address bar, and it contains a short list of preselected hyperlinks. You can add or remove links from this list.
- The Activity Indicator is at the far right of the menu bar and is animated when Internet Explorer is sending or receiving data.
- The main window displays the resource you most recently accessed.

- The status bar is at the bottom of the screen. When you choose a menu command, the status bar displays a description of what it does. When you point to a link, the status bar displays its URL. When you click a link, the status bar displays a series of messages related to the progress of finding and opening that resource.
- The security zone indicator is at the far right of the status bar and displays the currently active security zone. We'll discuss security zones in detail later in this chapter.
- Just to the left of the security zone indicator is a Privacy Report icon, if the site has a privacy report. Later in this chapter, we'll discuss privacy features of Internet Explorer and show you how to display the privacy report of a site.

In addition, Explorer bars are displayed in a separate pane to the left of the main window when you select one of them. Examples of Explorer bars include the Search Companion and the Favorites bar. We'll look at each of these later in this chapter.

Exploring the Web

Once you open Internet Explorer, you can start exploring the Web immediately. All you have to do is click a link or enter a URL you've gleaned from TV or someone's business card in the Address bar. You can, however, use several techniques to make the time spent connected to the Internet more efficient.

Using the Address Bar

You'll notice that sometimes when you start to enter a URL, it sort of completes itself for you if you've ever entered this URL before. This is the AutoComplete feature at work. If AutoComplete enters the URL you want, simply press Enter to go to that resource. If not, continue typing.

AutoComplete also works in other fields you fill in on a Web page, such as search queries, a list of stock quotes, information you supply when you purchase items over the Internet, and so on. The information you originally enter is encrypted (encoded) and stored on your computer. It is not accessible to Web sites.

TIP *A handy trick you can use to quickly go to a Web site that begins with* www *and ends in .com is to enter just the main part of the name (such as* microsoft*) and then press Enter. This fills in the* www *and .com for you.*

If you've entered a URL (perhaps a lengthy one) and then want to use only part of it to try to access a resource, place the cursor in the Address bar, hold down Ctrl, and press the right or left arrow key to jump forward or backward to the next separator character (the slashes, the dots, and so on).

You can use the Address bar to do more than find a resource on the Internet. You can also run a program from the Address bar (for example, type *C:\Program Files\Movie Maker*), and you can find a file. Enter a drive letter (such as *d:*), press Enter, and click the Show The Contents of This Drive link. You'll see something similar to Figure 9-2.

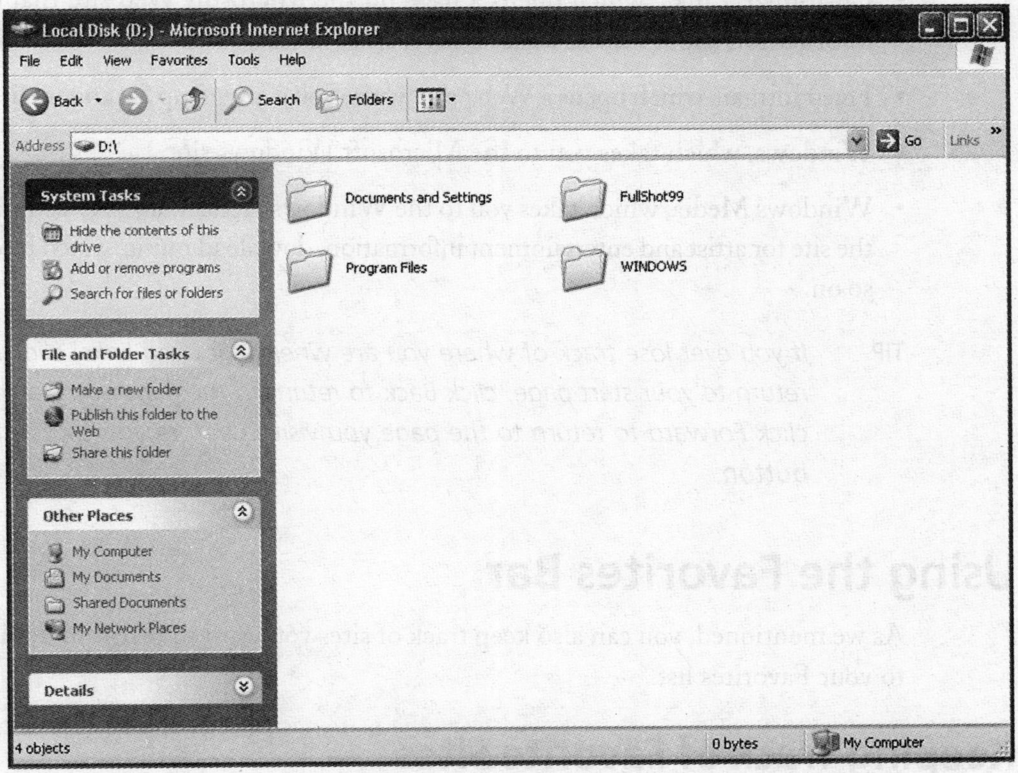

Figure 9-2 Looking for a file from the Address bar.

Navigating with Hyperlinks

A *hyperlink*, or simply *link*, can be a word, a phrase, an image, or a symbol that forms a connection with a resource that can be located on your local computer, your local network, or the Internet. In Internet Explorer, textual links are usually underlined and in a different color from normal text. You know something is a link if the pointer becomes a hand with a pointing finger when you place the mouse cursor over it.

To follow a link, of course, you simply click it. If you find something you know you'll want to revisit, you can place a link to it on the Links bar, or you can add it to your Favorites list, which we'll discuss next. To add a link to the Links bar, simply click it and then drag it there. To remove a link from the Links bar, right-click it and choose Delete from the shortcut menu. To rearrange items on the Links bar, drag an item to a new location.

By default, the Links bar contains the following links:

- Customize Links, which opens a page on the Microsoft Web site that contains information about how to add, remove, and rearrange items on the Links bar.
- Free Hotmail, which opens a Web page where you can sign up for an e-mail account.
- Windows, which takes you to the Microsoft Windows site.
- Windows Media, which takes you to the WindowsMedia.com site. You can search the site for artist and entertainment information, download music, watch movies, and so on.

TIP *If you ever lose track of where you are when following links, click Home to return to your start page, click Back to return to the page you last visited, or click Forward to return to the page you visited before you clicked the Back button.*

Using the Favorites Bar

As we mentioned, you can also keep track of sites you want to revisit by adding them to your Favorites list.

Keeping Track of Favorite Sites

You can add sites to your Favorites list in two ways: you can use the Favorites menu, or you can click the Favorites button on the toolbar.

To use the Favorites menu, follow these steps:

1. Open the Add Favorite dialog box, which is shown in Figure 9-3.

Click the Favorites menu, and then click Add To Favorites.

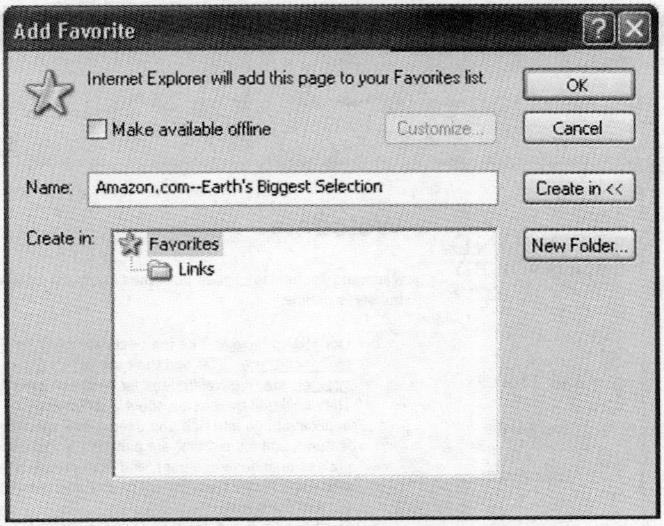

Figure 9-3 The Add Favorite dialog box.

2. **Add the site to the list.**

   In the Name box, accept the suggested name, or type another name and then click OK.

To store a favorite site in a particular folder, click Create In to open the Create In list and then select a folder. To create a new folder, click New Folder to open the Create New Folder dialog box, type a name for the folder, and click OK.

If you know that the contents of a site will not change, you can click the Make Available Offline check box. In this way, you can access the site when you aren't connected to the Internet. For example, suppose you find a lengthy report that contains facts and figures you want to be able to access easily and quickly. Make it available offline.

You can also add a favorite site by clicking the Favorites toolbar button to open the Favorites bar, as shown in Figure 9-4. Click Add to open the Add Favorite dialog box, and then follow step 2 above.

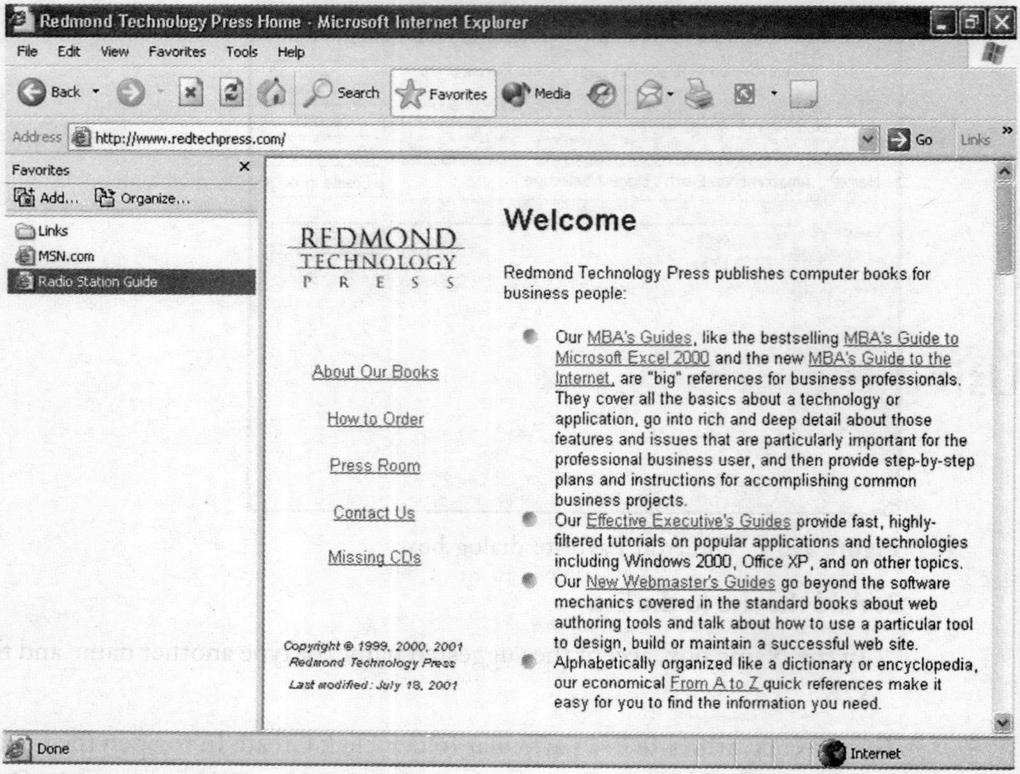

Figure 9-4 Using the Favorites bar.

Here are some other ways you can add sites to your Favorites list:

- Right-click a link, and choose Add To Favorites from the shortcut menu.
- Right-click the current page outside a link, and choose Add To Favorites from the shortcut menu.
- Drag and drop a link on a Web page to the Favorites toolbar button.

Organizing Favorites

If you just keep adding sites to the Favorites list without any sense of organization, you'll soon find that you have links to a lot of sites but that you can't put your cursor on one quickly. Here are some tips for managing the Favorites list:

- Create folders for collections of similar sites or for sites that you want to access for a particular project.
- Weed out sites that you no longer need to access. Right-click the item, and choose Delete from the shortcut menu.

- To move an item to another place in the list or to another folder, drag it to its new location.
- To create a new folder from the Favorites list, click the Favorites menu, click Organize Favorites, and then click Create Folder, or click the Organize button on the Favorites bar.
- To rename a favorite, right-click it, choose Rename from the shortcut menu, type the new name, and press Enter.

Using the History Bar

Another way to find out where you've been and return there is to use the History list. To do so, follow these steps:

1. Open the History Bar, which is shown in Figure 9-5.

Click the History button on the toolbar.

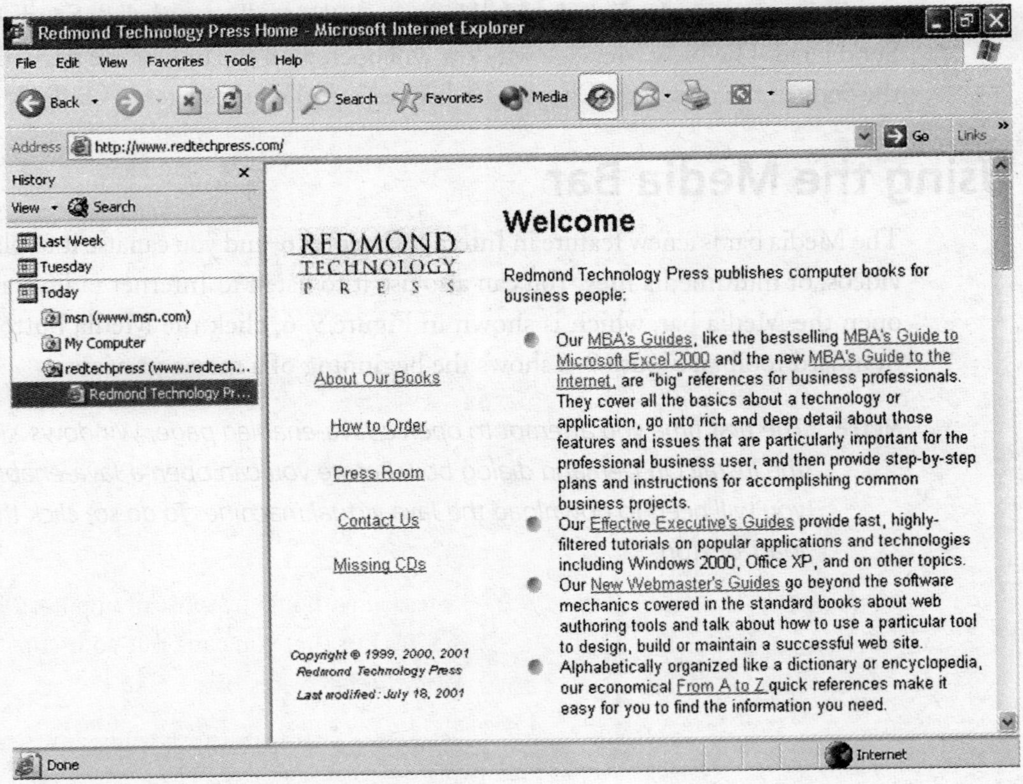

Figure 9-5 Using the History bar.

2. **Select a view.**

   Click the View button on the History bar, and then choose By Date, By Site, By Most Visited, or By Order Most Visited Today. You can also open a list of sites that you visited yesterday, last week, two weeks ago, and three weeks ago.

3. **Search for a site.**

   Click the Search button to open the Search For box, enter a term or a phrase, and click Search Now.

TIP *For really quick access to a site, place a shortcut to it on the desktop. With the page open in Internet Explorer, right-click an empty area, and choose Create Shortcut from the shortcut menu.*

E-Mailing Pages and Links

When you run across a page you want to share with a colleague, you can send the page or a link to it. Simply click the Mail button on the toolbar, and click Send A Link or Send Page. The New Message window will open with the link or the page inserted in the body of the message. (Chapter 10 discusses sending messages in Outlook Express.)

Using the Media Bar

The Media bar is a new feature in Internet Explorer 6, and you can use it to play music, videos, or multimedia files. You can also use it to listen to Internet radio stations. To open the Media bar, which is shown in Figure 9-6, click the Media button on the Standard toolbar. Figure 9-6 shows the beginning of a movie preview.

NOTE *The first time you attempt to open a Java-enabled page, Windows XP displays the Install On Demand dialog box. Before you can open a Java-enabled page, you will need to download the Java virtual machine. To do so, click the Download button.*

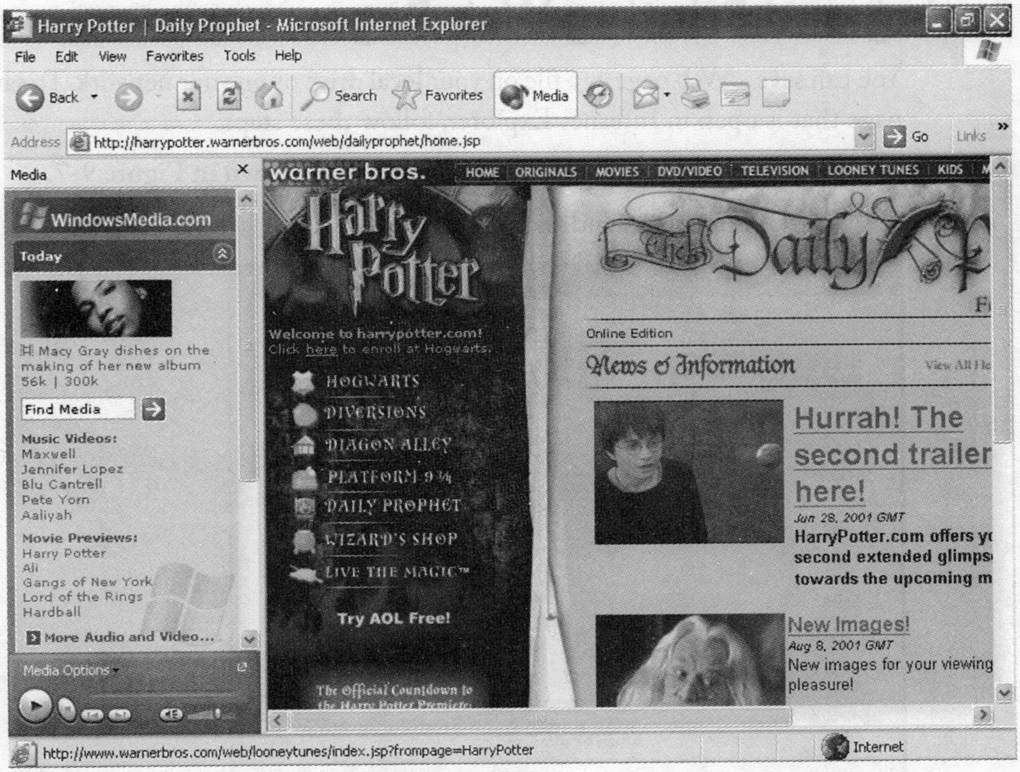

Figure 9-6 The Media bar in Internet Explorer.

The Media bar is a subset of Windows Media Player (see Chapter 5) and has the same controls as Media Player at the bottom of the bar. Point to a control to see a description of what it does. You can use the Media bar features as follows:

- Click a link in the Featured Artists section to open a page for that item. You can then click a link corresponding to the speed of your Internet connection to play the item.
- Click a link in Movie Previews to open a preview and play it.
- Click a link in the Radio Stations section to open that station's page and listen to what's playing.
- Click a link on the side of the Media bar to display more selections.

TIP *You'll find your listening or viewing pleasure enhanced with a fast Internet connection. A 56-Kbps modem is the minimum recommended standard and not really acceptable for most purposes.*

Saving and Printing Web Pages

You can save a Web page as a file on your local drive or on your network. To save a Web page that is open in Internet Explorer, follow these steps:

1. Open the Save Web Page dialog box, which is shown in Figure 9-7.

Click the File menu, and then click Save As.

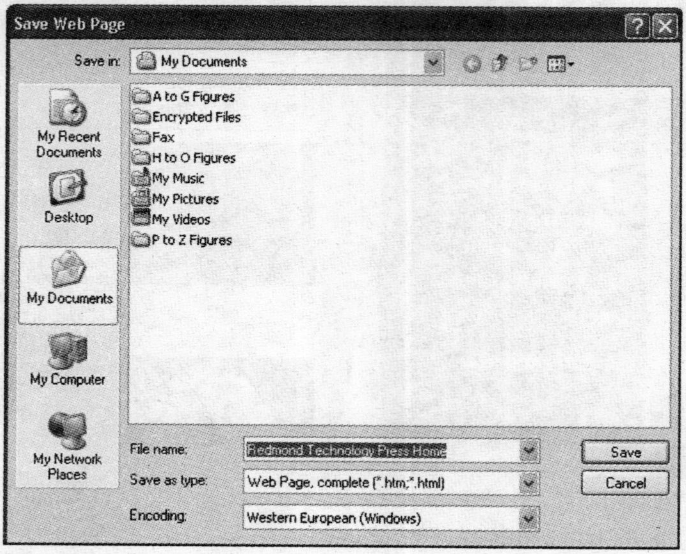

Figure 9-7 Saving a Web page.

2. Select a folder, a filename, and a type.

In the Save In box, select a folder in which to save the page. In the File Name box, accept the name that's suggested or enter another name. In the Save As Type box, select a file type. If you want to save a file with a character set other than Western European, click the drop-down Encoding list, and select a character set.

3. Save the file.

Click the Save button.

To save a Web page without opening it, right-click its link and choose Save Target As from the shortcut menu to download the file and open the Save As dialog box. Follow steps 2 and 3 above.

To save a portion of a page and place it in another document, follow these steps:

1. Make your selection, and copy it.

Select what you want, and press Ctrl+C.

2. **Insert your selection in another document.**

   Open the other document, place the insertion point where you want the text, and press Ctrl+V.

To save an image from a Web page, follow these steps:

1. **Select the image.**

   Right-click the image, and choose Save Picture As to open the Save Picture dialog box, as shown in Figure 9-8.

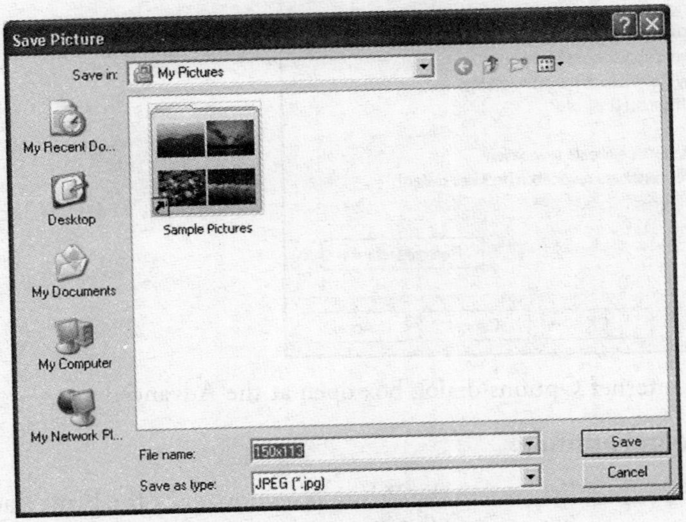

Figure 9-8 Saving an image.

2. **Save the file.**

   Select a folder, a filename, and a type, and then click Save.

To print a Web page you have open in Internet Explorer, simply click the Print button. By default, background colors and background images are not printed, which saves printing time, spooling time, and cartridge ink. If you want to print background images and colors, follow these steps:

1. **Open the Internet Options dialog box.**

   Click the Tools menu, click Internet Options, and then click the Advanced tab, as shown in Figure 9-9.

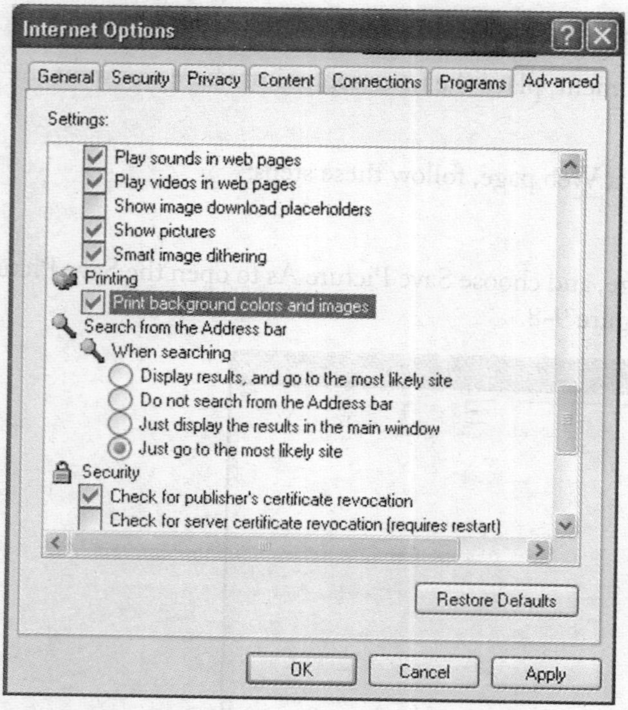

Figure 9-9 The Internet Options dialog box open at the Advanced tab.

2. **Enable background printing.**

   Scroll down the Settings list, and in the Printing section, click the Print Background Colors And Images check box. Click OK.

To print a Web page but to exercise finer control over what's printed, follow these steps:

1. **Open the Print dialog box.**

   Click the File menu, and then click Print. For the most part, you use this dialog box just as you would any Print dialog box in Windows.

2. **Specify your options.**

   Click the Options tab, as shown in Figure 9-10. If you want to print all the pages that are linked to the current page, click the Print All Linked Documents check box. (Be sure you really want to do this—you might need a lot of paper.) If you want to print a table that lists the links for this page, click the Print Table Of Links check box.

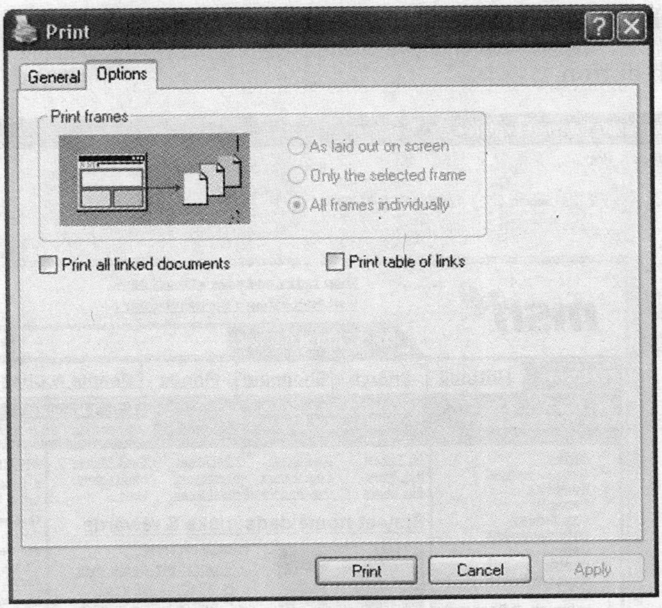

Figure 9-10 The Print dialog box open at the Options tab.

3. **Print the document.**

   Click the Print button.

To print the target of any link, right-click the link and choose Print Target from the shortcut menu to open the Print dialog box.

Searching the Web

If you've spent any time at all searching the Internet, you probably know about search services such as AltaVista, Google, and Yahoo!. You know that you can go to those sites and enter a search term or phrase to locate documents and other resources that contain references to your search item. You can also search the Web with Internet Explorer's Search Companion.

Doing a Basic Search

Before we get into all the options you can apply to a search, let's do a simple search. Although you may be annoyed by all the ad banners on Web pages, you may also find that the Internet is an effective marketing medium for your business products or services. Let's search for resources that might give us some information about advertising on the Internet. To do so, follow these steps:

1. **Open the Search Companion bar, which is shown in Figure 9-11.**

   Click the Search button.

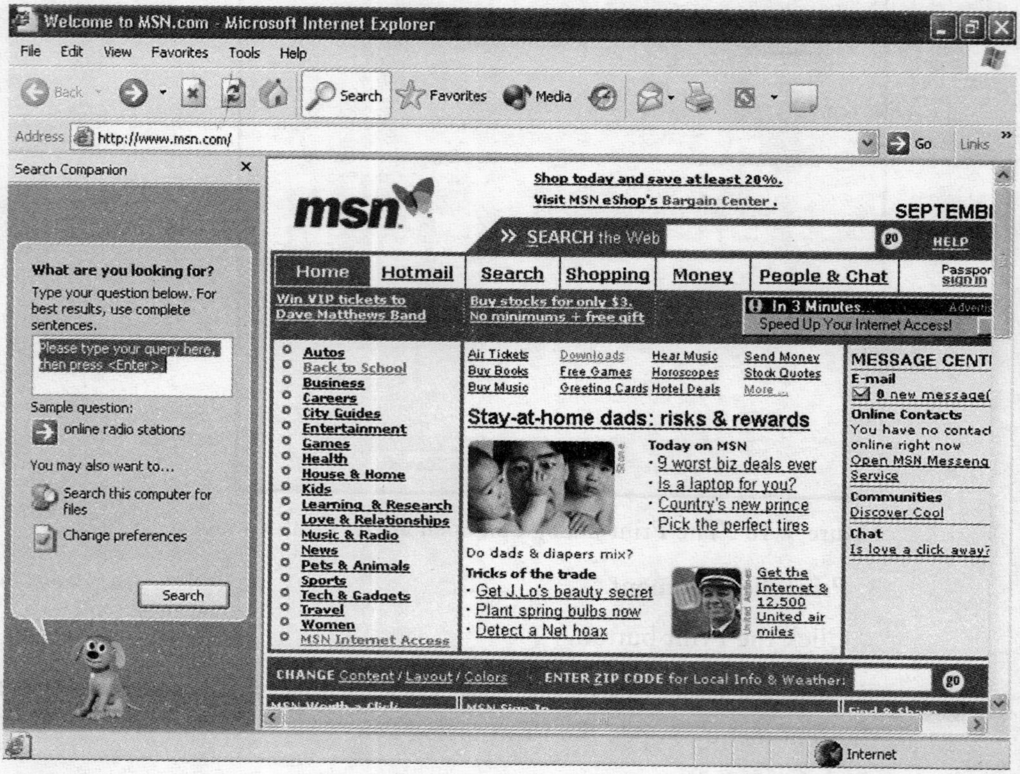

Figure 9-11 The Search Companion bar.

2. **Enter a search phrase.**

   In the box, type *advertising on the Internet*, and then click Search. Figure 9-12 shows the results of the search.

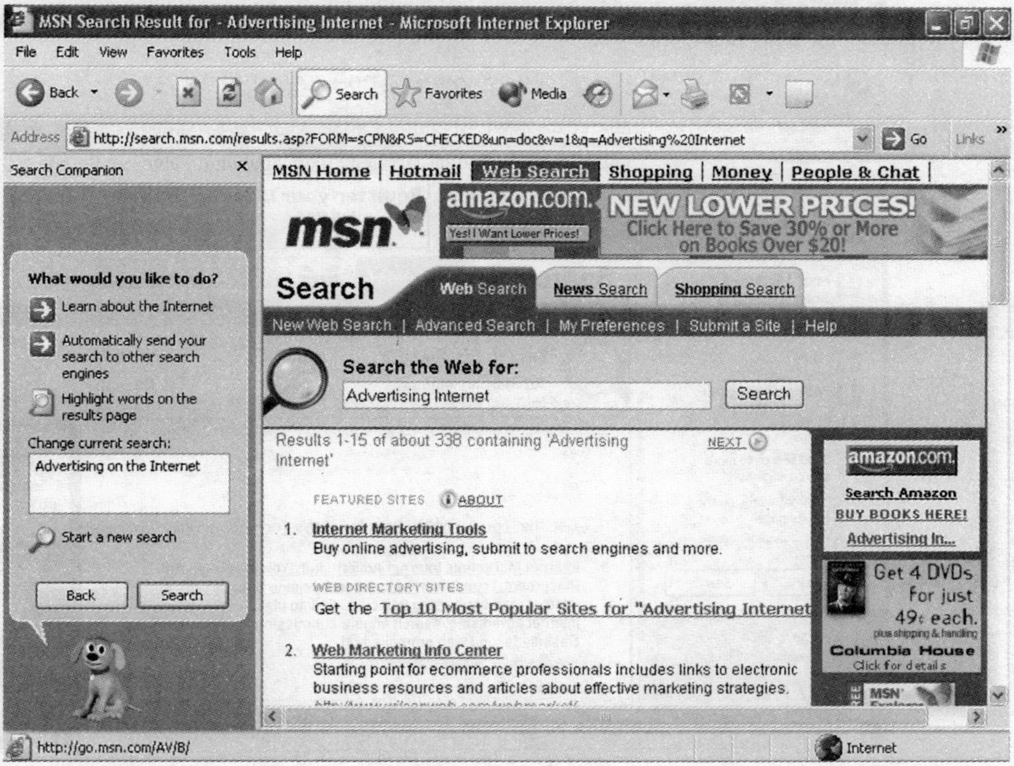

Figure 9-12 The results of a search.

To open a page, simply click it. To begin a new search, click Back.

TIP *You can also search by entering your search phrase in the Address bar. When you then press Enter, Internet Explorer automatically searches for your phrase and displays the results.*

Broadening a Search

When you use the Search Companion, you are searching with MSN Search. If you would like to see what other search services might turn up for your search, click the Automatically Send Your Search To Other Search Engines link in the Search Companion. Figure 9-13 shows the additional options that are then displayed on the Search Companion bar. As you can see, you can then select to search using other specific search services or even send your topic to even more search services.

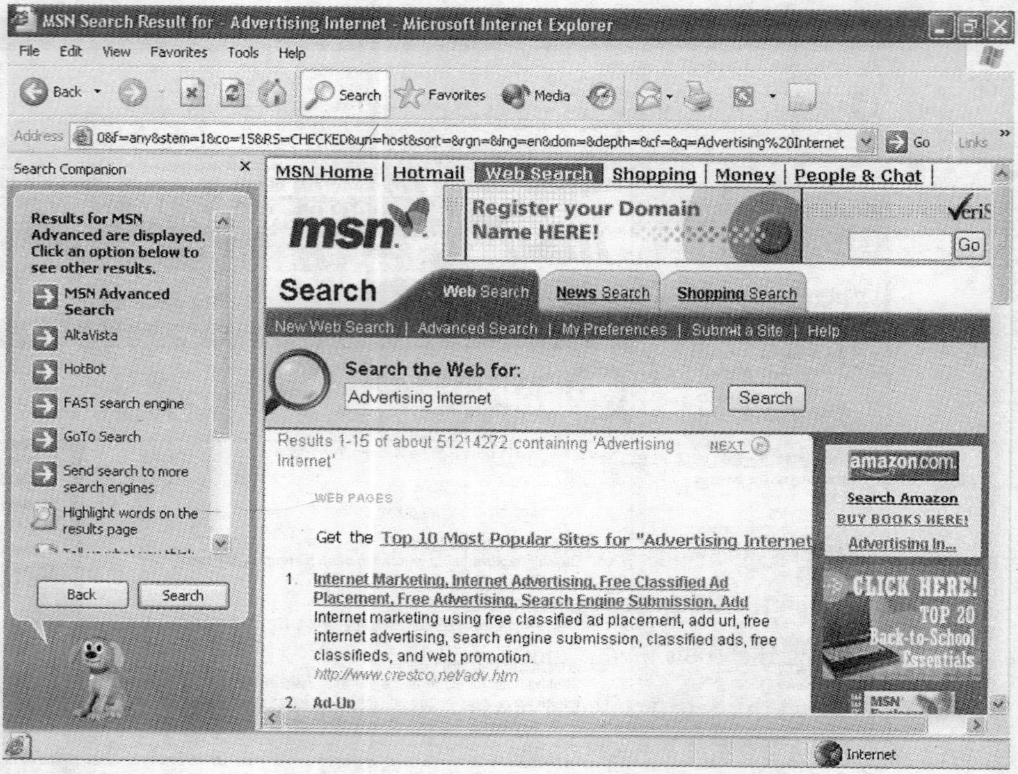

Figure 9-13 Searching with other search services.

You can also use the Search Companion to specifically look for pictures, music, or video, specific types of documents, all file types, and computers or people. In addition, from the Search Companion, you can search the Windows Help And Support Center. In the first Search Companion screen, click the Search This Computer link to display these further options.

To specify how you want to use the Search Companion, click the Change Preferences link at the bottom of the bar, and then click the links that apply to your situation.

Dealing with Cookies and Temporary Internet Files

A cookie is a file that is stored on your computer by the server of a site that you visit. A cookie is a simple data file that identifies you to the server. When you revisit the site, the cookie can be used to welcome you by name or to present you with a customized version of the page. Cookies are also used to make online shopping carts work. A cookie cannot see what's on your hard drive or local network, nor can it send any other information back to the server or run other programs on your computer. In a later section in this chapter, we'll discuss the available options regarding how you deal with cookies and maintain your privacy when using the Internet.

A temporary Internet file is a copy of a Web page that you have visited and is stored in the Temporary Internet Files folder on your hard drive, along with your cookies. When you access a site that you've visited before, Internet Explorer first checks to see whether the page is in your Temporary Internet Files folder. If it is, Internet Explorer then checks to see whether the page has been updated since being stored. If the page has not been updated, Internet Explorer opens it from your Temporary Internet Files folder (also called the cache), which is obviously faster than loading the page from the server.

To check out what's been stored in your Internet Files folder, follow these steps:

1. **Open the Internet Options dialog box.**

   Click the Tools menu, and then click Internet Options.

2. **Open the Settings dialog box, which is shown in Figure 9-14.**

   Click the General tab, and then in the Temporary Internet Files section, click the Settings button.

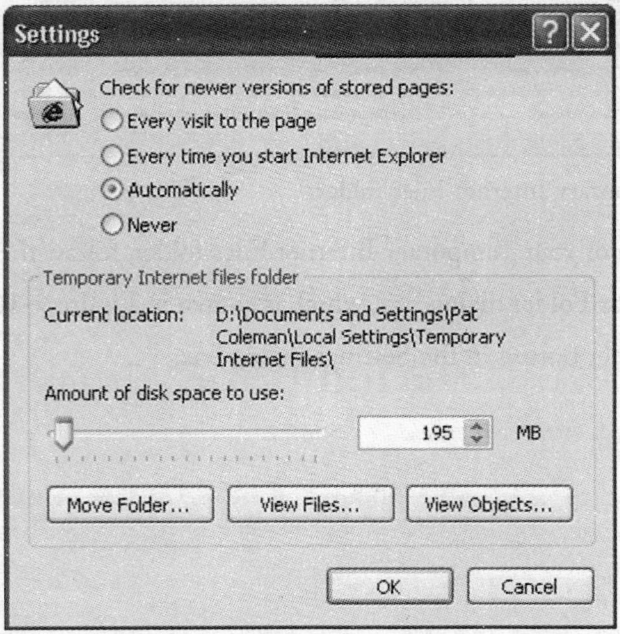

Figure 9-14 The Settings dialog box.

NOTE *You can specify when pages are stored in the Temporary Internet Files folder by selecting from the options in the top part of the Settings dialog box.*

3. Open the Temporary Internet Files folder, which is shown in Figure 9-15.

In the Settings dialog box, click the View Files button.

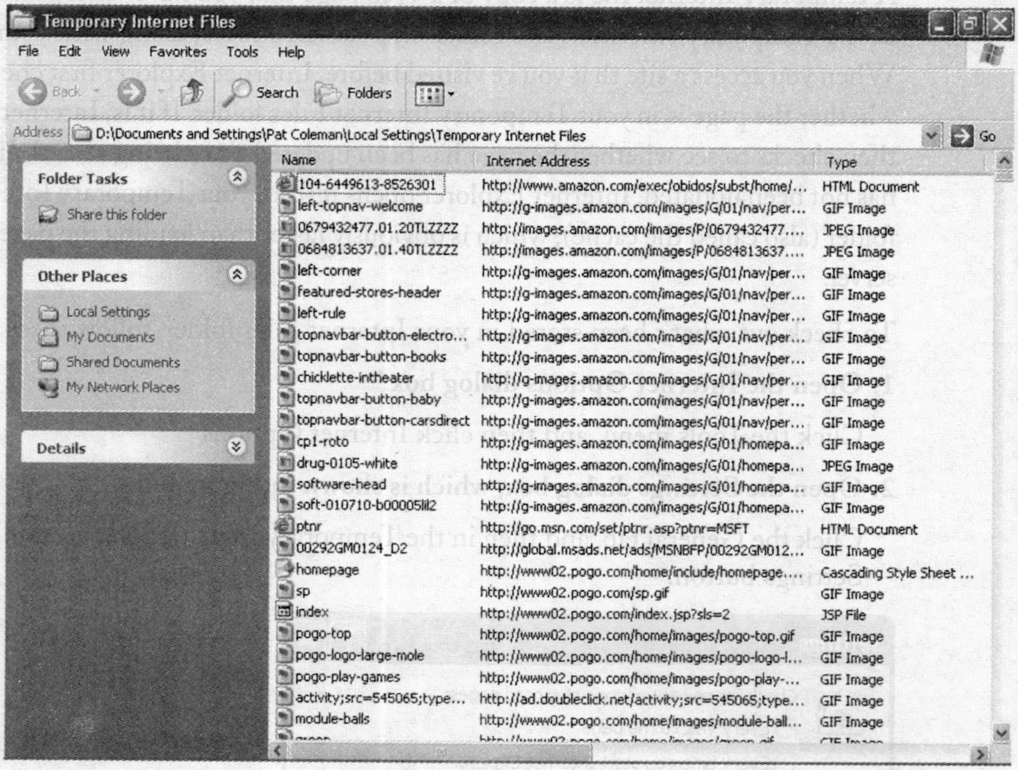

Figure 9-15 The Temporary Internet Files folder.

To change the location of your Temporary Internet Files folder, follow these steps:

1. Open the Browse For Folder dialog box, which is shown in Figure 9-16.

Click the Move Folder button in the Settings dialog box.

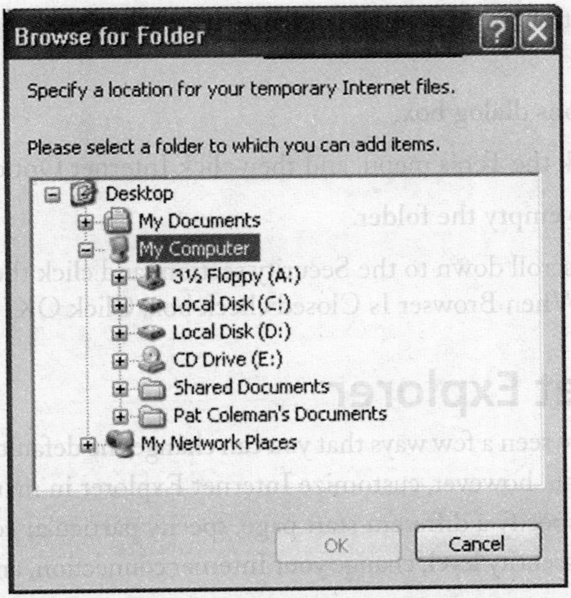

Figure 9-16 The Browse For Folder dialog box.

2. Specify a location.

Select a new folder, and click OK.

Sometimes when you open a Web page, a small program is needed to display the page. These programs are stored in your Downloaded Program Files folder. To view this folder, click the View Objects button in the Settings dialog box. If you want to delete one of these programs, right-click it, and choose Delete from the shortcut menu. Remember, though, that some pages might not be fully functional without the program.

To remove all cookies from your system, click the Delete Cookies button in the General tab of the Internet Options dialog box. To remove all temporary Internet files, click the Delete Files button. To increase or reduce the space for the Temporary Internet Files folder, move the slider bar in the Settings dialog box.

To empty the Temporary Internet Files folder automatically when you close Internet Explorer, follow these steps:

1. **Open the Internet Options dialog box.**

   In Internet Explorer, click the Tools menu, and then click Internet Options.

2. **Tell Internet Explorer to empty the folder.**

   Click the Advanced tab, scroll down to the Security section, and click the Empty Temporary Files Folder When Browser Is Closed check box. Click OK.

Customizing Internet Explorer

Already in this chapter, you've seen a few ways that you can change the default settings for Internet Explorer. You can, however, customize Internet Explorer in many other ways. For example, you can specify a different start page, specify particular colors for text and background, set the security level, change your Internet connection, and so on.

To do any of this, you open a dialog box that is called either Internet Options or Internet Properties. In Internet Explorer, click the Tools menu and then click Internet Options to open the Internet Options dialog box. In Control Panel, clicking the Internet Options icon opens the Internet Properties dialog box. Both dialog boxes contain exactly the same tabs and the same options. In this section, we'll open the dialog box from within Internet Explorer, so the illustrations will show the Internet Options dialog box.

Personalizing General Settings

As you just saw, you specify how to handle temporary Internet files using the options on the General tab of the Internet Options dialog box, which is shown in Figure 9-17. You also use this tab to change your start page and to manage your History list.

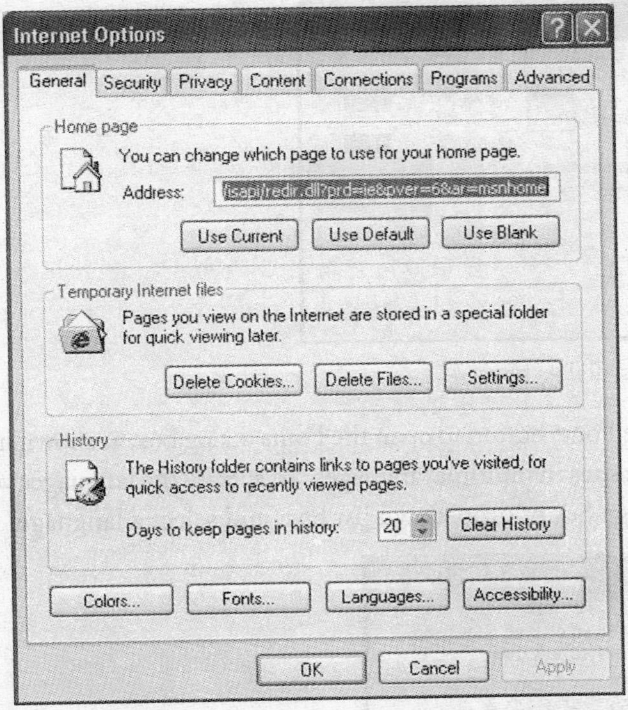

Figure 9-17 The Internet Options dialog box open at the General tab.

As you saw earlier in this chapter, by default Internet Explorer opens the MSN home page when you open Internet Explorer. To specify a different Web site as your start page, open the Web site, open the Internet Options dialog box, and then click Use Current, or enter a URL in the Address box. To specify a blank page, simply click Use Blank. Click OK, or click Apply. If you ever want to return to using the MSN home page as your start page, click Use Default.

Earlier in this chapter, we looked at how to use the History list to access pages you've visited previously. To specify how long to keep pages in history, click the spin box in the History section of the General tab. To empty the History list, click the Clear History button.

The creator of a Web page usually specifies the colors used on the page; otherwise, Internet Explorer automatically uses your Windows color scheme to display the page. For pages that the developer has not specified colors or fonts, you can specify what you want. To specify colors for text, background, visited links, unvisited links, and the hover color, click the Colors button to open the Colors dialog box, as shown in Figure 9-18.

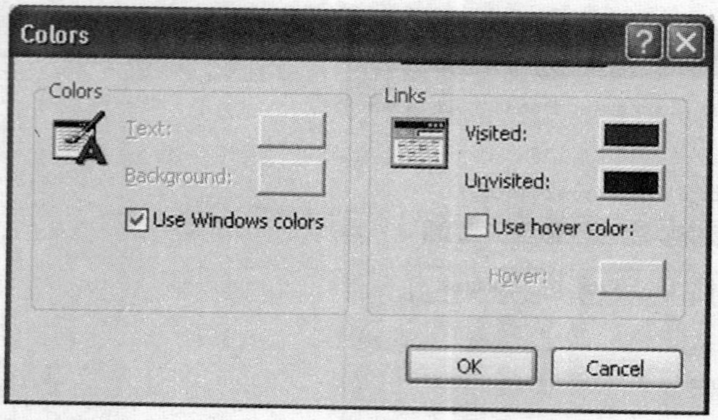

Figure 9-18 The Colors dialog box.

To specify fonts, click the Fonts button to open the Fonts dialog box, as shown in Figure 9-19. You can view some sites in multiple languages. To specify the languages you want to use, click the Language Script drop-down list box, and select a language.

Figure 9-19 The Fonts dialog box.

If you have a vision impairment and want to specify fonts and colors that make a Web page more accessible for you, click the Accessibility button on the General tab to open the Accessibility dialog box, which is shown in Figure 9-20. In the Formatting section of this dialog box, you can tell Internet Explorer to ignore colors, font styles, or font sizes on specified Web pages. You can also set up a style sheet that incorporates your formatting needs and have Internet Explorer use this style sheet.

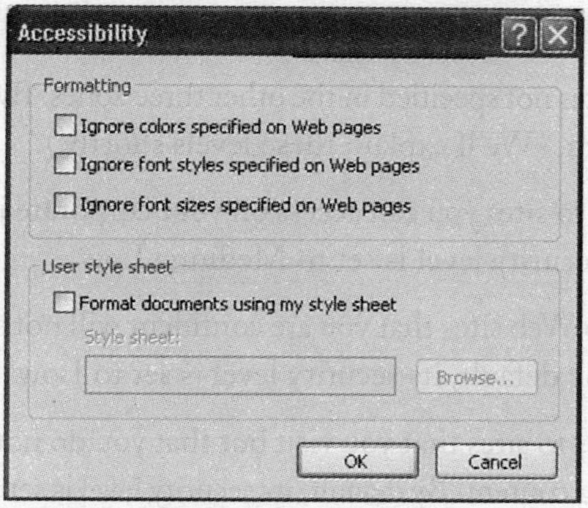

Figure 9-20 The Accessibility dialog box.

Establishing Security Levels for Zones

Internet Explorer establishes four security zones, and you can set the security level you want for each zone, using the Security tab in the Internet Options dialog box, which is shown in Figure 9-21.

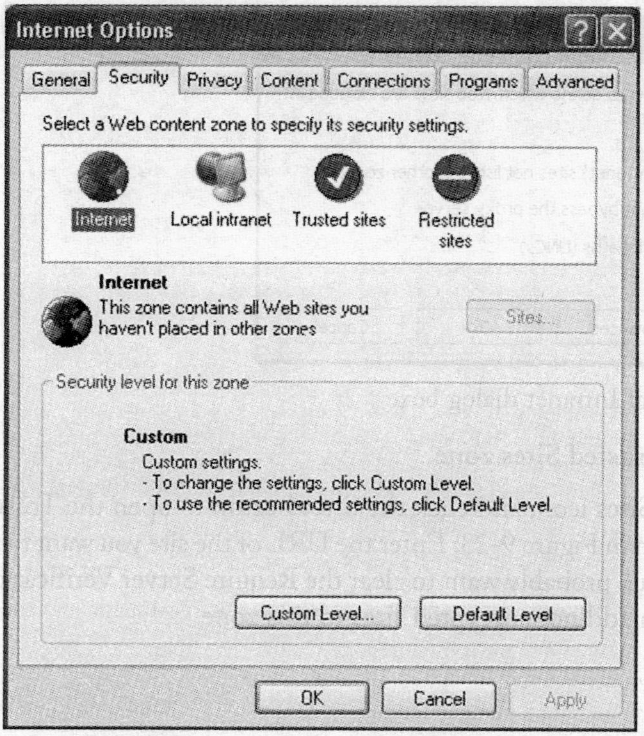

Figure 9-21 The Internet Options dialog box open at the Security tab.

Each zone pertains to specific kinds of sites:

- The Internet zone applies to all sites not specified in the other three zones. By default, its security level is set to Medium. (We'll explain these levels shortly.)
- The Local Intranet zone applies to sites you can access on your corporate intranet, if you have one. By default, its security level is set to Medium-Low.
- The Trusted Sites zone applies to Web sites that you are confident will not send you potentially damaging content. By default, its security level is set to Low.
- The Restricted Sites zone applies to sites that you visit but that you do not trust to not send you potentially damaging content. By default, its security level is set to High.

To add sites to any zone but the Internet zone, follow these steps:

1. Add a site to the Local Intranet zone.

Click the Local Intranet icon, and then click the Sites button to open the Local Intranet dialog box, as shown in Figure 9-22. Clear or check the check boxes to specify which sites to include. Click the Advanced button to open the Local Intranet dialog box to add and remove specific sites.

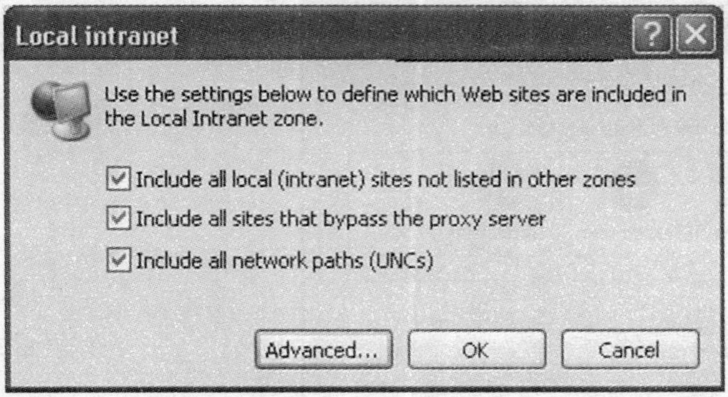

Figure 9-22 The Local Intranet dialog box.

2. Add a site to the Trusted Sites zone.

Click the Trusted Sites icon, and click the Sites button to open the Trusted Sites dialog box, as shown in Figure 9-23. Enter the URL of the site you want to add, and then click Add. You'll probably want to clear the Require Server Verification check box so that you can add nonencrypted sites to this zone.

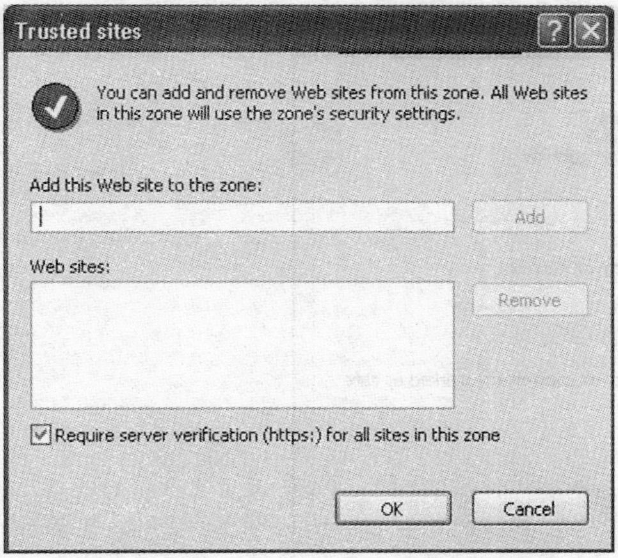

Figure 9-23 The Trusted Sites dialog box.

3. Add a site to the Restricted Sites zone.

Click the Restricted Sites icon, and click the Sites button to open the Restricted Sites dialog box, which contains the same options as the Trusted Sites dialog box shown in Figure 9-23.

To change the security level for a zone, select the zone and then move the slider bar. You have the following choices:

- High is the safest setting but also the most restrictive. Less secure features are disabled, including cookies, so you will not have access to all the features of a Web page.
- Medium is the next safest setting, and it allows more functionality. You are prompted before you download content that Internet Explorer considers potentially unsafe.
- Medium-Low is basically the same as the Medium setting, but you are not prompted before you download potentially unsafe content.
- Low is most appropriate for sites that you know you can trust. You are not prompted when downloading most content.

To establish a custom security level, click the Custom Level button to open the Security Settings dialog box, as shown in Figure 9-24. Click an option button to disable or enable an item or to specify that you be prompted before downloading a particular item, and then click OK.

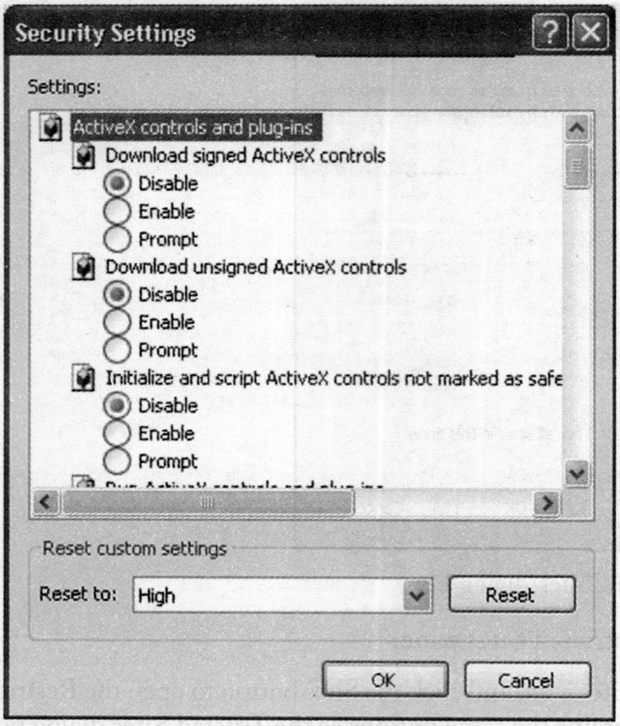

Figure 9-24 The Security Settings dialog box.

Protecting Your Privacy

Earlier in this chapter, we mentioned *cookies*—files that contain information about you and that are stored on your computer when you visit Web sites. To specify how you want to work with cookies, you use the options on the Privacy tab in the Internet Options dialog box shown in Figure 9-25.

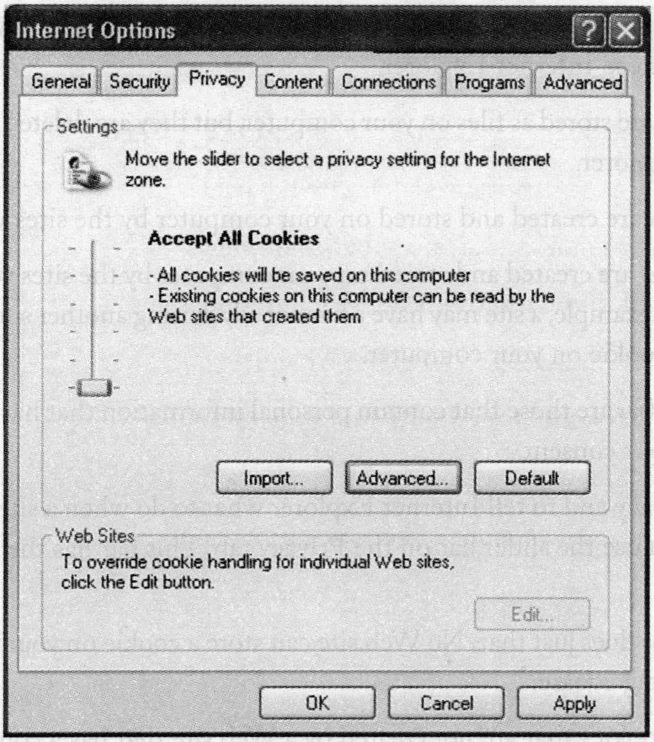

Figure 9-25 The Internet Options dialog box open at the Privacy tab.

Before we get into your choices, though, we need to look at the various kinds of cookies:

- *Persistent cookies* are stored as files on your computer, and they remain on your computer when you close Internet Explorer.
- *Temporary cookies* are stored as files on your computer, but they are deleted when you close Internet Explorer.
- *First-party cookies* are created and stored on your computer by the sites you visit.
- *Third-party cookies* are created and stored on your computer by the sites you visit or by other sites. For example, a site may have a banner advertising another site, and that site may store a cookie on your computer.
- *Unsatisfactory cookies* are those that contain personal information that has been collected without your consent.

To protect your privacy and to tell Internet Explorer what to do when a site attempts to store cookies, you use the slider bar on the Privacy tab. This bar has the following six settings:

- Block All Cookies does just that. No Web site can store a cookie on your computer or access an existing cookie.
- High blocks all cookies that are not created by a Web site that has a compact privacy policy and cookies that contain personal information that has been collected without your consent.

NOTE *A* compact privacy policy *is a statement in computer-readable form that outlines what personal information a Web site collects about you and how it does or does not disseminate that information.*

- Medium High blocks the following kinds of cookies:
  - Those created by Web sites that do not have a compact privacy policy.
  - Third-party cookies that include personal information collected without your explicit consent.
  - First-party cookies that include personal information collected without your implicit consent.

- Medium, the default setting, restricts first-party cookies that contain personal information collected without your consent and blocks the following kinds of cookies:
  - Those created by Web sites that do not have a compact privacy policy.
  - Third-party cookies that contain personal information collected without your implicit consent.
- Low restricts third-party cookies that do not have a compact privacy policy and third-party cookies that collect personal information without your implicit consent.
- Accept All Cookies saves all cookies on your computer and allows Web sites access to existing cookies saved on your computer.

Using the slider bar to restrict or block cookies applies the setting to all Web sites in the Internet zone. If you want to take a more specific approach, you use the other options in the Privacy tab. If you have a file of settings that you'd prefer to use instead of the settings available with the slider bar, click the Import button to open the Privacy Import dialog box. This dialog is really an Open dialog box in disguise and works exactly the same as an Open dialog box.

Another way to override the slider bar settings is to click the Advanced button to open the Advanced Privacy Settings dialog box, as shown in Figure 9-26. Click the Override Automatic Cookie Handling check box, and then apply the options you want for handling first-party and third-party cookies. If you want to allow session cookies, click that check box. When you've selected your options, click OK.

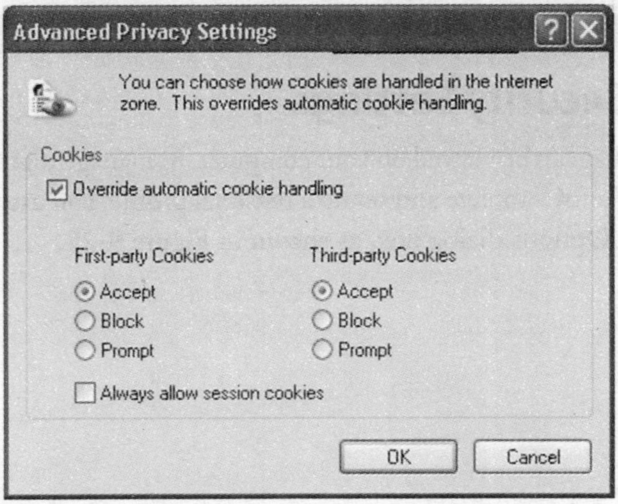

Figure 9-26 The Advanced Privacy Settings dialog box.

When you select any option on the slider bar except Accept All Cookies, you can set cookie options on a per-Web-site basis. Click the Edit button to open the Per Site Privacy Actions dialog box, which is shown in Figure 9-27. Enter the exact address of a Web site in the Address Of Web Site box, and then click Block or Allow. The name of the Web site and its setting will appear in the Managed Web Sites list. To remove a site from this list, select the site and then click the Remove button, or click Remove All to delete all sites.

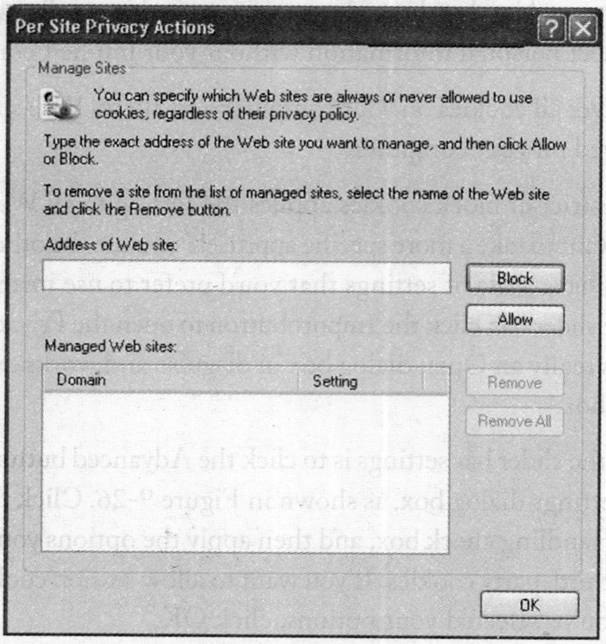

Figure 9-27 The Per Site Privacy Actions dialog box.

Establishing Other Security Settings

To specify the content that can be viewed on your computer, to manage digital certificates, and to configure AutoComplete and set up a personal profile, you use the Content tab in the Internet Options dialog box, as shown in Figure 9-28.

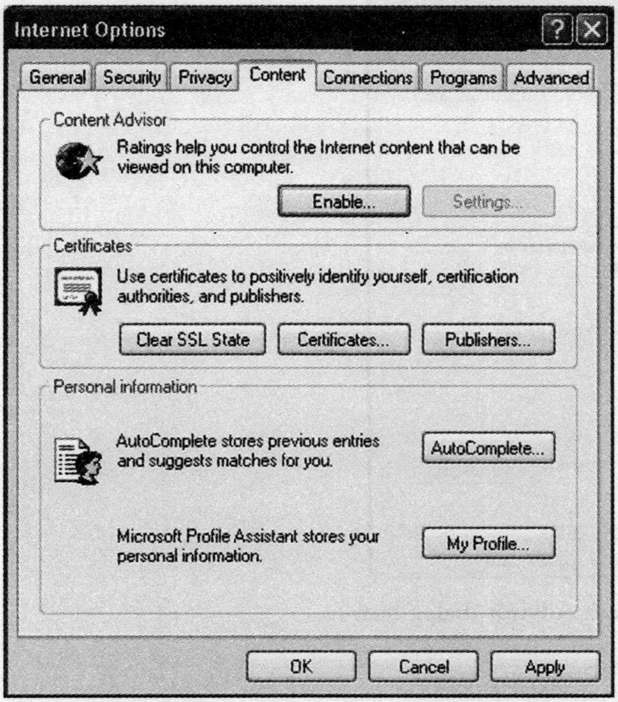

Figure 9-28 The Internet Options dialog box open at the Content tab.

Content Advisor is a feature that you can use to prevent access to certain sites that you consider inappropriate in your environment. By default, Content Advisor is set to the most conservative level; that is, if Content Advisor is enabled, you will be able to access only those sites that contain content that is the least likely to be offensive. To change this setting, you enable Content Advisor and then set up new viewing criteria. Of course, if Content Advisor is not enabled, your access is in no way restricted.

To enable the Content Advisor, follow these steps:

1. Open the Content Advisor dialog box, which is shown in Figure 9-29.

Click the Enable button.

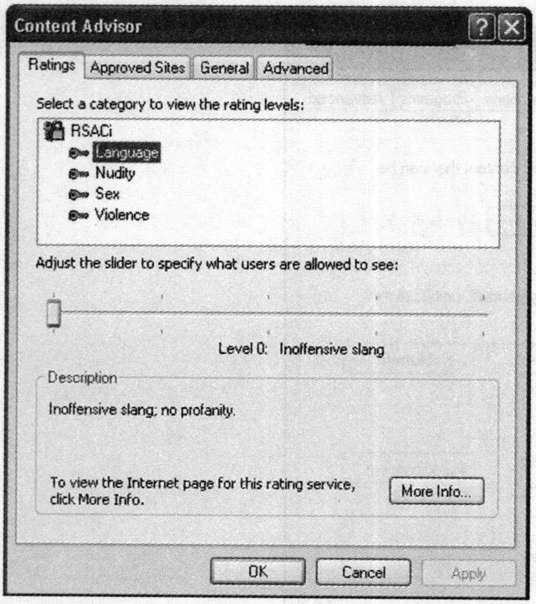

Figure 9-29 The Content Advisor dialog box.

2. **Configure your ratings.**

   Use the Content Advisor dialog box to configure your ratings and click OK when you're finished. The first time you do this, you'll be prompted for a password, as shown in Figure 9-30. Enter a password in the Password and Confirm Password boxes, and click OK. Now, anyone who wants to change the settings you specify must enter the password.

Figure 9-30 The Create Supervisor Password dialog box.

The ratings system in effect in Internet Explorer is that established by the Recreational Software Advisory Council and goes by the abbreviation RSACi. It is based on a system known as the Platform for Internet Content Selection (PICS). If Content Advisor is enabled and if you have set various rating levels, Internet Explorer first reads any PICS rating codes it finds in a page before opening that page. If the PICS rating exceeds the limit you've established, Internet Explorer does not open the page. To set a level for language, nudity, sex, or violence, select the category in the Ratings tab in the Content Advisor dialog box and then move the slider. You use the other three tabs in the Content Advisor dialog box to do the following:

- Click the Approved Sites tab to specify sites that can always be viewed or that can never be viewed, no matter how they are rated. Some businesses use this feature to prevent employees from accessing games sites, gaming sites, and so on.
- Click the General tab to specify that users can view unrated sites and that the supervisor can enter a password to let users view restricted content, to change the supervisor password, and to customize the rating system.
- Click the Advanced tab to view or modify the list of organizations that provide rating services.

A digital certificate is an electronic credential that verifies that you are who you say you are when connected to the Internet. Digital certificates are also used to guarantee the identity of a Web site or a downloaded program. You can acquire a digital certificate from a certificate publisher. One of the most popular is VeriSign, Inc., which you can find at *http://www.verisign.com*. To manage the digital certificates installed on your system and to specify certain software publishers as trustworthy, use the Certificates section of the Content tab in the Internet Options dialog box.

You'll also see a Clear SSL State button in the Certificates section. SSL stands for Secure Sockets Layer, and sometimes when you go to a secure site, you can ask for the SSL certificate to verify its existence. These certificates are saved on your computer until you reboot or click the Clear SSL State button to remove them.

Earlier this chapter mentioned the AutoComplete feature, which comes to your aid when you enter URLs. You can also use AutoComplete to automatically enter information you commonly supply at certain Web sites. To configure AutoComplete, click the AutoComplete button in the Content tab to open the AutoComplete Settings dialog box, as shown in Figure 9-31.

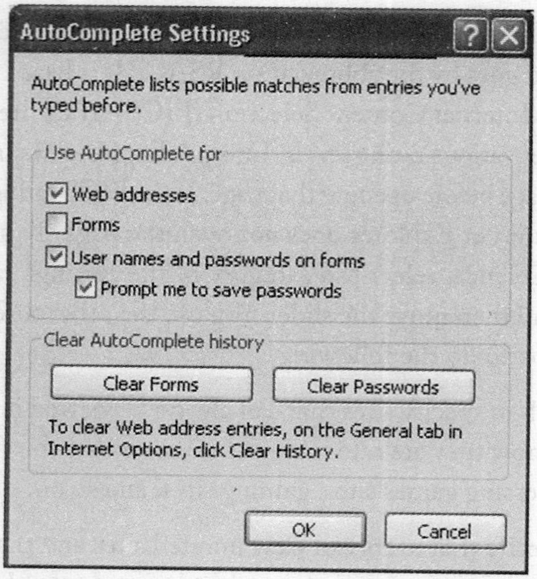

Figure 9-31 The AutoComplete Settings dialog box.

If you want to streamline the process of providing personal contact information to a Web site that requests it, you can set up a profile that will automatically be used. To do so, click the My Profile button in the Content tab to open the Address Book – Choose Profile dialog box. You use your Address Book to create a new entry or edit an existing one. When a Web site explicitly requests your personal information from the Profile Assistant (not that many sites do yet), Internet Explorer displays the information the site is requesting and asks your permission to send the information.

Modifying or Creating an Internet or Network Connection

You use the Connections tab, as shown in Figure 9-32, in the Internet Options dialog box to configure an Internet connection, dial-up settings, and local area network settings. In Chapter 7, we looked at how to create or modify an Internet connection using the New Connection Wizard. You can also start the New Connection Wizard by clicking the Setup button in the Connections tab.

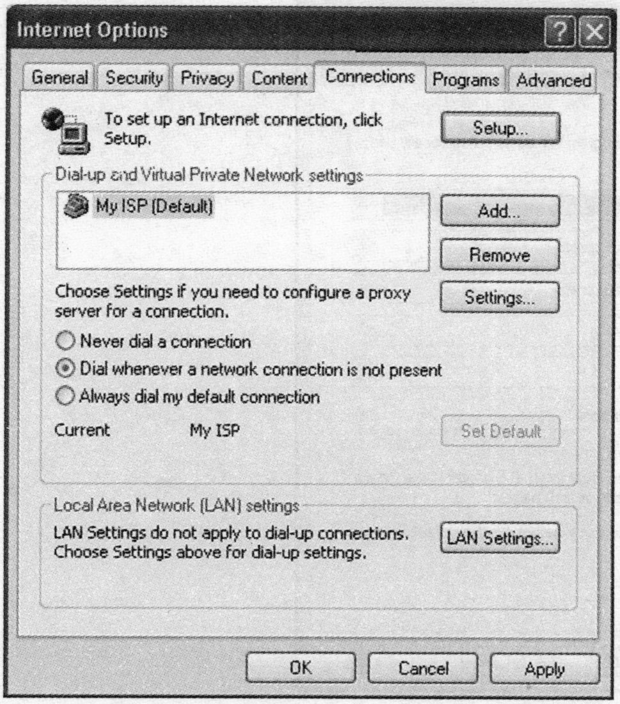

Figure 9-32 The Internet Options dialog box open at the Connections tab.

To add, remove, or change the settings for a dial-up connection, you use the buttons in the Dial-Up And Virtual Private Network Settings section. To add a connection, click Add to start the New Connection Wizard at the Type Of Connection screen. To remove a connection, select it and click Remove. To modify the settings for a connection, select it and click Settings to open the Settings dialog box for that connection. To modify the settings for a local area network, click LAN Settings to open the Local Area Network (LAN) Settings dialog box.

Specifying Programs to Use for Internet Services

E-mail, newsgroups, an Internet call, creation of a Web page, a calendar, and a contact list are all examples of Internet services, and you use the Programs tab in the Internet Options dialog box, as shown in Figure 9-33, to associate a program with a service. When you then want to access that service, the program you specify is always used.

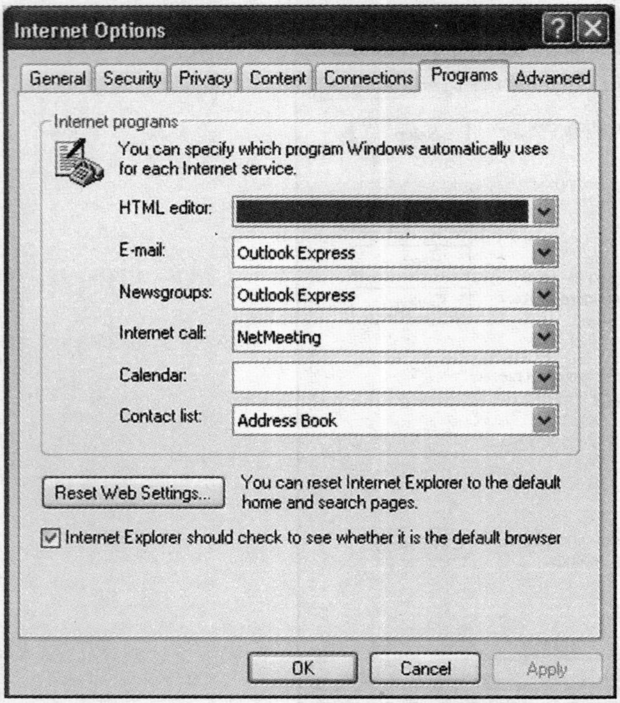

Figure 9-33 The Internet Options dialog box open at the Programs tab.

To change the associated program, click the down arrow in the list box for that service. To return to the programs that were assigned when you installed the operating system as well as the default start page, click the Reset Web Settings button. If you have more than one Web browser installed on your system, clear the check box at the bottom if you want to use another program as the default browser.

Specifying Advanced Options

Earlier in this chapter, we looked briefly at the Advanced tab in the Internet Options dialog box when specifying whether Internet Explorer prints background colors and images. You can also use the options on this tab to configure how Internet Explorer handles accessibility, browsing, HTTP settings, multimedia, searching from the Address bar, and security. Simply click a check box to enable a feature, or clear a check box to disable a feature. To return to the default settings, click the Restore Defaults button.

Summary

Of course, the most important thing about Internet Explorer is not how it works but how you can use it to access the resources that make you a more informed and better-equipped businessperson. You can certainly just point and click to your heart's desire, but you'll soon find yourself off track and probably wasting a good bit of time. Using the techniques described in this chapter, you can, for example, click a site from your Favorites list to go immediately to a site whose data you need to check every day or perhaps even more often (such as stock prices or weather conditions). You can quickly search for and find Web sites, business names and addresses, and all sorts of other business resources, and you can save the file, print it, and send it to a colleague or a client. You won't necessarily need to do all of these things every day, but you can refer to this chapter when a specific task presents itself.

Chapter 10

USING OUTLOOK EXPRESS

Featuring:

- Understanding How E-Mail Works
- Touring the Outlook Express Window
- Managing Messages
- Creating and Sending Messages
- Attaching Files to Messages
- Including a Personalized Signature
- Blocking Messages
- Using Identities
- Keeping Track of Contact Information
- Working with Newsgroups
- Customizing Outlook Express
- Taking Charge of Your Wired Office

Perhaps even more than the Web, electronic mail has become an essential business tool. Before the Internet was available commercially, we worked at companies that provided internal e-mail programs, and with all the right connections, you could access your office e-mail account from home. Within days, most new employees were so dependent on the e-mail system that they ceased to function if the server went down. And that was small potatoes compared with how the business world now relies on the Internet for e-mail.

Some business users consider e-mail both a blessing and a curse, and at the end of this chapter, you'll find some ideas about how to manage e-mail (and other components of your electronic office) rather than letting it manage you.

In this chapter, we look at how to use Microsoft Outlook Express. Outlook Express is an Internet standards e-mail reader, which means that you can use it to send and receive e-mail if you have an Internet e-mail account. An e-mail account is not the same thing as an account with an online information service, such as CompuServe or America Online. An Internet e-mail account provides services such as standards-based e-mail but does not provide services such as chat rooms, access to databases, conferences, and so on.

These days most Internet service providers (ISPs) provide you with an e-mail account as well as access to the Web. Before you can use Outlook Express to send and receive e-mail, you need to configure your e-mail account using the Internet Connection Wizard by following the instructions in Chapter 7.

Outlook Express is also a program that you can use to access newsgroups, and toward the end of this chapter, we'll look at how to use it for this purpose.

Understanding How E-Mail Works

You don't need to understand how e-mail works to use an e-mail program to send and receive messages. But if you know in general the steps involved in getting a message from your computer to another computer on the Internet, you'll become a more informed business user, and you'll have an idea of what's going on when you see, for example, a message that says "POP server unavailable."

After you create an e-mail message and click the Send button, your message travels the following route to get to its intended recipient:

- Your e-mail program, such as Outlook Express, contacts your ISP's computer and connects to an SMTP server program. SMTP stands for Simple Mail Transfer Protocol. The server program acknowledges that it has been contacted, and your e-mail program tells the server that it has a message it wants to send. The server program then says to send the message or to wait because it is busy.
- If it gets the green light, your e-mail program sends the message to the SMTP server and asks for confirmation.

- The server confirms that it has received the message and then asks the Domain Name Service (DNS) server for the best path through the Internet to the intended recipient.
- The DNS server replies with the best path, and the SMTP server sends the message on its way.
- When the message arrives at the recipient's SMTP server, it is transferred to a Post Office Protocol (POP), Internet Message Access Protocol (IMAP), or Hypertext Transfer Protocol (HTTP) mail server (such as Hotmail), which holds the message until the recipient requests it.
- When your recipient logs on to the Internet, opens his or her e-mail program, and checks for new mail, the message is downloaded to the recipient's computer.

Although this process sounds very involved, and technically it is, it can happen very quickly. We live in the United States and exchange messages with a colleague in Greece in a matter of minutes.

One exception to the process outlined earlier is America Online (AOL), the largest ISP in the United States. AOL uses proprietary protocols instead of the SMTP and POP protocols and then uses a gateway to translate the proprietary protocols into the standard e-mail protocols so that AOL users and users of standard e-mail programs can communicate. (A *gateway* is simply a software device that both transfers and converts information that originates from systems using different communication protocols, or rules.)

Touring the Outlook Express Window

You can open Outlook Express in the following ways:

- Click the Start button, and then click E-Mail.
- In Internet Explorer, click the Mail button on the Standard toolbar, and then click Read Mail or Read News.

Figure 10-1 shows what you'll see when you open Outlook Express the first time.

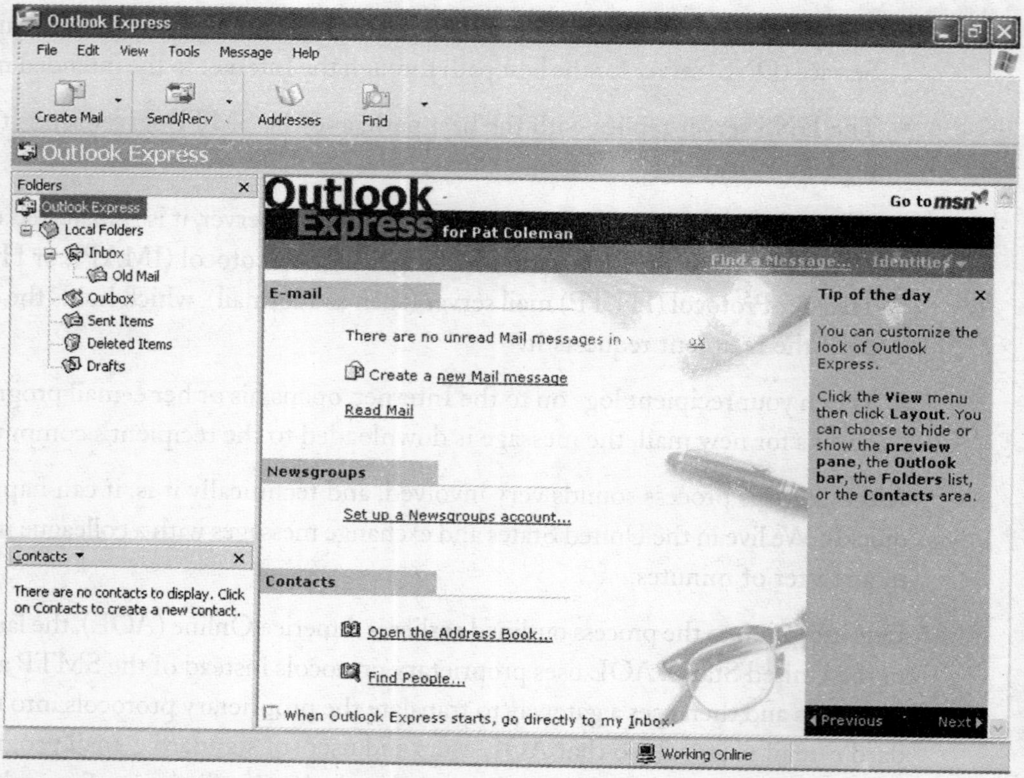

Figure 10-1 The opening screen in Outlook Express.

This window contains the usual Windows menu bar and toolbar. The Folders list is a tool for organizing messages and contains the following folders by default, although, as you will see, you can add your own folders to this list:

- The Inbox folder is the repository for newly received messages and messages that you haven't disposed of in some way.
- The Outbox folder contains messages that are ready to be sent.
- The Sent Items folder contains copies of messages that you have sent.
- The Deleted Items folder contains copies of messages that you have deleted. In other words, unless you tell Outlook Express to do otherwise, messages that you delete are not immediately removed but are placed in the Deleted Items folder.
- The Drafts folder contains messages that you are working on but aren't ready to be sent.

The Contacts list contains the names of people in your Address Book. For information on how to set up and use Address Book, see the section "Keeping Track of Contact Information," later in this chapter.

Managing Messages

From the Outlook Express Main main window, you can click the Read Mail link to open your Inbox folder and read messages. Figure 10-2 shows the Inbox folder in Preview Pane view. Message headers appear in the upper pane, and you select a message to open it in the lower pane. To view messages in a separate window rather than using the Preview pane, click the View menu, click Layout, and in the Window Layout Properties dialog box, clear the Show Preview Pane check box.

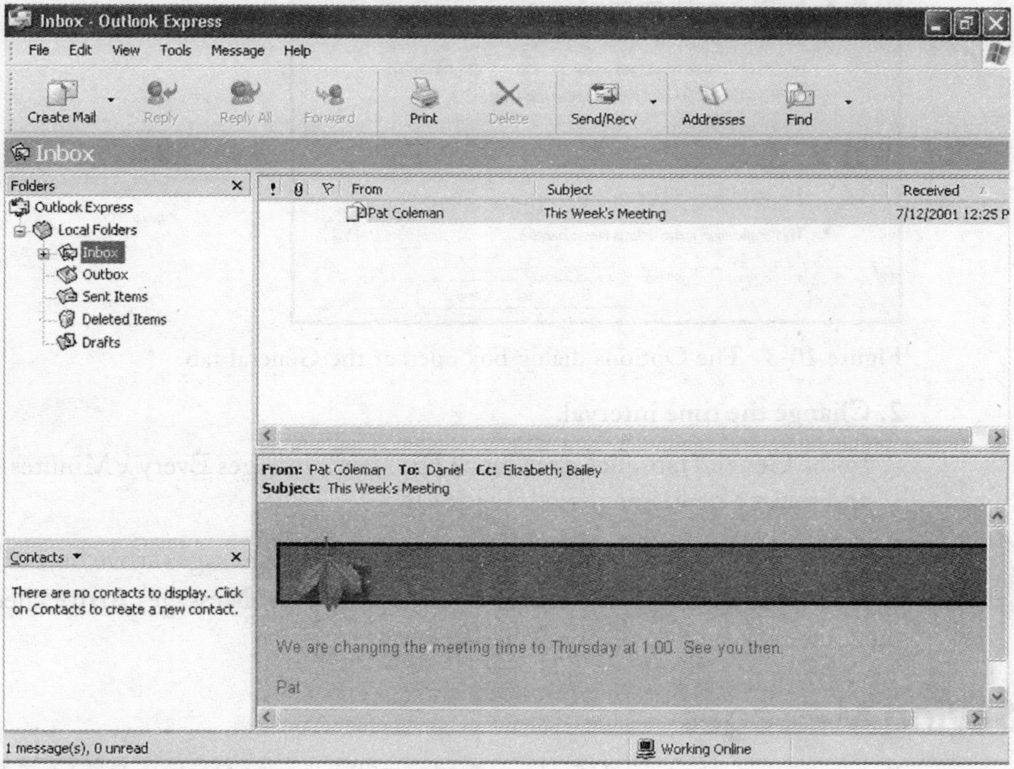

Figure 10-2 Reading a message in Preview Pane view.

If you are connected to the Internet, Outlook Express will automatically check the mail server for new messages and download them to your Inbox folder when you open Outlook Express. Thereafter, Outlook Express will check for new messages every 30 minutes as along as you are still connected to the Internet. If you want to check for messages more often or less frequently, follow these steps:

1. **Open the Options dialog box, which is shown in Figure 10-3.**

   Click the Tools menu, and then click Options.

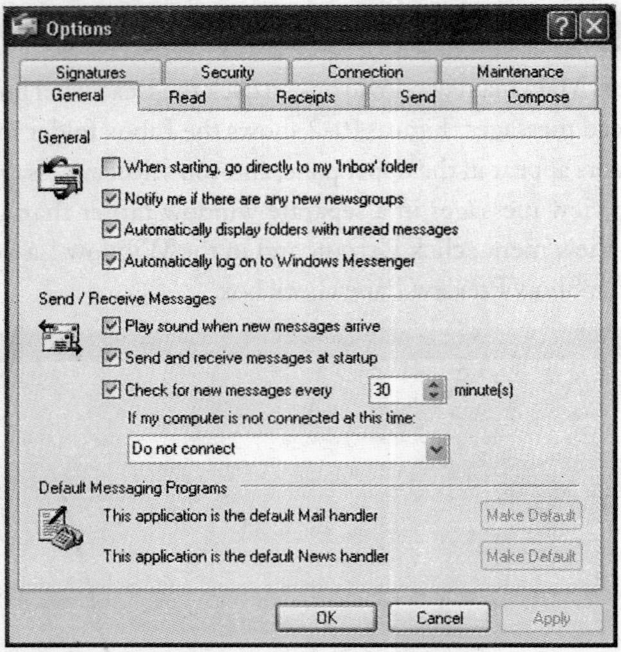

Figure 10-3 The Options dialog box open at the General tab.

2. **Change the time interval.**

   In the General tab, click the Check For New Messages Every *x* Minutes spin box, and select a new time period. Click OK.

By default, Outlook Express plays a sound when new messages arrive in your mailbox. If you prefer silence, clear the Play Sound When New Messages Arrive check box in the General tab of the Options dialog box.

Saving Messages

You can save messages in Windows Explorer folders or in Outlook Express folders, and you can also save attachments to messages. We'll look at attachments later in this chapter.

To save messages in Windows Explorer folders, open the message or select its header, and follow these steps:

1. **Open the Save Message As dialog box, which is shown in Figure 10-4.**

   Click the File menu, and then click Save As.

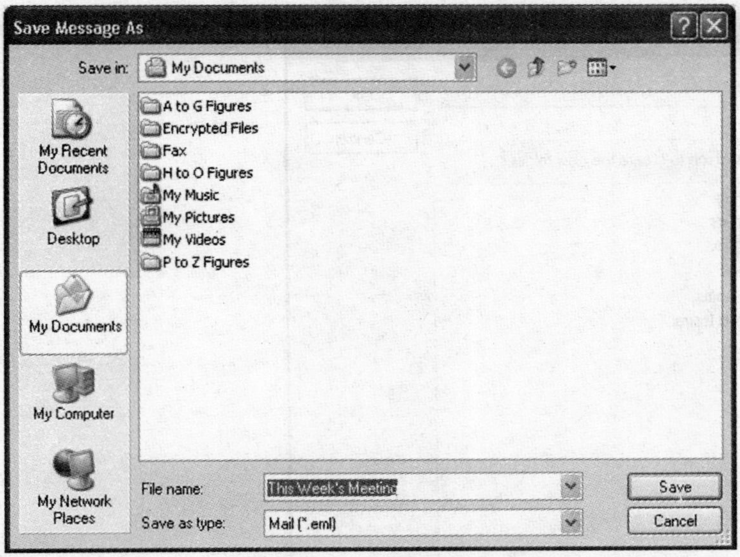

Figure 10-4 The Save Message As dialog box.

2. **Select a folder.**

   Select a folder, and then accept the filename that's suggested, or type a new filename.

3. **Select a file type.**

   In the Save As Type drop-down list box, choose how to save the message, and then click Save.

To save a message in an Outlook Express folder, simply drag its header to the folder. You can also create your own folders. For example, you might want to create a folder for a project and then place all correspondence related to that project in that folder. Or you might want to create a folder for a person and place all messages from that person in that folder. To create a new Outlook Express folder, follow these steps:

1. **Open the Create Folder dialog box, which is shown in Figure 10-5.**

   Click the File menu, click New, and then click Folder.

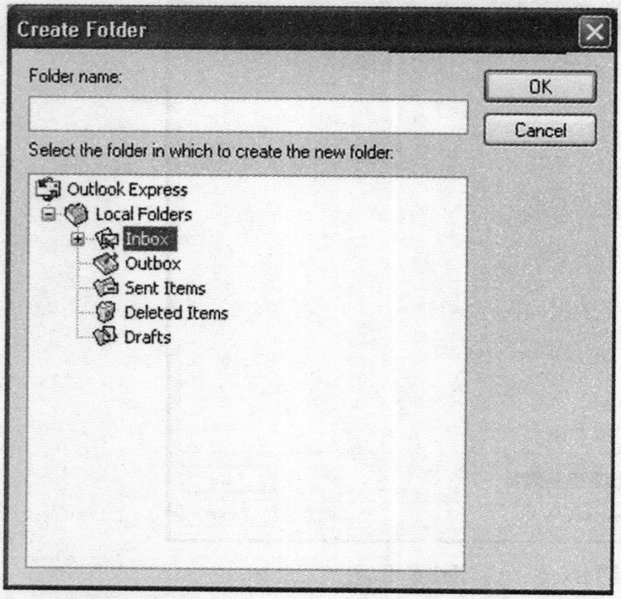

Figure 10-5 The Create Folder dialog box.

2. **Name the folder.**

   In the Folder Name box, enter a name for the folder.

3. **Select a folder in which to place the new folder.**

   You can place the folder as a main folder in the Local Folders list, or you can store it in any existing folder. Click OK.

Printing Messages

If you need a paper copy of a message, you can print it in the following ways:

- Select the header of the message, and click the Print button on the toolbar.
- Open the message, and then click the Print button in the Message window.
- Select the message or open the message, click the File menu, and then click Print.

Whichever method you use, you'll open the standard Windows Print dialog box.

Marking Messages

Although some of us may have a Pavlovian reaction to the mail notification alert, you don't need to read and process every message the instant it arrives in your Inbox. When you're checking mail, you can mark messages so that when you have time you can go back and deal with them. You can mark messages in the following ways:

- To identify a message as important, select the message header, click the Message menu, and click Flag Message to place a little red flag to the left of the header.
- If you've read a message but want to read it again later and respond, you can mark it as unread. Select the message header, click the Edit menu, and then click Mark As Unread. Now instead of an open envelope preceding the header, you'll see a closed envelope, and the header is in boldface.

Replying to Messages

To reply to a message from a single sender, you simply click the Reply button on the toolbar. If the message was sent to multiple recipients, you can reply to them as well as the sender by clicking the Reply All button. By default, Outlook Express places all the names of those you reply to in your Address Book—a quick and easy way to store e-mail addresses.

By default, Outlook Express includes the text of the original message in your reply. Sometimes this can be helpful, and at other times it can be a real nuisance, especially if you have to wade through several replies to get to the essence of the message. You have a couple of alternatives if you don't want the original message included in the reply:

- Click the Reply button, place your cursor in the body of the message, click the Edit menu, click Select All to highlight the message, and press the Delete key.
- Click the Tools menu, click Options to open the Options dialog box, click the Send tab, clear the Include Message In Reply check box, and click OK. Now, the message will never automatically be included in the reply.

Forwarding Messages

Sometimes it's handy to forward a message, and you can include your own comments in the forwarded message as well. As is the case with passing along anything that was created by somebody else, be sure that forwarding a message will not infringe on the original sender. Of course, some people maintain that you should never put anything in an e-mail message that you wouldn't want to see on the front page of the newspaper.

To forward a message, open it, click the Forward button, enter an e-mail address, add your comments if you want, and click the Send button.

Deleting Messages

You can delete a message in the following ways:

- Select the message header, and press the Delete key or click the Delete toolbar button.
- Open the message, and click the Delete toolbar button.

By default, deleted messages are placed in the Deleted Items folder, and they stay there until you manually delete them. To do so, select the Deleted Items folder, click the Edit menu, click Empty 'Deleted Items' Folder, and click Yes when you're asked if you want to delete these items.

To automatically clear the Deleted Items folder when you close Outlook Express, follow these steps:

1. **Open the Options dialog box.**

   Click the Tools menu, and then click Options.

2. **Open the Maintenance tab, which is shown in Figure 10-6.**

   Click the Maintenance tab, click the Empty Messages From The 'Deleted Items' Folder On Exit check box, and click OK.

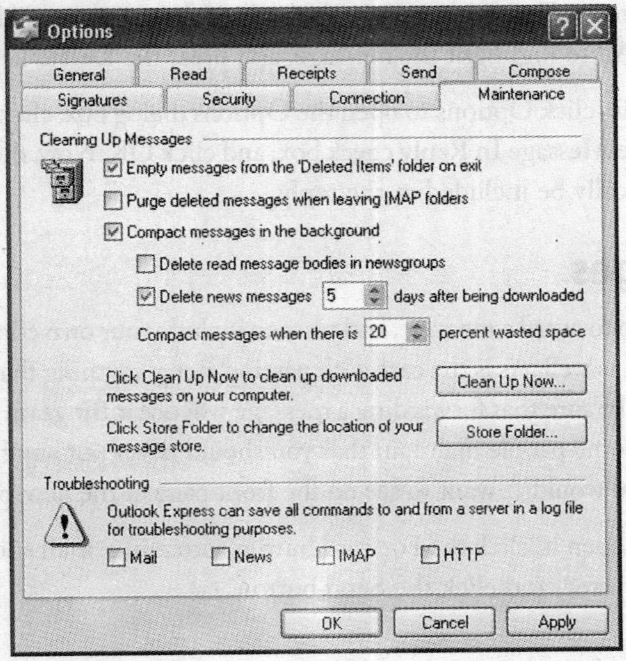

Figure 10-6 The Options dialog box open at the Maintenance tab.

Creating and Sending Messages

You can create a message in two formats: plain text and HTML. By default, Outlook Express uses HTML. As you'll see in the next section, not all e-mail programs can deal with HTML messages, so you'll want to use that with caution. To compose and send a message in plain text, follow these steps:

1. **Open the New Message window, which is shown in Figure 10-7.**

   Click the Create Mail button on the toolbar.

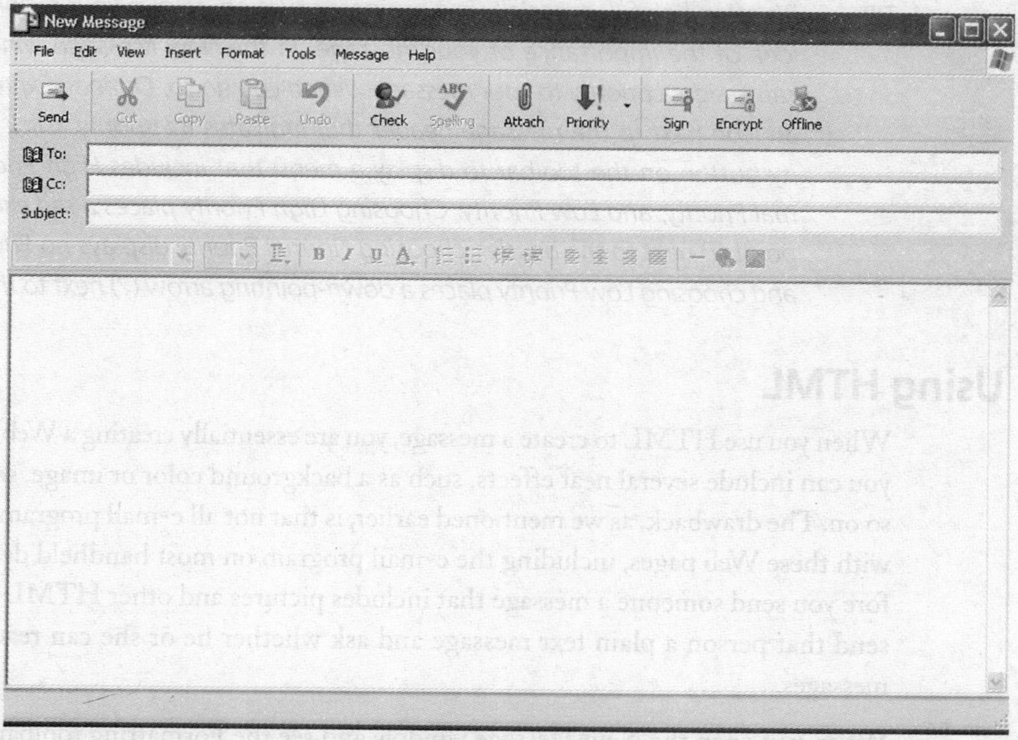

Figure 10-7 The New Message window.

2. **Specify plain text format.**

   Click the Format menu, and click Plain Text.

3. **Address and compose your message.**

   In the To line, enter an e-mail address, or click the icon to open your Address Book and select the address. Follow the same procedure to copy someone on the message. To send a blind carbon copy of the message, click the Cc icon to open the Select Recipients dialog box, select a name from the list, and click the Bcc button. Enter a subject in the Subject line, place the cursor in the message body, and type your message.

4. **Send the message.**

   Click the Send button.

By default, messages are sent immediately if you are connected to the Internet. If you want to wait and send a message later, click the File menu, and click Send Later. This places your message in the Outbox folder, and it is sent when you click the Send/Recv button. If you create messages offline (that is, when you aren't connected to the Internet), your messages are also stored in the Outbox folder.

TIP *It's often helpful, especially in a business situation, to give your recipient some idea of the importance of your message. In the New Message window, you can assign a priority to your message. When you do so, Outlook Express places an icon next to the message header that indicates its priority. Click the Priority button on the toolbar to display a menu that includes High Priority, Normal Priority, and Low Priority. Choosing High Priority places a red exclamation point (!) next to the header, choosing Normal Priority displays no Priority icon, and choosing Low Priority places a down-pointing arrow (?) next to the header.*

Using HTML

When you use HTML to create a message, you are essentially creating a Web page, and you can include several neat effects, such as a background color or image, sound, and so on. The drawback, as we mentioned earlier, is that not all e-mail programs can deal with these Web pages, including the e-mail program on most handheld devices. Before you send someone a message that includes pictures and other HTML elements, send that person a plain text message and ask whether he or she can read HTML messages.

When you open the New Message window and see the Formatting toolbar (see Figure 10-7), you know you're set up to compose a message in HTML. The Formatting toolbar contains many of the tools you see and use in your word processor. You can use it to do the following, among other things, in your message:

- Insert a bulleted list.
- Add effects such as boldface, italics, underline, and font color.
- Insert a numbered list.
- Format paragraphs as flush left, flush right, or centered.

- Insert a horizontal line.
- Insert a picture.
- Specify a font and font size.

Figure 10-8 shows an e-mail message that contains HTML elements.

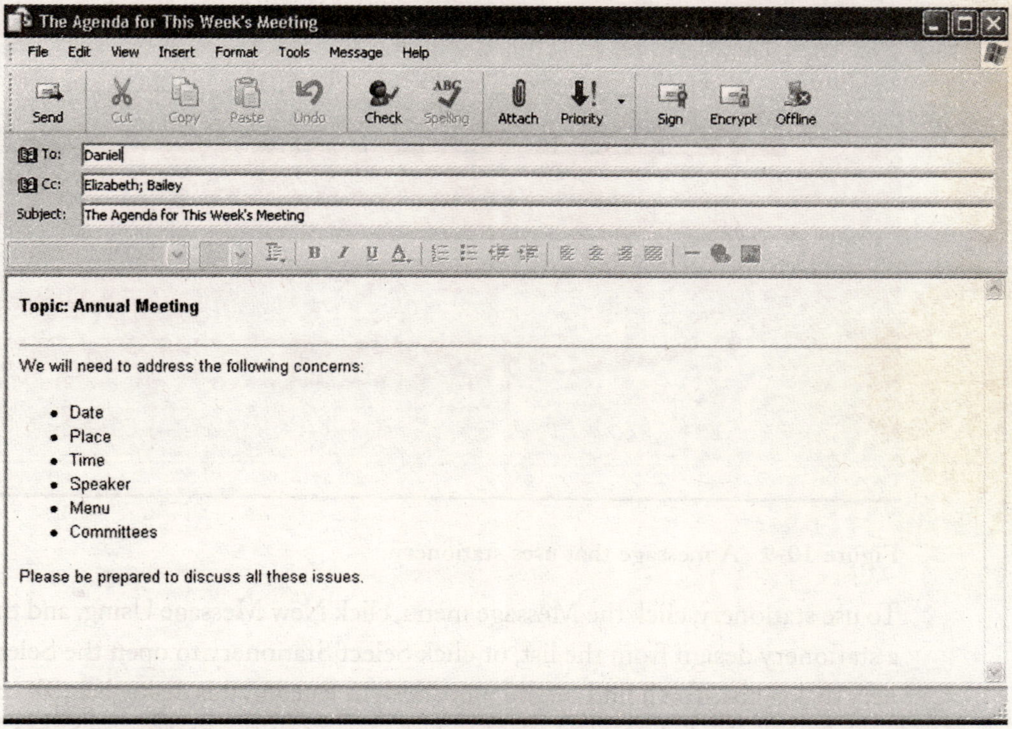

Figure 10-8 An e-mail message composed in HTML.

Using Stationery

You can also liven up your messages using stationery, or you can create your own stationery. Figure 10-9 shows a message that uses stationery that's included with Outlook Express.

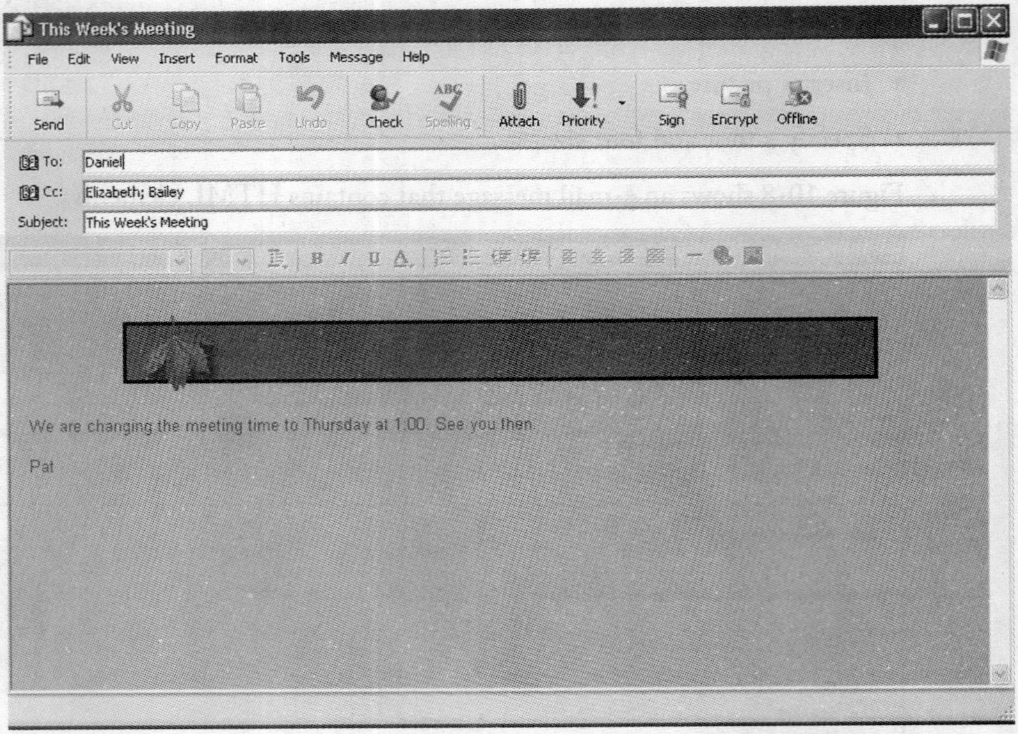

Figure 10-9 A message that uses stationery.

To use stationery, click the Message menu, click New Message Using, and then select a stationery design from the list, or click Select Stationery to open the Select Stationery dialog box. You'll find several more designs listed in this dialog box. To create your own stationery, click the Create New button to start the Stationery Setup Wizard.

Attaching Files to Messages

Earlier in this chapter, we mentioned that you can save files that are attached to messages. Obviously, you can also attach files to messages. Before getting into the details, though, we need to remind you that some serious computer viruses make the rounds via attachments to e-mail. Many businesses would cease to function these days if they couldn't e-mail files to colleagues and clients, so abandoning the use of file attachments is not an option. To be on the safe side, install virus protection on your system and configure it so that it will check all attachments for viruses before you open the files. If you don't have virus protection software, we recommend not opening an attachment if you don't know the source; just select the message header, and press the Delete key.

And we'd say to be particularly wary of an attachment that appears to have been forwarded, and forwarded, and forwarded.

When you receive a message that has a file attached to it, you'll see a paper-clip icon preceding the header. When you open the message, you'll see the filename of the attachment in the Attach line. If the file is in a format that a program on your computer can read, simply double-click the filename of the attachment to open it. To save the attachment, follow these steps:

1. **Open the Save Attachments dialog box.**

   Click the File menu, and click Save Attachments.

2. **Save the file.**

   In the Save To box, specify a folder into which to save the file, and click the Save button.

To attach a file to a message you are composing, follow these steps:

1. **Open the Insert Attachment dialog box, as shown in Figure 10-10.**

   Click the Insert menu, and click File Attachment.

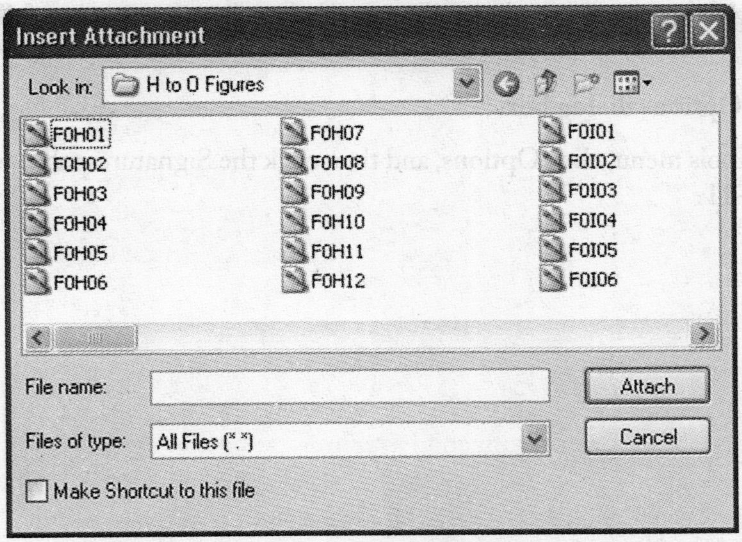

Figure 10-10 The Insert Attachment dialog box.

2. **Attach the file.**

   Enter the filename in the File Name box or browse to find it, select it, and then click Attach.

Your message now contains the name of the file in the Attach line.

When you attach a large file to an e-mail message, you'll want to compress it so that it transfers faster (if the file is not already compressed). To compress a file, right-click it in the Insert Attachment dialog box, choose Send To from the shortcut menu, and then click Compressed Folder. You'll now see a zipped icon in the file list. Simply select this file to attach to your message, and then click the Attach button. The recipient of your compressed file can uncompress the file and read it even if he or she has a different zip compression program. (For more information about compressed files and folders, see Chapter 2.)

Including a Personalized Signature

Many people never bother to sign their e-mail messages. After all, their name appears in the From line. Others create elaborate signatures that are automatically appended to all messages. Your business or organization may, in fact, have guidelines about what you should include in a signature. It's common to include your name, title, the name of your organization, perhaps its physical address, and your phone number.

To create a signature that is automatically appended to all your messages, follow these steps:

1. **Open the Options dialog box.**

   Click the Tools menu, click Options, and then click the Signatures tab, as shown in Figure 10-11.

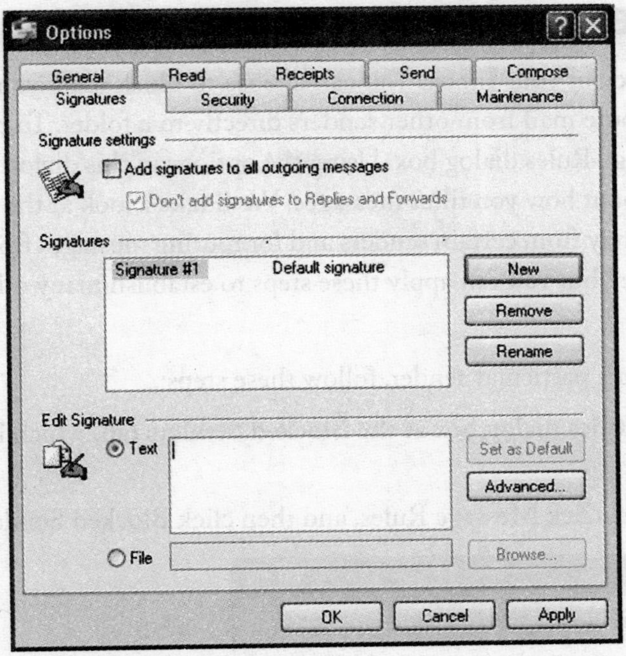

Figure 10-11 Creating a signature.

2. **Create a signature.**

   Click New, and then in the Text box, enter your contact information. If you have a file that contains the information you want in your signature, click the File option button, and then click Browse to locate the file.

3. **Specify the e-mail accounts for which you'll use this signature.**

   Click the Advanced button to open the Advanced Signature Settings dialog box. If you have a home e-mail account and a business e-mail account, for example, you might want to specify a different signature for each. Select the account, and click OK.

4. **Specify which messages will use the signature.**

   If you want the signature attached to all outgoing messages, click the corresponding check box. If you don't want the signature automatically added to all messages, leave this check box cleared. To add the signature to selected messages, in the New Message window, click the Insert menu, and then click Signature. When you have made your selections, click OK.

Blocking Messages

You are not at the mercy of your Inbox. You can choose to block mail from certain senders, and you can route mail from other senders directly to a folder. To do any of this, you use the Message Rules dialog box. Using the options in this dialog box, you can get very detailed about how you filter messages. We'll take a look at the steps for blocking messages entirely from certain senders and for routing messages from a particular person to a folder, but you can apply these steps to establish many other message rules.

To block messages from a particular sender, follow these steps:

1. **Open the Message Rules dialog box at the Blocked Senders tab, which is shown in Figure 10-12.**

   Click the Tools menu, click Message Rules, and then click Blocked Senders List.

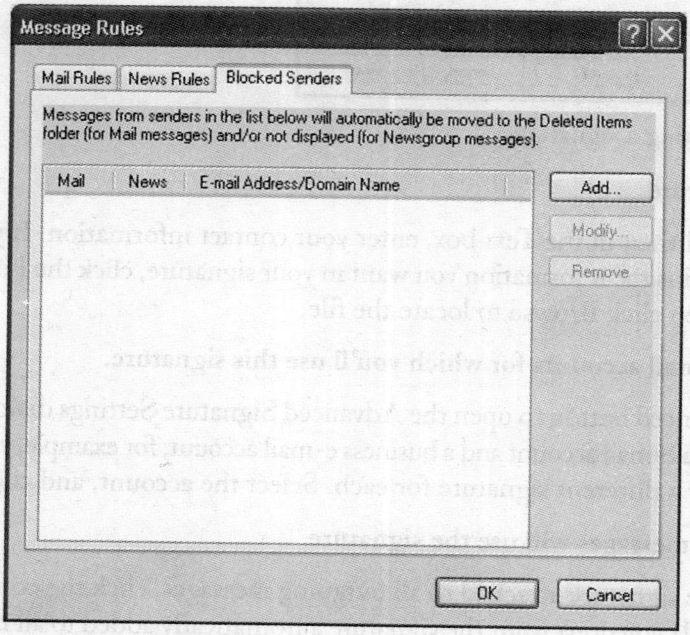

Figure 10-12 The Message Rules dialog box open at the Blocked Senders tab.

2. **Open the Add Sender dialog box, which is shown in Figure 10-13.**

   Click the Add button in the Message Rules dialog box.

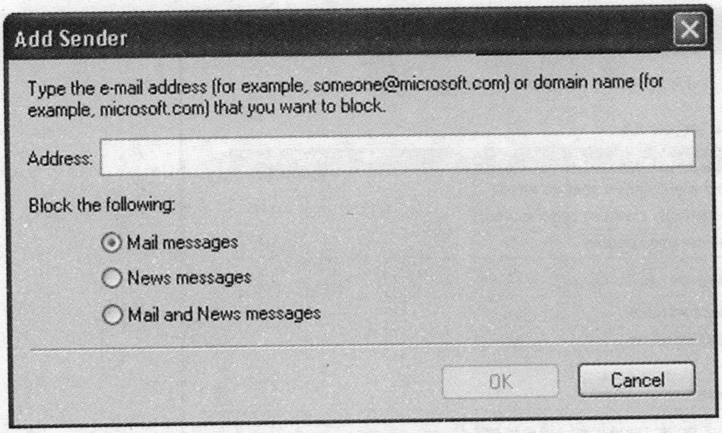

Figure 10-13 The Add Sender dialog box.

3. Specify who and what you want to block.

In the Address box, enter the e-mail address of the sender you want to block, and then select whether you want to block mail messages, news messages, or both. Click OK, and then click OK again back in the Message Rules dialog box.

Now all messages from that e-mail address will go immediately to your Deleted Items folder when they are downloaded to your system.

To establish a rule that sends all mail from a specific person to a specific Outlook Express folder, follow these steps:

1. Open the New Mail Rule dialog box, which is shown in Figure 10-14.

Click the Tools menu, click Message Rules, and then click Mail.

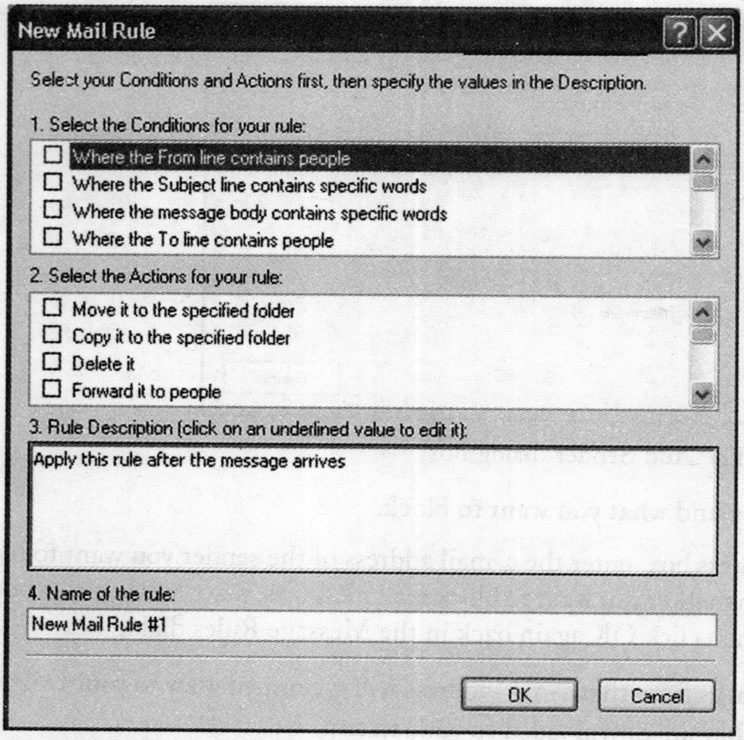

Figure 10-14 The New Mail Rule dialog box.

2. **Specify the conditions and actions for your new rule.**

   In the Select The Conditions For Your Rule section, click the Where The From Line Contains People check box, and in the Select The Actions For Your Rules section, click the Move It To The Specified Folder check box. You'll now see links in the Rule Description section that you can click to specify the person and the folder.

3. **Specify the person.**

   Click the Contains People link to open the Select People dialog box, as shown in Figure 10-15. Enter the e-mail address of the person, or select it from your Address Book, and click Add.

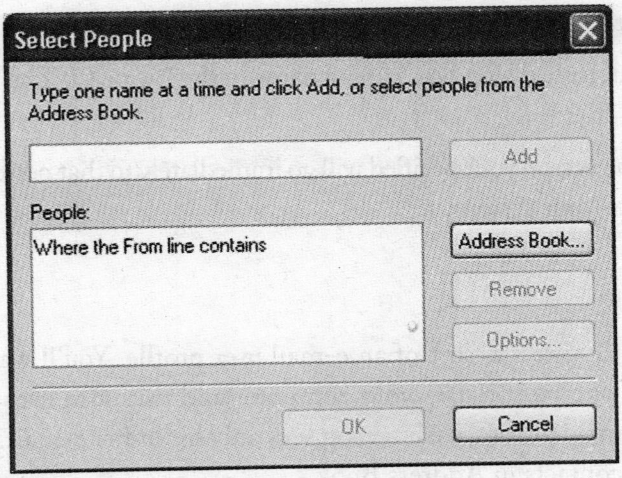

Figure 10-15 The Select People dialog box.

4. Specify the folder.

Click the Specified link to open the Move dialog box, as shown in Figure 10-16. Create a new folder, or select an existing folder, and click OK.

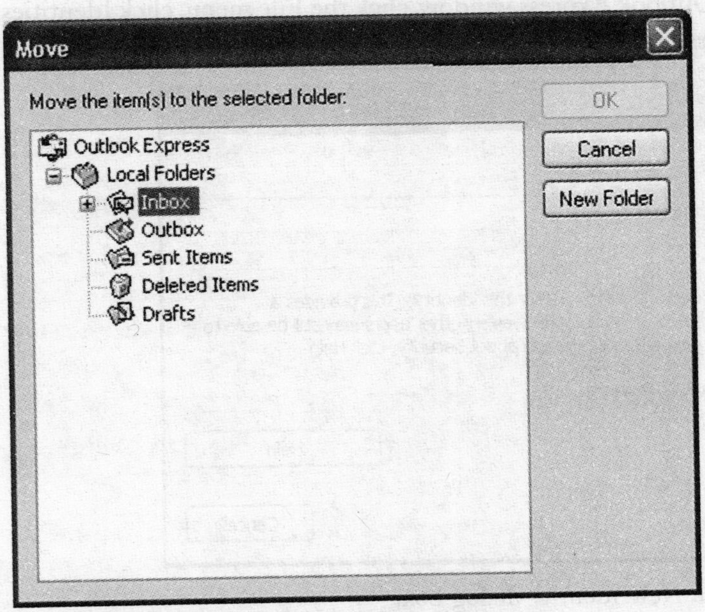

Figure 10-16 The Move dialog box.

5. **Name your new rule.**

   Back in the New Mail Rule dialog box, enter a name in the Name Of The Rule box, and click OK.

Now all the mail from the person you specified will go immediately to that person's folder when it's downloaded to your system.

Using Identities

An identity in Outlook Express is sort of an e-mail user profile. You'll want to use identities if more than one person uses your computer and thus also uses Outlook Express. When you set up identities, each person sees only his or her e-mail messages and has his or her own contacts in Address Book.

When you install Outlook Express, you are set up as the main identity. To set up other identities, follow these steps:

1. **Open the New Identity dialog box, which is shown in Figure 10-17.**

   In the main Outlook Express window, click the File menu, click Identities, and then click Add New Identity.

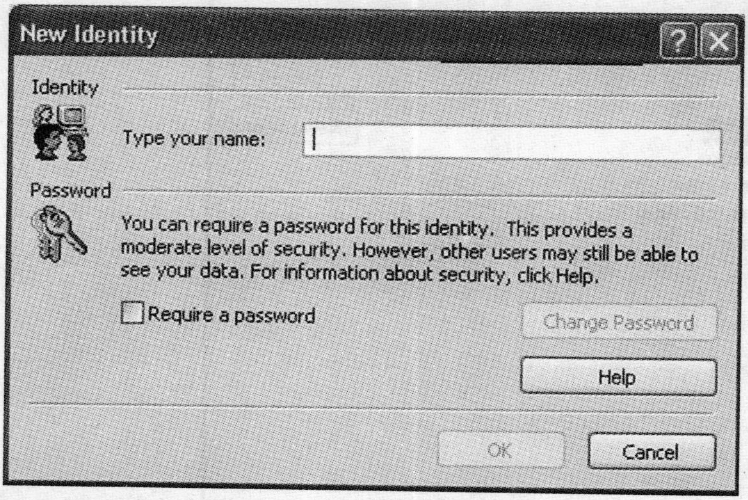

Figure 10-17 The New Identity dialog box.

2. **Specify a name and, optionally, a password for this identity.**

   In the Type Your Name box, enter a name for the new identity. If you want password protection enabled, click the Require A Password check box, which opens the Enter Password dialog box. Type the password twice—once in the New Password box and again in the Confirm New Password box—and then click OK.

The name of the new identity will appear in the Identities list in the Manage Identities dialog box, and you'll be asked whether you want to switch to the new identity now. If not, click No, and then click Close in the Manage Identities dialog box. The first time you log on as the new identity, you'll be asked for some information about your Internet connection.

To switch from one identity to another, follow these steps:

1. Open the Switch Identities dialog box, which is shown in Figure 10-18.

Click the File menu, and then click Switch Identity.

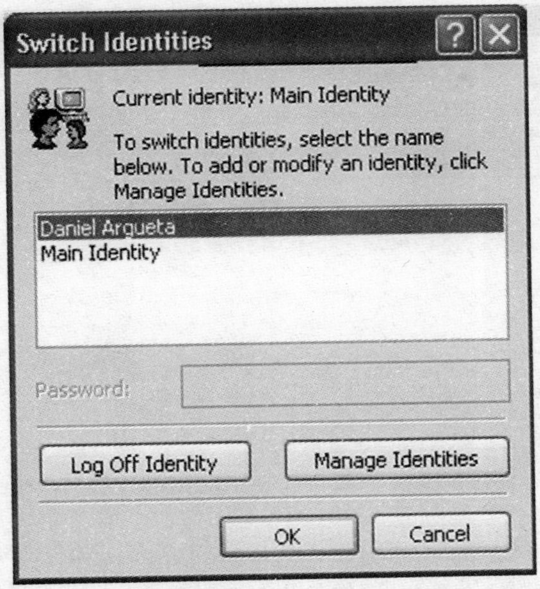

Figure 10-18 The Switch Identities dialog box.

2. Select the identity.

Select an identity from the list, enter a password if required, and click OK.

Once you set up more than one identity, you'll be asked to select an identity when you open Outlook Express.

Keeping Track of Contact Information

Earlier in this chapter, you learned that an easy way to enter an e-mail address in Outlook Express is to add it from your Address Book. This section gives you an overview of Address Book and shows you how to set it up to quickly locate contact information and to set up group, or distribution, lists.

You can open Address Book in a couple of ways:

- From the desktop, click the Start button, click All Programs, click Accessories, and then click Address Book.
- In Outlook Express, click the Addresses button on the toolbar in the Main window, or in the New Message window, click the To button (which opens the Select Recipients dialog box in Address Book).

Figure 10-19 shows an empty Address Book window, ready for you to add contact information. Notice that this Address Book is for the main identity.

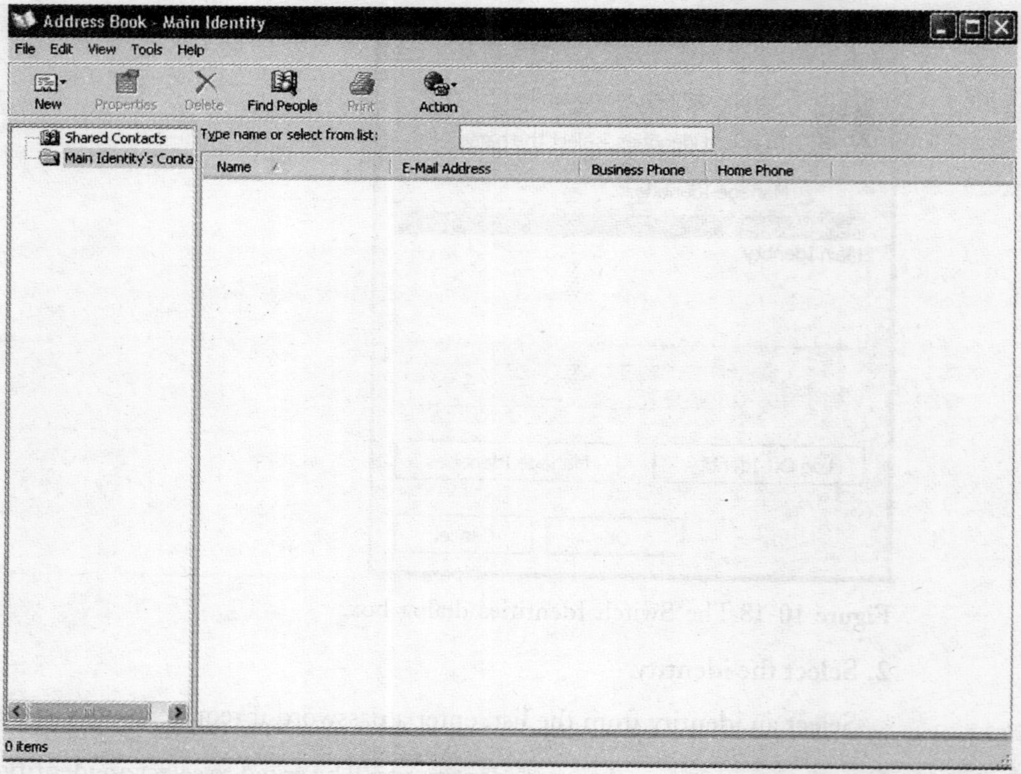

Figure 10-19 An empty Address Book window.

Adding Information for an Individual

To add contact information for an individual, open Address Book and follow these steps:

1. Open the Properties dialog box, which is shown in Figure 10-20.

Click the New button on the toolbar, and then click New Contact.

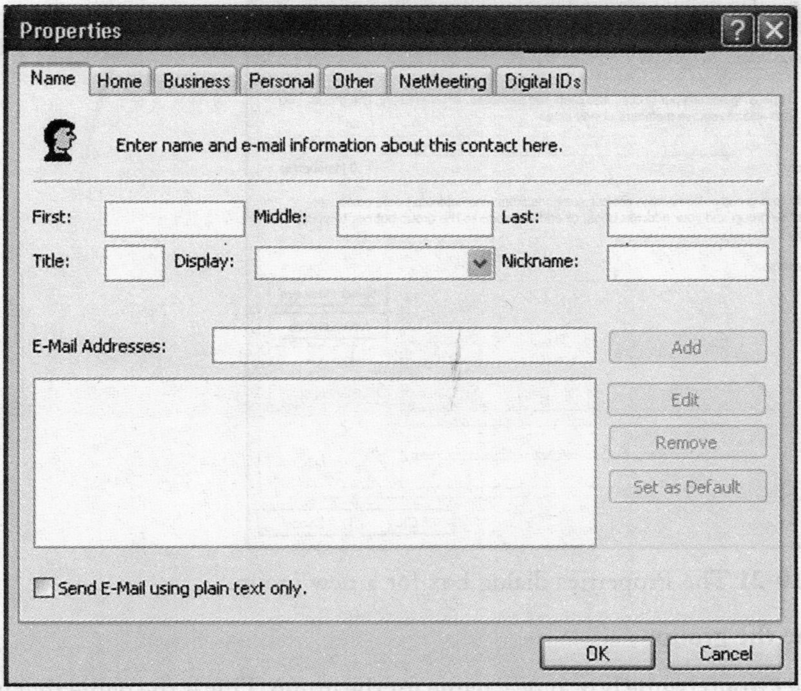

Figure 10-20 The Properties dialog box for a new contact.

2. **Add information for this person.**

   Use the Name, Home, Business, Personal, Other, NetMeeting, and Digital IDs tabs to add as much or as little information as you want. Press the Tab key to move from one box to another in a tab.

3. **Close the Properties dialog box.**

   Click the Close button. You'll see the new contact listed in the Address Book window. To send mail to this new contact, click the To button in the New Message window, double-click the name, and click OK.

Setting Up a Distribution List

In Address Book, a distribution list is called a *group*. To set up a group, follow these steps:

1. **Open the Properties dialog box for the new group, which is shown in Figure 10-21.**

   In Address Book, click the New button on the toolbar, and then click New Group.

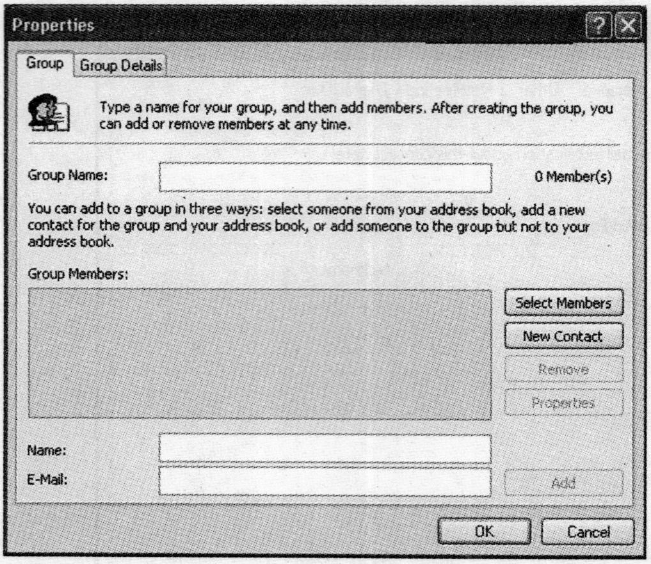

Figure 10-21 The Properties dialog box for a new group.

2. **Name the group.**

   In the Group Name box, type a name for the group. This is the name that will appear in the list in the main Address Book window.

3. **Add members to the group.**

   You can add members in the following ways:

   - Click the Select Members button to open the Select Group Members dialog box, select a name from the list, click the Select button, and then click OK.
   - Click the New Contact button to open the Properties dialog box for a new contact, enter contact information, and click OK to add a member to the group and to your Address Book.
   - In the Name and E-Mail boxes at the bottom of the window, enter information to add someone to the group but not to your Address Book.

   When you're finished, click OK.

The group name now appears in boldface in the main Address Book window.

Finding People

Using Address Book, you can find contact information for people using directory services such as Bigfoot Internet Directory Service, WhoWhere Internet Directory Service, and so on, if you are connected to the Internet. To do so, follow these steps:

1. **Open the Find People dialog box, which is shown in Figure 10-22.**

   In Address Book, click the Find People button on the toolbar.

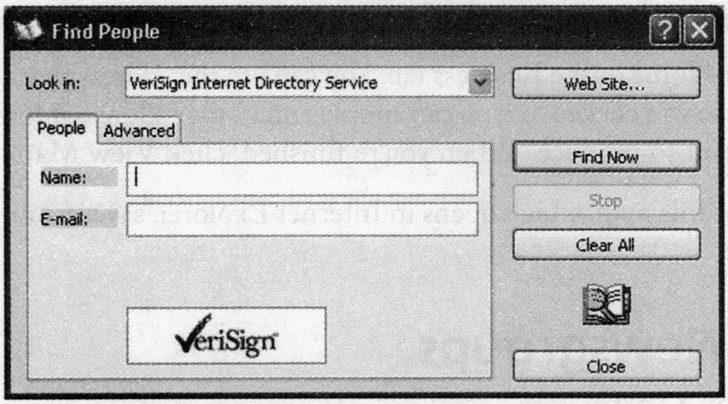

Figure 10-22 The Find People dialog box.

2. **Select a directory service.**

   Click the Look In drop-down list box.

3. **Enter some information.**

   In the People tab, fill in the information you know about this person, and then click Find Now.

Printing Your Address Book

You can print the contents of your Address Book in three formats:

- Memo prints all the information you have stored.
- Business Card prints the information you'd typically find on a business card.
- Phone List prints only the phone numbers.

To print in one of these formats, click the Print button to open the Print dialog box, select a print range, select a print style (Memo, Business Card, or Phone List), specify the number of copies, and click Print.

Creating and Printing a Map

If your organization is having an off-site retreat, if you're inviting your employees for dinner at your new house, or if you just need directions to a business meeting, you can use Address Book to create and print a map to the location. To do so, be sure you are connected to the Internet, and then follow these steps:

1. **Open the Properties dialog box.**

   In the Address Book window, double-click an entry in your Address Book.

2. **Enter an address.**

   Click either the Home or the Business tab. You can use the address that's stored for the person's name you clicked, or you can simply enter other address information for the map you want to produce. When you're finished, click View Map.

Now you can print this map, which opens in Internet Explorer, save it, or e-mail it to someone.

Working with Newsgroups

You can also use Outlook Express to access newsgroups. A newsgroup is not an electronic gathering of people who meet to discuss current events, but a collection of articles about a specific topic. The primary, but not only, source of newsgroups is Usenet, a worldwide distributed discussion system consisting of newsgroups with names that are classified hierarchically by topic. For example, alt.business.accounting is, theoretically, a newsgroup that discusses accounting subjects and practices. The first part of the name represents the largest hierarchical category, and the name gets more specific from left to right. Table 10-1 lists the major top-level newsgroup categories and explains what topics each discusses.

NEWSGROUP	WHAT IT DISCUSSES
alt	Free-for-all subjects outside the main structure of the other primary newsgroups.
comp	Computer science and related topics, including operating systems, hardware, artificial intelligence, and graphics.
misc	Anything that does not fit into one of the other categories.
news	Information on Usenet and newsgroups.
rec	Recreational activities such as hobbies, the arts, movies, and books.
sci	Scientific topics such as math, physics, and biology.
soc	Social issues and cultures.
talk	Controversial subjects such as gun control, abortion, religion, and politics.

Table 10-1 The major newsgroups.

In the previous paragraph, we used the word *theoretically*. In the early days of the Internet, newsgroups and Usenet were widely supported by educators, academicians, computer scientists, and other similar professionals. These days newsgroups seem to have degenerated into venues for get-rich-quick schemes and for discussion of topics that most of us in the business world would consider unseemly, whether at home or at work.

Thus, a caveat is in order. Newsgroups can be an excellent way to quickly get up-to-date opinions and information about a number of topics, such as computer hardware and software recommendations. However, most business users will find that they rarely use newsgroups except when searching for answers to specific questions that can't be found on the Web.

Setting Up a Newsgroup Account

Before you can access and read newsgroups, you need to set up a news account with your ISP. You access newsgroups by accessing the server on which they are stored. Get the name of your ISP's news server, and then follow these steps to set up an account:

1. **Start the Internet Connection Wizard.**

   In the main Outlook Express window, click Set Up A Newsgroups Account.

2. **Choose a name.**

   In the Your Name screen, shown in Figure 10-23, enter the name that you want displayed when you post a message to a newsgroup. You can use your own, real name, or you can use an alias if you want to remain anonymous. Click Next.

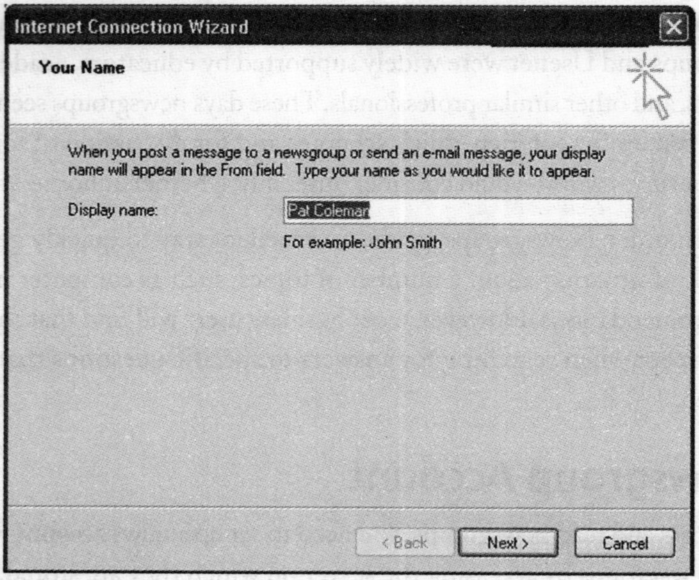

Figure 10-23 Enter your real name or an alias.

3. Enter your e-mail address.

In the Internet News E-Mail Address screen, shown in Figure 10-24, enter your e-mail address. If you don't want others in a group sending you e-mail, you can enter a fake e-mail address here. Check with your ISP first though, because some ISPs have policies prohibiting this practice. Click Next.

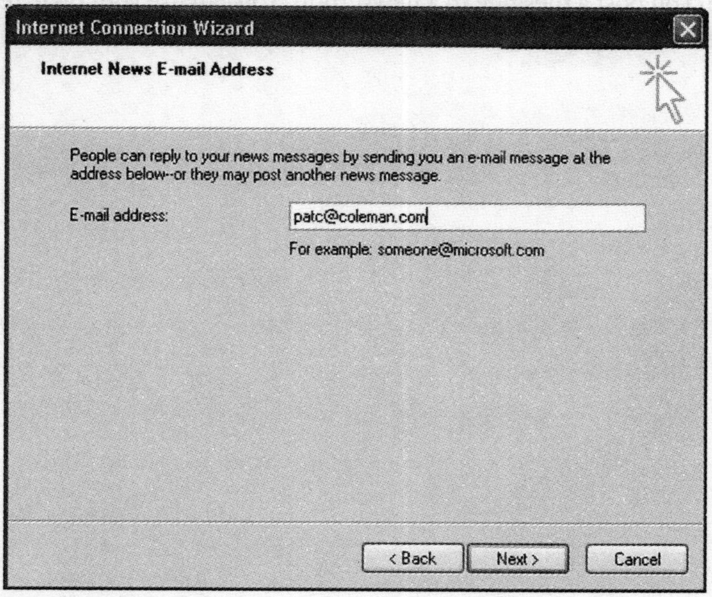

Figure 10-24 Enter your real e-mail address or a fake address.

TIP *Many people append the term* nospam *to their real e-mail address to prevent unscrupulous companies from adding them to a junk mail list. People that want to reply to your postings will need to manually remove the nospam from your e-mail address before replying.*

4. Enter the name of your news server.

In the Internet News Server Name screen, enter the name of the news server that you obtained from your ISP. This name will be something like *news.tw.net*. If your news server requires a special log-on in addition to your primary log on address, click the My News Server Requires Me To Log On check box. You will then need to enter this information in the next screen. If you don't select this check box, click Next, and then click Finish.

Connecting to Newsgroups

After you set up your news account, you are asked if you want to download the list of newsgroups from your ISP's server. Click Yes. While the list downloads, you'll see the dialog box.

This could take a while depending on the speed of your Internet connection—newsgroups number in the tens of thousands. But only the names are downloaded; the contents remain on the news server until you specifically access a newsgroup. When the list has downloaded, you'll see the Newsgroup Subscriptions dialog box.

Finding a Topic of Interest

You can select a newsgroup to read by scrolling this list (a time-consuming task) or by searching on a term.

With our earlier caveat in mind, enter a search term in the Display Newsgroups Which Contain box, and then simply wait. Soon you'll see a list of newsgroups whose names contain the search term. To read a newsgroup, select it and then click Go To. If you find a group that seems to have value for your business or profession, you can subscribe to it. Subscribing simply means creating a subfolder for a particular newsgroup in your news folder.

When you open a newsgroup by clicking Go To, a list of messages posted to this group opens in Outlook Express. Click a subject line in the top pane to open the message in the lower pane.

Posting to a Newsgroup

Replying to a newsgroup article or sending a message to a newsgroup is known as *posting*. To send an original message to a newsgroup, open the newsgroup and then click the New Post button. The New Message window will open with the group's name in the To line. To reply via e-mail to the author of a post, click the Reply button; to reply via a posting to the entire newsgroup, click the Reply Group button.

NOTE *In this chapter, we have been looking at how to use Outlook Express to access newsgroups. You can also access and participate in newsgroups using the deja.com Web site.*

Customizing Outlook Express

Earlier in this chapter, we looked at how to disable the new mail notification sound and at how to specify the interval after which Outlook Express checks for messages. In both cases, we used the Options dialog box. You can personalize a number of other features that concern e-mail and news, using the Options dialog box. To open the Options dialog box, click the Tools menu and then click Options.

NOTE *This section discusses the features in the Options dialog box that weren't discussed earlier in this chapter.*

Specifying General Options

The Options dialog box has either 9 or 10 tabs. (The Spelling tab is available only if you have installed a Microsoft Office program that includes the spell-checking feature, for example, Word, Excel, or PowerPoint.) By default, the Options dialog box opens at the General tab, which is shown in Figure 10-25.

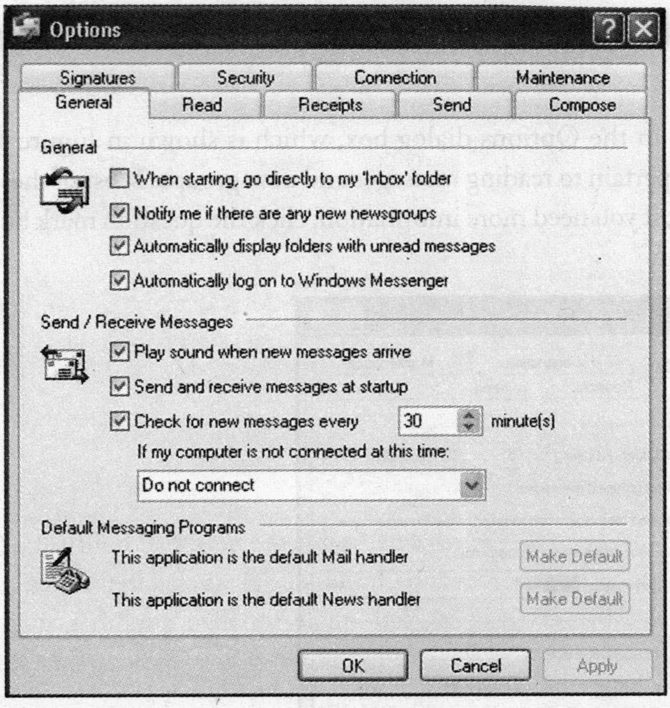

Figure 10-25 The Options dialog box open at the General tab.

To enable an option, check it; to disable an option, clear the check box. You use the options on the General tab to enable or disable the following features:

- Open Outlook Express at your Inbox.
- Let you know if there are new newsgroups.
- Display all folders that contain unread messages.
- Automatically log on to the Windows Messenger.
- Play a sound when you have new mail.
- Automatically send and receive messages when you open Outlook Express.
- Specify how often to check for new messages.
- Specify whether Outlook Express is to be used when you access mail or news features in your Web browser.

Specifying What Happens When You Read Messages or News

Click the Read tab in the Options dialog box, which is shown in Figure 10-26, to specify options that pertain to reading messages and newsgroups. Most of these options are self-explanatory; if you need more information, click the question mark button, and then click the option.

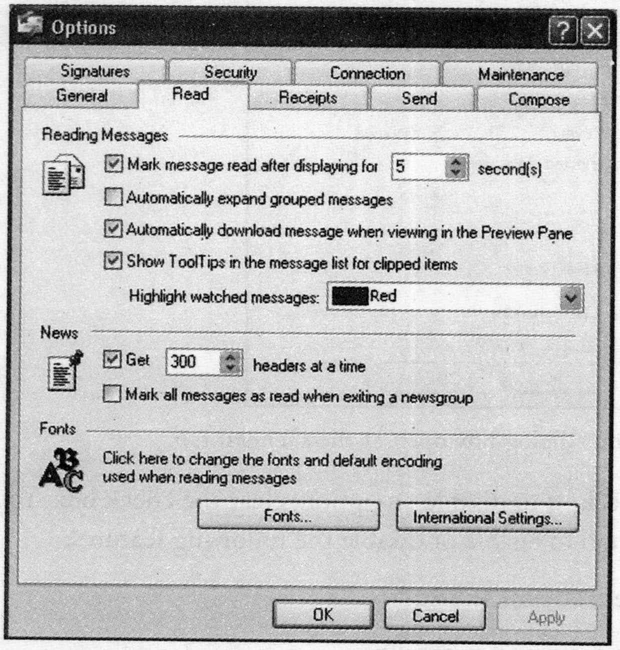

Figure 10-26 The Options dialog box open at the Read tab.

Handling Return Receipts

If you want to know when a recipient has received and read a message, click the Tools menu in the New Message window, and then click Request Read Receipt. If you want to know when all the messages you send have been received and read, you use the options on the Receipts tab in the Options dialog box, as shown in Figure 10-27.

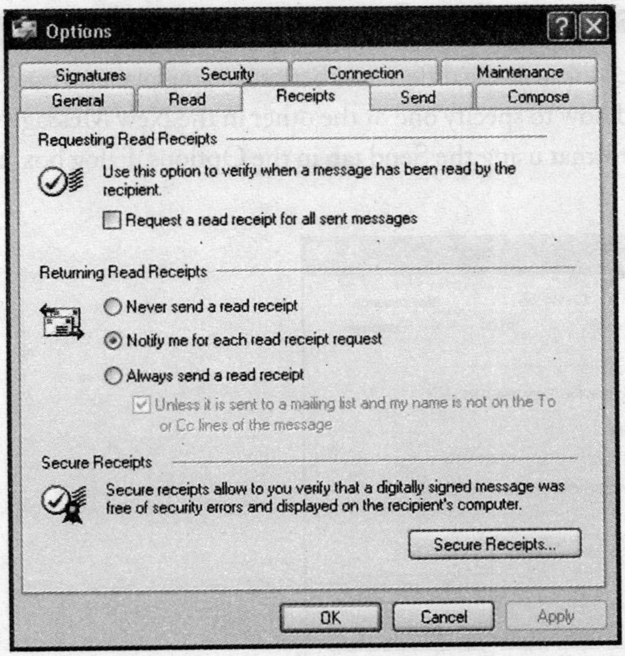

Figure 10-27 The Options dialog box open at the Receipts tab.

If you want to control how Outlook Express responds to requests for read receipts that you receive, use the options in the Returning Read Receipts section:

- Click Never Send A Read Receipt if you don't want a read receipt sent even though it was requested by the sender of a message.
- Click Notify Me For Each Read Receipt Request if you want to know that a read receipt has been requested for a message. You can then decide whether to let the sender know that you have received the message.
- Click Always Send A Read Receipt if you always want to know that your message has been received. The options in the Returning Read Receipts section are mutually exclusive. You must select one of the three options.

If you or the sender has a secure digital signature, you can specify that the signature be verified by clicking the Secure Receipts button and configuring the options in the Secure Receipt Options dialog box.

Managing How Messages Are Sent

Earlier in this chapter, we looked at the differences between using plain text and HTML formats for messages and how to specify one or the other in the New Message window. You can also specify the format using the Send tab in the Options dialog box, as shown in Figure 10-28.

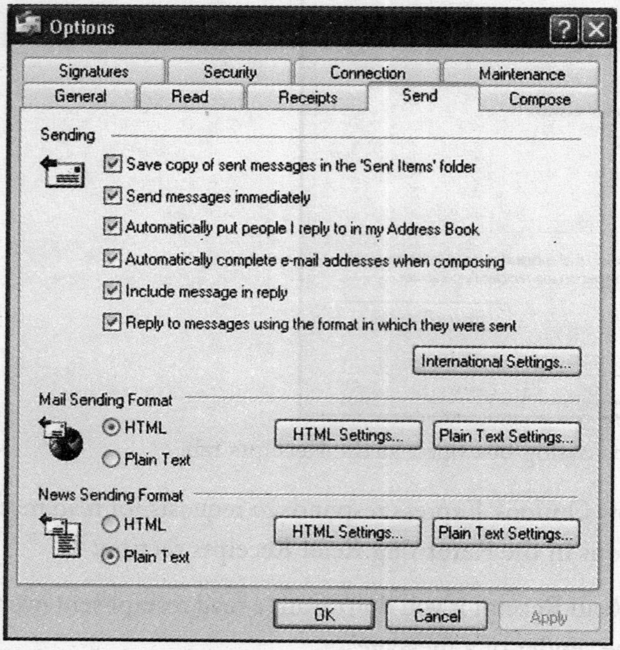

Figure 10-28 The Options dialog box open at the Send tab.

In addition, you can use the options in the Send tab to enable or disable the following features:

- Save a copy of every message you send in the Sent Items folder. This option is selected by default, and we suggest that you leave it that way. Having a record of what you said when and to whom is always a good idea in any business situation.

- Bypass the Outbox folder and send messages immediately. Composing messages offline and storing them in the Outbox folder was handy when we paid dearly for online time by the minute. In these days of always-on connections and low-cost unlimited connection time, it's probably simpler and easier to just compose the message and send it at once—unless you think you might want to edit it again before you send it. In that case, you can store it in the Drafts folder.
- Always put the names of senders that you reply to in your Address Book. Again, this option is enabled by default, and we suggest that you leave it that way. It's much easier to weed out your Address Book than it is to search for an e-mail address.
- Use AutoComplete for e-mail addresses. This is a handy feature, but even quicker is selecting the address from your Address Book.
- Include the original message when you reply to a message. This option is enabled by default, and if you ever want to do this, leave it enabled. Otherwise, you can't include the message in your reply. If you don't want to include the message, it's easy to delete it from your reply. Simply place your cursor in the body of the message, click the Edit menu, click Select All, and then press the Delete key.
- If you receive messages in both plain text and HTML format, you can reply in the format in which the messages were sent by enabling the last option in the Sending section.

Changing Fonts, Specifying Stationery, and Using Business Cards

To change the font in which you compose messages, to specify stationery that will be used when you compose a message or post to a newsgroup, and to specify that your business card is always attached to messages or posts, you use the options on the Compose tab in the Options dialog box, as shown in Figure 10-29.

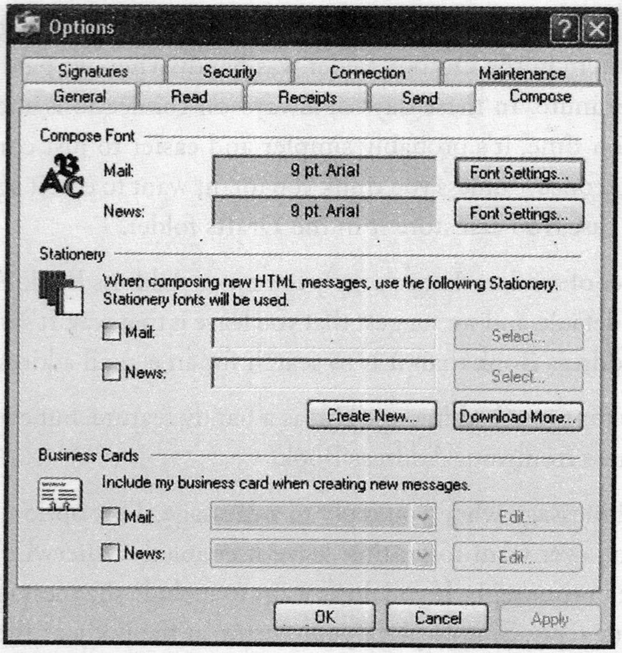

Figure 10-29 The Options dialog box open at the Compose tab.

A business card that you create in Outlook Express is actually a *vCard*, an electronic personal information card that you can exchange via e-mail. A vCard is an industry standard format for sharing contact information including your name, address, telephone and fax numbers, and e-mail address.

To create a business card and attach it to all your messages, follow these steps:

1. **Open Address Book.**

   Click Addresses in the toolbar in the Outlook Express Main window.

2. **Create an entry for yourself.**

   Click the New button, and then click New Contact to open the Properties dialog box. Fill in as much or as little information about yourself as you want to include on your business card, and then click OK.

3. **Save your business card to a file.**

   In the Address Book main window, select your name from the list, click the File menu, click Export, and then click Business Card (vCard) to open the Export *[Your Name]* As Business Card (vCard) dialog box. Save it in the location that Outlook Express suggests, or choose another location and click Save. Close Address Book.

4. Specify that your business card be included in all outgoing messages.

Click the Tools menu, and then click Options to open the Options dialog box. Click the Compose tab, click the Mail and News check boxes under Business Cards, and then click OK.

To attach a business card to a single message rather than to all messages, leave the Mail and News check boxes blank, and in the New Message window, click the Insert menu, and then click My Business Card.

Checking Spelling

Typically, e-mail messages have a bad reputation in the spelling, punctuation, and grammar department, and for good reason. One of our business contacts even sends stream-of-consciousness messages—they are in all lowercase letters, have no punctuation, no paragraph indications, contain a lot of abbreviations and misspelled words, and so on. Not impressive from a business point of view, or from any point of view for that matter.

True, e-mail has developed as one of the most important communications tools ever because it's quick and easy, but in a business environment you want to apply the same standards to e-mail that you apply to any other form of communication. You want to portray a professional image, and you want your customers, colleagues, and other contacts to trust you and your abilities.

At the very least, read through a message before you click the Send button. And if you want to avoid embarrassing typos and misspelled words, select the option in the Spelling tab of the Options dialog box to always check the spelling of a message before it is sent. (As we mentioned earlier, you won't have the Spelling tab unless you have an Office application installed that contains the spell-checking feature.)

The options in the Spelling tab are in general those found in other applications that can check spelling, but in addition you can also check Internet addresses and the original message in a reply or a forward.

Another Point of View

Currently, e-mail is the most popular online application, with more than 6.1 billion messages sent every day. You might never have a one-on-one meeting with the president of the United States or the CEO of your company, but you can send e-mail to both, a situation that seems to fulfill an early promise: that e-mail would be the great democratizing agent of corporate America.

A recent study, however, seems to indicate that e-mail messages signify the same kind of status that categorize senders in face-to-face meetings in corporations. David Owens, an associate professor of management at Vanderbilt University, spent a year attending meetings and interviewing employees of a research firm in California. He then analyzed some 30,000 e-mail messages sent within the company over a four-year period. Here's what he found:

- If your e-mail messages are late, unevenly capitalized, and sloppy, you're probably the CEO or CEO material. These sorts of messages convey the impression that the sender has better things to do with his or her time.
- If your e-mail messages are earnest and combative or if you spell-check them before you send them, you're probably middle management or destined for middle management.
- If you forward jokes, send greeting cards, or use happy face emoticons, you play an important role that tends to be underestimated—you are a low-status worker.

Enhancing Security

You can use the Security tab in the Options dialog box, as shown in Figure 10-30, to select an Internet security zone and to acquire and configure a digital certificate, which is also known as a digital ID. (For more on security zones, look back at Chapter 9.)

In the Virus Protection section in the Security tab, the Warn Me When Other Applications Try To Send Mail As Me check box is selected by default, and you should leave it that way. Certain viruses have been known to spread by sending themselves to everybody in your Address Book without your knowledge. In addition, you can check the Do Not Allow Attachments To Be Saved Or Opened That Could Potentially Be A Virus check box. To be on the safe side, however, you should install a third-party antivirus program and keep it enabled.

If your business involves sending and receiving e-mail that if intercepted by the wrong people could put your business at risk, you'll want to look into using digital certificates. Click the Tell Me More button for a complete explanation of how digital certificates work, and click the Get Digital ID button to go to a Web page that lists authorities from which you can obtain a digital certificate.

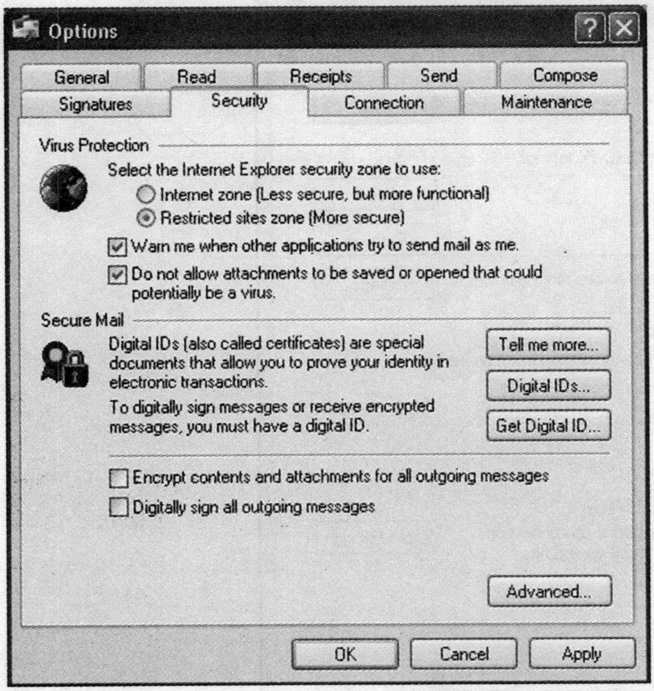

Figure 10-30 The Options dialog box open at the Security tab.

Configuring Your Internet Connection

You learned in Chapter 7 the various ways you can connect to the Internet, and you saw in Chapter 9 how to modify your connection using the Internet Options dialog box. If you have multiple dial-up connections, click the first option in the Dial-Up section of the Connection tab in the Options dialog box if you want to be notified before connections are switched. If you want your modem to hang up after you send and receive mail, click the Hang Up After Sending And Receiving check box.

Outlook Express and Internet Explorer both use the same Internet connection settings. You can modify those settings from within Outlook Express by clicking the Change button in the Connection tab, as shown in Figure 10-31, to open the Internet Properties dialog box at the Connections tab.

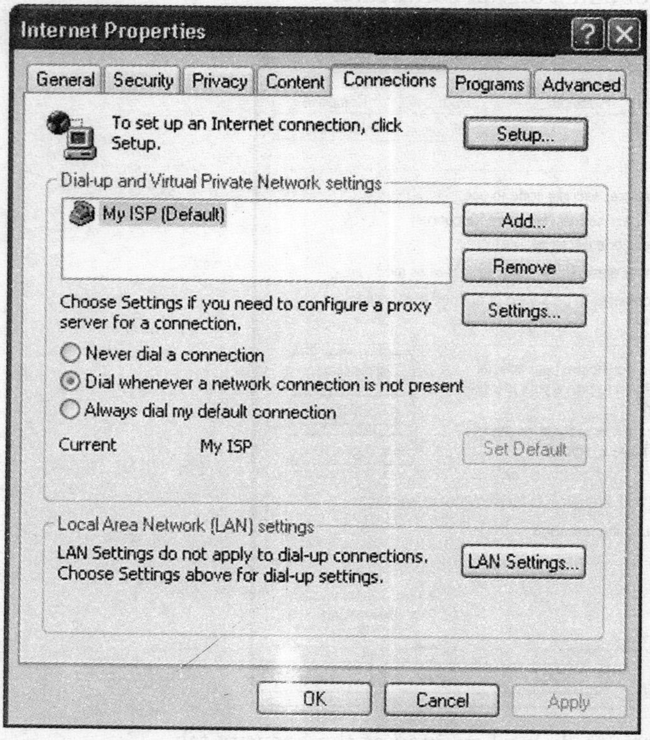

Figure 10-31 The Internet Properties dialog box open at the Connections tab.

Cleaning the Outlook Express House

You use the Maintenance tab in the Options dialog box, which is shown in Figure 10-32, to take care of various housekeeping chores, such as emptying the Deleted Items folder, compacting messages to save space, and changing the location of your message folders. To see where your message folders are stored, click the Store Folder button to open the Store Location dialog box. If you want to keep that location, click OK. If you want to change the location, click Change to open the Browse For Folder dialog box.

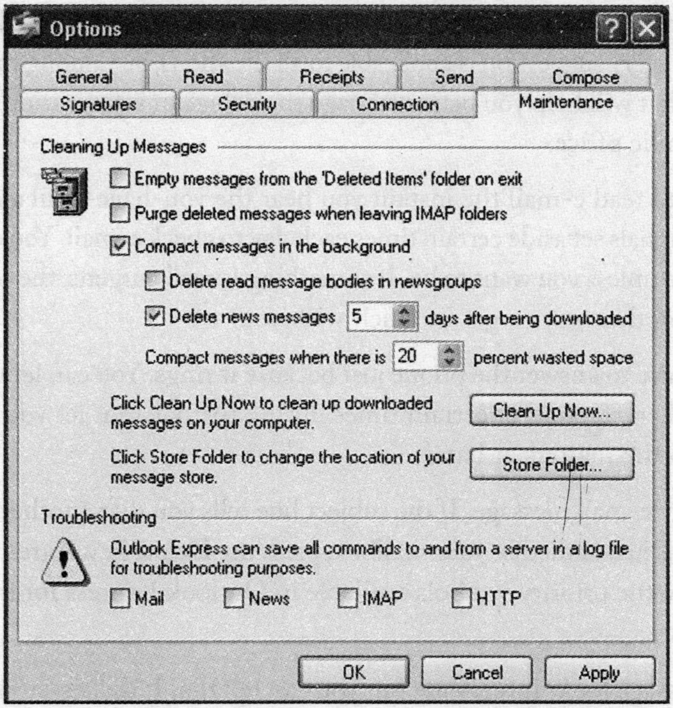

Figure 10-32 The Options dialog box open at the Maintenance tab.

If you are having trouble sending or receiving mail, click the Mail check box in the Troubleshooting section of the Maintenance tab. All commands sent to and from your mail server are then stored in a log file that you or a technical support person can peruse to see where the bottleneck might be.

Taking Charge of Your Wired Office

Do you ever wonder how you'd get by without the number of communications tools you currently have at your disposal? Phone, voice mail, fax, e-mail, pagers, the Internet and its vast supply of instant resources, even paper memos, reports, home-to-office network connections—the list seems endless. Or, maybe instead you wonder how to get your work done in the midst of all these tools.

A recent issue of *Harvard Management Update,* a newsletter put out by the publishing arm of Harvard Business School, had some suggestions that we've adapted for inclusion here. Not every suggestion is applicable to all situations, but among them you're sure to find some that will help you better manage the deluge of information that faces you in your electronic office.

- You don't have to read e-mail the instant you hear the you-have-mail alert. Some business professionals set aside certain times each day to check e-mail. You don't have to be interrupted unless you want to be. If something is really urgent, the sender will probably find another way to get in touch with you.
- You also don't have to answer the phone just because it rings. You can let voice mail pick it up and then respond at certain times during the day that let you give your full attention to the matters at hand.
- Don't open every e-mail message. If the subject line tells you that another get-rich-quick scheme has just landed in your mailbox, press the Delete key. Agree with your colleagues to use the priority symbols available in Outlook Express for things that are time-sensitive.
- If an e-mail message looks interesting but you can tell that it isn't essential, print it out and read it later or flag it in some way.
- Instead of using e-mail for team projects, set up an intranet (an internal Internet) or a newsgroup to which members can post messages.
- Take care of paper filing first, and then set up an electronic filing system for e-mail. Create folders for projects, people, and so on, and be diligent about moving messages into these folders.

- If you have tons of old messages lying around, just get rid of them. If you can't bear that thought, save them to a file somewhere.
- Multitask. Return phone calls while printing something, or check your paper organizer while downloading a file from the Internet.
- Don't waste time by following links that have nothing to do with the reason you're searching the Internet.
- Unsubscribe to newsletters (whether electronic or print) you no longer need or never get around to reading.
- Regularly evaluate your sources of information—journals, periodicals, reports, memos, and so on—and discontinue all that are not essential. Be on the lookout for new information sources that will keep you current.
- Set aside 5 to 10 minutes each day to learn something new about any of your electronic tools.

Summary

This chapter has covered a multitude of topics concerning electronic mail and, in particular, Outlook Express. Now you know how e-mail works; how to use the Outlook Express main window; how to read, process, create, and send messages; how to attach files to messages; and how to create a signature and filter messages. You also know how to access newsgroups and how to set up and use your Address Book to quickly insert e-mail addresses, and you know several ways to personalize Outlook Express so that it works efficiently in your business setting. And you have some tips about how to manage the slew of electronic devices that inhabit your office.

Chapter 11

USING THE SYSTEM INFORMATION TOOLS

Featuring:

- Finding System Information
- Looking at System Properties
- Using Computer Management
- Sharing Folders
- Using Disk Management
- Services Explained
- Task Manager Simplified
- Using the Desktop Cleanup Wizard
- Cleaning Up Your Hard Drive
- Checking for Disk Errors
- Defragmenting Your Files
- Optimizing Your System for Peak Performance

In this chapter, we are going to take a long look at all of the system evaluation and performance tools available to Windows XP Professional users. We'll peer into the basement and look at the Windows plumbing in a variety of different ways, and show you how to find fast answers to the tech-support person's questions, such as how much memory do you have, or what kind of modem do you use. Then we'll look at the tools you can use to find out exactly what is happening on your system, and we'll look at the tools you can use to restore, and in some cases, increase, system performance. But look out, here comes the tech-support guy with his questions.

Finding System Information

If you're having trouble with a computer and need the help of technical personnel, you'll want to have some information at hand. Depending on the nature of the problem, you might be asked how much free space is on your hard drive, what kind of modem do you have and how is it set up, or what type of video adapter is installed.

The System Information applet can give you a great deal of detailed information about the hardware and software on your system, and it can also give you a great one-page summary of the most essential information. Click the Start button, click All Programs, click Accessories, click System Tools, and click System Information. You will see the dialog box shown in Figure 11-1.

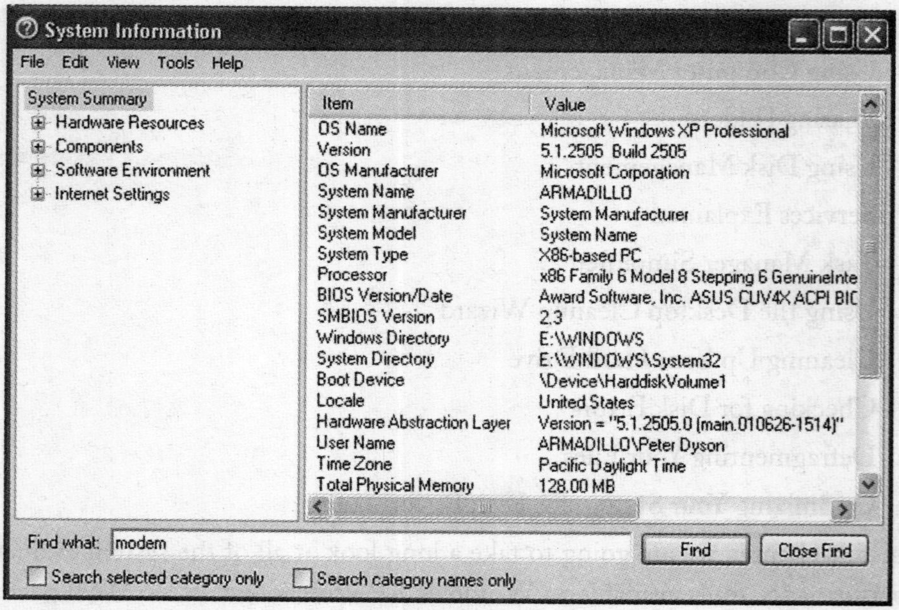

Figure 11-1 The System Information summary page.

What you'll see in this dialog box depends on what is installed on your computer and how it is configured. In the left pane, you will see several top-level categories:

- Hardware Resources includes hardware-specific details, such as memory-address information.
- Components lists information on the hardware installed on your system, such as the modem or the CD-ROM.
- Software Environment describes the system software running right now on your system, including device-driver information, any print jobs you are running, and any current network connections.
- Internet Settings lists the current configuration you have chosen for Internet Explorer.
- Applications includes information on the application programs you have installed on your computer.

To display more information about an item, click the plus sign (+) next to the item to expand it. For example, to display information about your modem, in the tree pane on the left, expand the Components folder, and then select Modem. Modem information is then displayed in the right pane.

If you are not sure where the item you are interested in is located, use the Find What box to help you. For example, type the word *modem* into the Find What box, and click Find. Detailed information about your modem will appear in the right pane.

Using the System Information dialog box, you can get details about every component in your system, including hardware, software, drivers, printers, and so on.

WARNING *Printing out the entire contents of System Information, including the information in all the subfolders, can take a ton of paper even for a modest computer system. A large complicated system can take up to 100 pages. So think before you print.*

Looking at System Properties

As always in Windows, there are other places you can look to find similar or related information. Click the Start button, click Control Panel, click Performance And Maintenance, and then click System. Alternatively, click the Start button, then right-click My Computer and choose Properties from the shortcut menu. Either way, you will see the System Properties dialog box.

We'll look at four of the tabs in this dialog box here, General, Computer Name, Hardware, and Advanced; the other three, System Restore, Automatic Updates, and Remote, we'll save for discussion in Chapter 16.

General Tab

The General tab, shown in Figure 11-2 lists basic information about your computer, including the operating system name and version, the registered user, the processor, the processor speed in megahertz (MHz), and the amount of memory installed.

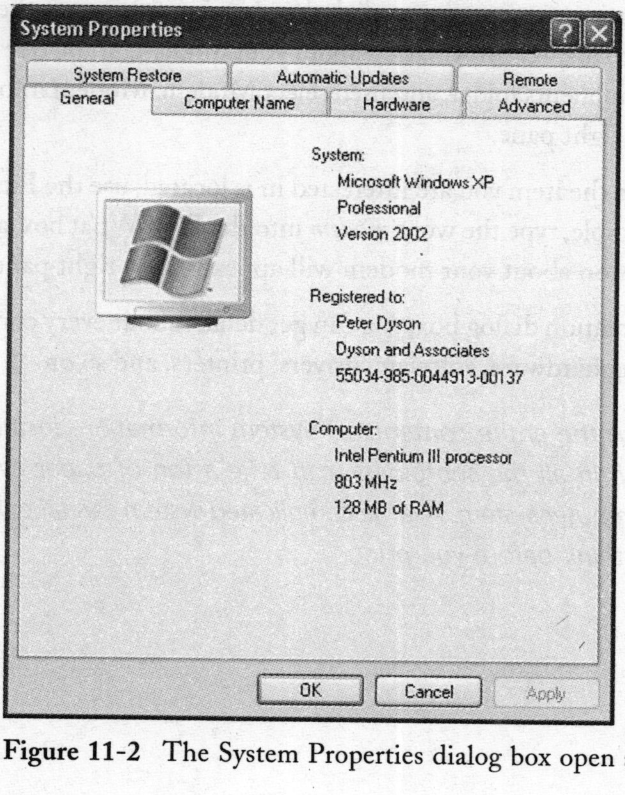

Figure 11-2 The System Properties dialog box open at the General tab.

Computer Name Tab

The Computer Name tab, shown in Figure 11-3, lists the information used to identify this computer to the network, the name of the workgroup to which you belong, and any relevant domain information.

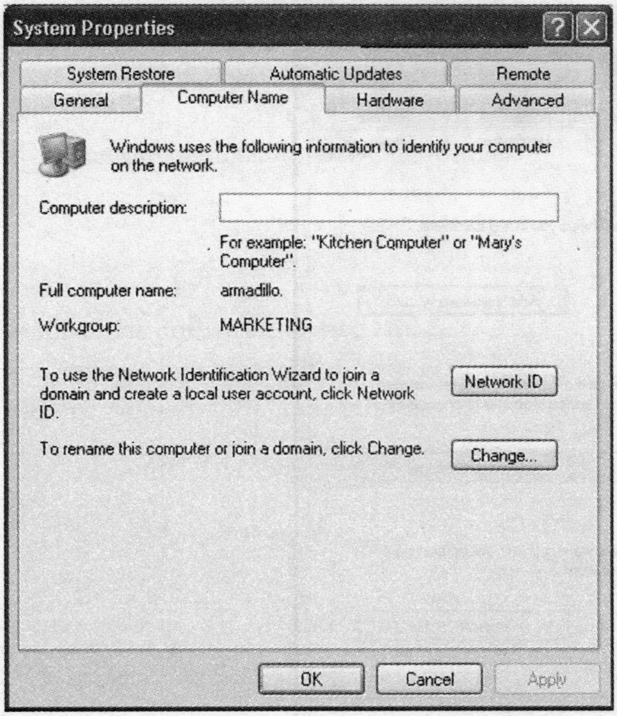

Figure 11-3 The System Properties dialog box open at the Computer Name tab.

Click Network ID to open the Network Identification Wizard to join a domain or create a local user account, or click Change to rename the computer or join a domain. If you are on a corporate network, be sure to consult your network administrator before you make any changes in this tab. You may cause your computer to become detached from the network if you make certain changes without the necessary go-ahead.

Hardware Tab

The Hardware tab, shown in Figure 11-4, gains access to the Add New Hardware Wizard if you want to add new hardware or remove existing hardware from your system. We'll look at Device Manager in Chapter 15. Hardware Profiles is used to create new hardware configurations for different users.

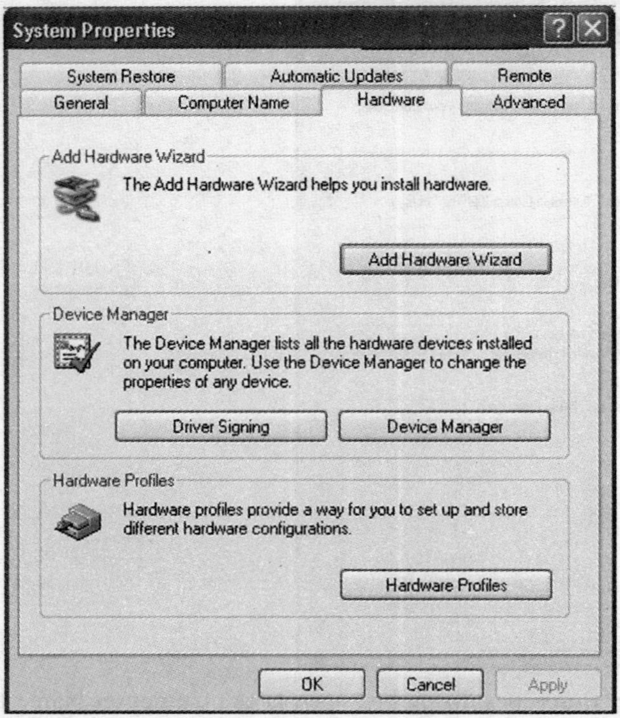

Figure 11-4 The System Properties dialog box open at the Hardware tab.

Advanced Tab

The Advanced tab contains three groups of options: Performance, User Profiles, and Startup And Recovery, as you can see from Figure 11-5. We'll look at the options available to you when you click the Performance Settings button in this tab under the heading "Optimizing Your System for Peak Performance" later in this chapter.

Click User Profiles Settings if you want to save different desktop configurations for different users. The options available to you when you click the Startup And Recovery Settings button will be covered in Chapter 16. The Environment Variables button lets you look at or change system variables, including the system path, and Error Reporting lets you turn on or off error reporting direct to Microsoft.

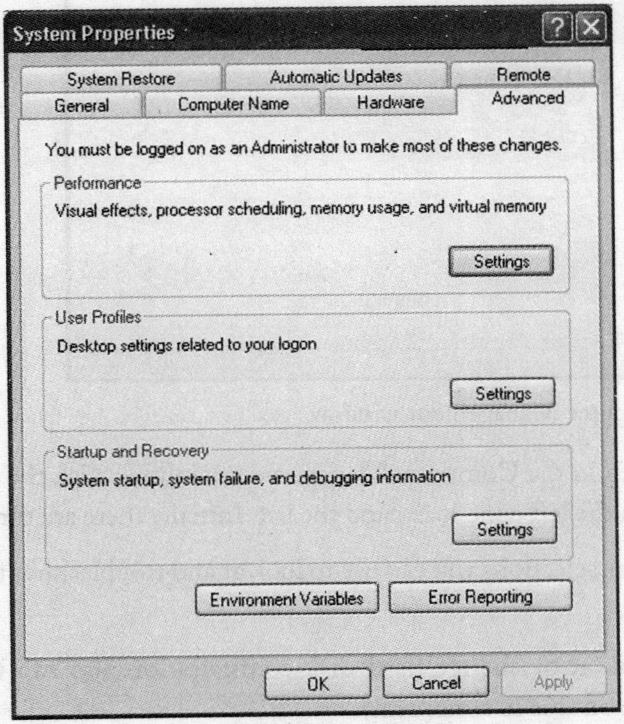

Figure 11-5 The System Properties dialog box open at the Advanced tab.

Using Computer Management

To find more detailed information, including potentially valuable status information, we have to use a more powerful tool; in this case, Computer Management. Click the Start button, click Control Panel, and then click Performance And Maintenance. Click Administrative Tools, and then click Computer Management and you will see the window shown in Figure 11-6.

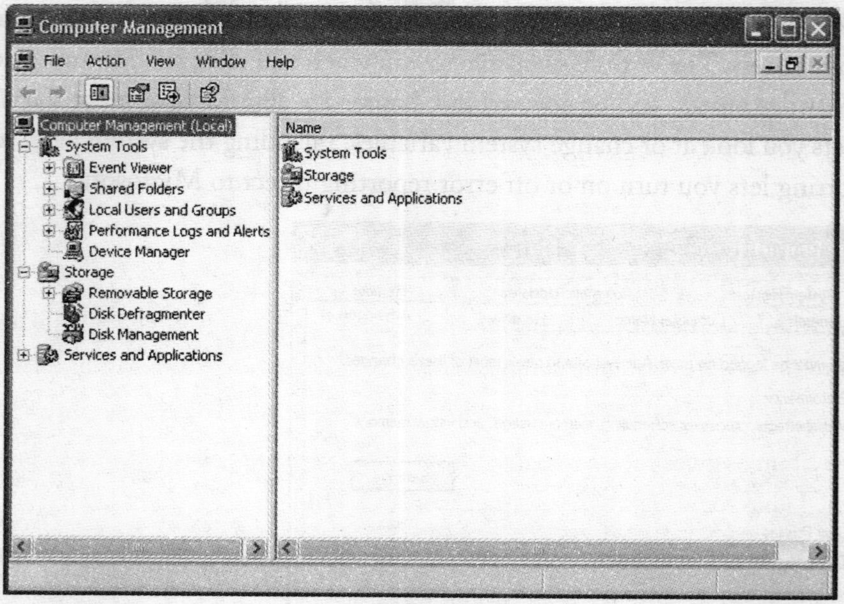

Figure 11-6 The Computer Management window.

Several options are listed in the Computer Management window; click the plus sign associated with items in the left pane to expand the list. Initially there are three items:

- System Tools contains selections you can use to look at and troubleshoot the hardware on your system.
- Storage lets you look at or change hard-disk configuration and run the Disk Defragmenter (more on this in a moment).
- Services And Applications allows you to look at the services running on your system.

We are not going to look at everything in Computer Management in exhaustive detail; instead, we're going to highlight the most important and useful elements. In this chapter we'll look at how we can use Computer Management to provide us with information, and in Chapter 15 we'll look at how to use the diagnostic tools available in Computer Management.

NOTE *Computer Management is a part of a much larger Microsoft initiative called the Microsoft Management Console (MMC) package, used to administer system components, networks, services, and individual computers. Each component of MMC is called a* snap-in. *Describing how MMC works is way beyond the scope of this book, but we'll give you sufficient information in this section so that you can use Computer Management and its components as effectively as possible.*

Administrative Tools Demystified

When you open the Administrative Tools folder, which is found in Control Panel, you will see several icons in addition to Computer Management, including the following:

- Component Services configures and manages Component Object Model (COM+) and Distributed COM (DCOM) applications. COM is a Microsoft Windows specification that defines how objects interact in the Windows environment. COM elements can be written in any language and can be added to or removed from a program without requiring recompilation of the source code.
- Data Sources gives access to database systems using Structured Query Language (SQL) via Open Database Connectivity (ODBC).
- Event Viewer lets you look at the system, security, and program event logs on your computer; see Chapter 15 for more details.
- Local Security Policy lets you look at or change several security policies, including Account Policies, Public Key Policies, and Software Restriction Policies.
- Performance lets you look at and evaluate a whole host of system performance parameters; see Chapter 15 for more details.
- Services lets you look at the system services available on your computer; see the section below called "Services Explained" for more information.

And depending on how your system is configured, you may see other icons in the Administrative Tools folder.

Sharing Folders

Click Shared Folders in the main Computer Management window, and you will see three items:

- Shares lists all the shared folders on your system; some of these folders are shared by default and you have no control over these folders. Other folders have been made available by their owners as shared folders; see Figure 11-7 for an example. If you want to stop sharing a folder, right-click the folder and choose Stop Sharing from the shortcut menu. If you want to see how a folder has been shared, right-click the folder, choose Properties from the shortcut menu, and then click the Share Permissions tab, shown in Figure 11-8. Folders in this list with a dollar sign ($) as the final character of their name are automatically shared by Windows and are hidden from view in Windows Explorer and My Network Places. If you add a dollar sign as the last character of a folder name, that folder will also be made invisible. You can still access the folder by typing the name, including the dollar sign, into the Run box or the Map Network Drive dialog box. If you hold down the Ctrl key as you choose Properties, you will also see a Security tab.

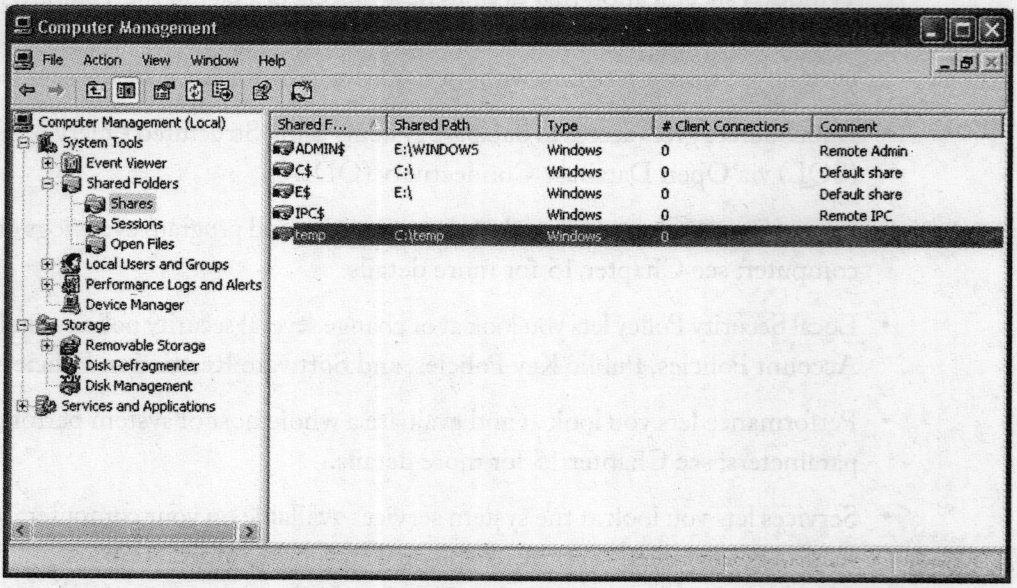

Figure 11-7 The Shares window in Computer Management.

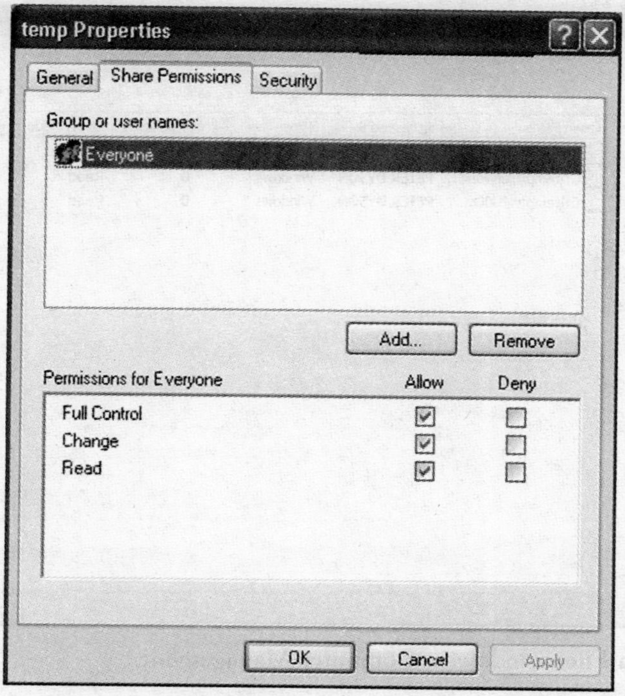

Figure 11-8 The Share Permissions tab.

- Sessions lists all the current sessions running on the system and includes the user name, the name of the computer he or she is using, the type of network connection in use, the number of open files, and the connect and idle time.
- Open Files, shown in Figure 11-9, allows you to look at all the currently open files, along with the name of the user accessing the file, the network connection they are using, and a list of the permissions granted when the file was first opened.

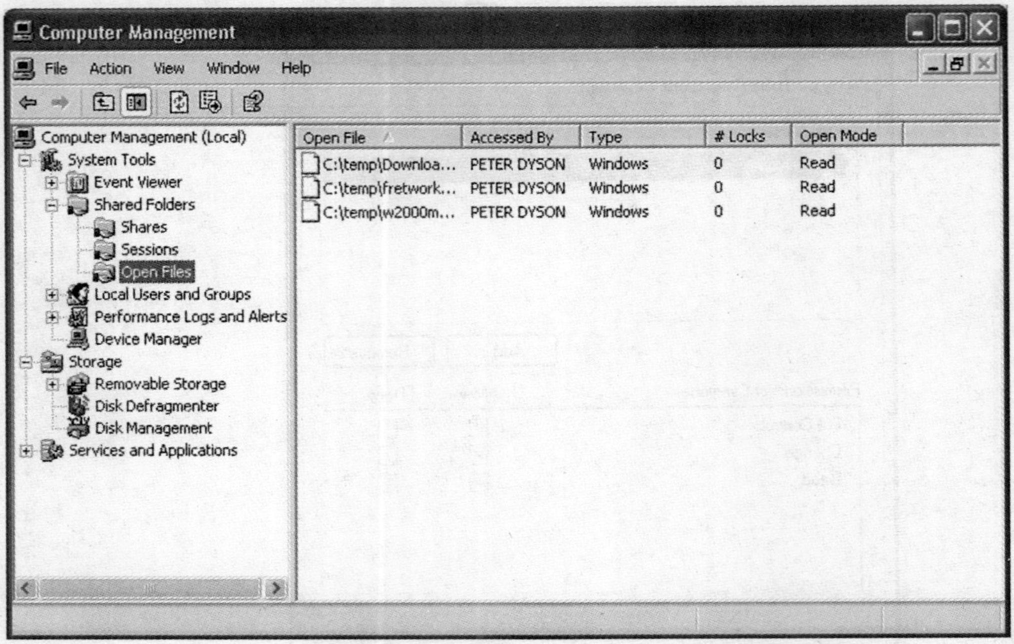

Figure 11-9 The Open Files window in Computer Management.

Using Disk Management

You can use Disk Management to perform a number of hard-disk-related tasks, including the following:

- Change a path.
- Change a drive letter.
- Format a disk or partition.
- Make a partition into an active partition.
- Upgrade a disk.
- Delete a partition.
- Create a partition.

To start Disk Management, click the Start button, click Control Panel, and then click Performance And Maintenance. Click Administrative Tools, and then click Computer Management. From the list in the left pane, click Storage to expand the list and then click Disk Management; you will see a window similar to that shown in Figure 11-10.

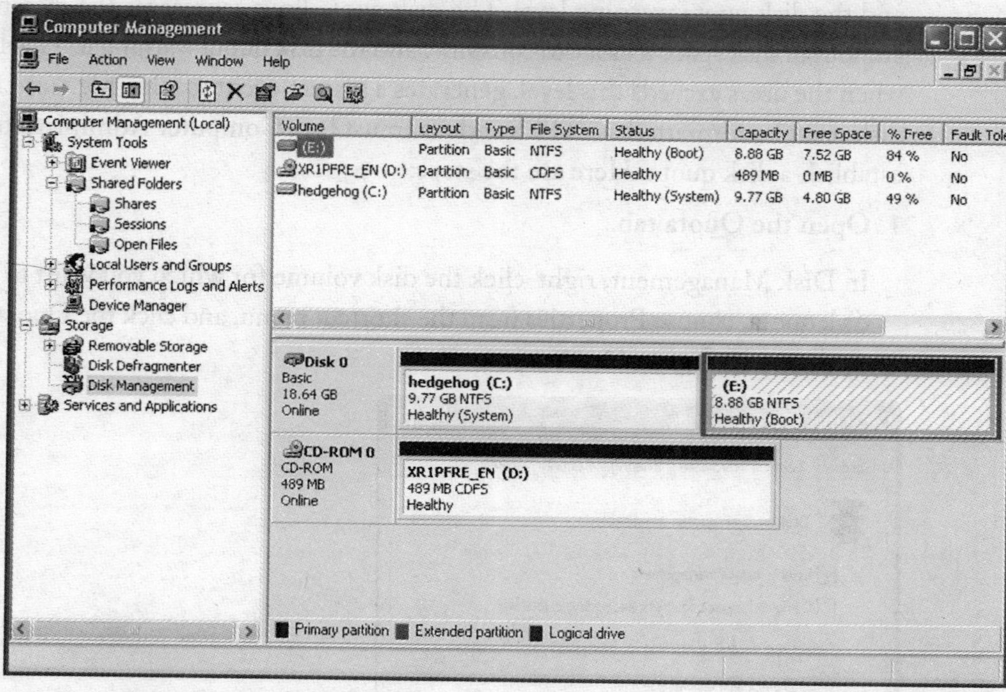

Figure 11-10 The Disk Management window.

The information displayed on your computer will be different from that shown in Figure 11-10. In the upper pane, you will see information listed for the hard-disk, CD-ROM, and DVD drives on your system, while in the lower pane, you will see a graphical representation of these same devices.

Right-click on any part of the graphical display to open a menu containing selections specific to that item; you can also right-click on the Volume name and open the same menu. Any items currently unavailable will be grayed out from the menu. Once you have chosen an activity, a wizard will take you through the process you selected; just follow the instructions on the screen.

Establishing Disk Quotas

You can set limits on the amount of hard-disk space a person can use by means of a disk quota. In Windows, a disk quota consists of two parts: the disk quota limit and the disk quota warning level. The disk quota limit represents the maximum amount of disk space a user can consume, and the disk quota warning level, which, when the users exceeds this level, generates a system event to a log file. Your hard disk must be formatted as NTFS and you must be a Computer Administrator to establish a disk quota. Here are the steps:

1. Open the Quota tab.

In Disk Management, right-click the disk volume for which you want to set a disk quota, choose Properties from the shortcut menu, and click the Quota tab, as shown in Figure 11-11.

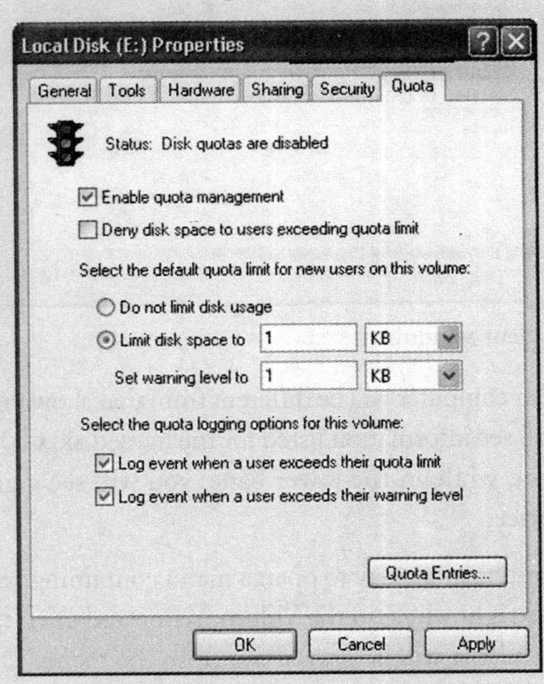

Figure 11-11 The Quota tab.

2. Enable quota management.

Click the Enable Quota Management check box, click Apply, and then click OK. You can also set the disk quota limit and the disk quota warning level on this tab.

When you enable disk quotas on a volume that already contains files and folders, Windows calculates the disk quota limit and the disk quota warning level for all current and future users based on this current usage. You can use the Quota tab to set different quotas.

Services Explained

If you click Service And Applications in the left pane of the Computer Management window, and then double-click Services in the right pane, you will see a display similar to the one shown in Figure 11-12. You can also open Services from inside the Administrative Tools folder in Control Panel.

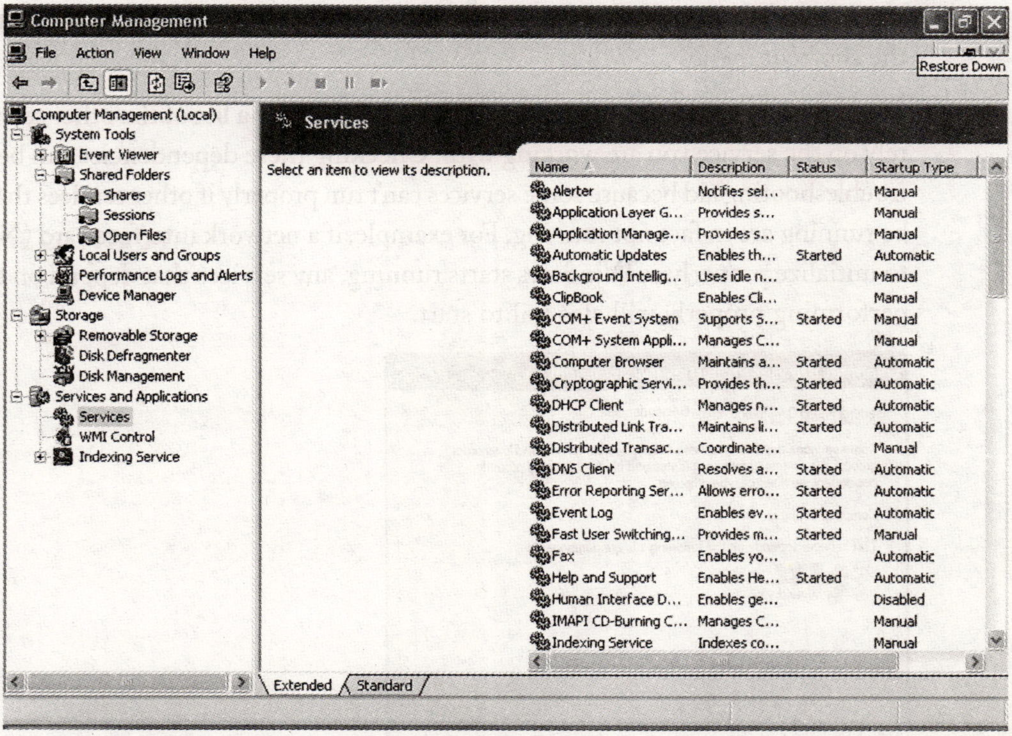

Figure 11-12 The Services window.

Figure 11-12 lists all the operating-system services running on your computer right now. These services represent all the behind-the-scenes tasks that keep your computer humming along smoothly. For the most part they are completely automatic; they rarely need input from us in order to function properly.

Click the Standard tab at the bottom of the right pane to compress the information shown in this window. You will see each service listed by name, followed by a brief description of its function. The Status column gives the current operating status of each service, which will be one of the following: Started, Stopped, Paused, Resumed, or Restarted.

The Startup Type column indicates which services are started automatically and which are started manually. The Log On As column shows the name under which the service is running.

To change the status of a service, right-click the service and choose Start, Stop, Pause, Resume, or Restart from the shortcut menu. It goes without saying that you do this only when you have a very good reason to change the status of a service. If you want to find out more about a particular service, right-click the service, and choose Properties from the shortcut menu.

Click the Dependencies tab, shown in Figure 11-13, for a list of the other services that rely on the service you are working with. Checking these dependencies can be a useful troubleshooting aid because some services can't run properly if other services that should be running are in fact not running. For example, if a network interface card (NIC) fails to initialize properly as Windows starts running, any services that depend on that card performing properly will also fail to start.

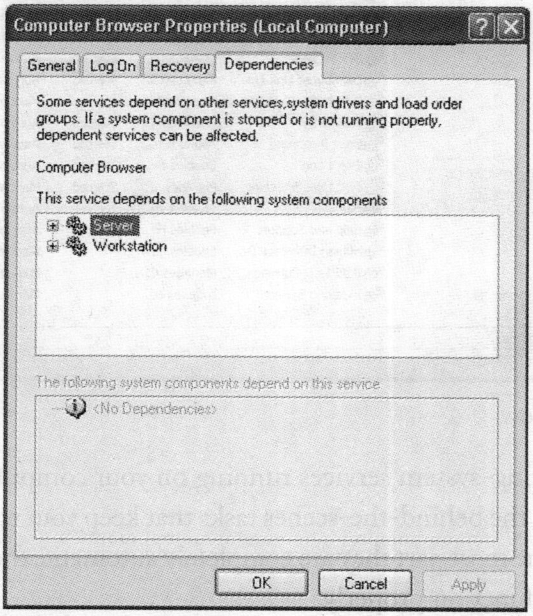

Figure 11-13 The Computer Browser Properties dialog box open at the Dependencies tab.

Task Manager Simplified

Another colorful way to display information about your system is to use Windows Task Manager. You can open Task Manager in the following ways:

- Right-click an empty area of the taskbar, and choose Task Manager from the shortcut menu.
- Click the Start button, click Run to open the Run dialog box, and in the Open box, type *taskmgr*.
- Press Ctrl+Alt+Del to open the Windows Security dialog box, and click the Task Manager button.
- Press Ctrl+Shift+Esc.

You can also start Task Manager from within Windows Help And Support Center.

Task Manager has five tabs, Applications, Processes, Performance, Networking, and Users, with the Performance tab displayed as the default.

Performance Tab

The Performance tab displays constantly refreshed totals for current and historic CPU and memory usage and is shown in Figure 11-14.

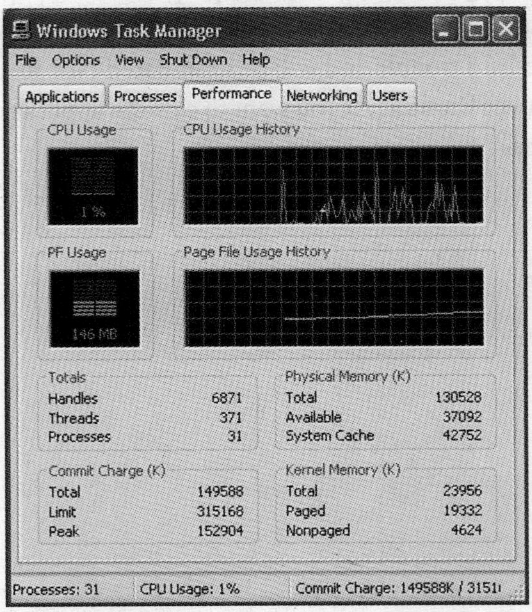

Figure 11-14 Windows Task Manager open at the Performance tab.

The two top boxes display current and historical CPU and memory usage in graphical form; as the load on your system changes, these displays will change immediately to reflect that load. Click the View menu, and then click Show Kernel Times to add a second graph in red to the usage history displays. This red graph indicates the resources consumed by Windows kernel activities.

A few large spikes in the Usage History boxes are nothing to worry about; you will see that sort of response when you start a large application, for example. But the usage level should drop back again once the application is running. Constant high-usage levels are an indication of poor system configuration, and you may need to change some or all of your virtual memory settings. We'll look at virtual memory later in this chapter.

The lower boxes give you numeric information about your system. The Totals box lists the number of handles, threads, and processes running on your computer. The Physical Memory box shows how the memory on your system is being used in terms of total and available memory, and how much memory is being used as system cache. The Commit Charge box displays the memory allocated to system and application programs, and the Kernel Memory box indicates the amount of memory being used by the Windows kernel.

Applications Tab

The Applications tab, shown in Figure 11-15, lists the programs running on your computer now and shows the status of each. The information in this window will tell you when an application has run into trouble and will be designated Not Responding rather than the normal description of Running. If you want to close an application, select it, and click the End Task button.

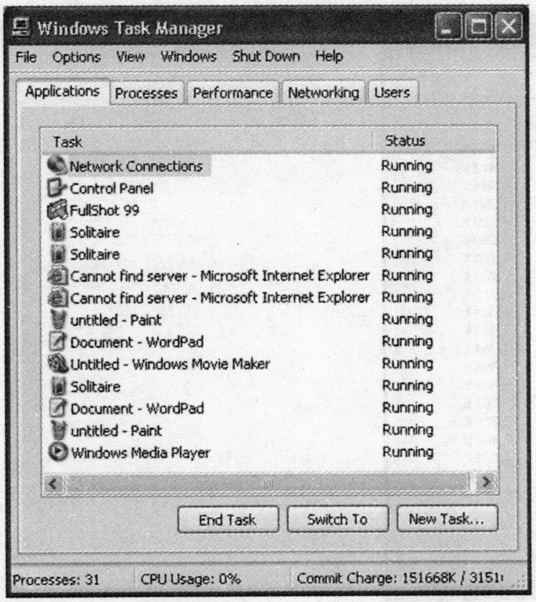

Figure 11-15 Windows Task Manager open at the Applications tab.

Processes Tab

The Processes tab, shown in Figure 11-16, lists the processes running on your computer by name, user name, and CPU and memory usage. Click the View menu, and then click Select Columns if you want to display additional information in the columns on the Processes tab; check a box to include a new column, clear a checked box if you want to remove that column. Click OK when you are finished.

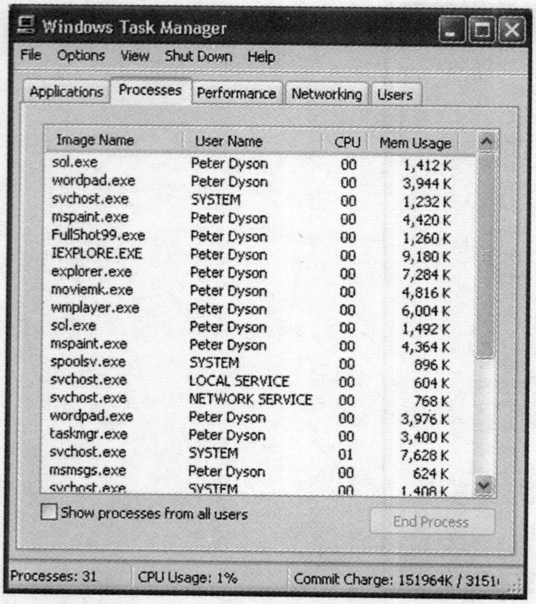

Figure 11-16 Windows Task Manager open at the Processes tab.

Networking Tab

The Networking tab, shown in Figure 11-17, is basically the Performance tab reconfigured for networks, and it displays constantly refreshed information about local area network (LAN) traffic, including network utilization, the speed of the link, and the number of bytes transferred across the network. The default display shows total network traffic in bytes as a green graph. Click the View menu, and then click Network Adapter History if you want to graph bytes sent (as a red graph) or bytes received (as a yellow graph). Click the View menu, and then click Select Columns if you want to change the information displayed in the area below the graph.

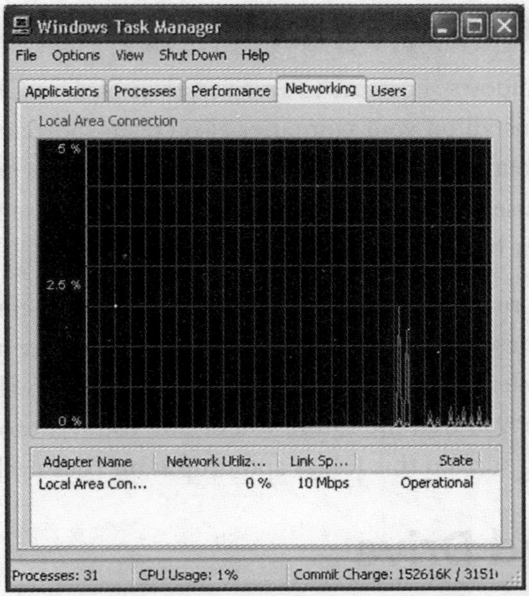

Figure 11-17 Windows Task Manager open at the Networking tab.

A few large spikes on the Local Area Connection graph are nothing to worry about; you will see that sort of response when you start a large application, for example, or when someone opens a large database file over the network. But the usage level should drop back again once the application is running or the file has been opened. Constant high levels are an indication of poor system configuration, and you may need to change some of your network settings or think about moving to a faster network.

Users Tab

The Users tab lists the names, IDs, and status of all logged on users. To display additional information, click the View menu and then click Select Columns; check a box to include a new column, clear a checked box if you want to remove that column. Click OK when you are finished.

Using the Desktop Cleanup Wizard

We looked at how to create Windows shortcuts to save you time back in Chapter 1. Many of the applications you install on your computer also create shortcuts. These shortcuts are supposed to make your life easier, but what they oftentimes do is just clutter up your desktop. A shortcut is useful only if you use it; if you prefer to use the Start menu, these shortcuts may never be used.

The Desktop Cleanup Wizard runs on your system every 60 days; it is completely automatic. The wizard checks these desktop shortcuts, decides that you are not using them, and copies them into a folder on the desktop called Unused Desktop Shortcuts. They are not deleted, just moved, so if in the future you decide you want to use one of them again, you can just drag it from this folder and drop it on your desktop.

Cleaning Up Your Hard Drive

In Chapter 9, we told you how to locate and delete temporary Internet files and cookies from your system. But in the process of managing your computer, Windows creates a number of other temporary files. Some speed the performance of the graphical interface, some are for setup purposes, and so on. If you're pressed for hard-drive space, you'll want to be diligent about getting rid of files that you no longer need. The tool you use to do this is Disk Cleanup.

To run Disk Cleanup, follow these steps:

1. Open the Select Drive dialog box, which is shown in Figure 11-18.

Click the Start button, click All Programs, click Accessories, click System Tools, and then click Disk Cleanup.

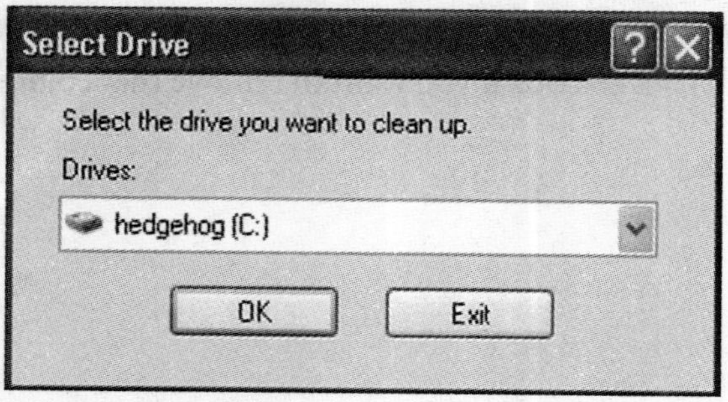

Figure 11-18 The Select Drive dialog box.

2. **Open the Disk Cleanup dialog box, which is shown in Figure 11-19.**

   Select the drive you want to clean up, and then click OK. Disk Cleanup checks the selected drive and then opens the Disk Cleanup dialog box.

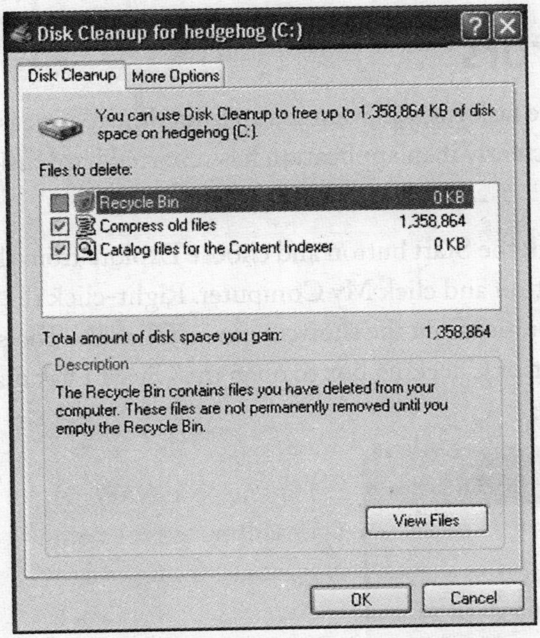

Figure 11-19 The Disk Cleanup dialog box.

3. **Select the files you want to delete.**

   Click the check box next to the category of files you want to delete, and then click OK. You can get rid of downloaded program files, including ActiveX and Java applets; you can delete temporary Internet files; and you can choose to empty the Recycle Bin. Also, you can delete temporary files and temporary offline files, compress little-used files (Windows will automatically uncompress them when you next access them, you'll never even notice), and you can also remove old Catalog files created by the Indexing Service.

If you want to remove Windows components or programs that you don't use, click the More Options tab. Clicking Clean Up in the Windows Components section starts the Windows Components Wizard, and clicking Clean Up in the Installed Programs section opens the Add Or Remove Programs dialog box. Clicking Clean Up in the System Restore section lets you remove old system restore points. If you have saved several restore points on disk, you may not need the older ones any more and you can remove them.

We recommend you run Disk Cleanup every two or three months. Even if you aren't pressed for hard disk space, getting rid of files that are totally and completely useless is always a good idea.

Checking for Disk Errors

Another hard-disk maintenance task you will want to run from time to time is to check your hard disk for errors, particularly if an application has reported hard disk reading or writing problems.

To check a hard disk, right-click the Start button and choose Explore from the shortcut menu, or click the Start button and click My Computer. Right-click the disk you want to check, and choose Properties from the shortcut menu. Click the Tools tab, and then click Check Now in the Error Checking box to open the Check Disk dialog box, as shown in Figure 11-20.

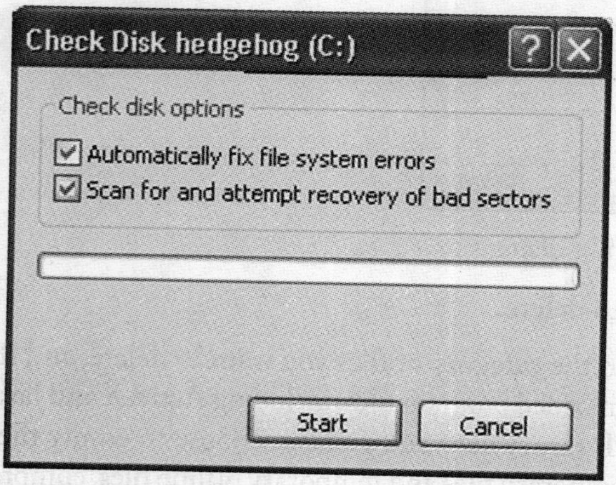

Figure 11-20 The Check Disk dialog box.

The Check Disk dialog box has two options:

- Automatically Fix File System Errors.
- Scan For And Attempt Recovery Of Bad Sectors.

Place a check mark in both of these boxes, and click Start to begin the checking process. A status bar at the bottom of the Check Disk dialog box displays the tests' progress, and you will see a final report when all the tests are complete.

Defragmenting Your Files

When Windows writes a file to your hard disk, it places the file wherever it finds room. Any one file can have a piece here, a piece there, a piece somewhere else, and so on. Windows always knows the location of these pieces and can access them when you want to open the file, but going to several locations takes longer than if all the pieces were in one place. Over time, this can lead to a slowdown in system performance as the level of fragmentation increases. Any process that reads a number of files will start to show the effects of fragmentation, including starting large applications and even restarting Windows after a shutdown.

Fragmentation occurs as you add and delete files and folders, download information from the Internet, and add or remove applications. In a similar way, the free space on your hard disk will also occupy more and more smaller and smaller spaces; the free space will itself become fragmented.

To speed up file retrieval, you can run Disk Defragmenter to round up the bits and pieces and organize them so that applications can find and load the file faster. And this is all done behind the scenes; the file fragments are moved from their original locations, but you will still find them in their original folders in Windows Explorer and My Computer. Here are the steps Disk Defragmenter takes:

- Locates the separate fragments of each file on the disk.
- Copies these fragments into a single contiguous section of the hard disk in a new location.
- Verifies that the copy is an exact copy of the original.
- Updates the Master File Table (MFT) or File Allocation Table (FAT) to record the new location for the file.
- Deallocates the old location and reclassifies it as free space.

NOTE *The MFT is that part of the NTFS file system that maps all files and folders stored on a disk. There is at least one entry in the MFT for every file on an NTFS disk; each entry contains information on the file size, time and date stamps, security attributes, and data location.*

To analyze the degree of defragmentation on your hard disk, and then defragment those files, make sure you are logged on as Computer Administrator and follow these steps:

1. **Open the Disk Defragmenter window, which is shown in Figure 11-21.**

   Click the Start button, click All Programs, click Accessories, click System Tools, and then click Disk Defragmenter. Alternatively, you can open Windows Explorer or My Computer, right-click the hard disk, choose Properties from the shortcut menu, click the Tools tab, and then click Defragment Now in the Defragmentation box. You can also click the Start button, click Control Panel, click Performance And Maintenance, and then select the task Rearrange Items On Your Hard Disk To Make Programs Run Faster.

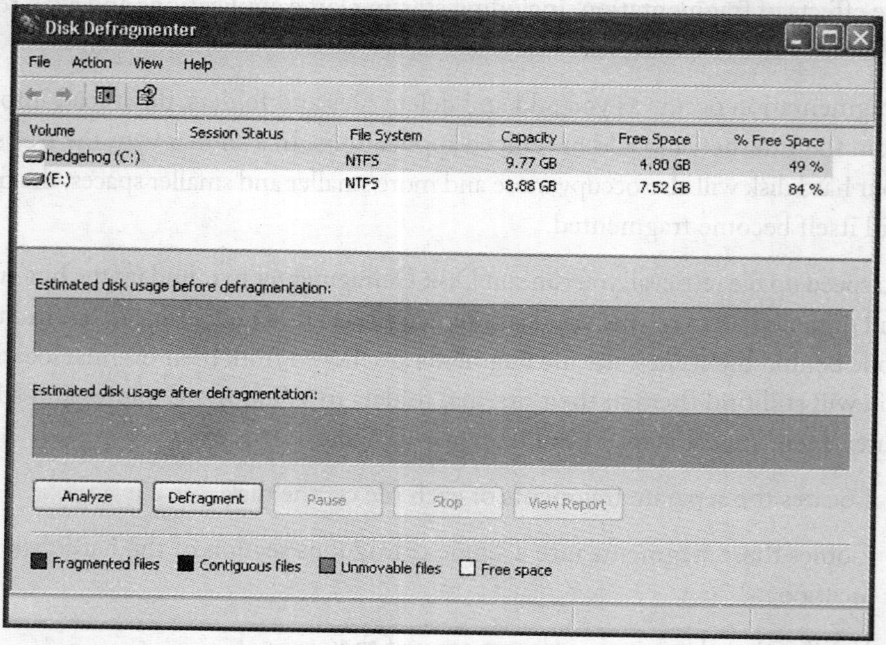

Figure 11-21 The Disk Defragmenter window.

2. **Analyze the disk.**

   Select the disk or volume you want to look at, and click the Analyze button. After a bit, you'll see something similar to the screen in Figure 11-22 and a message box that will tell you whether the drive needs to be defragmented. Notice the colored stripes at the bottom of the Disk Defragmenter window. The Analysis Display provides a graphical image of fragmented files (coded red); contiguous files (coded blue); system files, including the Windows Registry, the Hibernate file, the MFT and the Paging file (coded green); and free space (coded white). The size of each color stripe in the Analysis Display represents how much space each file occupies, and the location of the stripe indicates the file's approximate location.

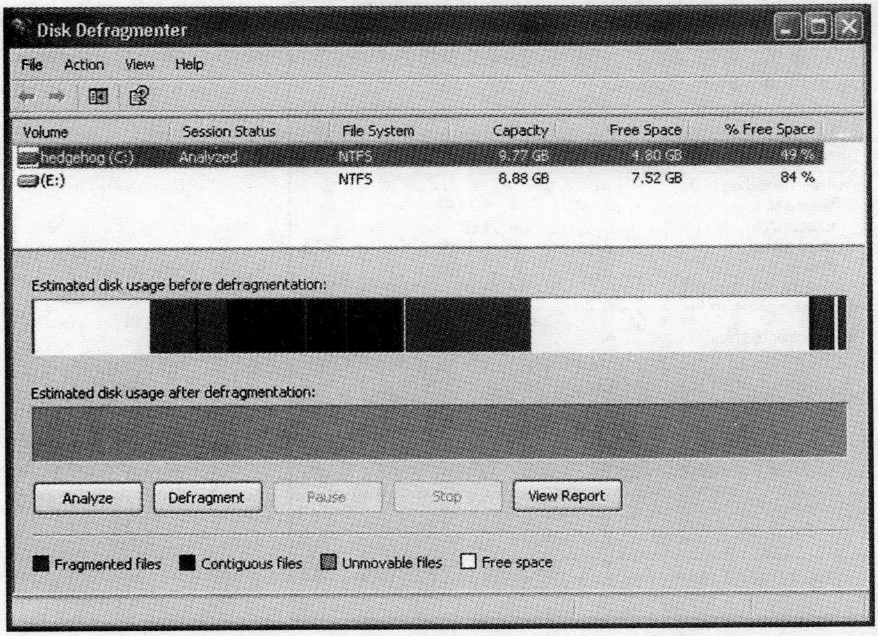

Figure 11-22 Analysis of a hard disk.

3. Get more information about the disk.

To get more information, such as the names of the fragmented files, their size, and the number of fragments, click the Action menu and click View Report. An example from a fragmented disk is shown in Figure 11-23. The report lists volume information for the disk you analyzed, as well as information about the most fragmented files on your system, giving the filename, file size, and the number of separate fragments the file contains.

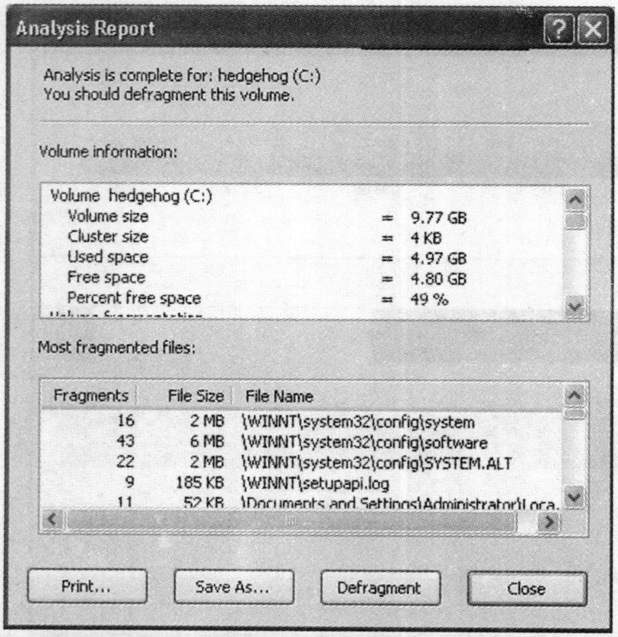

Figure 11-23 A Disk Defragmenter Analysis Report for a fragmented hard disk.

4. **Defragment the drive.**

   If both you and Windows decide that defragmenting is necessary, click the Defragment button to start the process.

5. **Select the next drive.**

   When defragmentation is complete, select the next disk drive or volume for analysis or defragmentation. When you are finished, close Disk Defragmenter.

Defragmenting a drive can take quite a while, depending on the size of the disk, the number of files it contains, and the degree to which these files are defragmented. The Defragmentation Display indicates progress as file segments are collected together and re-recorded into their new location.

If your hard disk is very badly defragmented and is also nearly full, there may not be enough free space available on your disk to complete the defragmentation because a complete contiguous copy of the file must be stored on your disk before the original dispersed segments can be safely erased. If this is the case, you may see a message displayed by Disk Defragmenter suggesting that you defragment the disk even though Disk Defragmenter has just finished running. If this happens to you, try copying a few very large files off onto another disk, or run Disk Cleanup to get rid of unwanted files and to empty the Recycle Bin.

NOTE *Plan to keep about 30 percent of your NTFS hard disk as free space; this should give you enough room to run Disk Defragmenter whenever you need to.*

You *can* do other work during the defragmentation process, but your system response will be much slower than normal. Also, whenever you save a file back to the hard disk, Disk Defragmenter will start all over again. So it's best to run Disk Defragmenter at a time when you don't need to be doing anything else on your computer, and doing so about once a month should be sufficient for normal users. If you are a heavy-duty user who adds tons of files during the course of your work, consider running Disk Defragmenter on a weekly basis. You should also run Disk Defragmenter as soon as you have finished the Windows installation, and after you finish installing any large applications.

The Challenge of Defragmenting an NTFS Volume

No matter what the file system, data has an inherent tendency to fragment as a file is written to and erased from a hard disk. In Windows, file fragmentation is present right from the start; the installation process leaves hundreds of fragmented files behind. And just to complicate matters, using the NTFS presents a special set of problems.

The smallest increment of data storage on an NTFS volume is the *cluster,* which in turn consists of one or more contiguous disk sectors. On our system, a cluster is 4 KB in size and consists of eight 512-byte sectors. This means that because 4-KB clusters are the smallest unit of storage on the disk, Windows writes files of 4 KB or less out to the hard disk as contiguous units. Files larger than 4 KB become fragmented if no group of contiguous clusters is available when Windows writes the file out to disk, and the larger the file, the greater the chance the file will be fragmented. If the free space on the hard disk is also fragmented, the chance of file fragmentation increases, as a smaller number of contiguous clusters is available.

Disk Defragmenter cannot move certain system files, and this decreases the efficiency of the defragmentation process. The Windows paging file is an essential part of the virtual memory management system (more on the paging file and virtual memory in the next section), but it also presents some serious obstacles:

- The Windows paging file is a big file. Windows typically allocates space on disk for the file that is approximately 150 percent of the real physical memory present in your system. The paging file might even be fragmented from the very beginning as a single block of disk space this big may not exist on your disk.
- The paging file is dynamic and expands to meet changing system requirements. As it expands, it may become fragmented. One trick to use here is to configure the paging file with a fixed size (called Custom Size) so that it can't expand.

Apart from the paging file, Windows also uses several other files connected to the NTFS that Disk Defragmenter can't move. When you format a volume as NTFS, the first part if the disk is reserved for Master File Table (MFT) information files. These files are hidden and can only be viewed with certain third-party utility programs. The NTFS file system also reserves several other files, including a transaction log (called $log), partition boot sector (called $boot), and the MFT mirror (called $MftMirr). The MFT mirror duplicates some of the information found in the MFT and acts as a backup in the event that the original MFT information is damaged in some way. The MFT mirror is always located in the logical center of the volume and can't be moved. Another obstacle.

A volume that contains a large number of small files will fill the original MFT faster than it will fill the free space, and this will cause the MFT itself to expand. To allow for this inevitable expansion, Windows creates a MFT reserved zone, but this is hidden and you won't see this area designated as used space when you look at your disk's Properties. The MFT reserved zone is listed as free space, when it is actually not free space that you (or Disk Defragmenter) can use. The reserved zone is also not available to Disk Defragmenter as free space during the defragmentation process.

Optimizing Your System for Peak Performance

Now that your hard disk is as clear of clutter and as optimized as it can be, we can turn our attention to other aspects of system tuning under Windows XP. First we'll look at some of the visual effects you can change, and then we'll delve into the arcane world of virtual memory.

Working with Visual Effects

In addition to the Display and Visual Themes we looked at back in Chapter 4, you can also look at and change the settings that govern how those visual elements work. Here are the steps:

1. **Open the Performance Options dialog box.**

   Click the Start button, click Control Panel, and click Performance And Maintenance. Then under the heading Pick A Task, choose Adjust Visual Effects to open the Performance Options dialog box shown in Figure 11-24.

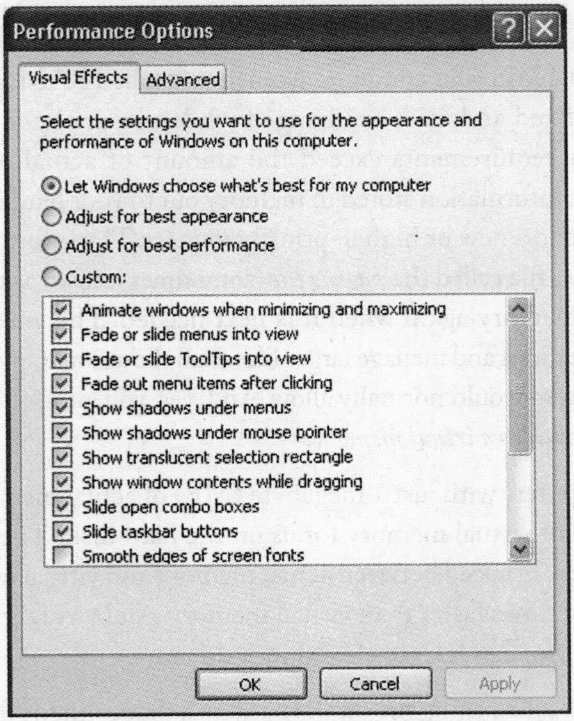

Figure 11-24 The Performance Options dialog box open at the Visual Effects tab.

2. **Choose between Best Appearance and Best Performance.**

   In the central portion of the dialog box, you will see a list of the current settings for a variety of effects used to define how windows open and close, how the taskbar is displayed, and so on. The current settings are a compromise based on your computer's hardware capabilities. Click Adjust For Best Appearance to turn all these effects on, and click Adjust For Best Performance to turn them all off. Click Custom if you want to choose your own settings.

This is the kind of thing you can experiment with to see whether you like the Adjust For Best Appearance settings, but can tolerate the inevitable system slowdown. Or you can go for the Adjust For Best Performance settings and see whether you like the speed increase at the expense of a less appealing user interface. Click Apply when you have made your choice, and then click OK to close the dialog box.

Managing Your System's Virtual Memory

For many people, just a simple mention of virtual memory is enough to send them running from the room screaming, but it's really not that complex. Let's take a quick look.

The amount of memory available in your computer (sometimes called RAM, short for random access memory) is fixed and can't be changed while you are busy with an application. When memory requirements exceed the amount of actual memory, Windows transfers the oldest information stored in memory out to your hard disk and makes that memory available to a new or higher-priority request. The information is written into a special Windows file called the *paging file* (sometimes known as the *swap file*) and can be restored to memory again when it is next needed. This means that Windows can run more applications and manage larger files than the amount of memory you have installed in your system would normally allow. And, yes, you guessed it, using a hard disk in this way is known as *virtual memory*.

So why don't we all buy computers with just 1 megabyte (MB) of actual memory and let Windows create 500 MB of virtual memory for us on the hard disk? The answer involves the relative differences in speed between actual memory and virtual memory; actual memory is hundreds of times faster than virtual memory. And virtual memory, when used to an excessive degree can start to slow things down.

Windows automatically creates the paging file on the hard disk that contains the other Windows system files, but if you have another hard disk on your system, which is bigger, has more free space, or is faster, then consider moving the paging file to this disk. To look at or change the virtual memory settings on your computer, log on as a Computer Administrator and follow these steps:

1. **Open the Performance Options dialog box.**

   Click the Start button, click Control Panel, and click Performance And Maintenance. Then under the Pick A Task heading, click Adjust Visual Effects. When the Performance Options dialog box opens, click the Advanced tab as shown in Figure 11-25.

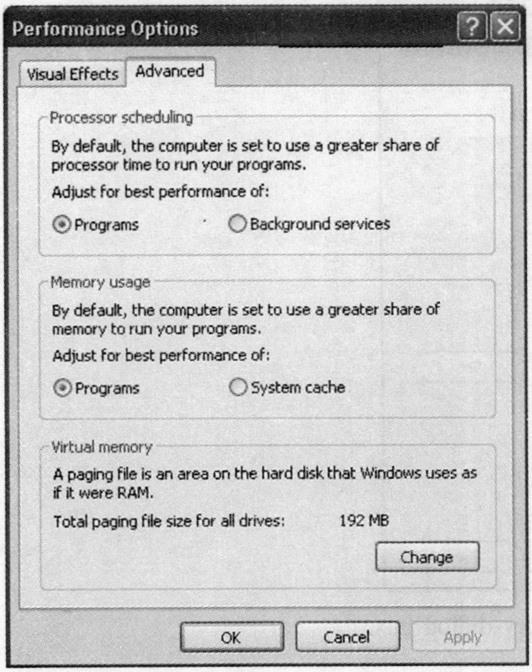

Figure 11-25 The Performance Options dialog box open at the Advanced tab.

2. **Choose a Processor optimization.**

   In the Processor Scheduling section, choose either Programs or Background Services. Most people want their applications to run as fast as possible and so choose Programs. (We looked at Windows services earlier in this chapter.)

3. **Choose a Memory Usage optimization.**

   In the Memory Usage section, choose either Programs or System Cache. Again, most people choose Programs.

4. **Look at your system's virtual memory settings.**

   In the Virtual Memory section, you will see the size of the paging file given in MB. Click Change to open the Virtual Memory dialog box shown in Figure 11-26.

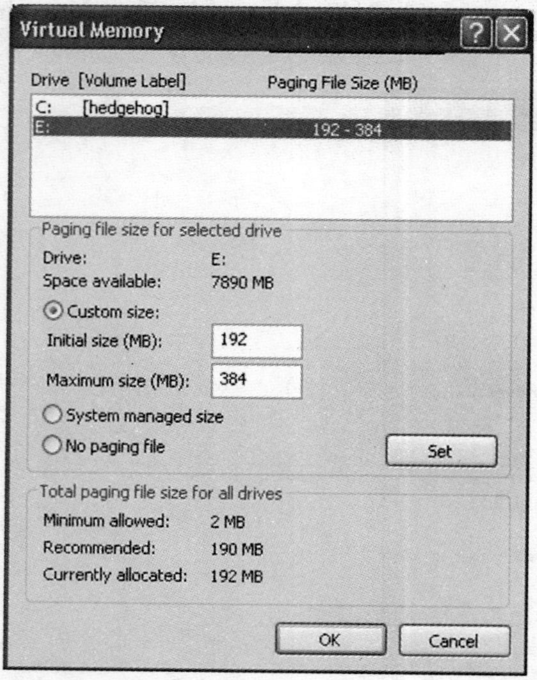

Figure 11-26 The Virtual Memory dialog box.

5. **Select a disk drive.**

   Select the disk drive whose settings you want to look at or change.

6. **Specify a new size for the paging file.**

   Choose between the three paging file options of Custom Size, System Managed Size, or No Paging File. If you selected Custom Size, you can enter an initial (or minimum) size and a maximum size you want to use for the paging file, in MB. If you do have lots of free disk space, you will definitely see a performance boost by specifying a large initial and large maximum paging file size.

NOTE *The paging file is actually called pagefile.sys, and it is always a hidden file, so you will not see it listed in Explorer or My Computer.*

Click OK to close the Virtual Memory dialog box, and you will be prompted to shut down and restart your computer if you made any changes to the paging file settings. And that's it; you are done with virtual memory.

Summary

In this chapter we have given you all the information you need to appear very knowledgeable the next time that bad-tempered tech-support guy barks his questions at you down the phone. You know where to find all kinds of detailed technical information about your computer, you can look at what is happening right now using the Windows Task Manager displays, and you can also keep your hard disks running at peak performance levels using the disk management tools in Windows XP.

Part 3

Business Projects

In This Part

Chapter 12

INSTALLING WINDOWS XP PROFESSIONAL

Featuring:

- Checking Windows XP Hardware Requirements
- Checking Hardware Compatibility
- Making a Backup
- Collecting Information
- Upgrading from an Earlier Operating System
- Looking at a Dual-Boot Installation
- Understanding File Systems in Windows XP
- Installing Windows XP
- Installing the Add-On Components
- Creating New User Accounts
- Turning Off the Guest Account

If you have just bought a new computer, there is a good chance that it arrived with Windows XP already installed. If this is the case, then you can skip this chapter; your work here is done. On the other hand, if you bought a copy of Windows XP to upgrade from an earlier version of Windows, or from another operating system, then read on.

Checking Windows XP Hardware Requirements

The official Microsoft hardware requirements that your computer must meet for Windows XP are as follows:

- 233 MHz Pentium microprocessor, or better.
- 128 MB of memory, or more; 4 GB is the maximum.
- At least 1.5 GB of free hard disk space on a 2-GB hard disk. If you are installing over a network, you will need more hard-disk space.
- VGA monitor.
- Keyboard.
- Mouse, or other compatible pointing device.
- CD-ROM, CD-RW, or DVD drive.

For a network installation, you will also need a network interface card and cable with which you can connect to the network, and access to the network share that contains the Setup files.

In terms of the official memory requirements, this is a case where more is definitely better, and we recommend that you load up your system with 256 MB of RAM. Most systems are sold with much faster processors than the above minimum requirements, so you will also see some performance boost there, too.

Checking Hardware Compatibility

The Windows Setup program automatically checks your computer hardware and lets you know of any possible problems that might crop up if you continue with the installation. You can also run this check separate from the installation process to evaluate your hardware before you start. Here are the steps:

1. Load the Windows CD.

Insert the Windows XP CD into your CD drive.

2. Check your system's compatibility.

Click the Check System Compatibility button and then click Check My System Automatically to run the hardware compatibility check on your computer system. You can also choose Visit The Compatability Web Site to go directly to Microsoft's Web site.

When the check is complete, a window opens on the desktop listing any potential problems on your system. Click Details to see more information on the topics listed, or click Finish to close the window.

You can also ensure your hardware is compatible with Windows XP by checking Microsoft's Hardware Compatibility List (HCL). You will find a copy of this list in the Support folder on the Windows XP CD; look for a file called hcl.txt. If you can't find your hardware in this list, the Windows XP installation might fail. To see the latest version of this list, go to *www.microsoft.com/hcl.*

Windows XP will run only on the hardware listed in the HCL; Microsoft is very clear about this. Previous versions of Windows would run on any hardware, but the same is not true of Windows XP. If your hardware is not listed in the HCL, contact the hardware manufacturer (try their Web site first) and ask them for a Windows XP device driver for your hardware. You don't need a special device driver if your hardware is Plug and Play.

Making a Backup

If you are upgrading from an earlier version of Windows, make a backup of all your important files to a floppy disk, CD, tape, or to a network hard drive before you begin the installation; you just never know when something might happen to damage those files.

If you are upgrading from Windows 95, 98, 98 Second Edition, or Windows ME, use the Backup program; if you are upgrading from Windows NT, use the Windows Backup program.

Collecting Information

If your computer will be connected to a network after the Windows XP installation, you will need to collect the following information:

- The name of your computer.
- The name of the workgroup or domain your computer belongs to.

Your network administrator can provide you with all this information.

Upgrading from an Earlier Operating System

Unless you have just purchased a new computer that came with Windows XP already installed, you will be upgrading from an earlier operating system, most likely from an earlier version of Windows. You can upgrade to Windows XP from the following operating systems:

- Windows 98
- Windows 98 Second Edition (Windows SE)
- Windows Millennium Edition (Windows ME)
- Windows NT 4 Workstation
- Windows 2000 Professional
- Windows XP Home Edition

Let's take a look.

Upgrading from Windows 3.1 and Windows 95

Upgrading from Windows 3.1 or Windows 95 to Windows XP is not supported by Microsoft. And for good reason, too. Windows 3.1 and Windows 95 computer systems are likely to contain older, legacy hardware not supported by Windows XP. The microprocessors will be too slow to manage the demands imposed by Windows XP, their hard disks will likely be too small to contain the operating system and associated files, and these systems will simply not have enough memory available. So don't even try; you won't get past the hardware compatibility tests performed at the beginning of the installation process.

Upgrading from Windows 98, 98 SE, and Windows ME

Upgrading to Windows XP from Windows 98, Windows 98 SE, and from Windows ME should be very straightforward. This will be the upgrade path chosen by most people, the computer systems should be capable of running Windows XP, processors will be fast enough to carry the load, and these systems will have sufficient memory available.

The main consideration here will be the choice of the most appropriate file system. Windows XP comes with a choice of three file systems, and we'll take a look at the pros and cons of using each of them in a later section in this chapter.

Upgrading from Windows NT 4 Workstation

Upgrading from Windows NT 4 Workstation will also be a simple upgrade. You are already using the New Technology File System (NTFS), so that choice has already been made for you. As long as your hardware passes the hardware compatibility tests, you are in good shape.

Upgrading from Windows 2000 Professional and Windows XP Home Edition

This is the easiest of all possible upgrade paths. If you can run Windows 2000 or Windows XP Home Edition on your computer, then your hardware is new enough and capable enough to run Windows XP Professional with ease. This upgrade will be a breeze.

Looking at a Dual-Boot Installation

Working with more than one operating system on your computer is known as a *dual-boot configuration;* if you have more than two different operating systems, you have a multiple-boot configuration. Such configurations, while they might not be all that common, do have advantages for certain situations. Once the dual-boot configuration is complete, you choose which operating system you want to use from an opening menu when you first boot up your computer. From that point on, all settings, applications, and files are kept separate.

Windows XP supports dual booting between the following operating systems:

- DOS
- Windows 3.*x*
- Windows 95
- Windows 98
- Windows NT Workstation 3.51
- Windows NT Workstation 4.0
- Windows 2000 Professional

Each operating system is installed in a separate volume on your hard disk so that files and configuration information remain separate. Also, you have to make sure that the boot volume is formatted with the appropriate file system. If you want to install Windows XP, Windows 2000, or Windows NT with Windows 95 or Windows 98, the boot volume must be formatted with the File Allocation Table (FAT) file system, not the NTFS file system. Windows 95, Windows 98, Windows 2000, and Windows XP can all support FAT32 volumes.

But if you format a Windows XP volume with anything other than the NTFS file system, you cannot use any of the NTFS-specific features, including the security features and disk quotas. Likewise, Windows 95 and Windows 98 cannot read an NTFS volume, so any files on that volume will be unavailable from Windows 95 and Windows 98.

To set up a dual-boot system between DOS or Windows 95 and Windows XP, make sure you install Windows XP last; otherwise, important Windows XP files may be overwritten. If you want to dual boot between any of the Windows 98 systems and Windows XP, you can install the operating systems in any order.

Understanding File Systems in Windows XP

A file system in an operating system is the overall structure that determines how files are named, stored, and organized. When you install Windows XP, you can choose to use any of three file systems:

- FAT, which stands for File Allocation Table and is the file system supported by DOS, Windows 3.*x*, and Windows 95 release 1 (16-bit operating systems).
- FAT32, which stands for File Allocation Table 32 and is the file system supported by Windows 95 release 2 and Windows 98 (a 32-bit operating system).
- NTFS, which stands for New Technology File System and is the file system supported by Windows NT and Windows 2000.

Which you choose depends in part on the size of your hard drive, how you plan to set up your network (if you intend to network your computers), and how secure you want your system to be.

NOTE *A 16-bit operating system can work with 2 bytes, or 16 bits, of information at one time. A 32-bit operating system can work with 4 bytes, or 32 bits, of information at one time.*

The FAT File System

The FAT approach to organizing your files is to create a database (the File Allocation Table) at the beginning of your hard drive. When you store a file on your hard drive, the operating system places information about it in the FAT so that you can later retrieve the file when you want it. You cannot use the FAT file system with a disk larger than 2.6 gigabytes. The FAT file system uses the 8.3 file-naming convention; that is, a file's name can be a maximum of eight letters. The three letters following the period are the file extension, which identifies the file's type. If you have a computer that uses the FAT file system and is connected via a network to a computer that uses the NTFS file system, you will not be able to see the files on the NTFS computer. The FAT file system does not provide any security.

The FAT32 File System

The FAT32 file system evolved from the FAT file system, but because of the way it is structured, you can use FAT32 with a hard drive as large as 2 terabytes. FAT32 also uses space on your hard drive much more efficiently. A few years ago when we converted a FAT drive to FAT32, the space available on the drive almost doubled. In addition, the FAT32 system lets you use long filenames; the maximum is 255 characters. The FAT32 file system is, therefore, a much better choice than FAT, but it still can't see the files on an NTFS system, and it does not provide any security.

The NTFS File System

Although you can use the FAT and FAT32 file systems with Windows XP, Microsoft recommends that you use NTFS for the following reasons:

- It has many security features, including password protection for files and folders.
- It provides better disk compression and file encryption. In other words, you can store more in less space, and you can encode data to prevent unauthorized access.
- You can use NTFS on a hard drive as large as 2 terabytes, and performance does not degrade as drive size increases.
- It provides better protection from viruses. Most viruses are written to attack systems formatted to FAT and FAT32, and they don't know what to do when they encounter NTFS.

- NTFS creates a backup of the Master File Table (MFT), which is the equivalent of the FAT database. If the boot sector of your hard drive becomes damaged, you can replace the information from the backup.
- NTFS includes features required for hosting Active Directory, so if your network uses Active Directory, you have to choose NTFS.

NOTE *A Windows XP installation that uses NTFS can see and access FAT and FAT32 files.*

Which File System Is Best for You?

One size does not fit all when selecting a file system, so here are some guidelines:

- If you are installing Windows XP on a standalone system or on a network that includes only Windows XP machines, go with NTFS. NTFS is a robust, secure file system, and though it causes the operating system to run a bit slower than it would using FAT32, it is your best bet if you want the additional features.
- If you are setting up a network that will be accessed by DOS, Windows 3.*x*, and/or Windows 95/98/ME machines, consider using FAT. Remember, FAT and FAT32 can't see NTFS files.
- If you are setting up a dual-boot configuration, for example, one partition uses Windows 98 and the other uses Windows XP, and it is important that each operating system be able to see the other's files, use FAT or FAT32.

Installing Windows XP

Installation generally takes from 60 to 90 minutes, depending on the options you choose. We made a custom installation that took just over an hour to complete. Windows automatically restarts your computer several times during the installation process; this is completely normal and nothing to worry about.

Insert the Windows CD into your CD drive, click Install Windows XP, and then choose between Upgrade and New Installation. Most people will choose Upgrade for a quick and easy installation, but if you want to have complete control over the installation, particularly if you want to create a dual-boot system, choose New Installation.

If your current version of Windows doesn't detect the Windows XP CD automatically, you can start the process manually by following these steps:

1. **Open the Run box.**

   Click the Start button, and then click Run.

2. **Enter the path to the installation program.**

   Type the following path to the setup file, using your own CD-ROM drive letter in place of the *d* shown here:

   d:\setup.exe and press Enter. Now, just follow the instructions on the screen.

The installation process goes through the following stages:

- Collecting Information
- Dynamic Update
- Preparing Installation
- Installing Windows
- Finalizing Installation

In the sections that follow, we'll look at what happens as the installation progresses through each of these stages.

Collecting Information

One of the most important pieces of information you need to complete this part of the installation is the Windows Product Key, which you will find on a yellow sticker on the back of the Windows CD jewel case. It's a 25-character key with letters and numbers grouped into five groups of five characters, separated by hyphens. Just type the characters into the five boxes on the screen; the cursor will skip to the next box at the right moment. Click Next.

In the next window, you can set up language options, review or change the default options for copying files, or use special accessibility options during the installation. Click Next.

Dynamic Update

To make sure that you have the latest copies of important Windows files, the dynamic update part of the installation process connects to a special Microsoft Web site and downloads the latest updates to Windows. This is well worth the little bit of extra effort required and takes only a moment to complete. If you use a dial-up connection with a modem, make sure your modem is connected to the phone line. Progress is shown on the screen. Click Next.

Preparing Installation

The Setup program checks your installed hardware, creates any required partitions, formats the partition according to the file system you choose, and copies the initial files to the Windows installation folder. This last part of the process usually takes several minutes to complete, and a bar graph on the screen indicates progress.

Installing Windows

Next, you will see the graphical Windows interface on the screen as more files are copied to your hard disk; as the files are copied, a small graphic indicates progress and displays the number of minutes it will take to complete your installation. This display is not updated minute by minute, but changes every few minutes, or when a major task completes, so don't worry if it stays on the same value for a while.

After a few minutes, the Installation Wizard asks you to choose your language and keyboard requirements, and then to enter your name and company name. Click Next.

The next window asks for a computer name. (Make sure you remember the name you type here; you'll need it later.) If you are on a company network, your network administrator will tell you the name you should use. You must also enter a password for the setup Administrator account. Choose something you will remember, but we'll come back and change this password later. Click Next.

Complete the modem dialing information in the next window with your area code and the number you use to get an outside line. Click Next. In the next Setup Wizard window, confirm or change the date and time settings; click Next. Setup now loads network settings and components so you can connect to other computers and to the Internet.

In the Networking Settings window, choose Typical Settings to create your network based on Client For Microsoft Networks, File And Print Sharing For Microsoft Networks, and TCP/IP with automatic addressing. Choose Custom Settings if you want to set up your network using a different configuration. We'll be looking at how to configure networking on both small home/office networks and large corporate networks in Chapters 13 and 14. Click Next.

In the Workgroup Or Computer Domain window, you can specify that you want this computer to be a member of a domain; check with your network administrator for the information to enter here. If the computer is not connected to a network or is not part of a domain, you can specify that the computer is a member of a workgroup. Click Next.

Finalizing Installation

Once all the Windows files have been copied to your hard disk, the installation program saves the appropriate system settings and removes temporary files and folders used during the installation process. And then Windows restarts for the last time.

The Welcome Screen

The Welcome screen guides you through five more steps in setting up your computer. Click Next, and select the method you plan to use to connect to the Internet. Most people in home offices will choose either Telephone Modem or Digital Subscriber Line (DSL) Or Cable Modem. In a larger office you might connect through the office network, so choose Local Area Network (LAN) in this case. Click Next. You must activate your copy of Windows within 30 days of finishing the installation; you can do it now or you can do it later, but don't forget to do it. We'll look at activation in the next section.

Click Next. Your computer is now ready for you to use, and in this last step, you can choose whether to set up your Internet connection now or do it later. We looked at all the connection options in Chapter 7, so we won't repeat the steps here. Click Next. Finally, if you will be sharing this computer with other users, you will want to create separate accounts for each person. You can create those accounts here, or you can use User Accounts in Control Panel to create them for you; it makes no difference. We'll look at creating new user accounts later in this chapter. Click Finish when you are done.

Activating Your Copy of Windows

If you don't activate your copy of Windows during the installation process and choose to do it later (you have up to 30 days), a small informational icon pops up on the desktop from time to time to remind you that time is running out; you will see a small Windows icon in the notification area. You can also click the Start button, click All Programs, and then click Activate Windows, or you can click the Start button, click All Programs, click Accessories, click System Tools, and then click Activate Windows.

No matter how you start it, Activate Windows allows you to connect to a special Microsoft Web site and also allows you to register your copy of Windows with Microsoft. Activation is anonymous and required, registration is not anonymous and is optional. You can also opt to receive informational mailings from Microsoft. Click Finish to close the Activate Windows dialog box.

NOTE *If you bought your computer from one of the big computer companies with Windows XP Professional already installed, activation was probably completed at the factory.*

So what's the difference between activation and registration? Activation creates a profile linking the hardware in your computer with the product key associated with the copy of Windows XP you installed. It allows Microsoft to lock each installed copy of Windows XP onto a specific computer. If you don't activate Windows and provide this information to Microsoft, your system will stop working after 30 days—except to remind you to activate, that is.

Product registration is different. Registration is the process whereby you choose to give contact and other information to Microsoft so that they can send you information about service packs and updates. You don't have to register your copy of Windows with Microsoft, but you do have to activate your copy or it will simply stop working.

If you try to install this same copy of Windows XP onto another computer, again, you will be prompted to activate, only this time the activation will fail, and you will be reminded that it is illegal to install one copy of Windows XP onto more than one computer.

Installing the Add-On Components

The Windows XP installation CD contains a number of optional elements that you can install on your system if you wish. To look at program information, or to install these add-on components, insert the Windows XP CD into your drive and then use Add Or Remove Programs in Control Panel to start the Windows Components Wizard. Optional components include the following:

- Accessories and Utilities
- Fax Services
- Indexing Service
- Internet Information Server (IIS)
- Management And Monitoring Tools
- Message Queuing
- MSN Explorer
- Networking Services
- Other Network File And Print Services
- Update Root Certificates

Select an item from the list and click Details to see more information, then follow the instructions on the screen to install the optional component you have selected.

Creating New User Accounts

The password you gave to the Installation program as Windows XP is installed gives you Administrator rights to the Windows XP computer system. Once the installation is complete, you can create normal user accounts for all the people who will have access to the Windows system.

Windows offers three types of user accounts on a standalone computer or a computer that is a member of a workgroup:

- Computer Administrator account gives you complete access to the whole Windows system. You can create, change, and delete other user accounts, you can install and uninstall hardware and applications, and you can access all files.
- Limited account is the most restricted account, allowing you only to change your picture and to change or remove your password.
- Guest account is not password-protected and allows anyone to access the computer, the network, even the Internet, from this computer. We'll turn this account off in the next section.

The person who is in charge of the Windows system should have both a Computer Administrator and a Limited account; other users should all have Limited accounts. Here are the steps to get them started:

1. Open the User Accounts folder.

Click the Start button, click Control Panel, and click User Accounts.

2. Name the new account.

Click Create A New Account, and then enter a name for the account. This can be the person's real name, and it will appear on the Windows Welcome screen and on the Start menu. Click Next.

3. Choose the account type.

Select the type of account you want this person to have. Click Create Account.

The account you have just created is displayed in the User Accounts folder, and the next thing we have to do is assign a password to this account. Click the account you just created, and you will see a User Accounts folder similar to that shown in Figure 12-1.

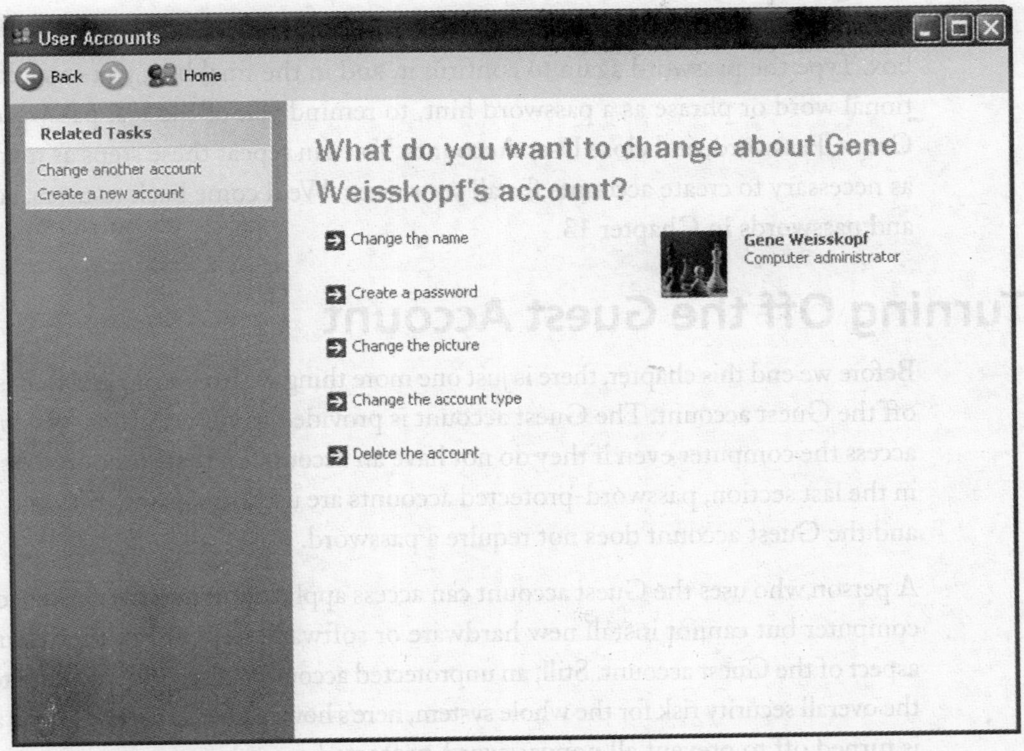

Figure 12-1 The User Accounts folder.

In this folder you can change all aspects of the account, including the following:

- Change the name of the account.
- Change the picture associated with the account.
- Change the account type.
- Create or change the password.
- Delete the account.

Click Create A Password, and then enter the password into the Type A New Password box. Type the password again to confirm it, and in the final box, you can add an optional word or phrase as a password hint, to remind you of the real password. Click Create Password, and close User Accounts. You can repeat these steps as many times as necessary to create accounts for all your users. We'll come back to users, accounts, and passwords in Chapter 13.

Turning Off the Guest Account

Before we end this chapter, there is just one more thing we have to do and that is to turn off the Guest account. The Guest account is provided to allow anyone, yes *anyone*, to access the computer even if they do not have an account on that computer. As we saw in the last section, password-protected accounts are used to separate files and folders, and the Guest account does not require a password.

A person who uses the Guest account can access applications and files installed on the computer but cannot install new hardware or software; neither can they change any aspect of the Guest account. Still, an unprotected account is a security risk, and to lessen the overall security risk for the whole system, here's how to check that the Guest account is turned off to prevent all nonpassword-protected access:

1. **Open User Accounts in Control Panel.**

   Click the Start button, click Control Panel, and then double-click User Accounts.

2. **Turn the Guest account off.**

   Click Guest, and if the guest account is turned on, click Turn Off The Guest Account.

When you return to the User Accounts folder, you will see that the Guest account is indeed designated as turned off. Keep it that way. We'll look at user accounts in more detail in Chapter 13.

Summary

Installing Windows XP is a pretty straightforward process once you understand some of the issues involved and the impact of the decisions you have to make. Making sure your computer hardware is listed on the Hardware Compatibility List (HCL) before you start the Windows XP installation can save you a lot of grief. Choosing the right file system to use is probably the most far-reaching of these decisions. Finally, we looked at how to create accounts for the people who will use the Windows XP computer system.

Chapter 13

SETTING UP A SMALL NETWORK

Featuring:

- Setting Up Your Peer-to-Peer Network
- Sharing an Internet Connection
- Bridging Between Two Different Networks
- Installing and Using a Networked Printer
- Working on Your Network
- Network Tips and Tricks
- Setting Up Users and Groups on Your Network

Setting up your own network is easy; that's all you have to remember. The networking world has come a very long way in recent years. These days, home networks are pretty common, most small businesses are networked, and you'd be hard-pressed to find a lone PC in a corporation that's not connected to a network of some type and to the Internet. A network will save you time, and therefore, save you money. As you will see in this chapter, you can easily use Windows XP Professional to set up a simple network based on easy-to-use standards in a small to medium-size office or to set up a network in your home office. You can also share one connection to the Internet between two or more computers on the network.

NOTE *Networking is one area of computer activity where you will find a lot of jargon and mysterious abbreviations. In this chapter, we will use some of that jargon, because it is useful shorthand. But if you find we have used a term that you don't understand, look in the Glossary at the end of this book and you will find it defined there.*

How do you know if a network could benefit your business? Well, take a look at some of the things that even a small network makes possible:

- You can open files, folders, and applications on one computer while you are sitting at another computer.
- You can share a single printer (and other devices) between several computers.
- You can share an Internet connection.
- You can back up important files and folders to a single network tape drive attached to another computer.
- You can create an e-business and run it off your network.
- You can play multiplayer games.
- You can access your corporate network from home and your home network from work.
- You can communicate with other users on the network with e-mail and applications such as NetMeeting.
- And, with Windows XP Professional, you can secure your system and thus your data.

And this list is far from exhaustive. Once you set up your network, you'll wonder how you ever got along without it. Long gone are the days of the floppy-disk shuffle, when you had to copy a file to a floppy and actually *carry* the floppy to another computer in order to print a file.

In this chapter, we'll take a look at setting up, configuring, and using a simple network, and then we'll give you some tips about troubleshooting your network.

Setting Up Your Peer-to-Peer Network

If you glance again at the list above, you'll see that the operative word is *sharing*. The real purpose of a network is to share resources. You don't need a printer for every computer in your office; you can set up one printer that everyone can share. Setting up a network can be cost effective as well as a productivity tool.

Before we get into the how-to-do-it part, though, we need to explain a bit about network structure and design. Just as you need to understand about the file systems you can use with Windows XP Professional before you install the operating system, you need to understand network structure and design so that you can set up a network that meets your specific needs. After all, that's why you're thinking about a network in the first place—so that your business operations run more efficiently and, in the long run, so that your business is more profitable.

Understanding the Network Types

In this section and the next, we're going to have to use some technical terms that you may not be familiar with. (Sometimes it seems that a technical term is basically just a new word for a concept or a thing that you don't know about or don't know much about.) Don't tune out. One of our colleagues describes the skill level needed to set up a network as about the same as making a pot of coffee. We don't know about that, but it's certainly easier than programming a VCR!

One of your first decisions is about network type, and you have two choices: peer-to-peer or client/server. In a *peer-to-peer network,* all computers are equals. Each computer has its own hard drive and can see and talk to all the other computers on the network. In addition, each computer can share its resources, such as a CD-ROM drive, a printer, files, folders, applications, and so on. A peer-to-peer network is fine until you reach a population of between 10 and 15 computers; at that point, things can get a little harder to manage. On a peer-to-peer network, each user decides which of their files and folders they want to share, and with whom.

In a *client/server network,* one or more computers stores resources and supplies, that is, *serves* them to the other computers. All the other computers are connected to this central computer(s), which manages applications, files, printers, and so on. In general, corporate networks are client/server networks and are managed by a system administrator. In this chapter, we are going to set up a peer-to-peer network, which is ideal for a small business or a home office. In the next chapter, we'll be looking at some of the issues involved in connecting to a larger client/server network in a corporate setting.

Designing Your Network

After you decide on a network type, you need to decide how your network will be designed physically. The technical term for physical design is *topology*, and you can choose from three basic topologies:

- Star, in which all the computers are connected to a central hub like the points of a star. A star topology uses 10BaseT cabling. (We'll explain cabling in the next section.)
- Bus, in which all the computers are connected to a single cable. The bus topology uses coaxial cable.
- Ring, in which all the computers are connected via a closed circle of cabling. This topology is not in common use.

Techie types love to discuss topologies and which physical design actually corresponds to a theoretical topology. We'll leave that to them and just say that the star design is the one that's best suited to a peer-to-peer network, and that's what we'll use in this chapter. We'll connect each computer on the network to a central hub.

There are lots of different ways you can connect your computers. Some systems use the electrical or telephone wiring already installed in your house or office, while others are completely wireless. These methods can be pretty expensive, and they also come with another significant drawback: they can be slow. Their major advantage is that you don't have to run cable to them. We'll look at how to connect a computer using a wireless adapter or a home phone-line network adapter (sometimes abbreviated to HomePNA or to HPNA) to our Ethernet network a bit later.

Far better to start with an industry standard, known and understood all over the world, called *Ethernet*. Ethernet is the driving force behind millions of computer networks, the hardware is well understood, readily available, reliable, fast, and cheap. You can buy the components you need from your local computer store, or you can shop around for the best price at Web sites such as PC Connection (*www.pcconnection.com*), ProVantage (*www.provantage.com*), or CDW (*www.cdw.com*).

So How Fast Is Ethernet?

Ethernet equipment is available in three different speeds; standard Ethernet that runs at 10 megabits per second (Mbps), Fast Ethernet that runs at 100 Mbps, and Gigabit Ethernet that runs at 1,000 Mbps. Your choice here is between standard Ethernet and Fast Ethernet; Gigabit Ethernet is still too expensive and is overkill for a network of modest proportions. These days all Fast Ethernet equipment is actually dual speed and can operate at 10 Mbps or at 100 Mbps; if you go with Fast Ethernet, make sure you use Category 5 cabling.

So how fast is 10 Mbps? A megabit is roughly equal to 1 million bits, where each bit can be a 1 or a 0. Your dial-up V.90 56-Kbps modem, for example, processes information at about 50,000 bits per second, a standard Ethernet network runs at 10 million bits per second, and a Fast Ethernet network runs at approximately 100 million bits per second. So a standard Ethernet network is about 200 times faster than your 56 Kbps modem, and a Fast Ethernet network is 2,000 times faster.

Shopping for What You Need

We mentioned a couple of network components earlier that we now want to explain—*cable* and a *hub*. Cabling and a hub are only two of the necessary components though; you also need a *network interface card* (NIC) for each computer you want to attach to your network. Here's your shopping list and a description of what each item does:

- 10BaseT cabling is the physical connection between the computers on the network and the hub. You can get two grades of 10BaseT cable—Category 3 UTP and Category 5 UTP. (UTP stands for unshielded twisted-pair.) Category 3 UTP cable length runs from a minimum of 8 feet to a maximum of 328 feet and transmits data at 10 Mbps. The maximum length for a Category 5 UTP cable is 165 feet, and it transmits data at 100 Mbps. So you can see that Category 5 UTP cable is faster, but if you need to connect computers that are more than 165 feet from the hub, you'll need to use Category 3 UTP. In large offices, installers run bulk cable through the walls and ceilings, and attach connectors where they are needed; for a small office, it is much easier to buy a cable of the right length complete with the connectors already attached. Cable lengths of 10, 15, 20, 25, and 50 feet are commonly available. The cable attaches to the network hardware with RJ-45 jacks, snap connectors that look like a wider version of the plastic jacks used by your phone system.
- A hub is the central device that connects all the computers on the network, and it is about the size of this book. The hub itself doesn't require any software or configuration; it is simply the device that allows all the computers to communicate. The number of connections on the hub, that is, the number of places to which you can connect a cable that's connected to a computer on the other end, determines the number of computers that can be on the network. Be sure to buy a hub that has enough connections for the number of computers you want to connect. Big companies use large rack-mounted systems. You might start with a hub that has five or eight ports (for less than $70) and expand from there. You can usually attach a second hub (up to a limit of four hubs for Standard Ethernet; some versions of Fast Ethernet limits you to just two), although you will have to use a special cable called a *cross-over cable*.
- A network interface card (NIC) goes into each computer on the network and connects to one of the slots on the computer's motherboard. (The motherboard is the main printed circuit board in a computer.) The slots on the motherboard are of two types: Industry Standard Architecture (ISA) and Peripheral Component Interconnect (PCI). A NIC will work with one type or the other, but not with both. Most newer computers have PCI slots, but you'll need to find out which type your computer uses. Also, if you don't want to open the computer case, you could use a Universal Serial Bus (USB) network card that you plug into the USB port on your desktop or portable computer. The manufacturer of the NIC assigns each Ethernet interface card a unique number known as the *Ethernet address*; this number cannot be changed and is used as a navigation aid by the networking software.

You can shop for these parts and pieces at your local computer store or on the Internet. Another option is to buy a starter kit that contains everything you need to connect a couple of computers—NICs, cable, and a hub—all for less than $100 from companies such as Intel (*www.intel.com*), Linksys (*www.linksys.com*), 3Com (*www.3com.com*), or Netgear (*www.netgearinc.com*). If you need to connect more than two computers, you could buy extra starter kits, but you'll probably save money if you buy the parts separately.

NOTE *When you buy your network interface cards and hub, make sure the packaging explicitly states that the hardware has been certified by Microsoft as being suitable for Windows XP Professional. If you are in doubt, check the Hardware Compatibility List at* www.microsoft.com/hcl.

Connecting Your Network Hardware

Okay—you've decided on the physical layout of your system, all the pieces are in place, and you have your starter kit or your components assembled. Get yourself a screwdriver, and follow these steps:

1. Insert a NIC into each computer that you want to connect to the network.

Turn off all computers and peripherals, and unplug them. Open the case (this is likely to be the hardest step), remove the slot cover from a free expansion slot, and insert the NIC in the empty slot, according to the manufacturer's instructions. Be sure that the card bracket is sitting snugly in the case and secure it with the screw that originally held the slot cover. Replace the case. If the NIC is a PC Card, insert the card into your portable computer.

2. Locate the hub.

Find a good central location for the hub, and plug the power adapter into a power socket. A central location helps to keep cable lengths short, and most of the time, you won't need access to the hub unless there is a problem with the network. Most hubs have small LEDs on the front of the case used to indicate network activity, and it can be comforting to glance across at them to see that the network is still running. Other lights on the hub may indicate connection speed (either 10 or 100 Mbps) and overall network bandwidth. Some NICs also have LEDs to indicate status or network activity, but because they are only visible from the back of the computer, they can be very hard to see.

NOTE *Installing network cabling through walls and ceilings in your house may fall under local building codes or fire regulations; check with your local planning office before you run any cables.*

3. Connect the cables.

Connect one end of the cable to the NIC, and connect the other end of the cable to the hub, starting with the first connection. Do this for each computer on the network. By the way, both ends of the cable are identical, so it doesn't make any difference which end you connect to the computer or the hub. Don't run cables across doorways where they will be walked on or tripped over, don't put furniture on top of them, and don't staple them to your baseboard using standard square staples. And keep them away from fluorescent light fixtures and large electric motors.

NOTE *If your hub has a port labeled* Uplink *or* Crossover, *don't connect a computer to that port; it is for connecting two hubs together or for connecting a cable or DSL modem to the network.*

4. Power up the system.

Turn on the hub and all connected computers. You should see a light or LED on the hub for each connected computer.

That's it—really, that's all there is to it. The first time you do this, it may take you a while, especially if you've never taken the back off your computer before. But the next NIC you insert will take you half that time, and soon you'll be inserting NICs like the guy at the computer store. Now you're ready to install and configure your network software.

Configuring Your Network with the Network Setup Wizard

Now you need to give Windows XP Professional some information about the network you've just set up. When you power up your system, the Windows XP Professional Plug and Play system loads the device drivers you need for the NICs. Your next order of business is to specify the network *protocols* that you will use. A protocol specifies the rules that will be used when you transmit and receive data over a network. The default protocol for Windows XP networks goes by the formidable name of Transmission

Control Protocol/Internet Protocol. It is the same protocol that powers the Internet; we'll just call it TCP/IP for short. By far the easiest and best way to configure TCP/IP on your system is to use the Network Setup Wizard. The wizard automates the following tasks:

- Setting up the network protocol.
- Configuring Internet Connection Sharing.
- Turning on the Internet Connection Firewall.
- Creating a network bridge if required. (We'll look at what a bridge is and why you might want to use one in a moment.)

NOTE *Internet Connection Sharing in Windows XP works with all types of Internet connections, including NICs connected to the local area network, LAN adapters connected to routers (including DSL, frame relay, and ISDN), and dial-up connections using a modem or an ISDN terminal adapter.*

Before you go much further, you should decide which of the computers on your network will host Internet Connection Sharing. In other words, which computer will share its Internet connection with the other computers on the network. The host computer must meet the following requirements:

- Run Windows XP.
- Be turned on at all times so that the other computers on the network can access the Internet.

If one of the computers on your network has an existing DSL hookup or a cable modem, that computer would be an excellent choice to be the Internet Connection Sharing host computer.

With Internet Connection Sharing turned on, you can use Internet Explorer and Outlook Express from the other computers on the network as though they were directly connected to the Internet. And if you change you mind, you can always disable Internet Connection Sharing on one computer and enable it on another.

To configure your network, make sure you are logged on as a Computer Administrator and then follow these steps:

1. Start the Network Setup Wizard.

Click the Start button, click Control Panel, click Network And Internet Connections, and then click Network Connections. Under Common Tasks, click Set Up Or Change Your Home Or Small Office Network. You can also click the Start button, click All Programs, click Accessories, click Communications, and then select the Network Setup Wizard. When the Welcome screen opens, click Next.

2. Review the checklist.

Click Checklist For Creating A Network to see a help page summarizing the steps in network planning that we detailed earlier in this chapter, or click Next.

3. Select a connection method.

In the Select A Connection Method screen, select This Computer Connects Directly To The Internet. This will allow other computers on the network to connect to the Internet through this computer. Click Next.

4. Choose a connection.

In the Select Your Internet Connection screen, choose the connection, by name, that you want to use when you connect to the Internet, as Figure 13-1 shows. Click Next.

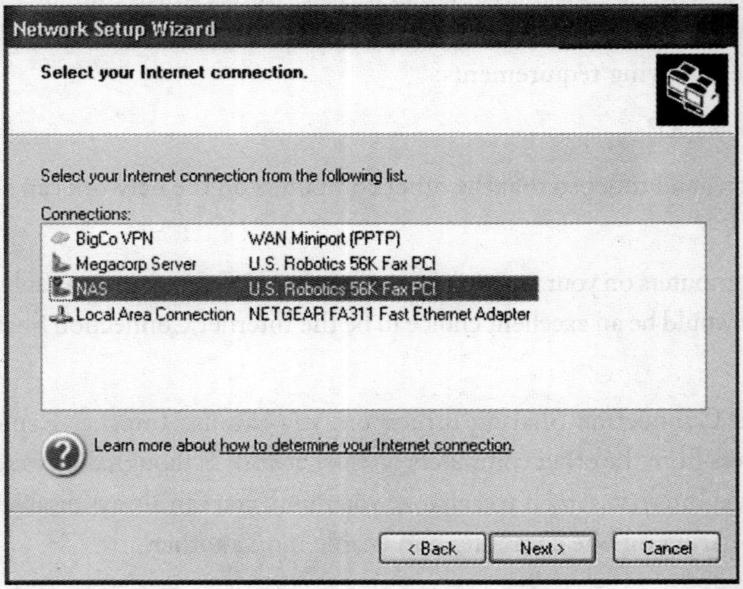

Figure 13-1 Selecting an Internet connection.

5. **Describe your computer.**

   In the Give This Computer A Description And Name screen, enter a short text description for the computer, something that will help you remember which computer this is. Call it Pat's Computer or Peter's Computer, but don't call it Office Computer; there are way too many computers called Office Computer already and we don't need any more. The Computer Name box holds the name you gave to this computer when you installed Windows XP. It is best to leave this name unchanged. Click Next.

6. **Name your network.**

   In the Name Your Network screen, enter a Workgroup name. We'll use the Workgroup called MARKETING. Click Next.

7. **Review the settings.**

   In the Ready To Apply Network Settings screen, shown in Figure 13-2, review the selections you have made. The wizard will apply these settings when you click Next. The process may take a few minutes and once it has started, don't interrupt it. Take a deep breath, and click Next. An animated graphic acts as a progress indicator.

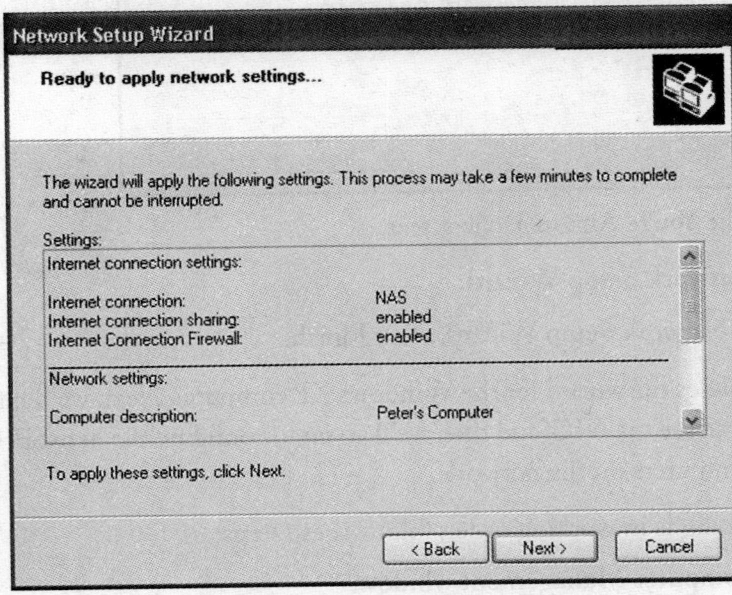

Figure 13-2 The Ready To Apply Network Settings screen.

8. Create a Network Setup Disk.

In the You're Almost Done screen shown in Figure 13-3, you can create a Network Setup Disk that you can use to configure the other computers on your network, or you can opt to use the Windows XP installation CD instead. We'll be doing this in a section later in this chapter, and we'll use the Windows XP installation CD in our example. Make your choice, and click Next.

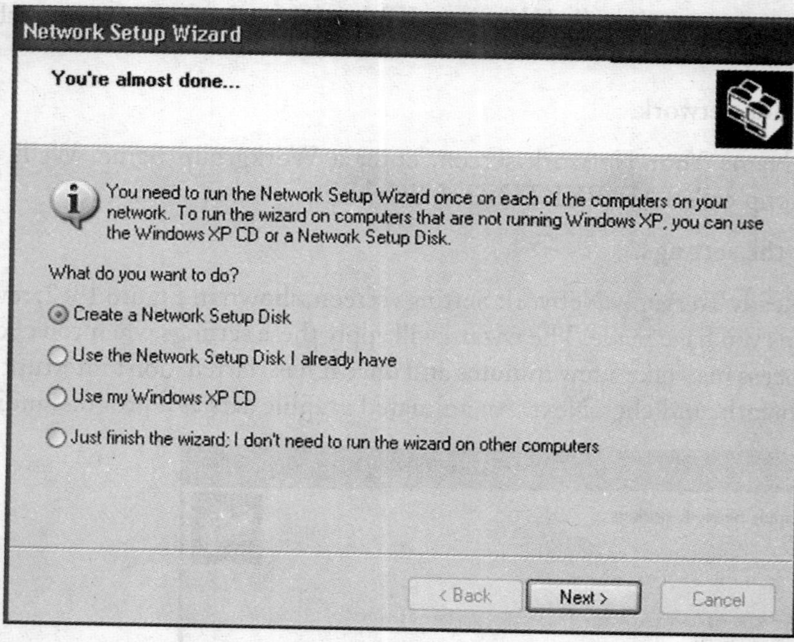

Figure 13-3 The You're Almost Done screen.

9. Close the Network Setup Wizard.

To close the Network Setup Wizard, click Finish.

That step completes the wizard for the Windows XP computer. Next, we'll make sure that Windows can see the NIC, and then we'll go on to configure the network settings for the other computers on the network.

To see if everything is in working order, follow these steps:

1. Open the Computer Management window.

Click the Start button, click Control Panel, click Performance And Maintenance click Administrative Tools, and then click Computer Management.

2. Display a list of the devices installed on your computer.

In the tree pane on the left, click System Tools to expand it (if necessary), and then click Device Manager to display a list of the devices installed on your computer in the right pane. You'll see something similar to Figure 13-4.

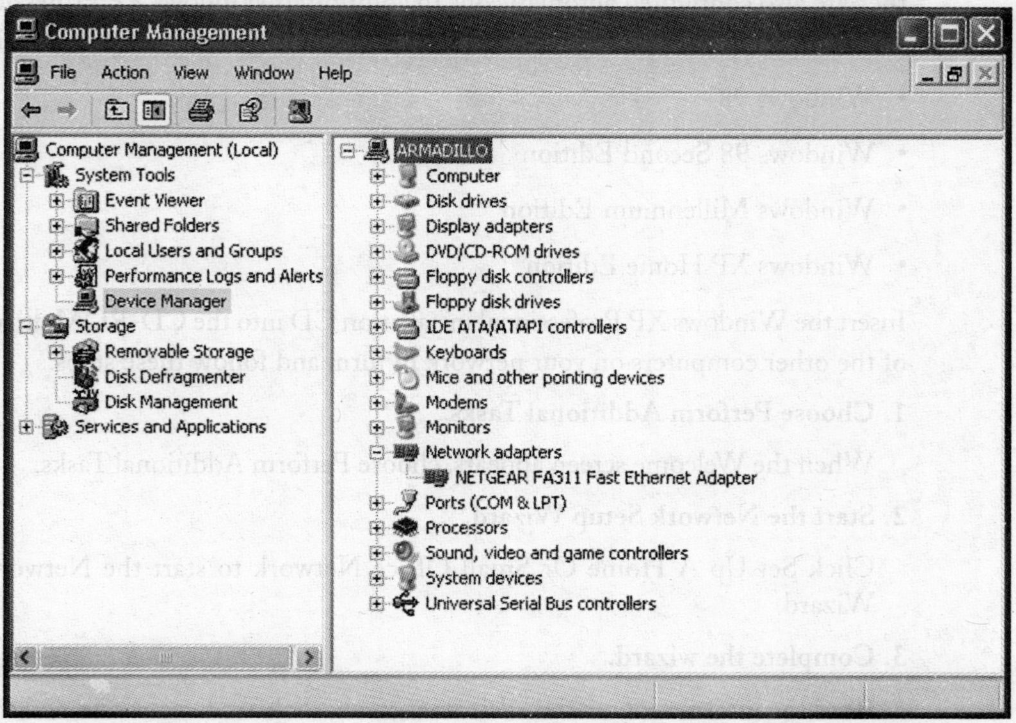

Figure 13-4 A list of the devices installed on one of our computers.

3. Expand Network Adapters.

Click the plus sign next to Network Adapters. If you don't see a yellow exclamation point or a red arrow next to the icon for your adapter, everything is working just as it's supposed to work.

Using the Network Setup Wizard on Other Windows Computers on Your Network

You can run the Network Setup Wizard on other computers on your network so that they are also configured automatically. In addition to Windows XP Professional, the Network Setup Wizard works with computers running these versions of Windows:

- Windows 98
- Windows 98 Second Edition
- Windows Millennium Edition
- Windows XP Home Edition

Insert the Windows XP Professional installation CD into the CD-ROM drive of each of the other computers on your network in turn, and follow these steps:

1. **Choose Perform Additional Tasks.**

   When the Welcome screen appears, choose Perform Additional Tasks.

2. **Start the Network Setup Wizard.**

   Click Set Up A Home Or Small Office Network to start the Network Setup Wizard.

3. **Complete the wizard.**

   Read the information on the Welcome screen, click Yes to continue, and then simply follow the instructions on the screen. The wizard will copy certain network support files onto the computer and may have to restart your computer to make sure the new configuration is loaded.

Repeat these steps for all the computers on your network to complete the setup and configuration process.

If you created a Network Setup Disk using the Network Setup Wizard, you can use that floppy disk instead of the Windows XP installation CD by following these steps:

1. **Insert the floppy disk.**

   Insert the Network Setup Disk into the drive of the next computer on your network that you want to configure.

2. **Open My Computer.**

   Click the Start button, and click My Computer.

3. Open the Network Setup Disk.

Open the Network Setup Disk in the A drive, and double-click the file called netsetup. If the system needs to restart, you will be prompted to remove the floppy disk from the drive first.

When your computer restarts, the Network Setup Wizard runs automatically. Just follow the instructions on the screen to complete the configuration. Your computer will restart a second time. Once that is done, the wizard has done its work, and you can repeat these steps for all the other computers on your network.

Phone-line, Power-line, and Wireless Networking Alternatives

In addition to Ethernet, several other technologies are available for use in a home or small office network, including phone-line networking, power-line networking, and wireless networking. When you come to make your decision, you will find that the three major considerations are capacity, cost, and convenience.

Home phone-line networking (abbreviated Home PNA, or HPNA) allows you to connect computers and printers using the telephone wiring and phone jacks already installed in your house. Connections are made using USB ports, and typically operate at a rate of somewhere between 1 and 10 Mbps. Home PNA kits are available from Intel (*www.intel.com*), D-Link (*www.dlink.com*), or 3Com (*www.3com.com*). Normal telephone connections are created with two-wire pairs. You can pair wires randomly without affecting phone operations, but for a network connection, specific wires must be paired. In other words, your phone wiring must be correctly wired. If you live in a house that has several phone lines (as most new houses do these days), make sure you connect all the computers to the same line.

Power-line networking lets you connect your computers through existing electrical sockets (this concept just makes us nervous). Again, connections are made using USB ports, and data rates are usually about 2 Mbps. Power-line networking is still pretty new, so there are not quite as many products to choose from, and kits are available from Compaq (*www.compaq.com*), Intel (*www.intel.com*), and 3Com (*www.3com.com*).

Wireless networking is becoming very popular, and the main reasons are cost and convenience; there are no cables to buy and no cables to run. You can connect to the network from your desk or from out by the pool. Two technologies are available, the 802.11b standard and the HomeRF standard. Equipment based on the 802.11b standard is faster with data rates in the 10 Mbps range, while HomeRF is cheaper but slower at about 1.5 to 2 Mbps. The Wireless Ethernet Compatibility Alliance (WECA) sponsors a logo program known as Wi-Fi to promote complete adherence to the 802.11b standard. All products with the Wi-Fi logo have passed a series of laboratory tests that confirm compliance with the standard. If a wireless network device encounters a certain level of interference, it will automatically cut back the data rate to about half, or 5.5 Mbps. When the interference gets to be too great, the device will stop working altogether. Wireless kits are available from Intel (*www.intel.com*), Lucent Technologies (*www.lucent.com*), and Proxim (*www.proxim.com*).

As time goes by, prices will fall and data rates will increase, and that, coupled with the convenience these technologies offer, will make them increasingly attractive alternatives to Ethernet.

Sharing an Internet Connection

Internet Connection Sharing (ICS) allows the computers on your network to access the Internet through the connection from the Windows XP computer, so if you have a fast DSL or cable-modem connection on that system, all the computers on your network can take advantage of its speed.

ICS settings are controlled by the Advanced tab of the connection used to access the Internet. To see these settings, click the Start button, click Connect To, and then select Show All Connections to open the Network Connections dialog box. Right-click the connection the Windows XP system uses to connect to the Internet, and choose Properties from the shortcut menu. Click the Advanced tab, and you'll see the dialog box shown in Figure 13-5.

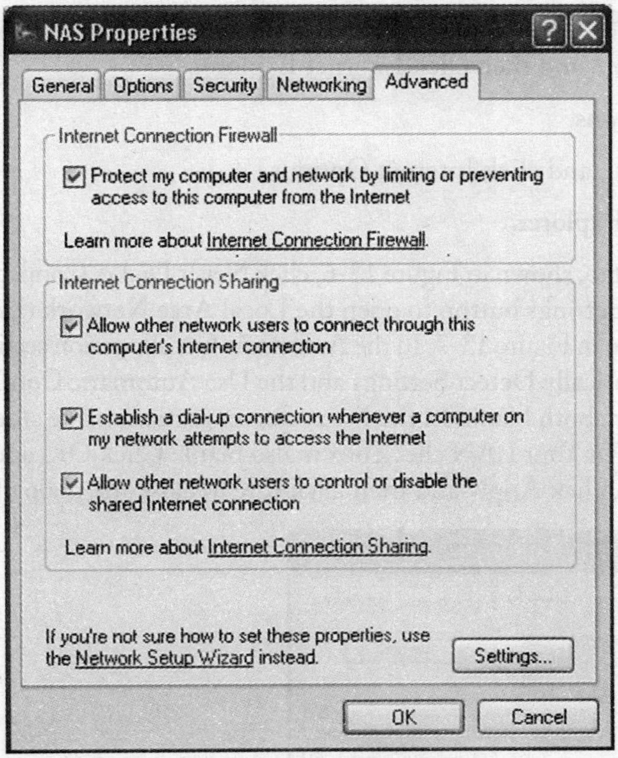

Figure 13-5 The connection Properties dialog box open at the Advanced tab.

Once the Network Setup Wizard has run, all of the check boxes on the Advanced tab will be checked. In other words, the Internet Connection Firewall will be turned on, and ICS will be available to all users on your network. To turn ICS off, clear the three check boxes in the Internet Connection Sharing section on the Advanced tab.

Setting Up Internet Explorer to Use Internet Connection Sharing

We have just one more step to take before we can access the Internet from any computer on the network. We have to make some changes to the way that Internet Explorer is configured on those other computers, and by the way, you must be using Internet Explorer version 5.0 or later for ICS to work. Follow these steps:

1. **Open Internet Explorer.**

   Click the Start button, and then click Internet Explorer.

2. **Open Internet Options.**

   Click the Tools menu, and click Internet Options.

3. **Configure Internet Explorer.**

   On the Connections tab, shown in Figure 13-6, click Never Dial A Connection, and then click the LAN Settings button to open the Local Area Network (LAN) Settings dialog box shown in Figure 13-7. In the Automatic Configuration section, make sure that the Automatically Detect Settings and the Use Automatic Configuration Script check boxes are both blank. In the Proxy Server section, make sure that the Use A Proxy Server For Your LAN check box is also blank. Click OK, and then on the Connections tab, click Apply and then click OK to close the dialog box.

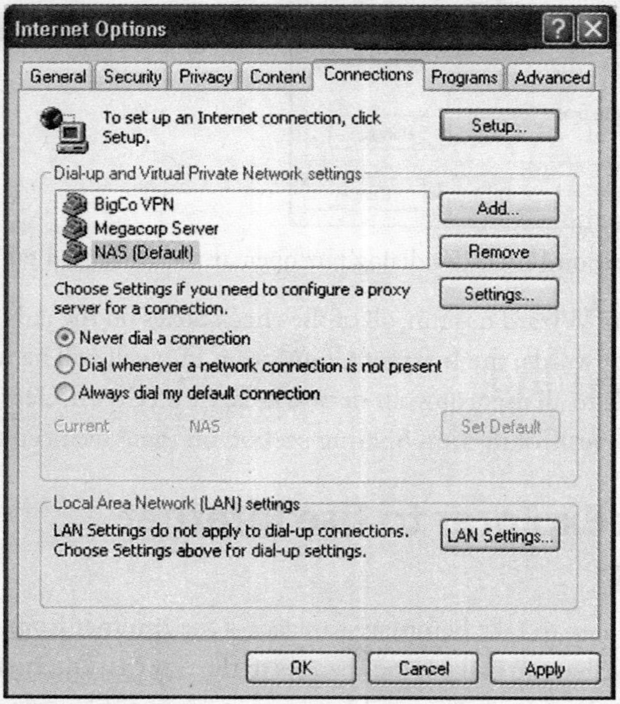

Figure 13-6 The Internet Options dialog box open at the Connections tab.

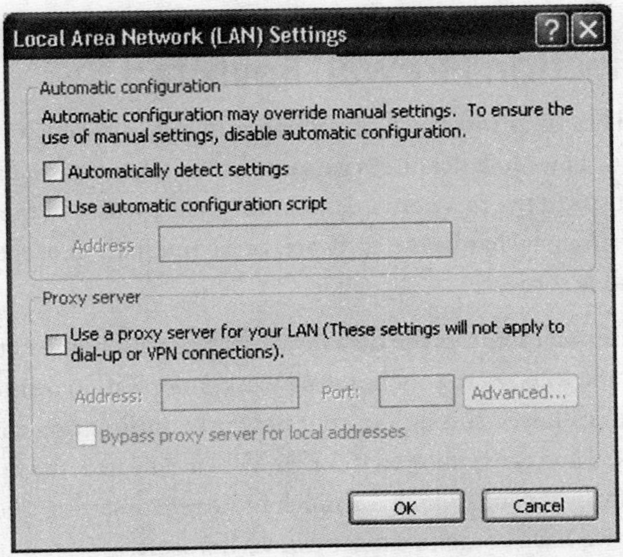

Figure 13-7 The Local Area Network (LAN) Settings dialog box.

4. **Close Internet Explorer.**

   Finally, close Internet Explorer.

The next time you start Internet Explorer on this client computer on the network, it will access the Internet through the connection being shared through the Windows XP computer, rather than dialing out using its own modem.

A Final Word of Warning

Internet Connection Sharing is designed for small office and home office use; don't use it on a large corporate network. ICS provides several important network support functions to a small network, after all, that's how it works. The problem is that these functions can interfere with similar services already provided by the corporate network, and then nothing works. So if you work on a large network that uses domain controllers, DNS servers, gateways, DHCP servers, or systems configured to use static (rather than dynamic) IP addresses, don't use ICS. Also, if your network uses Active Directory-based domains, don't use ICS, as these domains must include DNS services.

Internet Connection Firewall Revisited

In Chapter 7 we looked briefly at Internet Connection Firewall, and now it is time to look again, this time in a bit more detail. As we said back in Chapter 7, a *firewall* is a security system that sits between a network and the outside world in the form of the Internet. A firewall can be hardware, software, or a combination of the two; in Windows the firewall is software.

Internet Connection Firewall monitors the data flowing from your home network to the Internet and from the Internet to your home network. Information considered by the firewall to be safe is allowed through to your network; information considered to be unsafe is blocked and is not allowed through. When activated, the firewall denies all incoming traffic by default, which is a much more secure setting than the usual "allow all" default we have come to expect from Microsoft.

If you use Internet Connection Sharing to provide Internet access to several of the computers on your network, don't use the Internet Connection Firewall on these computers sharing the connection, just use it on the computer that actually connects to the Internet. Turning on Internet Connection Firewall on a computer on your network will stop all network communications to that computer.

If you have a single computer that is not part of a network and that connects to the Internet using a dial-up, DSL, or cable-modem connection, you can use Internet Connection Firewall to protect that connection. Don't use Internet Connection Firewall on a virtual private network (VPN) connection as it will impede certain VPN functions, such as file sharing.

Bridging Between Two Different Networks

In the last section, we set up our peer-to-peer network using Ethernet network interface cards, and now we have decided that we want to add our laptop to the network. The problem is that the laptop has a wireless network adapter rather than an Ethernet adapter, and we don't want to buy a docking station for the laptop just to gain an Ethernet connection. So how do we join these two different network technologies together to form a single network?

The answer is to buy a single wireless adapter, install it in one of the Ethernet computers, and use a technique known as *bridging* to allow both segments of the network—the Ethernet segment and the wireless segment—to interact. Bridging makes both network segments appear as one continuous network. And all this work is done within Windows.

Creating the Bridge

The Home Networking Wizard creates a bridge automatically when it finds two or more network adapters installed in the same computer running Windows XP Professional. Only one bridge can exist at a time, but that bridge can manage any number of network connections; the only limitation is the number of network adapters you can fit into the computer case. The Home Networking Wizard will not bridge a network interface card connected to a DSL connection or to a cable modem.

To create a network bridge manually, follow these steps:

1. **Open Network Connections.**

   Click the Start button, click Connect To, and then click Show All Connections to open Network Connections.

2. **Choose the connections to bridge.**

   Under LAN Or High-Speed Internet, right-click one of the connections you want to bridge, hold down the Ctrl key on the keyboard, and click any of the other connections you want to include in the bridge. A progress box tells you that the appropriate software, called *bindings,* is being loaded.

Back to our example. We now have one computer with an Ethernet NIC, one computer with both an Ethernet NIC and a wireless NIC (this computer is acting as the bridge), and the laptop, which just has its wireless NIC. They can all talk to each other on our network. By using the same technique of adding an NIC for each new networking technology you want to add to your network, you could roam all over the house using the Inter AnyPoint Wireless Home Network HomeRF NIC in the laptop, or you could add a HomePNA connection to a desktop computer to take advantage of the existing phone wiring in your house. There are quite a few possibilities, and they are all made possible by the bridging software in Windows XP Professional.

One final cautionary note about wireless networks. Wireless NICs all operate on the same frequency and use the same basic equipment, so it is possible that someone with a Windows laptop and a wireless NIC could drive into your company parking lot and as long as they are within range, they can access your network. There are methods you can use to stop this unauthorized access, including strong passwords and the use of virtual private networks (VPNs); we'll get to those in the next chapter.

Adding and Removing a Connection

To add another connection to the bridge, open Network Connections, right-click Network Bridge, and choose Properties from the shortcut menu. On the General tab, check the box of each adapter you want to add to the bridge. Click OK to close the dialog box.

NOTE *You must first create the bridge before you can add connections to it.*

Alternatively, you can right-click the connection, and choose Add To Bridge from the shortcut menu. You cannot add connections to the bridge that are currently being shared or are running Internet Connection Firewall. To remove a connection from the bridge, you just do the reverse. Open Network Connections, right-click Network Bridge, and choose Properties from the shortcut menu. On the General tab, clear the box of each adapter you want to remove from the bridge. Click OK to close the dialog box.

Enabling or Disabling the Bridge

To enable the network bridge, open Network Connections, right-click Network Bridge, and choose Enable from the shortcut menu. To disable the network bridge, open Network Connections, right-click Network Bridge, and choose Disable from the shortcut menu. If you choose Disable, the different network segments will no longer be able to talk to each other.

To remove the bridge altogether, open Network Connections, right-click Network Bridge, and choose Delete from the shortcut menu; again, if you delete the bridge, the different network segments will no longer be able to talk to each other.

Installing and Using a Networked Printer

One of the commonest reasons for setting up a network is to share a printer between a group of computers. You can physically connect a printer to your network in a couple of ways:

- If your printer does not have a NIC in it, connect the printer to one of the computers on the network and turn the printer on. (This is more common in a small network and is the kind of printer we will describe in this section.)
- If your printer has a NIC in it, you can connect it directly by running a cable to the network hub. (This is found more commonly in a corporate environment where the computer administrator would configure the printer, and we won't cover this kind of setup here.)

The printer must be physically connected to a computer, installed as a local printer on that computer, and then shared so that other computers can access it over the network. We'll look at how to install the printer as a local printer in this section, and then take a look at how to work with sharing in the next section.

After the printer is connected to the computer and turned on, log on to that computer as a Computer Administrator and follow these steps:

1. **Open the Printers folder.**

   Click the Start button, click Control Panel, click Printers And Other Hardware, and then click Printers And Faxes to open the Printers And Faxes folder, as shown in Figure 13-8.

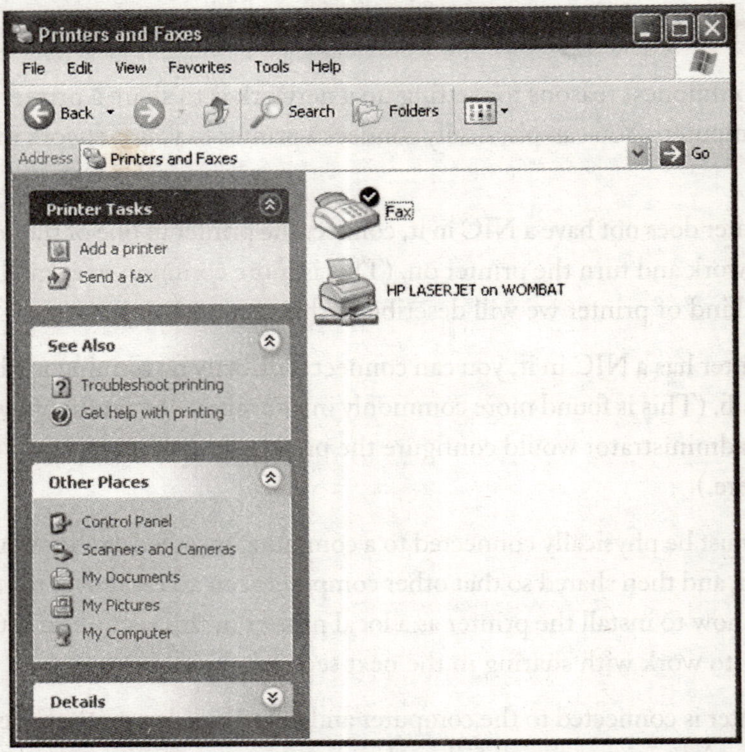

Figure 13-8 The Printers And Faxes folder.

2. **Start the Add Printer Wizard.**

   Click the Add A Printer link to start the Add Printer Wizard.

3. **Select local or network printer.**

   At the Welcome screen, click Next. On the next screen, shown in Figure 13-9, select the local printer option if the printer is physically attached to this computer. Select the network printer option if the printer is attached to another computer on your network. Before you can add this printer, you have to share it first; see "Sharing a Printer on the Network" in the next section for more on this topic. Click Next.

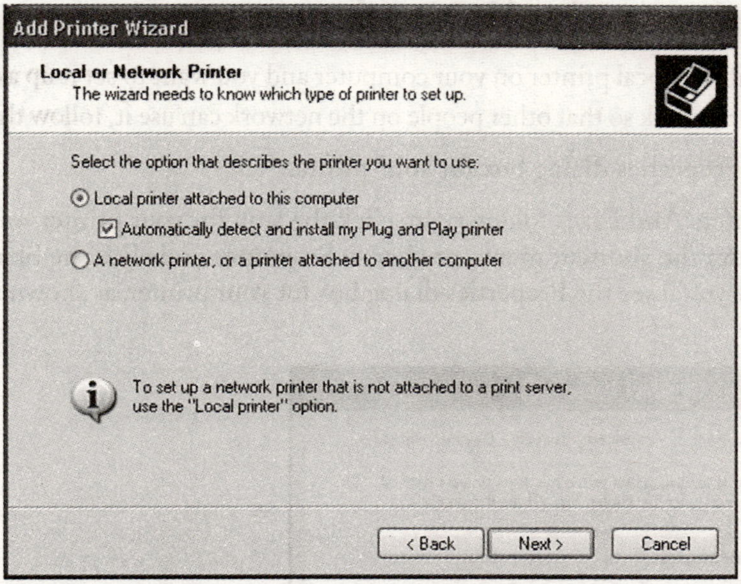

Figure 13-9 The Local Or Network Printer screen.

4. **Select the printer by name.**

   Enter the name of the printer you want to use. If you don't know the name, you can browse the available resources on your network. Find the printer, select it, and then click Next.

5. **Specify whether this printer is the default printer.**

   Click Yes if you want this printer set as the default. (You can always change the default printer by right-clicking the printer's icon in the Printers folder and choosing Set As Default Printer from the shortcut menu.) Click Next. Review your choices, and click Finish to close the wizard.

To remove a printer, to rename it, or to create a shortcut to it on the desktop, right-click its icon in the Printers And Faxes folder and choose the appropriate command from the shortcut menu. Once you have finished these steps and configured your printer, all you have to do is use the Print command from the File menu in an application; the printout will be sent to the printer automatically. See Chapter 3 for complete details.

Sharing a Printer on the Network

If you've installed a local printer on your computer and you want to set it up as a shared printer on the network so that other people on the network can use it, follow these steps:

1. Open the Properties dialog box for your printer.

In the Printers And Faxes folder, right-click the icon for your printer, and choose Sharing from the shortcut menu, or choose Properties and click the Sharing tab. Either way, you'll see the Properties dialog box for your printer, as shown in Figure 13-10.

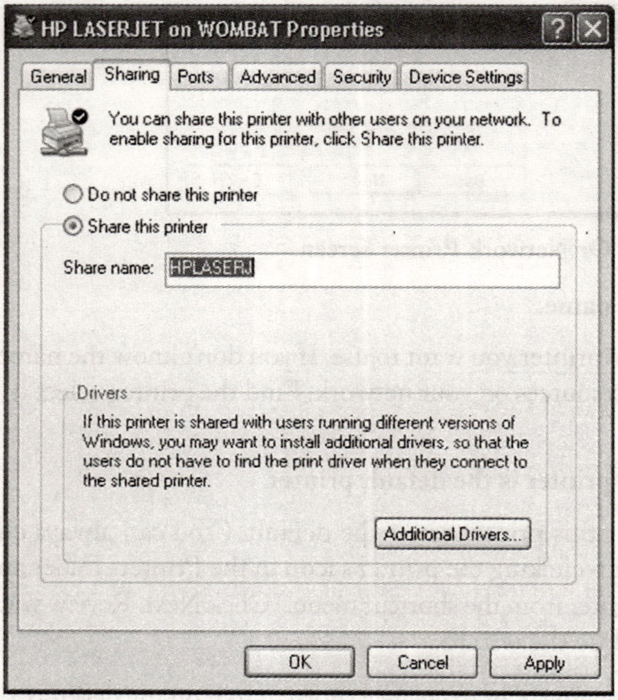

Figure 13-10 Using the options on the Sharing tab to share a printer.

2. Share and name this printer.

Accept the name that is generated, or enter a new name. Click the General tab if you want to enter a description of this printer in the Comment field. We sometimes use this field to describe the printer's physical location, such as in Room 321 on the third floor. Click Apply, and then click OK when you are finished.

You'll see a hand under the icon for this printer in the Printer And Faxes folder, indicating that this is now a shared printer.

If you are sharing a printer on a network where some of the computers will be running a different version of Windows, click the Additional Drivers button on the Sharing tab to open the Additional Drivers dialog box, which is shown in Figure 13-11.

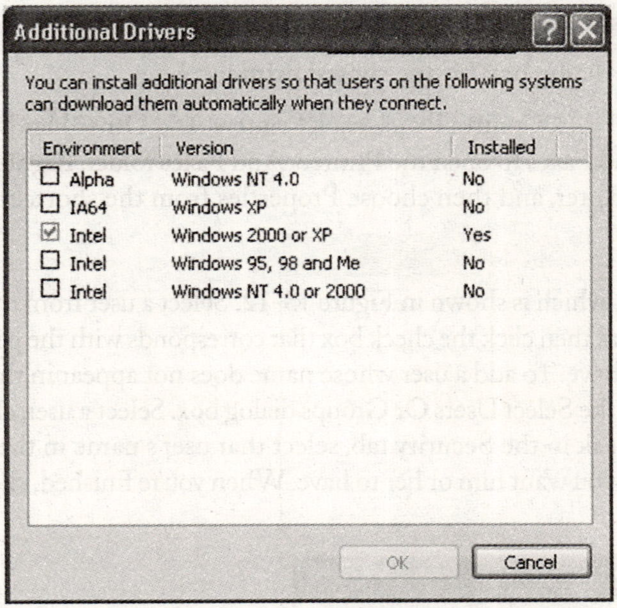

Figure 13-11 The Additional Drivers dialog box.

The computers running different versions of Windows need the right printer drivers, even if the printer is somewhere else on the network. The drivers that have already been loaded are listed in the Additional Drivers dialog box. Click the check box for all the versions of Windows that will be sharing this printer, and then click OK. Depending on the choices you made in the Additional Drivers dialog box, you may be prompted to insert the Windows XP Professional CD-ROM.

Setting Printer Permissions

When you install and set up a printer on your network that printer is available to everyone on the network. If you want to, you can set limits on who can access and manage a printer. You can specify the following permissions:

- Print is assigned to everyone by default and lets everyone print to the printer.
- Manage Printers lets a user pause or restart the printer, share the printer, and change the properties and the permissions.

- Manage Documents lets a user pause, resume, restart, or cancel print jobs submitted by other users but prevents the user him- or herself from printing documents on the printer.

To set up printer permissions, follow these steps:

1. **Open the Properties dialog box for the shared printer.**

   Click the Start button, click Control Panel, click Printers And Other Hardware, and then click Printers And Faxes to open the Printers And Faxes folder. Right-click the icon for the shared printer, and then choose Properties from the shortcut menu.

2. **Set the permissions.**

   Click the Security tab, which is shown in Figure 13-12. Select a user from the Group Or User Names list, and then click the check box that corresponds with the permission you want that user to have. To add a user whose name does not appear in the Names list, click Add to open the Select Users Or Groups dialog box. Select a user, click Add, and then click OK. Back in the Security tab, select that user's name in the list, and check the permissions you want him or her to have. When you're finished, click Apply and then click OK.

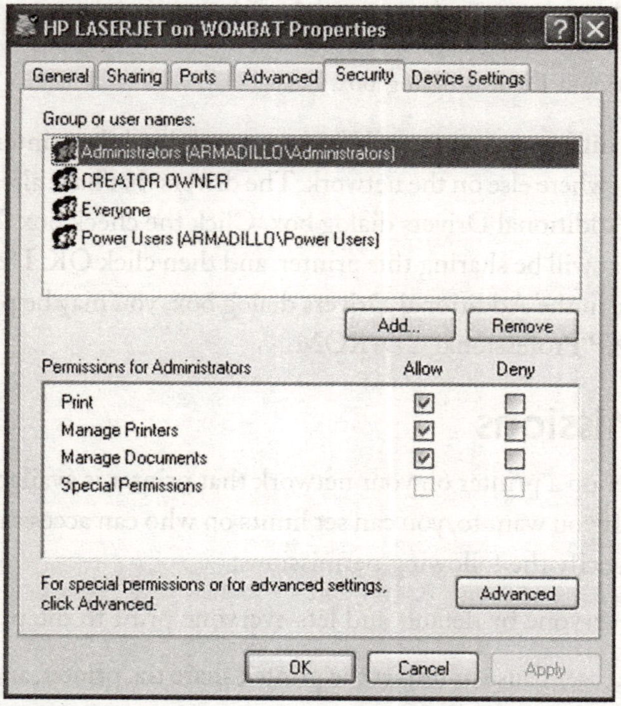

Figure 13-12 The Security tab for a shared printer.

Setting Up Separator Pages

A handy device to use for a printer on your network is a separator page. A separator page prints between each print job, making it easier for users to identify their particular documents. To set up a separator page, follow these steps:

1. **Open the printer's Properties dialog box.**

   Click the Start button, click Control Panel, click Printers And Other Hardware, and then click Printers And Faxes to open the Printers And Faxes folder. Right-click the printer, and choose Properties from the shortcut menu.

2. **Open the Separator Page dialog box.**

   Click the Advanced tab in the Properties dialog box, and then click the Separator Page button to open the Separator Page dialog box, as shown in Figure 13-13.

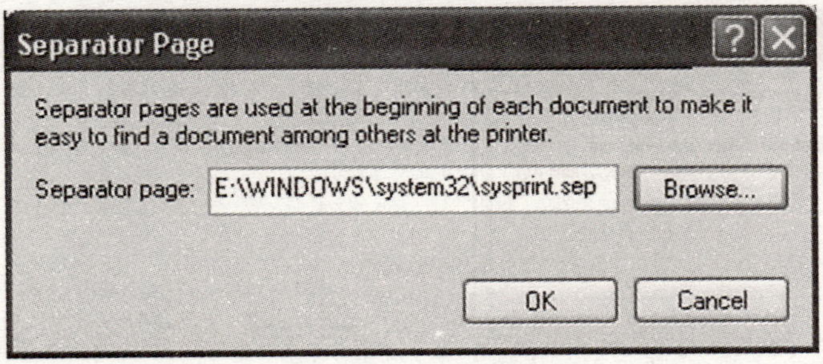

Figure 13-13 Creating a separator page.

3. **Select a separator page to use.**

   In the Separator Page box, enter a filename for a separator page, or click Browse to locate one. You'll find several separator page files listed in the System32 folder; they have the filename extension of .sep. Click OK after you've selected a page.

Working on Your Network

Now that we have set up the network hardware, configured the network software, and shared a printer, we're ready to get to the good stuff. Now we actually get to use the network.

The main purpose of the network is sharing—sharing hard disks, CD-ROM drives, folders, files, and as we saw in the previous section, sharing printers, too. All of these elements are usually grouped together by the term *shared resources,* or simply *shares.*

Sharing Resources on the Network

Before users on your network can share resources—drives, files, folders, applications, and so on—the resources must first be shared. On a peer-to-peer network, this means that the user at each workstation must specifically mark his or her resources as shared. To do this, follow these steps:

1. Open Explorer.

Right-click the Start button, and then click Explore.

2. Open the Properties dialog box for the resource you want to share.

Navigate to the resources you want to share, right-click it, and choose Sharing from the shortcut menu. You'll open a Properties dialog box at the Sharing tab and see something similar to that shown in Figure 13-14.

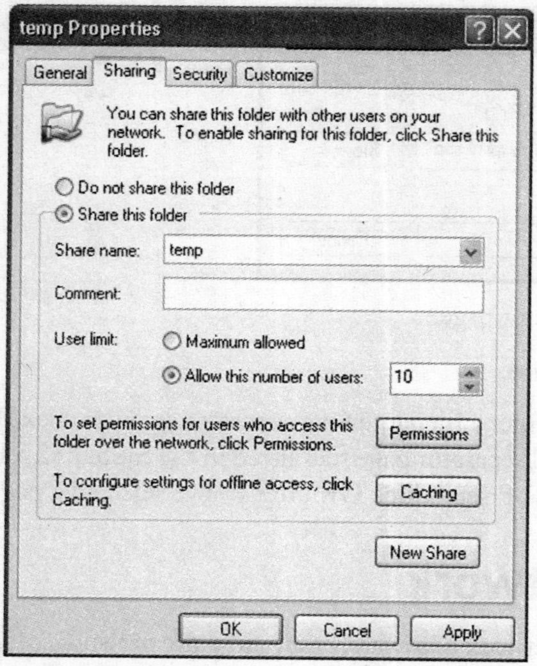

Figure 13-14 The Sharing tab of the Properties dialog box.

3. Share and name the resource.

First, click the Share This Folder option button. Then, in the Share Name box, you can accept the name that Windows suggests or enter another name. This name must be unique on this computer, and it is the name that others on the network will see when they browse this computer, so again, give some thought to how you name resources.

4. **Enter a comment.**

   In the Comment box, briefly describe the share. Users will also see this information when browsing the network.

5. **Specify the maximum number of users who can access this resource simultaneously.**

   In the User Limit area, click Maximum Allowed, or click Allow This Number Of Users and then specify the maximum number of simultaneous users. The maximum that Windows allows is 10 users. If the eleventh person tries to log on, he or she will see this message: "No more connections can be made to this remote computer at this time because there are already as many connections as the computer allows."

6. **Set the permissions for this resource.**

   Click the Permissions button to open the Permissions dialog box for this share. You'll see something similar to Figure 13-15, depending on the resource you are sharing. For information on the types of permissions and how to set them, look back at Chapter 2. Remember that you can set permissions on files and folders only if you are using the NTFS file system.

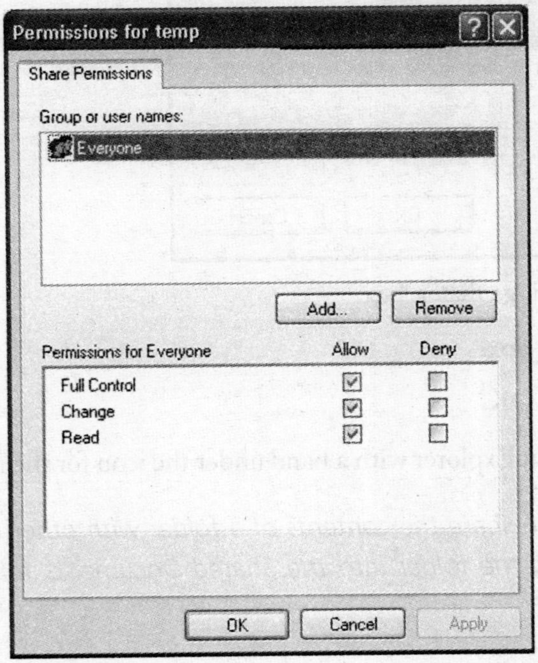

Figure 13-15 Setting share permissions.

7. **Set caching options.**

Offline Files, which we discussed in Chapter 2, stores a version of shared network files on the hard drive in an area called the *cache*. Your computer can access these files even if you are not connected to the network. To specify how files are cached, click the Caching button to open the Caching Settings dialog box, as shown in Figure 13-16. You allow or disallow caching of the shared resource, and you choose from Manual Caching Of Documents, Automatic Caching Of Documents, and Automatic Caching Of Programs. Select a setting, and then click OK.

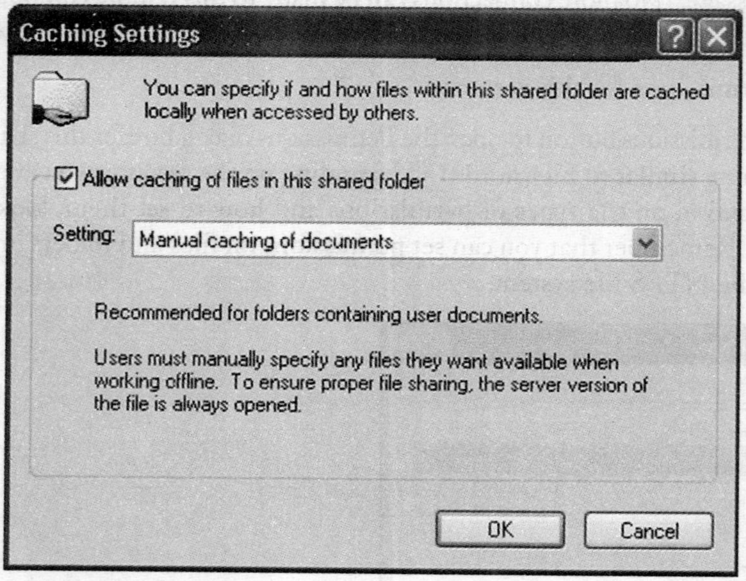

Figure 13-16 The Caching Settings dialog box.

8. **Close the Properties dialog box.**

Click Apply, and then click OK.

Shared resources are identified in Explorer with a hand under the icon for the resource.

NOTE *There is another way to share the contents of a folder with other users on the network: just drag the folder into the Shared Documents folder. See Chapter 2 for details.*

Networking Icons Demystified

Click the Start button, and then open My Network Places when you're looking for network resources. This is a good place to start because if you see an icon in My Network Places, that usually means the resource is shared and you can use it. Depending on how your network is set up, you will see some or all of the icons shown in Table 13-1.

ICON	WHAT IT REPRESENTS
	Displays the computers connected using Microsoft Windows networking.
	Displays the computers that make up a particular workgroup.
	Indicates a single computer on the network.
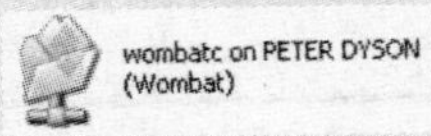	Indicates a shared drive.

Table 13-1 Icons found in My Network Places.

The icon in Explorer or My Computer for a shared folder or printer is shown with a hand under it to indicate that it's shared.

Accessing My Network Places

Getting to the file or folder you want to work with on the network can take quite a few clicks. To access shared resource on your network, follow these steps:

1. **Open My Network Places.**

   Click the Start button, and then click My Network Places or navigate to My Network Places in Explorer. You'll see the My Network Places window, as shown in Figure 13-17.

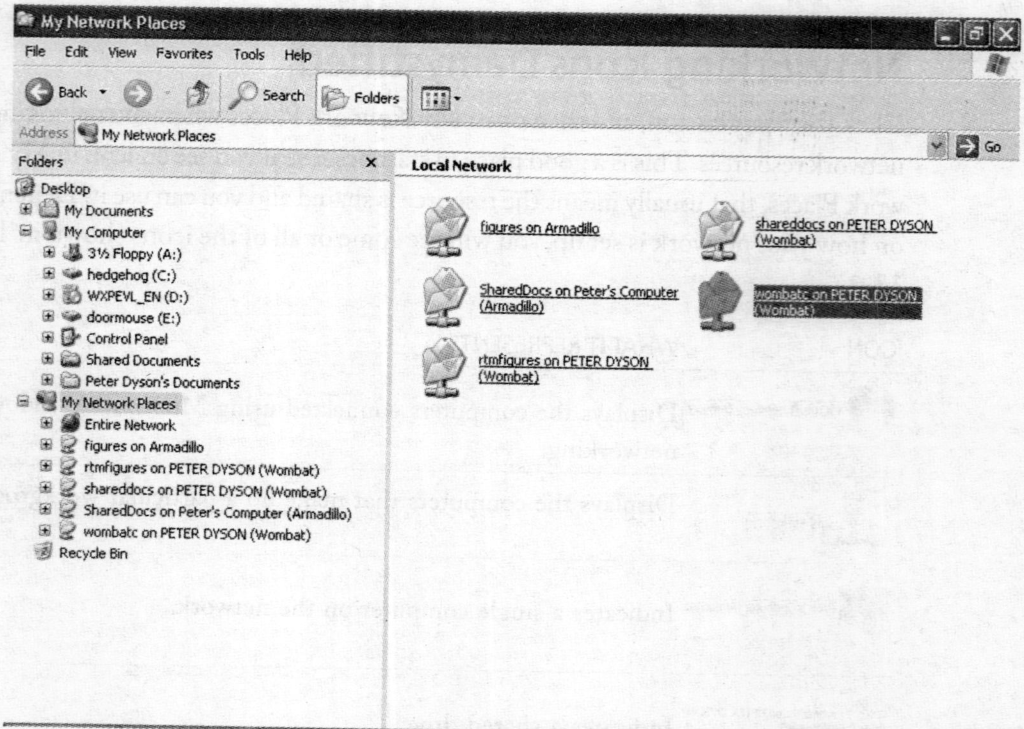

Figure 13-17 My Network Places window.

2. **Double-click a hard-disk or folder icon.**

   Double-click a hard-disk icon to display all the folders and files inside, and then browse until you locate the file, folder, or application you want to work with.

You can use the files and folders on the network just as though they were right there on your own computer.

Using Explorer

You don't have to use My Network Places if you don't want to; you can use Explorer instead. You'll see an entry for My Network Places in the left pane of the Explorer window, and if you click the plus sign to expand all the entries underneath, you'll see a list of all the computers, hard disks, and folders on them as Figure 13-18 shows.

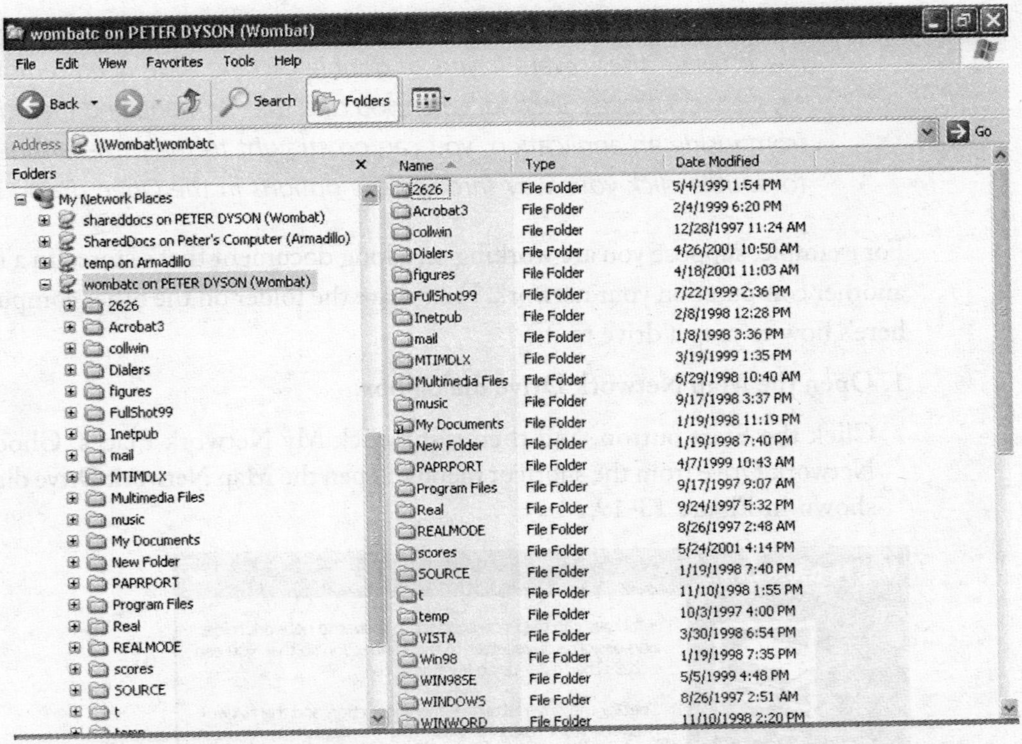

Figure 13-18 My Network Places in the Explorer window.

Using Explorer like this makes it very easy to copy a file from a network hard disk to your own local disk, because you can open and access files and folders on both computers from within the same Explorer window. Of course, all the Explorer techniques you learned earlier in this book work on network disks, too.

Mapping Network Drives

You can see that it might take quite a few steps to drill down all the way through the network to find a specific file. But don't worry, there is a faster way. If you use a particular network resource frequently, you can map a network drive to it in order to access it quickly. That resource then appears as though it were a drive on your own computer, just like the C drive and the A drive.

NOTE *Mapping a network drive brings two big benefits. First, you can access the drive much faster after several layers of double-clicking have been removed from My Network Places. Second, when you click the File menu and then click Open from inside an application, you can go straight to the drive without having to double-click your way through the options in the Open dialog box.*

For example, suppose you are working on a long document that's stored in a folder on another computer on your network. First share the folder on the other computer, then here's how to map a drive to it:

1. **Open the Map Network Drive dialog box.**

   Click the Start button, and then right-click My Network Places. Choose Map Network Drive from the shortcut menu to open the Map Network Drive dialog box, shown in Figure 13-19.

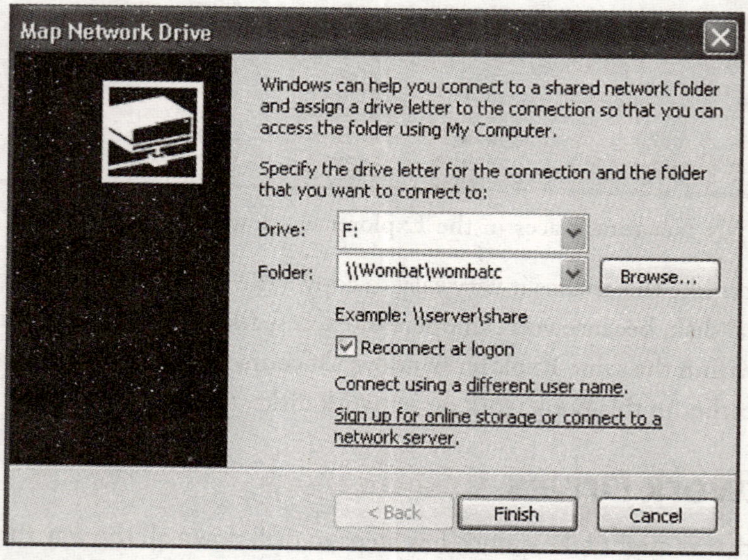

Figure 13-19 The Map Network Drive dialog box.

2. **Specify the drive letter.**

   In the Drive drop-down list box, click the down arrow, and select an unused letter. The default is the next drive in sequence. For example, in Figure 13-19, the default is F. We are already using C, D, and E for existing drives on this computer.

3. **Locate the share you want to map.**

   In the Folder drop-down list box, enter the path to the share, or click Browse to locate it. Click Finish.

Now, the mapped drive, in this case, the drive wombatc on the computer called Wombat, appears just like any other drive in My Computer and in Explorer, as shown in Figure 13-20.

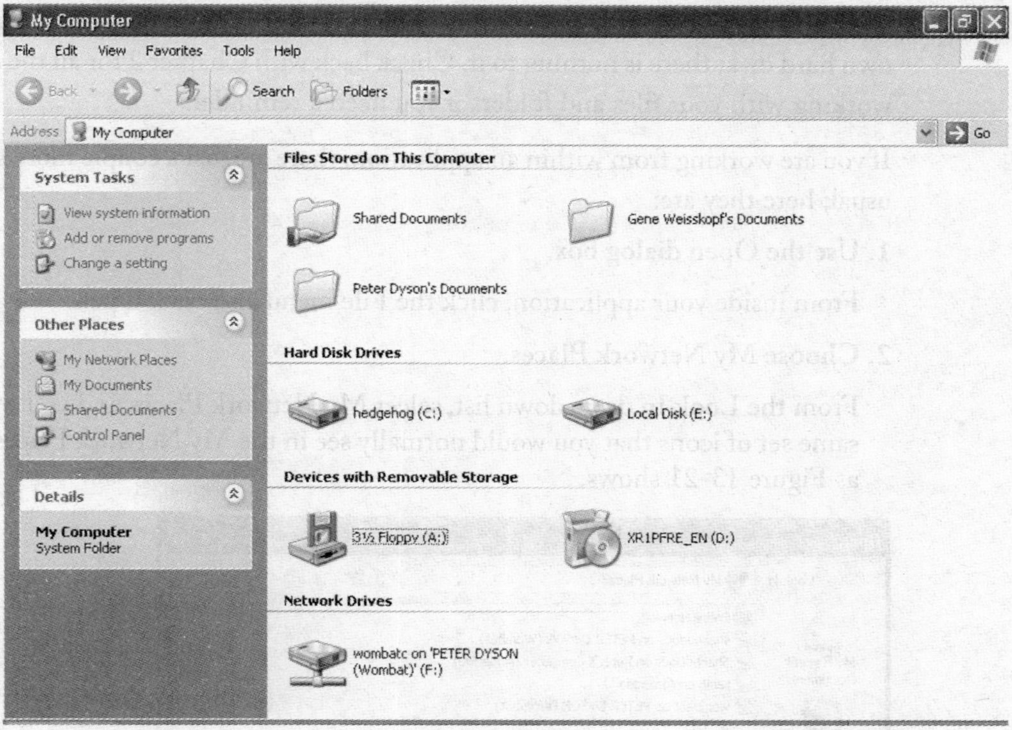

Figure 13-20 A mapped drive in My Computer.

Now opening a specific file on another computer is as easy as opening a file on your local computer. You no longer have to browse My Network Places to find it.

NOTE *A mapped drive is visible in My Computer, so when you right-click the Start button and choose Search from the shortcut menu, you can easily include mapped drives in your searches.*

Windows considers mapped drives to be *persistent,* or in other words, Windows automatically remaps drives automatically for you each time you log on. If you don't want to reconnect to this drive the next time you log on, clear the Reconnect At Logon check box. If you no longer need to connect to a mapped drive, open My Computer, right-click the drive, and choose Disconnect from the shortcut menu. You can always remap to the drive if you need to do so. Nothing happens to it when you disconnect—the resource is still right where it was to start with.

Working with Network Files

Once you have set up shared files and folders on your network, you can start to use them in your work. Given that you have the appropriate permissions, you can open applications, and copy, delete, and rename files on the network just as though they were on your own hard disk; there is nothing to it. Check back with Chapter 2 for all the details on working with your files and folders if you need a reminder.

If you are working from within an application, there are just a couple more steps than usual; here they are:

1. Use the Open dialog box.

From inside your application, click the File menu and click Open.

2. Choose My Network Places.

From the Look In drop-down list, select My Network Places and you will see the same set of icons that you would normally see in the My Network Places window, as Figure 13-21 shows.

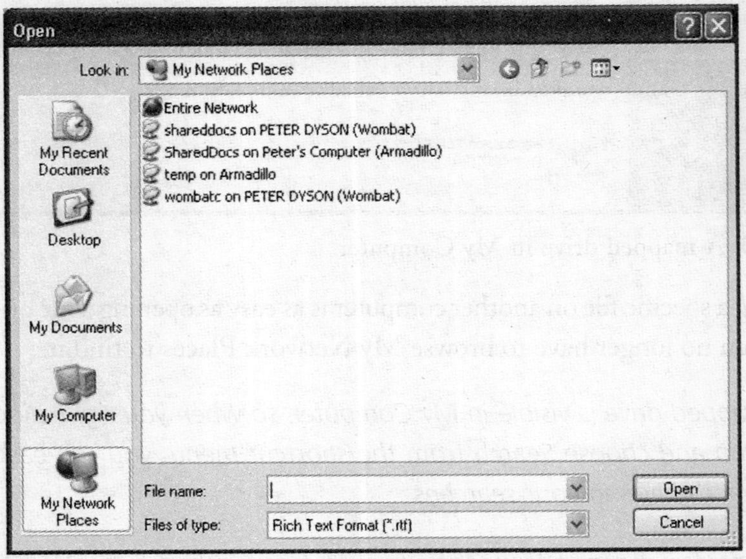

Figure 13-21 Network icons in the Open dialog box.

3. Find the file you want to open.

Double-click your way through the icons to the folder and file you want to work with. Double-click the file to open it, and the file opens just as though you were opening it from your own hard disk. Easy.

You can use the normal Save commands to save your changes back to the original file on the network, or you can use the Save As command if you want to make a local copy of the file on your own hard disk.

Network Tips and Tricks

Here are some reminders about things that are particularly important when working on a network and some tips that we've discovered working on the peer-to-peer network in our office:

- Be sure that everyone who uses your network is scrupulous about protecting his or password. A sticky note attached to a monitor or desktop is an open invitation for someone to attempt unauthorized access. And don't put the sticky note under the mouse pad either.
- Network administrators frequently have a policy of forcing users to change their passwords every 30 days or so, and it's a good idea to change passwords regularly on a small network, too.
- If you can't access a particular computer on your network, be sure the computer is turned on and then wait for a few minutes. Sometimes it takes a while for all the computers to appear in My Network Places after they've all been shut down. If you still can't access the computer, check the simple things first: cable connections and power sources. More on troubleshooting your network in just a moment.
- If you can't access a particular drive, folder, or file, verify that the resource has actually been shared by the owner.
- When you're finished with work for the day, shut down the computer properly using Turn Off Computer; don't just pull the plug out of the wall. The old notion that shutting down a computer risks data loss is simply no longer true.

Monitoring a Connection

Windows provides several tools to help you monitor a local area network (LAN) connection. Unfortunately, the default setting for the most useful of these tools is not on, as you might expect, but it is off. To enable the status monitor whenever the particular connection (in this case, our network) is active, follow these steps:

1. **Open Network Connections.**

   Click the Start button, click Connect To, and click Show All Connections to open Network Connections.

2. **Enable the status monitor.**

   Right-click the LAN icon, and choose Properties from the shortcut menu. In the General tab, click the Show Icon In Taskbar Notification Area When Connected check box, and click OK.

Now you'll see two small monitors in the desktop taskbar notification area by the clock. You'll see them flash their screens in response to network activity. This is very reassuring; you can just glance at the corner of your screen and see immediately that the network is running.

If you right-click these little screens and choose Status from the shortcut menu, you'll see the General tab, as shown in Figure 13-22.

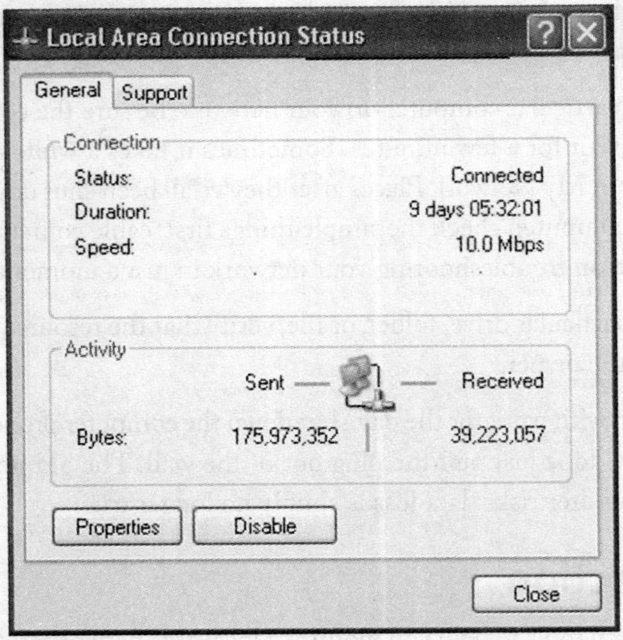

Figure 13-22 The Local Area Connection Status dialog box open at the General tab.

The Connection section describes the nature of the connection, including current status, duration of the connection, and current speed. The Activity section details the number of bytes sent and received over the network since the current connection was established.

The Support tab shown in Figure 13-23 details information specific to the connection, including type of address, Internet Protocol (IP) address, and subnet mask.

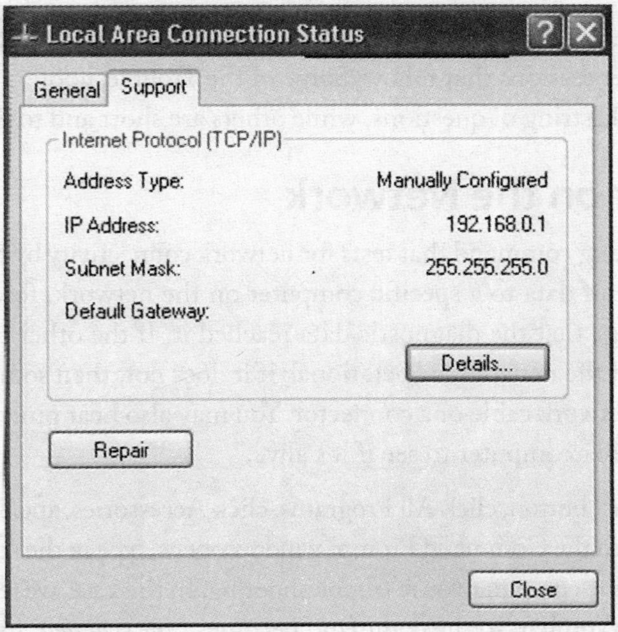

Figure 13-23 The Local Area Connection Status dialog box open at the Support tab.

If you just pass the mouse pointer over the little screens in the notification area, you'll see a small summary window that displays the name and speed of the connection. Handy for a quick check of network status.

Using the Network Troubleshooters

You can use several of the built-in Windows Troubleshooters to track down problems with network and network-related hardware. Click the Start button, and open Help And Support. Click Fixing A Problem, and then choose Networking Problems. Here you'll find the usual Windows Troubleshooters question-and-answer screens for the following topics:

- Internet Connection Sharing Troubleshooter
- Modem Troubleshooter
- Home And Small Office Networking Troubleshooter
- File And Printer Troubleshooter
- Terminal Services Troubleshooter

- Drives And Network Adapters Troubleshooter
- Diagnose Network Configuration And Run Automated Tests

Click the Troubleshooter that most closely relates to your problem, and work through the question-and-answer sessions that follow. Some of the Troubleshooters are quite extensive and ask a whole string of questions, while others are short and to the point.

Pinging a Computer on the Network

Ping is a special networking command that tests for network connectivity by transmitting a diagnostic packet of data to a specific computer on the network, forcing that computer to acknowledge that the diagnostic data reached it. If the other computer responds, that section of the network is operational; if it does not, then something is wrong, often with the network cable or a connector. You may also hear ping used as a verb, as in "Ping that other computer to see if it's alive."

To use ping, click the Start button, click All Programs, click Accessories, and then click Command Prompt. When the Command Prompt window opens, type in the command, followed by the name of the computer you're troubleshooting. In this case, we're working with a computer called Wombat, so the command becomes *ping wombat*. Figure 13-24 shows a successful result, with four diagnostic data packets sent from this computer to Wombat, four diagnostic data packets received back from Wombat, and no data packets lost.

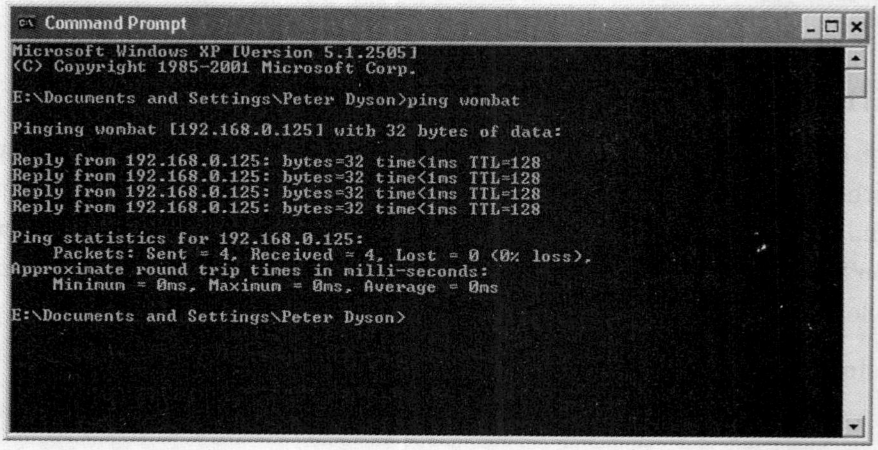

Figure 13-24 The results of a ping command sent to the computer called Wombat.

Ping was designed for network testing, troubleshooting, and performance measurement, and because of the large load it can impose on the network, don't use it unless you have to.

The Silence of the LANs

There are times when the tools in Windows cannot tell you what is happening on the network. One morning recently we arrived at the office to find two of the LEDs on our network hub flashing exactly in time, about a second apart. Very odd, very odd, indeed. Most of the time we don't even look at the hub; we just assume it is sitting there doing its job, and most of the time that is exactly what it does. But on this particular morning, the synchronized flashing was just too obvious to ignore.

One of the computers was running Windows XP and the other Windows 98 Second Edition. Both seemed to be working fine, we could access each computer from the other, and all was well until we tried to dial out to the Internet from a dedicated modem in the Windows 98 machine. Internet Explorer appeared to dial out, but nothing happened. Nothing at all. So we restarted the Windows 98 computer, and as we did so, the LEDs on the hub stopped their synchronized flashing, and went back to their normal indicators of network activity. Once the computer had booted up, we tried to use Internet Explorer again to dial out to a favorite Web site, and everything worked as we expected it to, network activity was normal, and the LEDs on the hub were fine.

So what happened during the night to cause this to happen? We have no idea, and it has not happened again, so we'll just have to put it down to the network gremlins.

Setting Up Users and Groups on Your Network

Because Windows XP Professional is a secure operating system, you must set up a user account on a system before you can do anything. As you may remember, when you installed Windows, you set up the Computer Administrator account, and you set up yourself as a user with administrative privileges. The user account is an integral part of Windows and has some great benefits, both on a standalone computer that is used by more than one person and on a network.

For example, if you and another person share a computer—maybe one of you works the early shift and the other works the late shift—you can set things up so that it is completely impossible to access each other's data unless you specifically give that person permission.

Understanding Users and Groups

The two broad categories of accounts in Windows are *users* and *groups*. A user account identifies a specific user by his or her user name and password. A group account contains other accounts that share common privileges.

User accounts are of these types:

- Computer Administrator gives the person full and complete rights to the computer. This means that an administrator can go anywhere and do just about anything to the computer. You cannot delete the Administrator account, and you must log on as Administrator when you need to create accounts, install software that will be available to everyone, and so on.
- Limited prohibits the user from changing computer configuration settings and deleting files.
- Guest lets a user log on to the computer even if he or she does not have an account on the system. This account presents a security risk. By default, it is disabled, and you should leave it that way. If a user needs access to the system and doesn't have an account, create a new one; don't use the guest account.

WARNING *Don't stay logged on as Administrator just because you can. Because you are all powerful, you can accidentally do something to damage your system that makes it necessary to completely reinstall Windows XP Professional. Create a user account for yourself, and use that until you need to do something that requires the rights of Administrator.*

So your user account determines exactly what you can and can't do on your own computer and on the network, including which Control Panel settings you can change; which files and folders you can open, change, or delete; and even which printer you can use.

By default, Windows contains a set of groups (although you can create other groups, as you'll see later in this section) with default sets of privileges. When a new person joins the company, you can just add her account to an existing group, say Accounting or Marketing, and you automatically grant her all the rights and permissions you have already granted to the group. Here is a list of the default groups and what each can do:

- Administrators can do just about anything to the computer, including loading and unloading device drivers, setting up an audit, and taking ownership of objects; they can even change their own permissions.
- Backup Operators can log on to the system, back up and restore the system or selected files (irrespective of the permissions that protect the files), and shut down the system.
- Guests have limited access to the system, and as we said earlier, these accounts should not be used.
- Power Users can share files and printers, change the system time, force a shutdown of the system, and alter the priorities of system processes.
- Replicators are involved in processes that involve a system connected to a Windows Server network, so we won't get into that here. Don't add any users to this group.
- Users can run programs, access data, shut down a computer, and access data over the network.

Groups are a great administrative tool, as they allow you to create associations of users very quickly, all with identical privileges.

Understanding User Rights

In Windows XP Professional, the ability to perform a certain function is a user *right*. User rights are an important aspect of security. To see a list of user rights and to whom they are typically assigned, follow these steps:

1. Open Control Panel.

Click the Start button, and then click Control Panel.

2. Open the Local Security Settings window.

In Control Panel, click Performance And Maintenance, click Administrative Tools, and click Computer Management. Click Local Security Policy to open the Local Security Settings window, which is shown in Figure 13-25.

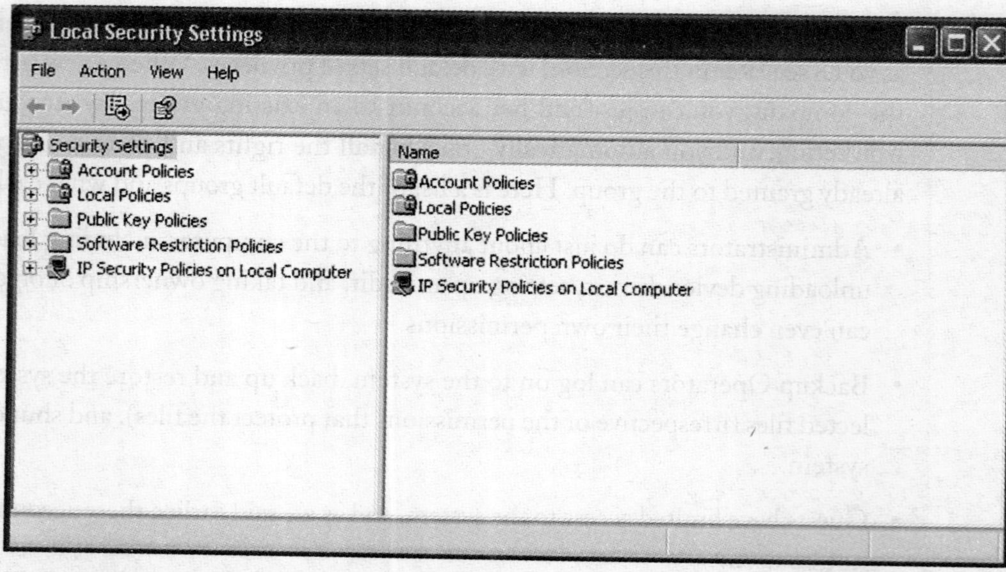

Figure 13-25 The Local Security Settings window.

3. Display the list.

In the tree pane, expand Local Policies, and then click User Rights Assignment. In the pane on the right, you'll see a list of user rights, as shown in Figure 13-26. Use the vertical scroll bar to see the rest of the list. In the Policy column, you'll see a list of security-related user rights, and in the Security Setting column, you'll see a list of the user groups associated with the policy.

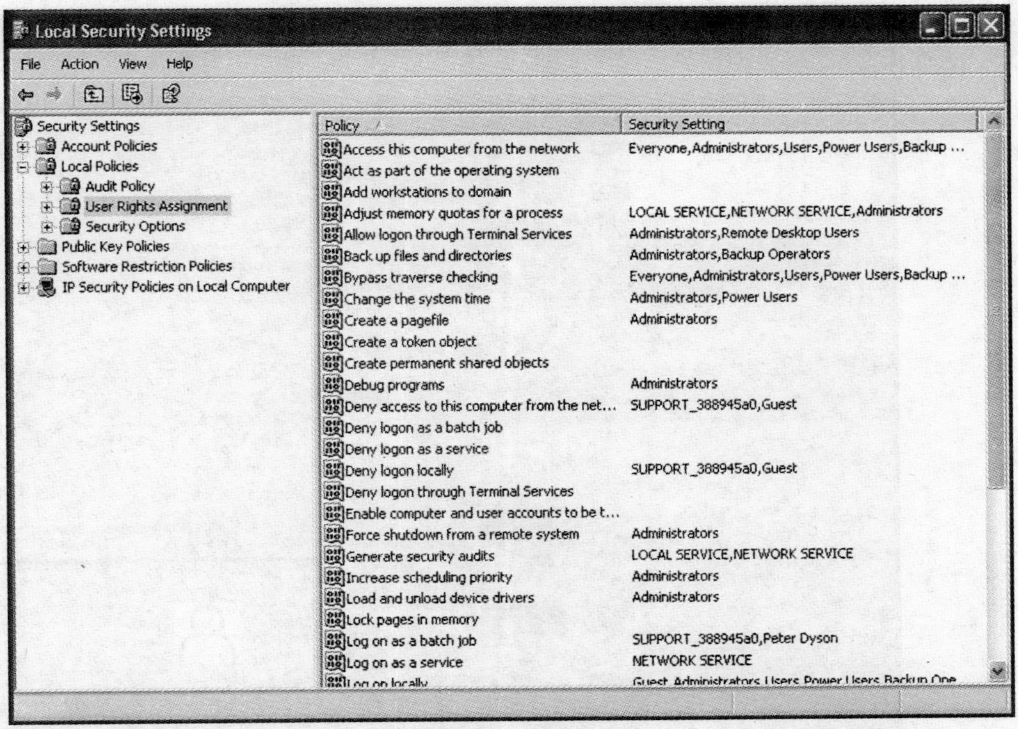

Figure 13-26 User rights in Windows.

Take a minute to peruse this list. Most of these rights are self-explanatory, but it's helpful to have an idea of what's included. Right-click an item, and choose Properties from the shortcut menu to look at or change the setting.

Creating a New User Account

To set up a new user account on your local computer, log on as Computer Administrator or as a Power User, and then follow these steps:

1. Open the User Accounts folder.

Click the Start button, click Control Panel, and then click User Accounts to open the User Accounts folder shown in Figure 13-27.

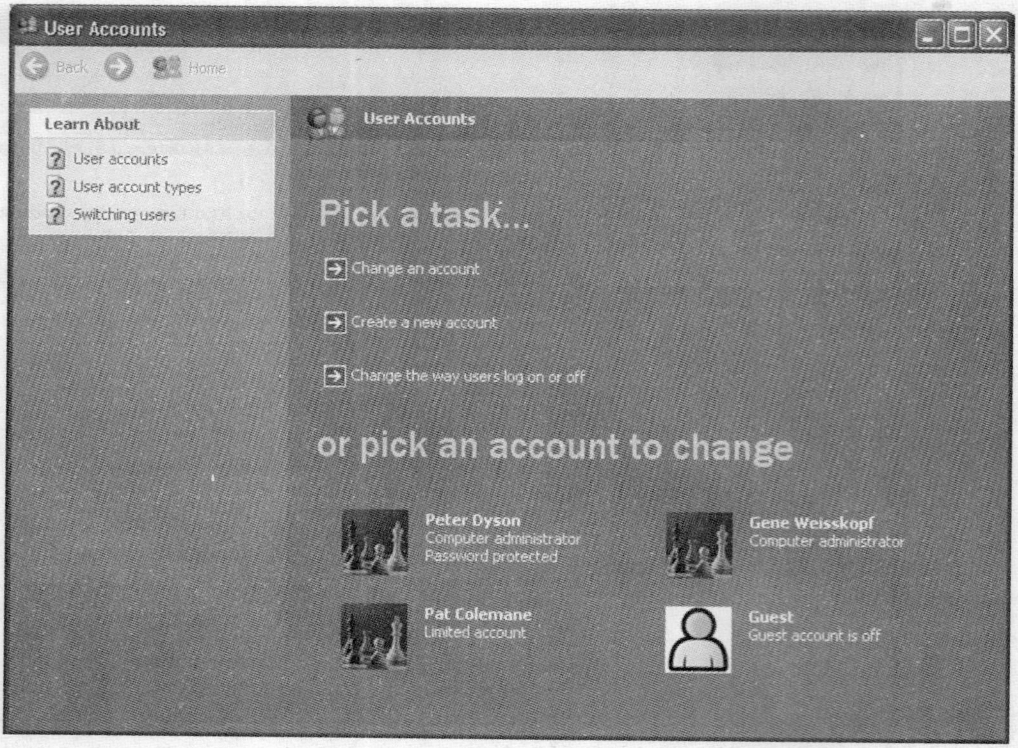

Figure 13-27 The User Accounts folder.

2. **Name the new account.**

   Click the Create A New Account button, and enter the name you want to use with this account. The name must be unique on this computer, can be a maximum of 20 characters, and is not case sensitive. Click Next.

3. **Pick an account type.**

   Pick the type of account you want to create, from Computer Administrator or Limited. Click Create Account. Now you will see an entry for this new account in the User Accounts folder. Select this new account, and click the Create A Password button.

4. **Assign the user a password.**

   In the Type A New Password box, enter a password for this user. (You'll see asterisks in place of the characters you type.) In the Type The New Password Again To Confirm box, retype the password, and then click Create Password. If your network includes only Windows XP Professional machines, the password can be a maximum of 127 characters. If your network includes Windows XP Professional machines and Windows 95/98 machines, the password should be a maximum of only 14 characters. Passwords are case sensitive, so if your password contains capital letters, you will have to type them the same way every time.

Changing an Existing Account

Once you have created an account, there are a number of items you can change if you wish. Open User Accounts, select the account you want to work with, and do one of the following:

- Change the name on the account.
- Change the picture associated with the account.
- Change the account type if you are logged on as a Computer Administrator.
- Change the password for the account.
- Remove the password altogether; this is not a good idea.
- Delete the account from the computer.

There are several user-account-related tasks that you can't do with User Accounts in Control Panel, and for those tasks we'll have to use Computer Management. Click the Start button, click Control Panel, click Performance And Maintenance, and click Administrative Tools. Click Computer Management, and then click the Local Users And Groups folder. In the right pane, double-click Users, and you will see a window something like that shown in Figure 13-28. What you actually see depends on how many of what kind of user accounts you have created on your computer.

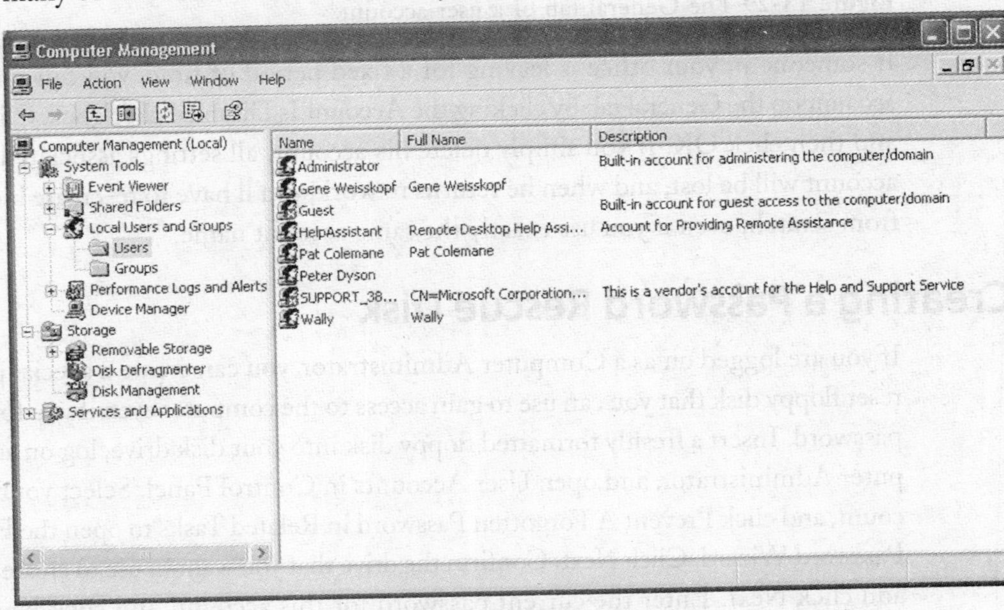

Figure 13-28 A listing of users in Computer Management.

Right-click a specific account, and choose Properties from the shortcut menu to open the account Properties dialog box shown in Figure 13-29.

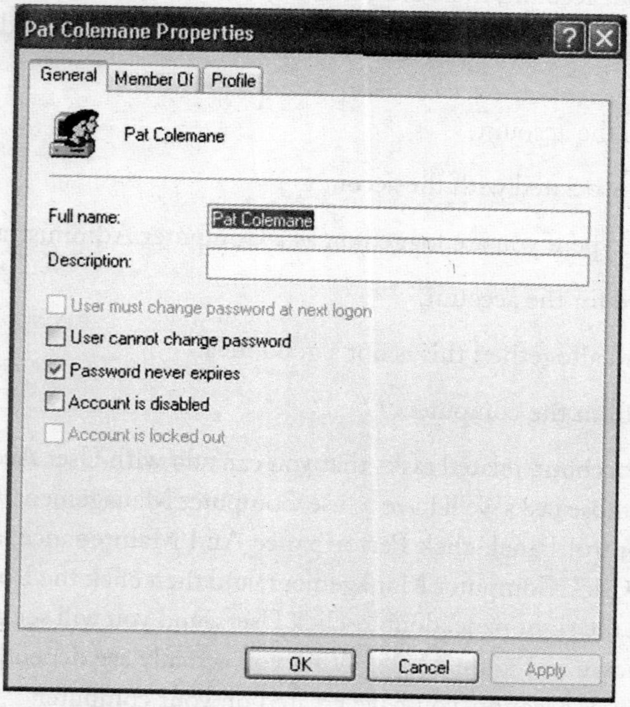

Figure 13-29 The General tab of a user account.

If someone in your office is leaving for a fixed period of time, you can turn off his account on the General tab by clicking the Account Is Disabled check box. Click Apply, and then click OK. If you simply delete his account, all settings associated with the account will be lost, and when he returns to work, you'll have to re-create his account from scratch, even if you use exactly the same account name.

Creating a Password Rescue Disk

If you are logged on as a Computer Administrator, you can create a special password reset floppy disk that you can use to gain access to the computer even if you forget your password. Insert a freshly formatted floppy disk into your disk drive, log on as a Computer Administrator, and open User Accounts in Control Panel. Select your own account, and click Prevent A Forgotten Password in Related Tasks to open the Forgotten Password Wizard. Click Next. Confirm the drive that you want to use to create the disk, and click Next. Enter the current password for this account, and click Next. Once Windows has finished writing to the floppy disk, label the disk and put it away in a safe place. You can use this disk at the Windows Welcome screen if you forget your password.

Setting Up Groups

As you saw earlier, by default Windows XP Professional creates several group accounts. You can, however, create other groups to satisfy organizational purposes. For example, you might want to create a group for a special project. To create a new group, follow these steps:

1. **Open Computer Management.**

   Click the Start button, right-click My Computer, and choose Manage from the shortcut menu.

2. **Open the Local Users And Groups window.**

   Select System Tools, click Local Users And Groups, and then double-click Groups. Figure 13-30 shows the result.

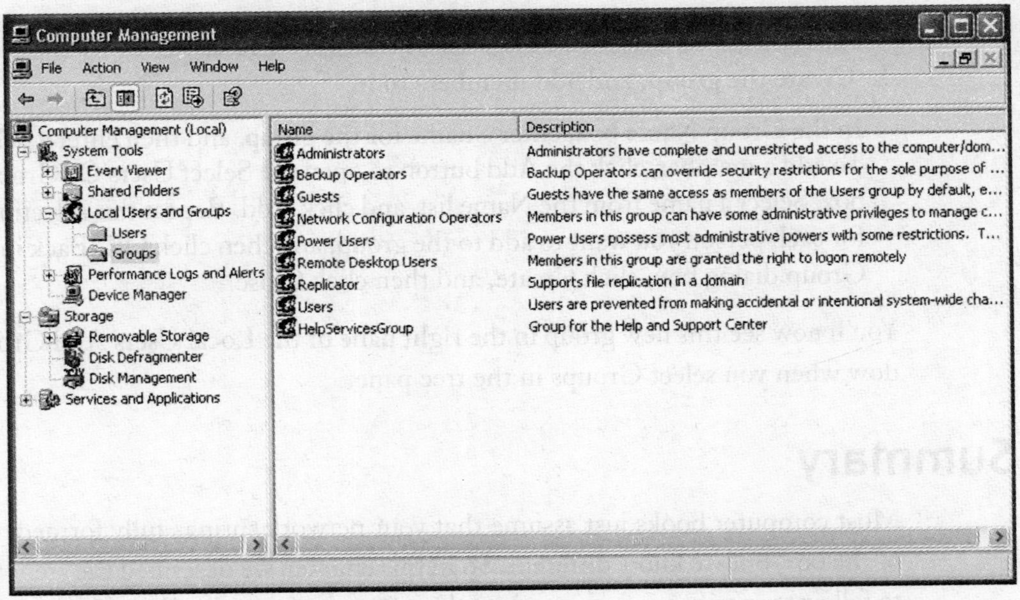

Figure 13-30 The Groups window.

3. **Open the New Group dialog box.**

   In the Local Users And Groups window, select Groups, click the Action menu, and then click New Group, or right-click Groups and choose New Group from the shortcut menu to open the New Group dialog box shown in Figure 13-31.

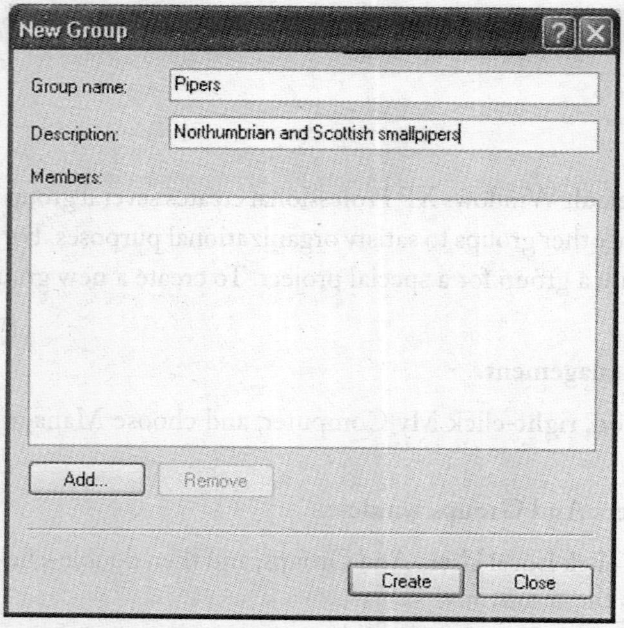

Figure 13-31 The New Group dialog box.

4. **Create the group, and add members to it.**

   In the Group Name box, enter a name for the group, and then enter a description. To add a member, click the Add button to open the Select Users Or Groups dialog box. Select a name from the Name list, and click Add. Repeat this selection process for each person you want to add to the group, and then click OK. Back in the New Group dialog box, click Create, and then click Close.

You'll now see this new group in the right pane of the Local Users And Groups window when you select Groups in the tree pane.

Summary

Most computer books just assume that your network springs fully formed, right out of the box, but we know different. So in this chapter, we described the steps you need to follow to specify, configure, and get the most out of a small office or home office peer-to-peer network. Then, after some networking tips, tricks, and troubleshooting steps, we took a good look at users and groups.

Chapter 14

WORKING WITH A CLIENT/SERVER NETWORK

Featuring:

- Connecting to a Corporate Network
- Connecting Over a Phone Line
- Setting Up a Calling Card
- Connecting with a VPN
- Connecting to a Windows XP Professional Computer Using Remote Desktop
- Disconnecting from the Network
- Synchronizing Offline Files
- Using Hardware Profiles
- Creating User Profiles

Corporate computer networks have been around for a long time. We first worked on one in the early 1980s at Encyclopaedia Britannica where each user tapped away at a 3270 terminal connected to the mainframe that sat in its sacred air-conditioned room on an upper floor. On the mainframe resided all the articles that composed the mother of all encyclopedias, and with the proper rights and permissions, you could access and edit those articles.

These days, a corporate network is more likely to be PC-based, with one or more central servers running one of the members of the Windows Server operating system. In this chapter, we'll look at some of the ways you can benefit from accessing a corporate network from Windows XP Professional, and we'll look at how you can dial in to your own Windows XP Professional system back at the office while you're on the road.

There are lots of reasons why you would want to connect to the network at the office or to your computer at home. According to IDC, a research company based in Framington, Massachusetts, the number of telecommuters in the United States is expected to grow from 10 million in 1999 to something like 13.5 million by 2003. So what will all those people be doing?

- Accessing your work e-mail while you are out of the office is one of the easiest and best ways to stay in touch while you are traveling. And if you keep up with your e-mail while you are on the road that means you won't have to spend your first two days back at the office digging your way through the pile of messages.
- Downloading the most current copies of documents such as sales figures or technical specifications so you can keep right up-to-date, even if the documents were changed after you left the office. You can also download any documents you forgot to take with you when you left on your trip.
- You will have a copy of PowerPoint or Word with you on your laptop, so you won't need to access the office copy, but many companies use custom applications that won't run on a portable computer. You can run these programs no matter where you are.
- You can send data back to the office network and update the database with new sales figures or projections.

Connecting to a Corporate Network

When you connect to your local area network (LAN) at your office, you are probably connecting to a client/server network. If you are running Windows XP Professional on your desktop, you could be connecting to a Windows XP Server, a Windows 2000 Server, or a Windows NT 4 Server back at the office. When your computer starts, you'll see a message that network communications are being established. You can then log on to the system.

But you can also log on to that LAN from your home network or while you're on the road, and you can do so in the following ways:

- Dial-up access over a phone line. You dial out using your modem and connect to special software known as a *remote access server* back at the office. This software is specially designed to accept incoming calls from your modem.
- Through a virtual private network (VPN). A VPN allows you to connect to the office computer using the Internet. And while many transactions on the Internet are not secure, data passed over a VPN connection is encrypted, and therefore is secure from prying eyes.

NOTE *Remote doesn't mean from some place far from civilization; it just means away from the office.*

Connecting Over a Phone Line

Perhaps the most common way to access a remote network is by modem. To do this most successfully, you'll first want to make sure that your modem and the modem at the office are compatible. Of course, you also need the permission of the corporate powers that be. For security reasons, some corporations don't allow remote access to the system, but as more and more people telecommute, this is becoming less common. You will also need to collect the following information before you leave the office:

- The telephone number of the receiving modem; this is the number you have to call to connect to the network.
- The network protocol in use; this will usually be TCP/IP, but check with your network administrator just to be sure.
- Your user name and password. If you are connecting to a Windows XP or NT server back at the office, you will be able to use the same user name and password that you use at the office. If the remote server does not use Windows, check with your network administrator which user name and password you should use.

NOTE *You can use a dial-up connection to connect to the office network by means of a phone line, an Integrated Services Digital Network (ISDN) line, or an X.25 network. The process is the same, although the technology used may be different.*

Once you have collected all this information, you can set up a dial-up connection by following these steps:

1. **Open Network Connections.**

   Click the Start button, click Control Panel, click Network And Internet Connections, and then click Network Connections to open the Network Connections folder shown in Figure 14-1.

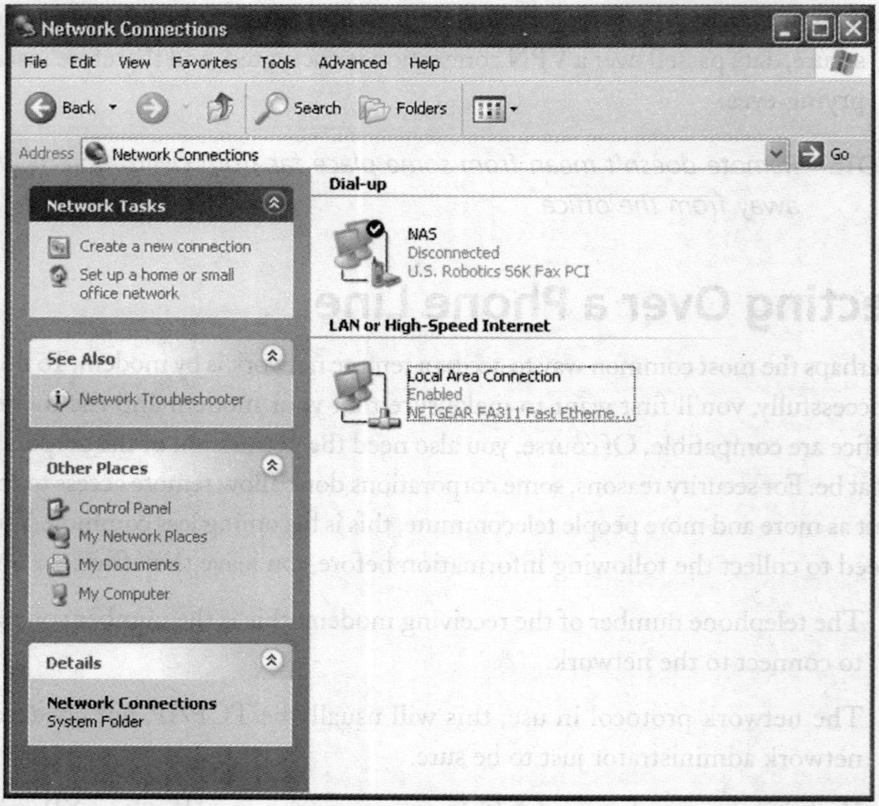

Figure 14-1 The Network Connections folder.

2. **Start the Network Connection Wizard.**

   Click the Create A New Connection icon to start the New Connection Wizard. Click Next.

3. **Select a network connection type.**

   Click the Connect To The Network At My Workplace option button, as shown in Figure 14-2, and then click Next.

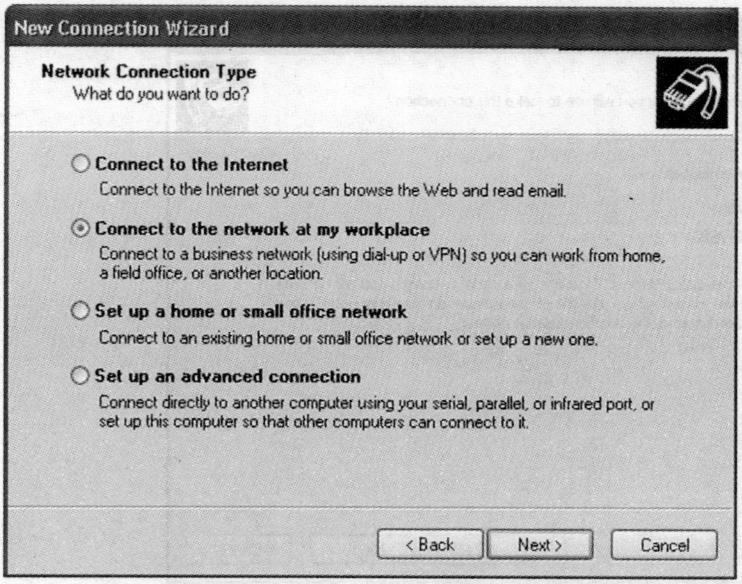

Figure 14-2 The Network Connection Type screen.

4. **Create the connection.**

   Click the Dial-Up Connection option button, and click Next.

5. **Name the connection.**

   Enter a name for this connection (a name that will appear in the Network Connections folder), and then click Next.

6. **Tell your modem which phone number to dial.**

   In the Phone Number To Dial screen, as shown in Figure 14-3, enter a phone number. Click Next.

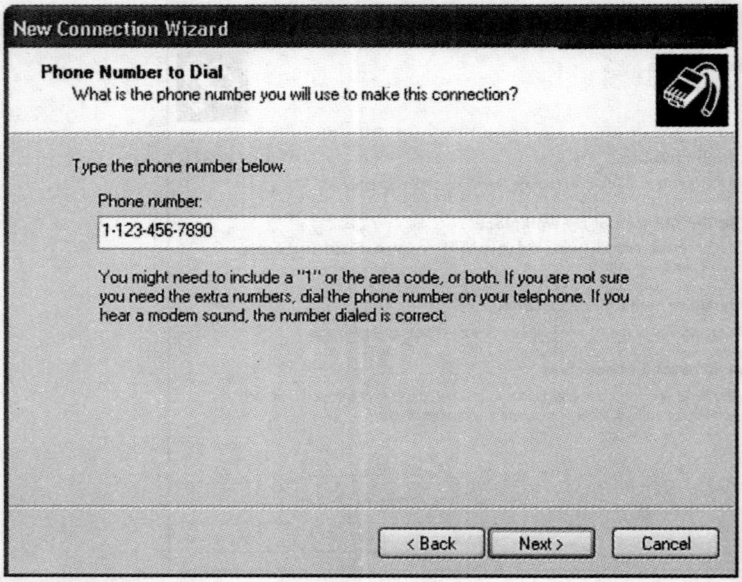

Figure 14-3 Entering a phone number.

7. Create a shortcut and then connect.

Click the Add A Shortcut To This Connection To My Desktop check box; then double-click the desktop icon when you want to connect. Click Finish.

If you want to connect immediately, enter your user name and password and click Dial in the Connect dialog box that now appears. If you want to connect later, click Cancel. To connect at any other time, click the icon for this connection in the Network Connections folder.

NOTE *To delete a connection, select its icon in the Network Connections folder and press Delete, or right-click the icon and choose Delete from the shortcut menu.*

Configuring Connection Properties

Now that we have created a new dial-up connection, you'll see a new icon in the Network Connections folder. Right-click this new icon, and choose Properties from the shortcut menu to open the Connection Properties dialog box, where you'll see several tabs you can use to fine-tune the settings for this connection.

General Tab

The General tab, shown in Figure 14-4, details the modem in use for this connection, as well as the phone number or numbers to use. Click Alternates to look at or change alternative phone numbers; you can also move numbers up and down the list. In many corporate settings, you will only ever need to dial one number; a modem pool at the receiving end will manage the problems associated with simultaneous access attempts.

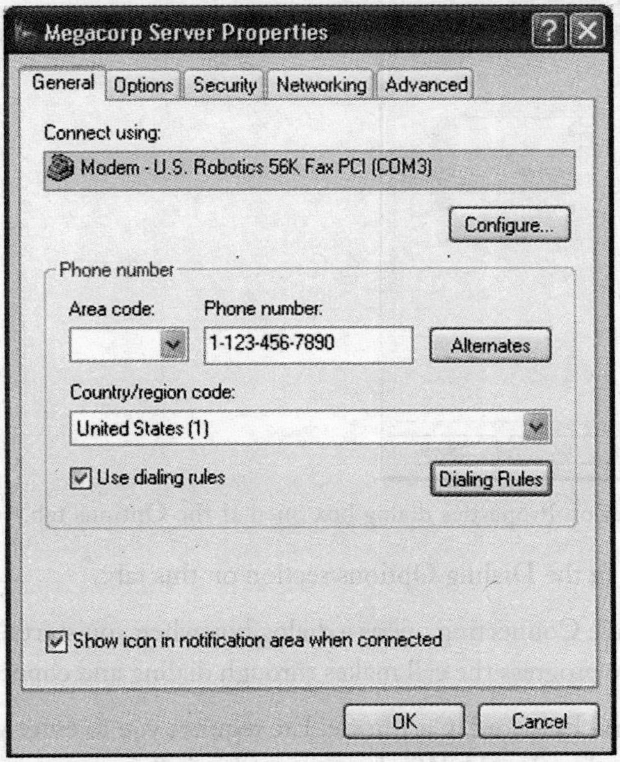

Figure 14-4 The connection Properties dialog box open at the General tab.

If you want your computer to decide how to dial in from various locations, click the Use Dialing Rules check box and click the Dialing Rules button to specify the rules you want to use. Dialing rules can be very useful if you need to switch between dialing 9 for an outside line from your office and dialing 8 for an outside line from a hotel.

Options Tab

The Options tab, shown in Figure 14-5, specifies how to manage dialing and redialing.

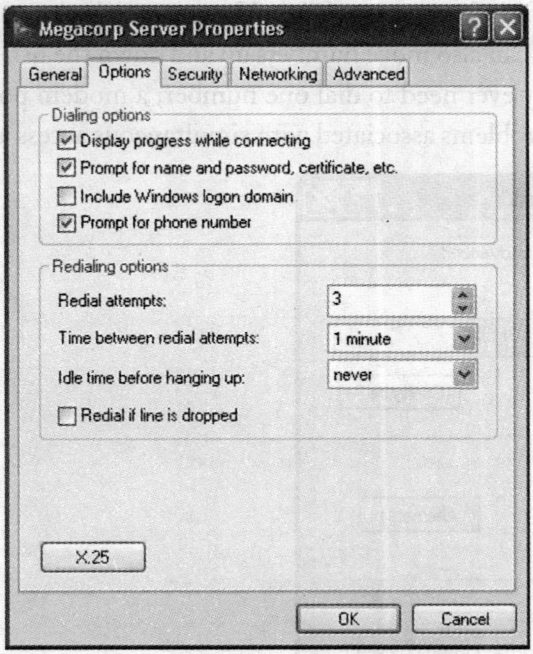

Figure 14-5 The connection Properties dialog box open at the Options tab.

You'll see these settings in the Dialing Options section on this tab:

- Display Progress While Connecting opens a dialog box when you start a connection that describes the progress the call makes through dialing and connecting.
- Prompt For Name And Password, Certificate, Etc requires you to enter your user name and password rather than let Windows remember it for you.
- Include Windows Logon Domain specifies whether to request domain information before trying to connect to the network. If you are working from your laptop that you also use at the office, it may already be configured to log on to the Windows Server domain. If you are connecting to a Windows Server domain from a computer that is not a member of the domain, click this check box.
- Prompt For Phone Number lets you look at or change the phone number before dialing out.

The settings in the Redialing Options section specify what you want to have happen when the line is dropped and the connection broken, or when you get a busy signal.

Security Tab

The Security tab, shown in Figure 14-6, controls authentication settings. If you are connecting to a Windows Server, click Typical, and then select Require Secured Password from the drop-down list. If your user name and password are the same for your office computer and your laptop, click Automatically Use My Windows Logon Name And Password (And Domain If Any).

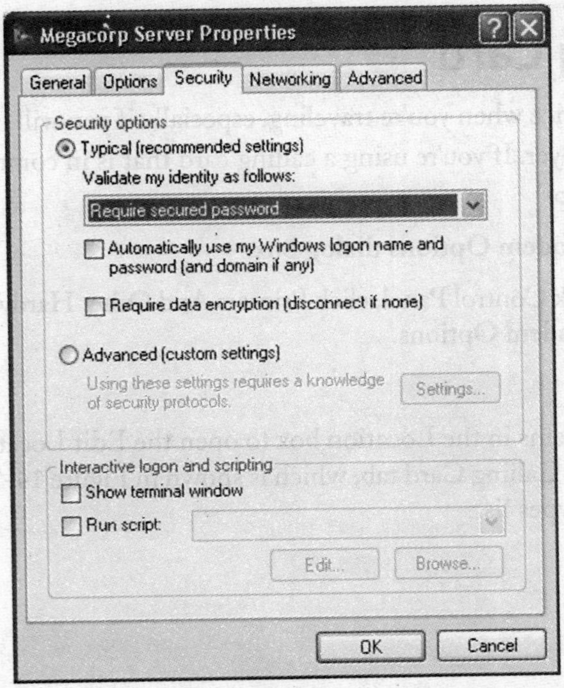

Figure 14-6 The connection Properties dialog box open at the Security tab.

The Require Data Encryption check box specifies whether or not to encrypt data. If you select this option, and data encryption is not used by the server you are connecting to, the connection disconnects automatically. If you clear this check box, your computer will encrypt data, but will not refuse to connect to the server if the server does not also use encryption. If in doubt about this setting, ask your network administrator before you leave the building.

If you are connecting to a non-Windows server, click the Advanced (Custom Settings) check box, and click the Settings button to open the Advanced Security Settings dialog box. It is best to confirm all of the encryption, logon, and protocol options required by the Advanced Security Settings dialog box with your network administrator as some of them are pretty complex; far more technical than we want to discuss here.

Networking and Advanced Tabs

The Networking tab gives more detail on the communications protocols in use and their settings. Your network administrator is the best person to advise you on which of these settings might need to be changed and what you should change them to so that they work in your specific networking environment. And finally, we looked at the settings on the Advanced tab in Chapter 13 when we looked at sharing an Internet connection.

Setting Up a Calling Card

A calling card is a handy device when you're traveling, especially if you will be billing expenses back to your employer. If you're using a calling card that is in common use, follow these steps to set it up:

1. **Open the Phone And Modem Options dialog box.**

   Click the Start button, click Control Panel, click Printers And Other Hardware, and then click Phone And Modem Options.

2. **Specify the card type.**

   Double-click one of the items in the Location box to open the Edit Location dialog box, and then click the Calling Card tab, which is shown in Figure 14-7. Select the card from the Card Types list.

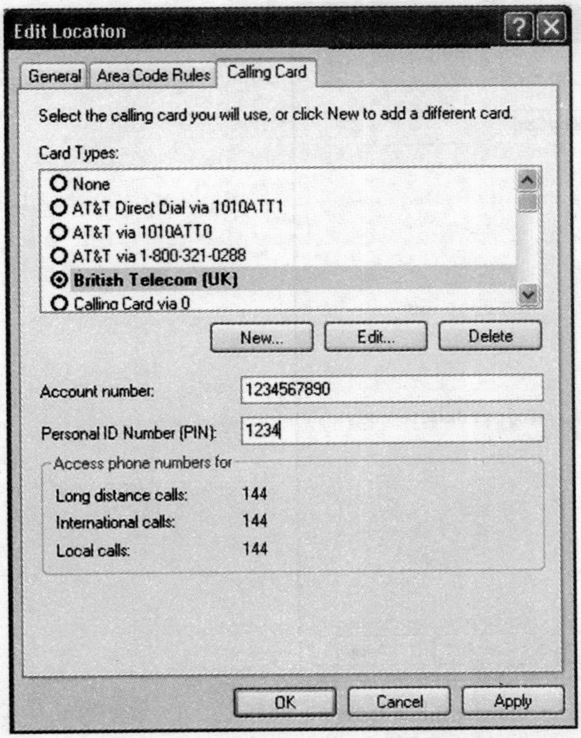

Figure 14-7 The Edit Location dialog box.

3. Enter the information about your card.

Enter your account number, and then enter your PIN number. Access numbers are entered automatically when you select the card type. Click OK.

If your card is not listed in the Card Types list, follow these steps:

1. Open the New Calling Card dialog box.

In the Calling Card tab, click New to open the New Calling Card dialog box shown in Figure 14-8.

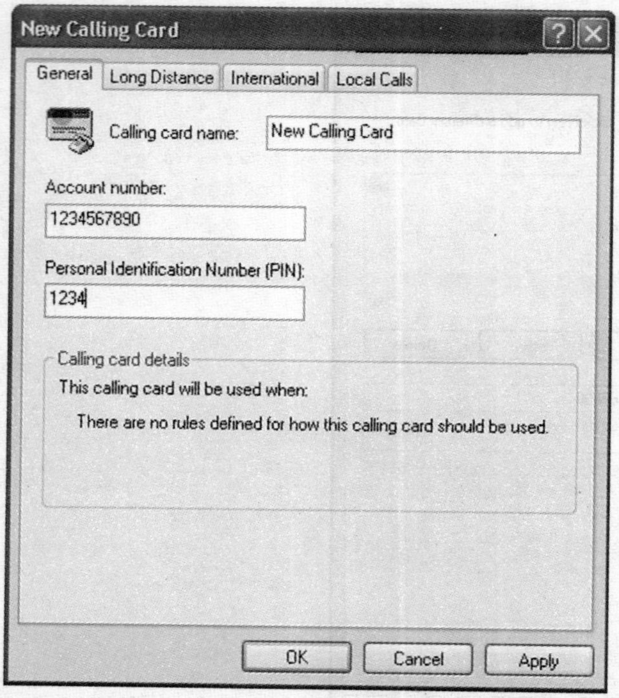

Figure 14-8 The New Calling Card dialog box.

2. **Enter information about the card.**

   In the Calling Card Name box, enter a name for the card, and then enter the account number and your PIN number.

3. **Enter the steps you must follow to make a call.**

   Click the International, Long Distance, or Local Calls tab, depending on how you want to use this calling card. Enter the number you dial to access the appropriate telephone service, and then in the Calling Card Dialing Steps box, enter the numbers in the exact order that you must enter them to make a call. For example, click the Access Number button, and enter the access number; click the PIN button, and enter the PIN number; and so on. To change the order of a step, click the Move Up or Move Down button. Click Apply, and click OK.

To use your calling card to make international or local calls, click the corresponding tab and follow step 3 above.

How a Virtual Private Network (VPN) Works

A VPN usually connects by means of the Internet, but in theory it could connect using any network. Rather than simply forwarding the data packets, a VPN encapsulates the original data inside another packet. The header information in this new packet provides the routing information needed to guide the data across the Internet. Data is also encrypted, so even if your message is intercepted, it is meaningless without the encryption key.

At the receiving end of the connection, the encapsulating information is removed, and the message is decrypted and made available. Windows XP Professional includes two industry-accepted encapsulating or tunneling protocols, both of which have long ungainly names: Point-to-Point Tunneling Protocol (abbreviated to PPTP) and Layer Two Tunneling Protocol (L2TP).

Connecting with a VPN

A VPN sounds complicated, but it isn't really. A VPN is a tunnel through the Internet that connects your computer to your corporate network. First you connect to the Internet, and then use the Internet to connect to your corporate computer. You can dial up almost any Internet service provider (ISP) and set up a VPN session. Data that is transmitted via the VPN tunnel is encrypted, so it is always secure. So not only is this cheaper as all calls are local calls (you don't need dedicated end-to-end leased lines) but a VPN is also much more reliable and can be configured very securely.

Configuring the receiving end of a VPN is a job best left to the experts; let your network administrator take care of that. Once this has been done, you just need the host name or IP address of your corporate network, which you can obtain from your system administrator if you don't know it. Follow these steps to set up the connection:

1. **Open Network Connections.**

   Click the Start button, click Control Panel, click Network And Internet Connections, and then click Network Connections to open the Network Connections folder.

2. **Start the Network Connection Wizard.**

   Click the Create A New Connection icon to start the Network Connection Wizard. Click Next.

3. **Select a network connection type.**

   Click the Connect To The Network At My Workplace option button, and then click Next.

4. **Choose how to connect.**

   Click the Virtual Private Network Connection button, and click Next.

5. **Name the connection.**

   Enter a name for this connection, which will appear in the Network Connections folder, and then click Next.

6. **Specify whether to automatically dial your ISP.**

   In the Public Network screen, which is shown in Figure 14-9, click the Automatically Dial This Initial Connection option button if you want to establish a connection to your ISP first before connecting to your corporate network. Otherwise, click Do Not Dial The Initial Connection. Click Next.

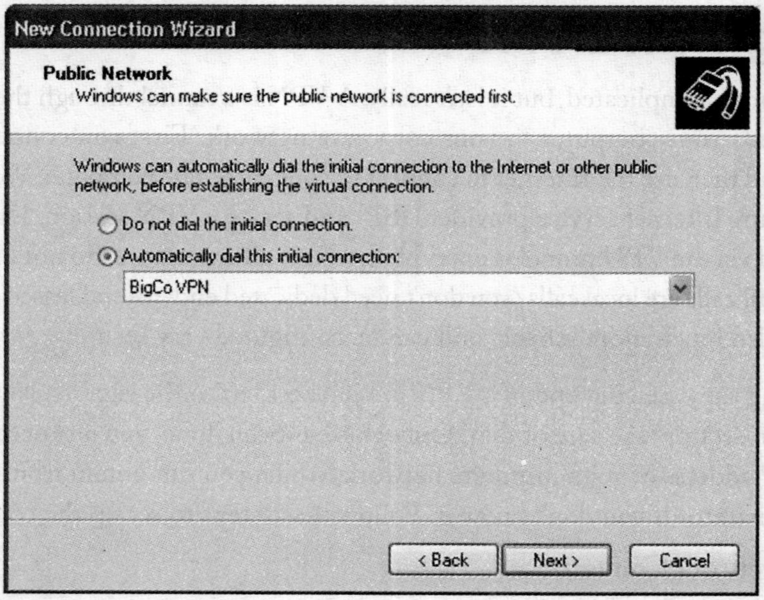

Figure 14-9 Choosing whether to dial your ISP automatically.

7. **Specify the destination address.**

   In the Host Name Or IP Address box, enter the host name or address you obtained from your system administrator. A host name is something like stephenlnelson.com, and an IP (Internet Protocol) address is a string of numbers, such as 123.45.6.78. Click Next. When the connection summary screen appears, check the information. If it is correct, click Finish to create the connection and close the wizard.

If you want to connect immediately, click Yes in the Initial Connection dialog box that now appears. If you want to connect later, click No. To connect at any time, click the icon for this connection in the Network Connections folder.

To delete a connection, select its icon and press Delete.

You can copy the connections you made for modem, ISDN, or VPN by right-clicking the connection and choosing Create Copy from the shortcut menu. You can then right-click the copy, and choose Properties from the shortcut menu to modify the connection for a particular situation.

Now all you have to do to connect using a VPN is to double-click the connection you just created in the Network Connections folder. The modem will dial out and connect to your ISP. Then you'll be prompted for the user name and password you used when you created the connection so you can access the remote access server back at the office. And bingo, you're in.

You can now use the network back at the office just as though you were sitting at your desk, but with one very obvious difference. Speed. Performing certain operations, such as opening that big sales database, can be agonizingly slow.

Configuring the VPN

When you right-click the VPN connection and choose Properties from the shortcut menu, you'll see that the Properties dialog box contains several tabs. Some of these tabs contain essentially the same information as the properties for the dial-up connection we looked at earlier in this chapter. Options specifies dialing and redialing configuration; Security covers passwords and encryption; Advanced details Internet Connection Firewall and Internet Connection Sharing settings. Two tabs, however, contain different information.

General Tab

The General tab, shown in Figure 14-10, lists the host name or IP address of the remote access server you want to connect to, and the name of the connection to your ISP. Click the Show Icon In Notification Area When Connected check box to display the small screens on the taskbar when this connection is active. Then you can right-click these icons to see connection status and activity information right from the desktop.

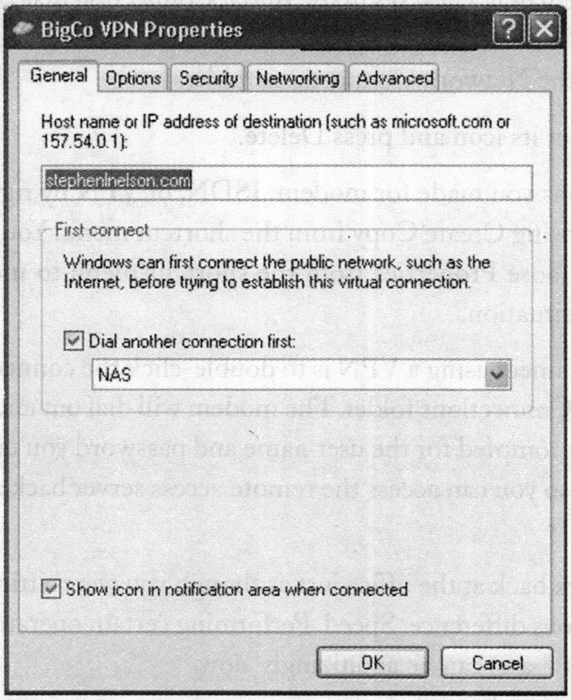

Figure 14-10 The VPN Properties dialog box open at the General tab.

Networking Tab

The Networking tab, shown in Figure 14-11, details the VPN communications protocol in use in the Type Of VPN box. Set this to Automatic if you're not sure which protocol to use. Windows will try to connect using L2TP initially, and if that is unsuccessful, will try PPTP instead. If you know which protocol is in use on your remote access server, select it from the list.

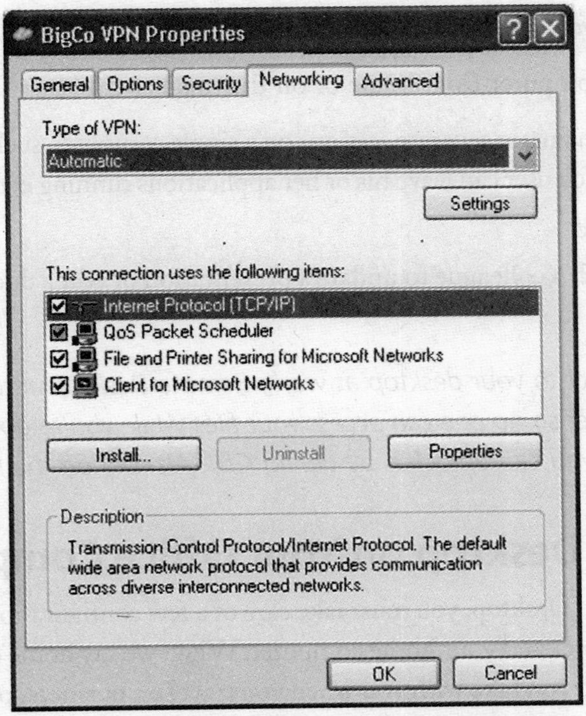

Figure 14-11 The VPN Properties dialog box open at the Networking tab.

To look at or change VPN configuration information, click the Settings button to open the Settings dialog box for the tunneling protocol you are using. Check with your network administrator before you change any of these settings.

Connecting to a Windows XP Professional Computer Using Remote Desktop

A corporate network isn't the only connection you can make from your laptop while you're out on the road. You can also connect to your computer running Windows XP Professional on your desktop back at the office. All you need is a modem in each computer and the software package built into Windows XP Professional known as Remote Desktop. Remote Desktop lets you connect from your home computer or from your laptop when you're traveling to your work computer, and access all the applications and files as though you were still at your desk.

Using Remote Desktop you can do the following:

- Work on your office computer from home or on the road.
- Allow several users to maintain separate sessions on a single computer, such as a sales point or a help desk. Each user can leave his or her applications running even as other users log on.
- Share your desktop with a colleague to update a presentation or edit a document or spreadsheet.

NOTE *When you connect to your desktop at work, Remote Desktop automatically locks the computer so no one can access your files while you're gone. When you come back, you can unlock it by typing Ctrl+Alt+Del on the keyboard.*

Configuring Remote Desktop on Your Office Computer

Before you can use Remote Desktop, you must take care of a few configuration settings on both your office computer and your home computer. When we say home computer here, we include the laptop you take with you when you travel on business, or in other words, we are referring to any computer that is not your office computer. Here are the steps:

1. **Log on as a Computer Administrator.**

   Log on to your office system as a Computer Administrator.

2. **Open System in Control Panel.**

   Click the Start button, click Control Panel, click Performance And Maintenance, and click System.

3. **Click the Computer Name tab.**

   Click the Computer Name tab shown in Figure 14-12, and write down the entry in the Full Computer Name field. Your computer name is all the text to the left of the first period. In Figure 14-13, the full computer name is *armadillo*. You will need this name to connect from another computer.

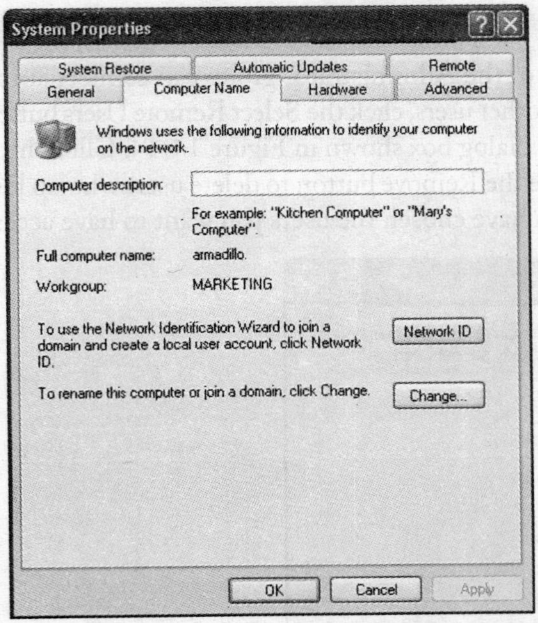

Figure 14-12 The Computer Name tab in System.

4. Click the Remote tab.

Now click the Remote tab shown in Figure 14-13, and click the Allow Users To Connect Remotely To This Computer check box.

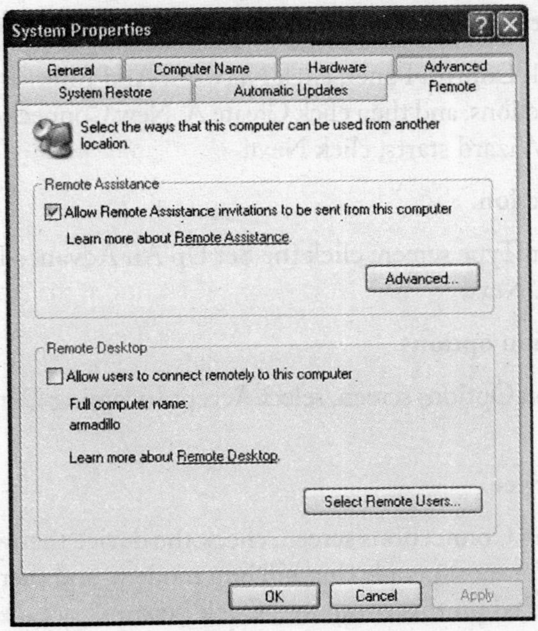

Figure 14-13 The Remote tab in System.

5. **Select users.**

   Any user who is a member of the Administrator group can connect automatically to this computer, but to add other users, click the Select Remote Users button to open the Remote Desktop Users dialog box shown in Figure 14-14. Click the Add button to add new users and use the Remove button to delete users who no longer need access. Click OK when you have chosen the users you want to have access.

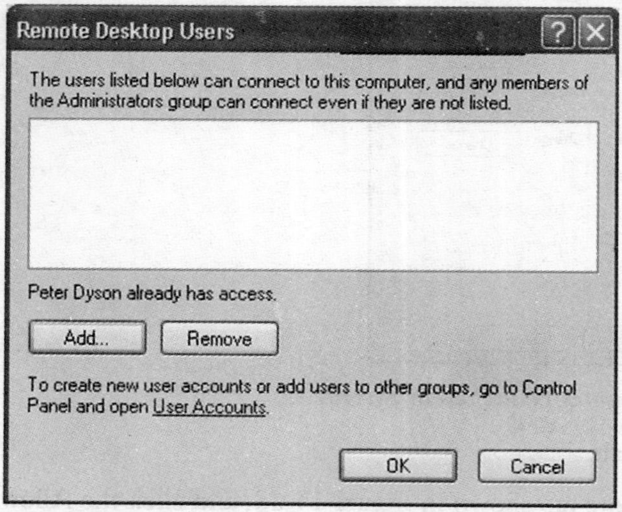

Figure 14-14 The Remote Desktop Users dialog box.

6. **Start the Network Connection Wizard.**

   Click the Start button, click Control Panel, click Network And Internet Connections, click Network Connections, and then click Create A New Connection. When the Network Connection Wizard starts, click Next.

7. **Choose Advanced Connection.**

   In the Network Connection Type screen, click the Set Up An Advanced Connection button, and then click Next.

8. **Select Advanced Connection options.**

   In the Advanced Connection Options screen, select Accept Incoming Connections, and click Next.

9. **Choose the connection device.**

   In the Devices For Incoming Connections screen, check the device that will accept the incoming connection. For most people this will be a modem, and there is probably only one modem installed on this computer. Click Next.

10. Allow a VPN connection.

If your computer will always have a permanently assigned IP address, you can choose to accept incoming VPN connections. If not, choose Do Not Allow Virtual Private Connections. Click Next.

11. Specify users.

In the User Permissions screen, shown in Figure 14-15, select the users who will be allowed to connect to this computer. Use the Add and Remove buttons to configure the list. For security reasons, you should keep this list as short as possible, one user, preferably. To specify a callback number, select a user, click the Properties button, and then click the Callback tab. A callback is a security measure that makes your computer immediately hang up an incoming call and then dial out to the number you give here or to another number specified by the caller. You must provide all the numbers for the callback number, including any prefixes you have to dial. Windows doesn't follow its own dialing rules for a callback.

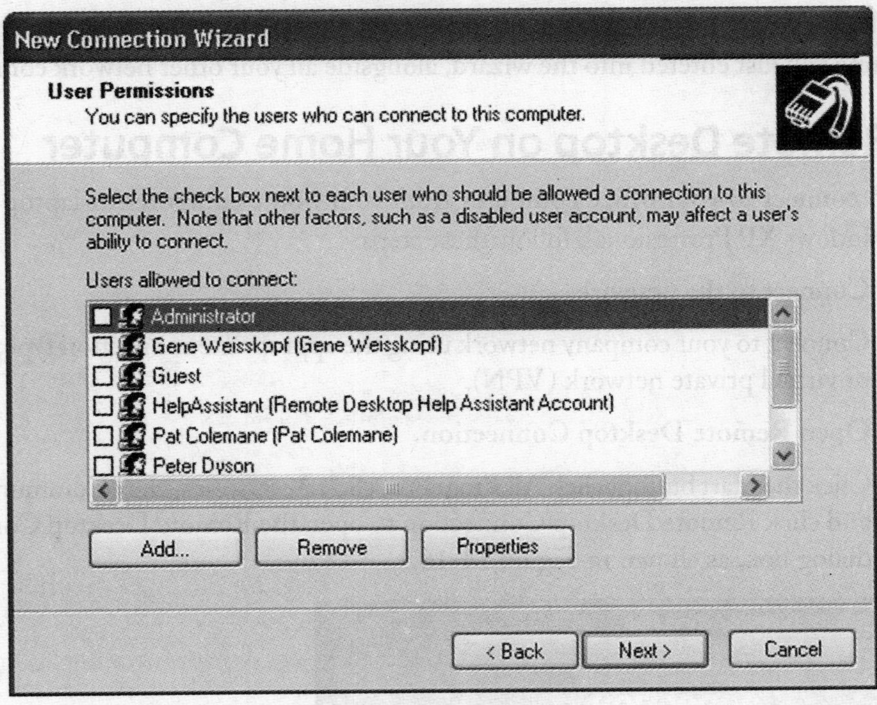

Figure 14-15 The User Permissions screen.

12. **Confirm networking software.**

    In the Networking Software screen, leave all the networking protocols selected. If this computer is connected to a network, anyone dialing in will have access to the network. If you don't want them to have that access, highlight a protocol from the Networking Software list and click the Properties button. Then clear the Allow Callers To Access My Local Area Network check box, and click OK. Click Next.

13. **Check the summary screen.**

    In the final screen of the Network Connection Wizard, check the summary information. If it is all correct, click Finish to create the connection and close the wizard.

14. **Leave your computer turned on.**

    To be able to connect to your computer while you are out of the office, make sure you leave it turned on.

After a moment, you will see a new icon in the Network Connections folder with the name you just entered into the wizard, alongside all your other network connections.

Using Remote Desktop on Your Home Computer

To connect to your office computer from your home computer or laptop running Windows XP Professional, follow these steps:

1. **Connect to the network.**

   Connect to your company network using the appropriate connection type, dial-up, or virtual private network (VPN).

2. **Open Remote Desktop Connection.**

   Click the Start button, click All Programs, click Accessories, click Communications, and click Remote Desktop Connection to open the Remote Desktop Connection dialog box, as shown in Figure 14-16.

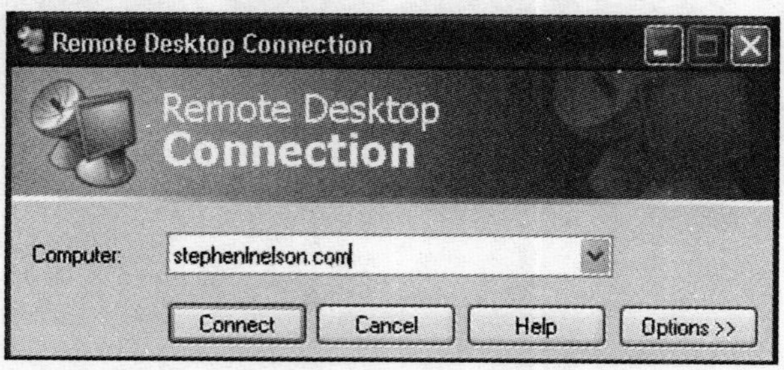

Figure 14-16 The Remote Desktop Connection dialog box.

3. **Connect to the remote computer.**

   Enter the name of the remote computer you want to connect to, and click the Connect button.

To connect to your office computer from your home computer or laptop running an operating system other than Windows XP Professional, follow these steps:

1. **Insert the Windows XP Professional CD.**

   On a computer running Windows 95, any of the versions of Windows 98, Windows NT 4.0, or Windows 2000, insert the Windows XP Professional installation CD into the CD-ROM drive.

2. **Perform additional tasks.**

   When the Welcome screen appears, click Perform Additional Tasks, and then choose Set Up Remote Desktop Connection. Follow the instructions that appear on the screen.

Configuring Remote Desktop on Your Home Computer

Click the Options button in the Remote Desktop Connection window to open the properties dialog boxes associated with Remote Desktop Connection. Figure 14-17 shows the General tab, which details the remote computer and your logon information.

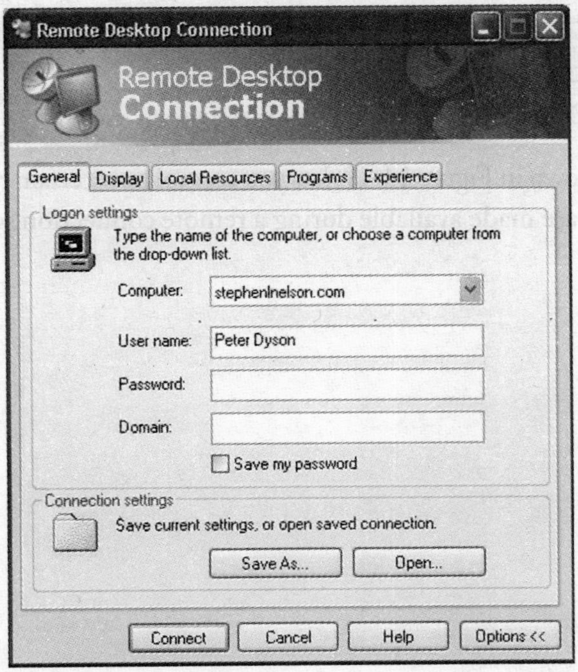

Figure 14-17 The Remote Desktop Connection properties General tab.

The Display tab, shown in Figure 14-18, lets you choose the size of the remote desktop, and the screen colors to use, although the settings in place on the remote computer may override your selection here.

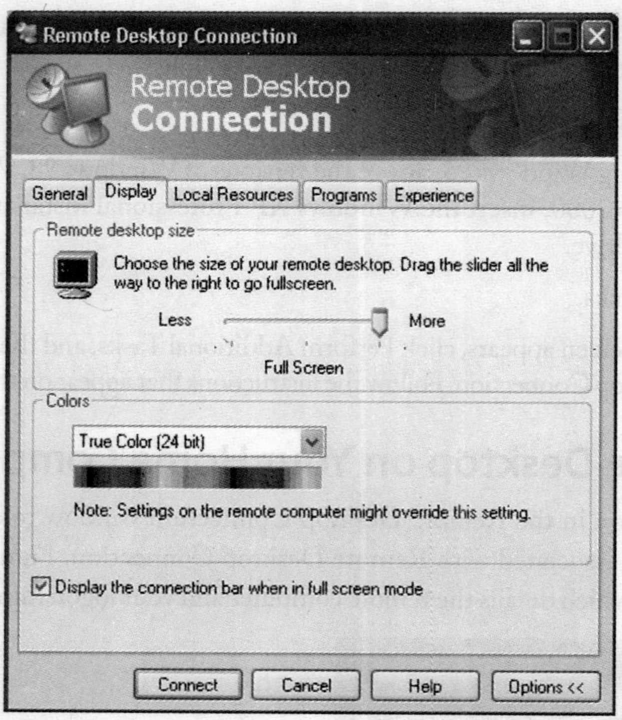

Figure 14-18 The Remote Desktop Connection properties Display tab.

The Local Resources tab, shown in Figure 14-19, lets you control how certain resources, including hard disk drives, are made available during a remote connection session.

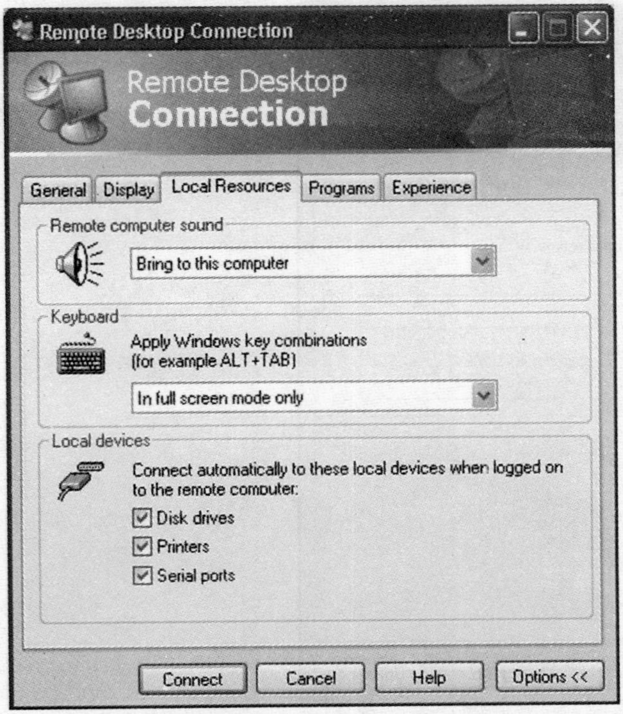

Figure 14-19 The Remote Desktop Connection properties Local Resources tab.

Sound is one feature you can well do without during a remote session (unless you want to work with the Media Player, of course), so choose Do Not Play from the Remote Computer Sound drop-down list, and both computers involved in the link will go quiet.

You can also choose whether or not Windows shortcut keys are turned on or not during a remote session. Finally, in the Local Devices section, you can specify that local disk drives, printers, and serial ports will be available during a remote session. Remember that your local area network policies may not allow local drive mapping during a session. If you choose not to make local disk drives available, the Remote Desktop Connection is still established, but the files and folders on these local drives are not available to the remote computer.

The Programs tab, shown in Figure 14-20, lets you specify a program that will start running on the remote computer once the connection is made. This option is available only if you are connected to a terminal server.

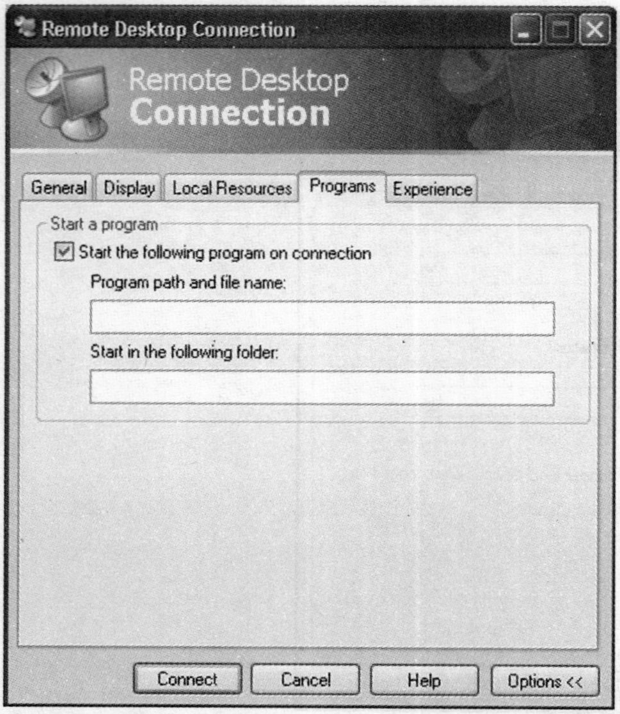

Figure 14-20 The Remote Desktop Connection properties Programs tab.

The Experience tab, shown in Figure 14-21, lets you specify how Windows will behave in a remote connection session. You can turn off many of the Windows display features, such as the desktop background or menu and window animation, to cut down on the volume of information that has to pass from the local computer to the remote computer. The configurable display features selected on this tab are related to your connection speed; the higher the connection speed, the more features are enabled. Clearing all the check boxes on this tab will ensure the best performance and fastest response.

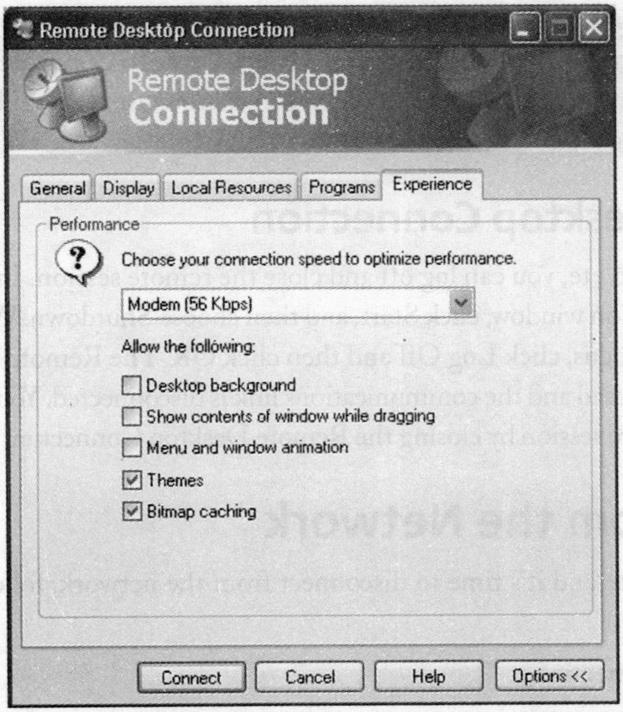

Figure 14-21 The Remote Desktop Connection properties Experience tab.

Remote Desktop and Security

Configuring your computer to accept incoming calls is certainly a security risk, but there are some things you can do to minimize the risk:

- Make sure you get permission from your company for this connection. In some commercial or government settings, opening an unauthorized connection is sufficient cause to get you fired.
- Add yourself to the Remote Desktop users group on your computer. This means that you won't have to log on to your computer as a Computer Administrator to access your system.
- Insist that all Remote Desktop users log on with a strong password, one that is at least eight characters long, combines letters and numbers, is not a real word or a name or a date, and one that is significantly different from the previous password.
- Keep to a minimum the number of people who can connect using Remote Desktop.

- Disable Remote Desktop when it is not being used. To do this, open System in Control Panel, click the Remote tab, and clear the Allow Users To Connect Remotely To This Computer check box. Click OK. When you want to use Remote Desktop, click the check box again.

Closing a Remote Desktop Connection

Once your work is complete, you can log off and close the remote session. In the Remote Desktop Connection window, click Start, and then choose Shutdown. When the Shutdown dialog box opens, click Log Off and then click OK. The Remote Desktop Connection session is closed and the communications link is disconnected. You can also disconnect from a remote session by closing the Remote Desktop Connection window.

Disconnecting from the Network

When your work is done and it's time to disconnect from the network, follow these steps:

1. **Open Network Connections.**

   Click the Start button, and then click Network Connections.

2. **Close the connection.**

   Right-click the appropriate open connection, and then choose Disconnect from the shortcut menu.

You can also right-click the small green icon for this connection in the taskbar notification area, and choose Disconnect from the shortcut menu. This action also disables the network interface card associated with this connection until you reactivate the connection.

Synchronizing Offline Files

We looked at how to use the Offline Files Wizard and how to use offline files in Chapter 6 as part of our discussion of laptop and portable computers. Now it is time to revisit offline files and how to synchronize them in a bit more detail here in a network context.

Programmers and designers have long wrestled with the problems associated with simultaneous updates to a file or document; here's the problem. When you take a file offline, a copy of the file is made to your laptop. You then update the file during a business trip, so now there are two different versions of that same file, one on the network and one on your laptop, and both different from the original. If several people take the same file offline, there could be many different versions of that original file.

Offline files (or Synchronization Manager) is the answer to this problem. When you reconnect to the network, the changes you made to the file while you were out of the office are updated to the network copy of the file. In other words, the two copies are synchronized.

Offline files are very useful when you spend most of your time working on your laptop and you only connect to the company network occasionally, or when you are connected to the network from home or your hotel room over a slow or unreliable connection.

Files that you specify are available for offline use are copied (or cached) from the network hard disk to the hard disk in your laptop. When you disconnect from the network, a message appears to let you know that the connection has been broken and a new icon appears in the notification area of the taskbar indicating you are no longer connected to the network.

Now that you are offline, you can open and change the files that have been cached to your laptop. You can work with the files as you normally would, and when you reconnect to the network at the office, or dial in from your hotel room, the Synchronization Manager compares your files with the original files on the network. If the Synchronization Manager finds differences in the files, it can update the files in both directions. Changes from your version of the file are made to the network version of the file, and changes in the network version of the file are made to the copy on your laptop. At the end of the process, both files are up-to-date and contain all the changes.

Setting Up Your Computer to Use Offline Files

Before you can work with shared files and folders offline, you have to set up a couple of things on your computer first. Here are the steps:

1. Open My Computer.

Click the Start button, and then open My Computer. Alternatively, you can also open any other desktop folder.

2. Click Folder Options.

Click the Tools menu, and click Folder Options.

NOTE *If you are using Fast User Switching, you can't use offline files; it is one or the other. To change your Fast User Switching settings, click the Start button, click Control Panel, click User Accounts, and click Change The Way Users Log On Or Off. Clear the Use Fast User Switching check box, and click Apply Options. That will do the trick.*

3. Click Offline Files.

Click the Offline Files tab, shown in Figure 14-22, and click the Enable Offline Files check box.

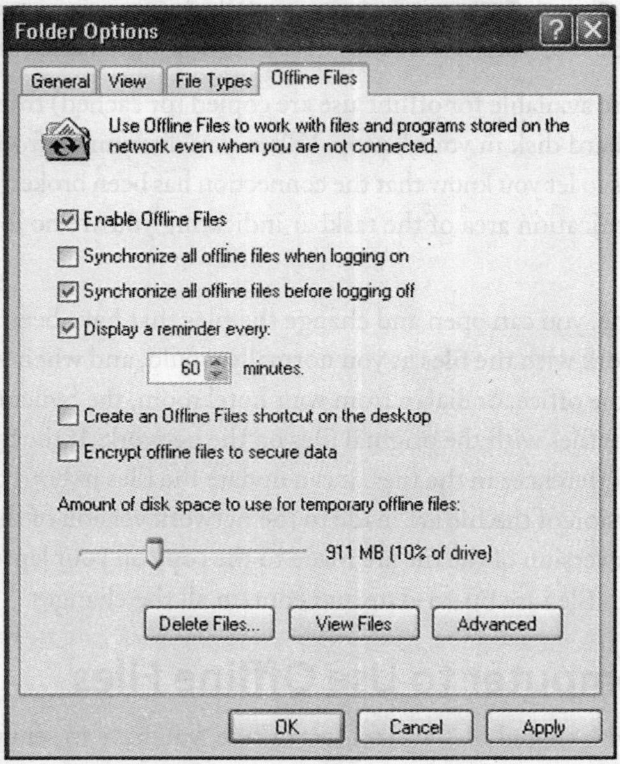

Figure 14-22 The Folder Options dialog box open at the Offline Files tab.

4. Choose a synchronization option.

Click the Synchronize All Offline Files Before Logging Off check box to make sure that you'll have the most up-to-date copies of the files and folders you need for your trip. Click Apply, and then click OK.

The Offline Files tab has several other important settings, including the following:

- Synchronize All Offline Files When Logging On will automatically start the synchronization process as soon as you log back on to the network.

- Display A Reminder opens a taskbar balloon reminder at the specified interval telling you that you are no longer connected to the network. This might be useful if you connect and reconnect to the network many times during the day, but if you are out of the office for a week, you don't need to be reminded that you are no longer connected. Instead, when you are out of the office, set this to the maximum of 9999 minutes, which is roughly about a week.
- Create An Offline Files Shortcut On The Desktop does exactly that; it creates a shortcut for you. When you open this shortcut, you'll see a folder like the one shown in Figure 14-23. Here you'll see a listing of every file that came from the network by name and type, as well as its synchronization status, current availability, access type, server status, original location on the network, size, the time and date it was last modified, and whether the file is encrypted or not.

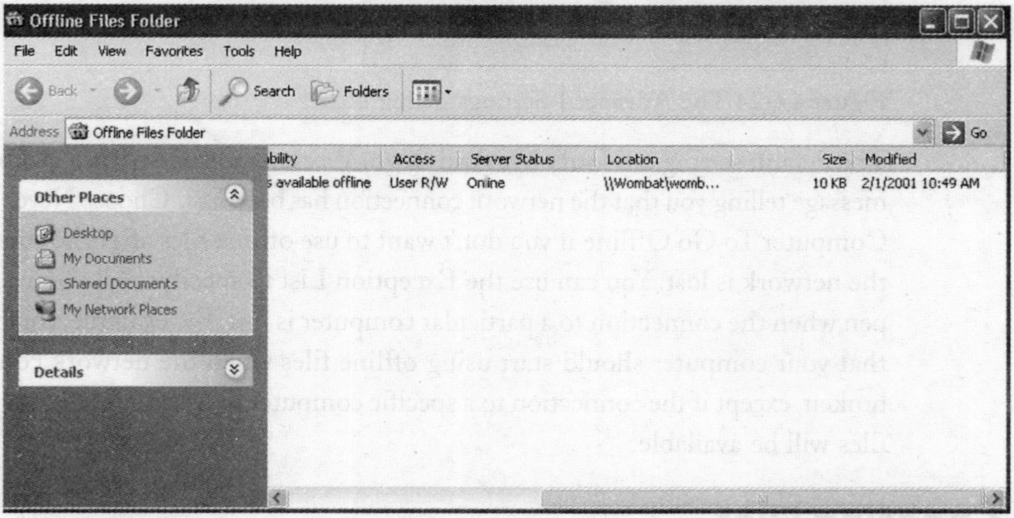

Figure 14-23 The Offline Files folder.

- Encrypt Offline Files To Secure Data is a good way to prevent prying eyes from looking at your files.
- Amount Of Disk Space To Use For Temporary Offline Files lets you specify how much hard disk space to set aside for the offline files cache. The cache is initially set at 10 percent of your hard disk's capacity. This may be too much or too little space, depending on how you use offline files, so use the slider to adjust the limit.

Click the Advanced button on the Offline Files tab to open the Advanced Settings dialog box shown in Figure 14-24. You can use these settings to tell your computer what you want it to do when the network connection is lost.

Figure 14-24 The Advanced Settings dialog box.

The default setting of Notify Me And Begin Working Offline posts a taskbar balloon message telling you that the network connection has been lost. Choose Never Allow My Computer To Go Offline if you don't want to use offline files after the connection to the network is lost. You can use the Exception List to specify what you want to happen when the connection to a particular computer is lost. For example, you can specify that your computer should start using offline files when the network connection is broken, except if the connection to a specific computer is lost, in which case, no offline files will be available.

Choosing Files

Selecting the individual files you want to work with offline is easy, just open Explorer or My Network Places, right-click the file you are interested in, and choose Make Available Offline from the shortcut menu. Alternatively, you can highlight the file, click the File menu in Explorer, and click Make Available Offline.

You can also make entire folders available offline too, but be careful with this as you can use up a tremendous amount of hard disk space on your laptop very quickly, and when you come back to the office, you will suffer very long synchronization times. Once you have made a file or folder available offline, a small arrow appears as part of the icon to indicate this, and the Make Available Offline menu selection has a tick on the left side to indicate that it is in effect.

Working with Offline Files

While you are connected to the network, you continue to work with the network copies of these files and folders. But when you disconnect, the Offline Files icon appears in the taskbar notification area (it looks like a little computer), and you'll see a red X on the network icon in the taskbar.

When you open one of these drives, you'll see that they contain only the files and folders that you've opted to make available offline. You can open the folders and work with the files just as you did back at the office, and you have the same rights and permissions for these files and folders as you did in the office.

Synchronizing Offline Files

When you return from your trip and reconnect to the network, Windows automatically synchronizes your offline files and folders with the copies on the network. If both your copy and the network copy of a file have changed, Windows asks for your help; the Resolve File Conflicts dialog box opens listing these options:

- Keep Both Versions.
- Keep Only The Version On My Computer. Replace The Network Version.
- Keep Only The Network Version. Replace The Version On My Computer.

Check the box for the option you want, and click OK. If you are unsure of the changes, use the View button to check the contents of the file.

Configuring Synchronization Manager

You don't have to synchronize offline files and folders when you reconnect to the network, there are many ways to configure the Windows Synchronization Manager. Open My Computer, Explorer, or Offline Files; click the Tools menu; and click Synchronize to open the Items To Synchronize dialog box shown in Figure 14-25.

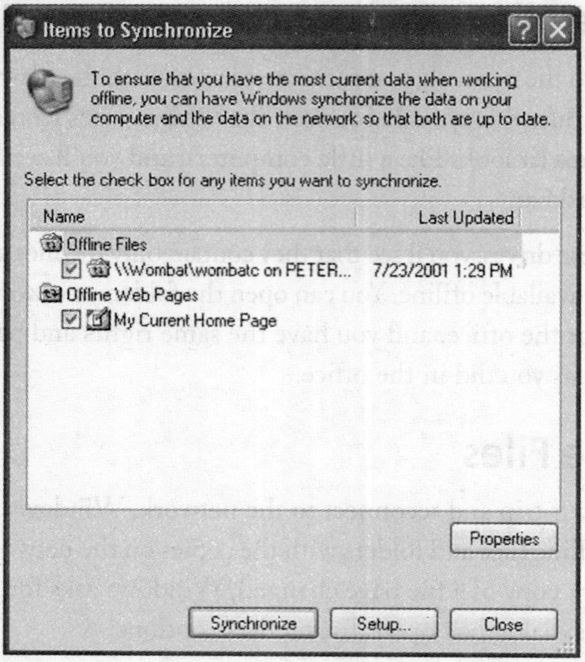

Figure 14-25 The Items To Synchronize dialog box.

Click the Synchronize button to synchronize the items listed in the Name box. Click Setup to open the Synchronization Settings dialog box at the Logon/Logoff tab, as shown in Figure 14-26.

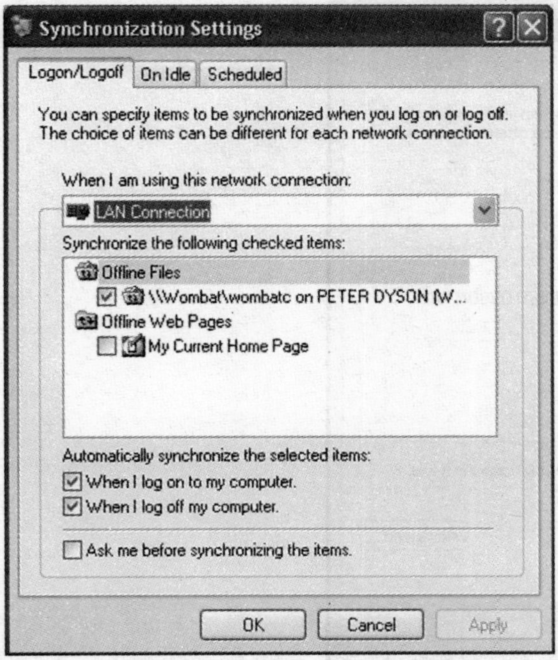

Figure 14-26 The Synchronization Settings dialog box open at the Logon/Logoff tab.

Specify the network connection first, and then check the items you want to synchronize. With this done, you can specify when you want to synchronize your offline files and folders. The default setting synchronizes when you log on and when you log off your computer. If you want Windows to ask your permission before synchronizing, click the Ask Me Before Synchronizing The Items check box.

Click the On Idle tab, shown in Figure 14-27, if you want Windows to synchronize items during periods when your computer is connected to the network but not doing very much.

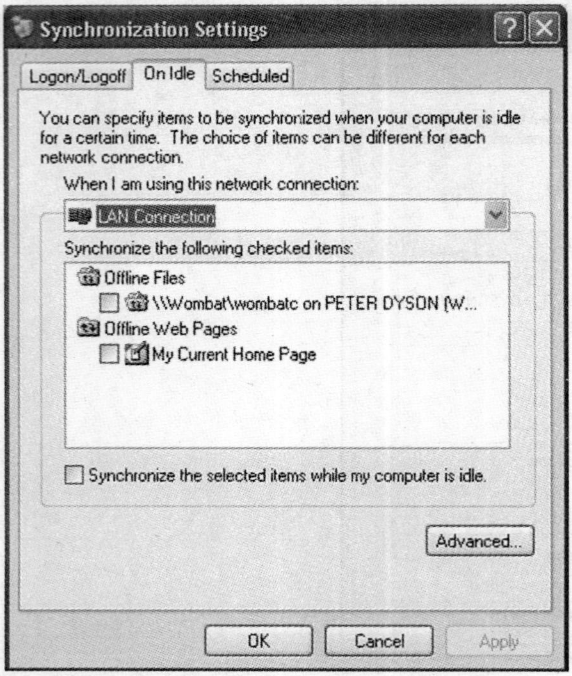

Figure 14-27 The Synchronization Settings dialog box open at the On Idle tab.

Choose the network connection first, check the items you want to synchronize, and then click the Synchronize The Selected Items While My Computer Is Idle check box. To specify exactly what idle means, click the Advanced button to specify a time period after which synchronization can begin and an interval after which you want to repeat the synchronization. You can also specify here that you don't want to perform any synchronization operations while your laptop is running on battery power. Click OK to close the Idle Settings dialog box.

You can also schedule a synchronization for a specific time on the Scheduled tab shown in Figure 14-28.

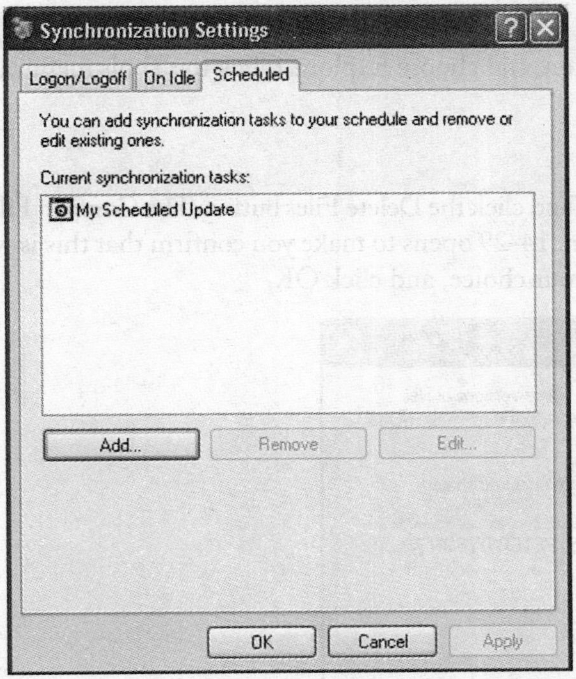

Figure 14-28 The Synchronization Settings dialog box open at the Scheduled tab.

Click the Add button to start the Scheduled Synchronization Wizard. Select the connection you want to use and the items you want to synchronize. You can also make Windows dial up the connection automatically if you wish. Specify a start time and date, specify a repeat frequency, and give the scheduled synchronization a name. Once the wizard finishes, you will see this scheduled synchronization listed on the Scheduled tab. To change the schedule, select the task and click the Edit button on this tab.

Clearing Out the Offline Files Cache

If you want to clear out your laptop's hard disk once a synchronization has finished, or you know you won't be taking any more sales trips for a while and want to reclaim your hard disk space, you can throw away your offline files and flush out the offline files cache. Here are the steps:

1. **Open Folder Options.**

   Right-click the Start button, and choose Explore. Click the Tools menu, and click Folder Options.

2. **Delete offline files.**

   Click the Offline Files tab, and click the Delete Files button. The Confirm File Delete dialog box shown in Figure 14-29 opens to make you confirm that this is what you really want to do. Make your choice, and click OK.

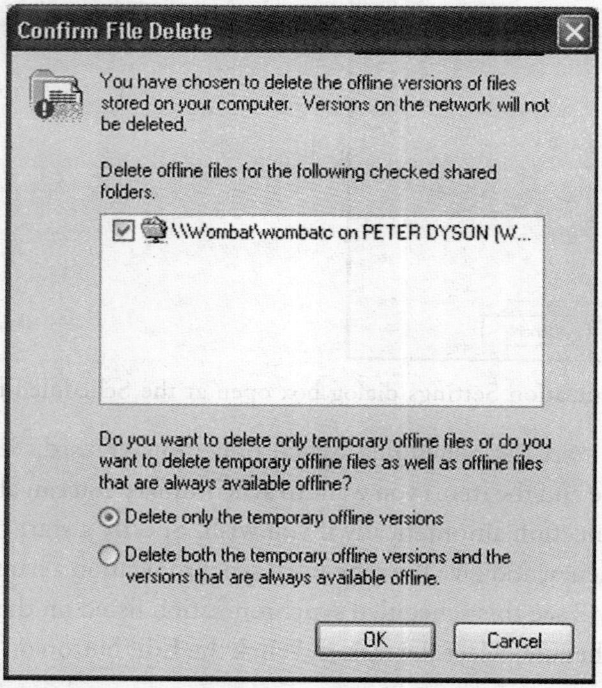

Figure 14-29 The Confirm File Delete dialog box.

3. **Clear the cache.**

   Back at the Offline Files tab, press the Ctrl and Shift keys at the same time, and click the Delete Files button again. The warning message shown in Figure 14-30 opens to tell you that any changes that have not been synchronized with the network will be lost and that your computer will be restarted. To clear the offline files cache, click Yes.

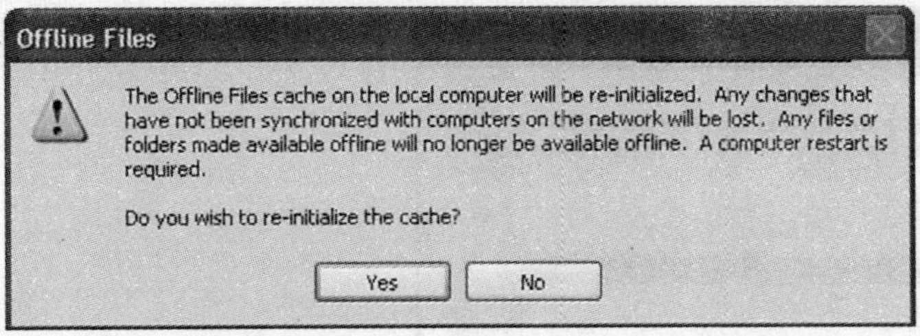

Figure 14-30 The Offline Files message box.

All of this has absolutely no effect on the copies of the files on the network; they remain unchanged. You can't undo a reinitialization of the offline files cache, but you can always go back to the network copies of these files and make them available offline once again.

Using Hardware Profiles

To close out this chapter, we need to look at two more network-related topics: hardware profiles and user profiles. We'll start with hardware profiles. A *hardware profile* is a canned set of configuration information, and it is particularly useful with a portable computer. You can create a hardware profile to use on your laptop when you're on the road and another when you're back at the office connected to your docking station. By switching from one hardware profile to another, you can quickly tell the laptop that its hardware configuration has changed.

To create a new hardware profile, follow these steps:

1. Open System.

Click the Start button, click Control Panel, click Performance And Maintenance, and then open System. Alternatively, you can right-click My Computer and choose Properties from the shortcut menu.

2. Open Hardware Profiles.

Click the Hardware tab, and then click the Hardware Profiles button to open the Hardware Profiles dialog box shown in Figure 14-31.

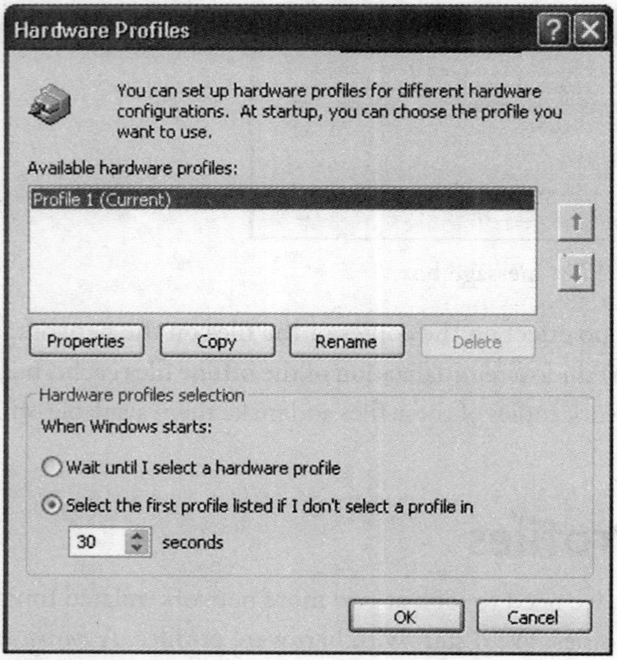

Figure 14-31 The Hardware Profiles dialog box.

3. **Configure Properties.**

   Click the Copy button to make a duplicate hardware profile, and then click the Properties button to configure your laptop's docking state. Click OK.

4. **Choose a hardware profile.**

   Back at the Hardware Profiles dialog box, specify what you want to have happen when Windows starts; you can select a hardware profile from the list, or you can tell Windows to load a profile itself if you haven't chosen one within a specified period of time. Click OK.

Now you can use the Windows Device Manager to customize the new hardware profile by enabling or disabling devices.

Creating User Profiles

In the same way that a hardware profile defines your current hardware configuration, a *user profile* defines your customized desktop environment, including your display, network, and printer settings. If you like a purple screen with green text, you can store those settings as part of your user profile.

Windows supports several kinds of user profiles, including the following:

- A local user profile is created the first time you log on to a computer and is stored on that computer's hard disk. Any changes you make to your local user profile stay on that computer.
- A roaming user profile is stored on the network server and is available to you whenever you log on to any computer on the network. Any changes made to a roaming user profile are always available no matter where you connect to the network.
- A mandatory user profile is a special type of roaming user profile that is set up by the network administrator and can be used to specify particular settings for a specific group of users.

When a new user logs on to the computer for the first time, Windows creates a new user profile based on the default user profile. To create a new user profile, follow these steps:

1. Open System.

Click the Start button, click Control Panel, click Performance And Maintenance, and then open System. Alternatively, you can right-click My Computer and choose Properties from the shortcut menu.

2. Click Settings.

Click the Advanced tab, and click Settings in the User Profiles box to open the User Profiles dialog box shown in Figure 14-32.

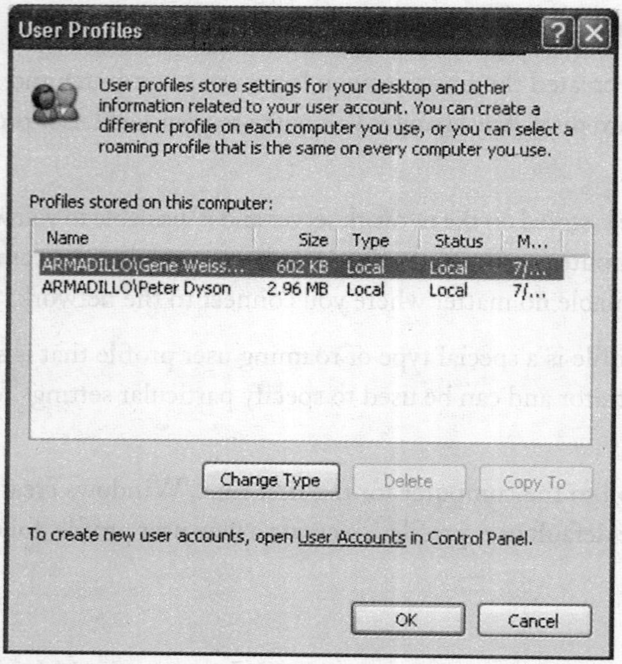

Figure 14-32 The User Profiles dialog box.

3. **Copy a profile.**

   You will see that the current user profile is selected from the list in the User Profiles dialog box. Click the Copy To button to open the Copy To dialog box, and enter a location for the new user profile, or click Browse to select the path. Click the Change button in the Copy To dialog box to open the Select User Or Group dialog box, select a new user, and click OK. Click OK to close the Copy To dialog box, and click OK to close the User Profiles dialog box.

Summary

In this chapter we looked at the various ways that you can connect to a corporate network, including dialing in over a phone line or using a virtual private network. We looked at how to create a calling card, and how to connect to your own Windows XP Professional computer at home or at the office while you're on the road. The Windows Synchronization Manager has solved many of the problems associated with multiple updates to the same file, and we looked at how to get the best out of Synchronization Manager and offline files. Finally, we closed out the chapter with a quick look at hardware and user profiles.

Chapter 15

TROUBLESHOOTING SYSTEM PROBLEMS AND ERRORS

Featuring:

- Protecting Your Computer's Health
- Tracking Events with Event Viewer
- Evaluating Your System's Performance
- Using the Windows Command-Line Utilities
- Getting the Most from Device Manager
- Looking at Device Driver Signatures
- Troubleshooting with Help And Support Center
- Fixing a Problem Using Help And Support Center
- Using the Windows Troubleshooters
- Looking at the System Configuration Utility
- Running Applications in Compatibility Mode
- Searching the Microsoft Knowledge Base

According to experts who have been running large and small networks with Windows XP, this operating system really is what it was cracked up to be—stable. And, as we mentioned in an earlier chapter, it has been described as "crashless." That doesn't mean, however, that it's maintenance free and that nothing will ever go wrong.

The first part of this chapter describes some practical environmental considerations that influence the well-being of your computer system. The next part describes some tools that come with Windows that you can use to gather detailed information about what is happening on your system right now. The last part of this chapter gives you some guidelines about what you can do when something does go wrong.

Protecting Your Computer's Health

You probably know that spilling a cup of coffee on your keyboard is not a good idea, but you may not know what room temperatures are safe for computers. Here are some tips about the physical setup of your computer system that can prolong its life and save on repair costs:

- Excessive heat can seriously damage your system. The recommended maximum room temperature is 85 degrees Fahrenheit, and the minimum is 60 degrees Fahrenheit. If these guidelines seem modest, remember that a typical computer may run 40 degrees hotter inside than outside.
- If you're serious about protecting your data, install an uninterruptible power supply (UPS). A UPS is basically a high-powered battery with an intelligent switch. When the main electrical power to your house or office is cut off, the UPS swings into action and powers the computer on the fully charged battery. The battery may last for a few minutes, giving you just enough time to log off and shut down Windows, or it may last long enough for you to close applications, save files, log off, and shut down the system. Check the specs of your UPS so you know how much battery life you have available to you *before* the power goes out.
- Keep cables and power cords routed away from foot-traffic areas, and use power strips, which typically have one cord running to the wall outlet and space for five or six plugs. Be sure, though, that the power circuit can handle the load.

- Don't place any piece of electronic equipment in direct sunlight.
- Clean the inside and outside of your machines periodically using a can of compressed air. And don't forget your printer—paper dust collects quickly in a printer.
- Minimize the effects of static electricity, for example, by raising the humidity with an evaporative humidifier or adding plants or an aquarium. Static electricity can shorten the life of a computer chip if not destroy it.
- Don't plug any heating element into the same outlet as a computer—no coffee maker or heater, for example, and make sure that you are not plugging your PC into the same electrical circuit as your home refrigerator or other large household appliance.
- Watch out for vibration sources; don't put the computer on the same table as an impact printer.
- Make sure that all connectors on the back of the computer are securely attached; if your printer uses a parallel screw-in connector, make sure it is actually screwed in.

If you follow these simple guidelines, you will save yourself and your computer lots of wear and tear in tracking down and fixing computer-related problems.

Tracking Events with Event Viewer

A very useful way to peek inside your Windows system is to open Event Viewer, which displays event logs and, if you are on a Windows 2002 Server network, directory services and file replication services.

To open Event Viewer, click the Start button, click Control Panel, click Performance And Maintenance, click Administrative Tools, and then double-click Event Viewer. Figure 15-1 shows the Event Viewer window.

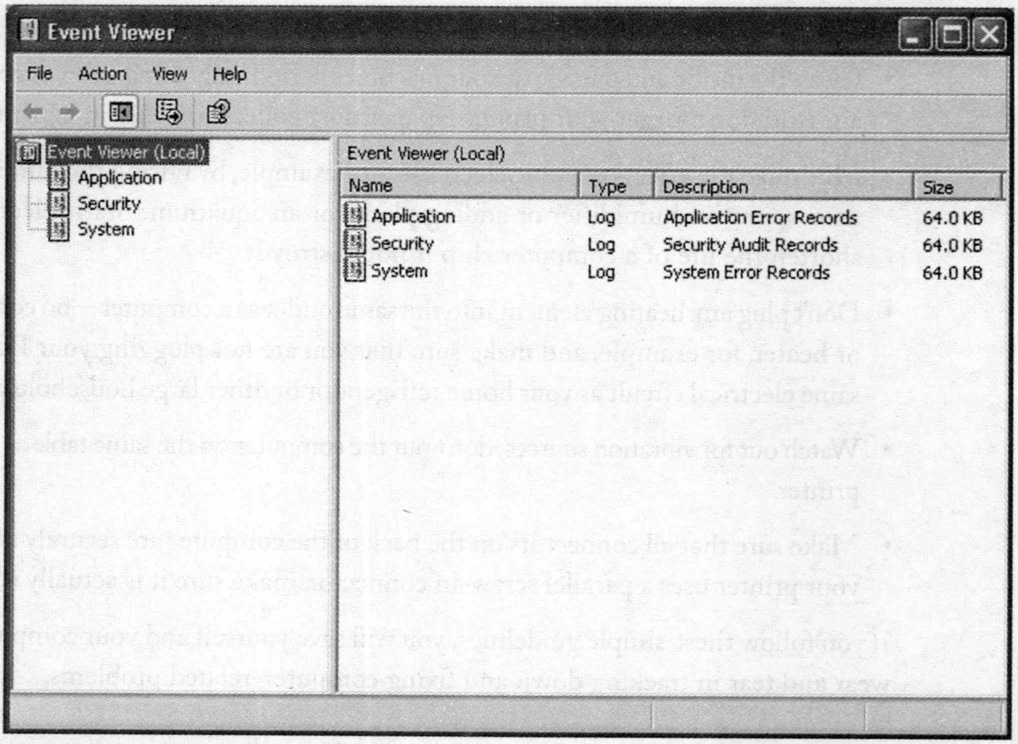

Figure 15-1 The Event Viewer window.

When you start Windows, Event Viewer begins to track events and stores them in three logs:

- The Application Log contains events that applications generate. The developer of the application specifies which events to log. Any user can take a look at the Application Log.
- The Security Log contains information such as failed logon attempts and successful and failed audits. Only an administrator can view the Security Log, and the administrator can specify which events are logged in the Security Log.
- The System Log contains events logged by Windows XP components. For example, if a device driver fails to load, that event will be noted in the System Log. Any user can view the System Log.

To view a log's contents, select it in the tree pane on the left. To view details about a particular event, right-click it, and choose Properties from the shortcut menu to display the event's Properties dialog box. Figure 15-2 shows the Properties dialog box for a Warning event in the Application Log.

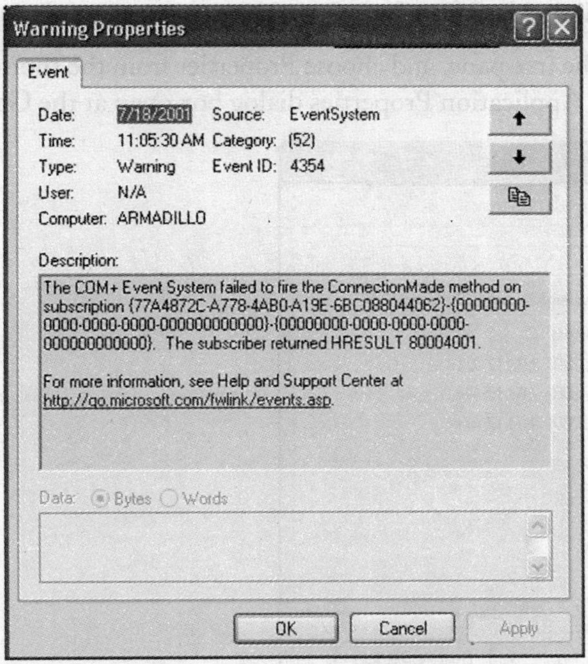

Figure 15-2 The Properties dialog box for a Warning event.

The Application and System Logs track three types of events, each with their own icon:

- An Information event is identified by the letter *i* in a bubble, which indicates that the event was successfully completed.
- A Warning event is identified by an exclamation point in a yellow triangle, which indicates that a condition is not yet crucial but could be in the future.
- An Error event is identified by a white *x* in a red circle, which indicates a problem.

The Security Log tracks successful events (such as a user logging on to the system) and failed events (such as a user typing an incorrect password). A successful event is identified by a yellow key, and a failed event is identified by a yellow lock.

Setting Up the Logs

Although you can specify which events are logged only if you are a Computer Administrator and only for the Security Log, you can specify the maximum size of the log file, how long to keep events in the log file, and which events are displayed for any log. Follow these steps:

1. **Open the Properties dialog box for a log.**

   Right-click the log in the tree pane, and choose Properties from the shortcut menu. Figure 15-3 shows the Application Properties dialog box open at the General tab.

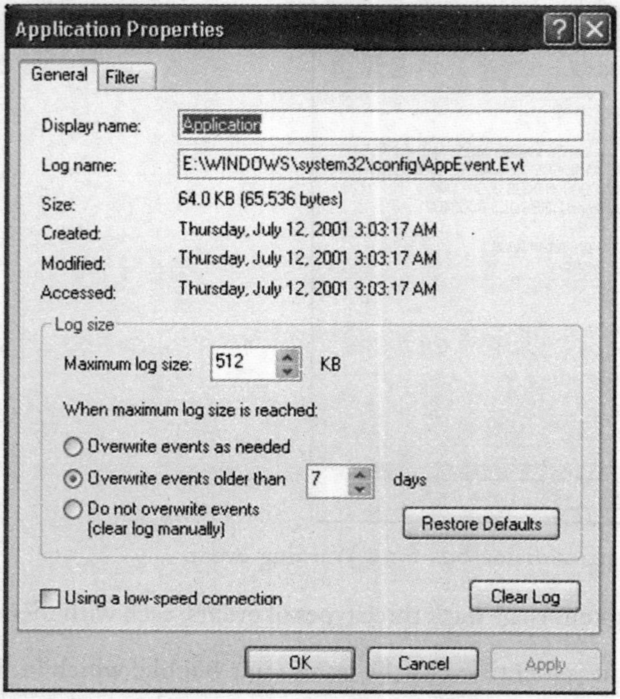

Figure 15-3 The Application Properties dialog box.

2. **Specify the log size.**

   In the Maximum Log Size spin box, select a size.

3. **Specify whether and when to overwrite events that have been logged.**

   In the When Maximum Log Size Is Reached section, click an option button.

4. **Specify which events to display.**

   Click the Filter tab, and clear the check box for the type of event that you don't want displayed. This can be helpful when you want to see only Error events, for example. You can use the other options in this dialog box to specify the event source, the category, the event ID, the user, the computer, and a time period. When you've made your selections, click OK.

Troubleshooting with Event Logs

Now that we have collected all this log information, how do we put the information to use? How do we find system problems? Here's how:

- If you notice that a specific event always seems to trigger a system problem, open the appropriate log in Event Viewer, click the View menu and click Find to search for other instances of the same event. In this way you can track problems back through the system.
- If you think a specific piece of hardware, such as a network interface card (NIC) for example, is the cause of all the problems, set up a filter to log only those events generated by the NIC to help you zero in on the problem quickly.
- Always make a note of the Event ID number; you can use this number when you talk to tech-support people.

Evaluating Your System's Performance

One of the best aspects of using Windows XP is that it is self-tuning and can make changes to itself automatically to reach optimum performance. And Windows also includes a tool you can use to find, display, and quantify system bottlenecks.

The Performance console is in some ways a rather esoteric tool, but you can use it to monitor and log hundreds of system variables, including random access memory (RAM) usage, how much CPU time an application is using, and repeated failed logons. Such information is useful in a number of ways. For example, if RAM usage is consistently high, you might want to consider installing more RAM in your computer. If a particular application is using excessive CPU time, that could explain a degradation in overall system performance. And if you see a number of repeated failed logons, you might suspect that a password-guessing program is attempting to crack your system.

To open the Performance console, click the Start button, click Control Panel, click Performance And Maintenance, and then click Administrative Tools to open the Administrative Tools folder. Now open Performance. Figure 15-4 shows the Performance console when you first open it.

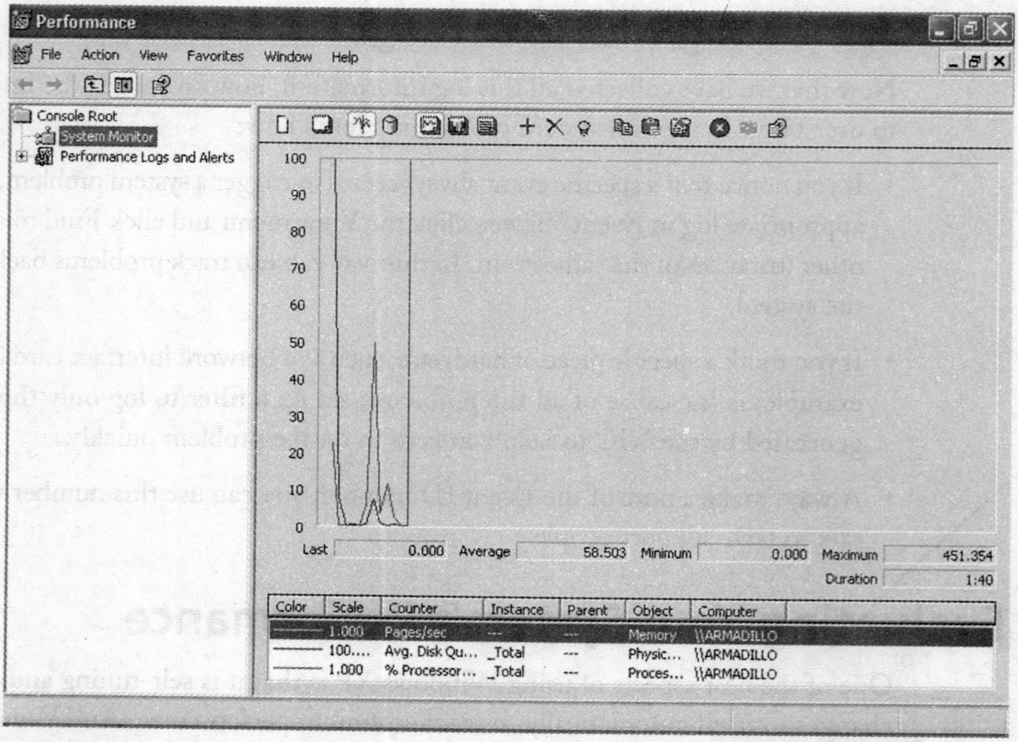

Figure 15-4 The Performance console.

The system and performance variables you monitor with the Performance console are known as *counters*. The values of the current set of counters are displayed as a graph in the main Performance window, and the moving vertical red line indicates the current data. Below the window, you will see the graph color, scale, and name of these counters, along with other information.

You use the buttons displayed on the toolbar above the graph in the right pane to work with Performance. From left to right, the buttons are as follows:

- New Counter Set lets you specify a new group of counters for display.
- Clear Display clears a refreshes the display.
- View Current Activity displays real-time data.
- View Log Data displays data you previously recorded into a log file.
- View Graph displays the information as a chart.
- View Histogram displays the information as a bar graph.
- View Report displays the information as a text report.

- Add lets you add a counter to a display.
- Delete lets you remove a counter from a display.
- Highlight lets you highlight a counter.
- Copy Properties lets you copy a set of counters to the Clipboard.
- Paste Counter List lets you copy a set of counters from the Clipboard.
- Properties opens the System Monitor Properties dialog box.
- Freeze Display stops the display of data.
- Update Data starts the display of data.
- Help opens the Performance help system.

To specify which counter or counters you want to monitor and display, you use the Add Counters dialog box, which is shown in Figure 15-5.

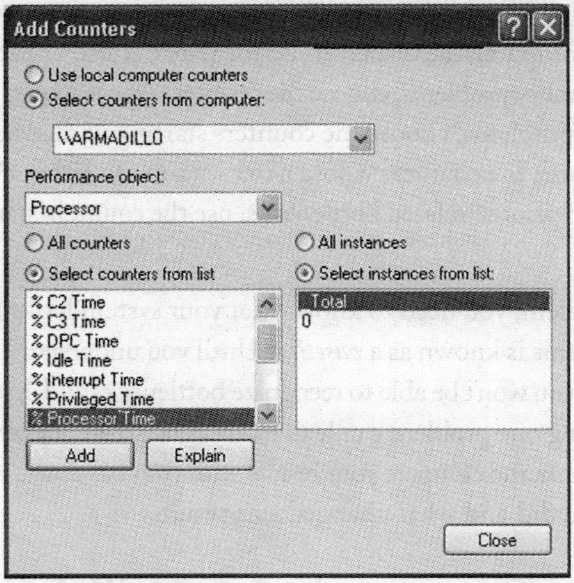

Figure 15-5 The Add Counters dialog box.

To open the Add Counters dialog box, click the Add button on the toolbar (it has a plus sign on it). In this section, we couldn't possibly get into all the counters you can monitor or all their many ramifications, but we can show you basically how to add and monitor a counter. For demonstration purposes, let's add a counter for the number of files that have been opened on your local computer and a counter that indicates how hard your processor is working. Open the Add Counters dialog box, and then follow these steps:

1. **Select a performance object.**

   The subsystem components of Windows XP are classified into objects, and each object has counters. In the Performance Object drop-down list, select Server.

2. **Select a counter.**

   Click the Select Counters From List option button, and then select Files Opened Total. To see a description of this counter, click the Explain button. Close the explanation, and then click Add.

3. **Add another object and a counter.**

   In the Performance Object drop-down list, select Processor, and then in the Select Counters From List box, select %Processor Time. Click Add, and then click Close.

Back in the Performance console, you'll see a graphic display of the counters you've just added. By default, information is displayed in Chart view. If you want a report instead, click the View Report button (it's a little notebook). If you want a bar chart, click the View Histogram button (it shows a little bar chart).

As things change on your computer, the display in Performance is also updated. If you are trying to track down memory problems, choose the counters whose names start with the word *Memory;* for disk problems, choose the counters starting with *Physical Disk;* for processor problems, choose the counters whose names start with either *Processor* or *System\Processor;* and to find printer-related bottlenecks, use the counters starting with *Print Queue*.

Before you can track a problem, you need to know what your system looks like when it is running routine tasks; this is known as a *baseline*. Until you understand how your system performs over time, you won't be able to recognize bottlenecks and system slowdowns. Sometimes, resolving one problem can lead to another, so whenever possible, change only one thing at a time and compare your results with your baseline. And always document exactly what you did and what changed as a result.

Using the Windows Command-Line Utilities

Some of the Performance tools are available from the Windows command prompt, but before we can describe them and how to use them, we need to look at how to use the command prompt itself.

You can do everything you need to do on the computer using the Windows graphical user interface, right? Yes, you can, but sometimes there are circumstances where you want to use a simple utility to look at the files in a folder rather than invoke the power and overhead of Explorer or My Computer, and that is where the command prompt comes in very handy.

NOTE *You might see the command prompt referred to as a* shell *or* command shell; *all these names are interchangeable.*

To open a Command Prompt window, click the Start button, click All Programs, click Accessories, and then click Command Prompt. You will see a window similar to the one shown in Figure 15-6.

Figure 15-6 The Windows Command Prompt window.

You can also choose the Run command from the Start menu, type *cmd* in the Open box, and press Enter. To close the Command Prompt window, type *exit* and press Enter, or click the Close button.

When you're working from the command prompt, you can get abbreviated help information if you type a command name followed by /?. So to see help information on the directory-listing command, type *dir /?* at the command prompt. If you have used the command line in previous versions of Windows, including Windows NT and Windows 98/95, or even DOS, many of the commands will be familiar to you. If not, click the Start button, click Help And Support, click Use Tools To View Your Computer Information And Diagnose Problems, and then click Command-Line Reference A-Z. Click a letter to see a list of the commands starting with that letter, or scroll down the list until you find the command you are looking for.

To customize the way the Command Prompt window looks and works, click the window's Control menu icon and click Properties to open the Properties dialog box. Or press Alt+Spacebar+P from within the Command Prompt window to open the Properties dialog box. You can change the Command Prompt window colors, font, cursor size, and several other options.

Using the System Monitor Command-Line Utilities

There are four command-line tools you can use to collect performance information without invoking the power and overhead of Performance:

- Logman lets you start, stop, and schedule performance counters on local or networked computers.
- Relog lets you extract information from an existing log file and create a new log file containing just the extracted data.
- Tracerpt allows you to generate trace-analysis reports and comma-delimited files from the data stored in binary log files.
- Typeperf lets you send performance-counter data to the Command Prompt window, or to a specific log-file format, at a user-specified interval.

Getting the Most from Device Manager

In Chapter 11 we looked at how to use System Information to display all sorts of technical information relating to the hardware and software available on your system. Now let's take a look at how Device Manager takes us a step further and adds the ability to do the following:

- Examine or change hardware configuration settings.
- Enable or disable hardware devices.
- Install or uninstall hardware devices.
- Identify system resource conflicts.
- Locate and identify individual device drivers.

To start Device Manager, choose one of the following methods:

- Right-click My Computer, and then choose Manage from the shortcut menu. Select Device Manager under Computer Management, System Tools, to display Device Manager in the right pane.

- Right-click My Computer, and then choose Properties from the shortcut menu. Click the Hardware tab, and then click the Device Manager button.
- Click the Start button, click Control Panel, click Performance And Maintenance, and then click Administrative Tools. From inside the Administrative Tools folder, open Computer Management and then choose Device Manager.
- Click the Start button, click Control Panel, click Performance And Maintenance, click System, and then click the Device Manager button on the Hardware tab.
- Click the Start button, click Run, type *devmgmt.msc* in the Open box, and then click OK.

You can also start Device Manager from within Help And Support Center, but no matter how you start it, you will see a display similar to the one shown in Figure 15-7.

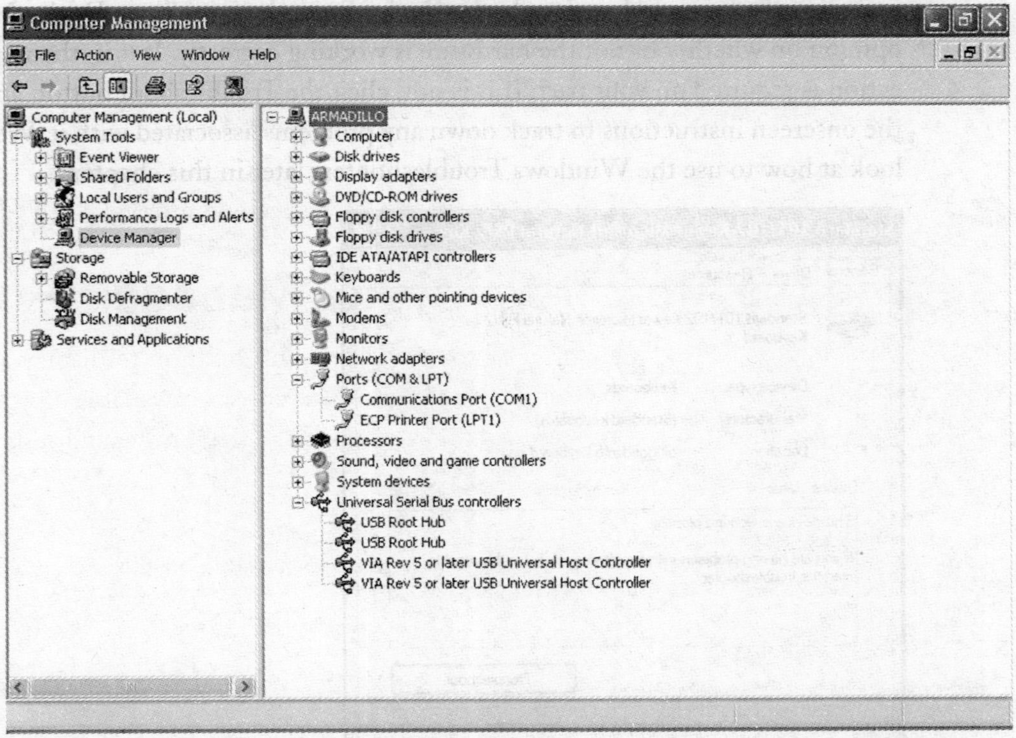

Figure 15-7 The Device Manager window.

In the right pane of the Device Manager window, you will see a list of the main groups of hardware components on your computer, listed in alphabetical order by device type; click the plus sign to expand the list. In Figure 15-7 you'll see that the Ports category and the Universal Serial Bus Controllers category have both been expanded to show more details. If a piece of hardware is experiencing problems or is not working correctly, you will see a yellow circle containing an exclamation point at the left end of the device name.

Next, we'll use the Keyboards category as an example to describe the most important Device Manager properties. Click the plus sign next to Keyboards to expand the category, then right-click the entry and choose Properties from the shortcut menu. The Standard 101/102-Key Or Microsoft Natural PS/2 Keyboard dialog box opens, showing (in our case, at least) three tabs, General, Driver, and Resources. We'll look at each of these tabs in turn, starting with the General tab.

General Tab

The General tab, shown in Figure 15-8, lists basic information about the keyboard, including the type and location. In the Device Status box, you'll see Device Manager's opinion on whether or not the hardware is working correctly. If it is, then no further action is required on your part. If it is not, click the Troubleshoot button and follow the onscreen instructions to track down any problems associated with it. We'll take a look at how to use the Windows Troubleshooters later in this chapter.

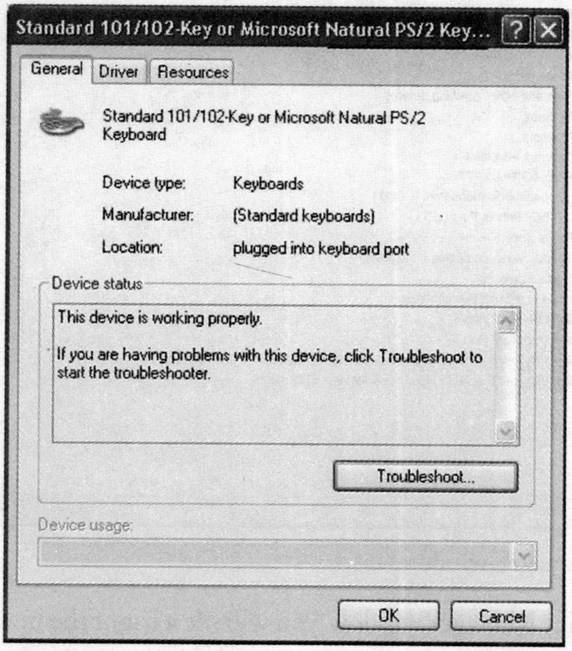

Figure 15-8 The Standard 101/102-Key Or Microsoft Natural PS/2 Keyboard dialog box open at the General tab.

Driver Tab

Click the Driver tab, shown in Figure 15-9, to bring it to the front. This tab lists important device driver information for the keyboard, including the device driver original provider, the date, version number, and digital signer.

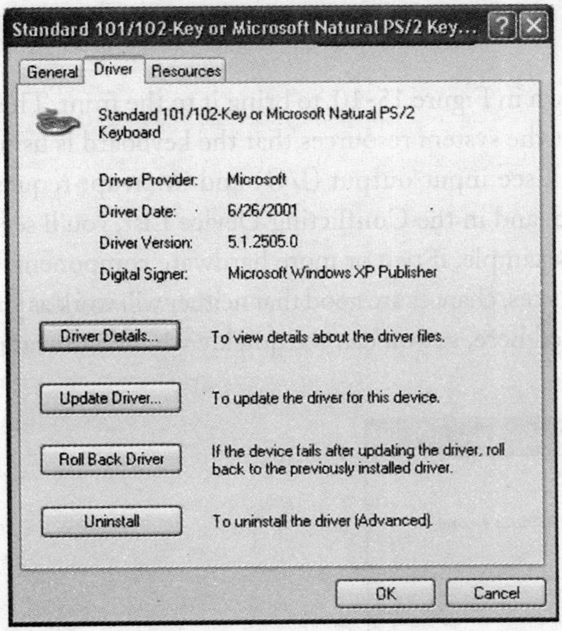

Figure 15-9 The Standard 101/102-Key Or Microsoft Natural PS/2 Keyboard dialog box open at the Driver tab.

NOTE *A device driver is a small program that lets Windows communicate with and control a specific piece of hardware. Windows contains a standard set of Plug and Play device drivers for the keyboard, monitor, and so on, but if you install a specialized piece of hardware that Windows doesn't know about, such as a digitizing tablet, you must also install the appropriate device driver so that Windows knows how to communicate with the new device.*

In addition, there are four buttons on this tab that you can use for this particular device driver:

- Driver Details displays more information about the device driver, including the location of the driver files on your hard disk.
- Update Driver lets you update the device driver.

- Roll Back Driver lets you go back to the previous version of the device driver. You can use this button if, after you installed an update to the device driver, the hardware did not work as you expected.
- Uninstall lets you uninstall this device driver.

Resources Tab

Click the Resources tab, shown in Figure 15-10, to bring it to the front. This tab lists important information about the system resources that the keyboard is using. In the Resource Settings box, you'll see input/output (I/O) and interrupt request (IRQ) information for the keyboard, and in the Conflicting Device List, you'll see an indication of conflict status. For example, if two or more hardware components are both assigned the same system resources, chances are good that neither will work as you expect. Conflicts such as this are listed here, so you can see quickly which hardware components need your attention.

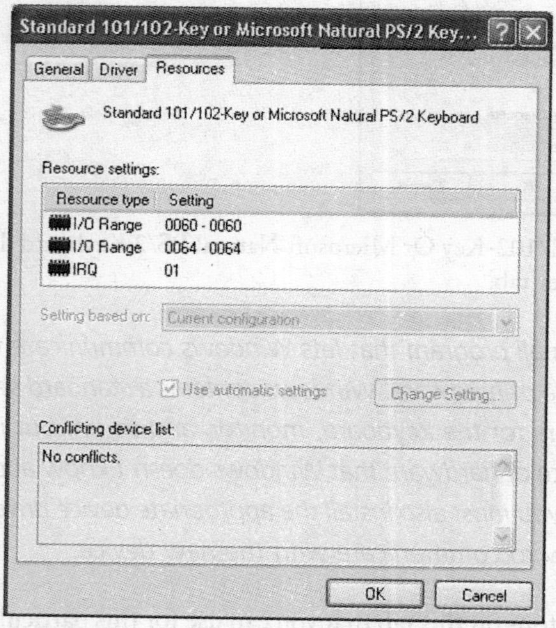

The Standard 101/10 - ey Or icrosoft atural S/ eyboard dialog box open at the Resources tab.

an in s ste resour es wit out nowin e a tl w at ou are doin an result in our s ste e a in in une e ted wa s so e areful Alwa s write down t e ori inal settin s efore ou an e t e

Other Tabs

All the hardware components listed in the Device Manager window will have General, Device, and Resources tabs, and some of them will have other tabs, too. The tabs available depend on the nature of the component. For example, open a disk drive, and you will see a Volumes tab; open a USB Root Hub (usbport) and you will see a Power tab.

If you expand the Modem category, right-click your modem, and choose Properties from the shortcut menu, you'll see a dialog box with several tabs, as Figure 15-11 shows:

- The Modem tab lists configuration information, including the name and speed of the communications port the modem is using.
- The Diagnostics tab lets you run a quick modem test. Click the Query Modem button to send a string of commands to your modem to test that it is working properly.
- The Advanced tab allows you to look at or change the modem port settings.
- The Power Management tab lets you specify that any modem activity brings the computer out of the power-conserving standby mode.

Figure 15-11 The Device Manager modem Properties dialog box.

Using the View Menu

By default, Device Manager hides several devices; to look at them, click the View menu and click Show Hidden Devices. On our system, this results in a new device appearing called Non-Plug and Play Drivers, and this expands to a long list of device drivers that support system services. On your system, you may see other drivers, depending on how your computer is configured. For example, with Show Hidden Devices selected, if you expand Network Adapters, you will see drivers such as the WAN Miniport drivers for Internet Protocol (IP), Point-to-Point Tunneling Protocol (PPTP), and Level 2 Tunneling Protocol (L2TP).

You can also rearrange the order in which Device Manager displays devices. Open the View menu and choose one of the following:

- Devices By Type is the default view you see when you first open Device Manager.
- Devices By Connection sorts the information according to the device's connection.
- Resources By Type sorts the information according to the resources attached to or available to each device.
- Resources By Connection sorts the list according to the resources that each connection type uses. This option is particularly useful if you are tracking down a resource conflict. Click the Interrupt Request (IRQ) device for a quick and easy way to list all the IRQ assignments on your system, as Figure 15-12 shows.

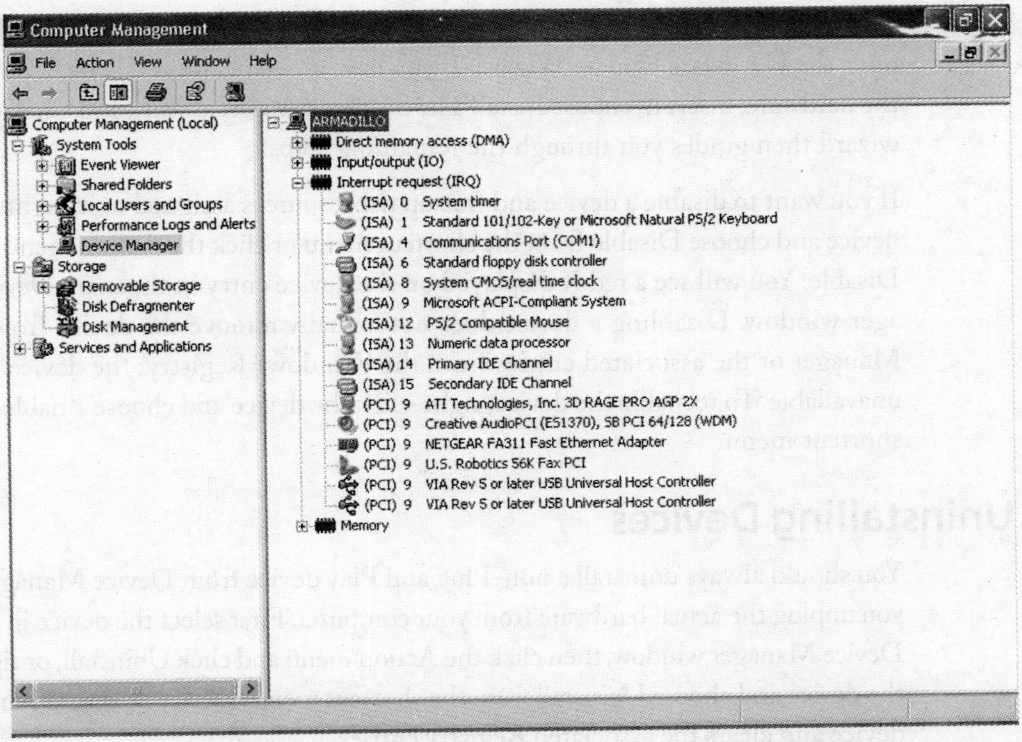

Figure 15-12 Interrupt Request (IRQ) assignment listing in Device Manager.

Configuring Devices

While some of the settings for certain devices are locked, you can use Device Manager to change and configure other devices on your system, and you can use Device Manager to enable or disable a device.

To change the resources for a device, right-click the device and choose Properties from the shortcut menu. Click the Resources tab, clear the Use Automatic Settings check box, and click the Change Settings button. What you see next depends on the device you are working with, but in general, as you choose settings, the dialog box displays messages about conflicts, either warning you that the setting you have specified conflicts with another device's settings or confirming that no resource conflicts exist.

To update a device driver, click the Driver tab and click the Update Driver button to open the Hardware Update Wizard. If you have an installation CD or floppy disk for the hardware, insert it, choose Install The Software Automatically, and click Next. The wizard then guides you through the remaining steps.

If you want to disable a device and free up the resources assigned to it, right-click the device and choose Disable from the shortcut menu or click the Action menu and click Disable. You will see a red X displayed on the device entry in the main Device Manager window. Disabling a device does not actually remove the device from Device Manager or the associated entries from the Windows Registry; the device is simply unavailable. To reenable the device, right-click the device and choose Enable from the shortcut menu.

Uninstalling Devices

You should always uninstall a non-Plug and Play device from Device Manager before you unplug the actual hardware from your computer. First select the device in the main Device Manager window, then click the Action menu and click Uninstall, or right-click the device and choose Uninstall from the shortcut menu. Device Manager removes the device and clears the associated Registry entries.

Searching for New Plug and Play Devices

If you attach a new piece of Plug and Play hardware to your computer while it is running (and you shouldn't do this anyway, but many of us ignore the rules when configuring printers, USB devices, or other external devices), Windows doesn't know about the new hardware. Windows checks around for new hardware only when the system first starts running. To make Windows look for new hardware without rebooting, connect the new hardware click the Action menu, and click Scan For Hardware Changes; Windows will find the new hardware. If Windows does not find it, then the hardware is probably not Plug and Play or is not configured for automatic Plug and Play operation. Many modems, for example, can be configured for automatic Plug and Play or for manual configuration. If this is the case, open Control Panel and use Add Hardware to make a manual installation.

Printing a Report

You can also print a report of the devices attached to your computer. Click the Action menu and click Print, or click the Printer icon on the taskbar. The Print dialog box offers these options:

- System Summary prints summary information for all the devices.
- Selected Class Or Device prints information about the devices you selected before you chose Print.
- All Devices And System Summary prints everything, usually more than you even want to know about your system. But if you do make this printout, it will be invaluable in the event you have to reconfigure your system after a major disaster.

You can also use the Print To File option in the Print dialog box to send the report information to a file. Remember that this file will be specific to the printer selected, and you won't be able to load the report into your word processor.

Looking at Device Driver Signatures

While we're on the subject of device drivers, there is one more topic we should touch on here. As a security precaution, Microsoft now stamps all Microsoft-written device drivers with a digital signature to prove their authenticity. Device drivers signed in this way have been rigorously tested and should work reliably with your hardware.

By using the System applet in Control Panel, you can tell Windows what course of action you want it to take when it encounters an unsigned device driver. Click the Start button, click Control Panel, click Performance And Maintenance, and then click System. Click the Hardware tab, and then click the Driver Signing button to open the Driver Signing Options dialog box, shown in Figure 15-13.

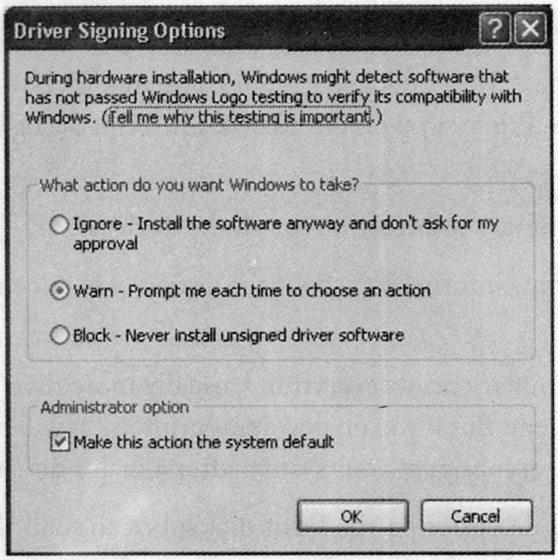

Figure 15-13 The Driver Signing Options dialog box.

This dialog box offers the following options in the What Action Do You Want Windows To Take section:

- Ignore allows Windows to install all device driver files, signed or not.
- Warn displays a dialog box telling you the device driver file is unsigned, and gives you the option of not installing it. This is the default setting.
- Block prevents the installation of all unsigned device driver files.

In most cases, Warn is the best choice here as it gives you the option of continuing the device driver installation or aborting the installation. If the device driver comes from a reputable source, it may work perfectly well, and with some uncommon or custom-built hardware, you may not have a choice other than to install the unsigned driver.

If you are logged on as a Computer Administrator, you will see another option at the bottom of the Driver Signing Options dialog box. Click the Make This Action The System Default check box to apply the setting you chose above as the default setting for all users of this computer.

Troubleshooting with Help And Support Center

Way back in Chapter 1, we looked at Help And Support Center; in this section, we're going to go quite a bit further and look at some of the more advanced options available to us under the help system. We'll start by looking at how you can work through the help system to find additional system information using the Tools Center, and then we'll look at how you can locate and fix problems in Windows using the Windows Troubleshooters. First, the Tools Center.

Using the Tools Center

To open the Tools Center, click the Start button, click Help And Support, and then click Use Tools To View Your Computer Information And Diagnose Problems. We'll look at three of these tools: My Computer Information, Advanced System Information, and the System Configuration Utility. You will find coverage of Disk Cleanup and Disk Defragmenter in Chapter 11, Network Diagnostics in Chapter 13, and Backup and System Restore in Chapter 16.

Using My Computer Information

Click My Computer Information in the Tools Center to open the My Computer Information screen, shown in Figure 15-14, where you'll see several additional options. Let's start with View General System Information About This Computer.

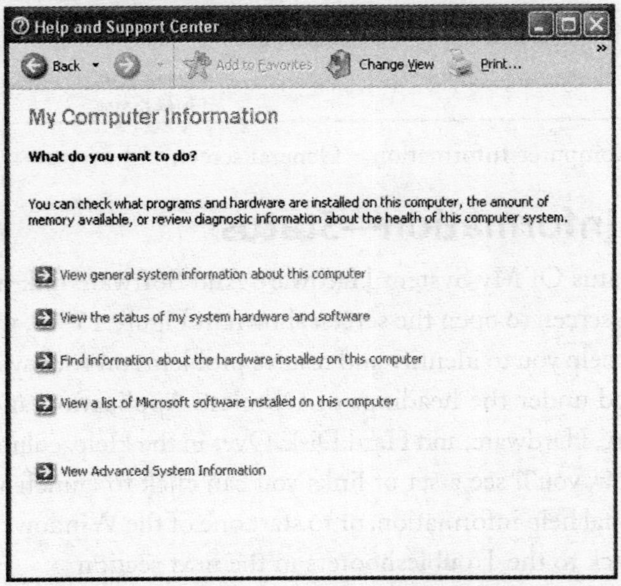

Figure 15-14 The My Computer Information screen.

My Computer Information—General

Click the View General System Information About This Computer link to open the My Computer Information – General screen shown in Figure 15-15. Here you'll find information about your computer grouped under several headings, including Specifications, Processor, Operating System, General Computer Info, Memory (RAM), and Local Disk.

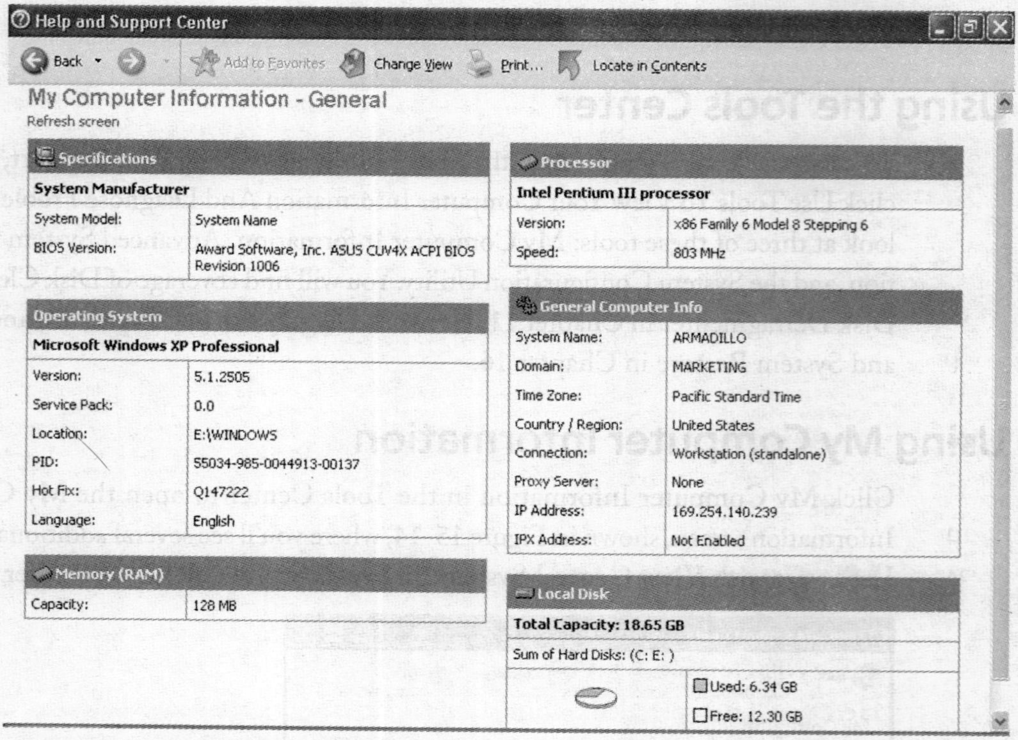

Figure 15-15 The My Computer Information – General screen.

My Computer Information—Status

Click the View The Status Of My System Hardware And Software link in the My Computer Information screen to open the screen shown in Figure 15-16, which lists information that might help you to identify and resolve problems on your system. The information is displayed under the headings of Obsolete Application and Device Drivers, System Software, Hardware, and Hard Disk. Over in the Help column on the right side of this window, you'll see a set of links you can click to launch Windows Update, to open additional help information, or to start one of the Windows Troubleshooters. We'll come back to the Troubleshooters in the next section.

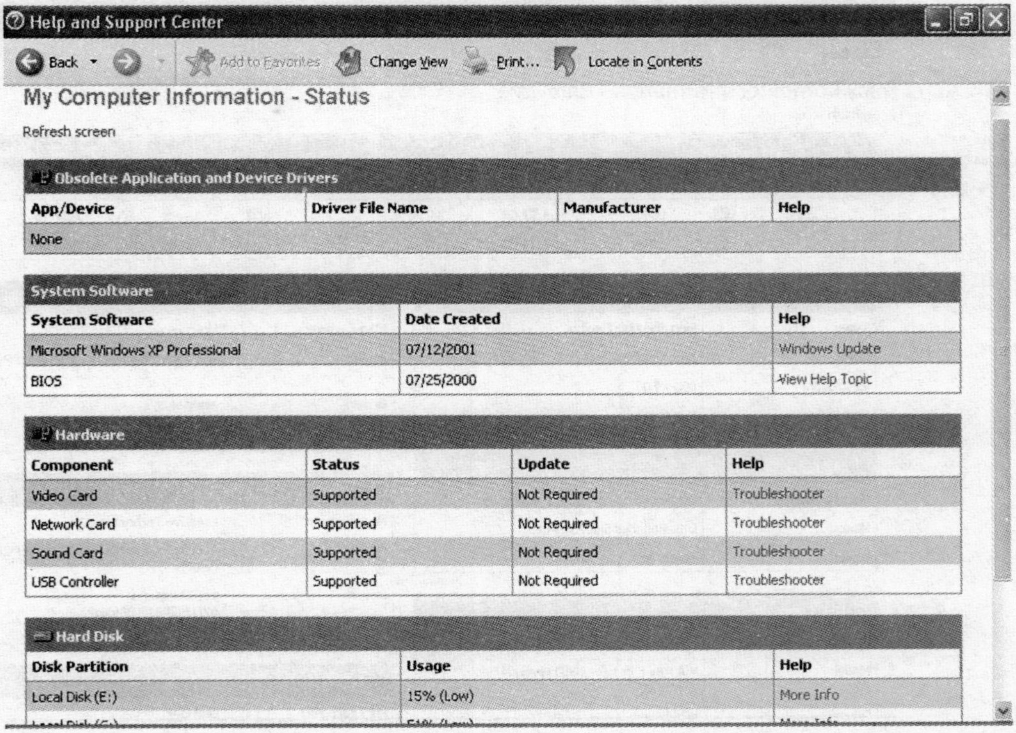

Figure 15-16 The My Computer Information – Status screen.

My Computer Information—Hardware

Click the Find Information About The Hardware Installed On This Computer link in the My Computer Information screen to open the screen shown in Figure 15-17. Here you'll find detailed information about the hardware and adapter cards installed on your computer under the headings Local Disk (Partitioned), Display, Video Card, Modem, Sound Card, USB Controller, Network Card (if you have one installed in your computer), CD-ROM Drive, Floppy Drive, and Printers. You may also see additional information if you have other hardware installed on your computer.

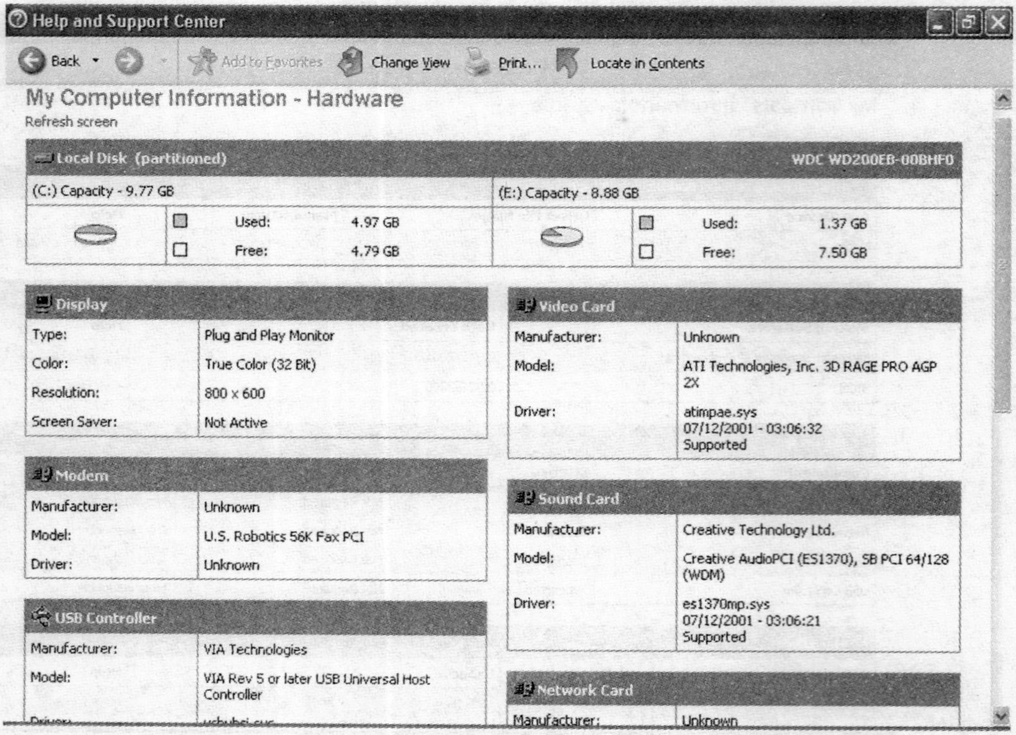

Figure 15-17 The My Computer Information – Hardware screen.

My Computer Information—Software

Click the View A List of Microsoft Software Installed On This Computer link in the My Computer Information screen to open the screen shown in Figure 15-18.

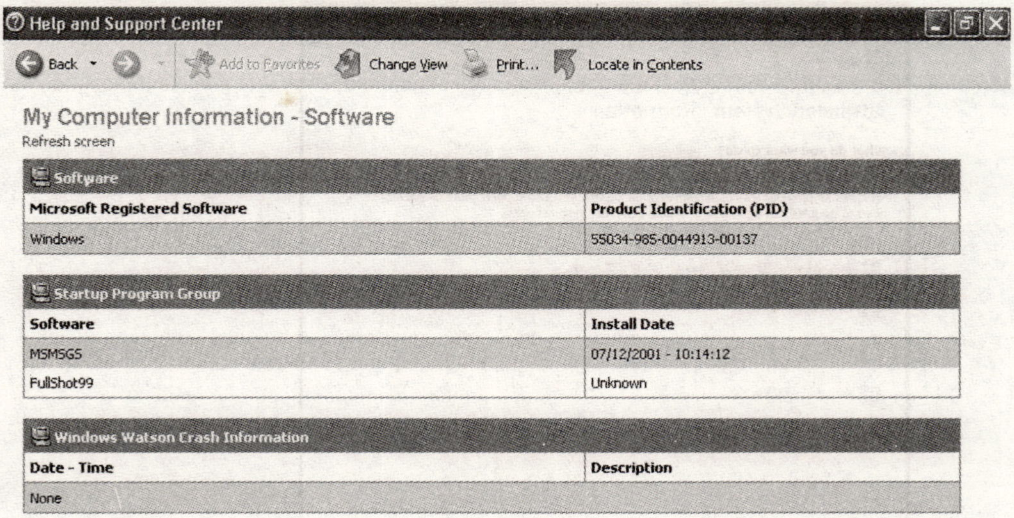

Figure 15-18 The My Computer Information – Software screen.

This screen lists the Microsoft-registered software loaded onto your system and associated product identification (PID), as well as any applications you have added to your startup program group, along with the date you installed them.

Using Advanced System Information

Click View Advanced System Information in Tools to open the Advanced System Information screen shown in Figure 15-19.

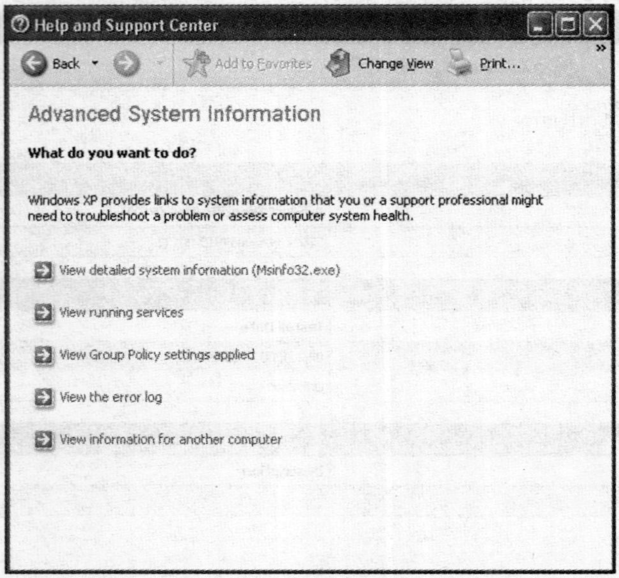

Figure 15-19 The Advanced System Information screen.

Click the View Detailed System Information link, and you will see the same information, displayed in the same format, that we looked at in Chapter 11 in the section "Finding System Information," so there is no need to spend any more time on it here.

Click the View Running Services link to see a list of the services on your system along with the name of the executable file, the service status, and the method used to start the service.

Click the View Group Policy Settings Applied link to see a lot of complicated information of interest to system administrators; we won't cover it here.

Click the View The Error Log link to look at the contents of the error log. Information is presented in three columns: the date and time the error occurred, the source of the error, and a text description of what happened to cause the error and a suggested course of action for you to take to fix the error.

And finally, click the View Information For Another Computer link to review system information about another computer on your network.

Fixing a Problem Using Help And Support Center

In addition to all the hardware and software information you can look at using Help And Support Center in Windows, you can also track down and then fix certain kinds of problems. Click the Start button, click Help And Support, click Fixing A Problem, and then click Troubleshooting Problems and you'll see the screen shown in Figure 15-20.

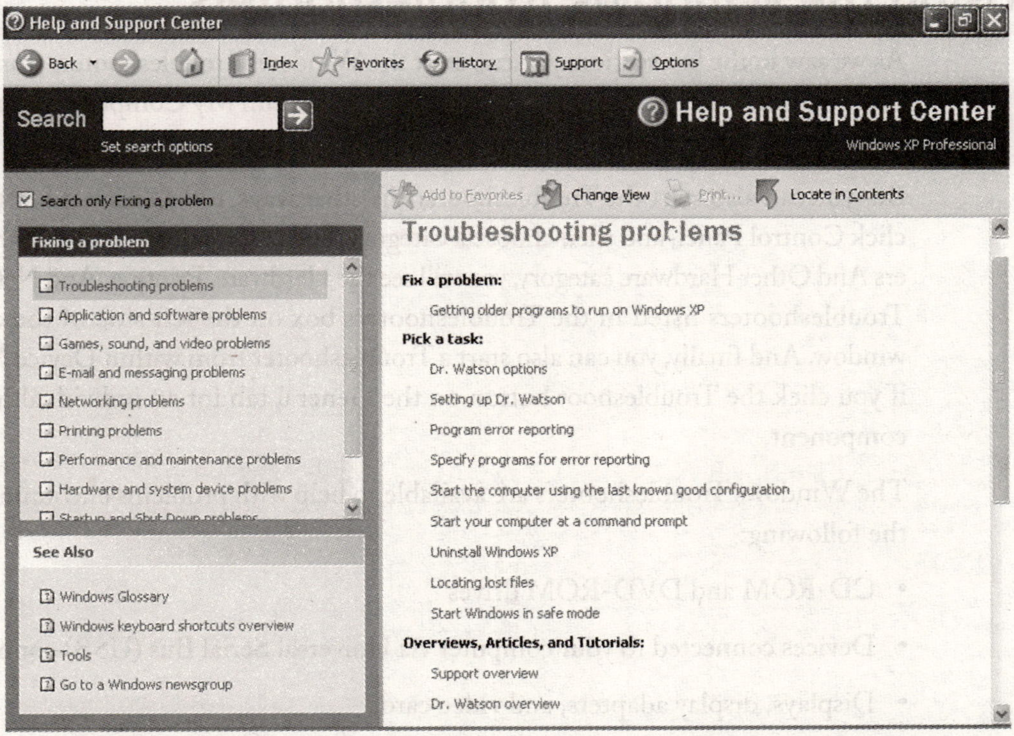

Figure 15-20 Help And Support Center open at the Troubleshooting Problems screen.

In the left pane you'll see a list of categories under the general heading Fixing A Problem, and then in the right pane you will see several options listed under the headings Fix A Problem, Pick A Task, and Overviews, Articles, And Tutorials.

- Fix A Problem starts the appropriate Windows Troubleshooter.

- Pick A Task lets you work through an interactive session designed to run down the problem or conduct a test on the ailing piece of hardware.
- Overviews, Articles, And Tutorials lists additional help information on the topic at hand that might contain pertinent information.

Not all of these options will be listed under all the Fixing A Problem headings, but you will usually find at least two of them.

Using the Windows Troubleshooters

As we saw in the last section, you can start the Windows Troubleshooters from several places within Help And Support, including from within My Computer Information, and from within Fixing A Problem.

But you can also start the Troubleshooters in other ways, too. Click the Start button, click Control Panel, and then choose a category. For example, if you choose the Printers And Other Hardware category, you will see the Hardware, Printing, And Networking Troubleshooters listed in the Troubleshooters box on the left side of the category window. And finally, you can also start a Troubleshooter from within Device Manager if you click the Troubleshoot button on the General tab for an individual hardware component.

The Windows Troubleshooters are available to help with problems encountered with the following:

- CD-ROM and DVD-ROM drives
- Devices connected to your computer via Universal Serial Bus (USB) connections
- Displays, display adapters, and video cards
- Floppy and hard-disk drives
- Game controllers and multimedia
- Hardware resource conflicts
- Home networking
- Input devices, such as keyboard, mouse, camera, or scanner
- Internet Connection Sharing
- Modems

- Network adapters
- Power management
- Printers and printing
- Sound cards
- Tape drives

Troubleshooters are also available for several applications, systems, and operational tasks, including the following:

- Backup
- DirectX
- E-mail and Outlook Express
- Faxing
- File and printer sharing
- Internet connection sharing
- Internet Explorer
- Microsoft Stop Errors
- Outlook Express
- Scheduled tasks
- Startup and shutdown
- System setup
- Terminal Services Client
- Transmission Control Protocol/Internet Protocol (TCP/IP)

Once you find a problem area and start the Troubleshooter, all you have to do is answer the questions asked by the Troubleshooter to arrive at a determination of the problem.

Figure 15-21 shows the opening screen for the Hardware Troubleshooter as an example.

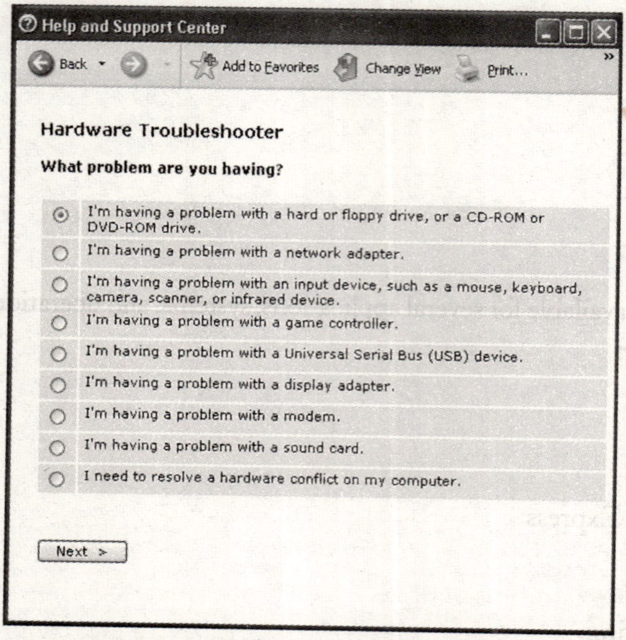

Figure 15-21 The Hardware Troubleshooter.

Some of the Troubleshooters are quite concise and ask only a few questions, but those that deal with very complex issues can take a long time to work through. Just be sure to follow all the steps suggested by the Troubleshooter; your answers will help Windows to help you find the solution to the problem.

Looking at the System Configuration Utility

Before we leave the area of hardware troubleshooting there is one more Windows XP element that we should look at, and that is the System Configuration Utility. Click the Start button, click Help And Support, and then click Use Tools To View Your Computer Information And Diagnose Problems. Inside the Tools Center, click the System Configuration Utility, then click Open System Configuration Utility, and you'll see a dialog box with a set of tabs like those shown in Figure 15-22.

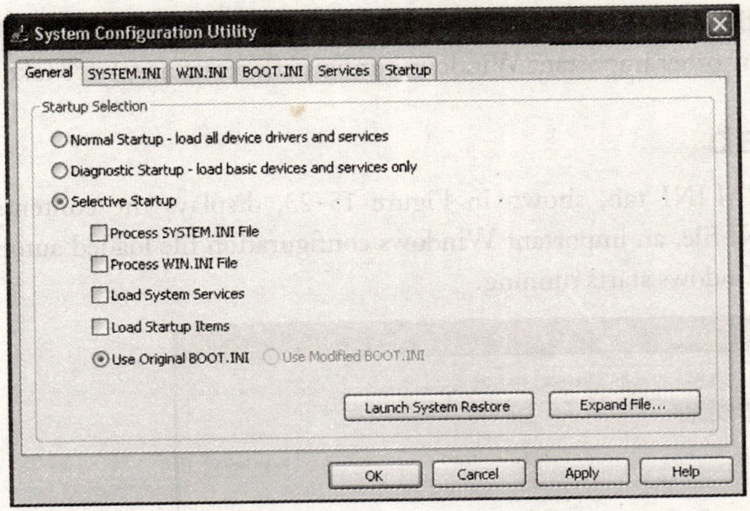

Figure 15-22 The System Configuration Utility dialog box open at the General tab.

The System Configuration Utility automates some of the troubleshooting steps that a technical support person might follow in tracking down a Windows configuration problem. In the old days, you would have to edit the Windows configuration files by hand using a word processor, save the file, and then re-boot the computer to see the effects of the changes you made. These days we can use the System Configuration Utility to do the same job, but to do it quickly and with fewer possibilities for error.

On the General tab, you'll see three options in the Startup Selection section:

- Normal Startup loads Windows, including all device drivers and operating system services.
- Diagnostic Startup loads just the basic device drivers and services needed to operate the system. In this mode, your monitor's color palette will be reduced to 16 colors.
- Selective Startup lets you choose which of the Windows startup files you want to process as well as which applications and operating system services you want to load.

Under most circumstances, the Normal Startup setting is appropriate, until something goes wrong, of course. Then you might try using the Diagnostic Startup mode to see if you can isolate the problem when you restart Windows. Finally, use the Selective Startup mode to load and process the Windows configuration files one at a time in an attempt to isolate the problem still further.

You can use the other tabs in the System Configuration Utility dialog box to look at or refine many other important Windows configuration settings. Let's take a look.

SYSTEM.INI Tab

The SYSTEM.INI tab, shown in Figure 15-23, displays the contents of the SYSTEM.INI file, an important Windows configuration file loaded automatically every time Windows starts running.

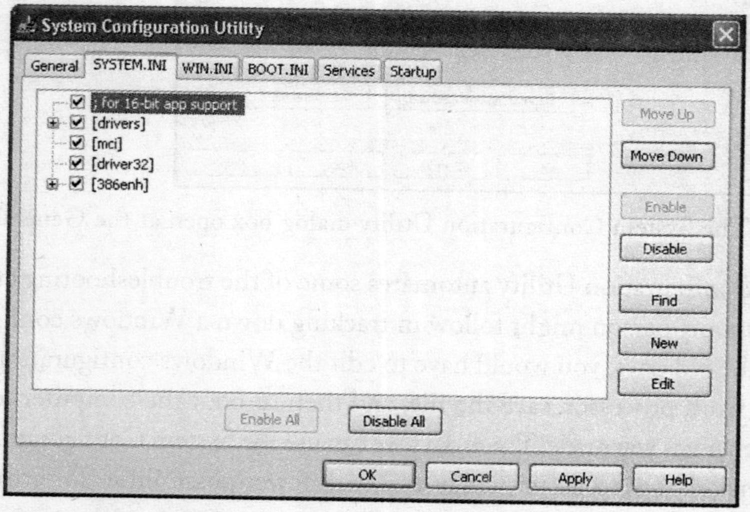

Figure 15-23 The System Configuration Utility dialog box open at the SYSTEM.INI tab.

You can use the buttons on the right side of this tab to change the order in which entries appear in the SYSTEM.INI file, as well as enable or disable selected elements, edit the contents of the file, or create a new version of the SYSTEM.INI file.

WIN.INI Tab

The WIN.INI tab, shown in Figure 15-24, is much the same as the previous tab, but contains the contents of the WIN.INI configuration file. You can use the buttons down the right side of the tab to edit the contents of the WIN.INI file.

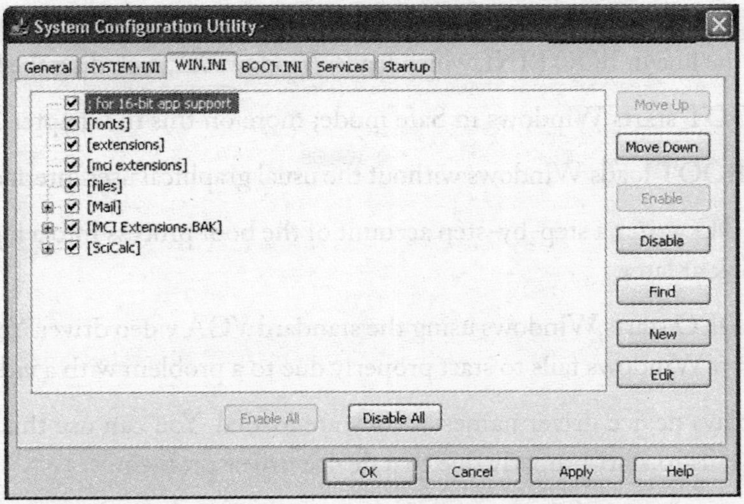

Figure 15-24 The System Configuration Utility dialog box open at the WIN.INI tab.

BOOT.INI Tab

You will see the BOOT.INI tab, shown in Figure 15-25, only if you have Windows XP installed in dual-boot mode with another operating system.

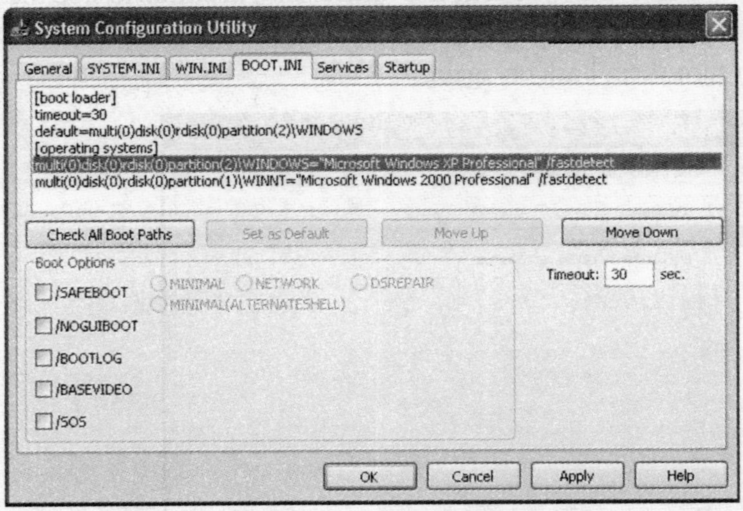

Figure 15-25 The System Configuration Utility dialog box open at the BOOT.INI tab.

The BOOT.INI file contains the operating system information displayed in the boot menu that you see when you start Windows in dual-boot mode as well as the location of the Windows XP system files. The file also contains the timeout value (in seconds) that the boot loader must wait before loading the default operating system in the event that no choice is made from the boot menu.

In the Boot Options box you will see a set of check boxes you can use to add commands to the end of the line in BOOT.INI, which loads Windows XP, including the following:

- /SAFEBOOT starts Windows in Safe mode; more on this in Chapter 16.
- /NOGUIBOOT loads Windows without the usual graphical user interface (GUI).
- /BOOTLOG writes a step-by-step account of the boot process into a log file that you can look at later.
- /BASEVIDEO starts Windows using the standard VGA video driver. You can use this switch if Windows fails to start properly due to a problem with a video driver.
- /SOS displays device driver names as they are loaded. You can use this switch if Windows fails to start properly due to a device driver problem.

Click the appropriate box to add a command. Next time you start Windows, the new command will be executed.

Startup Tab

The Startup tab, shown in Figure 15-26, lists the applications that start automatically on your system when Windows starts. Use the Disable All button to stop them all from being loaded if you suspect a problem. Once the problem is resolved, use the Enable All button to turn them back on again.

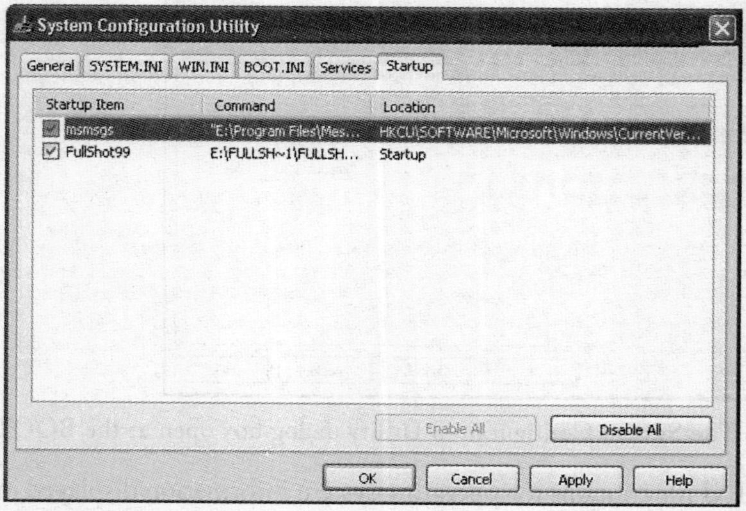

Figure 15-26 The System Configuration Utility dialog box open at the Startup tab.

Services Tab

The Services tab, shown in Figure 15-27, lists all the low-level services available on your system; we looked at services in some detail in Chapter 11, you will remember. Use Hide All Microsoft Services to remove all the Microsoft-created services running on your system. This will leave a listing of only the third-party services running on your system. Again, Enable All and Disable All buttons are available on this tab.

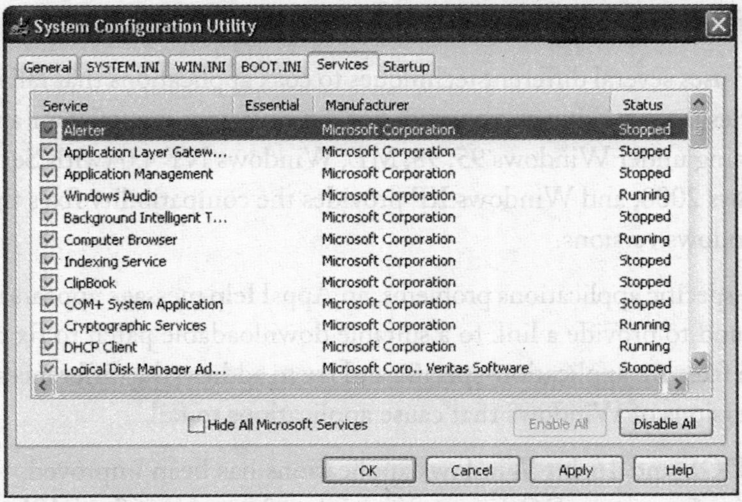

Figure 15-27 The System Configuration Utility dialog box open at the Services tab.

We'll come back to the topic of troubleshooting certain aspects of Windows operation in Chapter 16, particularly how to handle unresponsive applications and what to do when you see the "Blue Screen of Death."

Running Applications in Compatibility Mode

In the last section we looked at ways you can track down hardware and system-related problems, but what can you do if your applications don't run as you expect? In the past, one of the main reasons companies and individuals installed Windows as a dual-boot system was to preserve application compatibility. Keeping the older version available allowed people to run applications that refused to work on the new operating system. With Windows XP, you can run applications designed to run on previous versions in a special mode.

Three different kinds of applications have historically caused compatibility problems:

- Platform-specific applications that were designed to run on a specific version of Windows; when users upgraded to the next release of Windows, these applications stopped running.
- Applications that used to work on the last version of Windows, but now they don't work; something in the new operating system broke the program.
- Legacy applications that were never designed in a general enough way to work on later versions of Windows.

Windows XP uses several different techniques to coax applications that fall into these three categories into working as expected. For example, you can tell your application that it is running under Windows 95, 98, ME, Windows NT 4.0 (with Service Pack 5), or Windows 2000, and Windows XP provides the compatibility fixes that mimic the older Windows versions.

For platform-specific applications problems, an AppsHelp message appears to explain the problem and to provide a link to a suitable downloadable patch to fix the application. These fixes are application-specific and try to address the differences between the various versions of Windows that cause applications to fail.

Support for DOS and 16-bit Windows applications has been improved, too. DOS applications (and yes, even DOS games) can take advantage of SoundBlaster audio capabilities as well as VESA video mode support. So you can play Doom and Castle Wolfenstein on Windows XP, either full screen or in a window. Now that's progress.

NOTE *Application fixes can be collected dynamically using Windows Update.*

There are certain classes of programs that you should not run on different versions of Windows, and you should not attempt to run these programs in Compatibility mode either. These programs often contain warnings about running them on versions of Windows other than the one for which they were designed. Such programs include many system-level utilities, disk management tools, virus detectors, and the like, and because they run at a very low level, you can do some serious damage to your system if you try to run them in Compatibility mode. The best known of these programs will simply be blocked by Windows and will not be allowed to run under Compatibility mode.

So you have an application that used to work on the last version of Windows you used, but it does not work as expected with Windows XP; what do you do. You run the Program Compatibility Wizard, that's what, and here are the steps:

1. **Start Compatibility mode.**

   Click the Start button, click All Programs, click Accessories, and then click Program Compatibility Wizard. Read the cautionary text on the opening screen, and click Next.

2. **Choose the application.**

   Choose the application from a list, specify that you want to run the program from your CD drive, or locate the program manually. Once you have found the program, click Next.

3. **Select the appropriate operating system.**

   Choose the operating system under which your application ran as expected:

   - Microsoft Windows 95
   - Microsoft Windows NT 4.0 (Service Pack 5)
   - Microsoft Windows 98/ME
   - Microsoft Windows 2000

   You can also opt to run the program under Windows XP if you choose Do Not Apply A Compatibility Mode. Click Next.

4. **Specify display settings for the application.**

   Choose the appropriate display settings recommended for use with your application. You can also turn off Windows XP visual themes just to be safe, because they might accidentally change the appearance or behavior of the program.

   Enter the full pathname to your application, or click Browse to go and look for it manually. Once you have selected the operating system and selected the application, as Figure 15-28 shows, click Next.

5. **Test the application.**

   In the next screen, you'll see the complete path to your application, the name of the Windows operating system you will be using for the compatibility test, and your chosen display settings, as Figure 15-28 shows. Click Next to start your program running in this mode. Your screen may blink once or twice as it changes screen mode, but don't worry, this is only to be expected. Once you have determined that the application works as expected in this mode, close your application and click Next. If the application did not work as expected, choose No, Try Different Compatibility Settings, or No, I Am Finished Trying Compatibility Settings.

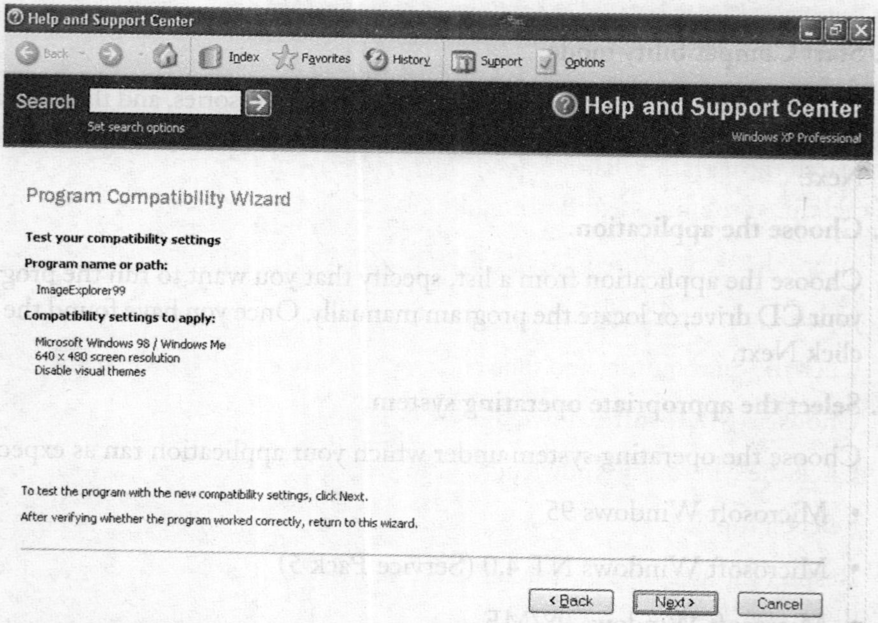

Figure 15-28 The Program Compatibility Wizard settings summary screen.

6. **Configure the application to run in Compatibility mode every time it starts.**

   If your application worked as expected, you can make Windows start the application in Compatibility mode automatically every time you start the program. Choose Yes, Set This Program To Use These Compatibility Settings. If the application you are working with is not in Microsoft's application database, you can choose to send the compatibility information to Microsoft. Choose either Yes or No. Click Next. Click Finish and you are done.

Compatibility mode represents a great step forward in Microsoft's thinking on how people and companies use applications, and it shows that application compatibility was not just an afterthought on the part of the system designers, but that it has been a major consideration since the very start. And that is good for all of us.

Searching the Microsoft Knowledge Base

In times past, the Windows Resource Kit contained a database of all the system error messages and error ID numbers. The trouble was that most people didn't know what the Resource Kit was or how they could use it. In Windows XP, a special advanced search option in Help And Support lets you connect to the Microsoft Web site and perform what is clumsily known as a Knowledge Base article search. For many years, Microsoft has published articles on its Web site in what it calls the knowledge base. These articles range from the informational to extremely technical explanations of what is happening in the Windows plumbing, but until now there hasn't been a quick and easy way to search through this dense mass of knowledge right from the desktop. Now you can use Help And Support to do the job for you.

Here are the steps to use to search Microsoft's online Knowledge Base articles:

1. **Open Help And Support.**

   Click the Start button, and then click Help And Support. Click Set Search Options.

2. **Choose a Microsoft Knowledge Base search.**

   Click the Microsoft Knowledge Base check box.

3. **Select a topic.**

   Restrict the area of your search by selecting a Microsoft product or a topic from the drop-down list.

4. **Select the type of search.**

   Specify the kind of search you want to run. You can choose from the following:

   - Search for the exact phrase.
   - Search for all the words.
   - Search for any word.
   - Perform a Boolean search.

   And then choose between searching just the title or searching the full text of the Knowledge Base article.

Type your query in the Search box, and click the Search button to connect to the Microsoft Web site and run the search. When the search is complete, you may have to click the Microsoft Knowledge Base bar in the Search Results box to see the list of found topics. When you see a topic that looks promising, click the title in the Search Results box and the text of the article will appear on the right side of the Help And Support Center screen as Figure 15-29 shows.

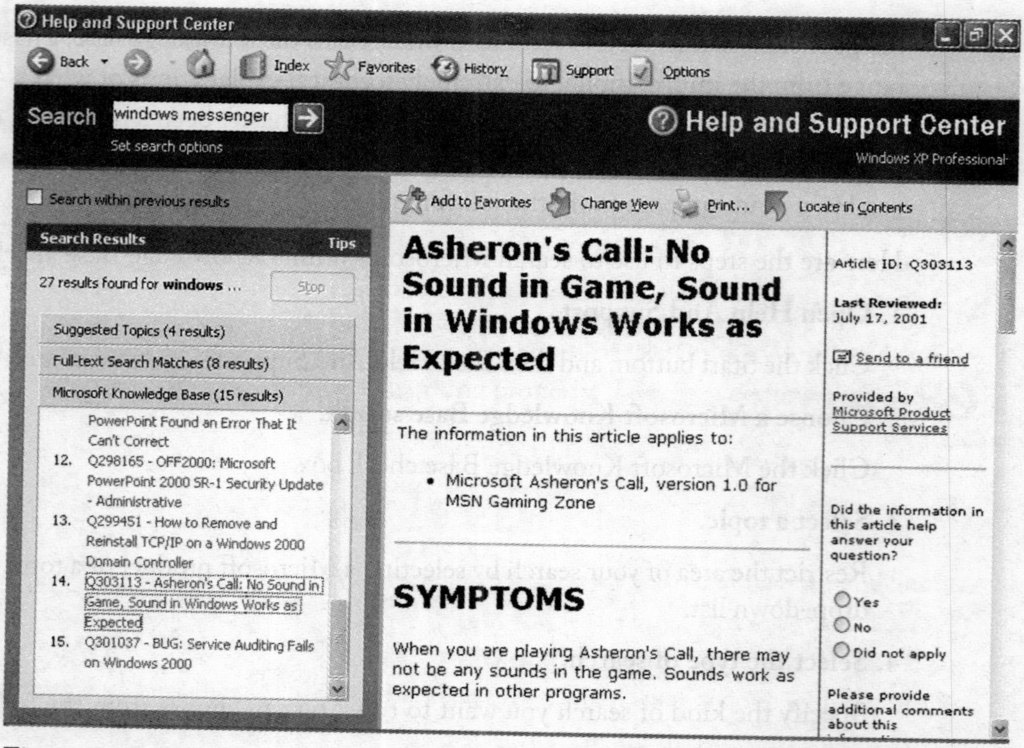

Figure 15-29 The text of a Microsoft Knowledge Base article displayed in Help And Support Center.

Summary

In this chapter we looked at some of the simple steps you can take to protect your computer's health. We also looked at how you can find out what is going on inside your computer by tracking events with Event Viewer and evaluating system performance. Then we moved on to finding problems with Device Manager, and fixing them with Help And Support Center and the Windows Troubleshooters. Finally, we looked at how to run legacy applications that won't run as you expect on Windows XP by running them in Compatibility mode, and how to search the Microsoft Knowledge Base.

Chapter 16

CREATING AND EXECUTING A DISASTER RECOVERY PLAN

Featuring:

- Backing Up Your Files and Folders
- Restoring Your Files and Folders Using the Restore Wizard
- Working with Windows System Data
- Working with Recordable CDs
- Protecting Your System from Viruses
- Keeping Everything Up-to-Date
- Scheduling Maintenance
- Using System Restore
- Rolling Back Device Drivers
- Handling Nonresponsive Applications
- Oh No, It's the Blue Screen of Death!
- Starting Windows in Safe Mode
- When All Else Fails…

In this chapter, we're going to look at some of the bad things that can happen to your computer. Your hard disk can (some would say, *will*) crash or a virus strikes or some other disaster occurs, and you lose everything. In order to protect your computer, you must make regular backups, install the latest virus-protection software, and make sure you have the most recent, up-to-date security patches installed.

Backing Up Your Files and Folders

A backup is an up-to-date copy of your computer files, and the importance of backing up cannot be overstated. If you work on a corporate network, your system administrator has probably gone to considerable time and expense ensuring that the data on your network is backed up on a regular schedule and stored in a safe place—probably even off site.

Unfortunately, experts estimate that 95 percent of all small office/home office (SOHO) workers do not have a current backup. These same experts go so far as to say that if you don't have a current backup and you also don't have a current version of virus protection software running, don't even turn on your computer! (We'll talk a lot more about virus protection later in this chapter.)

You have to lose only one important document—and we all have—to become obsessed with making backups. In Windows XP Professional, not just anyone has backup rights. You have to be logged on as a Computer Administrator, you must own the files you want to back up, or you must have one or more of the following permissions: Read, Read & Execute, Modify, Full Control.

In Windows, you can back up using the Backup Wizard, or you can make a manual backup, which gives you slightly more control. We'll give you the steps for backing up both ways, look at a Web storage alternative, and then complete the discussion by talking about how to restore what you've backed up.

A Word About Backup Media

Choosing the right backup media is always a tradeoff between capacity, speed, convenience, and cost. You could back up to floppy disks, but to make a backup of a 10 GB hard disk would take over 7,000 floppies and it would probably take the rest of your life to complete. So depending on how much data you want to back up, and how much time you have, you may want to buy hardware specifically for backup purposes. Here are some of the possibilities:

- If your system includes a CD ReWritable drive (a drive that lets you "burn" your own CDs) and you need to back up lots of data, you can back up to a CD. You can use CD-R (recordable) discs that you can use just once, or CD-RW (rewritable) discs that you can use and then erase as many times as you like.

- Another possibility for storing large amounts of data is a Zip or Jaz drive. A Zip drive uses 3.5-inch removable disks (Zip disks) that can store 100 megabytes (MB) or 250 MB of data. These drives are slower than hard disks, but faster than tapes.
- You can also back up to a tape drive if you have one. Tape drives have long been popular for backing up corporate networks because they are reliable, fast, and the tapes are relatively cheap. Restoring a single file, however, means you have to search through the tape to find it, and that can be a long, slow process.
- If you're on a network, you can back up to a drive on another computer on the network, but be sure to tell your network administrator if you plan to do this on a regular basis.

Recordable CDs or Zip Disks for Your Backup?

So which is the best backup media, a Zip disk or a recordable CD (a CD-R or a CD-RW)? Both are good candidates and both have their merits. A Zip disk can hold either 100 MB or 250 MB of information depending on the model of your Zip drive. A recordable CD can hold much more; approximately 650 MB.

If you buy them in quantity, blank CDs are cheaper than blank Zip disks. A 100 MB Zip disk costs about $10, and a 250 MB is $12. A blank CD-R is about 50 cents per disk, and even the more expensive rewriteable CD-RW blanks are only a dollar or two each.

To make a financial comparison between Zip disk and CD-R backup costs, you can calculate the cost per megabyte by dividing the cost of a disc by its capacity in megabytes. Zip disks come out at about 10 cents a megabyte, while CD-R disks are so cheap that you can throw them away once the backup is out of date.

You don't have to use the Backup program to back up your information. You can save files to either a Zip drive or a recordable CD using the Save As command from the File menu in an application, and if you right-click a file, you can use the Send To command to send the file (or a group of files) to the CD. You can also simply select a bunch of files and drag them to the CD-R, as we'll see in a later section in this chapter.

Developing Your Backup Plan

Making a backup is a pain, and if it is too much of a pain, you just won't do it. So in developing your backup plan, you should try to simplify and automate as much of the process as possible. To do that, you need to think about how you work and how often your files actually change. Or to put it the other way 'round, if your hard disk crashes one minute from now, how much data have you lost and how much time will it take you to re-create that work? And how much will it cost your business to re-create that work? For a backup plan that fits the way you work, consider these questions:

- How often do your data files change? Every day? Once a week? Once a month? In some settings, making a backup at the end of the week is sufficient. In other cases, you should make a backup every night as part of the process of closing the office and heading home. We make a backup of current working files four times every day; in other words, every time we take a break from work.
- How much data do you have to back up? The volume of data you have to back up may help determine the backup device you use, as we saw in the previous section. If you don't have too much data to back up at any one time, the data may fit onto one tape or disk, and you may be able to automate the backup and run it unattended; something you can't do if you have to be present to manually change tapes or disks.
- How long will the backup take? If you have a ton of data to back up and only a short time in which to make the back up, get yourself a faster tape drive.
- How vital are your files to the day-to-day operation of your company? Can you work without them? How long will it take you and your staff to re-create them?
- What will be the cost to the company to replace or re-create the lost files? Costs can be calculated in terms of time spent or in terms of business lost.

It can take weeks of intensive work to arrive at a department budget spreadsheet that everyone can agree to, or a Web page that has just the right look, but either one can be lost or destroyed in milliseconds. All it takes is a hard-disk glitch, a mistaken delete command, or overwriting the file with an earlier version to destroy those weeks of work, not to mention the natural disasters of fire, flood, or earthquake. As we said earlier, all it takes is losing one important file to make you an instant convert to regular, planned, backups.

Choosing a Backup Type

You will see mention of the *archive bit* in any discussion of backing up files. The archive bit is a piece of housekeeping information set automatically by Windows when a file is first created or when it is changed, and cleared again by many of the operations in the Backup program. In other words, the current status of the archive bit tells the Backup program whether or not it has to back up the file. A file whose archive bit is set to On is copied to your backup medium and then the archive bit is reset to Off so that it is not copied again; not until its contents change, that is.

In Windows Backup, there are several different types of backup that you can use in combination to create the best backup strategy to fit your needs. They treat the archive bit in different ways, too.

- Normal (usually called a full backup) is a complete backup of all the selected files, and once the files are backed up, the archive bit is set to Off. Your first backup should be a normal backup.
- Copy is useful for a quick backup of selected files between other backups. The archive bit is not changed.
- Differential backs up the files created or changed since the last Normal or Incremental backup but does not turn off the archive bit. If you have to restore files after an accident, you will have to restore the Normal backup and then only the most recent Differential backup.
- Incremental backs up the files created or changed since the last Normal or Differential backup, and resets the archive bit to Off. If you have to restore files after an accident, you will have to restore the Normal backup and then each of the Incremental backups in turn in chronological order.
- Daily backs up the files that have changed the day you make the backup, and does not change the archive bit.

So how can you transform these options into a backup strategy that works for you? One option is to make a Normal backup on the first day, say Monday, and then on the other days of the week you make a partial backup, either a Differential backup or an Incremental backup. On the following Monday, you start all over again with a Normal backup, and so the process continues.

Businesses should contract with a storage company and store backups off site in a secure facility; the chances are good that the same fire that destroys your computer at work will also destroy the backup tapes you have made so carefully and stored in that box under your desk. Most storage companies will pick up tapes or CDs for storage and return used backups for recycling. Don't take backup copies of work files home; because of the liability issues involved, it just isn't worth the risk.

Backing Up with the Backup Wizard

The easiest way to get started backing up your files is to use the Backup Wizard. To do so, follow these steps:

1. **Start the Backup Wizard.**

   Click the Start button, click All Programs, click Accessories, click System Tools, and then click Backup. At the Welcome screen, click Next.

2. **Select an operation.**

   Click the Back Up Files And Settings option button, and click Next.

3. **Specify what to back up.**

   In the What To Back Up screen, choose what you want to back up. You can back up everything on your computer; only certain files, drives, or data. When you've made your selection, click Next.

4. **Select the items you want to back up.**

   In the Items To Back Up screen, which you'll see if you didn't choose to back up everything, click the files, folders, and drives you want backed up, and then click Next. You can back up files and folders from your own computer or from network drives for which you have the appropriate permissions.

5. **Specify the destination of the backup.**

   In the Backup Type, Destination, And Name screen, specify the type of medium you'll be backing up to, or browse for the backup's filename. The options you see here will depend on the hardware you have attached to your computer; if you select a tape drive, you can choose between using a new tape or adding to the end of an existing backup on a tape you have used before. The File option lets you make a backup to a single large file that you can save later to another computer on your network. Click Finish to start the backup process, or click Advanced to make the additional backup configuration choices described in the next four steps.

6. **Select the type of backup to make.**

   In the Type Of Backup screen, choose Normal, Copy, Incremental, Differential, or Daily backups. See the previous section for detailed information on all these backup types. Click Next.

7. **How to back up.**

   Check the appropriate box for any additional options you want to use, including data verification, compression, and volume snapshots. Data verification checks the backed up data by comparing the copy against the original to ensure that nothing went wrong during the backup. If your tape drive supports hardware compression, click the check box to turn compression on, and your backup will occupy less physical space on the tape as a result of the compression. Volume snapshots allow files to be backed up even though the files are open and in use by an application. Click Next.

8. **Select media options.**

   In the Backup Options screen, you can specify whether you want this backup to overwrite an existing backup or append it to the end of the tape, disk, or file. Click Next.

9. **Set up a schedule.**

   In the When To Back Up screen, you can choose to run the backup now or to run it later. Select Now, and click Next. We'll come back to scheduling a backup job to run in the future in a later section in this chapter.

The final screen shown in Figure 16-1 summarizes your options. To change any of them, click the Back button to return to the previous screens. If the information is correct, click Finish to start the backup. The Backup Progress window will track the backup as it proceeds, showing the filenames as they are backed up, as well as an estimate of the time remaining to complete the backup. Once the backup is complete, click Report to view a detailed description of the backup, or Close to close the Backup Progress window.

Figure 16-1 Completing the Backup Wizard screen.

Backing Up Manually

To back up using a more hands-on approach, start the Backup Wizard as we did in the last section, clear the Always Start In Wizard Mode check box, and close the wizard. The next time you start Backup, you'll see the dialog box shown in Figure 16-2.

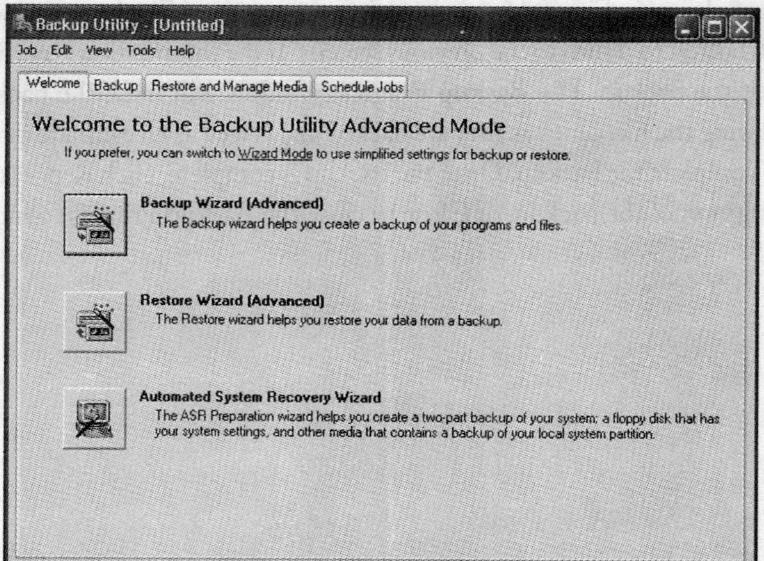

Figure 16-2 The Backup opening dialog box.

Click the Backup tab to open the Backup window, and then follow these steps:

1. **Select what to back up.**

   In the Backup tab, which is shown in Figure 16-3, click the check boxes next to the files, folders, disks, and so on that you want to back up.

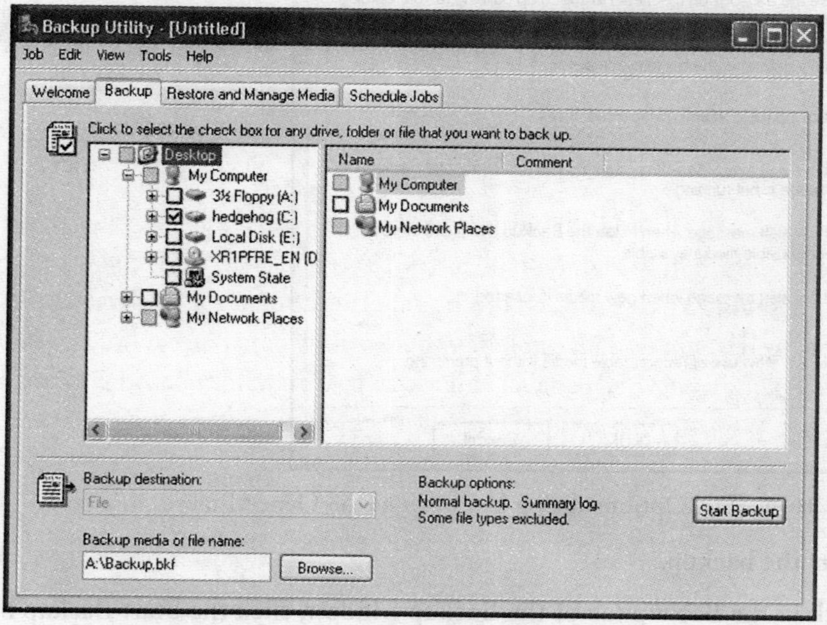

Figure 16-3 The Backup tab of the Backup window.

2. **Select where to back up.**

   In the Backup Destination box, specify where to back up to.

3. **Specify the name of the medium or the file.**

   In the Backup Media Or File Name box, enter or browse to the filename.

4. **Verify your backup configuration settings.**

   Click the Tools menu, click Options to open the Options dialog box, as shown in Figure 16-4, and then click the General tab. If the options are to your liking, click OK.

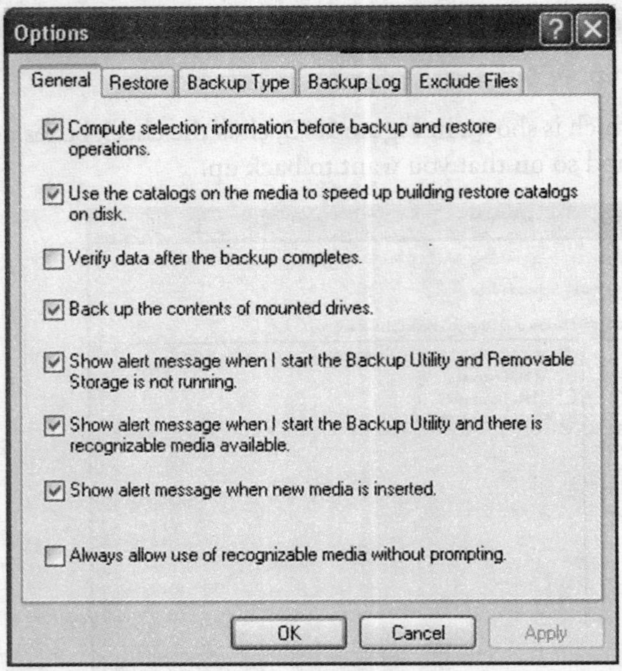

Figure 16-4 The Options dialog box open at the General tab.

5. Start the backup.

Back in the Backup tab of the Backup window, click the Start Backup button.

You can exercise even more control over your backup using the other tabs in the Options dialog box:

- Restore specifies what happens when duplicate files are found while you are restoring a backup.
- Backup Type lets you specify the backup type.
- Backup Log specifies whether and what type of information to store about the backup.
- Exclude Files lets you specify the file types you want to exclude from the backup.

Scheduling a Backup

As we saw a couple of sections earlier in this chapter, on the When To Back Up screen, you can choose to run the backup right now, or if you click Later, you can choose the time and date for the backup.

Make sure that the Task Scheduler service is running before you schedule a backup. Click the Start button, and click Run. Enter *net start schedule* in the Open box, and click OK.

Then set up your backup as you would normally, and in the When To Back Up screen, choose Later. Enter a name for this backup job in the Job Name field, and click Set Schedule to open the Schedule Job dialog box shown in Figure 16-5.

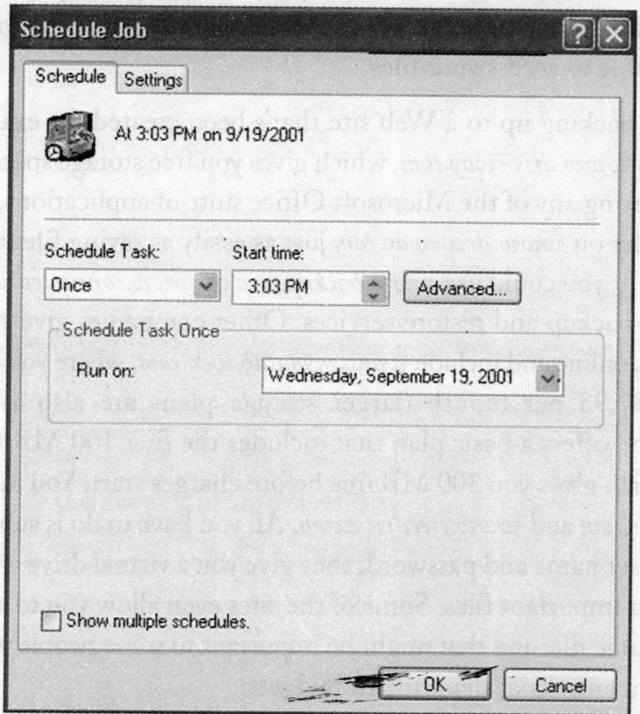

Figure 16-5 The Schedule Job dialog box.

In the Schedule tab of the Schedule Job dialog box, you can choose how frequently you want the backup to run as well as specify a start time and date. Click the Settings tab to make scheduled task, idle time, and power management specifications (if your computer is a laptop). Click OK to return to Backup.

When the Set Account Information dialog box opens, specify the user account you want the backup job to use when it runs; make sure the user account you specify has the appropriate permissions to access the drives, folders, and files you want to back up. Finally, check the details on the Completing The Backup Wizard screen, and click Finish when you're happy with all your backup settings. Windows adds the backup job to the queue of jobs waiting for execution; when the appointed time arrives, the backup job will run automatically.

Backing Up to a Web Site

For still more protection, you can back up to a Web site, either instead of or as well as another medium. For starters, you might check with your Internet service provider (ISP) to see if your Internet account includes storage space. Be sure to verify that others on the Internet won't be able to access your files.

Another possibility is backing up to a Web site that's been created for exactly that purpose. One option is *www.driveway.com*, which gives you free storage space just for signing up. If you are using any of the Microsoft Office suite of applications, you can save files to a Web folder on *www.driveway.com* just as easily as saving files to a local hard drive. Alternatively, you could use *www.backup.com* or *www.connected.com*, both of these sites focus on backup and restore services. Other companies give you more conventional hard disks online and include *www.mydatahaven.com*, where you can store up to 100 MB for $7.95 per month (larger storage plans are also available); *www.xdrive.com*, which offers a basic plan that includes the first 100 MB free; and *www.myspace.com*, which gives you 300 MB free before charges start. You might also check out *www.i-drive.com* and *www.freedrive.com*. All you have to do is subscribe to the site and specify a user name and password; they give you a virtual drive where you can store copies of your important files. Some of the sites even allow you to store different versions of the same file, and that might be important to some people who need to preserve project benchmarks or department budgets.

The advantage of using a Web-based service is that you can access your backed up files 24 hours a day from anywhere you can access the Internet. The disadvantage is that unless you have a very small number of files to back up, sending files to a Web site using a dial-up link is not very practical; the link is just too slow. You'll need DSL or a cable-modem connection to take full advantage of the service. And make sure you review the site's terms and condition statement; you don't want to find out the hard way what happens to your precious files if *their* hard disk goes down!

Restoring Your Files and Folders Using the Restore Wizard

Windows XP Professional has been described as crashless by some industry commentators, and that certainly seems to be the case when you compare it with previous versions of Windows. But when the inevitable happens, such as a hard disk giving up the ghost, you're prepared if you've been ruthlessly adhering to a backup schedule, and you can restore your lost information. And restoring files is a whole lot easier than backing them up was.

To restore your files and folders using the Restore Wizard, follow these steps:

1. Start the Backup program.

lick the tart button, click All Programs, click Accessories, click ystem Tools, and then click Backup.

. Start the ar .

n the Welcome tab, click e t, and then click Restore iles And ettings.

. Se ect a ackup e ce.

n the What To Restore screen, choose the device you want to use with the restore. lick e t.

. Se ect the e ou a t to re tore.

heck the bo es for the files and folders you want to restore, and click e t. The Restore Wizard then displays a summary page, ompleting The Restore Wizard, shown in igure - , detailing the settings you have chosen. lick inish to start restoring your files and folders.

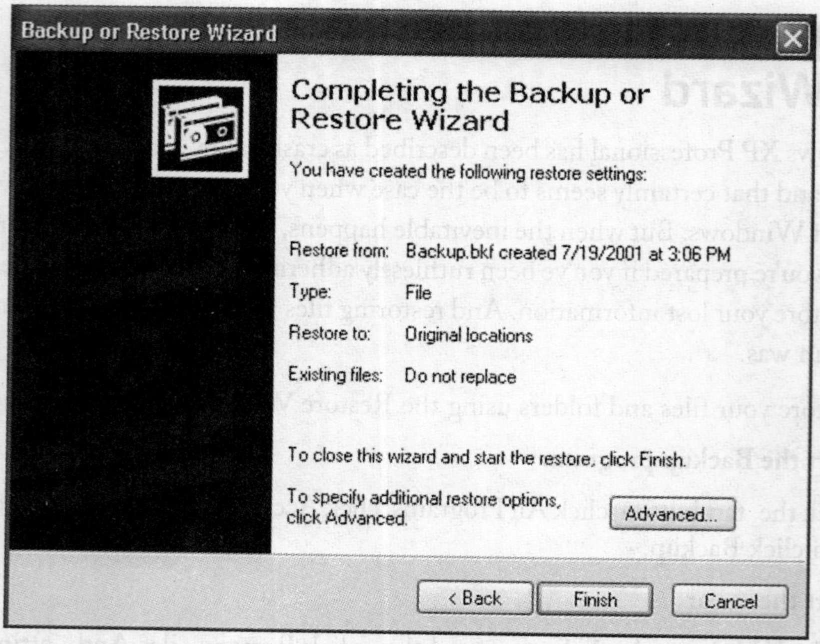

Figure 16-6 The Completing The Restore Wizard screen.

The Backup program usually restores each backed up file into the same folder that it originally came from, but if you want to restore the file to a different folder, you certainly can do so. Click the Advanced button in the Completing The Restore Wizard screen and in the Where To Restore page, choose the folder you want to use. When you choose Alternate Location, Backup tries as best it can to re-create the original folder structure; if you choose Single Folder, all the files are dumped into one folder in a big heap with no folder organization. Click Next. In the How To Restore screen, you will be presented with three options to deal with files that are already on the hard disk:

- Leave Existing Files (Recommended).
- Replace Existing Files If They Are Older Than The Backup Files.
- Replace Existing Files.

The first option is usually the safest one to choose; click Next. Review the summary page once again, and if everything looks good, click Finish and the restore will proceed.

Restoring a Backup Manually

Restoring a backup manually involves essentially the same steps that the Restore Wizard walks you through, but you use the Restore And Manage Media tab in the Backup window. Select the drive, folder, or file that you want to restore, specify where to restore the backup, and click Start Restore to begin.

Working with Windows System Data

You can also use the Backup program to make backup copies of essential Windows system files, including:

- The Windows Registry, the database that holds all the configuration information for users, applications, documents, property settings, hardware, and so on.
- Windows boot files, the system files needed to start the operating system running when it first boots up.
- Windows system files, the files used to load, configure, and start the operating system.

If your system is seriously damaged, you can use this backup to restore your system settings and then use the Restore Wizard to reload all your files and folders. Best of all, it's done using a wizard. Let's take a look.

Backing Up System State Data

Click the Start button, click All Programs, click Accessories, click System Tools, and then click Backup. In the Welcome tab, click the Automatic System Recovery Wizard button, or if you are already in the Backup program, click the Tools menu and click ASR Wizard. The ASR Wizard helps you to create a two-part insurance policy consisting of a floppy disk holding your system settings and a file holding a backup of your local system partition. When the Welcome screen opens, click Next to start the wizard, and select a destination for the backup of your system files. Click Next, and then click Finish. The Backup Progress window shows you where you are in the process. Insert a blank floppy disk when prompted.

Restoring System State Data

You can also use the Restore Wizard to restore system state data. The Restore Wizard will restore the backed up system files to their original location, erasing the current files, unless you specify an alternative location. Certain system files are location specific on your hard disk, and these files must be restored to the correct location in order for them to function correctly.

There is certainly an element of the old which came first, the chicken or the egg conundrum here, because you can't run the Backup program unless Windows is working properly, and if Windows isn't working properly, there are very few shortcuts you can use to get 'round that fact.

Working with Recordable CDs

Another way you can make a backup of important data files is to use the normal Windows file-copying methods to select a bunch of files and then copy them to a recordable CD, either a CD-R or CD-RW. As we said earlier in this chapter, blank CD-RWs are now so cheap that you can store files on them, and then when you are done with the project, just reuse them for backups of the next project. Here are the steps to follow:

1. **Open Explorer.**

   Right-click the Start button, and choose Explore from the shortcut menu.

2. **Select the files to backup.**

   Use the normal Windows methods to find and then select the files you want to copy to the disk.

3. **Drag the files to the CD.**

   Arrange the Explorer window so you can drag the files to the CD. Initially, the files are copied to a temporary area known as the *staging area,* which looks just like any other folder. Click the Write These Files To CD button on the left side of this folder.

4. **Run the CD Writing Wizard.**

   When the CD Writing Wizard opens as Figure 16-7 shows, name the CD or let Windows choose a name for you, and click Next.

Figure 16-7 The CD Writing Wizard.

5. Write the files to the CD.

The CD Writing Wizard then writes the selected files to the CD. A bar display indicates progress, and the CD is ejected when the copy is complete. You can choose to copy the same files to another CD, or click Finish to close the wizard and clear the temporary copies of your files from the CD staging area. If you are copying a music file, such as an MP3 file, you may be asked to choose between creating an audio CD you can play on a standard CD player or a data CD you can use on your computer.

CD-ROM, CD-R, CD-RW, and DVD Explained

It's turning into alphabet soup, what with CD-ROM, CD-R, CD-RW, and now DVD, DVD-R, and DVD-RW, so let's just start at the beginning and work our way through.

On a CD or CD-ROM, data is recorded mechanically; a master is prepared with a spiral track of pits and smooth areas that hold the encoded data, and this is stamped onto the surface of a blank disk. The disk is then coated for protection and the label is added to the top of the disk. A CD-ROM drive reads data by shining a laser beam at the disk, and the amount of light reflected back is decoded as data.

A CD-R (recordable) disk is created as a blank so that users can add their own data. A thin coating of light-reflective dye changes color when illuminated by the laser as data is written, and because this color change is not reversible, you can write on a specific area of a CD-R only once.

A CD-RW disk uses a different light-reflective layer with reflective properties that can be altered, so CD-RW drives support read, write, and erase operations. And as a result, the read-head technology that works with a CD or a CD-ROM, may not be sensitive enough to read data from a CD-R or CD-RW. The effect of this is that you can read a factory-manufactured CD such as an encyclopedia on your older CD drive, but you may not be able to read a duplicate of that same disk if the duplicate was made on a newer CD-RW drive.

You should be able to use blank disks from any manufacturer on any of these drives. If you see read errors when you read these disks on drives other than the drive the disk was originally created on, try a better-quality blank or contact the manufacturer of the drive to see if they recommend a specific brand.

DVD disks have much higher capacities than CDs: 4.7 GB compared with 650 MB. To fit all this extra data on the disk, the tracks must be much narrower, and to read both CD disks and DVD disks, DVD drives use two lasers of different wavelength, one for CDs and the other for DVD disks. By using dual lasers, DVD drives can read DVD disks, CD-RW, CD-R, and CD-ROM disks. Of course, this doesn't work the other way round; normal CD-ROM drives can't read DVD disks.

The Pioneer DVD-R drive used by Compaq can also record one-time DVD-R disks and when they are available it will be able to record onto blank, multi-use, DVD-RW disks. There are competing DVD recording standards being promoted at the moment, and the final specification may in fact be incompatible with the Pioneer drive. We'll have to wait and see.

Erasing Files from a CD-RW

If you are working with a CD-RW, you can also erase files from the disk once they are no longer of use. Insert the disk into the CD drive, and when the window opens, click Erase Files On CD-RW. This is only present if your drive is a CD-RW; you won't see it if you have a CD-R or CD-ROM. The CD Burning Wizard opens reminding you that all files will be deleted; click Next. A bar display indicates progress, click Finish to close the wizard.

Setting CD Drive Properties

A CD-R or CD-RW drive has different properties that you can look at or change if you right-click the drive in Explorer or My Computer, and choose Properties from the shortcut menu. You will see four tabs in the Properties dialog box:

- General lists basic information for the disk, including name, file system, and the capacity, the amount of used space and the amount of free space that remains.
- AutoPlay lets you select a content type and then choose an action you want Windows to take when you insert a disk containing that content. For example, if you select video files as the content type, you can choose between automatically playing the video files with the Windows Media Player or opening a folder window with Explorer so you can view the files.
- Hardware lists the basic hardware information for the drive, and you can access the Troubleshooter if you are having problems with the drive.
- Sharing allows you to share the drive with other users on the network.
- Recording, shown in Figure 16-8, lets you specify the settings Windows will use when writing to this drive. Click the Enable CD Recording On This Drive check box to allow you to drag and drop files and folders to this CD. You must also select a hard disk with at least 700 MB of free space to use as the temporary staging area where files are placed before they are copied to the CD-R or CD-RW. And finally, you can set the recording speed. It makes good sense to select the Fastest option until you see a dialog box open during a file copy operation telling you that there have been errors writing to the disk. At this point, come back here and select a lower speed. The copying process will take longer, but you won't get any errors. The optimum speed to use depends on many factors, but on slower computers you should close any other applications until you have finished writing to the CD.

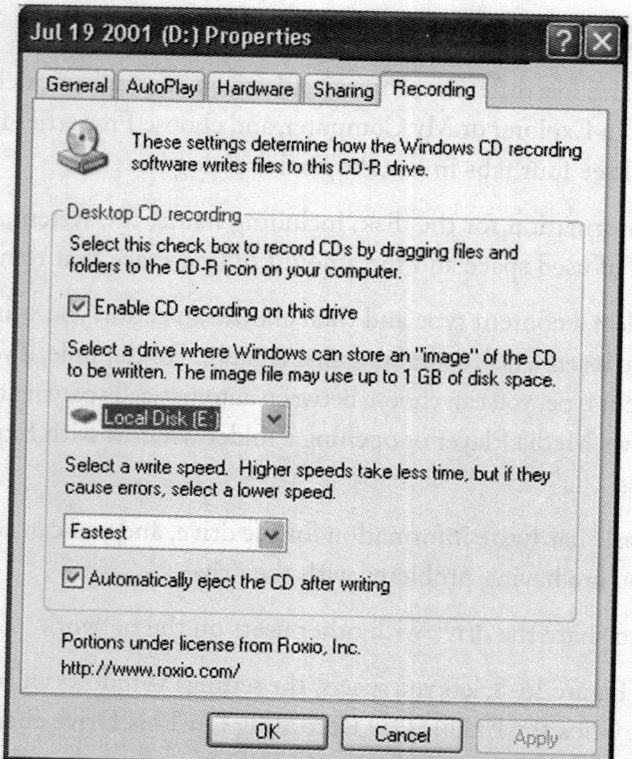

Figure 16-8 The CD Drive Properties dialog box open at the Recording tab.

Speeding Up the Process

There is one more thing you can consider to speed up the CD copying process, and that is actually changing the priority of the application writing to the CD. Here's how it's done:

1. **Open Task Manager.**

   Right-click the taskbar, and choose Task Manager from the shortcut menu.

2. **Check the priority.**

   To look at the current priority of all running programs, click the View menu, click Select Columns, and click the Base Priority check box. You will now see a new column in the Task Manager window listing the current priority of each program.

3. **Select the program, and change the priority.**

   On the Processes tab, right-click the program whose priority you want to change, and choose Set Priority from the shortcut menu. Change the priority from Normal to High, and the application will get all the CPU time it needs.

And you should leave it at that; don't set the priority to the highest setting, Realtime, unless of course, you don't want Windows to do anything else.

Protecting Your System from Viruses

A virus is a malevolent program that can attach itself to your computer system without your knowledge or permission and wipe out all your work in less than a minute. Computer viruses are not airborne; they travel via infected floppy disks, e-mail, files that you download from the Internet, and even shrink-wrapped software. Many recent viruses replicate themselves by reading a recipient's address book and mailing themselves to all the people in it. It is very hard to estimate the total number of viruses that have been released, but experts put the number at somewhere between 60,000 and 100,000.

NOTE *According to an International Computer Security Association study, viruses infected 14 computers per thousand in January 1997, but by January 1999 that number had reached 88 per thousand.*

A Trojan horse is slightly different in that it is malicious software masquerading as a useful application. A Trojan horse might be attached to free software, such as a game or a utility you download from the Internet; when you run the application, the Trojan horse also runs on your computer.

Some viruses are benign; they might send you to a Web site or post a message on your screen. Others carry a malicious payload that can wipe out your system, destroying files and making it impossible to boot your system.

Finding and Using Antivirus Software

In addition to faithfully adhering to your backup schedule, what can you do to avoid falling prey to computer viruses? Here are some ideas:

- Buy and use anti-virus software. A simple step, but one that many people ignore. Good antivirus software will check vital system files as you boot up your computer, monitor your system for suspicious activity, scan memory when you run an application, check programs when you download them from the Internet, and scan e-mail attachments before you open them. Two popular antivirus packages are Norton AntiVirus by Symantec (*www.symantec.com*) and VirusScan from McAfee (*www.mcafee.com*). If you are looking for virus protection and content-filtering software for a Microsoft Exchange system, check out Trend Micro products at *www.antivirus.com*.
- Keep your antivirus software upgraded by checking your antivirus software vendor's Web site once a week. New viruses are being discovered all the time, somewhere between 500 and 700 a month, and your antivirus software needs to have the latest virus detection information, known as virus definitions.
- Protect the integrity of your home computer/network and your office computer/network. It is common to catch a workplace virus and bring it home or to acquire a virus at home and then infect the office network.
- Never download a file or a software program if you don't know and trust the source.
- If an application supports it, turn on Macro Virus Protection. For example, in a Microsoft Office application, click the Tools menu, click Macro, click Security to open the Security dialog box, select High or Medium, and click OK.
- Don't believe everything you hear. There are as many hoaxes about viruses as there are viruses. To stay current, go to one of the antivirus software vendor's sites. The Symantec AntiVirus Research Center at *www.symantec.com/avcenter* lists well over 100 hoaxes and so-called jokes, programs that only pretend to perform a malicious action (pretty funny, huh?). You will also find a list of hoaxes at *www.mcafee.com* and on their e-business Web site at *www.avertlabs.com*.
- Never open an e-mail attachment without pausing to think, even if it appears to be from somebody you know. Some viruses spread through e-mail attachments that the sender doesn't even know were sent. Be very suspicious of any e-mail attachments with filename extensions of .exe, .com, or .vbs, and don't open the attachment until you have verified who sent it and what the attachment contains.

Protecting Against Macro Viruses

Until the Melissa worm struck in 1999, it was widely assumed that it was impossible to spread viruses automatically by e-mail. Unfortunately, Melissa took advantage of Microsoft Office's Visual Basic for Applications (VBA) scripting language to send a copy of itself to the first 50 people in each recipient's address book. In the process, Melissa slowed e-mail servers all over the world to a dismal crawl. A year later, the May 4, 2000, attack of the "ILOVEYOU" macro virus hit almost 45 million computers and cost an estimated $10 billion in damage, mostly as a result of lost work time. So macro viruses are a serious risk; before you can defend yourself against macro viruses, you need to know just a little about how they work.

A conventional virus may require you to run an executable file to trigger an infection, but a macro virus can be triggered by much more mundane activities, such as opening a document. This is possible due to the power built in to VBA for automating common tasks, and the Windows Scripting Host extends this power across applications, so that one macro can manipulate several applications. For example, you can write a VBScript program to look up data in an Access database, and send e-mail to people in your Outlook address book based on the results. This capability is enormously powerful but is open to abuse by virus writers. The fundamental problem is that the computer can't tell the difference between a script that you want to run to automate a set of tasks and a virus that you don't want to run.

But there are some precautions you can take against macro viruses:

- Never open an e-mail attachment without pausing to think, even if it appears to be from somebody you know. Yes, we know we just said this in the last section, but it is worth repeating. Don't do it.
- Use the Virus Protection settings in Outlook Express (click the Tools menu, click Options, and then click the Security tab shown in Figure 16-9) to alert you to any scripting activity that is trying to send out an automatic e-mail, and to prevent attachments that could contain a virus from being opened or saved.
- Because some viruses will attack files on any shares they can find on your network, don't share whole drives. Instead, just share specific directories, and give permission only to those users who need access.

- If you decide to share directories, don't allow unlimited access and always use a strong password to protect the share.
- Don't use persistent mapped network drives (mapped drives that are reconnected every time you log on) if possible, as they are an easy target for viruses.

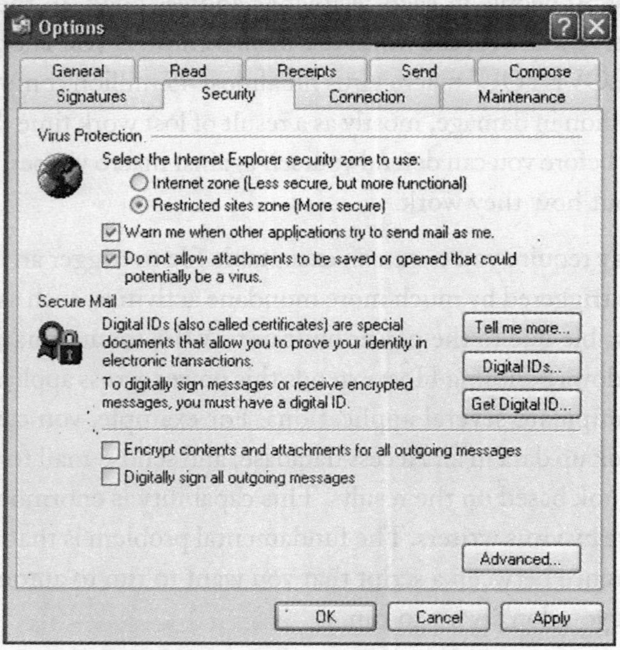

Figure 16-9 Outlook Express open at the Security tab.

Keeping Everything Up-to-Date

Another aspect of keeping your system as safe as possible is to make sure you have the latest software releases, patches, and security fixes installed on your system. Experts estimate that 80 to 90 percent of all security breaches take advantage of vulnerabilities for which software makers have already issued patches. Microsoft continuously issues *security bulletins* outlining problems with software, and *security patches* designed to fix these problems. In the sections that follow, we'll share with you some of the most useful Windows Web sites we have found that you can use to stay current.

Microsoft Web Sites

The place to start is with the Microsoft TechNet Security Web site at *www.microsoft.com/technet/security/notify.asp* to subscribe to Microsoft's Product Security Notification Service. This is a free e-mail service used to provide accurate and timely information to users of Microsoft products. When you receive a security bulletin, it will contain information on a specific issue or vulnerability, the affected software product, what measures you can take to protect yourself, details of Microsoft's plan to fix the problem, any caveats associated with the fix, and links to other associated resources.

Once you have the bulletin, you are ready to find the security patch. Many times, the simplest way to find the patch is to use the links contained in the bulletin. Sometimes an initial patch with a manual installation will be issued to fix a problem immediately, and then a follow-up patch with an automated installation might be issued some time later. Fixing broken software is always a fine balance between immediacy and convenience, and with security-related issues, time is obviously of the essence.

The Microsoft Download Center is the next place to look. Because of the way this Web site works, patches can be posted here very quickly indeed. You will find the Download Center at *www.microsoft.com/downloads/search.asp?*, and here you can search by product name, operating system, or keyword. Results are listed by title or by date, and include the affected product version numbers and an estimate of the length of time it will take to download the patch.

Windows Update Web Site

You can connect to the Windows Update Web site at *www.windowsupdate.microsoft.com* manually, or you can click the Start button, click More Programs, and then click Windows Update. Either way, you end up at the Windows Update site, as Figure 16-10 shows, which is one of the best-designed and easiest to use of all Microsoft's Web sites.

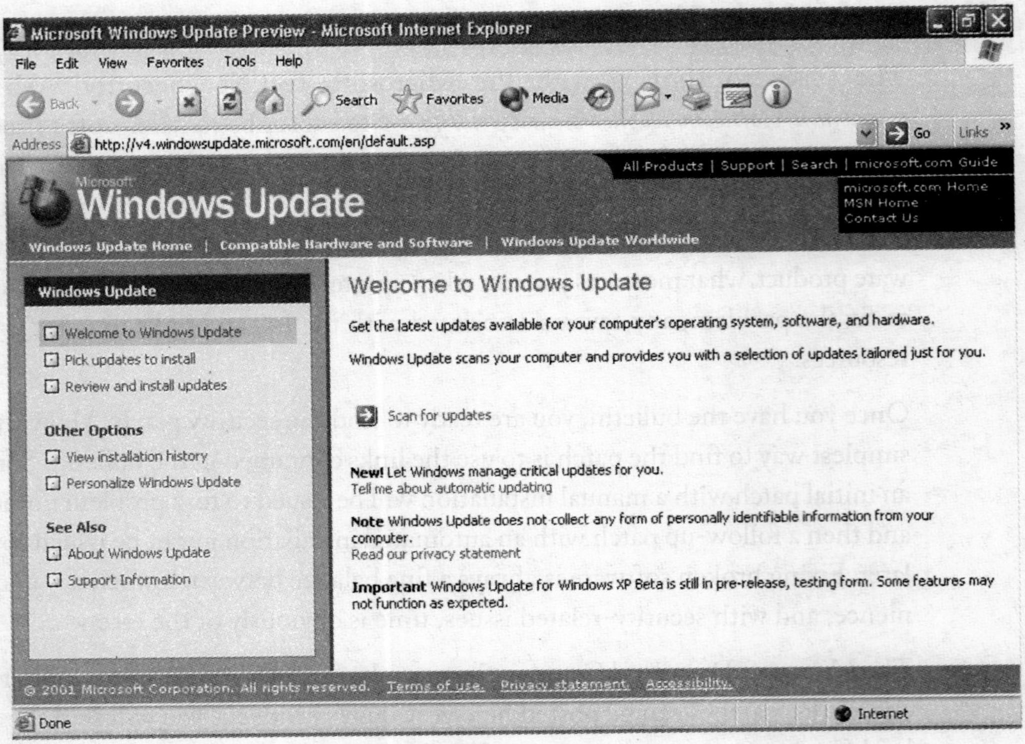

Figure 16-10 The Windows Update Web site.

Use the settings on the Automatic Updates tab in the System applet to specify what you want to happen when you connect to the Windows Update Web site. To open System, click the Start button, click Control Panel, click Performance And Maintenance, and then click System. Click the Automatic Updates tab, shown in Figure 16-11, and in the Notification Settings box, choose one of the following settings:

- Download The Updates Automatically And Notify Me When They Are Ready To Be Installed.
- Notify Me Before Downloading Any Updates And Notify Me Again Before Installing Them On My Computer.
- Turn Off Automatic Updating. I Want To Update My Computer Manually.

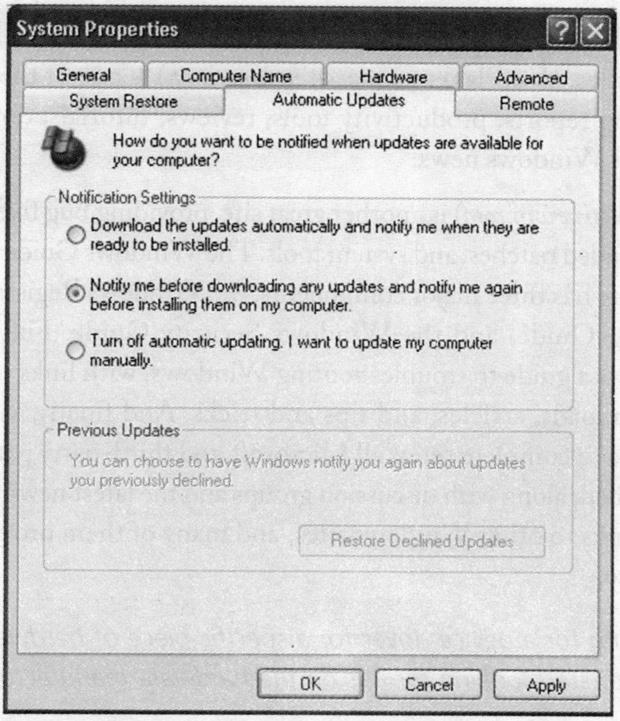

Figure 16-11 The Automatic Updates tab.

The Windows Update site will automatically list the updates, patches, and useful additions for your version of Windows, and arrange them in priority order, telling you which are critical and which can be put off for another day. Check the ones you want, then you can download and install them all at the same time. Because of the complexity of this site, security patches may take a few weeks to appear here; if you are in a hurry, go to the Download Center.

Make sure your Internet Explorer security settings are set to Medium before you access the Windows Update site. To look at or change your settings, click the Tools menu in Internet Explorer and click Internet Options. Click the Security tab, click the Internet Zone icon, and then move the slider to Medium. You may have to click the Default Level button if you have made custom settings in the past.

The Windows Update Web site also has an excellent technical support section that includes device drivers, service packs, patches, and FAQs, as well as links to the main Microsoft Windows Web site and the Office Update Web site. The Office Update site contains patches and updates for Outlook, Word, Excel, PowerPoint, Access, FrontPage, Project, Visio, and all other Office products.

Other Useful Web Sites

Of the non-Microsoft sites, WinPlanet (*www.winplanet.com*) is one of the best designed with utilities, bug reports, productivity tools, reviews, tutorials, downloads, drivers, and all the latest Windows news.

Active Network (*www.activewin.com*) is another great site, providing bug fixes, service packs, articles, recommended patches, and system tools. The Windows Guide Network (*www.winguides.com*) site has three major components, the Windows Registry Guide, the Windows Scripting Guide, and the Windows Security Guide. FixWindows (*www.fixwindows.com*) is a guide to troubleshooting Windows, with links to drivers, technical support, downloads, articles, and tips and tricks. And finally, WinPortal (*www.winportal.com*) has a complete set of all Microsoft and third-party patches and updates all clearly described, along with discussion groups and the latest news. All these sites contain pages of links to other Windows sites, and many of them provide a free e-mail newsletter service.

NOTE *If you are looking for a device driver for a specific piece of hardware, often the best place to start looking for it is on the hardware manufacturer's own Web site.*

CERT (*www.cert.org*), operated by Carnegie Mellon University, provides security advisories, technical tips, and other recommendations. SecurityFocus.com (*www.securityfocus.com*) offers a calendar of security conferences and seminars, and the SANS Institute (*www.sans.org*) provides security information, access to a reading room of technical articles, and an excellent free newsletter. We have received their weekly security newsletter SANS NewsBites for several years now, and it is definitely one of the best.

Scheduling Maintenance

As you have seen from earlier chapters in this book, you can clean up your hard drive or defragment it whenever the need arises, but you can also schedule these tasks to be taken care of automatically, perhaps after the work day or on the weekend. To schedule maintenance tasks, follow these steps:

1. Open the Scheduled Tasks folder.

Click the Start button, click All Programs, click Accessories, click System Tools, and then click Scheduled Tasks to open the Scheduled Tasks folder as shown in Figure 16-12. Here you will see a list of any previously scheduled tasks by name, schedule, next run time, last run time, and status.

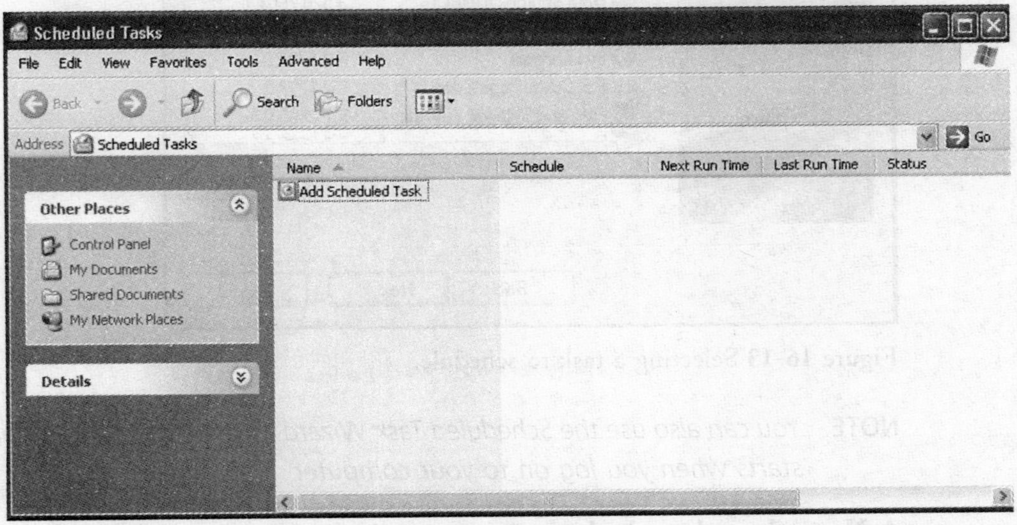

Figure 16-12 The Scheduled Tasks folder.

2. Start the Scheduled Task Wizard.

Click Add Scheduled Task, and at the opening screen of the wizard, click Next.

3. Select a task.

Click the name of the application you want to schedule, as shown in Figure 16-13, and click Next.

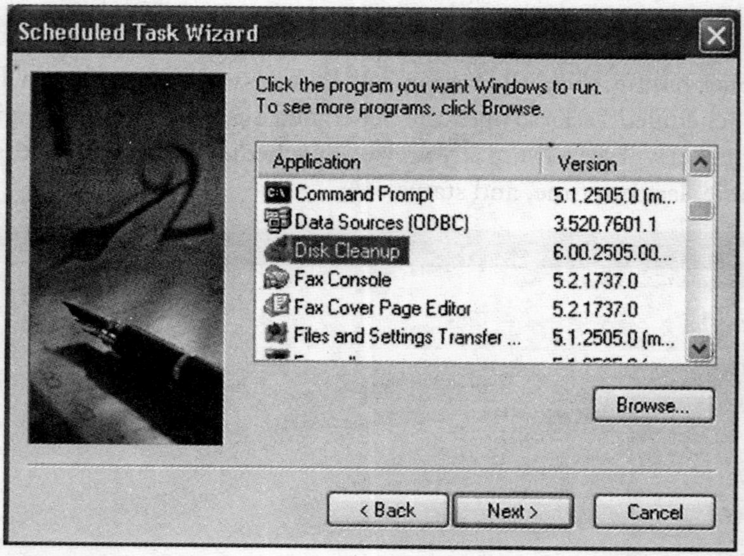

Figure 16-13 Selecting a task to schedule.

NOTE *You can also use the Scheduled Task Wizard to specify a program that always starts when you log on to your computer.*

4. **Name the task, and select a time to run it.**

   Accept the suggested name or enter another name for this task, and then click the option button that corresponds to when you want the task to run. Click Next, and further specify the exact time and dates to run the program. Click Next.

5. **Specify a user and a password.**

   Enter a user name, enter a password, and confirm the password. The task will run as if that user started it. Click Next.

6. **Add this task to the Scheduled Tasks folder.**

   Click Finish.

To add other tasks, just repeat steps 1 through 6.

NOTE *Make sure the system time and date are correct on your computer as Schedule Tasks uses the computer clock to start tasks. The quickest way to change the system time is to double-click the time indicator on the taskbar.*

If you click the Open Advanced Properties For This Task When I Click Finish check box in the last screen of the wizard, you can set more configuration options for the task you are working with, including command-line switches if the task supports them. Some applications have a large group of command-line switches, while others may have none at all.

Using System Restore

All of us at some point have installed a new device driver, or downloaded an application from a Web site, only to find that Windows doesn't work properly afterwards. And all of us have wished that we could return to the point just *before* we installed the new software and carry on working. Well, with System Restore, you can now do exactly that.

System Restore lets you return your computer to a previous state in the event of a problem, without the loss of important saved data files, e-mail, or other documents you were working with at the time. System Restore actually monitors changes to your system configuration and to certain application files, creating easily recognizable restore points, so you don't have to remember to run the Backup program quite so carefully. These restore points are created automatically every day, and also at significant events, such as the installation of a new device driver. You can also make your own restore points at any time, if you know you are about to do something that will change the system configuration in a significant way.

NOTE *One thing System Restore cannot do is recover your lost or damaged data files or documents.*

Creating a Restore Point

To make a restore point, start System Restore from one of the following locations:

- Click the Start button, click All Programs, click Accessories, click System Tools, and then click System Restore.
- Click the Start button, click Help And Support, click Use Tools To View Your Computer Information And Diagnose Problems, and click System Restore.
- Click the Start button, click Control Panel, click Performance And Maintenance, and then click System Restore.

In the Welcome To System Restore screen, click System Restore Settings to open the System properties dialog box at the System Restore tab as shown in Figure 16-14.

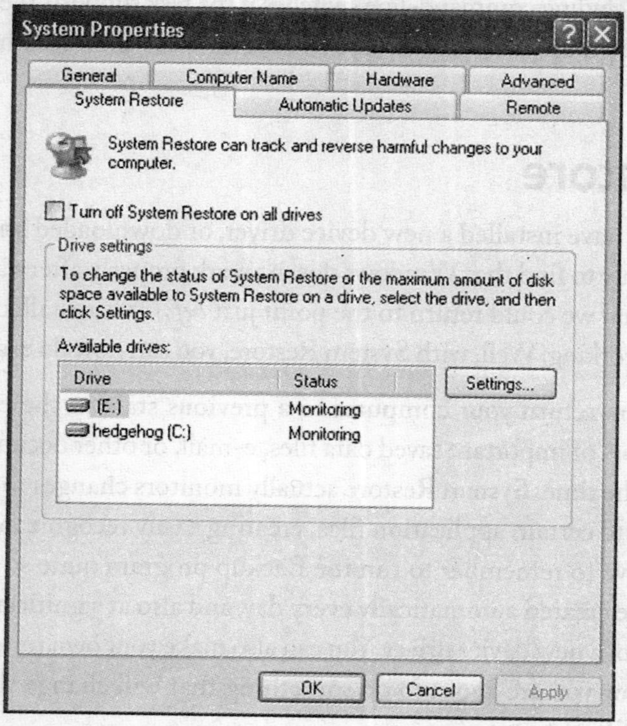

Figure 16-14 The System properties dialog box open at the System Restore tab.

To change the maximum amount of disk space available to System Restore on any of your hard-disk drives, select the drive, and then click the Settings button. Use the slider to change the amount of disk space. Click OK to close the Settings dialog box, and click OK to close the System Properties dialog box. Click Create A Restore Point in the Welcome To System Restore screen, and click Next.

Enter a name to use with this restore point, making it easy to remember by associating it with whatever operation you are about to perform on your computer; the time and the date will be added automatically. Click Create. The final screen lists the day, date, time, and name of the restore point. Click the Close button to end System Restore.

Starting a System Restore

If the application you downloaded from the Internet did not work as you expected and you want to return to a previous configuration, open System Restore using one of the methods described in the previous section and choose Restore My Computer To An Earlier Time. Click Next.

In the Select A Restore Point screen, shown in Figure 16-15, you will see a calendar with certain days displayed in bold type.

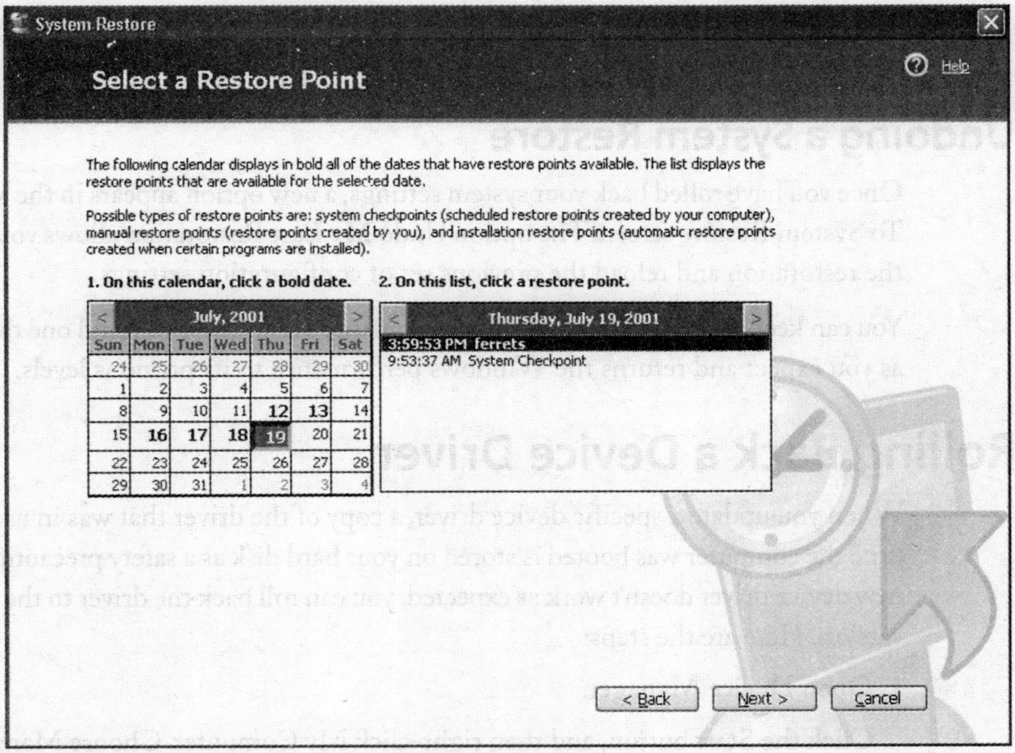

Figure 16-15 The Select A Restore Point screen.

These are the days associated with a restore point, and these restore points can be one of three types:

- A scheduled restore point (called a *system checkpoint*) automatically created by your computer.
- An installation restore point automatically created when your computer detects a change associated with a certain application.
- A manually created restore point.

Once you choose a date on the calendar, you will see the restore points for this date listed in the window on the right. Choose one of the restore points, and click Next. During the restoration process, System Restore will shut down Windows, and then restart Windows using the settings from the restore point you specified. Be sure to close all open applications and save all your work; when you are ready, click Next. A bar graph indicates progress until Windows shuts down. When it restarts, System Restore opens automatically, reminding you of the name and time of the restore point you have just used. If this restore point is not successful in restoring Windows performance, you can always use a different restore point and try again. Click OK to return to the Windows desktop.

Undoing a System Restore

Once you have rolled back your system settings, a new option appears in the Welcome To System Restore screen. The option Undo My Last Restoration allows you to undo the restoration and reload the previous set of configuration settings.

You can keep loading and testing different restore points until you find one that works as you expect and returns the Windows performance to its previous levels.

Rolling Back a Device Driver

When you update a specific device driver, a copy of the driver that was in use the last time the computer was booted is stored on your hard disk as a safety precaution. If the new device driver doesn't work as expected, you can roll back the driver to the previous version. Here are the steps:

1. **Open Device Manager.**

   Click the Start button, and then right-click My Computer. Choose Manage from the shortcut menu, and then click Device Manager.

2. **Select the appropriate hardware.**

   Expand the list of elements in the right pane until you can see the piece of hardware whose device driver you want to roll back.

3. **Roll back the device driver.**

   Right-click the hardware component in question, and choose Properties from the shortcut menu. Click the Driver tab, and then choose Roll Back Driver to reload the previously saved version of the device driver.

Handling Nonresponsive Applications

It is very rare for Windows XP to just stop working, to *hang up* or to *freeze*; after all Windows system stability is one of the biggest selling points to the business world. Windows XP is much more stable than Windows 95 and all the variations of Windows 98.

Some of the common indications that a program has crashed include the following:

- Everything freezes; you can move the mouse pointer but clicking the mouse button has no effect and the keyboard doesn't do anything.
- A warning dialog box opens telling you a program has performed an illegal operation and is going to shut down—whether you like it or not.
- Some of your programs are working just fine, but when you move the mouse pointer over another program, it always turns into the hourglass symbol.

If Windows XP does hang up, it is usually a problem with an application or a poorly written device driver. Check that any new device drivers you install have been certified by Microsoft for use with Windows XP. If the problem is with a device driver, you can use Device Driver Rollback, described in the last section, to return to the previous version of the driver.

If the problem is with an application, just wait for a minute or two; sometimes Windows can sort out problems all by itself. If nothing happens after a couple of minutes, press Ctrl+Alt+Del to open the Task Manager, and then click the Applications tab, shown in Figure 16-16, to bring it to the front.

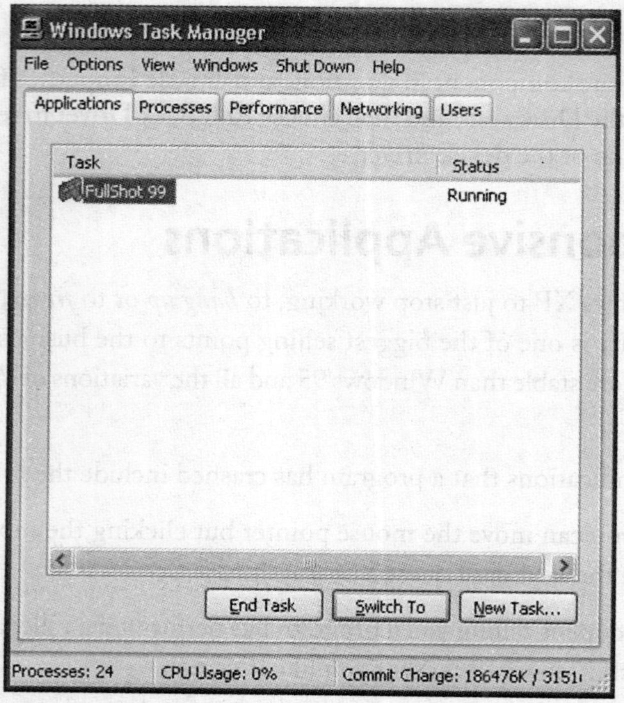

Figure 16-16 The Applications tab in Task Manager.

The Status column on this tab may list an application as Not Responding, and that application is the one causing the problem. Once an application is listed as Not Responding, it is not going to do anything more; you will have to end the task manually to get things back to normal again. Select the offending task and click End Task. If you were working in an application, any work you did since the last save will probably be lost and you will have to do it over. On the other hand, Windows is so good at keeping applications separate that the failure of one application will probably not bring down other applications or the operating system itself.

Oh No, It's the Blue Screen of Death!

Sometimes Windows will come to a crashing halt, and that is when you will see the screen known as the Blue Screen of Death, technically, a stop error or a fatal system error. In other words, Windows was so badly compromised that it was impossible to continue running.

The Blue Screen of Death lists all sorts of technical information about the stop, including the stop error message (which you should write down), and device drivers loaded into the system at the time of the crash. It is very unlikely that an application will cause a system stop; it is much more likely to be hard-disk corruption or failure, or a hardware failure such as a problem with the circuitry inside a CD-ROM drive, for example.

If you can restart Windows after the stop error, check the Event log (described in Chapter 15) to see if the stop is listed there. If you find an error message in the system log, you can search the Microsoft Knowledge Base for that message; you may well find an article containing information you can use to fix the problem. Given the huge number of people using Windows, it is unlikely that you are the first person to see this particular stop error.

Specifying Options for a Stop

You can specify what Windows does when it encounters one of these stop errors on another tab in the System applet. To start System, click the Start button, click Control Panel, click Performance And Maintenance, and click System. Click the Advanced tab, and under Startup And Recovery, click Settings to open the Startup And Recovery dialog box shown in Figure 16-17.

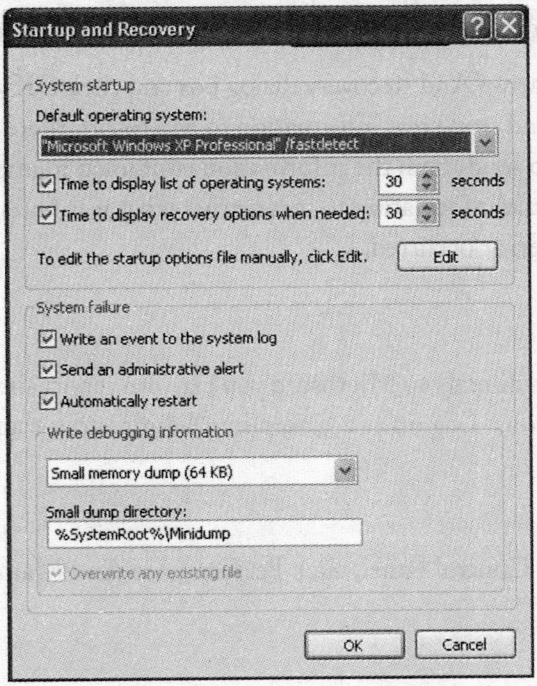

Figure 16-17 The Startup And Recovery dialog box.

In the System Failure box, you have the following options:

- Write An Event To The System Log specifies that information about the error will be written into the system log.
- Send An Administrative Alert sends a message to the Computer Administrator.
- Automatically Restart specifies that Windows will attempt to reboot automatically.

And in the Write Debugging Information box, you can choose what Windows will record in the event of a stop error:

- None specifies that no memory dump be taken.
- Small Memory Dump specifies that the smallest set of data be recorded. You will need a paging (or swap) file of at least 2 MB on the boot volume of your computer if you select this option.
- Kernel Memory Dump specifies that only kernel memory be saved. This option requires 50 to 800 MB of disk space depending on the amount of physical memory installed on your computer.
- Complete Memory Dump copies the entire contents of system memory. If you choose this option, you must have enough disk space to hold a copy of all the physical memory installed on your computer, plus one MB for management information.

Make your choices from the Startup And Recovery dialog box and click OK when you are done. If you do decide to send stop error information to Microsoft, there is a good chance that they will ask you to send them the information contained in one of these memory dumps. They can use the information to reconstruct what was happening on your computer when the stop error occurred.

Reporting Errors

You can report these stop errors directly to Microsoft; you can also report similar fatal errors with Microsoft applications. Log on as a Computer Administrator and follow these steps:

1. **Open System.**

   Click the Start button, click Control Panel, click Performance And Maintenance, and then click System.

2. **Click Error Reporting.**

   Click the Advanced tab, and then click the Error Reporting button to open the Error Reporting dialog box shown in Figure 16-18.

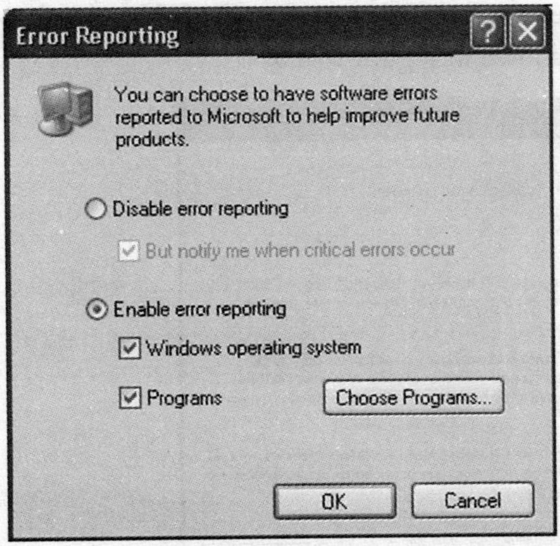

Figure 16-18 The Error Reporting dialog box.

3. **Select components.**

   Click the Enable Error Reporting check box to turn error reporting on, and then select Windows Operating System to report system errors and select Programs to report application errors. Use the Choose Programs button to select the applications you want to report on. Click OK to close the Error Reporting dialog box.

Next time your system restarts after a stop error or a Windows component freezes, a dialog box opens asking if you want to send a report on the problem directly to Microsoft. Figure 16-19 shows the Microsoft Hang Error Reporting dialog box that opened when Help And Support Center stopped responding.

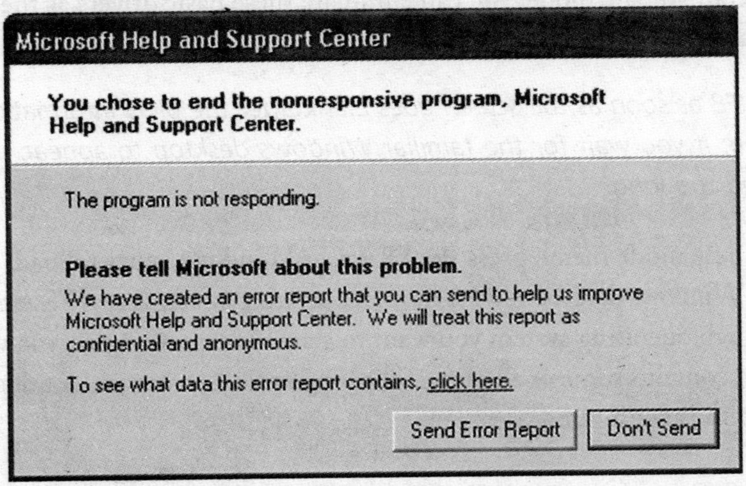

Figure 16-19 The Microsoft Hang Error Reporting dialog box.

To see the information that the report contains, use the Click Here button. You will see a screen similar to the one shown in Figure 16-20.

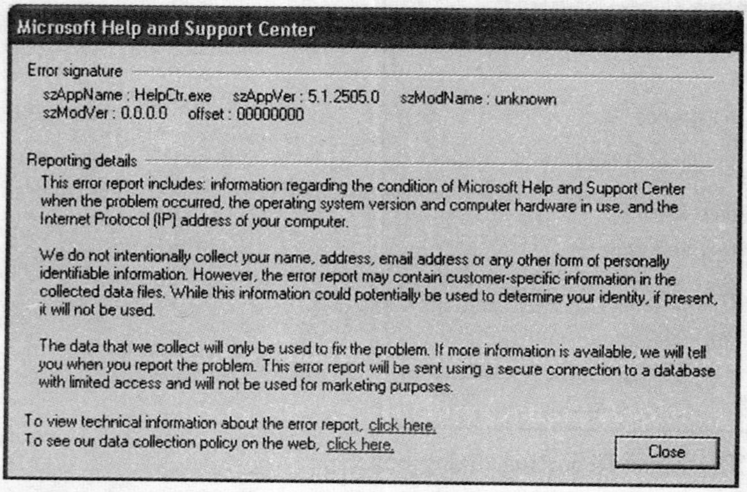

Figure 16-20 Error Signature And Reporting Details dialog box.

Click Close to return to the Microsoft Hang Error Reporting dialog box, and click Send Error Report to send details of the problem directly to Microsoft.

Starting Windows in Safe Mode

If you are having a problem with Windows, you can use a mode known as *Safe mode* to try to isolate the cause. When you start Windows in Safe mode, only the basic device drivers needed for a minimum level of service are loaded, so if the symptom goes away when you operate in Safe mode, you can eliminate these basic drivers as the cause of the problem and look elsewhere.

NOTE *Press F8 as soon as the screen goes blank after the BIOS information is displayed; if you wait for the familiar Windows desktop to appear, you have waited too long.*

To get to the Safe mode menu, press the F8 key as Windows starts to load, or if you have installed Windows dual-boot with another operating system, press F8 at the menu asking you which operating system you want to start. After a moment, you will see a text menu that contains some or all of the following options; what you see depends on how your system is configured:

- Safe Mode starts Windows with the minimum number of device drivers needed for a very basic level of service. The drivers loaded include mouse and keyboard, hard disk, basic video, and monitor. No network connections are supported.
- Safe Mode With Networking adds network connections to those listed above.
- Safe Mode With Command Prompt starts Windows at a command prompt rather than at the graphical desktop.
- Enable Boot Logging writes each event during the boot process, both successful and unsuccessful, into a text file. The boot log can be very helpful in determining the exact cause of a system problem
- Enable VGA Mode starts using a basic VGA device driver. This mode is most useful when you have installed a new video driver that is preventing Windows from loading properly.
- Last Known Good Configuration starts up using the Registry information and device drivers that Windows saved during the last normal shutdown. This mode is most useful in cases of incorrect configuration.
- Directory Services Restore Mode is for the server members of the Windows family acting as a domain controller.
- Debugging Mode starts Windows while at the same time sending debugging information to another computer via a serial cable.
- Boot Normally loads Windows in the normal way.
- Reboot restarts Windows.
- Return To OS Choices Menu goes back to the dual-boot menu without doing anything.

At this stage, tracking down a problem is often a repetitive process; try this and if it works, go on and try the next thing. If Windows seems to work well in Safe mode or in Safe Mode With Networking, reboot normally to see if Windows will run as you expect. If you have a piece of hardware that you suspect is failing, power down the computer, remove it, replace it if possible, and try to run Windows again.

If you suspect you have a problem with the Windows Registry, use the Last Known Good Configuration option. You will lose any changes you have made to the Registry (including changed system settings or applications you have installed), but if Windows starts, that's the thing that counts. And if Windows still doesn't start? Well, we have one more option.

When All Else Fails...

Yup, you guessed it. When all else fails, your only remaining option is to reinstall Windows. This is not nearly as awful as it sounds, and it might take you as long as an hour to complete. You can reinstall Windows as an upgrade, in which case all your applications and configuration settings will be kept intact, or as a clean install, which means you will have to reinstall all your applications software. See Chapter 12 for full details of both of these installation options.

Summary

In this chapter we looked at some of the bad things that can happen to your system and some of the things you can do to recover. We looked at backing up and restoring files, folders, and Windows system data. We looked at all the different kinds of CD you can use as part of your backup strategy, and how to protect your computer from attack by several different kinds of virus.

And in the second half of the chapter, we examined some the Windows tools you can use to help recover an ailing system, including the System Restore tool, rolling back device drivers, handling nonresponsive applications, starting Windows using Safe mode, and how to handle the Blue Screen of Death.

GLOSSARY

Accessibility Options

Features that can be used to customize Windows so that it is easier to use for people who have visual, mobility, hearing, or cognitive and language impairments.

Administrators

A group of **users** who can do just about anything to the computer, including loading and unloading **device drivers,** setting up an audit, taking ownership of objects, and even changing their own **permissions.**

application

A program that is designed for a specific task, for example, a word processor or a database.

attachment

A file that travels along with an e-mail message.

backup

An up-to-date copy of the files on your system.

Backup Operators

A group of **users** who can log on to the system, back up and restore the system or selected files, and shut down the system.

boot

The process of starting or restarting a computer system.

bridging

A technique that allows **network** segments of different types, for example, an **Ethernet** segment and a wireless segment, to connect.

bus topology

A **network** design in which all computers are connected to a single cable.

cable modem

A high-speed connection that uses the wiring provided by your cable TV company.

Category view

The default view of Control Panel, which places Control Panel applets in categories.

chat room

An area on a **Web site** where you can communicate with others in real time by typing on the keyboard or, if you have the necessary equipment, speaking into a microphone and listening through speakers or earphones.

Classic view

The view of Control Panel that was used in several versions of Windows prior to Windows XP. To switch from **Category view**, which is the default, to Classic view, click the Switch To Classic View link in the Control Panel bar.

ClickLock

A feature that lets you select or drag without holding down the mouse button continuously.

client-server network

A **network** in which one or more computers stores resources and supplies them to the other computers. All the other computers are connected to this central computer.

command prompt

A character or a group of characters on the screen, for example, C:\WINDOWS>, that appears in a window in Windows. You can enter a command at a command prompt.

Compatibility mode

A feature that allows you to run an **application** as if it were running in Windows 95, Windows 98, Windows Me, Windows NT 4 (with Service Pack 5), or Windows 2000.

Computer Administrator

The **user account** in Windows XP that gives you unlimited control over the system.

Computer Management

A Windows XP Professional tool that lets you view detailed information about the status of your computer system.

cookie

A file that is stored on your computer by the **server** of a **Web site** that you visit. A cookie is a data file that identifies you to the server.

desktop

The screen you see after you **log on** to Windows. Sometimes the desktop is called a **shell.**

Desktop Cleanup Wizard

A tool that runs automatically every 60 days to remove unused desktop **shortcuts.**

device

Any hardware peripheral that can send and receive information, for example, a printer, a **modem,** and a CD-ROM drive.

device driver

A program lets a **device** communicate with the computer.

device driver signature

A digital stamp that verifies that a **device driver** is authentic and that it has been rigorously tested by Microsoft.

digital certificate

An electronic credential that verifies that you are who you say you are when connected to the Internet.

directory

A feature of a **search service** that categorizes and catalogs **Web sites** and their contents. A directory is created by people rather than by software.

Disk Cleanup

A system tool that you can use to identify and delete files that you no longer need.

Disk Defragmenter

A system tool that you can use to reconstitute the bits and pieces of files stored in various locations on your hard drive into contiguous units.

DNS

An abbreviation for **domain** name **server,** a set of databases that are distributed among servers and store the numeric addresses of **Web sites.**

domain

The description of a single computer, a department, or a complete network that is used for administrative and naming purposes.

drive mapping

Assigning a drive letter to represent a file, folder, or drive on the **network.** The resource then appears as if it is local to your computer.

DSL

An abbreviation for Digital Subscriber Line, a high-speed connection to the **Internet** that uses existing telephone lines but that transmits at higher frequencies than those used to transmit voice.

Dynamic HTML

A version of HTML that introduces movement and the ability to react to a **user's** actions on a Web page.

encryption

Encoding information so that unauthorized persons cannot access it.

Ethernet

A computer networking **protocol** that can transfer data at a rate of 10 megabits per second. It is the most popular networking protocol in use today.

Ethernet address

A unique number that is assigned to each **NIC** by its manufacturer.

Event Viewer

A program that displays event logs and indicates any problem that occurs with an event.

Explorer bar

A bar in an Explorer-type window or other windows that contains items you can click to quickly accomplish a task.

Fast User Switching

A feature that allows multiple **users** of a single computer to open their individual accounts without **logging on** or off the computer and without closing any **applications** that the previous user was running. (Fast User Switching is not available on computers that are connected to a network **domain**.)

FAT

An abbreviation for File Allocation Table, the file system supported by DOS, Windows 3.*x*, and the first release of Windows 95.

FAT32

An abbreviation for File Allocation Table 32, the file system supported by Windows 95 release 2 and Windows 98.

favorite

A site whose **URL** you've placed in a list in **Internet Explorer** so that you can quickly and easily return to it. The **Netscape Navigator** equivalent is *bookmark.*

file system

The overall structure in an operating system that determines how files are named, stored, and organized.

firewall

A **device** (hardware, software, or both) that establishes a barrier that controls the traffic between two **networks,** usually a private local network and the **Internet.** Windows XP Professional comes with a personal firewall called **Internet Connection Firewall** (ICF).

folder

The container for files on your system. In earlier versions of Windows and in some other operating systems, a folder is called a **directory.**

FTP

An abbreviation for File Transfer **Protocol,** which you can use to download files from or upload files to an FTP site.

gateway

A **device** that links **local area networks** and also translates information from one kind of **network** to a different kind of network.

group account

Contains **user** and **group accounts** that share common privileges.

Guest

An account on a computer or a **network** that has limited access and that, for security purposes, should not be used.

Guests

A group of **users** who have limited access to the system. For security reasons, the Guests group should not be used.

Help And Support Center

The Help system in Windows XP that gives you access to the help files on your local system as well as access to the Microsoft Knowledge Base, which you can search via the **Internet.**

home page

The opening page of a **Web site.**

Home PNA

An abbreviation for home phone-line networking, which uses telephone wiring and jacks to connect computers and printers. Also sometimes abbreviated HPNA.

HTML

An abbreviation for HyperText Markup Language, the language used to create Web pages.

HTML tags

The basic building blocks used to create an **HTML** document.

HTTP

An abbreviation for Hypertext Transfer Protocol, the rules that specify how a **Web browser** and a Web server communicate.

hub

The central **device** that connects all the computers in a **network.**

HyperTerminal

Terminal emulation software that is included with Windows and that you can use to connect to public access **servers.**

IAB

An abbreviation for the **Internet** Architecture Board, an organization coordinated by the Internet Society. The IAB works out issues of standards, network resources, and so on.

IANA

An abbreviation for the **Internet** Assigned Numbers Authority, which is a clearinghouse for Internet addresses, **protocol** variables, and **domain** names.

ICANN

An abbreviation for the **Internet** Corporation for Assigned Names and Numbers, a nonprofit organization that assigns **domain** types.

ICS

An abbreviation for **Internet** Connection Sharing, a Windows feature that allows multiple computers to share the same **modem** or **ISDN** connection to the **Internet.**

identity

In **Outlook Express,** a type of mail **user profile** that you can set up if multiple people use your computer and, thus, Outlook Express.

IETF

An abbreviation for the **Internet** Engineering Task Force, which handles day-to-day issues of Internet operation.

IMAP

An abbreviation for Internet Mail Access Protocol, which defines how **users** can access and store incoming e-mail messages.

Internet

The world's largest computer **network,** connecting tens of millions of users.

Internet Connection Firewall

Personal **firewall** software that is included with Windows XP Professional.

Internet Explorer

The **Web browser** that's included with Windows.

Internet service provider

Abbreviated ISP. An organization that provides dedicated or dial-up access to the **Internet.**

intranet

A private corporate **network** that uses **Internet** technology.

IP address

A unique number that identifies a computer on a **network** or on the **Internet.**

IRTF

An abbreviation for **Internet** Research Task Force, which creates long- and short-term research groups that concentrate on **protocols,** architecture, and technology issues.

ISDN

An abbreviation for Integrated Services Digital **Network,** a digital connection that is available through the telephone company that can be considerably faster than a **modem** connection.

ISOC

An abbreviation for **Internet** Society, a group of volunteers that promote cooperation and coordination for the Internet, Internet **applications,** and Internet technologies.

keyword

A word or term that you enter in a field in a **search service.** Multiple keywords form a search string, a phrase that the search service compares with information it finds in its database.

LDAP

An abbreviation for Lightweight Directory Access **Protocol,** which searches a **directory** of e-mail addresses.

Limited

A type of **user account** that prohibits someone from changing computer configuration settings and deleting files.

link

Short for hyperlink. A word, a phrase, an image, or a symbol that forms a connection with a resource that can be located on your local computer, your local **network,** or the **Internet.**

list address

The address you use when posting messages to a **mailing list.**

Listproc

A **mailing list** program. Listproc is short for *list processor.*

Listserv

A **mailing list** program. Listserv is short for *list service.*

local area network

Abbreviated LAN. A group of connected computers and other **devices,** such as a printer, that can share files, **applications,** and other resources.

local printer

A printer that is physically attached to your computer by a cable.

logging off

Signing off on a **network** or a computer.

logging on

Identifying yourself to a **network** or to a computer.

Magnifier

A device that displays a magnified portion of your screen in a separate window.

mailing list

An e-mail discussion group.

Media bar

A feature in **Internet Explorer** that you can use to play music, videos, and multimedia files.

Media Player

A program you can use to play and organize digital sound and video files that are stored on your computer or on the **Internet**.

message rule

A filter that you can apply to block mail from certain senders and route mail to specific **folders**.

meta-search engine

A **search engine** that searches multiple other search engines simultaneously.

meta-search software

A program that is stored on your computer and that you can use to search multiple **search services** simultaneously if you are connected to the **Internet**.

MFT

An abbreviation for Master File Table, the part of the **NTFS** file system that maps all files and **folders** stored on a disk.

modem

A **device** that lets you transmit and receive information to and from other computers using a telephone line.

Mosaic

The first graphical **Web browser.** Mosaic was released in 1992.

Narrator

A synthetic voice that reads aloud the contents of a dialog box.

natural language query

A plain English question.

NetMeeting

A conferencing **application** included with Windows that you can use to finger chat over the **Internet,** audio conference, videoconference, share applications, collaborate on documents, transfer files, and draw on the whiteboard.

.NET Passport

Contains your personal information and a **password** that you can use to gain access to Passport-enabled services and **Web sites.**

Netscape Navigator

A **Web browser** that was first released by Netscape Communications in 1994.

network

A group of computers and peripherals **devices** (such as printers, **modems,** and so on) that are connected in some way so that **users** can share files and other resources.

network printer

A printer that is attached to another computer on your **network.**

network topology

The physical design of a **network.**

newsgroup

A collection of articles on specific topics that you can access from the news server of your ISP.

NIC

An abbreviation for **network** interface card, an adapter that plugs into a slot on the motherboard of a computer and then is connected to the network **device,** such as a hub.

NNTP

An abbreviation for **Network** News Transfer **Protocol,** which distributes **Usenet** news articles.

notification area

The area at the far right end of the **taskbar** that, by default, contains the volume icon and the clock. The notification area may also contain other icons.

NTFS

An abbreviation for New Technology **File System,** the file system supported by Windows NT, Windows 2000, and Windows XP.

object

Any component of Windows.

OCR program

An abbreviation for optical character recognition program. This type of program can convert a scanned document into text that can be used in a word processing program or a Web page editor.

offline file

A file that is stored on the **network** but that you make available to you while not connected to the network.

On-Screen Keyboard

A keyboard that displays on the screen and on which you can type by clicking keys with the mouse.

Outlook Express

The news and mail reader that's included with Windows.

packet

A chunk of information. Information is broken into packets before it is sent out over the **Internet**.

password

A combination of secret characters you enter during the process of **logging on** to Windows.

peer-to-peer network

A **network** in which all computers are equals. Each computer has its own hard drive and can see and communicate with all the other computers on the network. In addition, each computer can share its resources.

Performance console

A tool you can use to monitor and log system variables.

permissions

The rights assigned to **user accounts.** You need permission, for example, to change the system date and time.

ping

A command that tests for **network** connectivity by transmitting a diagnostic packet of data to a specific computer on the network, forcing that computer to acknowledge that the diagnostic data reached it.

Plug and Play

A feature of Windows that automatically configures a new piece of hardware when you install it in your computer.

POP

An abbreviation for Post Office **Protocol,** which retrieves messages from an e-mail **server.**

port

The interface through which information passes between a computer and a **device,** such as a printer or a **modem.**

portal

A large **Web site** that includes a **search service** but also other features such as free e-mail, online chat rooms, instant messaging, news about current events and sports, and so on.

post

To send an e-mail message to a newsgroup or a **mailing list.**

Power User

A group whose members can share files and printers, change the system time, force a shutdown of the system, and change the priorities of system processes.

PPP

An abbreviation for Point-to-Point **Protocol,** which connects a computer to the **Internet.**

printer driver

A small program that lets a computer communicate with and control a printer.

printer port

The interface through which information between the computer and the printer passes.

print server

A **network** printer.

properties

Characteristics of an **object** or a **device.**

protocol

A formal specification that defines the rules whereby data is transmitted and received.

Recovery Console

A program that advanced **users** can run to attempt to repair a system.

Recycle Bin

The container that holds deleted items until they are permanently deleted from your system.

Registry

A Windows database that contains all the configuration information about your system.

Remote Assistance

A feature that lets you log on to someone else's computer and view the **desktop** or allows some else to log on to your computer and view your desktop. In either case, the other person can look at your work and, with your permission, control your computer.

repeater

A **device** that amplifies the information going across the **Internet** at various intervals so that the signal doesn't weaken.

Replicators

A group of **users** who are involved in processes that concern a system connected to a Windows server **network.**

right-clicking

The process of using the right mouse button rather than the left. You can right-click almost anywhere in Windows and produce something useful.

ring topology

A **network** design in which all the computers are connected via a closed circle of cabling.

router

A **device** that ensures that packets always arrive at the destination for which they are intended.

Safe mode

A configuration in which you can start Windows if it won't boot otherwise and attempt to locate the source of the problem.

screen resolution

The number of pixels on the screen and the number of colors that can be displayed at the same time. Some typical resolutions are 640 by 480, 800 by 600, and 1024 by 768.

screen saver

A utility that displays a specified image on the screen after the computer has been idle for a certain amount of time. Originally, screen savers prevented images from being permanently etched on the monitor's screen. Today's monitors need no such protection.

Search Companion

An **Internet Explorer** device that you can use to search the **Internet** or your local computer.

search engine

A program that indexes resources on the **Internet** and puts that information into a searchable database. Search engines are also known as search tools.

search service

A program that can search a file, a database, or the **Internet** for **keywords** and retrieve resources in which those words are found.

security

Operating system controls that limit **user** access. Security is one of the most important features of Windows.

security zone

An **Internet Explorer** setting that specifies the types of **Web sites** that a **user** of your computer can access.

separator page

A page that prints between each print job on a **network** printer and makes it easier for **users** to identify their documents.

server

A **network** computer that provides services, such as printing, storage, and communications.

services

All the behind-the-scenes operating system tasks that keep your computer running smoothly.

sharing

Making a resource available to others on the **network**.

shell

The **user's** environment as opposed to what's going on inside the computer that makes it work. Sometimes the Windows **desktop** is referred to as a shell.

shortcut

An icon on the **desktop** that represents an **application,** a file, a document, a printer, or any other object in Windows.

shortcut menu

A menu of related commands that appears when you **right-click** an object; also sometimes referred to as a context menu or a right-click menu.

signature

In **Outlook Express,** a text file that you can append to the close of your e-mail messages. A typical business signature contains your name, title, the name of your organization, perhaps its physical address, and your phone number.

SMTP

An abbreviation for Simple Mail Transfer **Protocol,** which sends messages to an e-mail **server.**

SSL

An abbreviation for Secure Sockets Layer, a way of **encrypting** data that is transferred to and from a **Web site;** typically used for credit card transactions over the **Internet.**

star topology

A **network** in which all the computers are connected to a central hub like the points of a star.

Start menu

The primary tool for accessing programs and documents on your computer.

start page

The **Web site** you see when you first open **Internet Explorer.** You can choose any site you want as your start page.

stationery

A preformatted background that you can use to compose messages in **Outlook Express** using HTML. You can also create your own stationery.

subscription address

The address you use when sending a message to subscribe to or unsubscribe from a **mailing list.**

T1

A long-distance circuit that moves data at incredibly fast speeds and is very expensive.

taskbar

The toolbar at the bottom of the **desktop** that contains icons you can use to quickly access programs.

Task Manager

A tool you can use to display information about your system.

TCP/IP

An abbreviation for Transmission Control **Protocol/Internet** Protocol, a set of communication protocols that is best suited to large **networks,** including the Internet.

Telnet

A program that allows you to log on to a remote computer as if you were a terminal attached to it.

temporary Internet file

A copy of a Web page that you have visited and that is stored in the Temporary Internet Files folder on your hard drive.

topology

The physical design of a **network.**

transaction processing

A system in which transactions, such as buying and selling, are executed immediately. Transaction processing lets you use the Web as a virtual store, a salesperson, or a distribution facility.

Troubleshooter

A tool included with Windows Help that you can use to solve problems with various **devices,** such as printers, **modems,** network adapters, and so on.

Unicode

A character-encoding standard that lets all written languages be represented using a single character set.

UPS

An abbreviation for Uninterruptible Power Supply, a battery source of power that swings into action when your computer loses power, such as in a brownout.

URL

An abbreviation for Uniform Resource Locator, an address for a resource on the **Internet.**

Usenet

An international, noncommercial **network** that distributes news articles.

user

Any person who is allowed to access a computer or a **network.**

user account

Identifies a **user** on a **network** or on a computer by his or her user name and **password.**

user account picture

The picture that appears next to your name in the Welcome screen.

user profile

A collection of settings that are applied each time you **log on** to the system.

Users

A group of **users** who can run programs, access data, shut down a computer, and access data over the **network.**

vCard

An electronic personal information card that you can exchange via e-mail or during a teleconference.

virus

A malevolent program that can attach itself to your computer system without your knowledge or permission and wipe out your hard drive.

VPN

An abbreviation for Virtual Private **Network,** a tunnel through the **Internet** that connects your computer to your corporate network.

wallpaper

A graphical image that serves as a background on your **desktop.**

Web browser

A program that you can use to explore **Internet** resources.

Webcast

A radio broadcast that you can tune in to and listen to over the **Internet.**

Web site

A collection of Web pages that are connected by means of hyperlinks.

wide area network

Abbreviated WAN. Any **network** that crosses metropolitan, regional, or national boundaries.

Windows Messenger

A program you can use to send and receive instant messages, see if friends or associates are online, transfer files, communicate via audio and video, and share **applications** and the whiteboard.

wizard

A Windows component that steps you through a process, such as setting up a **network** connection, connecting to the **Internet,** and so on.

XML

An abbreviation for Extended Markup Language, which provides a way to give detailed content information about a Web page, allowing for more meaningful searching and information gathering.

Index

B

C

D

E

F

I

J

K

L

M

N

O

P

R

S

T

U

V

W

X

Z

The manuscript for this book was prepared and submitted to Redmond Technology Press in electronic form. Text files were prepared using Microsoft Word 2000. Pages were composed using PageMaker 6.5 for Windows, with text in Frutiger and Caslon. Composed files were delivered to the printer as electronic prepress files.

Project Editor

Paula Thurman

Layout

Minh-Tam S. Le

Indexer

Julie Kawabata